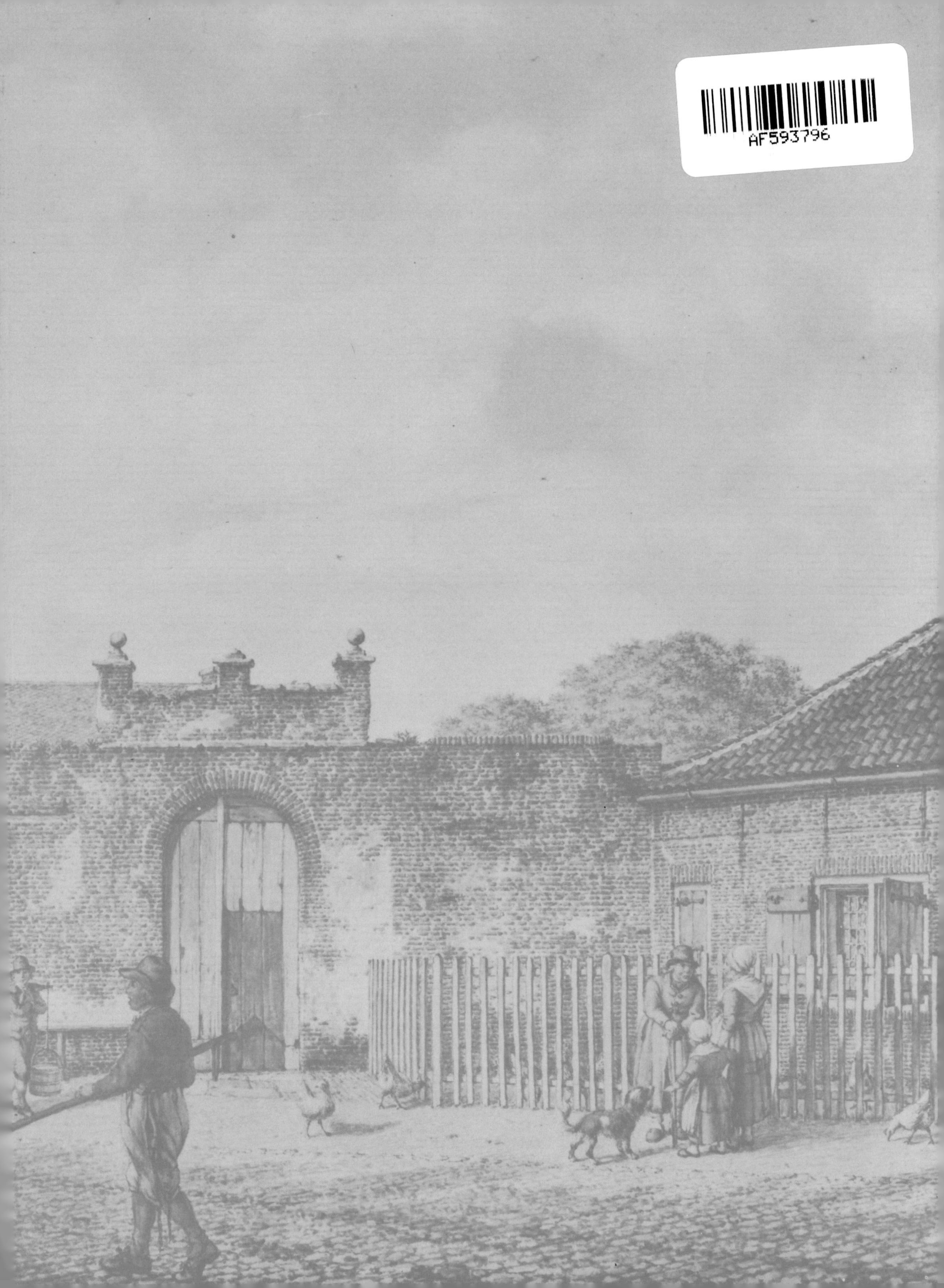

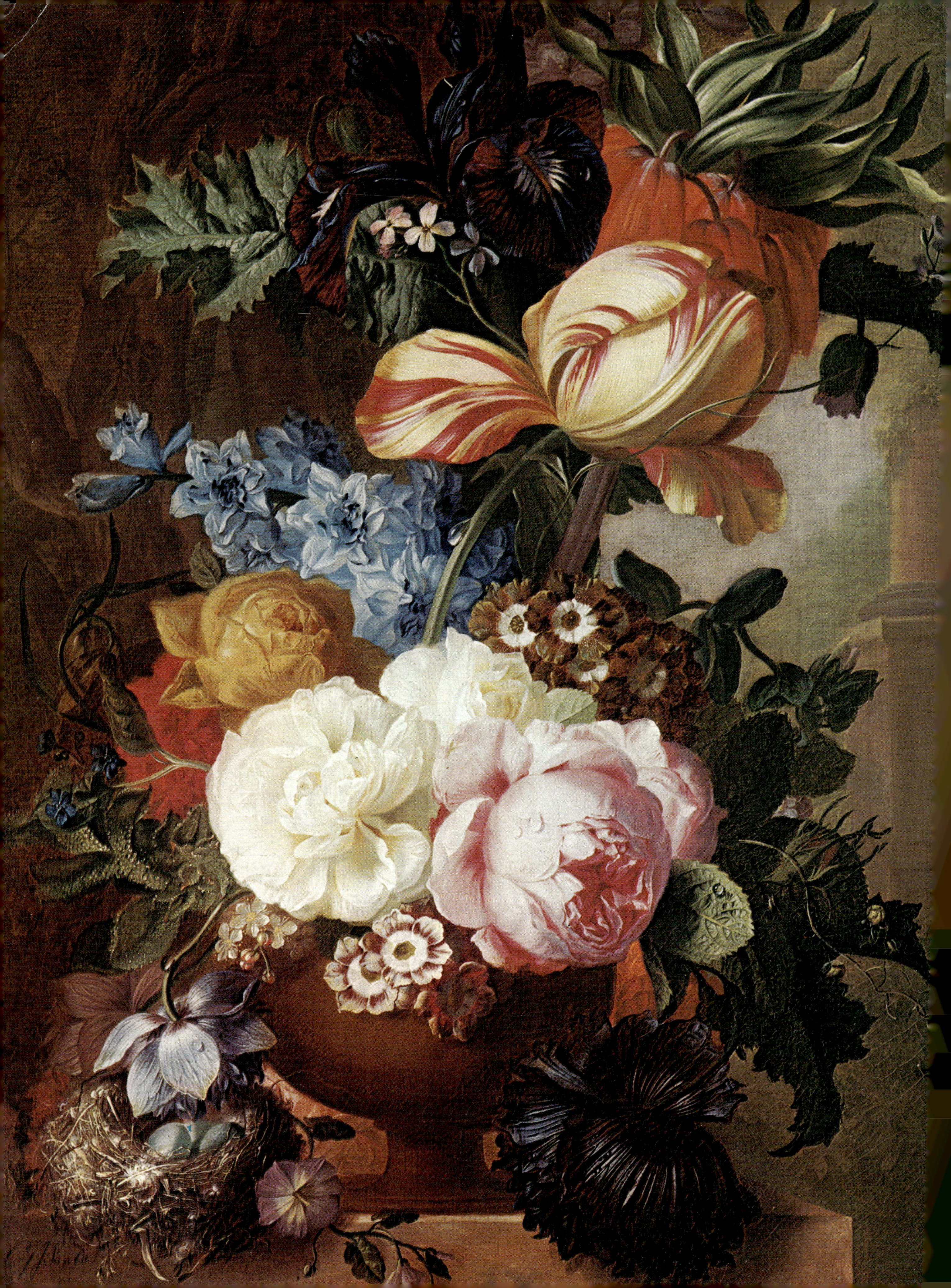

DUTCH PAINTERS

of the

19th Century

DUTCH PAINTERS
of the
19th Century

MARIUS

edited by Geraldine Norman

ANTIQUE COLLECTORS' CLUB

ISBN 0 902028 21 9

First published in Dutch in 1903.
English translation 1908.

Printed in England by
Baron Publishing, Church Street,
Woodbridge, Suffolk.

Frontispiece. **Georgius Johannes Jacobus van Os (1782-1861).** *"Still life of roses, tulips and peonies in an urn." (18 x 14ins.)* Photograph courtesy of Richard Green.

Antique Collectors' Club

The Antique Collectors' Club was formed in 1966 and now has a five figure membership spread throughout the world. It publishes the only independently run monthly antiques magazine *Antique Collecting* which caters for those collectors who are interested in widening their knowledge of antiques, both by greater awareness of quality and by discussion of the factors which influence the price that is likely to be asked. The Antique Collectors' Club pioneered the provision of information on prices for collectors and the magazine still leads in the provision of detailed articles on a variety of subjects.

It was in response to the enormous demand for information on "what to pay" that the price guide series was introduced in 1968 with the first edition of *The Price Guide to Antique Furniture* (completely revised, 1978), a book which broke new ground by illustrating the more common types of antique furniture, the sort that collectors could buy in shops and at auctions rather than the rare museum pieces which had previously been used (and still to a large extent are used) to make up the limited amount of illustrations in books published by commercial publishers. Many other price guides have followed, all copiously illustrated, and greatly appreciated by collectors for the valuable information they contain, quite apart from prices. The Antique Collectors' Club also publishes other books on antiques, including horology and art reference works, and a full book list is available.

Club membership, which is open to all collectors, costs £9.95 per annum. Members receive free of charge *Antique Collecting,* the Club's magazine (published every month except August), which contains well-illustrated articles dealing with the practical aspects of collecting not normally dealt with by magazines. Prices, features of value, investment potential, fakes and forgeries are all given prominence in the magazine.

Among other facilities available to members are private buying and selling facilities, the longest list of "For Sales" of any antiques magazine, an annual ceramics conference and the opportunity to meet other collectors at their local antique collectors' clubs. There are nearly eighty in Britain and so far a dozen overseas. Members may also buy the Club's publications at special pre-publication prices.

As its motto implies, the Club is an amateur organisation designed to help collectors get the most out of their hobby: it is informal and friendly and gives enormous enjoyment to all concerned.

For Collectors — By Collectors — About Collecting

The Antique Collectors' Club, 5 Church Street, Woodbridge, Suffolk

Contents

List of Colour Plates

Acknowledgements

We are grateful to the following for permission to reproduce the illustrations contained in this book:—

Mak van Waay, Amsterdam; Richard Green; Sotheby's; Rijksmuseum, Amsterdam; Williams & Son; M. Newman Ltd.; Spenser S.A.; Rijksmuseum Hendrik Willem Mesdag, the Hague; Christie's; Stedelijk Museum, Amsterdam; Kröller-Müller Museum, Otterlo; MacConnal Mason; Haags Gemeentemuseum; The Wallace Collection; Dordrechts Museum; Piccadilly Gallery; Boymans Museum, Rotterdam; King & Chasemore; Phillips.

Standardisation of Artists' Dates

Approximately a dozen dates have been altered from those given in Marius's text as later scholarship suggests that they may not be correct. The dates of births and deaths have accordingly been made to conform to those quoted by Pieter Scheen in his "Lexicon Nederlandse Beeldende Kunstenaars 1750-1950".

Introduction

The story of Dutch painting in the nineteenth century has not yet been tackled by modern art historians; it has been neither sifted, sorted through nor reassessed in terms of current aesthetic values. It is more than likely that, as I write, someone already has this project in hand. For the last decade has seen a growing awareness in all countries that the nineteenth century can no longer be dismissed as an aberration. Its art and its artists have as great a right to study and admiration as those of any other century – and this goes as much for the more conservative artists as for the experimentalists such as Goya, Delacroix or the Impressionists.

This book by G.H. Marius is now, and will remain when more has been written on the subject, a basic work of reference. This book was first published in Dutch in 1903 and in an English translation (that which we have used here) in 1908. Marius was a friend or acquaintance of many of the later artists discussed in these pages, and was himself a man of the nineteenth century. This gives his anecdotes and discussion of what painters were at the time trying to achieve the immediacy of first hand knowledge.

The point of view from which the book is written is, however, essentially of its time. At the turn of the century high fashion among wealthy collectors and art connoisseurs centred on the work of the French Barbizon painters (Corot, Millet, Daubigny et al) and the Dutch artists of the Hague school, Israëls, the Maris brothers and Mauve. Public taste is always a little behind the times; the great years of Barbizon dated from the 1840s and 50s while the closely related artists of the Hague school made their most important contribution to art in the 1860s to the 1880s. In 1973 Picasso, Matisse, Modigliani, working in the early decades of the twentieth century, are similarly reverenced as the great masters of "modern" art, although the period of their most important activity is already a long way in the past.

It is impossible to read this book today without being constantly startled by Marius' point of view. But it must be remembered that he was writing before public taste had even caught up with the great achievement of the French Impressionists. He is to be congratulated for his appreciation of the immensely important contribution of Van Gogh standing as he did so close to him in time.

Indeed, it is fascinating to read his comments on the pressures excessive American popularity exerted on the Hague school artists. "That degrading market" he calls America which "asks one year for "Sheep going to pasture" and the next for "Sheep returning" and the year after for something else, much as the height and breadth of our hyacinths is laid down for us by the exigencies of Anglo-American taste." In the first decade of the twentieth century paintings by Jacob Maris made £3,000 and £4,000 at Christie's in London. The same paintings would be hard put to make the same sums today even in the grossly devalued pounds sterling of the 1970s.

With the rise to fashion of the Impressionists after the First World War the Hague school was progressively forgotten. The interest of the English speaking world in Dutch painting of the nineteenth century, which had ensured the translation of Marius' book in 1908, was dead and buried. Even Van Gogh, the wild Dutch genius of the late nineteenth century, was looked on essentially as a master of the French school.

At last interest is reviving but, inevitably, the qualities which we admire today do not coincide with those valued by G.H. Marius and his friends in 1900. It is the achievements of the Romantic landscape school, mostly of the earlier part of the century, which are being rediscovered and justly valued for the first time since 1850 or so.

These painters, the Koekkoek family, Leickert, Springer, the Hulks et al leant heavily on the great tradition of the Dutch seventeenth century. Prosperous Protestant Holland, with its many burghers, enriched by the leading role of their small country in international trade, was the first country in Europe where painting was enthusiastically patronised by the middle classes. The walls of a palace or great public institution make different demands on a painter to the walls of a comfortable family sitting room. The Dutch artists of the seventeenth century were the first to develop an art adapted to the ordinary family home. Their landscapes, townscapes, genre scenes and marine views are a supreme achievement in the realm of paintings to be lived with rather than lived up to.

Their influence on Gainsborough, Constable, Crome and the English landscape school of the nineteenth century reflects among other things the rise of middle class patronage in England following the industrial revolution. The English also wanted paintings to live with and what better model could be found than that of Holland? The appeal of this sort of painting is timeless. While the cohorts of Classicism clashed with the Romantics, the Impressionists with the Symbolists, the abstract expressionists with the Surrealists, the art market has demonstrated no wavering in demand for the Dutch little masters of the seventeenth century.

Today most of the finest works of this period have found their way to the walls of museums. Those that are still available to the collecting public are either in very poor condition or exorbitantly expensive. The stage has been set for the rediscovery of the great achievements of the little masters of the nineteenth century, so close in mood and style to their seventeenth century predecessors. The link is underlined by Marius who tells us how the *oeuvre* of Jacob van Strij has become hopelessly muddled with that of Aelbert Cuyp. This, no doubt, explains why van Strij's work is seldom seen at auction today – his paintings have literally become Cuyps. He also tells us of the van der Laen landscape which became a Vermeer but was changed back again by the art historian Bredius in 1883.

These are extreme examples but one can find innumerable parallels even where no actual confusion of attribution exists. The relationship between B.C. Koekkoek's summer landscapes and Hobbema, Schelfhout's ice skating scenes and Avercamp, the Hulks' marine views and those of van der Velde or van de Capelle, the Dutch interiors of Hubertus van Hove and Pieter de Hoogh, the pastoral landscapes of Kobell and Paul Potter . . . . . The list could be almost indefinitely extended.

But just as each of the seventeenth century little masters has his own distinctive vision, so do their nineteenth century followers. There is a rich field for study here, investigating the different mood and approach of the various artists and the different influences that formed them. Although the Romantic school is now being enthusiastically collected, little is known about the background of their work and its place in art history. Individual artists may be looked up in Pieter Scheen's comprehensive "Lexicon Nederlaandse Beeldende Kunstenaars 1750-1950" but this provides no general picture of how the artist fitted into the unfolding story of Dutch art.

Marius provides much of this missing background. He tells the story of Dutch nineteenth century art linking it with the achievements of the seventeenth and eighteenth century at one end of the scale and with Van Gogh, Toorop and the Dutch Symbolists at the other. The Romantic landscape and genre painters whom we tend to think of as a group are divided into generations and we can see that universal nineteenth century trend towards a broader and freer brushwork (Schelfhout and Leickert) leading on to the Hague school and the Dutch version of Impressionism.

When a school is out of fashion, it always becomes difficult to study – the pictures disappear into attics and store rooms. Marius was clearly confronted with this problem in the context of the Romantic school. "When occasionally we come upon those somewhat antiquated landscapes in a museum, at a dealer's, at an auction sale" he writes "we are struck by their vigour and love of nature, by that healthy vigour which was always reserved for the greatest."

Nevertheless, he has unearthed the story of the school and introduces us to the leading figures of the day, their lives and their pupils. But some of the artists whose work has been rediscovered in recent years he can have known only slightly. Both Charles Leickert and Cornelis Springer are only mentioned in passing. The fine work which has appeared on the market in recent years leads us today to rate them much higher than did Marius.

For this reason we have added an addendum including a selection of artists not mentioned by Marius whose work is of a quality to deserve greater attention. The names of their masters and pupils will give the reader a general idea of where they fit into Marius' story of Dutch art.

For the rest, the book speaks for itself. It provides a timely reminder of the fickleness of fashion – of how fundamentally aesthetic judgements can change from one generation to another. It is also full of suggestions for new areas of collecting interest. This edition is much more heavily illustrated than the original. The captions to the illustrations are entirely my own work. I have tried to make them both add to and complement the text. I apologise for any cases where I have done an artist less than justice.

Geraldine Norman

Chapter I

Introductory

The seventeenth century bequeathed to the eighteenth three painters all of whom – and two in particular – heralded the spirit of the new age in matters of conception, colour and execution. The greatest of the three, Jacob de Wit, who was called the Rubens of his time, is esteemed as an historical painter – he executed a part of the Orange Room at the House in the Wood – and is world-famous for his painted bas-reliefs, the so-called *witjes,* in the Royal Palace in Amsterdam and elsewhere. These not only excel as extraordinary imitations of marble, to which De Wit owes his popularity, but the natural attitudes and grouping of the cherubs prove him to be, without a doubt, the greatest Dutch decorative artist of the eighteenth century. The second was Jan M. Quinckhard, who, as Van der Willigen says, "was a very good, yes, we venture to say, in many respects an excellent portrait-painter; he was particularly fortunate in his likenesses, his drawing was accurate, his brushwork good and his colouring soft and delicate." He, like De Wit, belongs entirely to the eighteenth century in ideas and his work did little to contribute towards the transition of the painted portrait from the seventeenth century to the nineteenth. The same may be said of the third painter, Cornelis Troost, who, in spite of certain drawings that remind us of the seventeenth century and, in particular, of the somewhat artificial elegance of Nicolaas Maes, was essentially a man of his time. All his work in various mediums is too strongly imbued with the eighteenth-century spirit to permit us to regard him as a result or consequence of the previous century. Not that he can have troubled much about the matter, for abundant fame was his portion, so much so that he was known, in his day, as the Dutch Hogarth, a comparison which, like most of its kind, contained but a minimum of truth.

If, nevertheless, we insist upon considering these three painters as offshoots of our great century, then

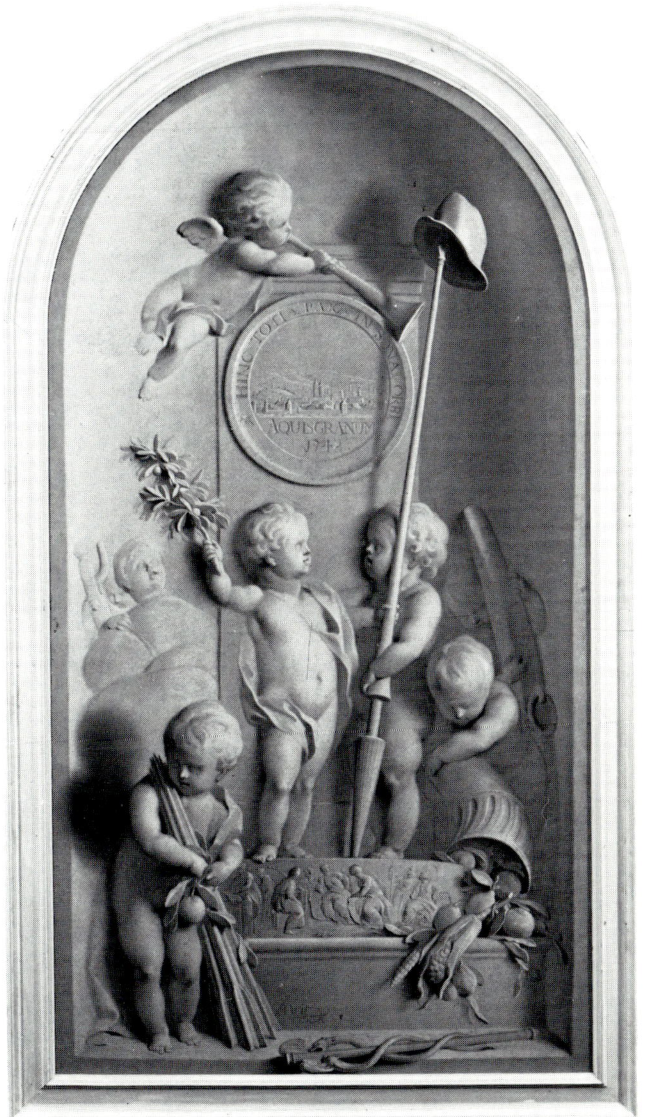

Jacob de Wit (1696-1754). *His greatest claim to fame rested on his painted bas-reliefs, although he was also hailed as "The Rubens of his time". This "Allegory of the Treaty of Aix-la-Chapelle" is a clever example of this* Trompe l'Oeil *technique on a grand scale (84 x 46 ins.) and is dated 1848.* Photograph courtesy of Christie, Manson & Woods.

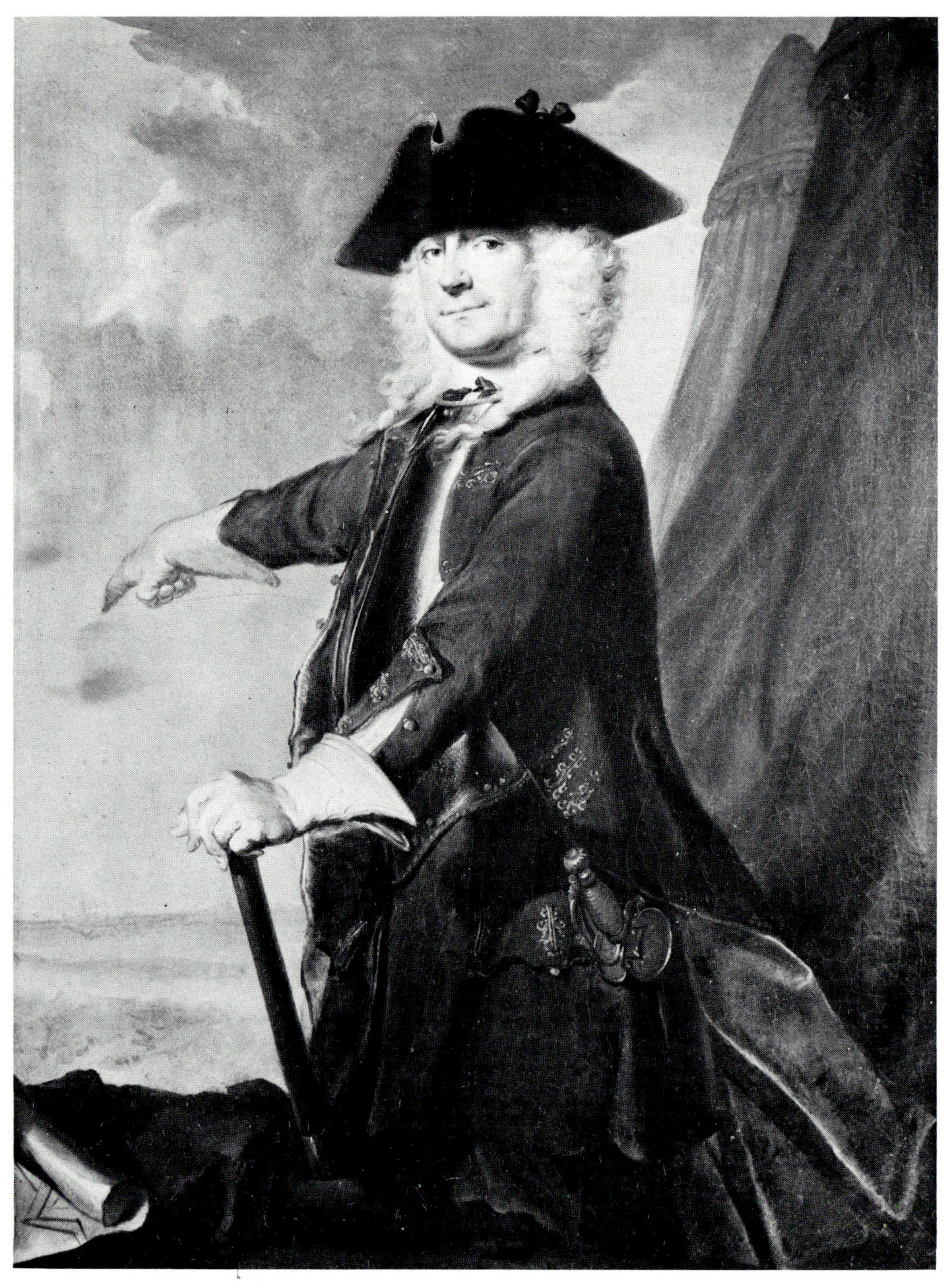

Cornelis Troost (1697-1750) *was one of the most distinguished Dutch portraitists of the 18th century. The Rijksmuseum took advantage of this portrait being recently on the market to add it to their collection (69½ x 56½cms.).* Photograph courtesy of Mak van Waay, Amsterdam.

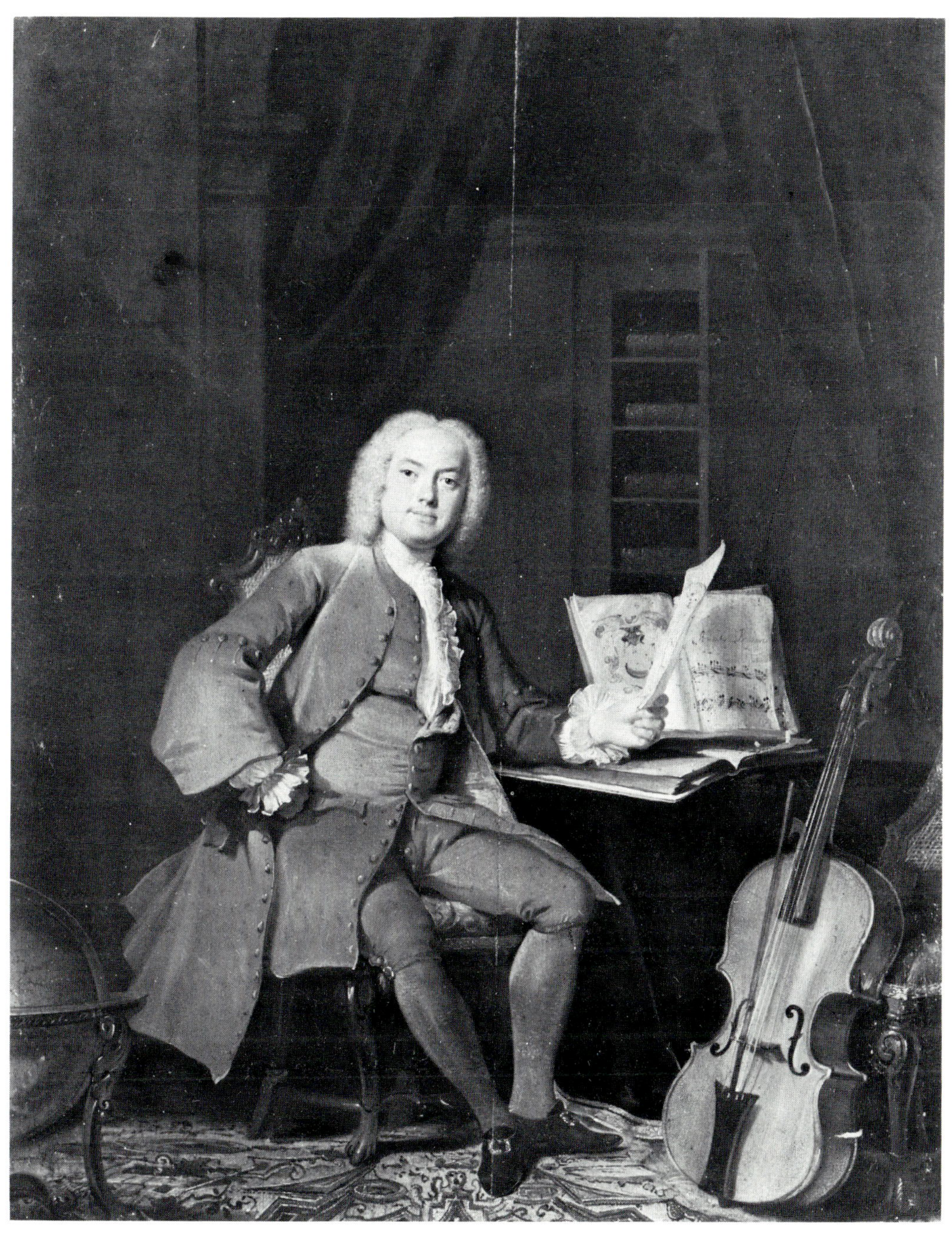

This portrait by **Cornelis Troost** *depicts a musician of the day with a still life attention to detail.*

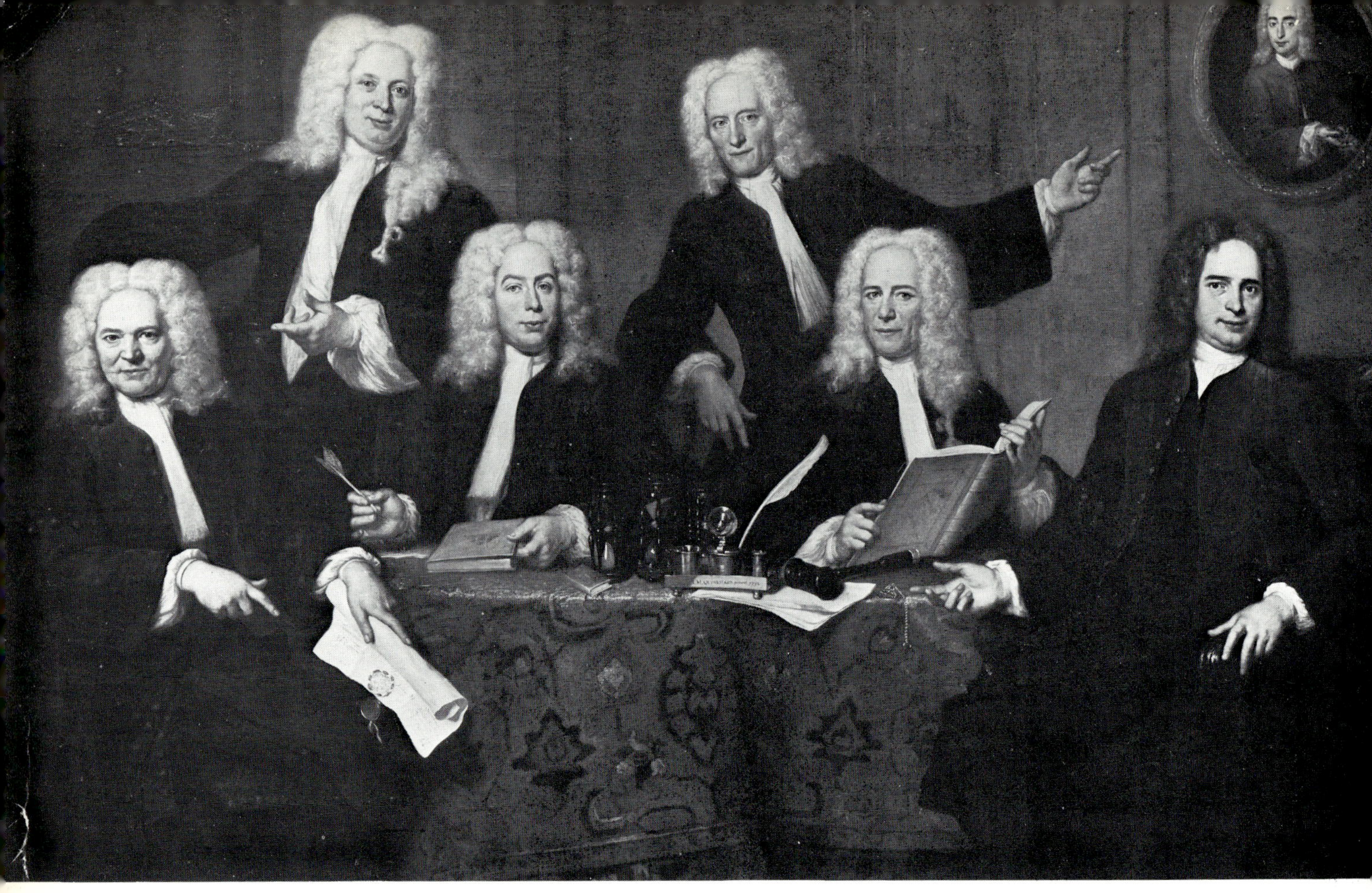

Jan Maurits Quinckhard (1688-1772) *painted this group portrait of the guild of chemists in 1752. (176.5 x 273cms.).* Photograph courtesy of the Rijksmuseum, Amsterdam.

we must needs add that they were the last effort of an exhausted soil. The art of painting declined into the art of decoration or scene-painting, the painter's workshop was transformed into the tapestry-factory. The minute, concentrated charm of our so-called little masters expanded itself into painted hangings; the stately portraits of the time degenerated, with few exceptions, into the pale, powdered pastels that seemed deliberately designed for the representation of the caricatural periwig.

Still, if only for the reason that the eighteenth century contains the predecessors or, at any rate, the teachers of the painters of the nineteenth century, it is well worth while to consider these decoration-painters from another point of view than that of the applied art which owed its prosperity to the luxury of the merchant-princes of Amsterdam, Rotterdam, Dordrecht and Middelburg. For not only had the best of these decoration painters learnt their art as real painters and merely altered the character of their productions in obedience to the whims of the day: most of them did paint or draw landscapes or portraits and prove that they had it in their power to satisfy a demand for real painting, should it ever arise. For instance, in the Foder Museum in Amsterdam, certain drawings by the tapestry-painter and manufacturer, Jacob Cats, display a strength, an old-Dutch quality, an originality which we should hardly have expected to find in those days. This Jacob Cats was born in 1741 at Altona and came with his parents, at an early age, to Amsterdam, where he achieved considerable success with both his hangings, and drawings; and, although the tapestries are no longer easy to find, his drawings go to show that he lacked the affection, if not the prolixity, that clung to many of those painters, especially towards the end of the century. They are very pleasantly executed, were greatly esteemed in their day and still fetch good prices under the hammer. Cats died in 1799.

Another tapestry painter of note is Hendrik Meijer, born in Amsterdam in 1737, who also drew landscapes in body-colour, sap-colour and Indian ink.

Andreas Schelfhout (1787-1870). *"Frozen river landscape with figures skating, a windmill and town in the distance." Signed and dated 1850. (21½ x 29½ ins.).* Photograph courtesy Richard Green.

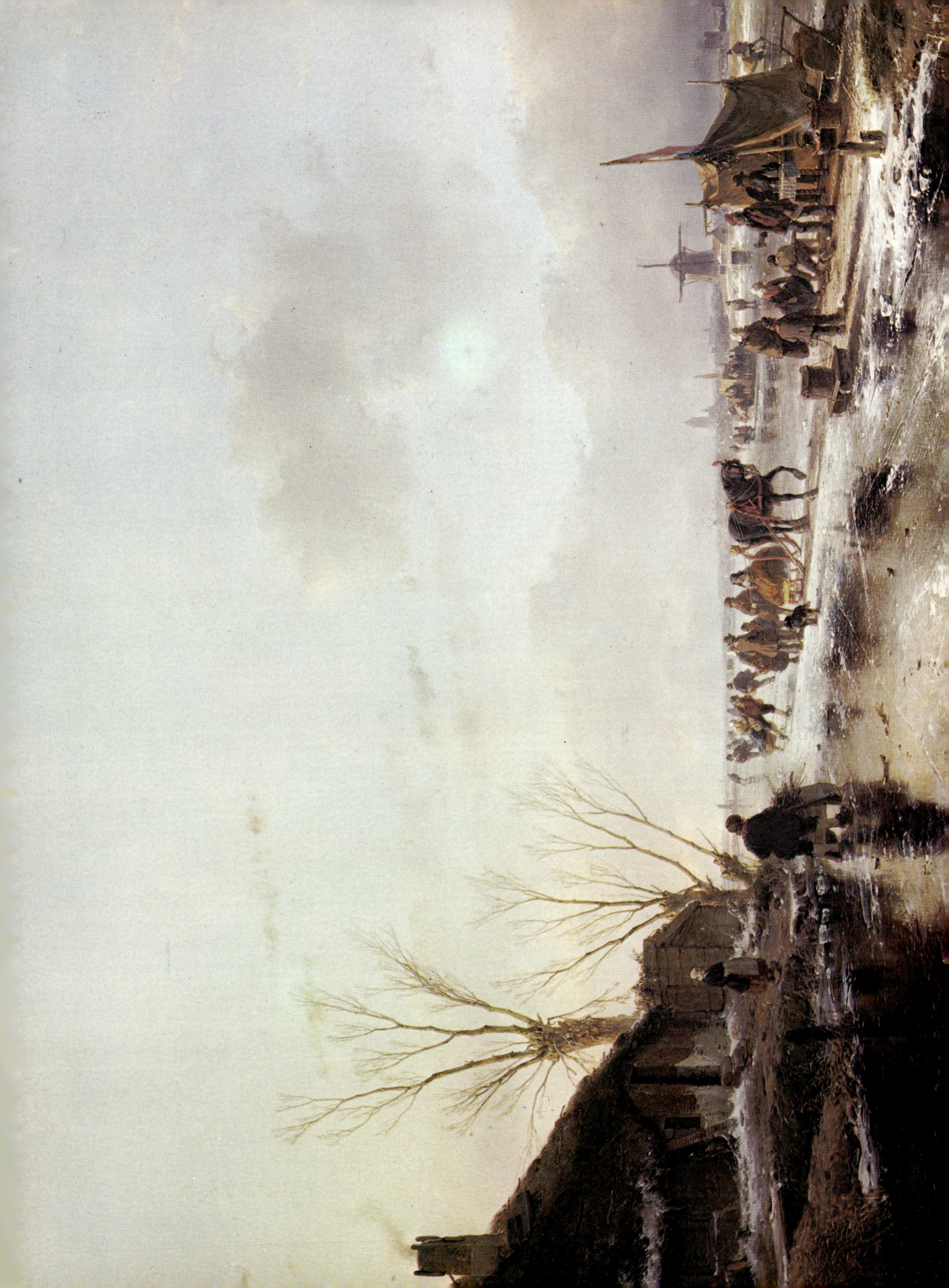

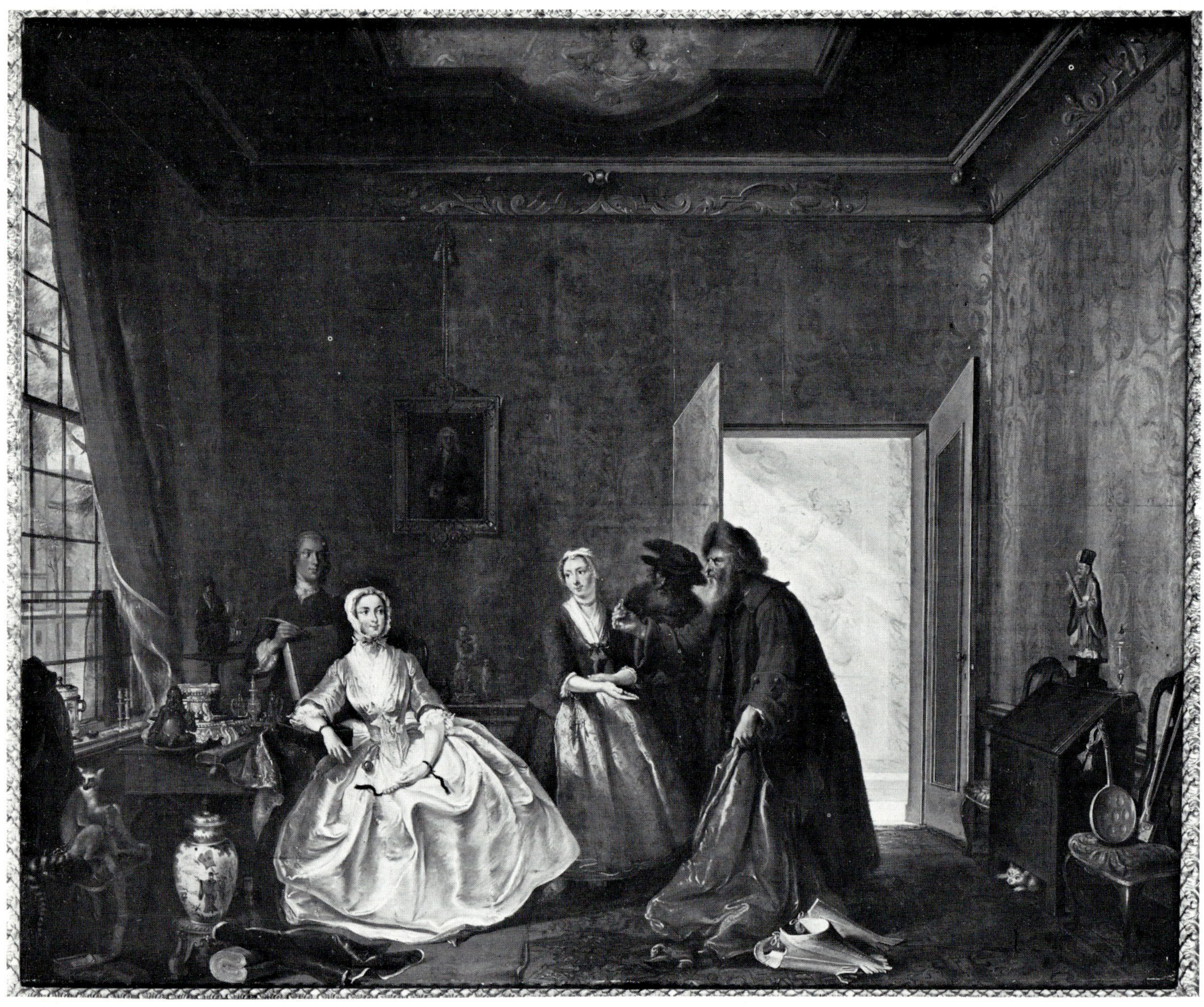

This brilliant interior with a pedlar indicates how **Cornelis Troost** *earned his reputation as the "Dutch Hogarth" (86.1 x 68.5cms.)* Photograph courtesy of the Rijksmuseum, Amsterdam.

His *Schevening Beach,* a picture that formed part of the Des Tombe collection of the Hague, is said to have been his master-piece and to be preferable in many respects to a sea-piece by Schotel. From our point of view, however, this painter's chief claim to importance lies in the fact that he was the teacher of various nineteenth-century artists. He died in London in 1793.

Aart Schouman, an eighteenth-century painter living at Dordrecht, preserved the seventeenth-century traditions more intrinsically, in so far as externals were concerned, and continued to paint corporation-pieces, which, if they cannot be reckoned among the finest of their kind, are at least able to hold their own. The fact is that many of these painters retained the arrangement of the old masters and copied them so industriously, often in water-colour or pastel, that they ended by making their style their own and frequently lapsed into contenting themselves with the production of but slightly altered copies. It is even said that Boymans, the famous collector, was induced to buy an interior by Laqui, one of those painters, under the impression that he was purchasing a Gerard Dou. We may take it, then, that these painters were still connected by a fine thread with the landscape-painters of the seventeenth century. On the other hand, so great were the demands of decoration-painting upon their strength and energy, that they had sunk remarkably low in the matter of portrait-painting. And yet portraits were asked for not only

Louis Verboeckhoven (1802-1889). *"Shipping off the coast." (28½ x 37¾ ins.).* Photograph courtesy of Richard Green. *Verboeckhoven, a highly successful Belgian animal painter, frequently collaborated with Dutch colleagues, notably Daiwaille, Verveer, Klombeck and M.A. Koekkoek.*

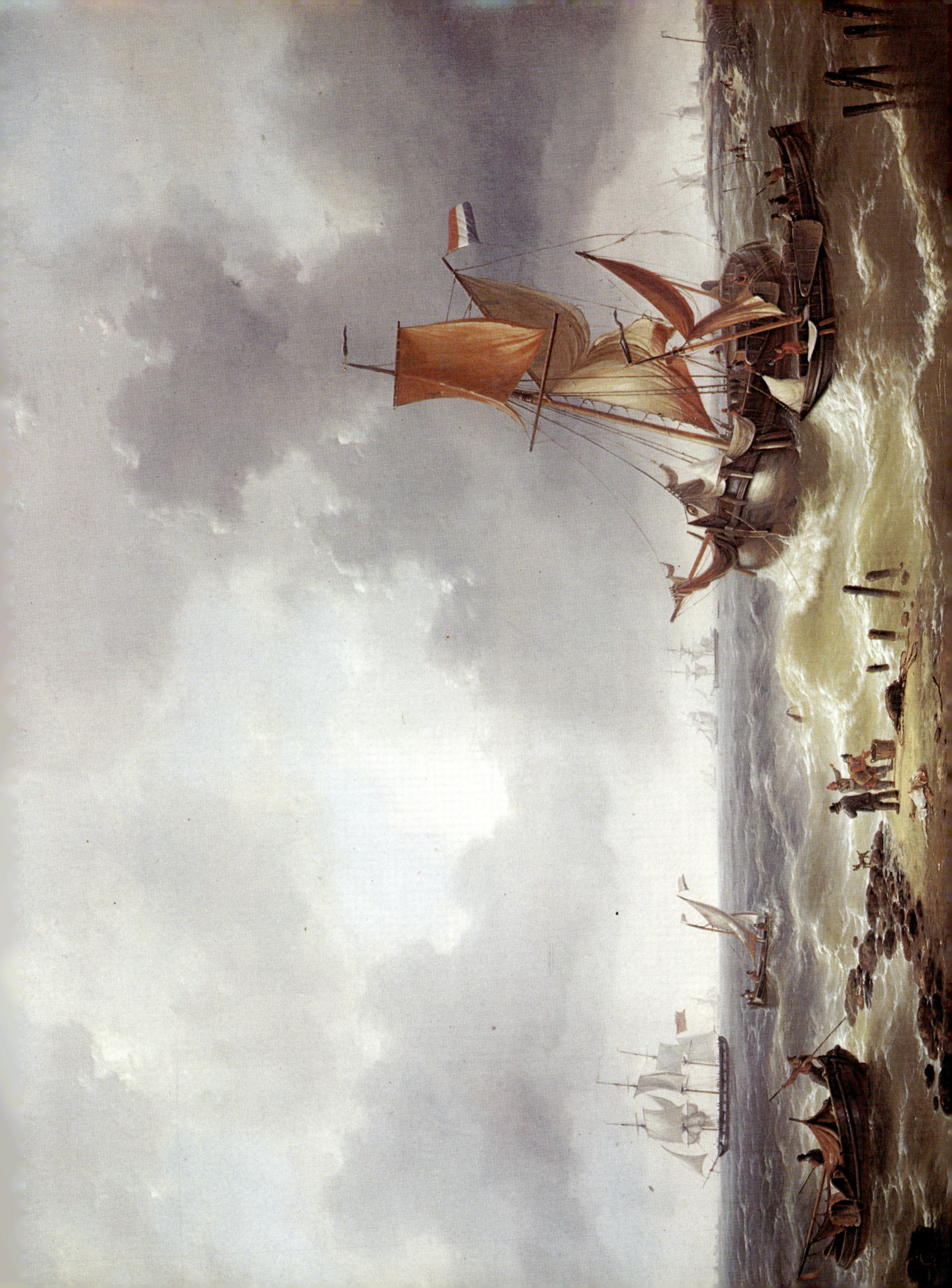

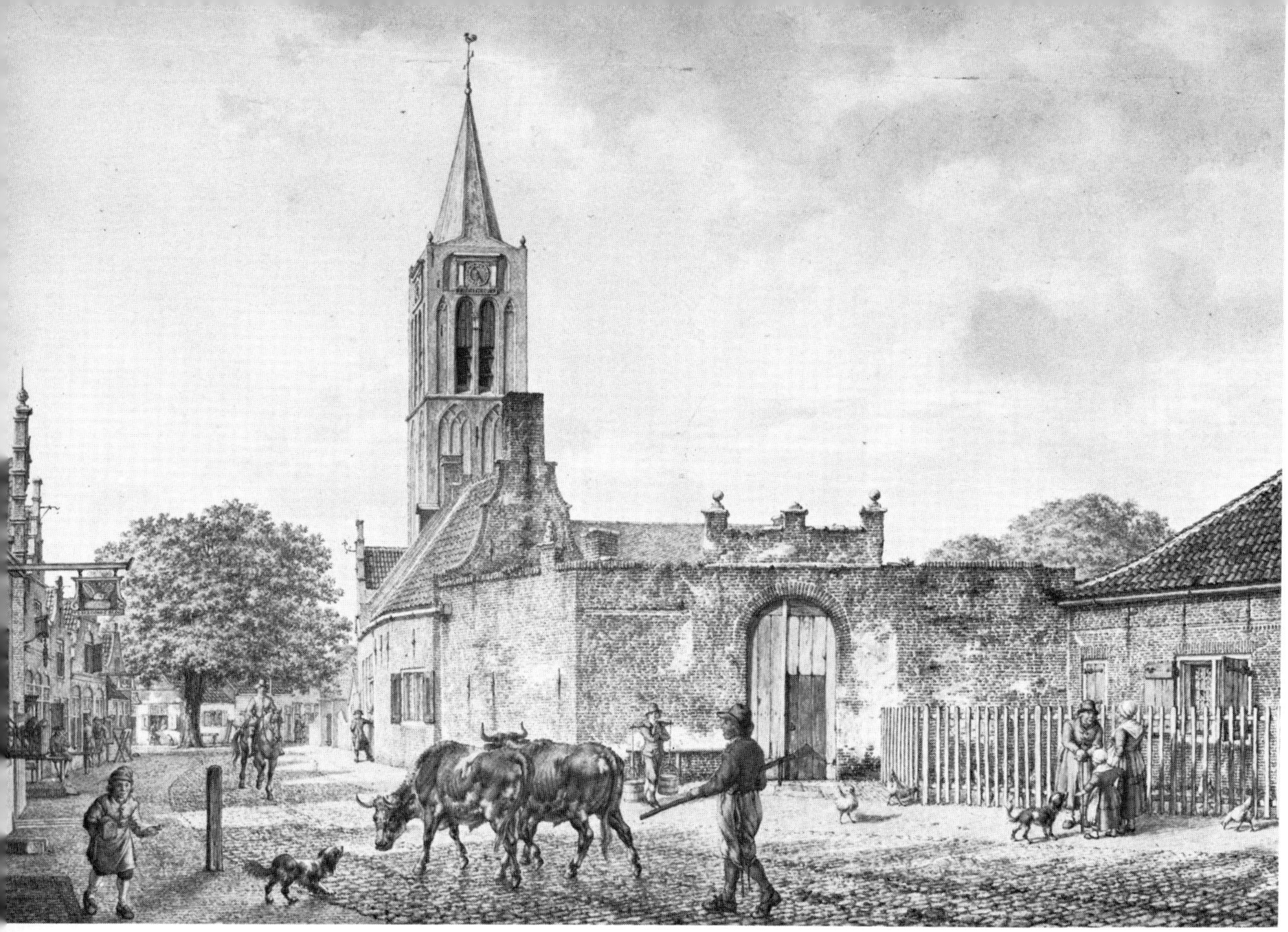

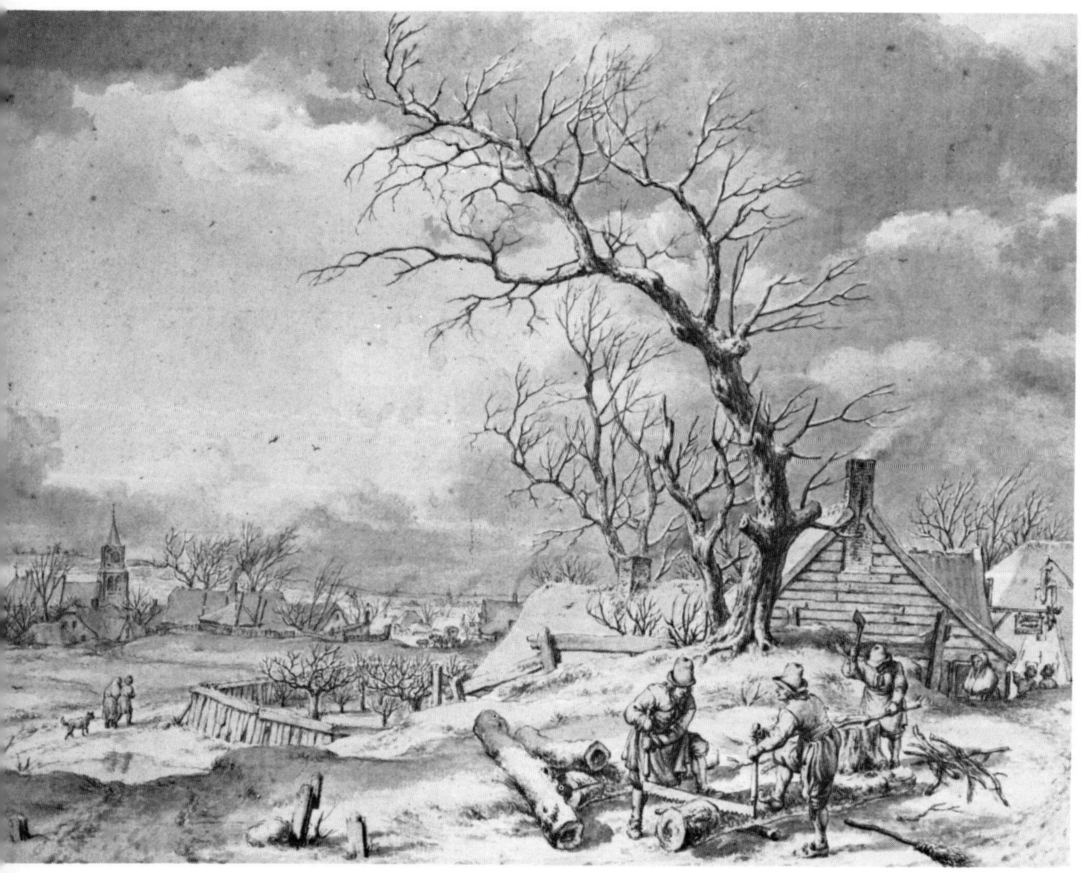

Above: **Jacob Cats. (1741-1799).** *The 18th century townscapists loved to render the tiny bricks that add a distinctive flavour to Holland's old buildings – in this they followed the example of Van der Heyden in the 17th century. Jacob Cats has been very successful with it in this watercolour, (31 x 44½ cms.) which is dated 1793.* Photograph courtesy of Mak van Waay, Amsterdam.

Left: **Jacob Cats'** *skill with a winter landscape, as in this sepia drawing, is also inherited from the 17th century Dutch Masters. It is dated 1796 and measures 27 x 35½cms.* Photograph courtesy of Mak van Waay, Amsterdam.

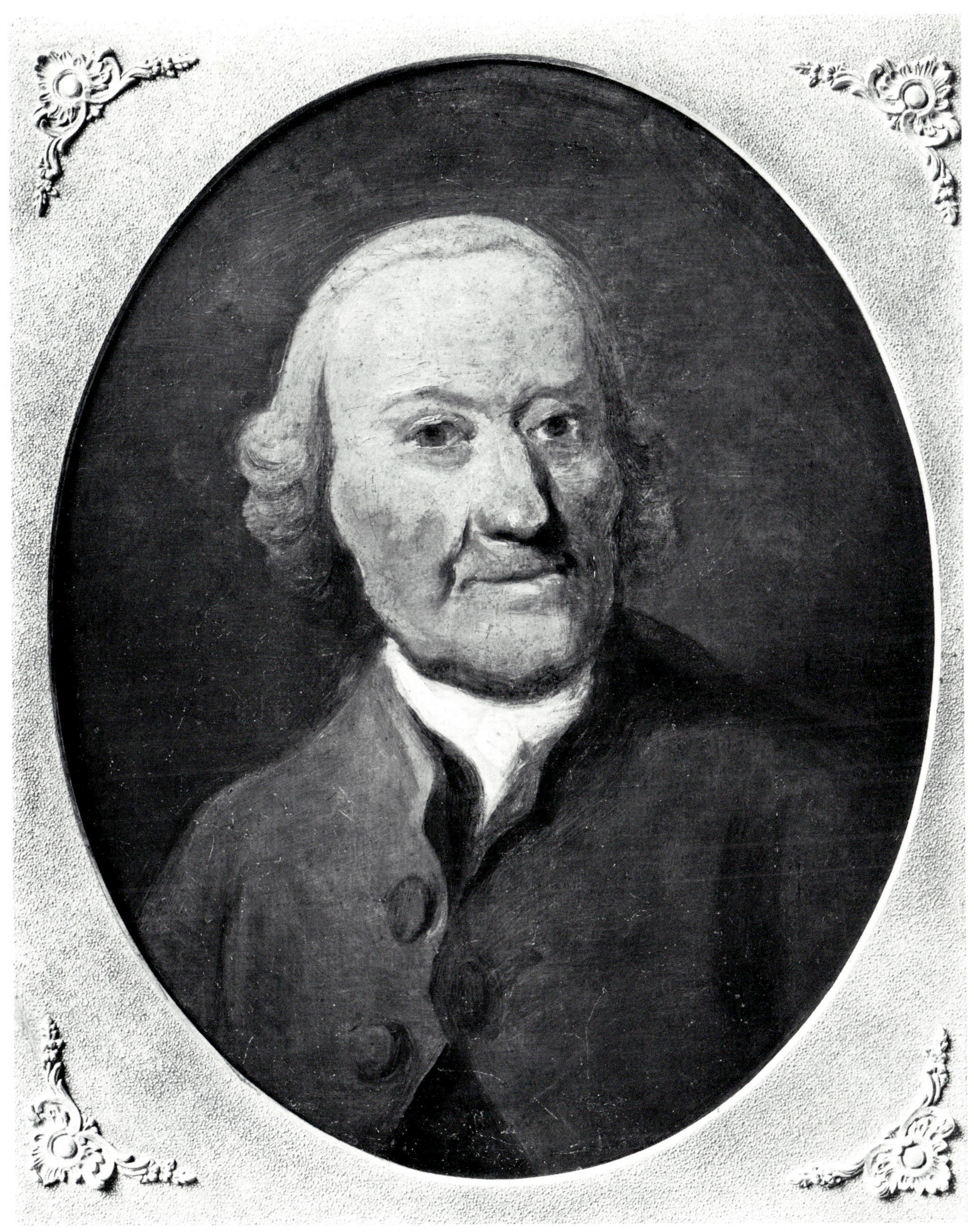

A self portrait of **Aart Schouman** *(45 x 37cms.).* — Photograph courtesy of the Rijksmuseum, Amsterdam.

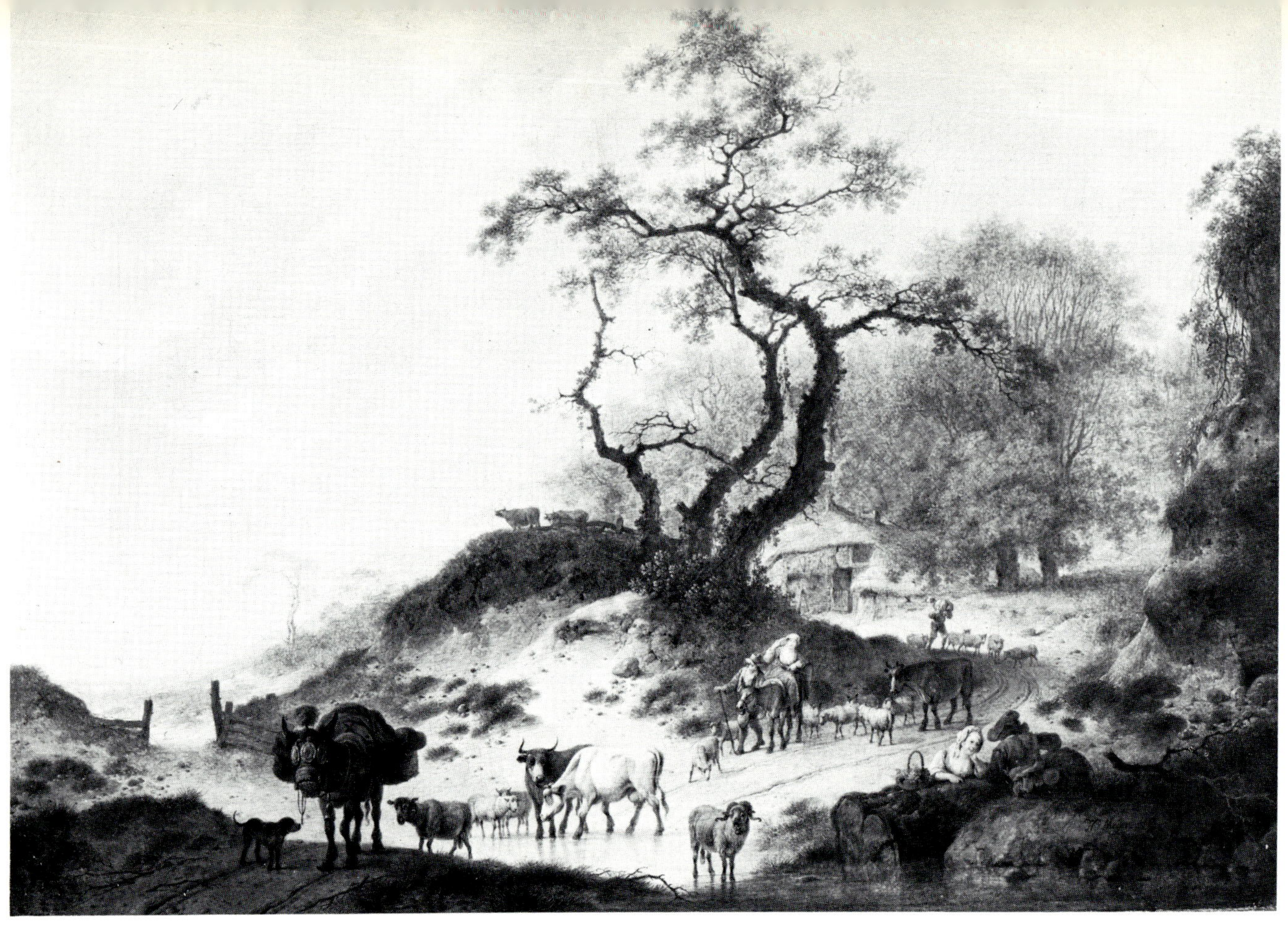

Hendrik Meijer (1737-1793) *continued the landscape tradition in addition to his work as a tapestry painter.* **Photograph courtesy of Christie, Manson & Woods.**

by the princes and the aristocracy, but also by the well-to-do middle-class. The tapestry-painters produced a number of small family-portraits, mostly naive and weak, although occasionally distinguished by a certain delicacy of conception. In addition to Adriaan de Lelie, Jean Augustin Daiwaille and others, part of whose work comes within the nineteenth century, and a few miniature-painters, of whom Temminck was one of the foremost, portraits were executed, for the greater part, by travelling portrait-painters, including Rienk Jelgerhuis, who has no fewer than 7,763 standing to his credit. Or, again, people would sit for their portraits in the course of the endless journeys which it was at that time their custom to take. This applied especially to miniatures, which were painted, so as to be easily portable, in lockets, on watch-keys, rings or snuff-boxes. And, although these were affected by the general decline, they sometimes displayed a daintiness of draughtsmanship, a softness of colouring and, above all, a certain "distinction" to which few of the larger portraits of the time can lay claim.

The French painters who frequented the luxurious Courts of the Bourbons or who followed in the wake of Napoleon and had more orders within the limits of the empire than they were able to execute were much too busy to visit less favoured countries on the chance of picking up commissions for portraits. The case was the same with the great English painters; so that this branch of industrial art was reserved, for the most part, for the Germans. Their portraits were stiff and expressionless. The grouping of the small family-portraits, usually in pastel, suggested the traditional semi-circle in which Molière is played at the Théâtre Français. They seemed, however, to give pleasure to the purchasers; and, to tell the truth, on looking into these unpretentious little family-groups, we find that they present a more general family-resemblance and are more lifelike than most of the photographic portraits of thirty years ago.

The two principal portrait-painters who came from foreign countries at the end of the eighteenth century were Tischbein and Hodges. Johann Friedrich August Tischbein, although born at Maastricht in 1750,

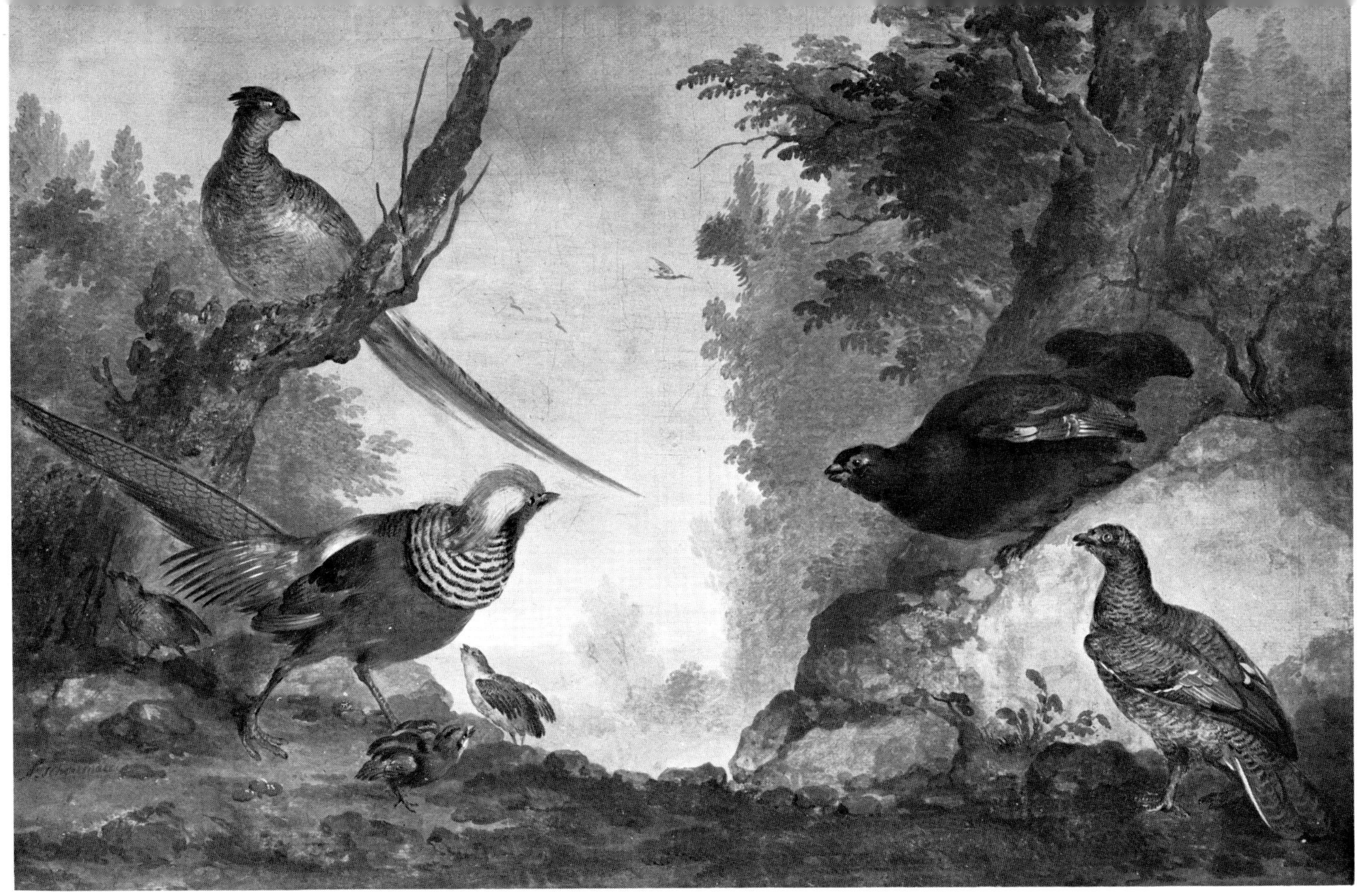

Aart Schouman (1710-1792) *follows the 17th century example of Hondecoeter in this painting of pheasants but sets them in romantic parkland redolent of 18th century taste (99 x 151cms.).* **Photograph courtesy of the Rijksmuseum, Amsterdam.**

belonged entirely to the German school. He was one of the few younger men who escaped the prevailing classicism of his time. His preference for portrait-painting drove him to foreign Courts; and for fourteen years he painted at the Hague, at the Court of the Stadtholder and his family. He was a competent and pleasant painter, who reproduced the powdered wigs and the features of his sitters in a refined manner. His portraits of women are of value for our time; and the many pictures which he painted of Wilhelmina of Prussia, the consort of William V, with her powdered hair, vivacious features and the fine colouring of the green dresses, in which he excelled, are in good taste on the whole.

He was famed for the naturalness of his ideas, but, as times were, was unable to exercise any influence upon the nineteenth century. The eighteenth century, with its sensibility, its gallantry, its powder, patches and pastels, had retreated before the harshness of the heroic emotions, decked in classic garb, with which David opened the nineteenth. Tischbein died in 1812.

The other, Charles Howard Hodges (1764-1837), was a painter of greater importance, a man of excellent gifts, whose portraits strike one at once by their elegance, their bright colouring and their supple, if somewhat weak workmanship. Kramm, in his *Lives and Works of the Dutch and Flemish Painters,* praises him for the subtle manner in which he flattered his sitters. To us he is the portrait-painter of the Empire period; and, although, at a later date, he painted King William I, he also gave us the portraits of Grand pensionary Schimmelpenninck and of Mrs. Ziesenis-Wattier, the famous actress of the time. If he is not to be compared with the great English portrait-painters of the eighteenth century, the fact remains that he possessed something of their taste and especially something of the supple method, the easy, fluent modelling that so greatly distinguished Sir Thomas Lawrence. Hodges was a member of the commission which, after the restoration of Dutch independence, brought back from Paris the paintings that had been taken from us by the French.

It must needs arouse surprise that this portrait-painter did not become the head of a school in his

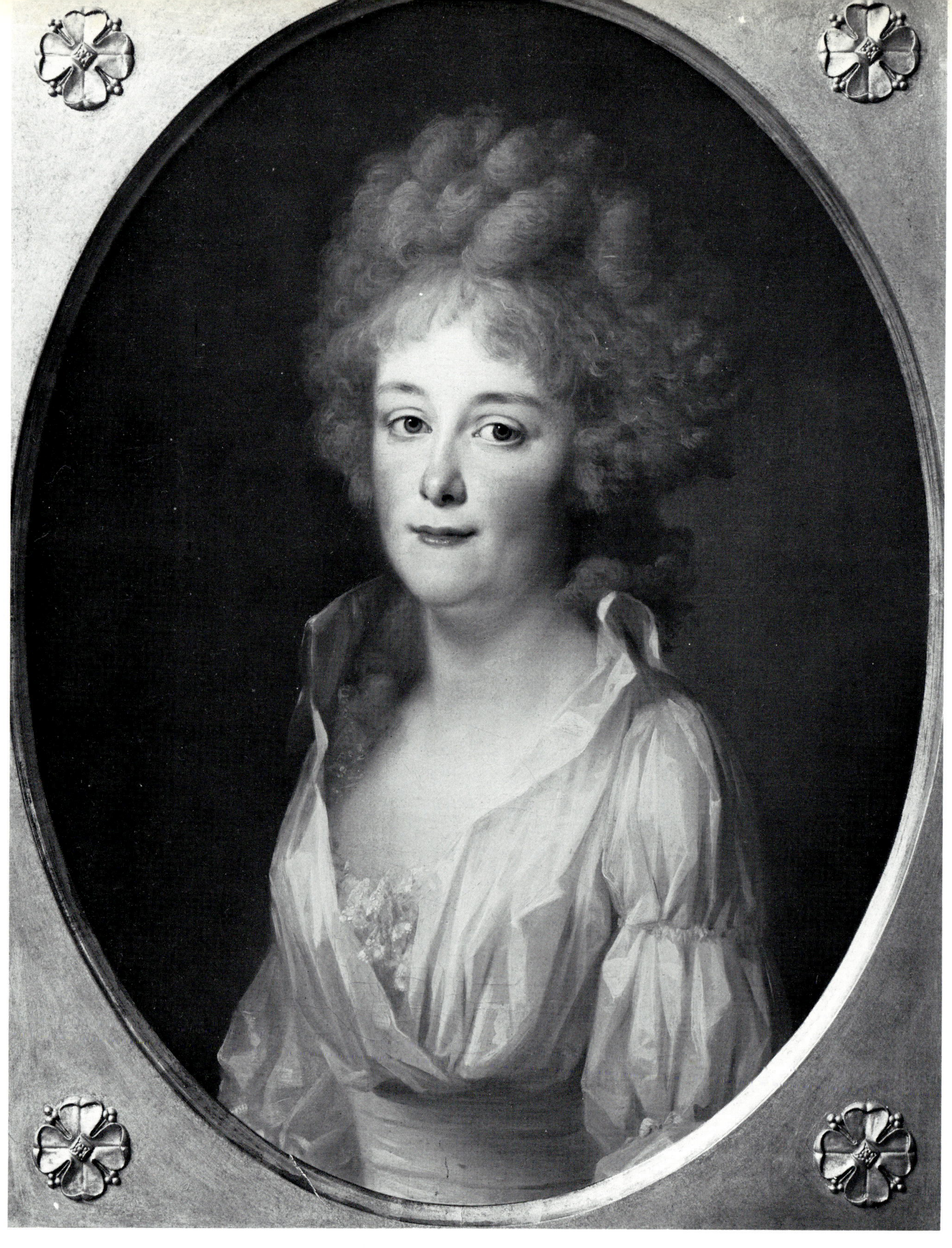

Johann Friedrich August Tischbein (1750-1812) *came to Holland from Germany. This portrait of Ferdinanda van Collen is typical of the style which rendered him so popular at the Stadholder's court at the Hague (68 x 5cms.).* Photograph courtesy of the Rijksmuseum, Amsterdam.

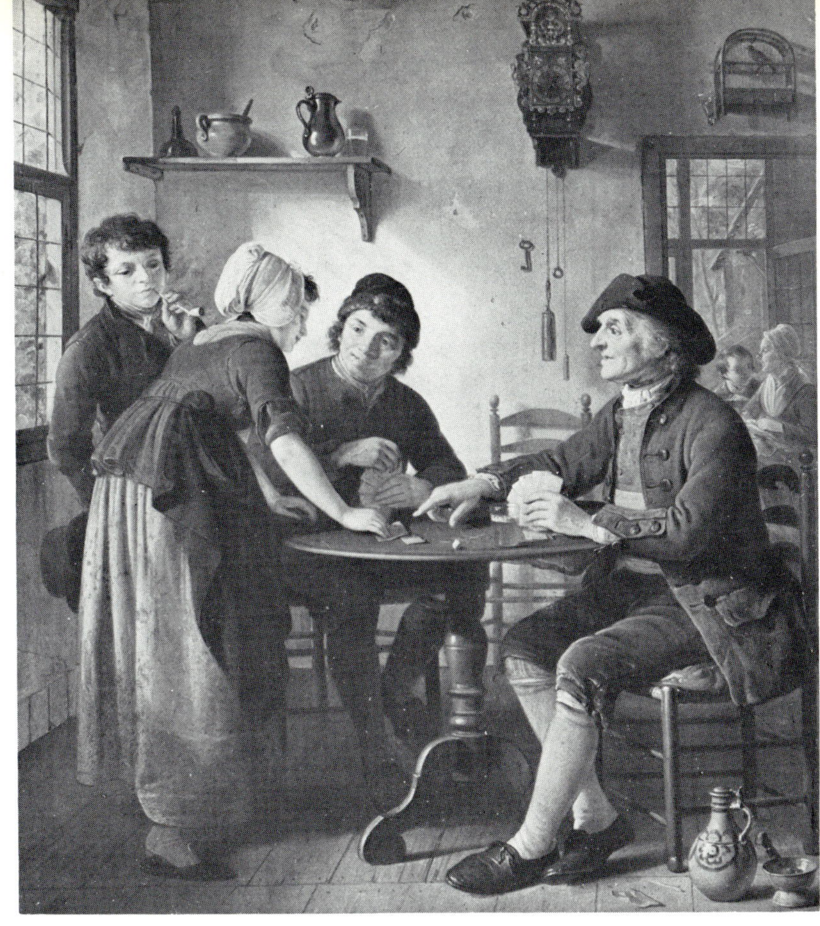

Adriaan de Lelie (1755-1820) *excelled at portraits and genre in the true Dutch tradition. This interior looks back to Jan Steen in the 17th century but was painted in 1820 (61 x 52cms.).* Photograph courtesy of Mak van Waay, Amsterdam.

day. True, his talent was distinguished rather than powerful; but, indeed, the polish and refinement of his work are not to be despised, especially when we consider at what a low ebb our fortunes then were. His chief pupil was Cornelis Kruseman, who failed to acquire or, at least, to retain his bright colouring, his supple and natural draughtsmanship or his qualities of distinction. Nevertheless, Hodges may have exercised an indirect influence upon his contemporaries. For instance, we find in Pieneman's *Battle of Waterloo* a cast of features which seems related to those which Hodges portrayed. On the other hand, this may be simply the English type; for Pieneman painted portraits for this picture in England. Perhaps J.A. Kruseman, Cornelis Kruseman's kinsman and pupil, preserved more of Hodges' characteristics than anyone else.

England, the land of the poets, was at that time rejoicing in a school of painting which, although mainly based upon the old Dutchmen and Italians, had recently, under Reynolds and Gainsborough, developed into a purely English school. Followed the passionate figure of the poet-painter William Blake, who stood at the entrance to a new century in which Constable and Turner wrought their artistic revolution. Germany had found in Beethoven the loftiest expression of her period of musical creation, an expression which was so brilliantly to influence the whole of the musical and also of the pictorial life of the nineteenth century. On the other hand, Germany was celebrating the heyday of her civilization in the little States where, amid this general budding of great minds, Goethe introduced the experimental novel into literature, Novalis wrote his *Hymns to Night* and Heine, a little later, proclaimed the eternity of romance, while in the art of painting, overshadowed by the theories of Winckelmann, she was able to point to his disciple Anton Rafaël Mengs and the fortunately more independent Chodowiecki. In Spain, the country where great painters appear like meteors, Goya had opened a new era. In France, weary of the carnage that had marked her Revolution, David, the man of iron ability, after glorifying the Republic under Robespierre, called into being, on the ruins of the eighteenth

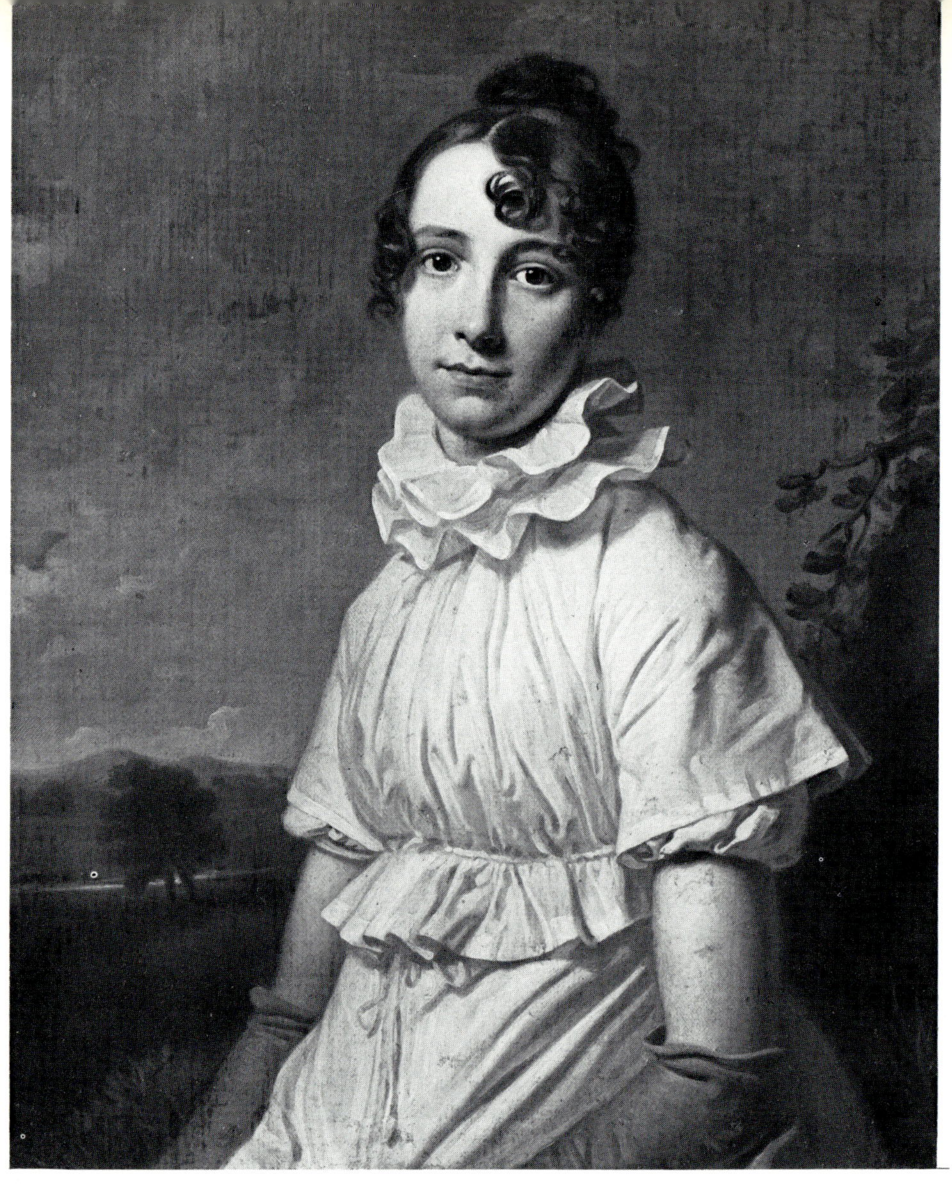

Charles Howard Hodges (1764-1837) *brought to Holland something of the supple, fluent brushwork of the contemporary English portrait school. This portrait of his daughter Emma Jane Hodges is a particularly relaxed and successful example of his style (77 x 62cms.).* Photograph courtesy of the Rijksmuseum, Amsterdam.

century, an imperial art which came to maturity under Napoleon and became the foundation of a school of painting that kept France at the head of the artistic world for well-nigh a century.

To us, who had lost our liberty, our independence, our strength and who possessed so very little in the domain of art, the beginning of the nineteenth century brought nothing but humiliation upon humiliation. Our national existence appeared to be wiped out. We were without power of action or, consequently, of reaction. True, the seventeenth century had borne fruit in such superabundance that two successive centuries have not sufficed to make us realize it fully. The soil had exhausted itself in producing the miraculous figure of Rembrandt, the epitome of all latent, conscious and unconscious forces, of all the instincts of a people, of the gospel of a nation rejuvenated by its newly-acquired liberty; of Rembrandt, in whom for us the seventeenth century is personified and incarnate. And a long period of rest was needed before the soil would once more become fertile and produce an artist, a dreamer whose genius should fall like a ray of light into a scientific age.

Chapter II

The History–Painters

It would be impossible to write the history of Dutch painting in the nineteenth century without naming Jan Willem Pieneman as its founder, even though it were only because he was the valued master of Jozef Israëls. This opinion may be regarded as hackneyed and antiquated; and it may be argued that Pieneman and Kruseman and their like did more harm than good to Dutch art, inasmuch as they led it into strange paths. But, apart from the fact that this extraneous tendency was the prevailing one in every country, Pieneman may be credited with having, by the strength of his personality, raised painting to the position of an independent art, able to produce a more powerful school than could ever hope to arise from the continual copying of seventeenth-century masterpieces.

Pieneman was born at Abcoude in 1779 and destined for a commercial career, for which, however, he was disinclined. He therefore resolved to enter a factory of painted hangings, intending at the same time to learn something of the painter's trade. In the evenings, he drew from the antique and the nude at the Amsterdam Academy, which appears to have been very deficiently equipped, so much so that, according to Van Eynden and Van der Willigen, Pieneman's chief instructor was his own genius. To provide for his maintenance, he began to give lessons at an early date and had to accept commissions to colour prints. In 1805, he was appointed drawing-master to the School of Artillery and Engineering, then still at Amersfoort, and although he had, in the meantime, won prizes and painted portraits and landscapes, he continued to fill the post until 1816, when King William I gave him the directorship of the royal collection at the Hague. Four years later, he was appointed the first president of the Royal Academy of Fine Arts.

Neither his landscapes nor his portraits brought Pieneman the fame which was soon to resound beyond the frontiers of our country. His first success was his *Heroism of the Prince of Orange at Quatre-Bras,* a large picture, twenty feet by thirteen, painted by order of the government for presentation to the prince. Before reaching its final destination in the palace at Soestdijk, it was exhibited in Amsterdam, Brussels and Ghent and, according to Immerzeel, was praised for its broad and powerful style, its accurate drawing and its fidelity to nature.

This was followed by *The Battle of Waterloo,* the sketch for which is in the Duke of Wellington's possession. The picture, which is twenty-seven feet wide by eighteen high, represents the moment at which the Prince of Orange is being carried, wounded, from the battle-field. The chief figures are painted with attention to details and the wounded prince is thrown into much less prominence than the figure of Wellington himself, who stands like an equestrian statue in the centre of the picture, which serves as an apotheosis of the British field-marshal. Pieneman paid several visits to London to paint portraits for this historical piece: during one of these, 1819 to 1821, he was the guest of the Duke of Wellington and, in addition to the necessary studies, painted a number of portraits of the leading nobility. In order to produce his large picture, for which he had no commission, he built a studio outside Amsterdam, beyond the Leiden Gate. Here he was visited by King William I, who bought the painting for forty thousand guilders for presentation to the Prince of Orange. It was exhibited in Ghent, Brussels and London and altogether earned about one hundred thousand guilders for the artist.

Pieneman painted many portraits in Holland as well as in England and in these his artistic temperament is most strongly displayed. One might say of him that he had little of the refined classicism which is to be met with in neighbouring countries; that he possessed

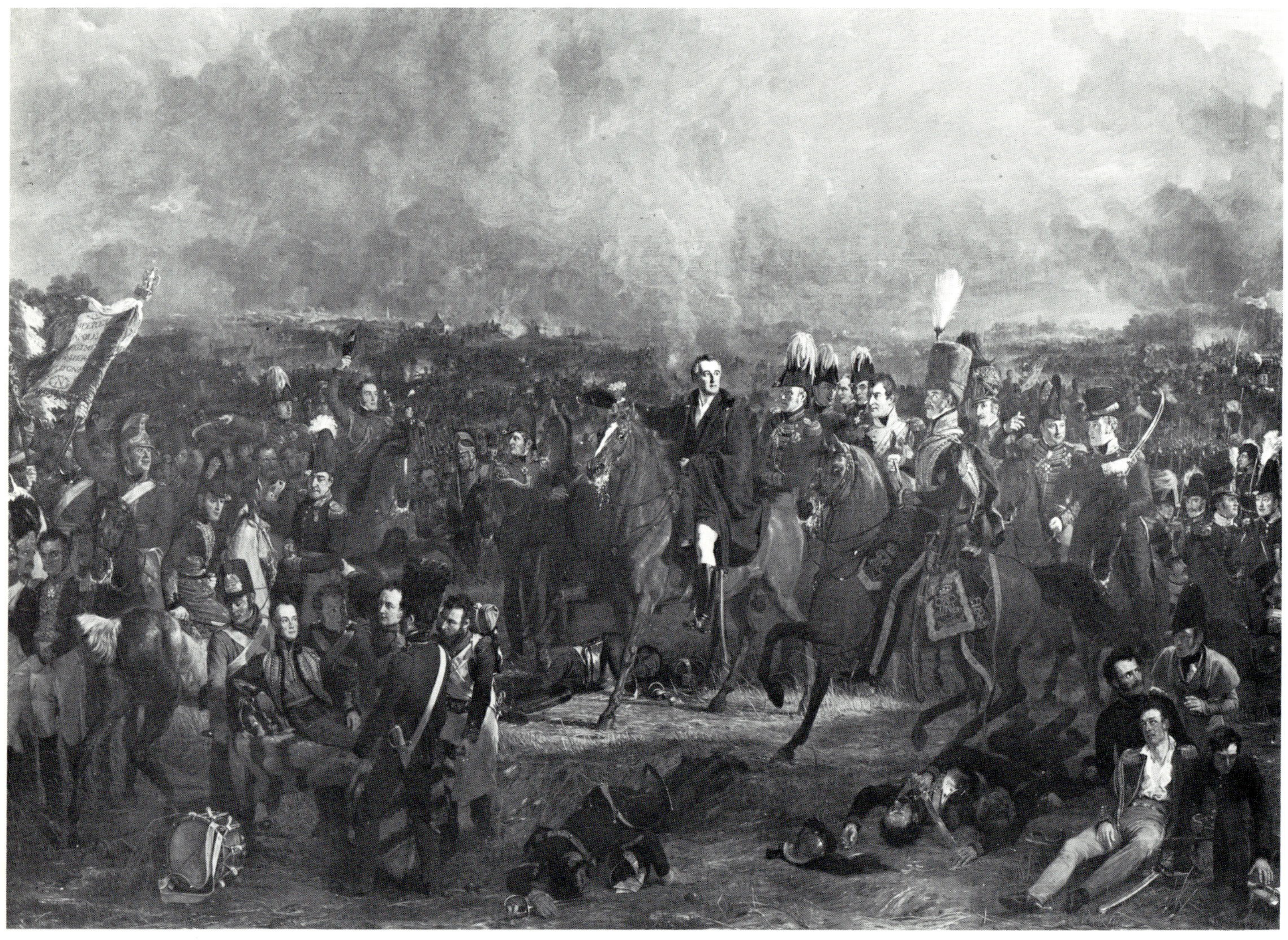

Jan Willem Pieneman (1779-1853) *The Napoleonic Wars inspired artists of many countries; in Holland the most notable example was Jan Willem Pieneman. This painting of "The Battle of Waterloo" is 18 feet high and 27 feet wide. The Prince of Orange is being carried wounded from the field while the equestrian Wellington dominates the scene. Pieneman paid three separate visits to London to ensure the accuracy of his portraits while he was painting the picture. It was an immense success and exhibited in Ghent, Brussels and London.* Photograph courtesy of the Rijksmuseum, Amsterdam.

more temperament than education, more common sense than intuition and that he was entirely devoid of the pictorial sense which was never lacking in the seventeenth century. But that he possessed a real artist's temperament is proved by his often rough, but always forcible portraits; and, although far from being a quick draughtsman, he had a good idea of the construction of a head, which enabled him to turn out his portraits rapidly enough. He died in 1853.

The Battle of Waterloo shows none of those passions, of that hatred born of impotence, which urged the Allies forward on that summer's day. The figures of the Duke of Wellington and the other persons in the foreground are good portraits; but neither their attitude nor their action conveys the impression that a fierce and critical contest is taking place. Nor has Pieneman's drawing the suppleness necessary to express a great moment. And yet he possessed what the born artist who, with scanty means, conquers for himself a place in a barren period must needs possess: he had energy and influenced his times. Jozef Israëls has said of him that he was a genius who grew up in an inartistic age; and it was not his fault if the times in which he lived prevented him from developing himself. In a society in a state of transformation, where,

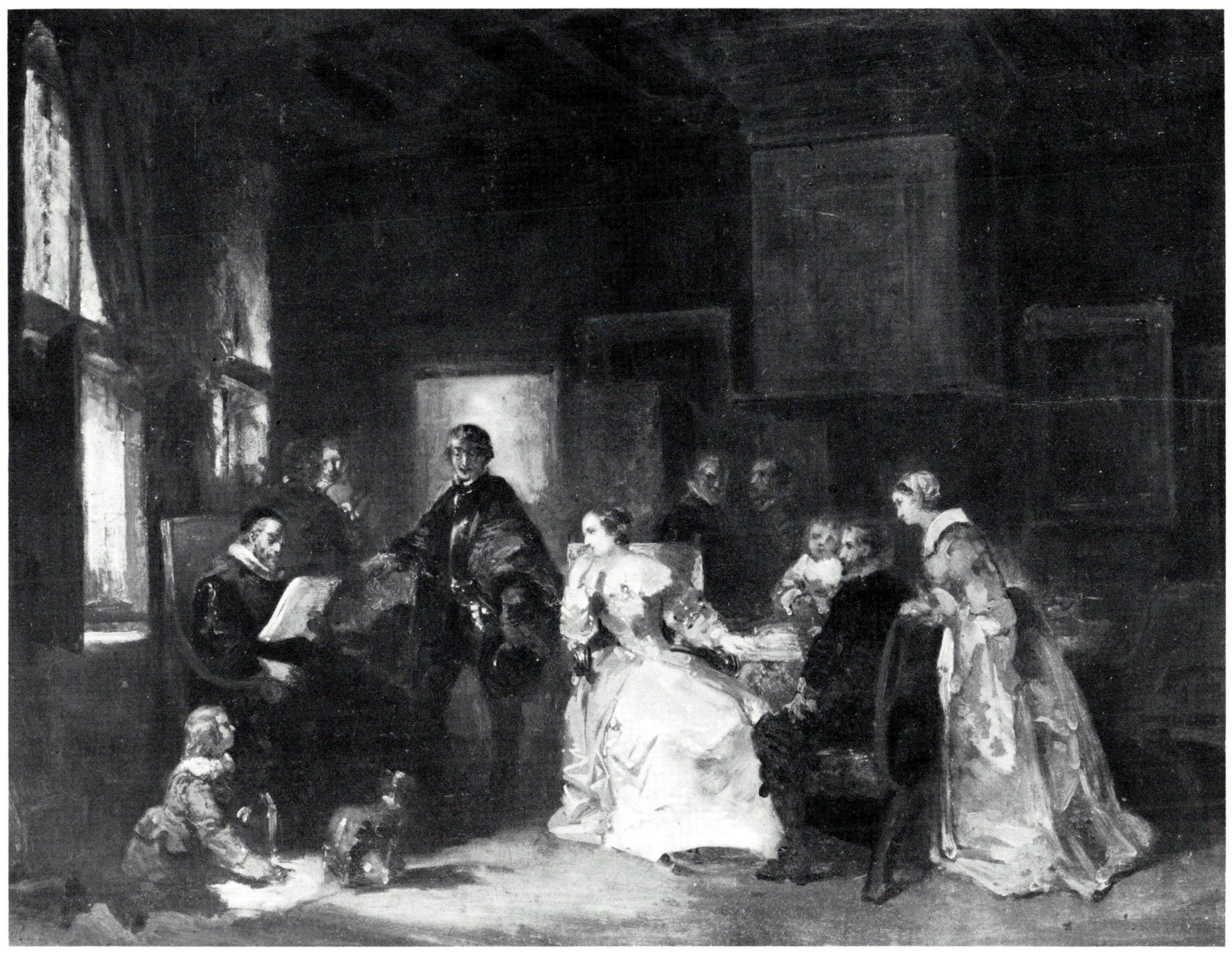

Nicolaas Pieneman (1809-1860) *achieved international fame with his portraits of the Dutch Royal Family. He lived in the age when history painting was high fashion and here he has achieved a charming and relaxed historical scene with William the Silent as its central character (73 x 101.5cms.).* Photograph courtesy of the Rijksmuseum, Amsterdam.

on the one hand, men, proud of their recovered nationality, asked for topical pictures representing the heroic deeds of the day, while on the other hand, a pious tendency held sway and called for religious or kindred subjects strictly confined to the limits of the middle-class virtues, there was no opportunity for the exaltation of painting pure and simple and *l'Art pour l'art* for once became a misplaced maxim.

And then think of the makeshifts with which Pieneman had to content himself. Burdened by an early marriage, he painted his *Quatre-Bras* in a small upper-part in the Nes, where he had to roll up one half of his enormous canvas, crammed with life-size equestrian figures, in order to paint the other half. He must have possessed a certain strength of will, a remarkable power of representation, to complete a work of this kind in circumstances such as these. And yet, though he was honoured in his time and distinguished by his sovereign, though he was socially esteemed and lived in "a stately house on a canal," though one may say of him that he was a great man in a slack time, he will never occupy a place in the ranks of our great painters nor even stand among our "little masters." His chief services to art were rendered

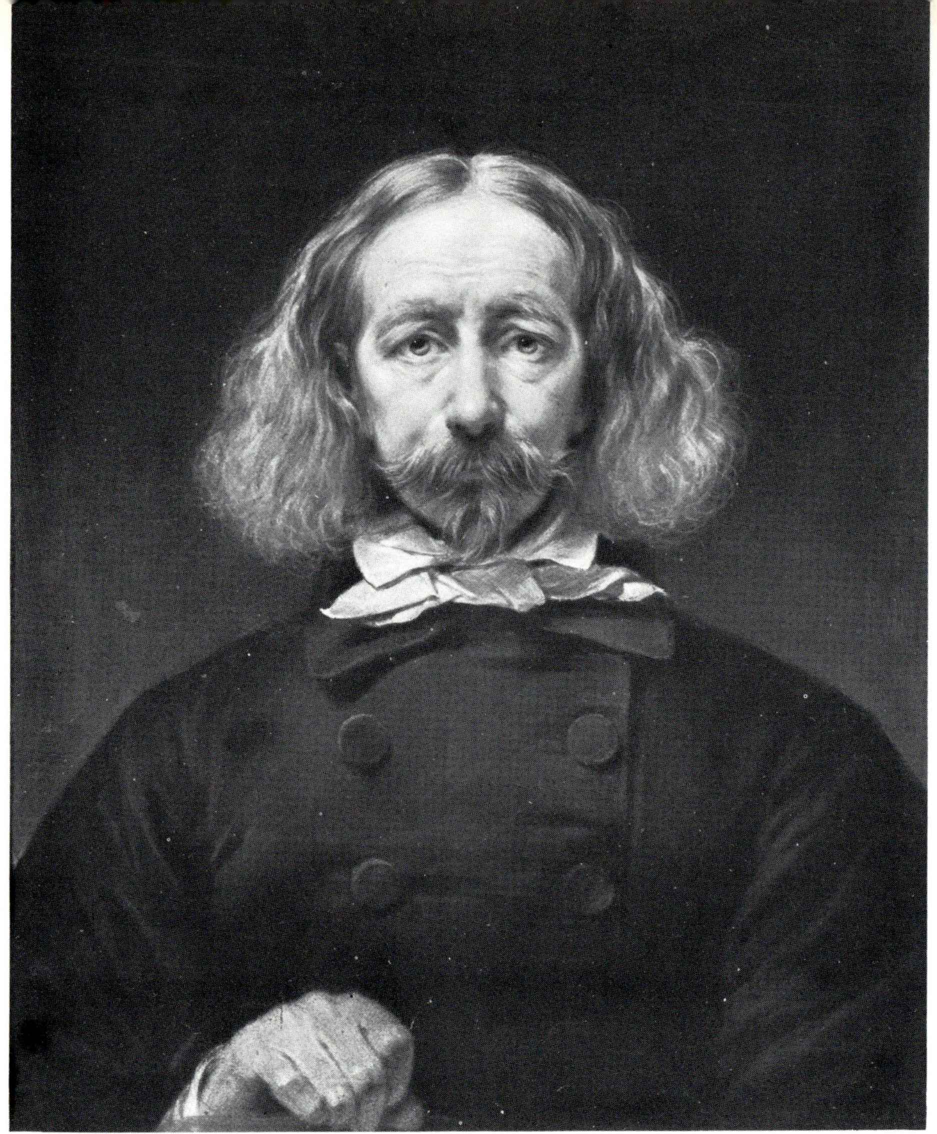

Jean Augustin Daiwaille (1786-1850) *depicts in this self portrait – according to Marius – "the melancholy face of one whose nature was his own worst enemy". (38.5 x 31 cms.).* Photograph courtesy of the Rijksmuseum, Amsterdam.

as director of the Amsterdam Academy. Israëls describes him as an excellent drawing-master, thoroughly acquainted with the mathematics of the nude and unrivalled in the suggestion of an outline with a bit of chalk or charcoal. And it is certain that, as the master of Jozef Israëls, who drew for seven years under his guidance and never speaks of him other than with respect and esteem, he deserves an honourable place in the memory of us all.

Nicolaas Pieneman, his son and pupil, was born at Amersfoort in 1809, died in 1860 and enjoyed – chiefly at the Hague, where he lived – an even greater favour than his father, thanks to his many portraits of the royal family. It is a pure delight to hear Jozef Israëls reply, when asked how the younger Pieneman painted:

"Klaas Pieneman was a courtier; at an exhibition, he used to walk arm in arm with William the Third!"

He had neither his father's temperament nor vigour and, possibly by way of a reaction against the latter's frequent want of polish, he painted in a soapy and feeble style, especially his royal portraits, which are smooth and insipid and devoid of all life. On the other hand, he must not be judged entirely by his royal portraits: the portrait of his father in the Rijksmuseum and a *Head of a Man* in the Municipal Museum of Amsterdam are better, although in these too he misses the naturalness that distinguished his father. And, if he had not that charming *Portrait of a Child* in the Fodor Museum standing to his credit, there would be little to say about him but that he was greatly liked and lived in a fine house in the Hague. This portrait,

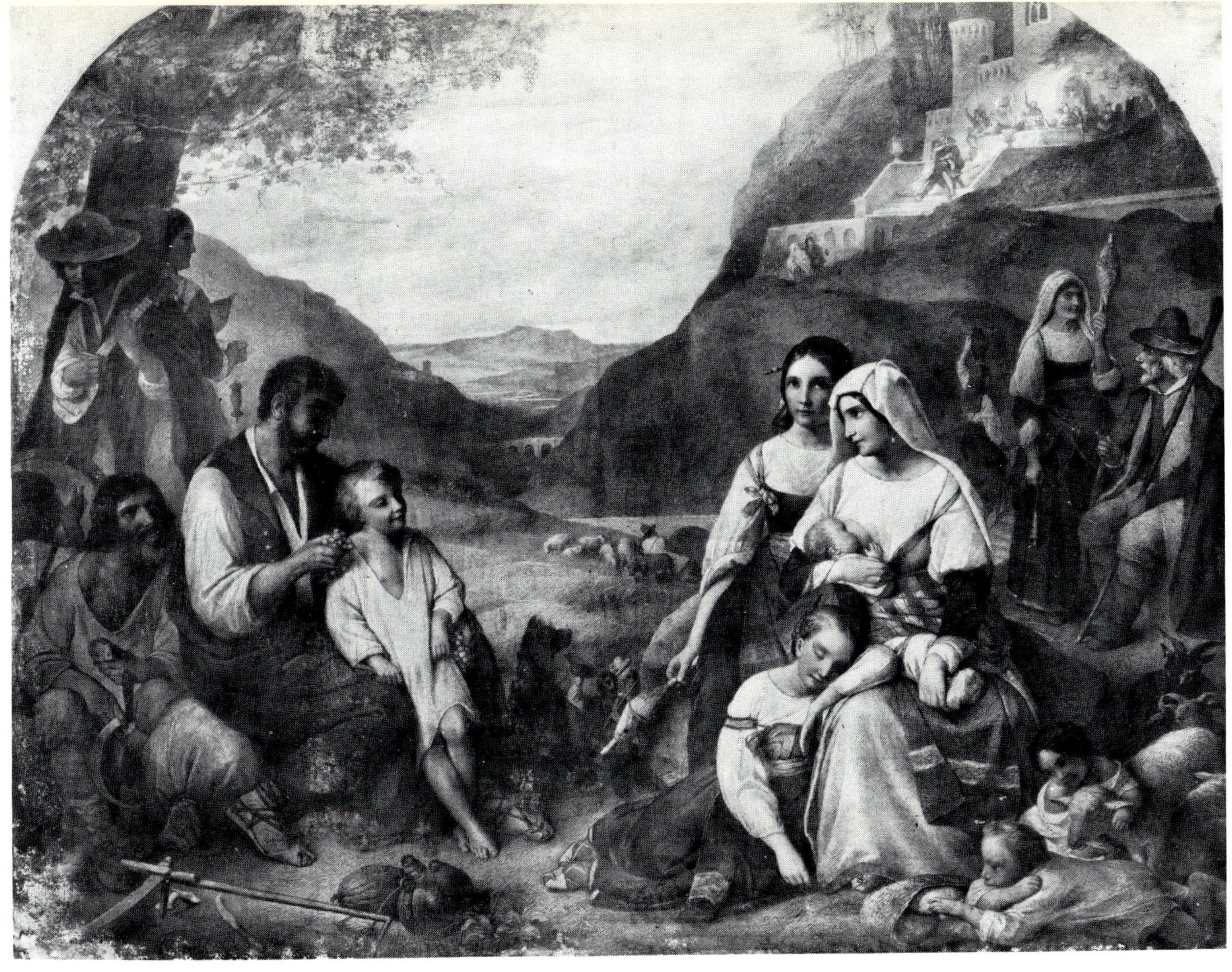

Cornelis Kruseman (1797-1857). *This "Rustic Idyll" by Cornelis Kruseman shows the subversive influence of Rome on the Dutch temperament. He spent three formative years in Italy. The influence of Raphael filtered through that of Overbeck and Nazarene religious painting (high fashion in Rome at the time) can be clearly discerned in this painting (50 x 64ins.).* Photograph courtesy of Sotheby's.

however, places him in a different category and we will gladly forgive him his smooth official portraits for the sake of the great feeling in this little picture.

His contemporaries judged differently. Kramm writes:

"It is a pleasure to me to be able to write a page in the history of art which greatly increases the fame of the Dutch school of painting of our own times. It concerns the brilliant talent of that celebrated painter, Nicolaas Pieneman, who has achieved an European reputation with his many famous master-pieces."

He mentions a whole array of royal presents, of gold snuff-boxes richly adorned with brilliants and enamels, and enumerates an endless series of portraits of King William II, of the Crown-prince, afterwards William III, of the latter's sons the Princes William and Alexander, of Princess Sophie, of the suites of the King and the Crown-prince. Nicolaas Pieneman was the first painter to receive the Order of the Netherlands Lion; and it must be added that he was honoured not only in his own country, but also – or was it his royal models? – in Paris, for, at the International Exhibition of 1855, he was given the Legion of Honour for his life-size portrait of William III, in naval uniform, and of his royal father.

Jean Augustin Daiwaille was born at Cologne in 1786 and, as a child, accompanied his parents to Holland, where he was educated for a painter by Adriaan de Lelie. Although his little genre-pieces met with considerable favour in their time, he was valued by his contemporaries mostly as a painter of portraits distinguished for their breadth of execution and their resemblance to the originals. He became director of the Amsterdam Academy of Plastic Arts and resigned his appointment in order to accompany an agent of the Dutch Trading Company to Brazil. Upon maturer consideration, he abandoned this plan and founded a lithographic establishment. Later, he settled at Rotterdam, where he occupied himself with portrait-painting until his death in 1850.

There is a certain want of definiteness about this short biography by Immerzeel and it is repeated in the account of Daiwaille's pupil, Cornelis Kruseman, who is said to have learnt his broad brushwork from Hodges, whereas Daiwaille, who was never satisfied with his work and never succeeded in finishing it, is supposed to have taught him only how not to paint. However, it often happens that later generations pass a different judgment; and many will discover finer qualities in the hesitations of this painter and pastellist than in the work of his over-praised pupil. Daiwaille's *Portrait of Himself* at the Rijksmuseum confirms the first impression: it shows us the melancholy face of one whose nature was his own worst enemy. The modernity of the analysis is astonishing in the pale-blue eyes; and the whole face is painted with a sincerity which none but a sensitive character would offer. The *Portrait of Himself* at Boymans' Museum is a more pleasant picture; and the same museum contains his very dainty *Portrait of a Woman,* in pastel. His best portrait, however, is that of H. van Demmeltraadt.

Although Cornelis Kruseman dates back to the end of the eighteenth century (he was born in 1797 and died in 1857), he can hardly be considered a man of Jan Pieneman's generation. Not that the elder Kruseman helped Dutch painting forward: on the contrary, while Pieneman preserved, if not the artistic culture, at least the simplicity of the eighteenth century, Kruseman, endowed with less temperament, a greater desire for refinement and less vigour, displayed a hankering after more pronounced forms and, in the absence of a natural gift of colour, employed hard tones for his biblical or Italian subjects and, in general, turned the art of painting into an uncouth classicism.

Meanwhile, it appears that Kruseman showed a decided aptitude for painting at a very early age; anyway, in 1819, he made a great success at an exhibition at the Hague with a picture representing a blind beggar, lighted by a paper lantern, whose appearance had always impressed him as he went down the Spui of an evening. People thought that they had found a Dou, a Schalcken Redivivus; and he received many orders for candle-light effects, all of which he refused, because it was not his object in life to imitate candle-light and he took no pleasure in such things. He strove to express the loftier matters in human nature and he felt offended that it had not been recognized at once that he had painted this picture only because of the venerable head of the beggar. He aimed further than the Dutch genre-painters, whose manner he considered insignificant and undignified. This was the time when David was decking out his heroes in the form and garb of antiquity; it was also the time when Italy was regarded as the land of promise, as the cradle of art and when Raphael's smooth outlines were held to possess a distinction by comparison with which Rembrandt was often considered vulgar: an opinion shared by some of the younger literary men until as late as 1880.

In 1821, Kruseman went *via* Paris to Italy, stayed three years in Rome and came back confirmed in his predilections. He began by painting biblical subjects and Roman peasants, the latter supplying him with the classical models which he had sought in vain in his own country. Nevertheless, he sacrificed himself in his turn to the national enthusiasm which had made the elder Pieneman the history-painter of Quatre-Bras and Waterloo and which drove Kruseman to paint a later episode: *H.R.H. the Prince of Orange at the moment when his horse was wounded at Bauterzen, 12 August 1831,* a picture which, like Pieneman's, may be looked upon as a sort of continuation of the *doelen-* or corporation-pieces. But this interlude had no influence upon the remainder of his work. The culture which he had acquired during his stay in Paris and his Italian journey had gradually alienated him from his own nationality. A long stay in Italy has never proved other than detrimental to any of our painters. It simply meant that they returned home seeing things from a point of view quite at variance with our national feeling. Ecclesiastical art brought into a Protestant country by a Protestant Dutchman must needs become theatrical. And in technique also Kruseman was doomed to fall short; for, though his ideas were formed upon the Italian masters of the Renaissance and upon Raphael in particular, he lacked the feeling and the technical knowledge necessary to emulate the peculiar qualities of those masters. All that we can say, therefore, is that Kruseman knew how, at a given moment, to give to a certain public exactly what it demanded, namely, an ideal conception of biblical figures, devoid of sensual charm or passion. And the result was that, although theologians wrote in indignant terms to protest that this great man was indulging in anachronism in his

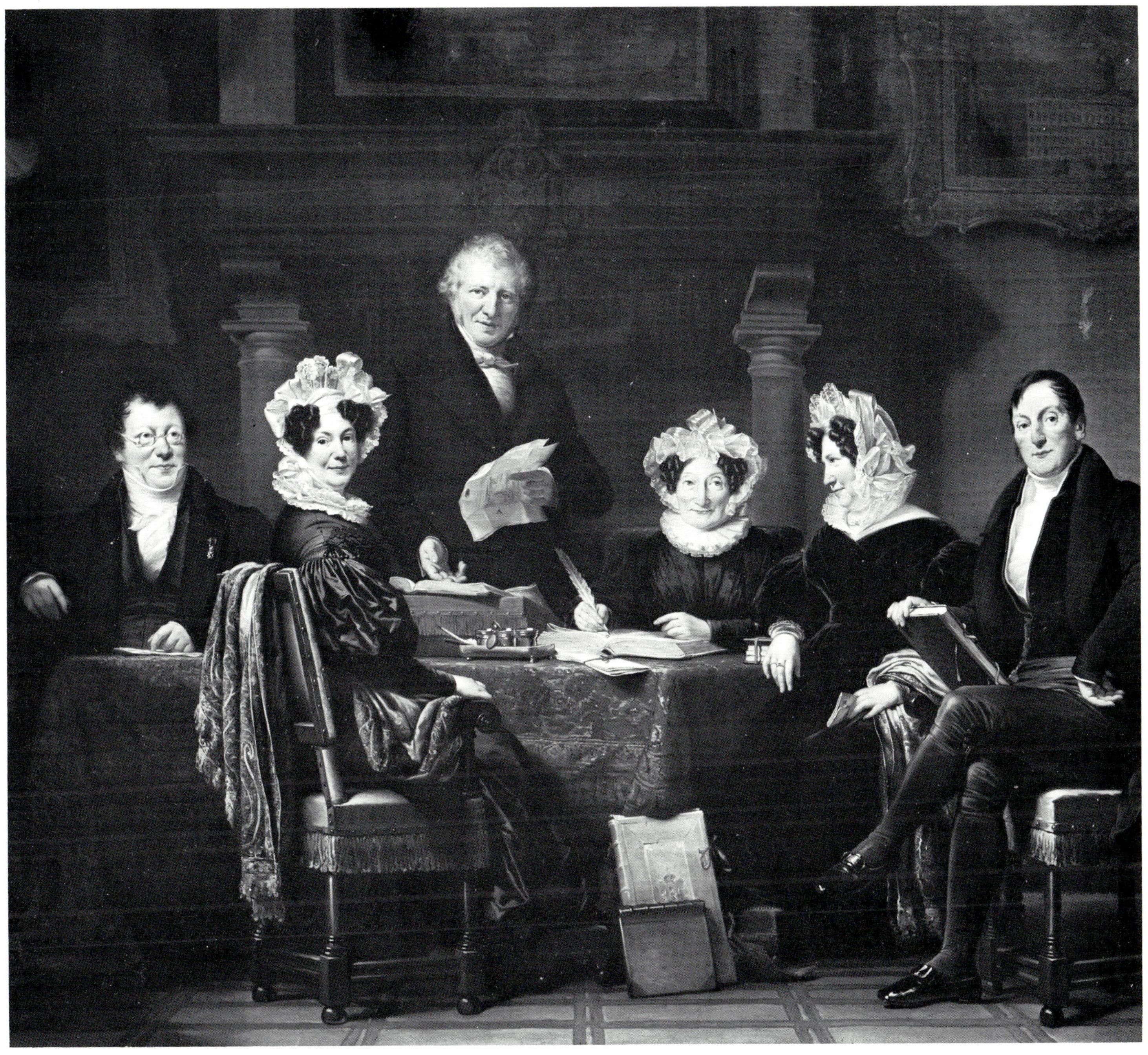

Jan Adam Kruseman (1804-1862) *was greatly valued as a portrait painter and director of the Amsterdam Academy. He had full scope to demonstrate this limited talent in this group portrait of the "Governors of the Amsterdam Leper Colony". (255 x 285cms.)* Photograph courtesy of the Rijksmuseum, Amsterdam.

biblical subjects and in spite of virulent criticism, he enjoyed a fame so universal as to exceed that ever known by Jozef Israëls, Jacob Maris, or even by Hendrik Willem Mesdag, who was so much more easily understood outside his own painting-room than either of the others.

Nor can this be called unnatural. The pictorial art of the Pienemans, of the Krusemans and, in particular, of Cornelis Kruseman was a direct echo of their time. As an historical painter in a period of newly-awakened national consciousness, Pieneman was the right man in the right place and he owes his reputation to his delineation of Quatre-Bras and the battle of Waterloo, which set the seal upon our liberty and renewed our compact with the House of Orange, to which the episode of the wounded Crown-prince lent an emotional side.

Kruseman, who had begun with a similar subject, devoted himself later on, after the peace had restored the ancestral Calvinism in a stricter form, mainly to the painting of Bible subjects, which were greatly admired for their "idealistic conception," to use the then prevailing phrase so popular in pious circles:

"Probably no people has at any time been more devoted to home-reading of an edifying character than our Protestant fellow-countrymen," says A.C. Kruseman in his *History of the Book-trade.*

Cornelis Kruseman's phlegmatic ideas were in the taste of the day: any passion would have disturbed the tranquillity of a view of life which demanded that everything should be gentle, pious and noble. The seventeenth-century paintings and prints, selected by a few, were thought low and common compared with the engravings published in the elegant almanacks of those days and accompanied by letterpress by serious authors. And the scenes of Italian peasant-life, the Neapolitan women, the *pifferari,* with their dark features, their sharp outlines against a blue sky, had what was known as a certain "nobility" of line which formed a great contrast with the vulgar Dutch people, the vulgar old-Dutch paintings, and which pleased the ladies.

And yet it was not only the women who formed the ranks of Kruseman's worshippers; these included practically everybody: the King, the Queen and, more, the painters. In connection with his *St. John the Baptist,* a painting which he had executed for the most part during his second stay in Rome, the Hague artists united to offer him a lasting memorial of the admiration with which they were seized at the contemplation of that work. This testimonial took the form of a silver cup, with cover and dish, beautifully designed and chased in the style of the sixteenth century and engraved with a suitable inscription in rhyme immortalizing the homage paid by the Dutch school to Kruseman after seeing his *St. John,* while a vellum document with Gothic illuminations spoke in well-chosen words of the painter's imperishable fame.

Public favour is fickle. The lasting duration which the inscription prophesied was fulfilled neither figuratively nor literally. Most of his great works no longer exist. Thanks to his habit of continual repainting — Kruseman was not easily pleased with himself — and of constant treatment with some siccative or other, a process to which perhaps he did not give enough care, it happened that the paint, which was never quite dry under the surface, began to sink, so that the upper portion became unrecognizable, and, while the hands of the Baptist of the picture, at that time in the collection of King William II, had dropped to the ground, the head hung where the hands should be and great lumps of paint were heaped up at the bottom against the frame. The case is not without parallel: the same thing is told of English painters insufficiently acquainted with the secrets of their craft. Only a few of Kruseman's pictures escaped this fate, including the four religious paintings in Mrs. Labouchère's *château* at Zeist, his best work; a portrait of *Three Sisters;* and some of his other portraits and smaller pictures.

But the lasting fame that makes us mourn what is lost the more we admire what has been preserved, this also was denied him. His was not an art that excelled in artistic merit or originality of ideas: it owed its existence and its success to the conception of the subject, which, being the product of his time, was bound to die with the spirit of that time.

His chief pupils were Jan Adam Kruseman, his cousin, in whose studio Jozef Israëls was to work in later years, Vintcent, who, although he died young, turned with all his soul towards the romantic movement, Jan Hendrik and Johan Philip Koelman, of whom the latter was to prove the last adherent to classicism, David Bles, whom one would not expect to find here, Herman ten Kate, De Poorter, Elink Sterk and Ehnle.

Jan Adam Kruseman, born at Haarlem in 1804, is best known as a portrait-painter. His portraits were praised as good likenesses and excellent pictures. The fact is that, without showing the artistry of the old Dutchmen, they do impress us by their simplicity and a certain style. Jan Kruseman did not try to complete his education in Italy, but, after the departure of his master, Cornelis, for that country, worked for two years in Brussels under the great David and went from there to Paris, whence he returned in 1825 and made a start with *The Invention of Printing by Laurens Koster.* He also began to paint corporation-pieces for the Baptist community at Haarlem and the Amsterdam Leper Hospital. Although, in his historical and biblical subjects, we are able to recognize a love of pronounced forms showing the influence of David or perhaps even more of Ingres, he possessed neither the vigour nor the tenacity of these painters. On the other hand,

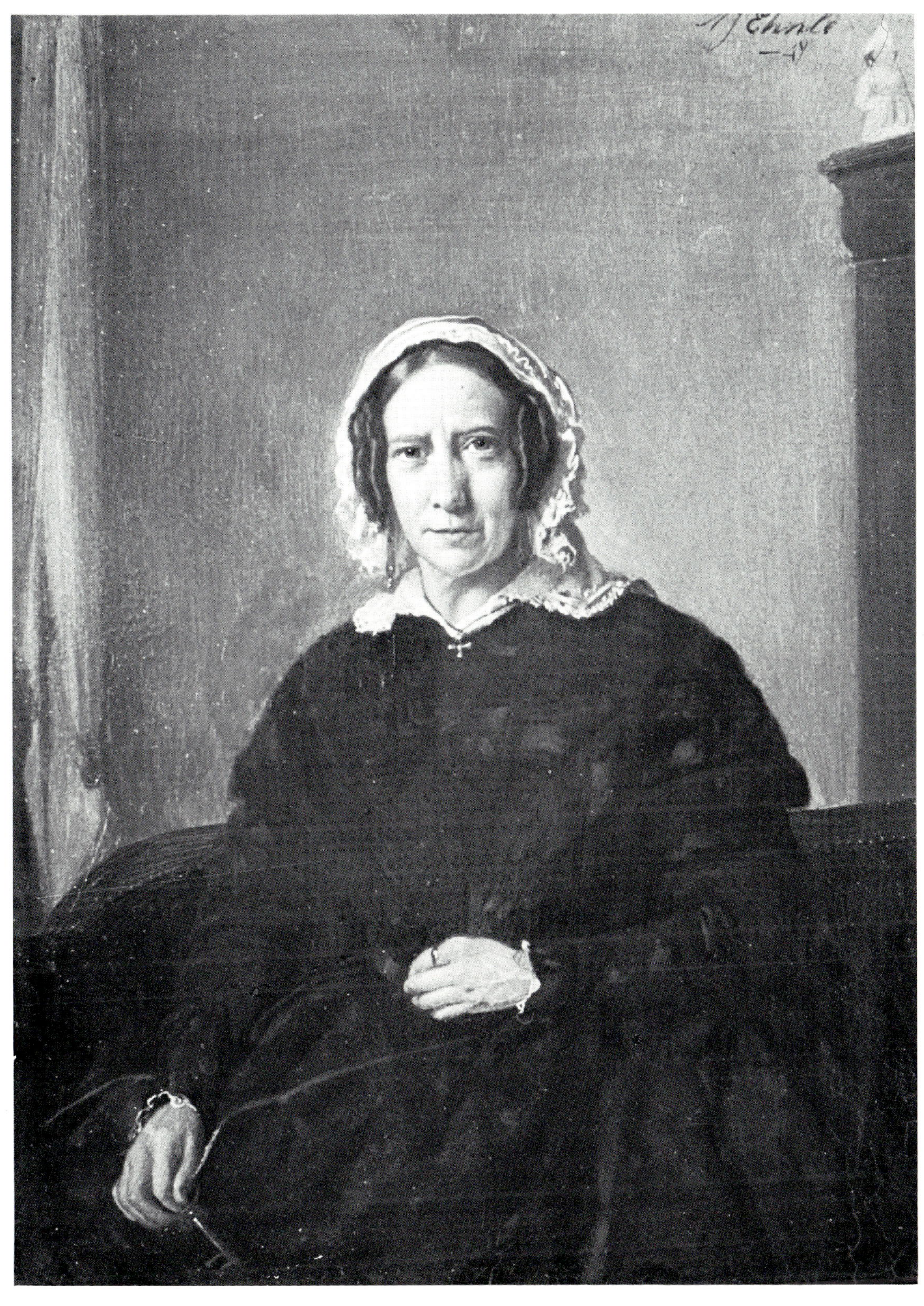

Adrianus Johannes Ehnle (1819-1863) *was one of the pupils of Jan Adam Kruseman. This is a portrait of a lady from his hand (32 x 25½cms.).* Photograph courtesy of the Kröller-Müller Museum, Otterlo.

there was something in his colouring and his modelling that was more free and natural than in the elder Kruseman's and yet not to so great an extent that these pieces can be valued by posterity apart from historical associations. The case is different with his portraits, although in these he is terribly uneven. His simple and natural portrait of Adriaan van der Hoop, his *Portrait of Himself* in the museum at Haarlem, conceived in the style of Ingres, and a portrait of a more pictorial character exhibited under his name in the same gallery might have been painted by three different artists.

He had a great name as a painter and was especially valued as a portrait-painter, in which capacity, according to his contemporaries, he made thirty thousand guilders a year. He led an excellent life in Amsterdam, was a jolly companion, kind to his brother-artists, helping them when he could, and later, as director of the Academy, a zealous teacher. Together with Tétar van Elven, he founded the society known as Arti et Amicitæ and, with it, the Artists' Widows and Orphans Fund. He died in 1862.

The best-known of his biblical subjects is *The Widow's Mite,* popularized through Steelink's engraving. De Genestet wrote a poem on it and the grave conception – we do not know the painting itself – and popular subject made it a favourite ornament for the sitting-room. He had as little romanticism in him as the elder Kruseman; only his ideas were a little less uncouth, less prejudiced, less hard, though quite as passionless.

Of all Cornelis Kruseman's pupils, the Koelmans alone remained faithful to the principles which their teacher proclaimed. Johan Philip Koelman (1818–1893) stood like a solitary on the ruins of classicism and became the more fanatical the more he saw his fellow-students and his own pupils departing in another direction. Jan Hendrik (1820–1887), the second of the brothers, went straight from Kruseman's studio to Rome and continued to live there till the day of his death. He painted many portraits and was, according to Vosmaer, who knew him in Rome, "a great artistic expert, a philosophical spirit, a most important man, yes, the type of a certain sort of artist: practical, experienced and positive in his execution, he is, at the same time, by nature a philosopher, whose deep-felt artistic speculations find utterance in fluent words and thoughts." Jan Daniel (1831–1857), a younger brother, the talented pupil of J.B. Tom the animal-painter, made excellent studies of draught-oxen in the South, went on to paint Dutch pastures with cattle and gave cause to expect that, had be not died at the early age of twenty-six, he might have developed into an independent and accomplished landscape-painter.

Johan Philip was born at the Hague and was brought up to his father's trade as a carpenter. He soon showed a taste for painting, studied under Kruseman and followed the latter to Rome, where he remained for fifteen years, painting, drawing and modelling. On his return to the Hague, he painted Roman scenes, some of them with all the delicacy of a miniaturist. Later, when he succeeded Van den Berg at the Academy, he was more of a sculptor and an architect than a painter. Vosmaer calls his draughtsmanship severe. In these latter days, we should be inclined rather to call it unfeeling, at once hard and slack. At a time of more widespread culture, his lack of depth and originality would have been more apparent. He had nothing whatever in common with our seventeenth-century masters, who above all were good painters, as were the Hague landscape-painters after them. But, notwithstanding his theories, notwithstanding the complete set of thoughts, principles and opinions which he had acquired from the Italian masters, Koelman was great enough, as a teacher, to inspire independent pupils.

The doom of classicism had come. No words, no theories are able to impede the progress of imperious life or to arrest the spirit of the age. Our country, in its turn, underwent the influence of the romantic movement, which came to us *via* Belgium and showed itself first in literature. The painters followed in the wake of the poets and novelists. But it was essentially a foreign movement and, therefore, imperfect in its manifestations.

Henri Beyle, in his *Histoire de la peinture en Italie,* says that what our soul asks of art is the portrayal of the passions and not of deeds provoked by the passions. And it was just this passion, which, in literature, was destined not to flame up until after 1870, that these natures were unable to render, either because they were over-polished by education or because they considered it incompatible with the calm belief of the time. Even the religious contests, surely the outcome of the most impetuous passion that could take fire in the Netherlands, had become dissolved in a calm, pious, conscientious life.

When all is said, did not all the romanticism of that time, with one or two great exceptions, consist rather

Johan Philip Koelman (1818-1893) *remained faithful to the Classical tradition. Even in this portrait of Johannes van Rossum he has added a classical urn and a distant ruin. (133.5 x 100cms.).* Photograph courtesy of the Haags Gemeentemuseum.

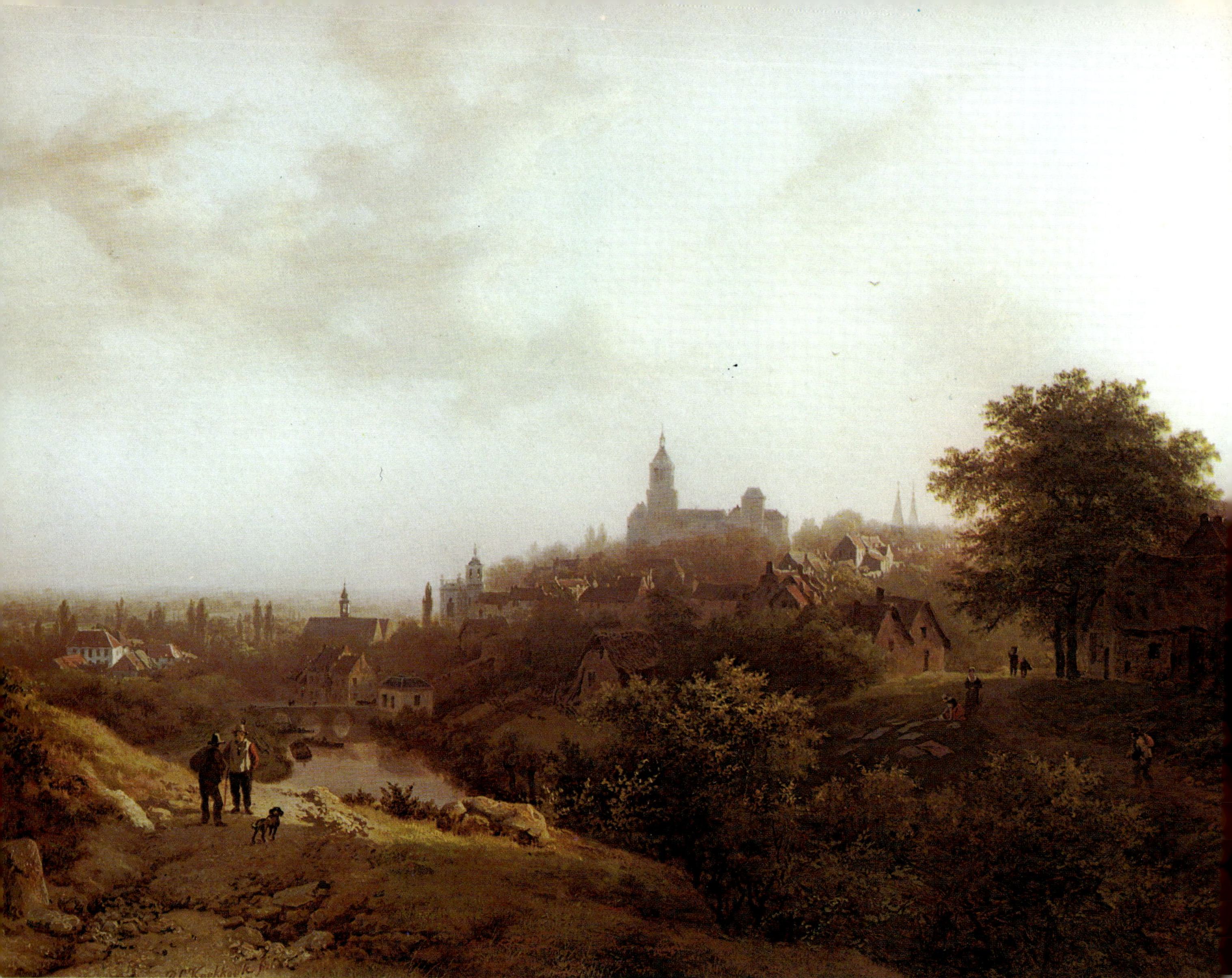

Barend Cornelis Koekkoek (1803-1862). *"View of Cleves with figures in the foreground."* Photograph courtesy of MacConnal-Mason & Son.

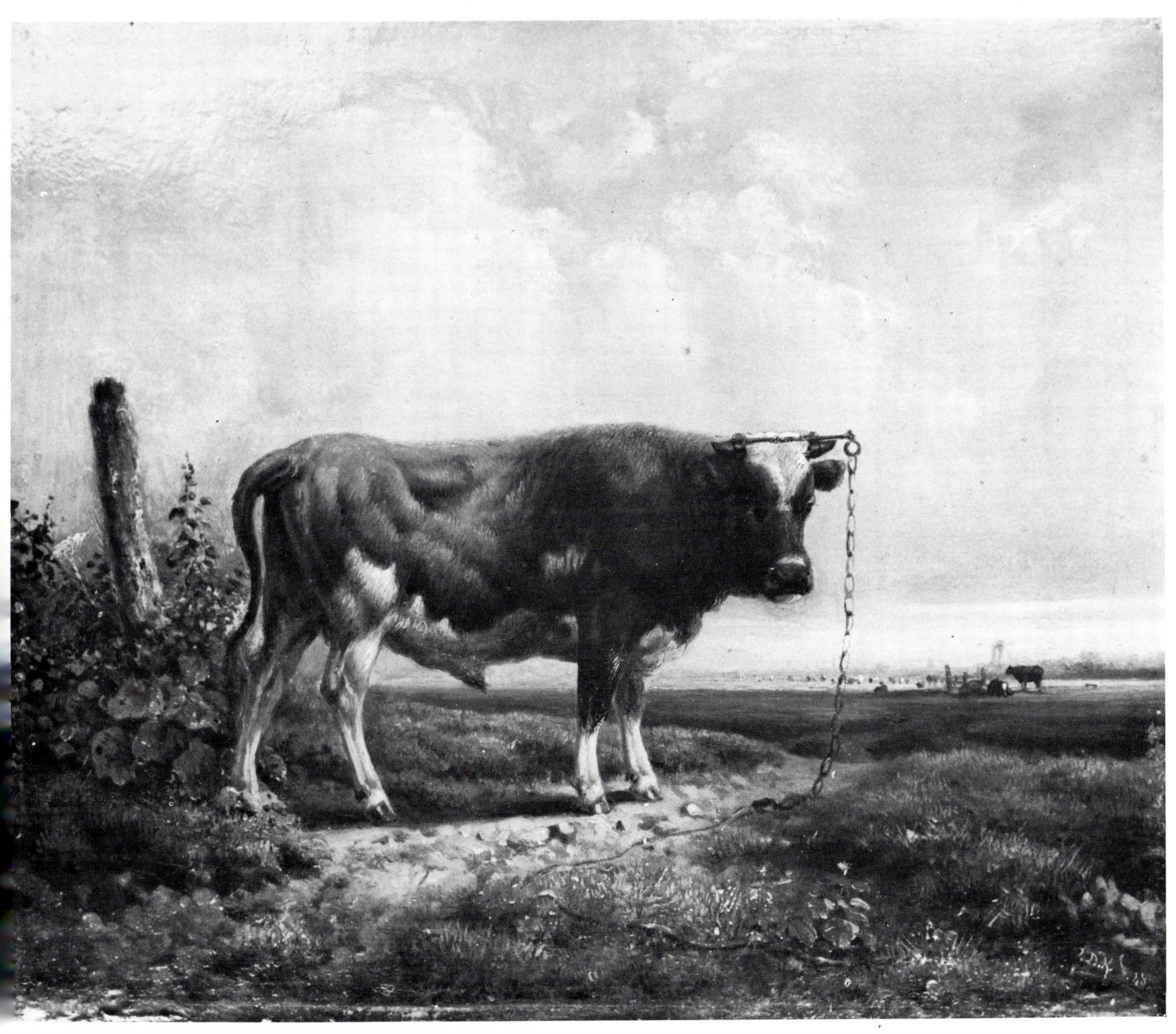

Jan Daniel Koelman (1831-1857) *a pupil of J.B. Tom, the animal painter, was noted for his Dutch pastures with cattle such as this "Bull in a field".* Photograph courtesy of the Haags Gemeentemuseum.

in the painting of deeds provoked by passions than in the portrayal of passion itself? And did not the Dutchmen of that time lack just the inspiring vigour with which a Delacroix translated romanticism into the purely pictorial, while, on the other hand, they lacked the expressive line with which the German painters conveyed the emotional side of romanticism? The passion of the first was to be kindled with us later in the bursts of colour of the Hague school, in the visions of beauty of Matthijs Maris, to blaze most brightly in that not yet fully understood visionary Vincent van Gogh. The views of the second were shared (although the Germans showed more nervous lines) by that Dutch Parisian, Ary Scheffer, the artist in whom the weak, but also the emotional aspect of romanticism found a more than enthusiastic spokesman.

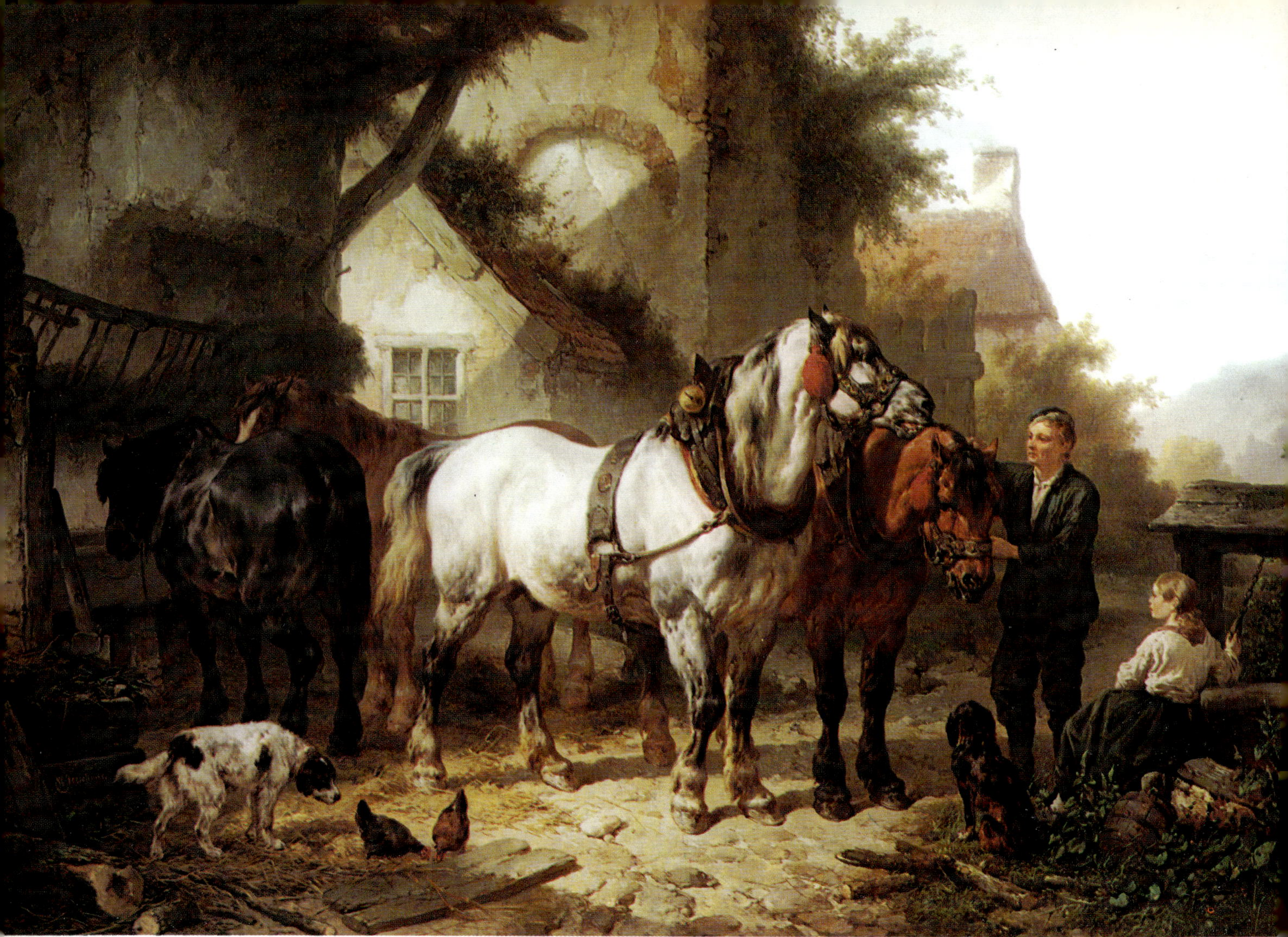

Wouterus Verschuur (1812-1874). *"Farmyard scene with horses and figures." (24 x 34ins.).* Photograph courtesy of Richard Green.

Chapter III

The Romanticists

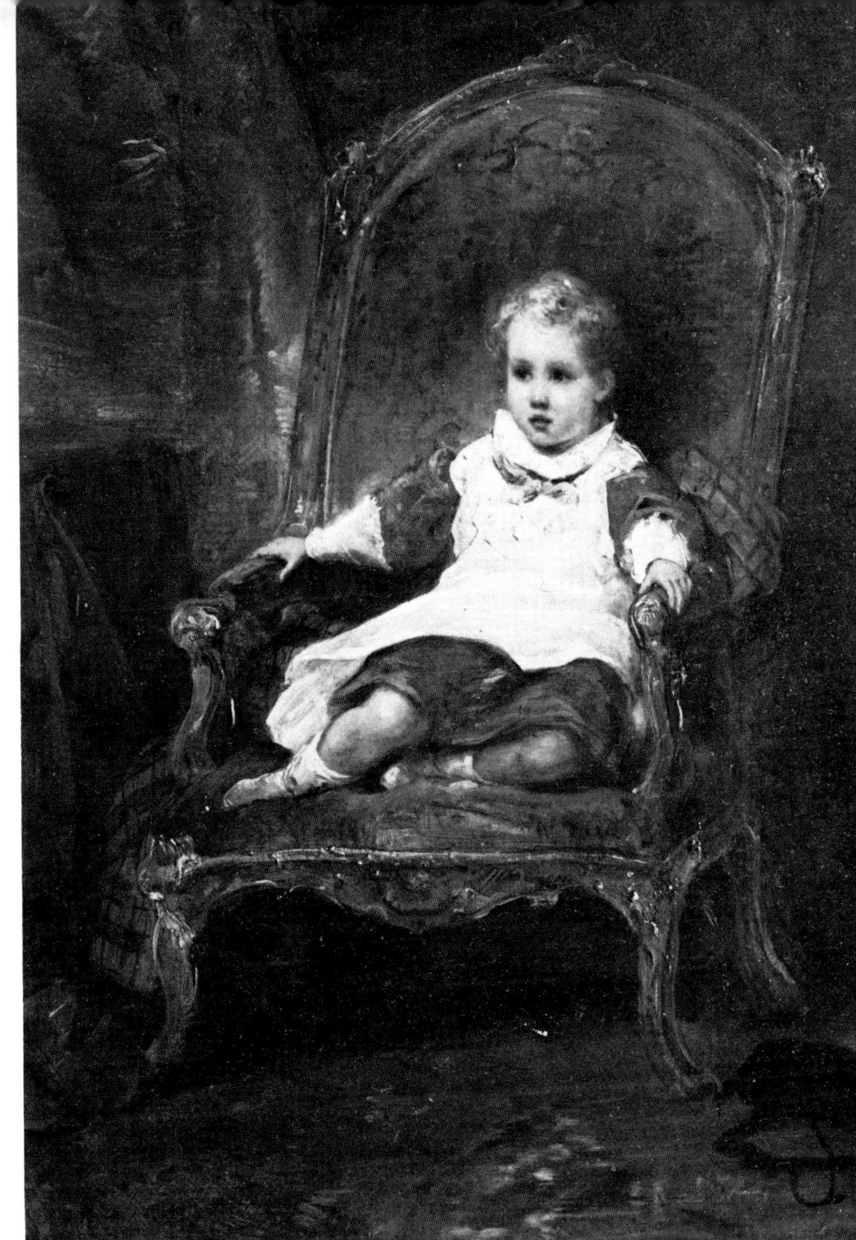

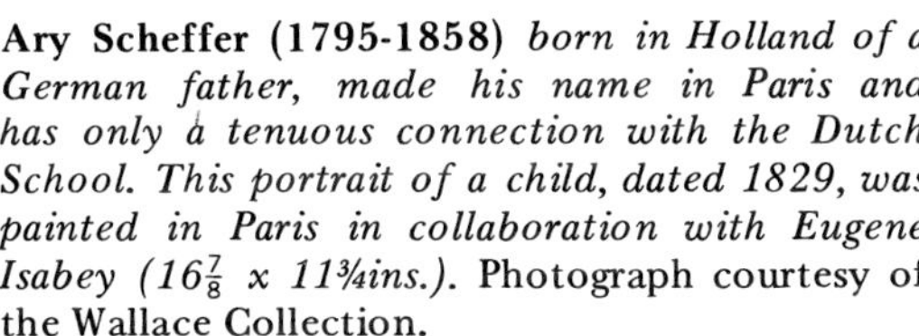

Ary Scheffer (1795-1858) *born in Holland of a German father, made his name in Paris and has only a tenuous connection with the Dutch School. This portrait of a child, dated 1829, was painted in Paris in collaboration with Eugene Isabey (16⅞ x 11¾ins.).* Photograph courtesy of the Wallace Collection.

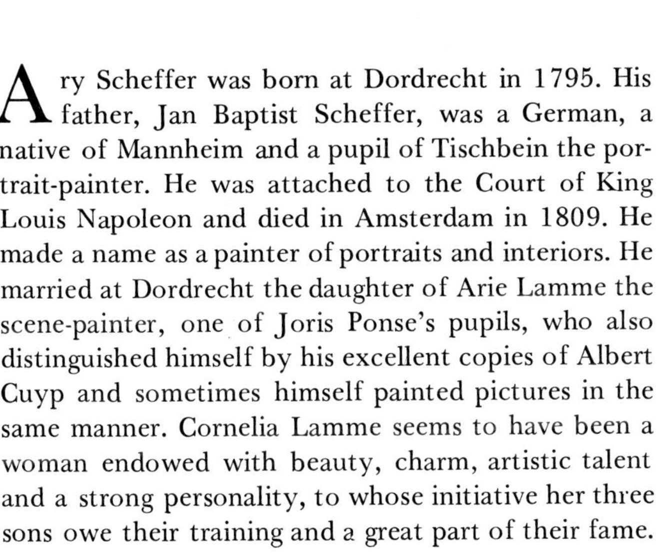

Ary Scheffer was born at Dordrecht in 1795. His father, Jan Baptist Scheffer, was a German, a native of Mannheim and a pupil of Tischbein the portrait-painter. He was attached to the Court of King Louis Napoleon and died in Amsterdam in 1809. He made a name as a painter of portraits and interiors. He married at Dordrecht the daughter of Arie Lamme the scene-painter, one of Joris Ponse's pupils, who also distinguished himself by his excellent copies of Albert Cuyp and sometimes himself painted pictures in the same manner. Cornelia Lamme seems to have been a woman endowed with beauty, charm, artistic talent and a strong personality, to whose initiative her three sons owe their training and a great part of their fame. History, including the history of painting, shows a whole array of mothers who, through their firm belief in their sons' talent, their indefatigable maternal solicitude, their utter self-sacrifice, have smoothed for their sons the difficult road of art. Ary received his first training at his father's hands and, when the latter died, at a time when the art of painting in Holland had sunk very low, Mrs. Scheffer resolved to take her children to Paris, where Ary and Henri could receive a good education. In 1810, the year before their departure, when Ary was in his fifteenth year, he exhibited in Amsterdam a portrait that was ascribed to the brush of a past master in the art. It has been regretted, by Frenchmen as well as by ourselves, that he did not remain in Holland and paint in accordance with the traditions of his own country. But, at that time, when all eyes were turned to Paris, it was only natural that those who could should make for this centre of civilization and refinement. In any case, it was not easy for the unknown Dutchman, with his defective education, to conquer a place in the city of those experts in technique, Ingres, Delacroix and Géricault; and, until he made a name with his *Gretchen at the Spinning-wheel,* his lack of a firm groundwork of knowledge often caused him to be looked upon as an amateur or dilettante painter.

In the meantime, he exhibited, in 1825, a portrait of M. Destuit de Tracy which was approved in every respect and considered a master-piece of draughtsmanship. And, after his *Defence of Missolonghi,* in which he employed the palette of Delacroix, after *The Suliote Women,* in which, while adopting the same colouring, he first displayed the feminine charm of his talent, he exhibited, in 1831, the *Gretchen* aforesaid, one of his best works, regarded by some as his master-piece, a work, at any rate, with which he secured a place of his own in the painting world of Paris. The picture is well known through the reproductions. It was admired for the delicacy of feeling, the expression, the composition and it was considered affecting, as a whole. It was said that no one had interpreted Goethe's Gretchen as Ary Scheffer had done: no painter, no poet, no actress. Heinrich Heine, who wrote his impressions of the Salon of 1831 in the *Allgemeiner Augsburger,* devoted a whole chapter to *Gretchen at the Spinning-wheel* and to its fellow-picture, a *Faust,* which was not so greatly admired by the painters, but which roused Heine's enthusiasm; he called it *eine schöne Menschenruine:*

"One who had never seen any of this artist's work," he wrote, "would be at once struck by a certain manner that speaks from his arrangement of colours. His enemies declare that he paints only with snuff and green soap. I do not know how far they do him an injustice. His brown shadows are often affected and hence miss the Rembrandt effect of light intended. His faces mostly display that fatal colour which has so often made us take a dislike to our own face when, after long sleeplessness, we look at it in those green mirrors which we find in any inn at which the diligence stops in the morning . . . .

"If we look into Scheffer's pictures more closely and longer, we become familiarized with his mannerism, we begin to think the treatment of the whole very poetic and we see that a serene mood peers through these melancholy colours like sunbeams through the clouds . . . .

"Really, Scheffer's Gretchen is indescribable," continues Heine, a little lower down. "She has more mind than face. It is a painted soul. Whenever I went past her, I used involuntarily to say, *'Liebes Kind!'* . . A silent tear runs down the pretty cheek, a dumb tear of melancholy."

The women especially doted on Ary Scheffer, so much so that it became an act of courage to publish any hostile comment on his work. They recognized the heart in the painter and fell into ecstasies over his sensitive and emotional nature. *"Une larme aux yeux ne ment jamais,"* says Alfred de Musset; and the somewhat feminine Scheffer, the man of sentiment, the man grown up in the mutual cult of mother and son, the man who never really knew what it was to be young, the man of melancholy poetic ideas, passionless and devoid of real sorrow, was just the man to draw that tear.

He understood the emotional side of painting; what he lacked was technical knowledge. And yet, notwithstanding his deficiency in that pictorial quality which we Dutch regard as the one and only essential of good painting, notwithstanding the feeble sentiment and often somewhat barren lines of his pictures, this painter of mixed Dutch and German origin, brought up from his childhood under the great French masters of romanticism, has always represented to us an important talent. It is a talent that stands, for the most part, outside the Dutch tradition, even though foreigners are inclined to see a certain striving after Rembrandt effects in the arrangement of the light. And the golden brown that may be so looked upon is no doubt far preferable to the feeble brown medium which one perceives glancing everywhere through the pale colours; and, though this blends best with the pale blues of his Gretchens, it makes the facial colouring seem very *unheimisch.*

When Scheffer came to Holland in 1844 as a famous man, he wrote, after visiting the Mauritshuis:

"I have seen wonderful pictures of the old Dutch school. Meanwhile, I am beginning to have a higher opinion of my own talent . . . . I believe that I have touched a string which the others have never played upon."

Therein lies his merit.

The two large pictures in Boymans' Museum, *Count*

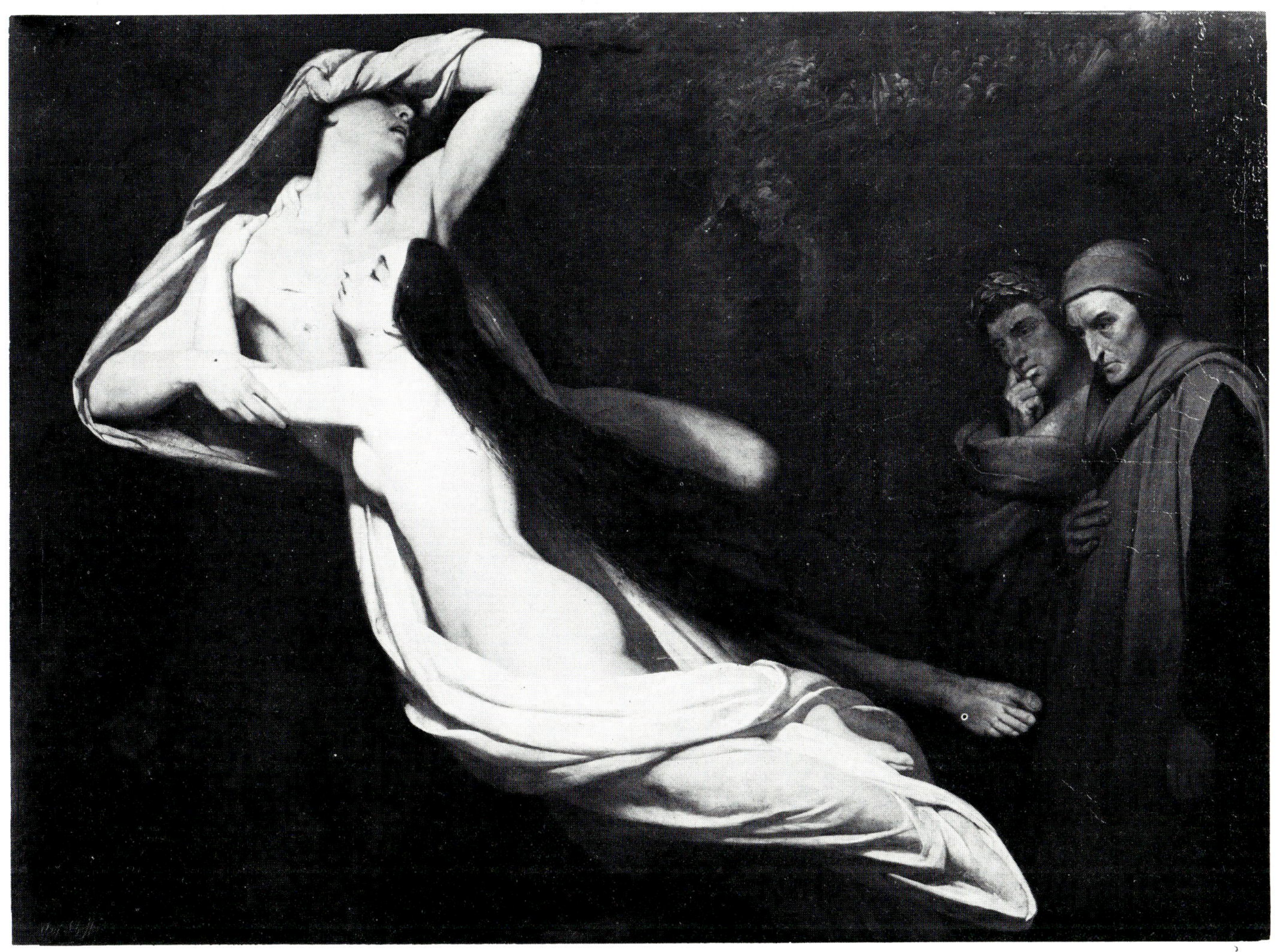

Ary Scheffer's *"Paolo and Francesca" was considered in Marius' time as his masterpiece – by those who could still stomach the Romantic movement. It depicts Dante's vision of the fate of the lovers (Inferno Book V) and dates from 1835. (66¾ x 93¾ins.).* **Photograph courtesy of the Wallace Collection.**

Eberhard of Wurtemberg cutting the Table-cloth between himself and his Son and *Count Eberhard by the dead Body of his Son,* life-size subjects taken from Uhland's ballad, are painted under Dutch influence in the matter of colour; but this causes us to miss the atmosphere all the more. Scheffer was more powerful in pictures which he painted from nature, such as the portrait of Reynolds the engraver, in the Dordrecht Museum, which, with its fluently-painted design, seems inspired by the English painters. Towards the end of his life, in painting his biblical subjects he underwent the influence of the Italian masters, which produced the more vigorous colour-scheme and the more positive, although still very sensitive conception of the *Christ bearing the Cross* at Dordrecht.

To many and also to those Dutch painters who are still able to take account of the works of the romantic movement his *Paolo and Francesca* is his master-piece. The well-known engraving does not do justice to this picture, whose value consists in the vigour of the diagonal line by which the painter lets the figures soar on high. It is well painted and is not so shadowless as his *Gretchen at the Fountain* which, like the *Paolo and Francesca,* is in the Wallace collection and which, in the arrangement of its lines, suggests a cartoon by Overbeck.

The sensitiveness of Scheffer's character is easily perceived in his work. But in daily life he was so gentle that he could not endure to see a cloud or a wrinkle on the faces of those who were with him.

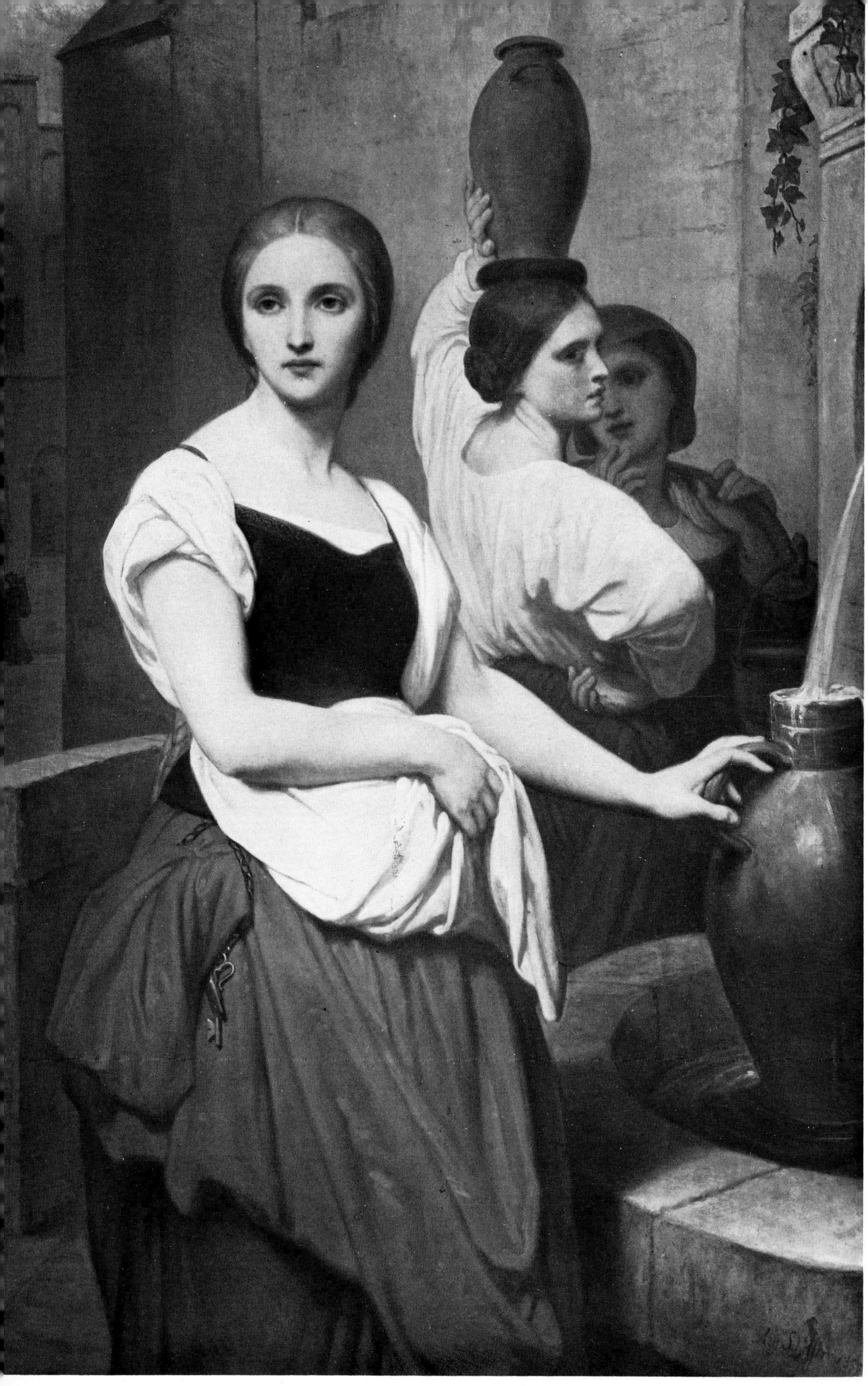

Scheffer's *"Gretchen of the Fountain" of 1858 is a subject taken from Goethe's Faust. The style as well as subject is very German in flavour. ($64\frac{1}{8}$ x 40½ ins.).* Photograph cour tesy of the Wallace Collection.

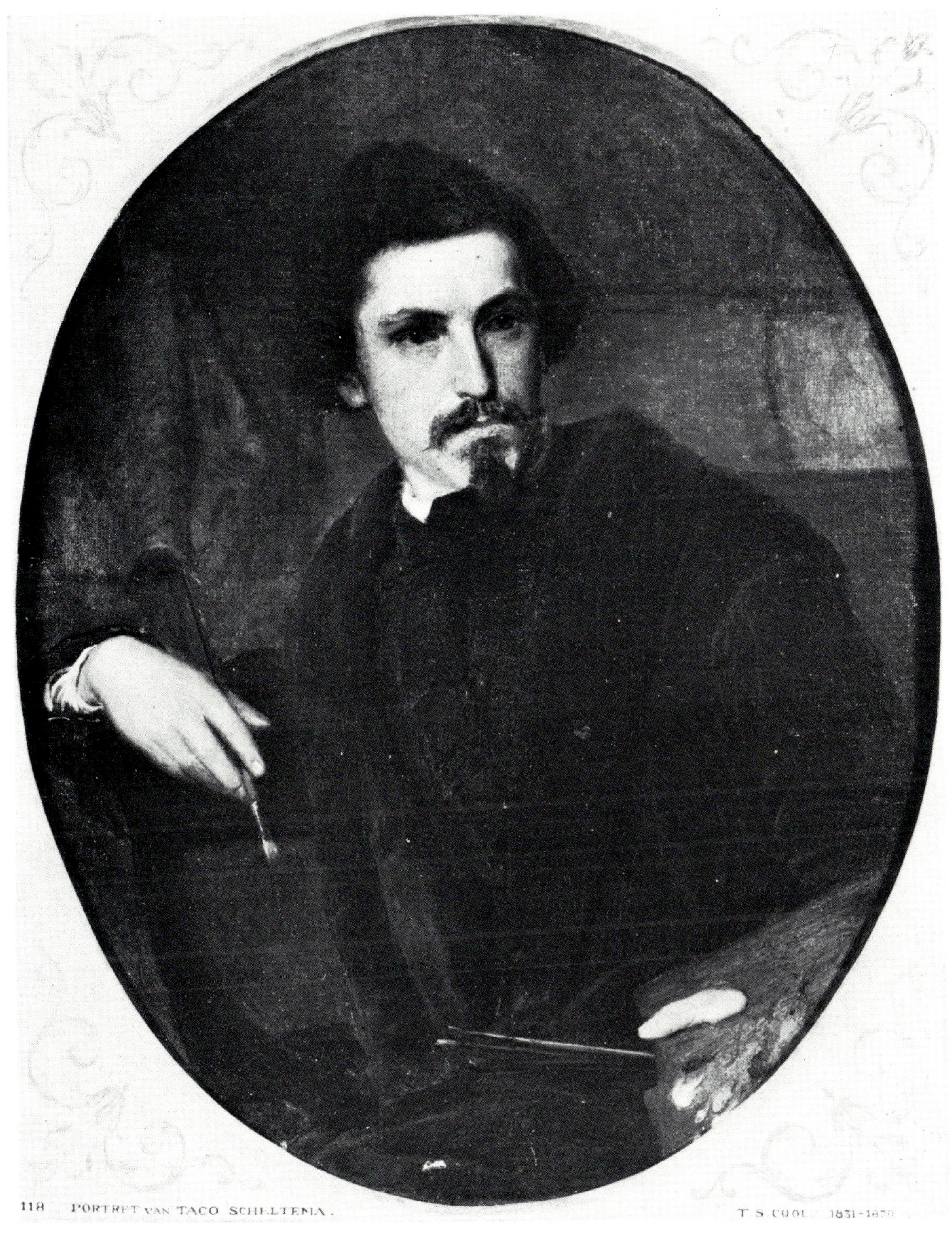

Thomas Simon Cool (1831-1870) *after flirting with romantic history painting reverted to old Dutch interiors and portraits. This portrait is of Taco Scheltema (40.5 x 33.5cms.).* Photograph courtesy of the Haags Gemeentemuseum.

Many abused this quality of his, so that he was forced to work ever harder in order to satisfy the many demands upon him. His benevolence knew no bounds nor did he ever spare pains to assure his mother's comfort.

His studio was difficult of entrance. Mrs. Grote, who is not always to be trusted in her remarks upon his work, tells how he refused admission to almost everybody. Still, he sometimes yielded to the prayers of his numberless admirers of the other sex. Then, on a Sunday morning, everything would be prepared; the visitors entered with hushed voices, as into a church; an organ played in the distance . . . . but the painter himself, meanwhile, was riding his horse in the Bois!

Ary Scheffer died at Argenteuil in 1858. His brother Henri, who was also a pupil of Guérin's, was thought by some to be the better painter, although he achieved nothing like the same celebrity. His *Charlotte Corday,* an excellent painting, in the Luxembourg, was copied there no fewer than twelve hundred times before the year 1849. There is a *Lying-in* of his at Boymans' Museum. More in Ary's style is his *Joan of Arc* in the historical collection at Versailles; but he excelled most of all in portrait-painting. Ernest Renan married his daughter.

Generally speaking, Ary Scheffer exercised no great influence upon the Dutchmen of his time: the strongest of them avoided his influence rather than fall under it. Nevertheless, it may be said that the same emotionalism that characterizes the work of Ary Scheffer is repeated sporadically, in other forms, in the painting of a later date, including the art of our own country. And, although the figure of the great Dutch master, Jozef Israëls, is too vigorous to allow us a comparison, still it was his same seeking for poetry, in another domain, that made Duranty, the French critic, say of his *Alone in the World* that it was painted *d'ombre et de douleur.* And do we not sometimes find moments in Toorop which Scheffer, had his line been firmer, would have loved to paint? And, generally speaking, the younger generation of painters often seems to exhibit a reaction against a landscape which it considers not sufficiently thoughtful or, rather, not sufficiently literary.

Thomas Simon Cool, born at the Hague in 1831, was an exponent of a more vigorous romanticism. In 1853, he painted his *Atala,* with its life-size figures, a bold feat for a youth of two and twenty; in 1859, his *Last of the Abencerrages.* Standing before the Chactas in the former picture at the Hague Museum, we find it difficult to imagine what the painter could have seen in this subject. And yet, though we may now consider it an unattractive picture, it was described in its time as a promising work by a young painter and was thought much of in Paris also. And, even now, notwithstanding the emptiness of the composition and the harshness of the colouring and the workmanship, it shows signs of conviction. Later, his art turned in a more national direction: he took to painting portraits and intimate scenes of Dutch life. But he was never certain of himself, never satisfied with himself. Towards the end of a very short life, he became drawing-master at the Military Academy, where he did well and was held in high account. He died, suddenly, in 1870.

Another and even shorter-lived artist, Lodewijk Anthony Vintcent (1812-1842), never turned his back upon romanticism, in which lay all his strength and all his weakness. He worked first under B.J. van Hove and later under Cornelis Kruseman. He excelled in romantic little genre-pieces: Savoyards, with eyes of exaggerated size, and the like. His master-piece is said to be *The City Apothecary,* which was painted in the cholera year and represents a crowd of sick and poor waiting for medicines. The grouping of the figures is lifelike: two dogs are fighting for a bone in the foreground; round the corner, in the distance, in a street drawn in fine outline, is a hearse. They say that Vintcent was slightly colour-blind – he confused red and green – and that this defect was not apparent in the grey-brown tones of this particular picture, which harmonized so well with the subject. Still, these genre-pieces do not make the romanticist. It was rather the feeling, the combination, the conception, the gruesomeness, as in the case again of his illustrations to *Macbeth,* that gave the necessary suggestiveness. And yet we cannot believe, when we contemplate the false and sentimental feeling displayed in these Savoyards with or without marmots or mouse-traps, that, even if he had lived, the young painter would easily have overcome this romantic condition of soul.

The Rotterdam history-painters, Willem Hendrik Schmidt and Arnold Spoel, were of much more importance, in their day, than Vintcent. The former was the intimate friend of Bosboom, who nursed him through his last illness; he was also the master of Christoffel Bisschop and was generally so honoured that he used to be ironically described as the Allah of Dutch painting, with Spoel, his pupil, for his prophet. This celebrity extended beyond his own

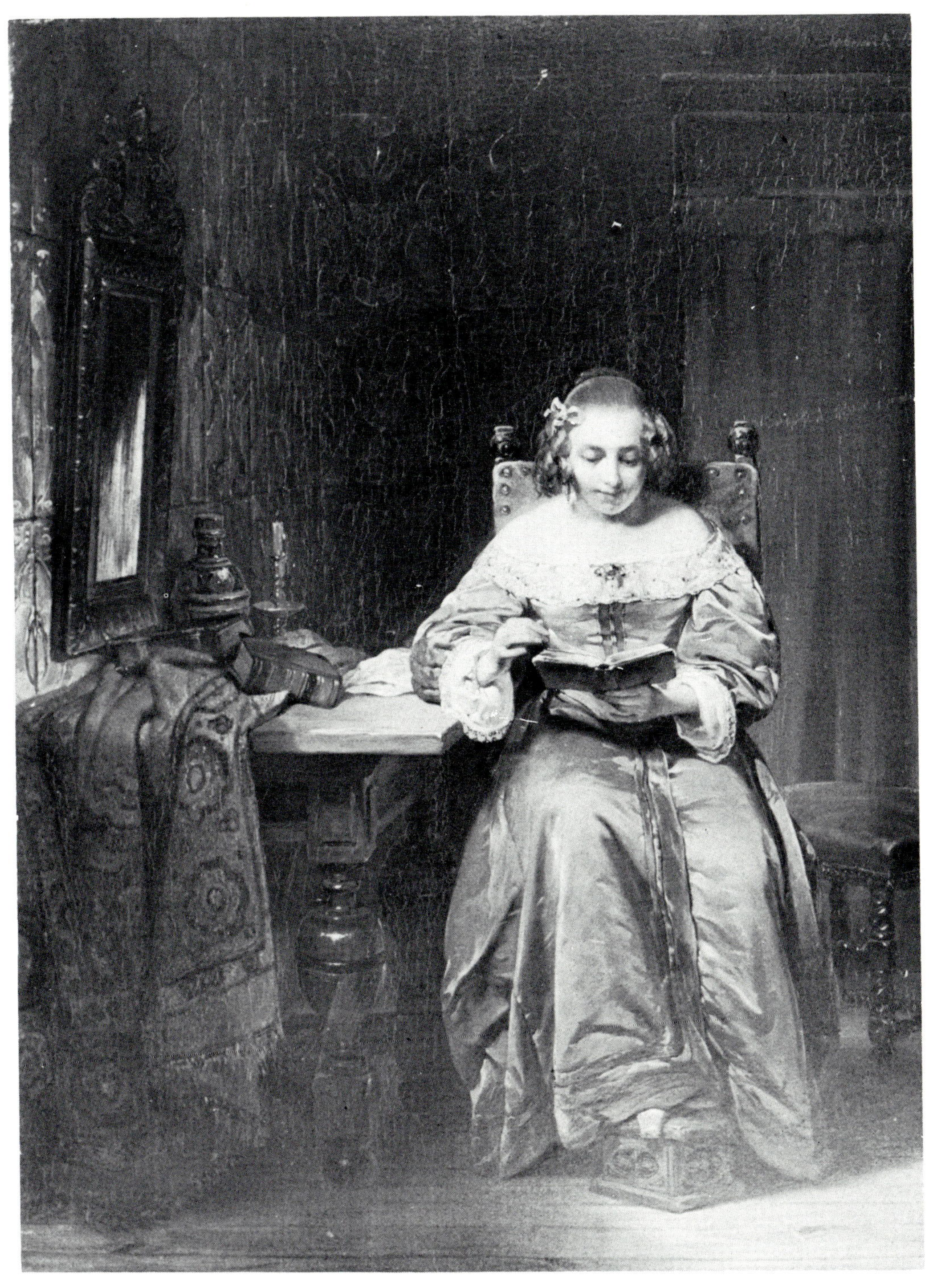

Willem Hendrik Schmidt (1809-1849) *was briefly revered among the history painters of Holland's romantic movement. He was ironically named "the Allah of Dutch painting" by his contemporaries. In this small painting he has gone back to the 17th century to show a young girl reading at a table. It is dated 1839. (46 x 36cm.).* Photograph courtesy of Mak van Waay, Amsterdam.

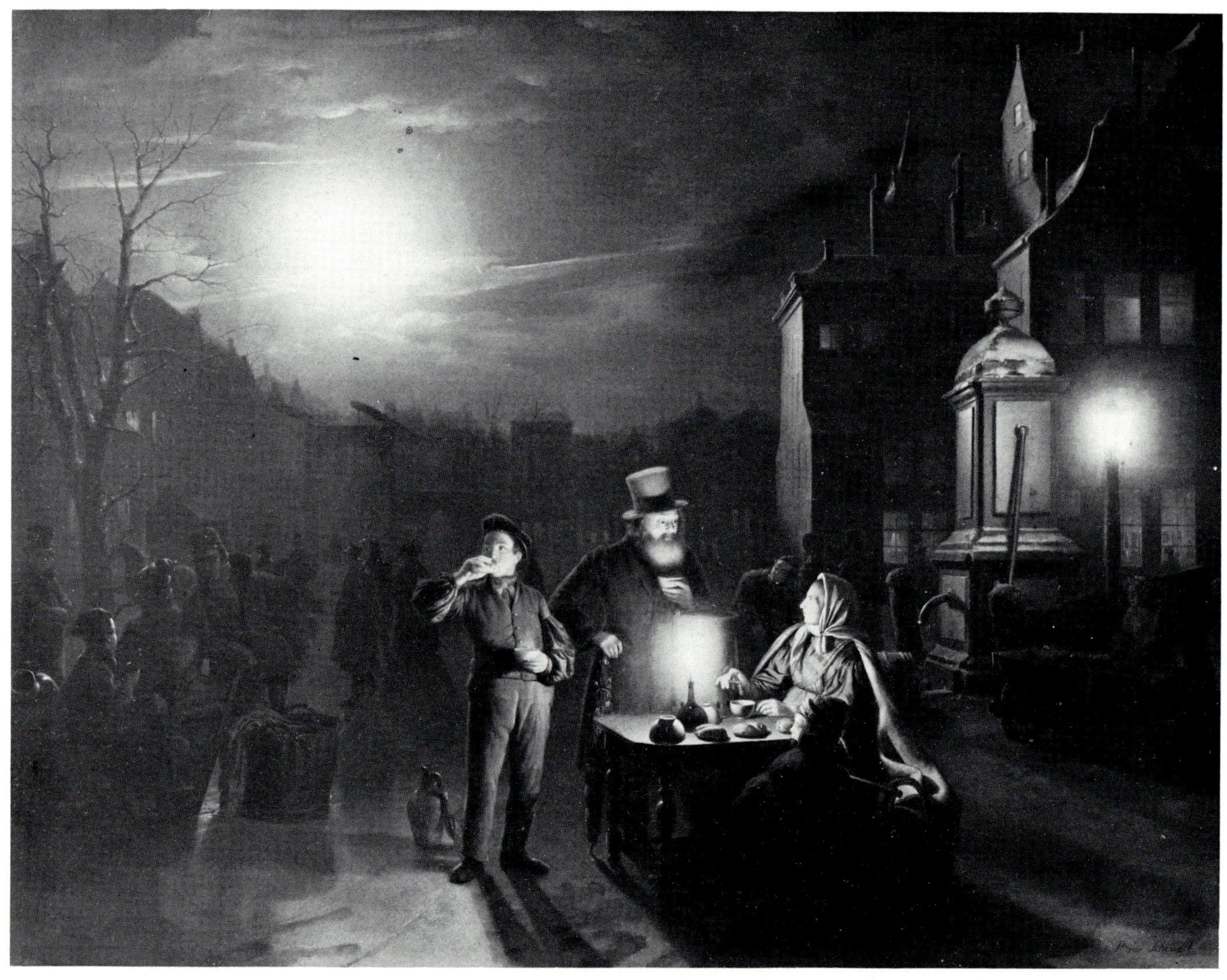

Petrus van Schendel's (1806-1870) *candlelight market scenes were as popular in the 19th century as they are again today – though he also distinguished himself as a portrait and history painter. These examples measure respectively 32 x 40ins. and 22½ x 30¼ins., the second (over page) being dated 1861.* Photograph courtesy of M. Newman Ltd., and Williams & Son.

country, so much so that, when he showed *The Raising of the Daughter of Jairus* at Cologne, his work was spoken of as the first in the exhibition and Degas' *Cain and Abel* as the second. He was born in 1809 at Rotterdam, received his first lessons from Gilles de Meyer, another Rotterdammer, who was more of a teacher than an independent artist, for the main part formed himself and, later, in 1840, acquired, in the museums of Düsseldorf, Berlin and Dresden, that culture which cannot be denied him. When he died, in 1849, at Delft, where for some years he had taught drawing at the Training-school for Engineers, people wrung their hands in despair for the future of Dutch painting after such a loss.

He is said to have possessed an original manner, to have succeeded in giving colour, dignity and charm to his works, especially in the painting of fabrics and all sorts of accessories, which reminded one of the old masters. And yet how intensely tedious are just those very qualities in the painters of so-called old-Dutch interiors! It would appear as though they all excelled in this, for we become sick and tired, in these shiny little pictures, of those "excellently limned" accessories and stuffs and silks. Still, Schmidt demanded

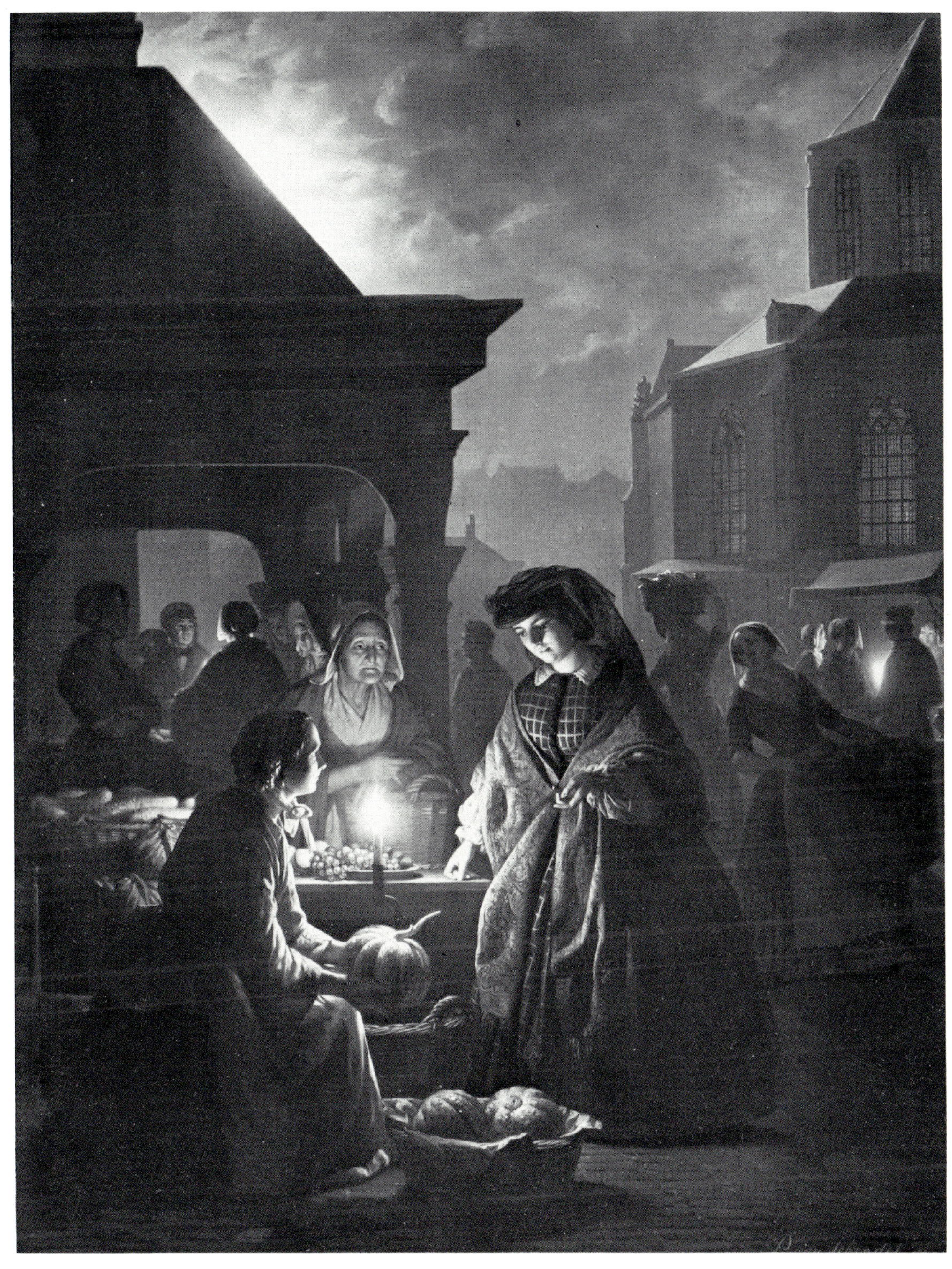

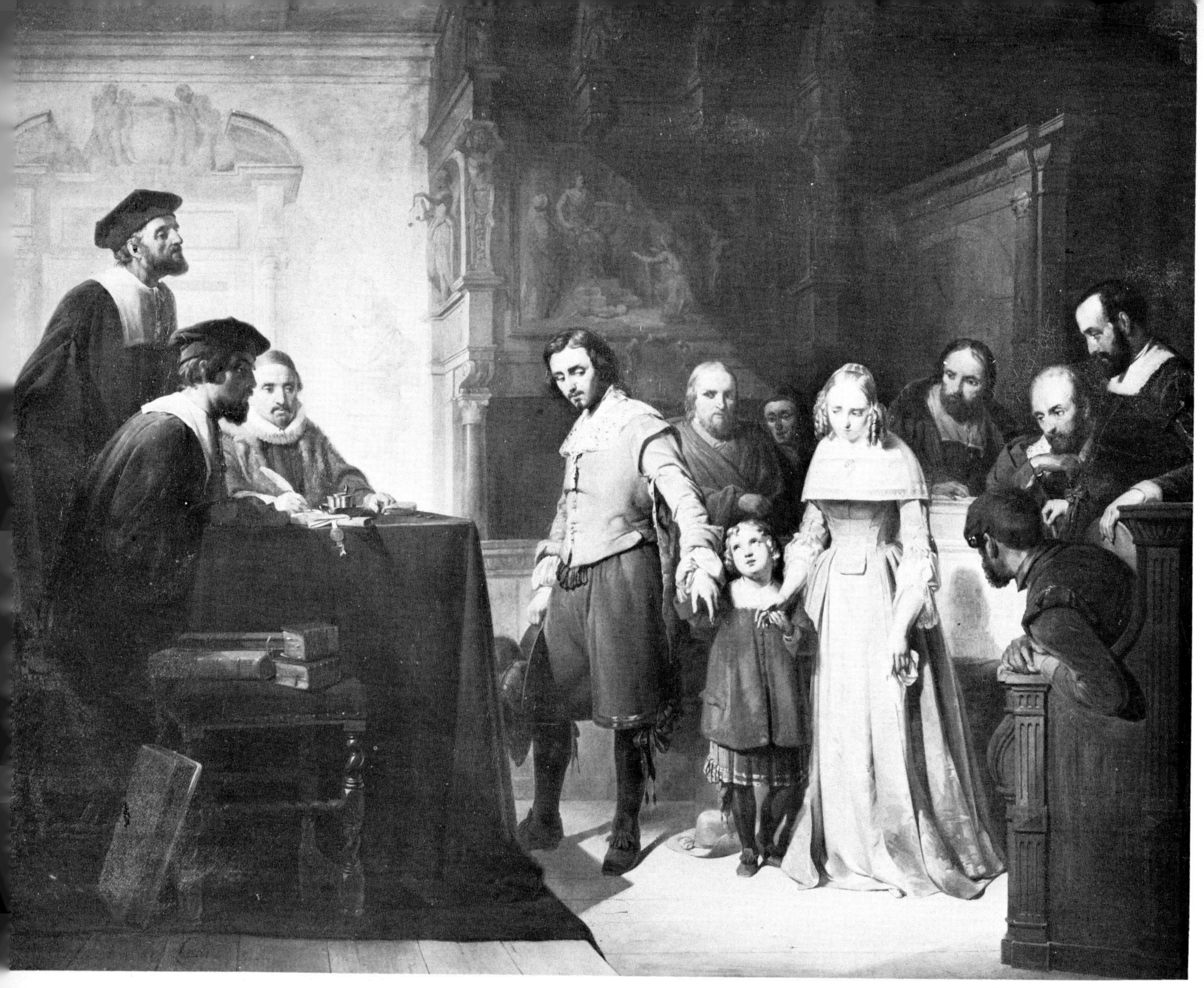

Jan Hendrik van de Laar (1807-1874) *sought his inspiration in Walter Scott and the Romantic poems of Tollens. Marius comments that this depiction of "The Divorce" "overflows with middle-class sentimentality".* **Photograph courtesy of the Boymans Museum, Rotterdam.**

more of art – and here we see his romanticism come peeping round the corner – began to feel that art must become something nobler and more exalted. We, who really know little of his work besides the picture of the monks in Boymans' Museum, in which naturally we cannot expect to find any lively colouring, see in him merely a good painter, with a rather wearisome method, a narrow modelling and a notable lack of harmony. His great, if short-lived fame must have rested on more important work than this.

It would appear that the history-painter Spoel is a little closer to us than his master. This impression is perhaps due to the engraving of his *Procession of the Rotterdam Rhetoricians on the occasion of the progress of the Queen of England, 19 March 1642,* which was published as a prize of the Society for the Encouragement of the Plastic Arts and distributed in every corner of our country. Westrheene says of the original picture that it unites all Spoel's good qualities and, moreover, displays a strength of colour, an ease and firmness of touch of which he did not often give proof. Jacob Spoel was born at Rotterdam in 1820 and died in the same town in 1868.

Another contemporary of Jan Kruseman, of Klaas Pieneman, of Hendrik Schmidt, of Van de Laar is Petrus van Schendel, who was born in 1806, in a little village near Breda, and studied at the Antwerp Academy under Van Bree. He resided consecutively at

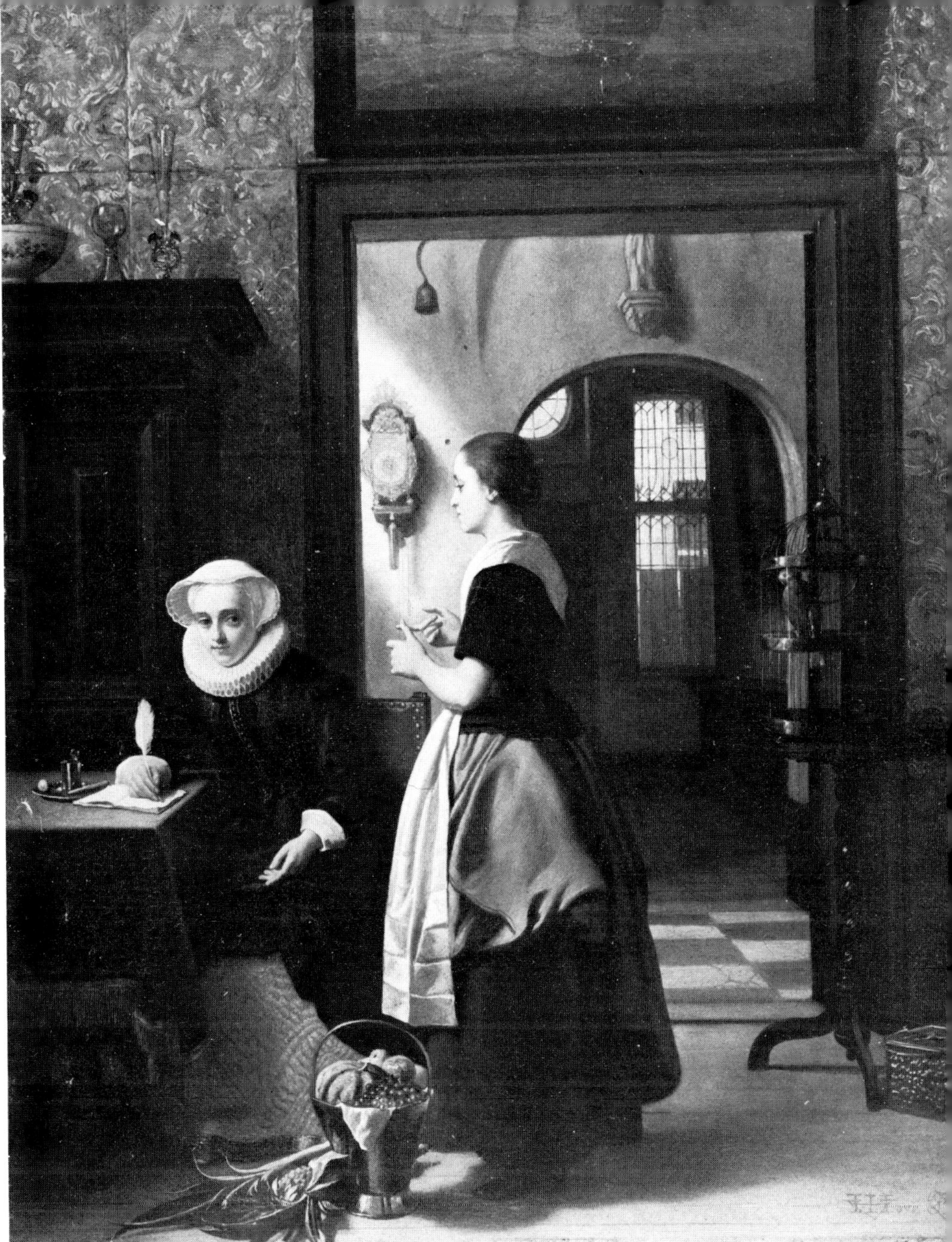

Hubertus van Hove (1814-1864) *came closest, among Dutch romantic painters, to emulating the colour and style of Leys and the Belgian School of historical genre. This interior combines history with sensitive still life painting in the details of the scene.* Photograph courtesy of Sotheby's & Co.

Rotterdam, Amsterdam, the Hague and Brussels, painted portraits, historical pictures and genre-pieces and excelled in his little candle, lamp or torch-light scenes, which were thought much of in his day. As an historical painter, he did not object to big canvases: his *Birth of Christ* measured three Dutch ells by four. The distance between Van Schendel and Da Vinci is great, but he had one thing in common with Leonardo: the love and success with which he practised the science of mechanics. He patented, among others, an important improvement in the propelling of locomotives. Petrus van Schendel died in 1870.

A much more genuine adherent of the romantic movement was Jan Hendrik van de Laar, born at Rotterdam, in 1807, a pupil of the miniature-painters C. Bakker and G. Wappers. Although, once in a way, he felt drawn towards historical subjects, as when he painted an *Heroic Death of Herman de Ruiter,* he preferred to move among the romantic episodes of Walter Scott or the romantic poems of Tollens, who provided the subject of his picture in Boymans' Museum. And yet his art has really as little in common with the romantic movement as has Tollens' poem. Van de Laar's *Divorce* overflows with middle-

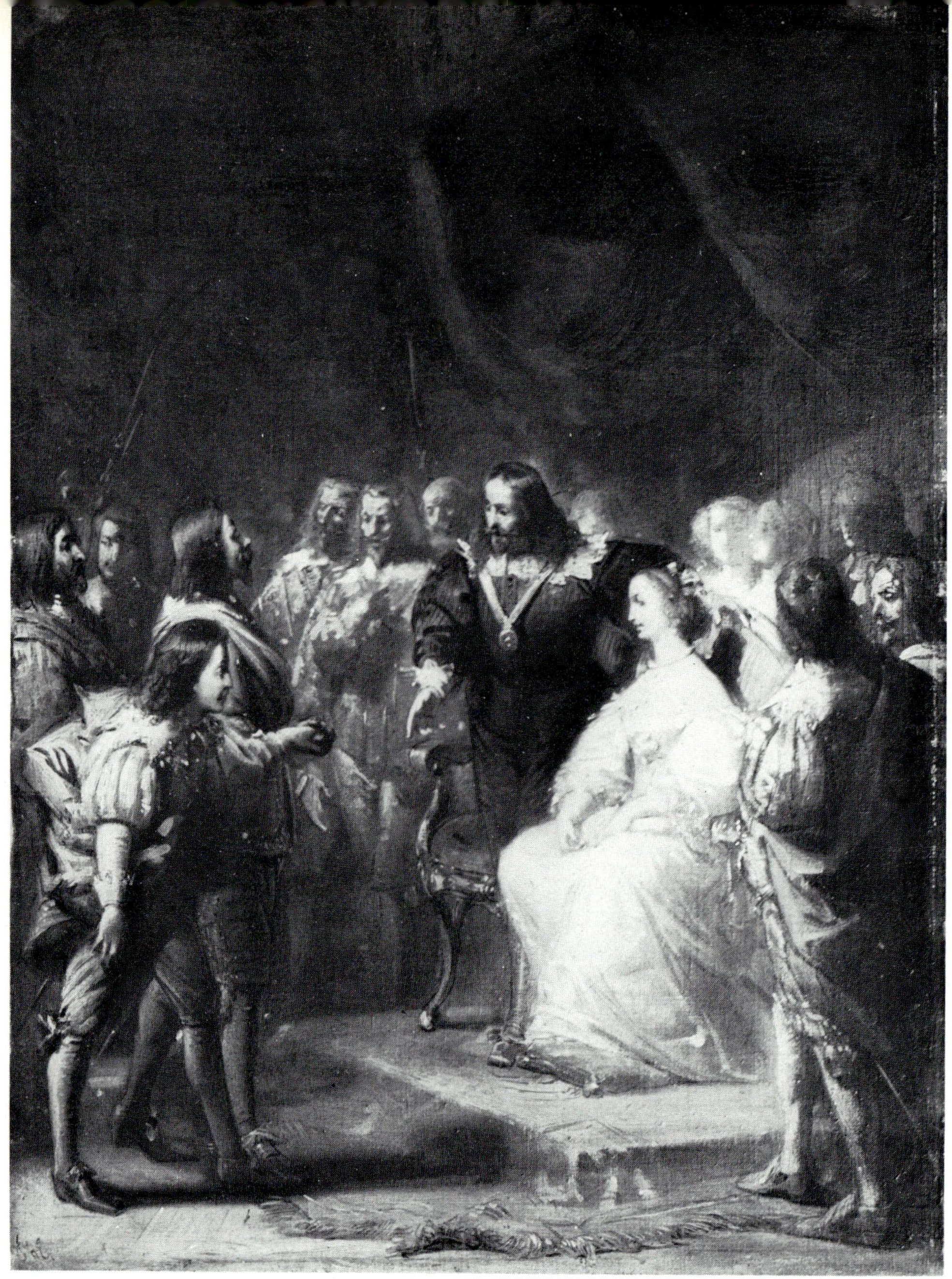

Johannes Hinderikus Egenberger (1822-1897), *a history painter much given to the theatrical, is in peaceable mood in this "Arrival of Prince William in England".* Photograph courtesy of the Stedelijk Museum, Amsterdam.

class sentimentality, with unnatural, feeble staginess. He died in 1874.

This is how things stood in those days: as in Belgium, men were genre-painters in the style of the old masters; or historical painters – but here Belgium had the advantage, inasmuch as she shared French ideas more strongly and therefore was more powerfully moved; or painters of biblical subjects – and here, again, Belgium had the advantage, inasmuch as she was a Catholic country and her painters therefore were bound to observe a certain decorum and found a place for their work in the Catholic churches;[1] or else – and in this they were always more or less excellent – they painted portraits, or they painted fashionable interiors, which were generally somewhat sugary and insipid, or they painted landscapes – but this was a separate tendency – or else they painted all these subjects by turns. We had no Leys, who united colour and style in his renascence, even though Huib van Hove, in his little vistas, often gave good evidence

[1] Whereas we had only the Frisian painter Otto de Boer, who painted *The Raising of Lazarus* for the church at Woudsend (where he was born in 1797) and *The Sermon on the Mount*, his best work, for the church at Heerenveen and, who therefore, like the painters in Catholic countires, was not obliged to adopt a flabby sentimentality in order to flatter the taste of the Pietistic Protestants. De Boer died in 1856.

of these two qualities; with us, everything was covered with a sauce of romanticism, which expressed itself in somewhat uncouth contrasts and which showed a decided preference for scenes with monks in them. One of the most sickly and self-satisfied instances of this is a boudoir with a lady and a monk behind her, by Charles van Beveren (1809-1850), that feeble painter who is so richly represented in the Fodor Museum. Schmidt also shared this predilection, as witness his *Five Monks in Meditation* at Boymans' Museum, and even Bosboom, that always eminent and distinguished painter, who from the beginning saw his way clear before him, took part in the fashion in his grand manner with *Cantabimus et psallemur* and *The Carmelite playing the Organ.*

The painters of that time, including Cool and Van Trigt, nearly all began by sacrificing to romance or history, although many of them soon returned to the traditions of their race. The Mæcenases asked for historical painting. Amsterdam, the ever serious city, in whose daily life nature does not play so great a part as in that of the Hague, continued to place before the painters what it considered to be a useful and worthy aim.

This historical romanticism is displayed in the most comical and, at the same time, in the most surprising light in many of the little pictures in the Historical Gallery, the outcome of the running commission given by Mr. de Vos, to which any painter could contribute lavishly and to which, although the payment was but

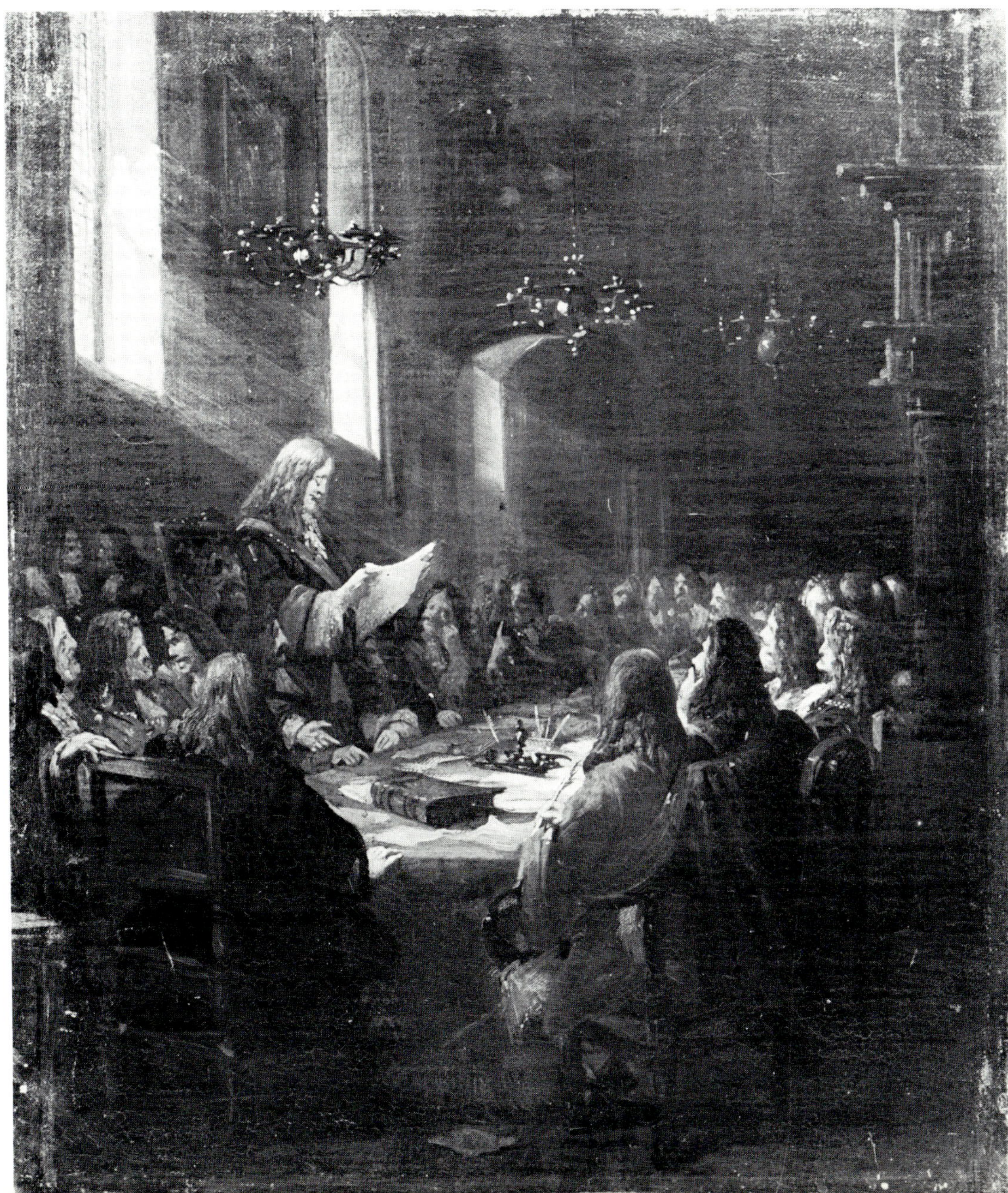

Barend Wijnveld Jnr. (1820-1902) *combines the fashion for history painting with bastardised echoes of Rembrandt in "The peace of Rijswijk."* Photograph courtesy of the Stedelijk Museum, Amsterdam

modest, a large number of painters did contribute with commendable readiness. For it was as sure as that twice two are four that whosoever stood in need of ready money at that time would paint one of these pieces in a day or two, although there are a few fortunate exceptions.

The contents of this Historical Gallery, now accommodated in the Municipal Museum of Amsterdam, were painted between 1848 and 1863 to the order of Mr. J. de Vos Jzn., of Amsterdam, a lawyer and a well-known collector, who, in addition to the 253 little pictures, all of the same size and shape, which form the gallery, possessed an important collection of which the acme consisted of drawings by the old Dutch masters, now partly housed in the Rijksmuseum. The historical plan, embracing the whole national history for A.D. 40 to A.D. 1861, the year of the great floods, was, if I am not mistaken, arranged with much taste and insight and described in the catalogue by a well-known author, Mr. Jacob van Lennep.

All that remains of any value to posterity, besides an attractive lesson in the history of the motherland for the youth of Amsterdam, is represented by the pictures of Allebé, Alma Tadema and Jozef Israëls and the twenty-six pieces by Rochussen, which excel in colour, style and, in the case of the last, in unity of treatment and great facility. Johannes Hinderikus Egenberger (1822-1897), first a professor at the Amsterdam Academy, afterwards director of the Academy at Groningen, divided the lion's share with Barend Wijnveld Jr. (1820-1902), who succeeded him in the former appointment. Their contributions, except in those cases where Egenberger confined himself to the eighteenth century, in which he is sober and deserving, all belong to the most violent kind. The diagonal lines of the battlesome arms in *The Heroic Death of Jan van Schaffelaar* are perhaps the most characteristic instance of that rude, theatrical system of historical painting which, like popular historical melodrama, is content to emphasize the hero, the traitor or the coward without troubling about the claims of the art concerned. As for the *Kenau Hasselaar* painted in collaboration by the two artists for the Town-hall at Haarlem, the violence of the Dutch Amazons, in view of the nature of the defensive weapons employed, is well worthy of the descriptive pen of a Huysmans.

In the midst of all these painters bound to their period, in the midst of so many mediocrities, in the midst of a long array of "famous masters" whom we should nowadays find it impossible to enjoy, De Bloeme stands apart as a sturdy painter, showing neither the influences of his own time nor those of the seventeenth century, but entirely himself, honest and simple. Born in 1802 at the Hague, where he died in 1867, Hermanus Anthonie de Bloeme started under J.W. Pieneman, working in his studio at the Hague and afterwards following him to Amsterdam when Pieneman was appointed director of the Academy. It was inevitable that he should sacrifice to the spirit of the time and begin by painting historical, followed by biblical subjects, of which his *Mary Magdalen* is considered the best. Nor do I see any reason to believe that he excelled his contemporaries in this regard, for his best portraits also were painted during the last twenty years of his life. What was most remarkable at that period was that he did not go to Italy in search of what he could find at home and this is the more noteworthy inasmuch as the fact, fortunate for him as it was, arose not so much from any convinced idea as from his strong affection for his parents' house and its ways; nay more, when he had to take part in the great competition at the Amsterdam Academy, he purposely sent in his *Adam and Eve by the body of Abel* in an unfinished state to escape an award which would have taken him for four years far from home. Probably the sheer artistic merit which he so unconsciously betrayed in a bad period is partly due to this, even though it is also probable that he brought home an occasional idea from his shorter journeys. For it must be admitted that the delicious *Portrait of a Lady* in the Hague Museum and that of Baron van Omphal in the Rijksmuseum, his best portraits, show some conformity of conception with a portrait by Gallait in our Municipal Museum, even though it be true to say that the comparison is to the disadvantage of the once so renowned Belgian. The drawing is thoughtful and compact, without the superfluous flourish with which his contemporaries used to fill in their portraits. Moreover, the attitude of the head in the portrait of Miss Huyser above-mentioned displays an engagingness which we do not expect to find in that period. De Bloeme's colouring is simple and refined, as is his workmanship; and everything is so nicely balanced that we forget to analyze. He was not easily pleased and would rather smear out an almost completed portrait with a couple of smudges than deliver it against his will, a habit which necessitated endless patience on the part of his sitters. We are told how, after many sittings, Princess Marianne of the Netherlands, on

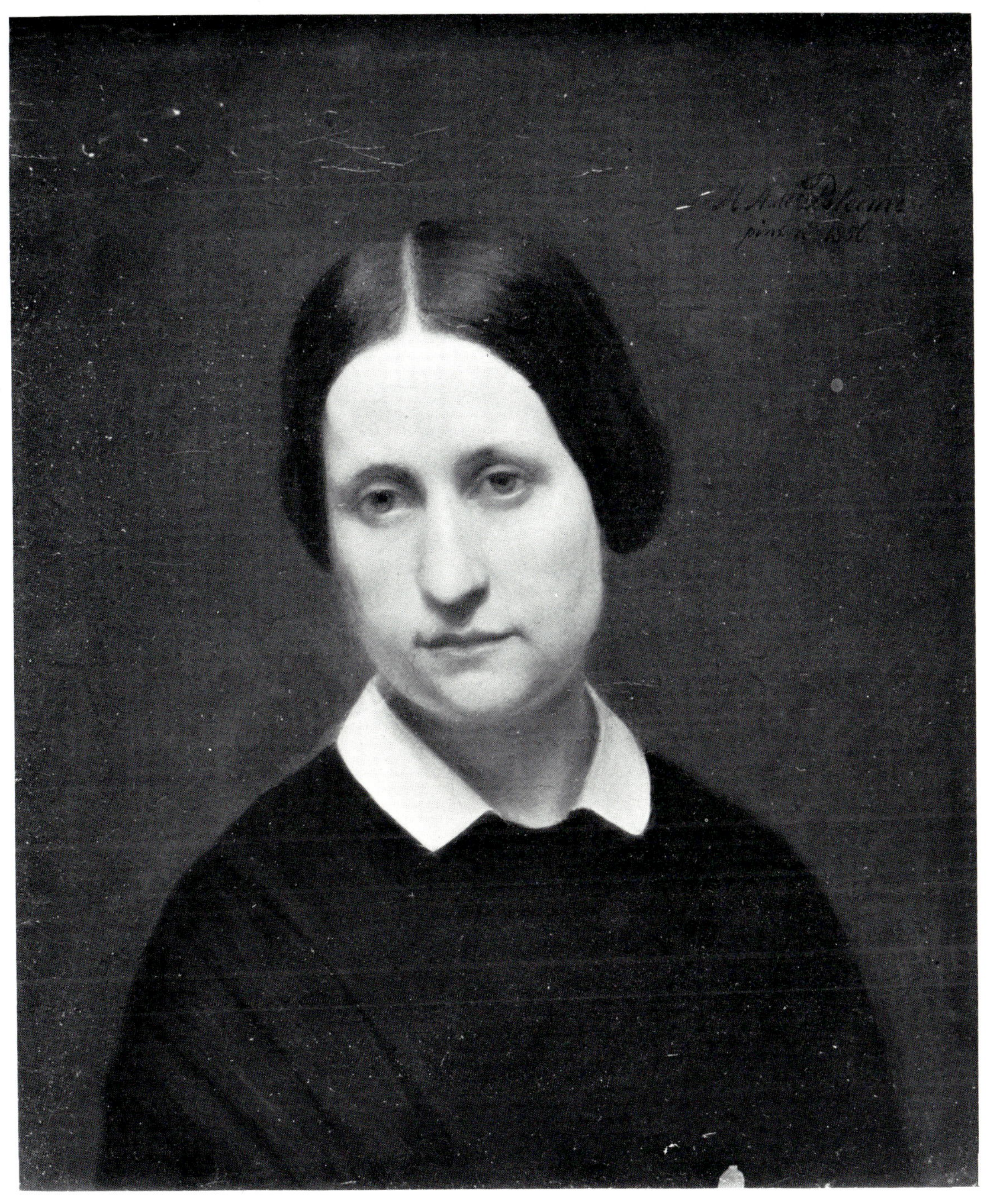

Hermanus Anthonie de Bloeme (1802-1867) *was a thoughtful realist in the midst of the romantic generation and a noted portraitist – as is shown in this portrait of a lady (dated 1856, 53.5 x 46.5cms.).* Photograph courtesy of the Haags Gemeentemuseum.

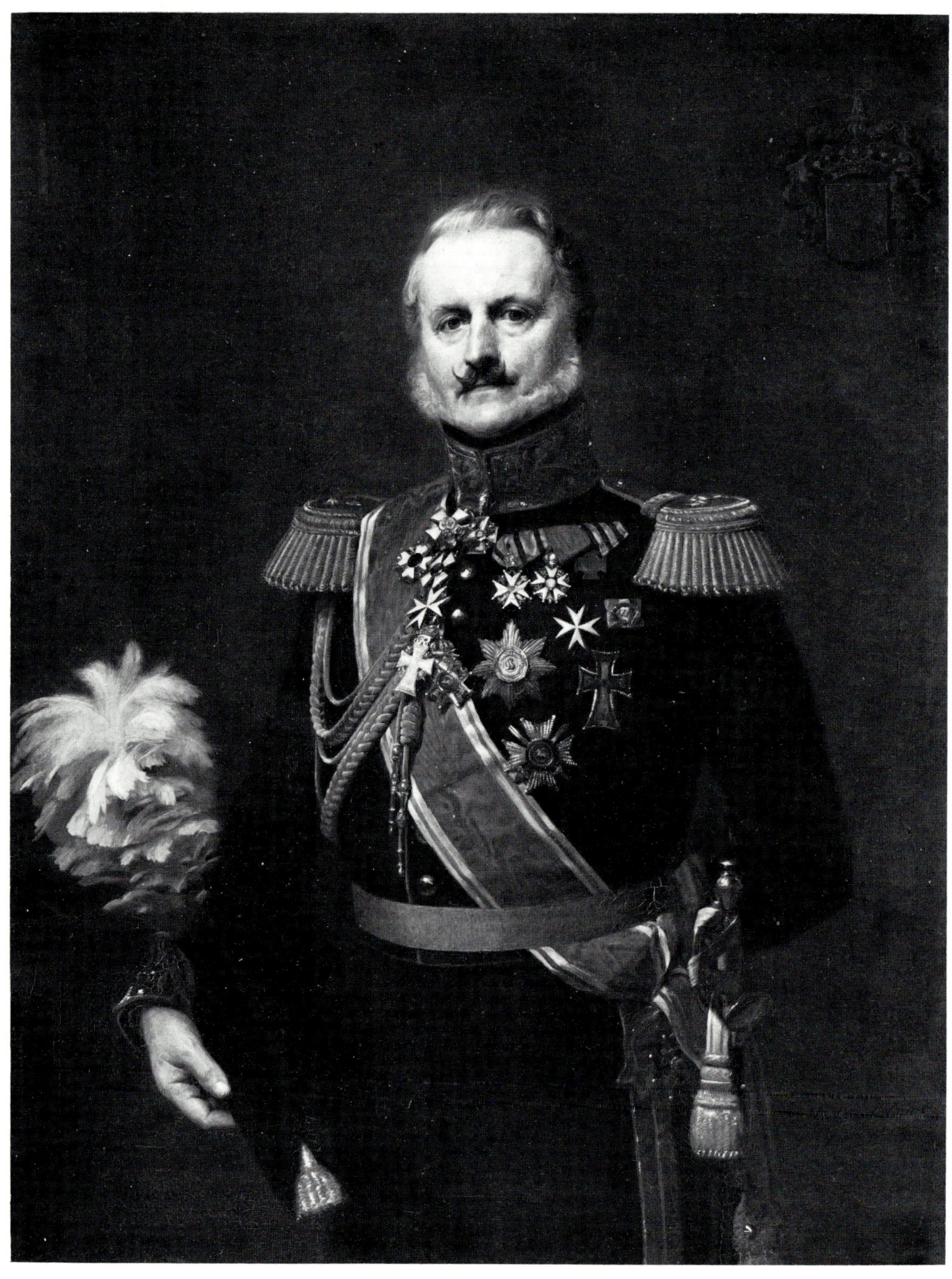

This glittering military portrait of "Baron Van Omphal" is accounted one of **de Bloeme's** *best. (131 x 106 cms.).* Photograph courtesy of the Rijksmuseum, Amsterdam.

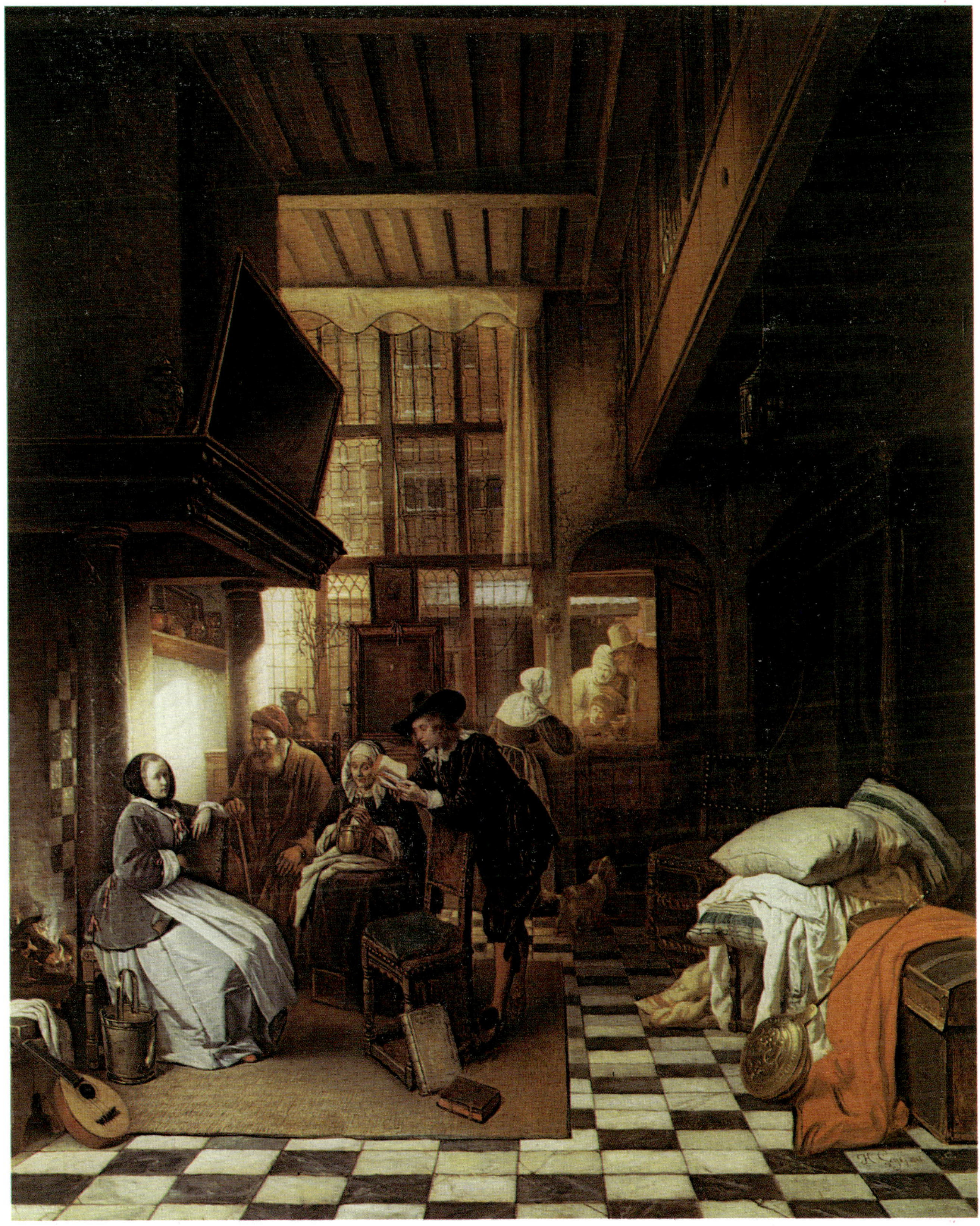

Baron Hendrik Leys (1815-1869). *"Interior scene with a Dutch family around the fire." Signed and dated 1848. (Panel 30 x 30ins.).* Photograph courtesy of Richard Green.
The Belgian genre painter Baron Leys enjoyed a high reputation throughout Europe and his influence was nationally felt across the frontier with Holland. Many Dutch artists studied with him, notably Alma Tadema.

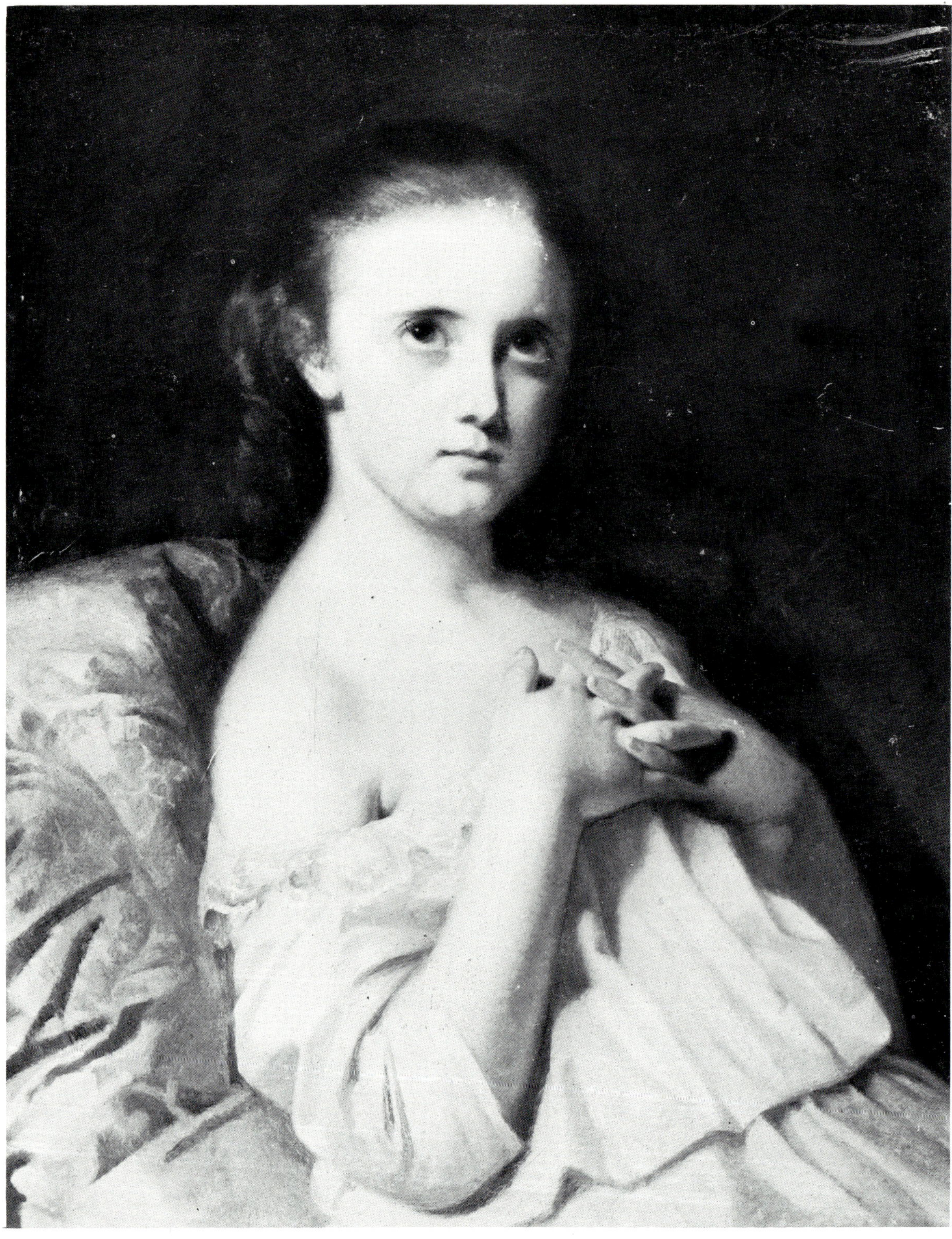

Johan George Schwartze (1814-1874) *was Amsterdam's most favoured portraitist at the mid-century. His romantic leanings are displayed in this dewy eyed "Girl at Prayer".* Photograph courtesy of the Stedelijk Museum, Amsterdam.

paying her last visit to the studio at the appointed hour, found the painter engaged in smudging out her portrait, whereupon there followed a "scene" which did not subside until mutual promises had been exchanged to start again from the beginning.

There is a great contrast in temperament between the simple Hague portrait-painter and the somewhat younger romanticist Johan George Schwartze, his rival in Amsterdam. Thanks to a wider conception, to a certain tendency towards romanticism, to a search after not only the outer but also the inner aspect of his sitters, Schwartze may be said to have aimed higher in his portraits than the less complex Hague artist. And, in view of these qualities, one would be disposed at once to allot the first place to this Rembrandtesque painter, whose *Portrait of Himself* is in many ways so charming, so distinguished, so soulful. But, when we look at it again, the thing becomes different: from under that soulful performance peeps something weaker, even though it be a very lovable weakness, against which De Bloeme's simpler excellence is well able to hold its own.

The fact that Schwartze, for all his great and attractive qualities, did not exercise a greater influence over his younger contemporaries is perhaps due to this very inclination towards romanticism, to this very striving to imbue his portraits with characters. Mental and moral characteristics too strongly emphasized can captivate us, in the long run, only when they are there unconsciously, or as an important piece of painting, or at any rate executed in a certain style. When Jozef Israëls painted the portrait of his brother artist, Roelofs the landscape-painter, full of suggestion as it is, while seeking for the man under the social varnish, he emphasized no single quality at the expense of any other; perhaps only a painter could recognize the painter in the eyes of the portrait; and even this is quite subordinate to the intense life that breathes through the wide-open nostrils, under the high forehead, in the eyes beneath the bushy brows. Whereas, when Schwartze painted the portrait of Professor Opzoomer, the philosopher, a portrait the conception of which was so greatly admired by the professor's friends because Schwartze painted the thinker as Faust, in a moment of despair, of powerlessness, he was condemned by a later generation, which sees that there is something so theatrical in the attitude, something so much of an actor playing his part, that the portrait resembles a rhetorical phrase rather than a human being.

We are not saying that Schwartze was not an excellent painter or that in him, as in the later Lenbach, the painter was sacrificed entirely to the psychologist; for, although of German origin, he shows in his painting the pure Dutch characteristics: fine, warm shadows, strong half-tones and boldly modelled light, solid workmanship, thought in the execution, fulness, completeness. His own portrait is certainly one of the very finest expressions of Dutch romanticism; the portrait of his wife, with which he made a great success at the time, possesses that charm which we always value in a woman's portrait, however much the forms may alter; in a certain sense, his portrait of Dr. Rive may be described as powerful; while his portraits of children are also conceived in an interesting way.

Schwartze left his native Amsterdam as a child, with his parents, for Philadelphia, whence he returned to Europe in 1838, at the age of twenty-four, and spent six years at the Dusseldorf Academy under Schadow and Sohn. At the same time, he took private lessons from Lessing, the well-known landscape-painter. In 1846, he settled in Amsterdam, because he had made so great a success in that city with his first portrait. Here he began by painting *The Prayer, Puritans at Divine Service* and *The Pilgrim Fathers,* which was lost on the way to America, but which is known through Allebe's lithographic reproduction. He made a name with these subjects and people are said to have regretted that he was obliged to abandon this style in order to execute his many commissions for portraits. We prefer, however, to think that the many and great admirers of his portraits will have regretted this decree of fate as little as did the subsequent generation, for this is certain, that, in his later years, his reputation was exclusively that of a sensitive portrait-painter, capable occasionally of genius. His great merit lies in this that, although of German descent, he chose Rembrandt, whom he admired above all other Dutchmen, as his model from the start.

Schwartze died in 1874. His chief pupil was his talented daughter, Miss Thérèse Schwartze, so well-known as a portrait-painter to-day.

Chapter IV

The Landscape and Genre-Painters

It is fairly well established nowadays that landscape-painting for its own sake is mainly of Dutch origin. And, although we are not prepared to go all lengths with Taine's theory of environment, or, at any rate, while admitting it in general, to apply it to individuals and artists, the cause does probably lie in the fact that nowhere, unless it be in Venice, do the natural conditions, the climate, the atmosphere, the light, the sky and their reflection in the endless pieces of water of which the most picturesque regions of the Netherlands, the provinces of North and South Holland, are as it were composed, nowhere do these conditions influence life so strongly as with us. The incessant changes of sunshine and clouds, the broad shadows of the latter over the flat fields, the long twilight, which is never quite dispelled indoors, unless a lighted cloud throws a sharp reflection from without: these all give a movement to the landscape, which, just because of this endless alternation, remains ever charming to the eye and offers to the eye of the painter in particular the greatest and most continuous interest.

Another reason to prove that landscape-painting is of Dutch origin lies in the fact that no country was so independent of both religious influences and princely patronage as the northern portion of the Netherlands; and, even though this does not apply to the fifteenth and a part of the sixteenth century, the fact that artists were free to paint what found favour in their eyes must have had its influence.

Seeing how closely nature and landscape-painting are bound up with the very existence of Dutch art, it can be no matter for surprise that, at a time of a decline such as that into which official painting in general had fallen in our country, there were painters at the beginning of the eighteenth century who had succeeded in keeping their art untouched by foreign influences and who, refusing to deny their kind or the traditions of the great centuries, looked at nature through their own eyes, through their own masters.

For, although, after 1870, the Hague school of landscape-painting attained a height which one could hardly have expected ever to behold again after the rich growth of the seventeenth century, there were very talented landscape-painters in the earlier part of the nineteenth century also; and, though it be true that the new generation but rarely admits the worth of that which precedes it, a time was bound to come when we should learn to appreciate those painters who worthily continued the seventeenth-century traditions and who were the precursors of the new florescence. If we go further into the lives of those painters, we shall find that fame and consideration were their portion, both here and abroad. And we, who have followed the magnificence of the Hague masters with so great an admiration, but who have also seen it fade away in feeble imitation of a misunderstood emotional power, when occasionally we come upon those somewhat antiquated landscapes in a museum, at a dealer's, at an auction sale, in the midst of those imitations, of the weaker works of to-day, we are struck by their vigour and love of nature, by that healthy vigour which was always reserved for the greatest. The composition may have become a little old-fashioned, the thing represented may remain within the limits of an anecdote, the influence of the light on the landscape may not in general have been so very much the one and only moving power as in the last thirty years of the nineteenth century, the subject itself may have been heavier, the colouring browned over with a yellow varnish or blackened through the bitumen employed, the filling in may have been made too much a matter for separate treatment: this was, when all is said, done in obedience to the taste of the public, which preferred to buy landscapes with figures and animals, water with accurately-detailed ships upon it. None of the painters of that time would have been capable of making the reply which Willem Maris gave

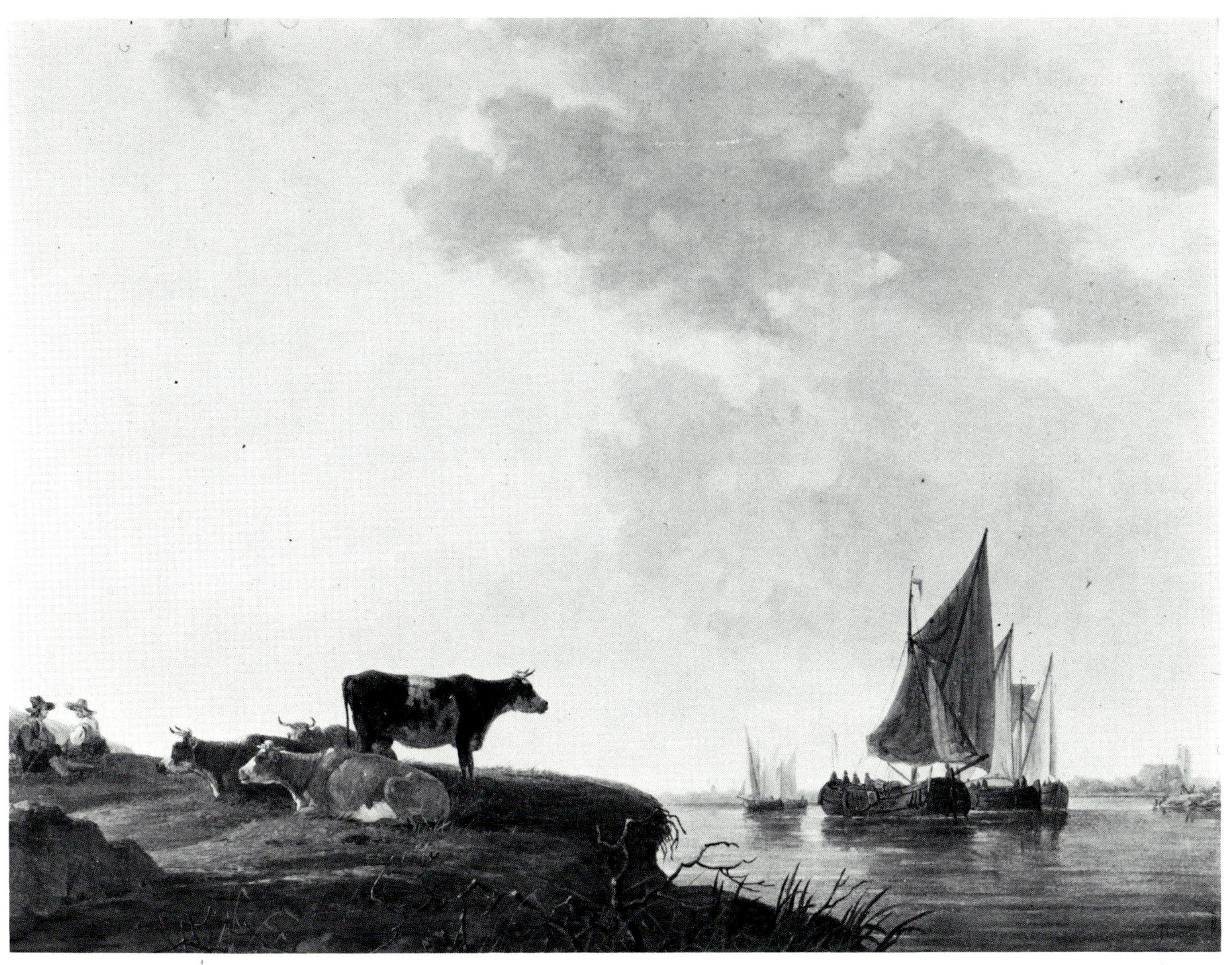

Jacob van Strij (1756-1815) *followed the 17th century artist Aelbert Cuyp so closely in style that many of his paintings have now become "Cuyps". This river landscape is more 17th century than 19th in feel. (22 x 29ins.).* Photograph courtesy of Christie, Manson and Woods.

to one who asked him why he always painted cows:

"I never paint cows, but only effects of light."

The nineteenth century set in with five landscape-painters who have shown by the work which they left behind them that they never ceased to admire and study the painting of the seventeenth century. And so greatly was this the case that we receive no impression of the eighteenth century at all in the better part of their work and but little in the remainder. The colour and workmanship of two of them was entirely in the beautiful manner of the old masters, while the arrangement of all of them was quite free of that rhetorical side which makes later landscape-painters, for all their skill, seem antiquated. Their names are, in the order of their births, Jacob van Strij, Dirk Jan van der Laen, Jan Kobell, Wouter Joannes van Troostwijk and George Pieter Westenberg.

Jacob van Strij was a native of Dordrecht. He was born in 1756 and died in 1815. His work is imbued with admiration for Aelbert Cuyp and he introduced Cuyp's colour-schemes so cleverly into his work that their pictures were often mistaken for one another. Also, the works left behind at his death included eleven copies after Cuyp, although it was not always a literal copying that he applied to his own work. Immerzeel says, as an instance of Van Strij's energy:

"His longing to give a faithful rendering of nature was so strong that, however great his physical pain (he

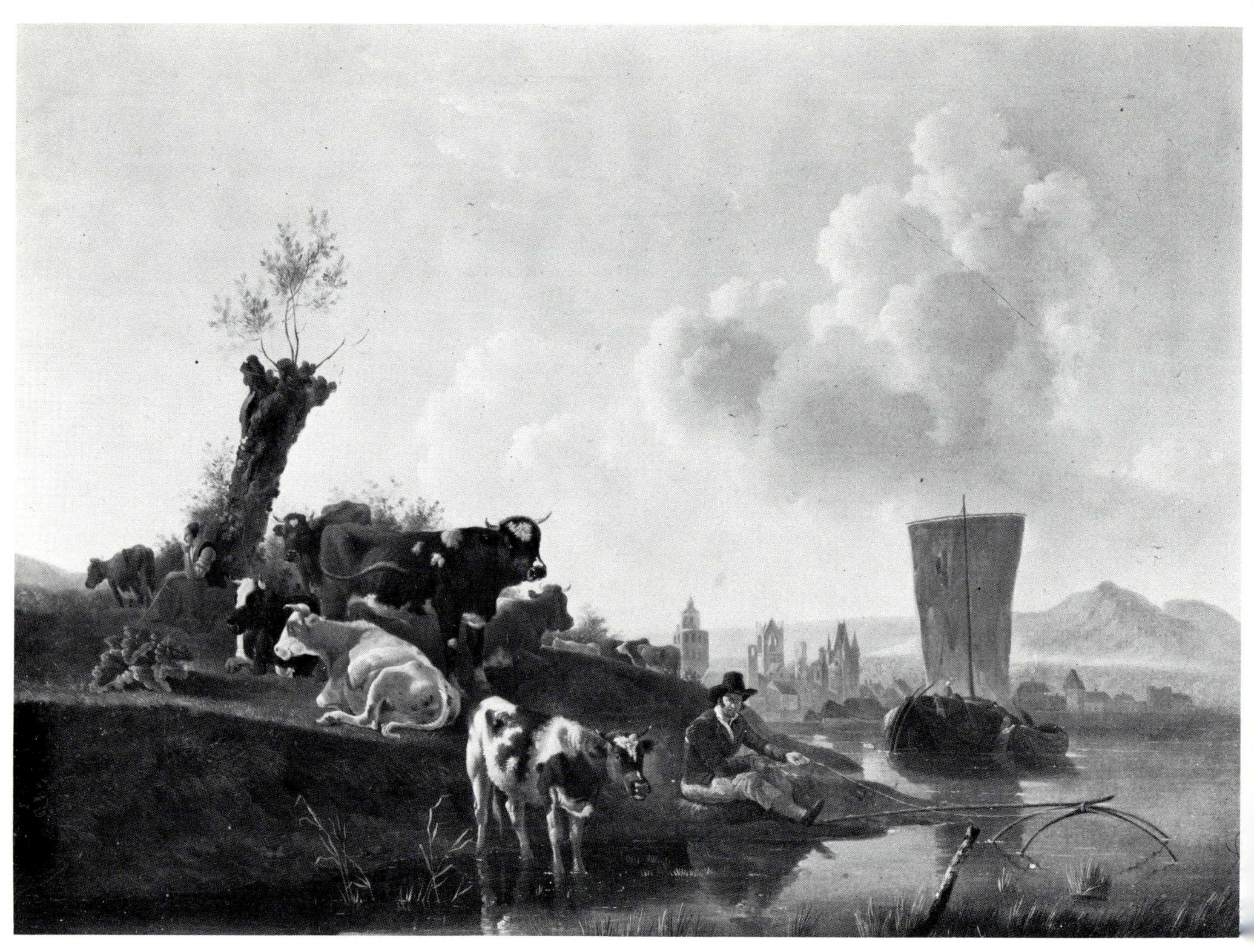

Above and right: **Jan Kobell's** (1778-1814) *calm and poetic landscapes with cattle reminiscent of Paul Potter, were an important contribution to the Rotterdam School in the early years of the 19th century. These contrast with his stormy inner life; over-ambitious and dissatisfied, his mind broke down and he died at 36. These paintings measure 20½ x 28½ins. and 41½ x 55cms. respectively.* Photographs courtesy of Christie, Manson and Woods, and Mak van Waay, Amsterdam.

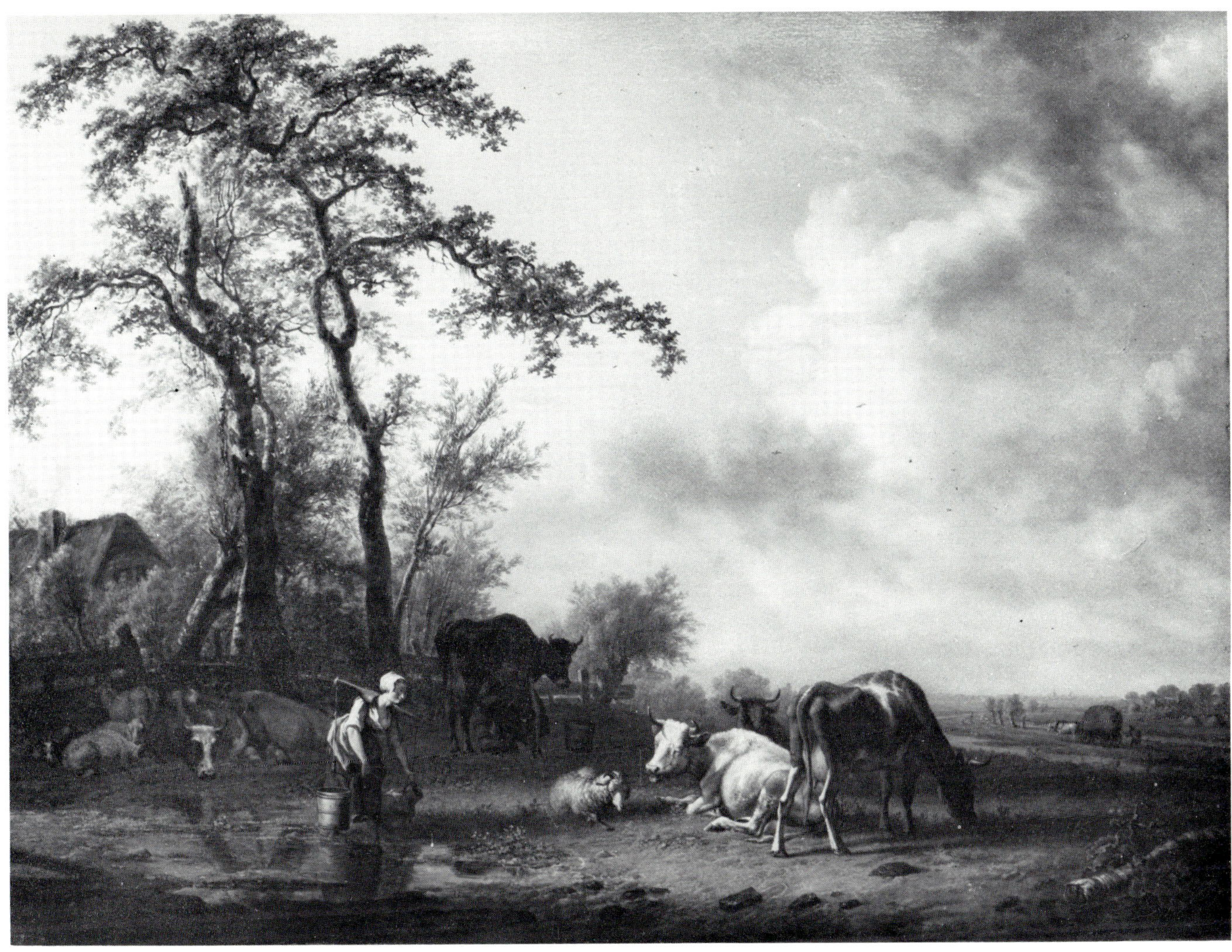

suffered for many years from gout), he would drive over the ice in a sleigh in bleak winter to make sketches for pictures which he subsequently painted."

His landscapes with cattle excel through the warm colouring of their sunlight. In a small upper room at the Rijksmuseum is a *Going to Market,* by Jacob van Strij, which displays in all its purity the bright atmosphere of his vigorous predecessor, although the composition is a little too much filled in after the Van Berchem manner. He was a pupil of the Antwerp Drawing Academy and of the history-painter Lens, but he formed himself principally upon his studies of nature and the old landscape-painters. His work was greatly valued in its day.

The second, D.J. van der Laen, was born at Zwolle in 1759. He was a member of an old and considerable family and was educated at Leiden, where, however, he soon left the university for Hendrik Meyer's manufactory of hangings. He began by painting genre-pieces, but soon confined himself more closely to landscape, in which he came to excel in so remarkable a degree that Thore, when visiting the Suermondt collection at Aix-la-Chapelle, took one of his landscapes for a Vermeer of Delft.[1] The little old house in the

[1] Dr. Bredius, in 1883, published in *Das Zeitschrift für bildende Kunst* an article entitled *Ein Pseudo-Vermeer in der Königliche Gemälde-Gallerie,* in which he showed that this fine little landscape was not a seventeenth-century picture, but was painted about 1800 by Van der Laen.

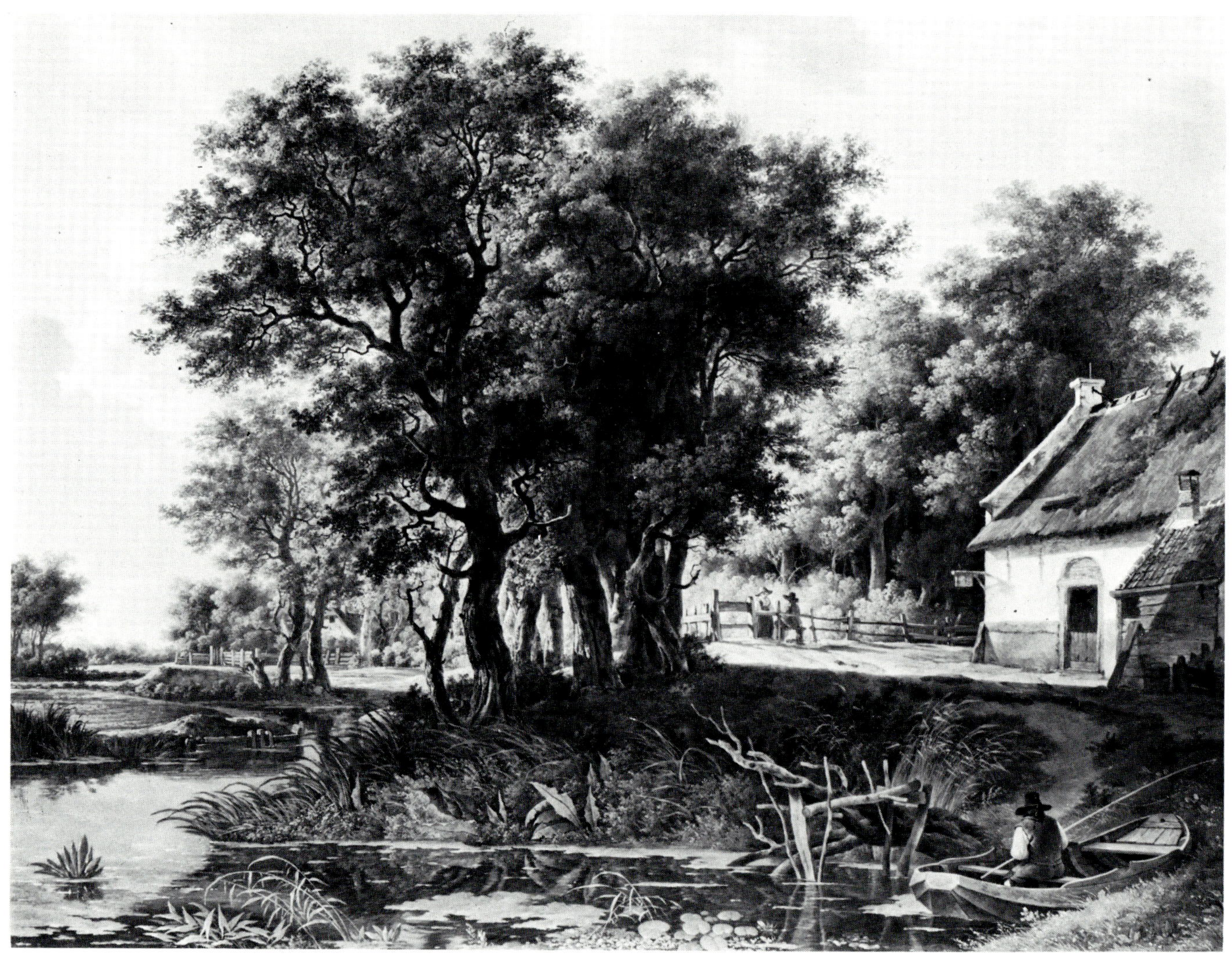

Working on this landscape in collaboration with the younger artist **Adrianus van den Koogh,** (1796-1831) *Strij emerges more as a figure of his time – with a lesser debt to Cuyp. (28 x 36ins.).* Photograph courtesy of Sotheby's.

middle does certainly resemble the little old houses of the great Delft artist in the Six Museum, only the composition is fuller and the house is overshadowed by a tall tree, behind which appears a stretch of dunes in the manner of Wijnants, who was much imitated at that time. In the foreground, to the left, is an inoffensive "set-off," very usual at the period, in the shape of a splintered tree-stump. To the right is an outbuilding, set at right angles to the house itself and grown over with a vine. Although it reminds one most particularly of Vermeer, this little picture, which was bought at the sale of the Suermondt collection, suggests by turns Ruysdael, Hobbema and Cuyp. But no one suspected that it was painted about 1800. The painting in the Rijksmuseum is greatly inferior. Van der Laen was a friend of Rhijnvis Feith and drew some illustrations for his *Fanny.* He died in 1829.

Jan Kobell belongs to a whole generation of Rotterdam artists, all of whom were talented, energetic landscape-painters, greatly in demand in their time, and all of whom died young, at thirty or forty. Jan Kobell, the chief of them, was born at Rotterdam in 1778 and educated at the Jansenist orphan asylum at Utrecht. He received lessons in painting at the school kept by W.R. van der Wall, a son of the Utrecht sculptor and himself a painter of landscapes with cattle. After achieving a considerable name in his native country, he sent a *Meadow with three small animals* for exhibition in Paris in 1812, which is praised by Landon in his *Salon* of the same year. He now received commissions from France and was really successful, but he was over-ambitious and dissatisfied. His mind broke down in the following year and he died in 1814.

When we look at Kobell's little pictures in the Rijksmuseum, with their charming presentation, their careful execution, their restful composition and a certain elegiac quality peculiar to his best work, we find it difficult to understand this ending to his life. He seemed to combine the calm execution of Paul Potter with something in the composition that reminds one of Dujardin or of Adriaan van de Velde. This is certain, that he was a cultured painter, who, even if he did not look for a certain poetry of expression in his landscapes with cattle, achieved it in spite of himself. In 1831, one of his paintings, in Professor Bleuland's collection, fetched 2,835 guilders. He left a number of drawings and a few sensitive, delicate little etchings.

It has been observed, in connection with Potter's early death, that artists who have been allotted but a short span of life often produce as much, or even more, in those few years than others who live much longer. It is as though they intuitively feel a need for haste. This applies not only to Kobell, but also to W.J. van Troostwijk, a member of the well-to-do class, born in Amsterdam in 1782. He is said to have painted for his amusement; but, whether we regard him as an amateur or a professional, there is no doubt but that he employed his time well. He was taught by the brothers Andriessen, of whom the elder had had Quinckhard for his master, and began by painting portraits, which he soon abandoned for the Potter style, which attracted him more. Two of his landscapes in the Rijksmuseum make a really astonishing impression in the surroundings amid which they are placed. Like Van der Laen's landscape, they impress one with their sheer artistic merit, their fine, wholesome conception, their true Dutch compactness. But, as against the study of the old masters which is apparent in the others, we find here something more modern, a greater freedom of workmanship and ideas. And, although the vigorous colouring, the positive conception, the manner of execution all betray the proficient painter, there is something so very different, so much less artificial in the independent choice of subjects as naturally to suggest an enthusiastic amateur rather than an experienced studio-painter. Again, the sultry blue of a summer sky, the deep green of the heavy thatch of a sheepfold and the white of the cows display a richness of colour which very closely approaches the modern and which is found (true, in a more complicated scheme) in the Barbizon school. Van Troostwijk possessed an originality of ideas that made him say:

"I admire Potter, Dujardin and Van der Velde, but I follow only simple and beautiful nature. If you wish to compare my work, compare it with my earlier efforts or, rather, compare it with nature."

And, notwithstanding his great dissatisfaction with his work, which often he completed only at the bidding of his friends, he knew quite well what he wanted:

"In Potter himself," he once said, "there is something which, it seems to me, ought to have been different and which Potter himself must have felt. But how far ahead of me was this same Potter, who died in his twenty-eighth year!"

Later investigations have shown that Potter lived one year longer. Van Troostwijk, however, did die in 1810, before attaining the age of twenty-eight. He was a talented and, for his period, an astonishing painter. His drawings also were in great request and, towards the end of his life, he produced a few etchings.

The fifth of the group, George Pieter Westenberg, offers for our admiration, in his *View of Amsterdam under Snow,* all those qualities of good painting which have distinguished landscape-painters at any given time. The picture is painted with directness and sobriety; is simply and yet broadly observed, firm and even in workmanship, without being laboured, and has the depth of penetration of a Ruysdael. Nor need we be acquainted with the fact that Westenberg was a great expert in the works of our old masters, whom he studied here and abroad, to arrive at this knowledge; for, whereas this little picture reminds us of Ruysdael and, more particularly, of the wintry view in the Dupper collection, the town-view in Teyler's Museum as powerfully suggests Vermeer of Delft, not only through the character and treatment of the little old houses, but also through a certain yellow and blue in the jackets of the women sitting on the door-steps.

Westenberg was born at Nijmegen in 1791 and came to Amsterdam in 1808, where he was taught by Jan Hulswit (1766-1822), a tapestry-painter whose drawings in the style of Ostade and Beerstraten were often greatly appreciated. He, in his turn, had as his pupils his kinsman Kasper Karssen (1810-1896), a deserving painter of landscapes and town-pieces, George Andries Roth (1809-1887), Hendrik Gerrit ten Cate (1803-1856) and Hendrik Jacobus Scholten, mentioned in the following chapter. In 1838, he was appointed director of the Museum of Modern Art in the Pavilion at Haarlem. We do not know whether he failed

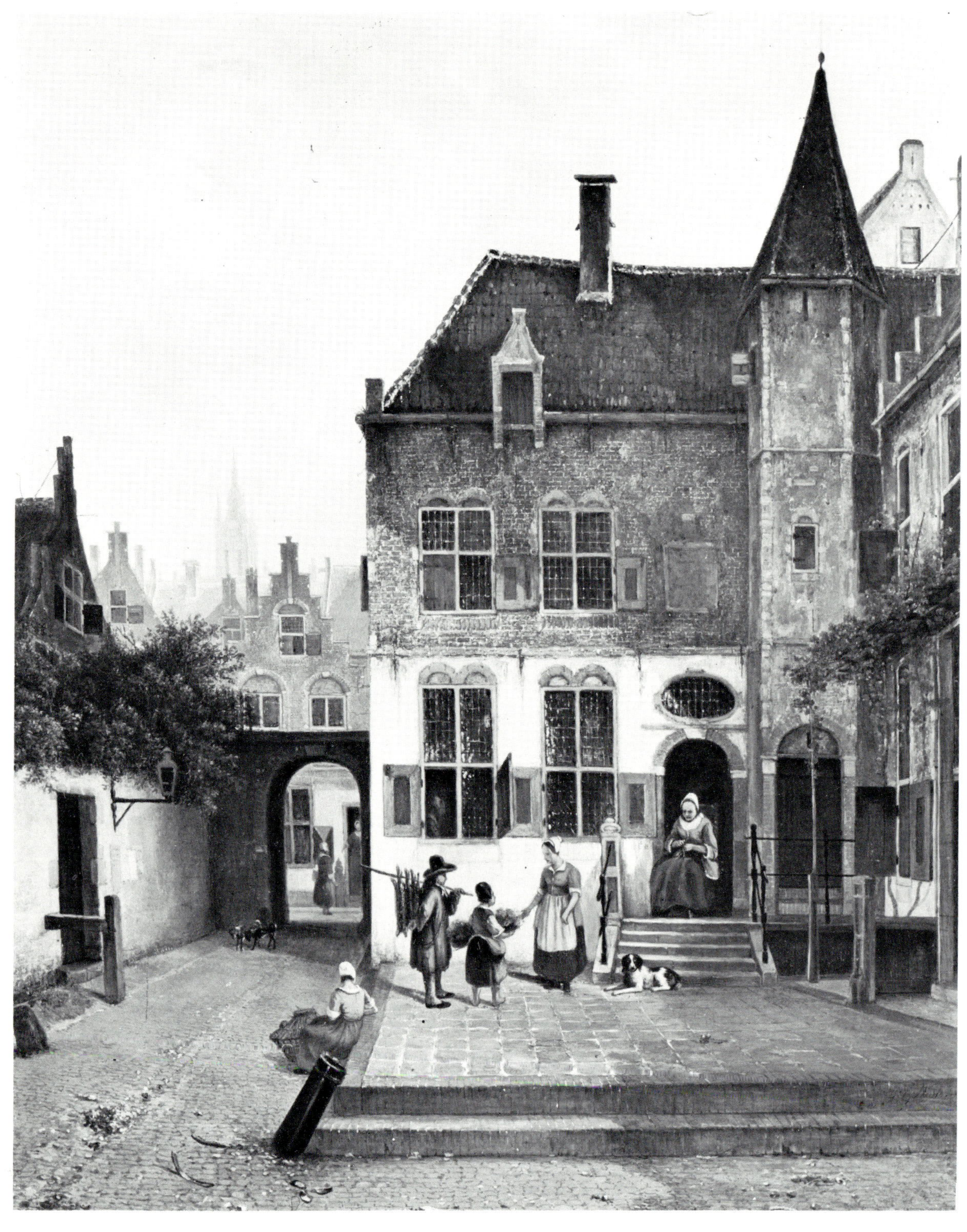

Above and right: **George Pieter Westenberg** (1791-1873) *was a great expert in the works of the older masters. These two views of Delft dated 1834 show him firmly grounded in the 17th century townscape tradition. (Each 31 x 26inches).* Photographs courtesy of Spenser S.A.

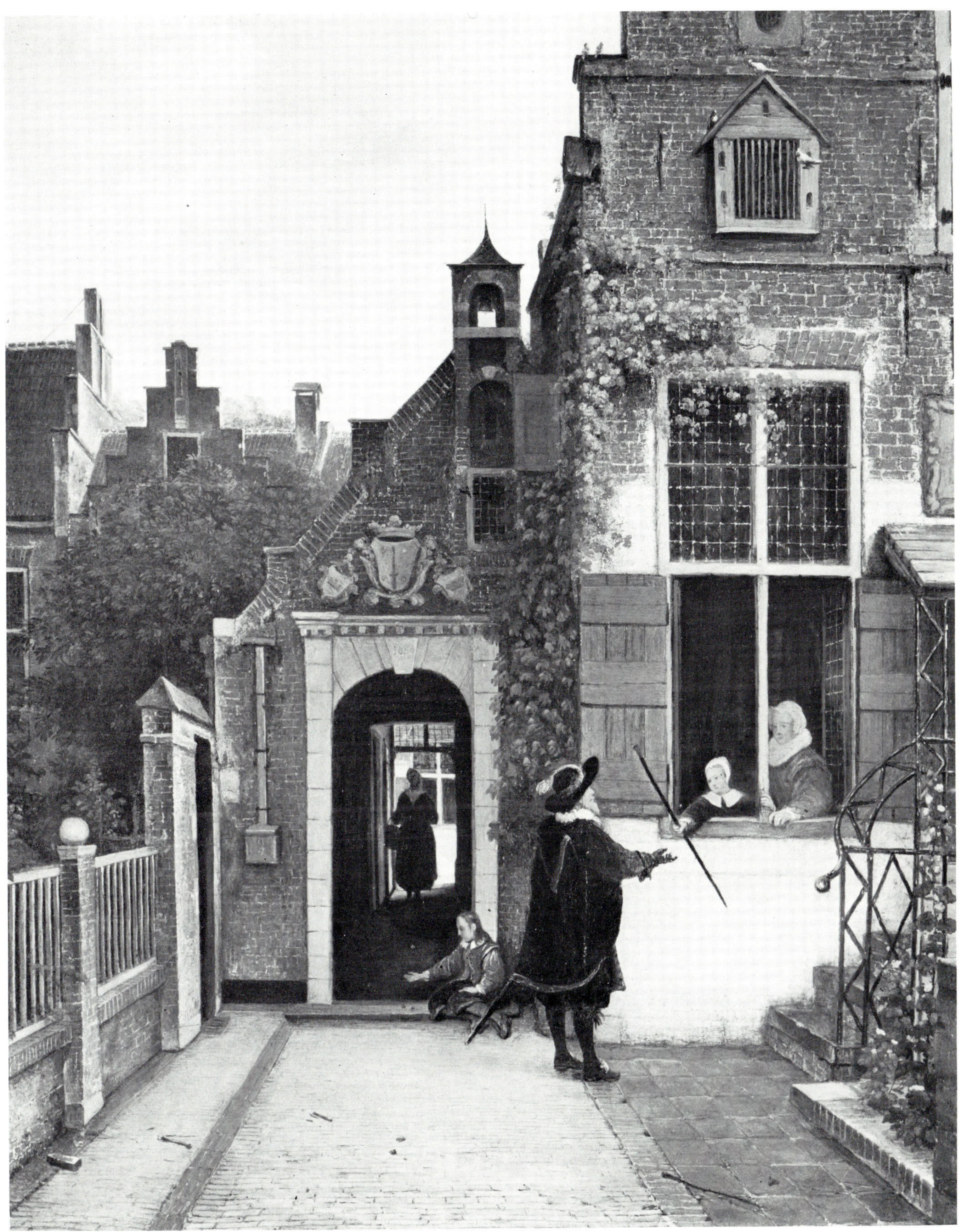

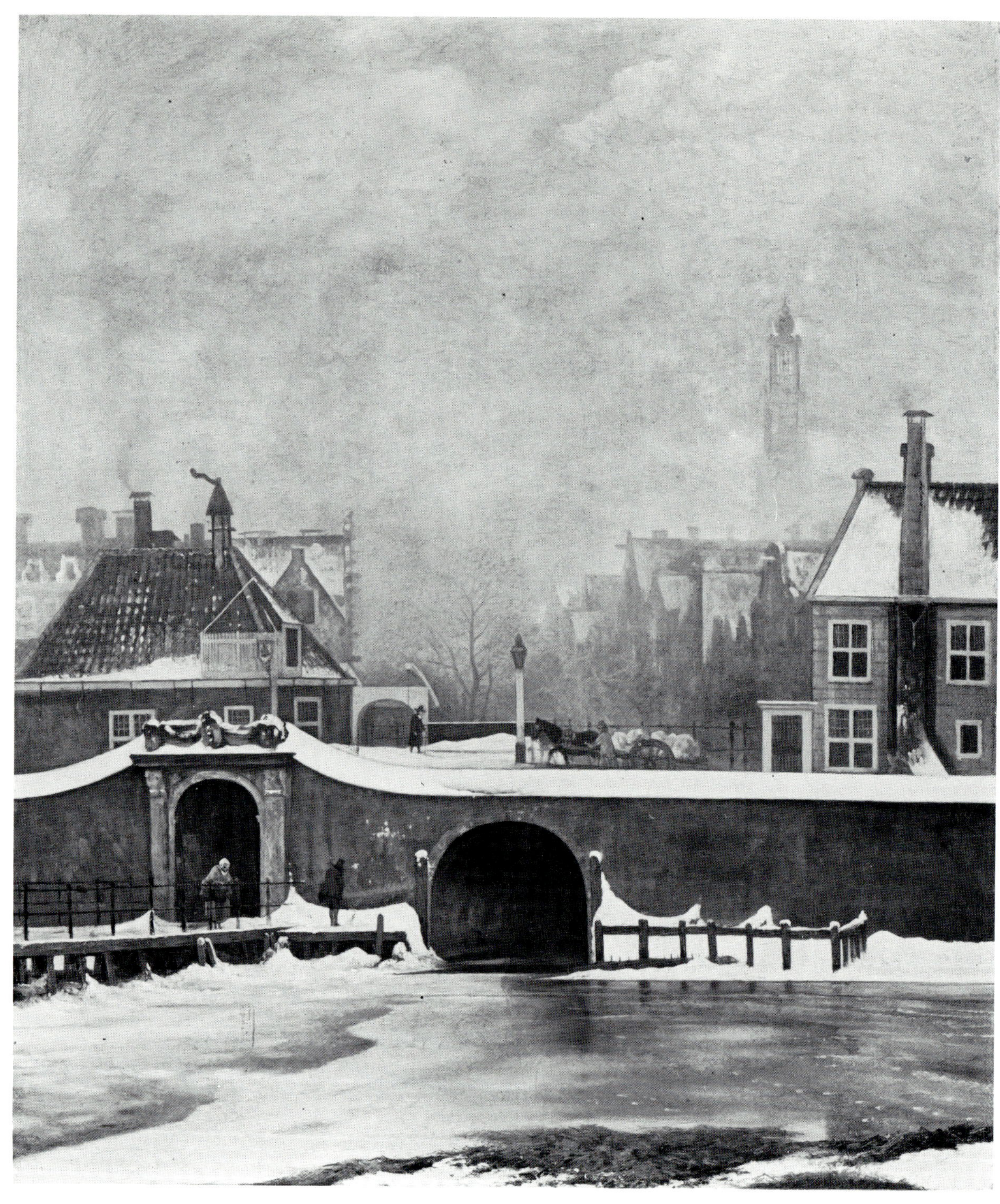

W.J. van Troostwijk (1782-1810). *This fine winter scene in Amsterdam by W.J. van Troostwijk in the Rijksmuseum has much more in common with the late 19th century than with his contemporaries. Painted in 1809 it combines strong planes of contrasting colour, a mist effect of which Monet would have been proud, and a simple realism at odds with the Dutch tradition – and the dawn of romanticism.* Photograph courtesy of the Rijksmuseum, Amsterdam.

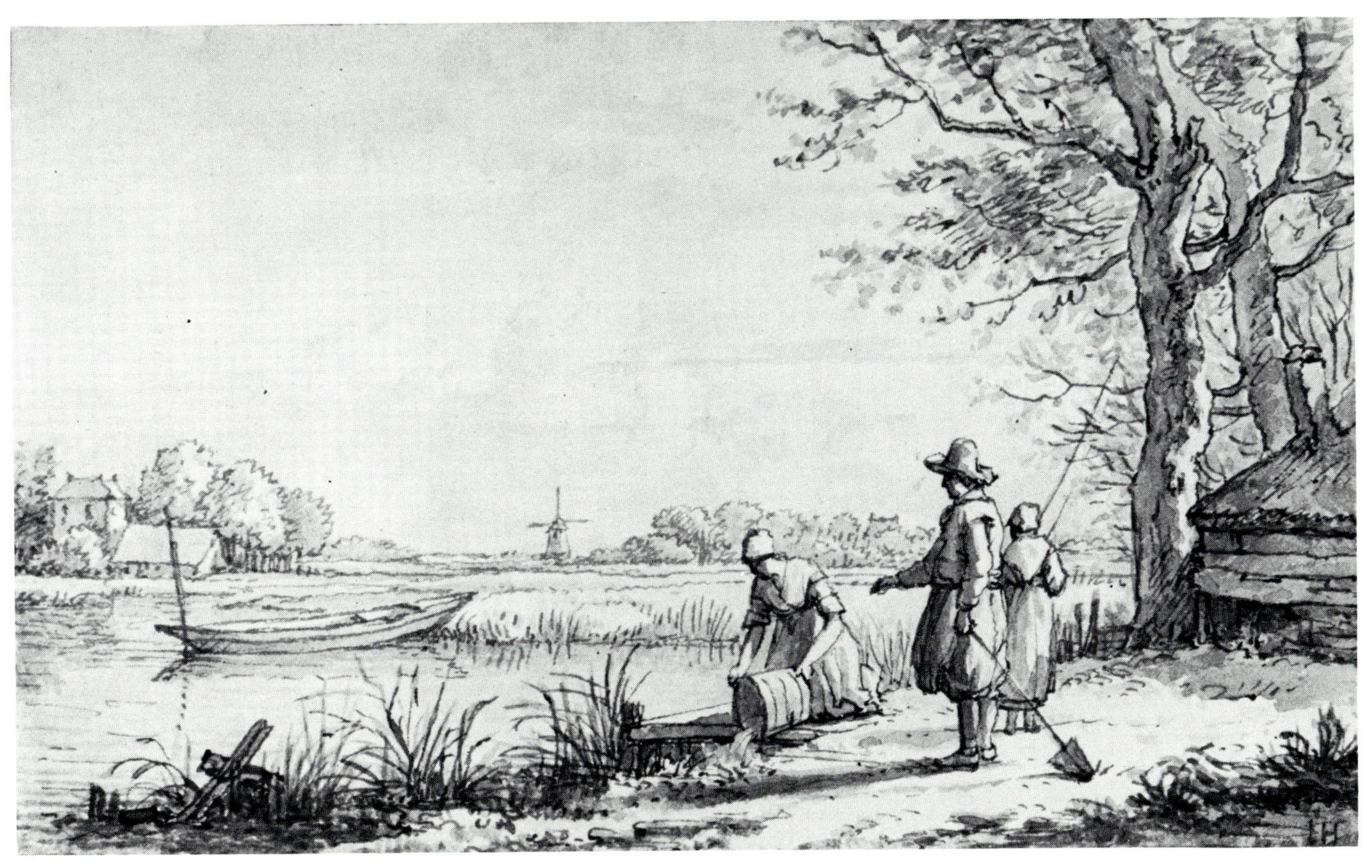

Jan Hulswit (1766-1822) *was Westenberg's teacher in Amsterdam. His own drawings, like this sepia landscape, were based on Ostade and Beerstraten and much sought after in his time. (9½ x 16cms.).* Photograph courtesy of Mak van Waay, Amsterdam.

to make a sufficient living as a painter, but in 1857 he resigned his post and went to Java with his family to fill a civil appointment in Batavia. He died at Brummen in 1873.

More important than Westenberg is Nicolaas Bauer, who was born at Harlingen in 1767 and died at the same Frisian village in 1820. He was taught by his father, a portrait-painter, began his career as a tapestry-painter, but afterwards painted town-views and landscapes. A view of Amsterdam seen from the IJ and one of Rotterdam from the Maas belong to his best works. There is a pleasant freshness and movement in these little pieces, combined with a striking originality of conception and colour.

There were many Frisian painters at that period, including Willem Bartel van der Kooi, who was born at Augustinusga in 1768 and who made a name as a portrait-painter at the Hague and Ghent. His masters were, first, a skilful amateur called Verrier and, later, Beekkerk, the painter. Things went differently in those days: it appears that concentration upon one's deliberately chosen profession was not always deemed essential; at any rate, he abandoned his art in 1795 to become the representative of the electors of Friesland and afterwards in favour of various political appointments. These, however, may have belonged to the sinecures that were very common at the end of the eighteenth century; for, in 1804, Van der Kooi went on an art-journey to Düsseldorf, where he copied portraits by Van Dijck and made so much progress that, in 1808, his picture, *A Lady with a Footman handing a Letter,* won the 2,000-guilder prize at the exhibition.

This piece is now at the Rijksmuseum and is no more than pale coloured plaster. The Town-hall at Haarlem has a portrait by him which has something in common with Jan Adam Kruseman's *Portrait of Himself,* although it is much weaker. He died in 1836.

Johannes Jelgerhuis Rienkzn was born in 1770 at Leeuwarden and was taught drawing by his father, Rienk Jelgerhuis, and painting by Pieter Barbiers Pz.

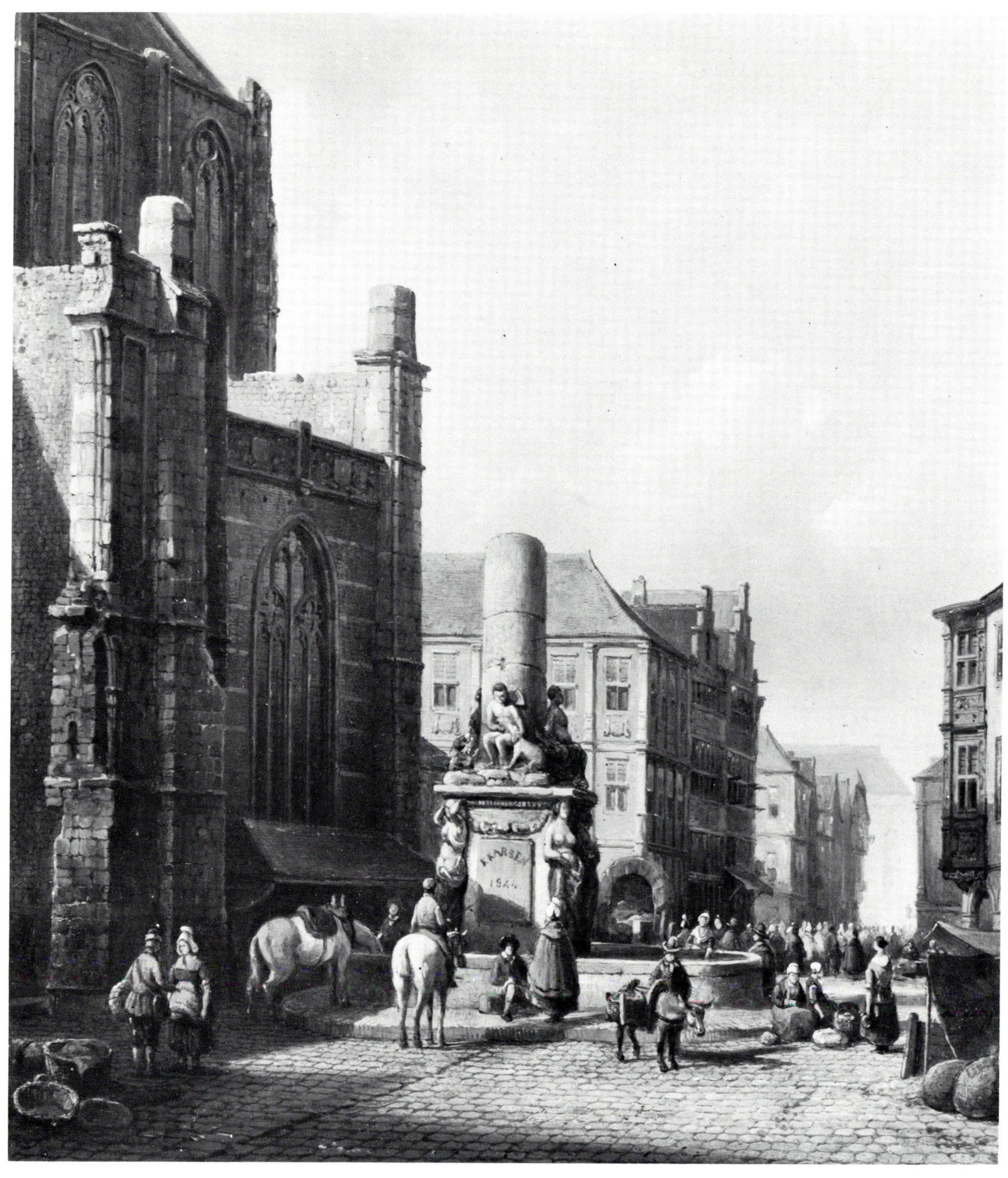

Kaspar Karssen, (1810-1896) *a pupil of Westenberg, shows his master's influence in his fine landscapes and townscapes. This Dutch street scene is painted on panel, measuring 11 x 9¾ins.* Photograph courtesy of Richard Green.

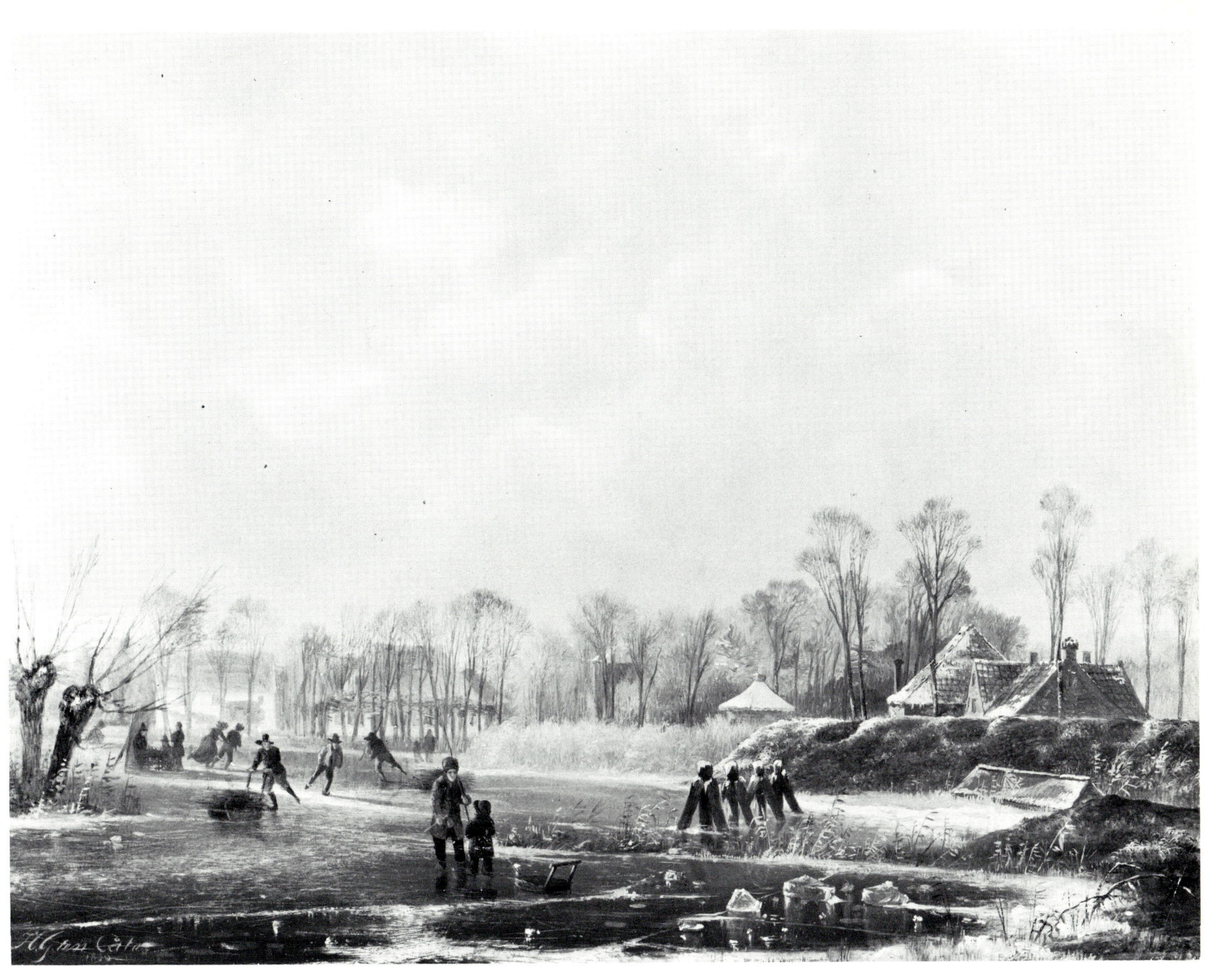

Hendrik Gerrit ten Cate (1803-1856) *was another pupil of Westenberg's. This winter landscape is painted on panel (11¼ x 14ins.) and dated 1839.* **Photograph courtesy of Richard Green.**

(1748-1842), the landscape-painter. The father, as I have said in an earlier chapter, was best known for his pastel and crayon portraits; the son painted portraits and interiors. We find pictures and drawings by this artist in different collections and even at this date his picture in the Rijksmuseum, *The Bookshop of P. Meijer Warnars*[1], strikes one by the typical representation, which, although simpler, does not differ greatly from the concrete manner in which De Brakeleer treated similar subjects. His *Apothecary* is in the same manner, entirely excellent, very graphically and at the same time concretely executed and yet astonishingly simple. His *View of the Choir in the New Church, Amsterdam* was greatly praised at the time. He died at Haarlem in 1836.

Less stimulating than Jelgerhuis, but excellent

[1]Johannes Jelgerhuis, who for many years was an actor at the Amsterdam Theatre as well as a painter, wrote a work on gesticulation and mimicry which was published by Meijer Warnars in 1827.

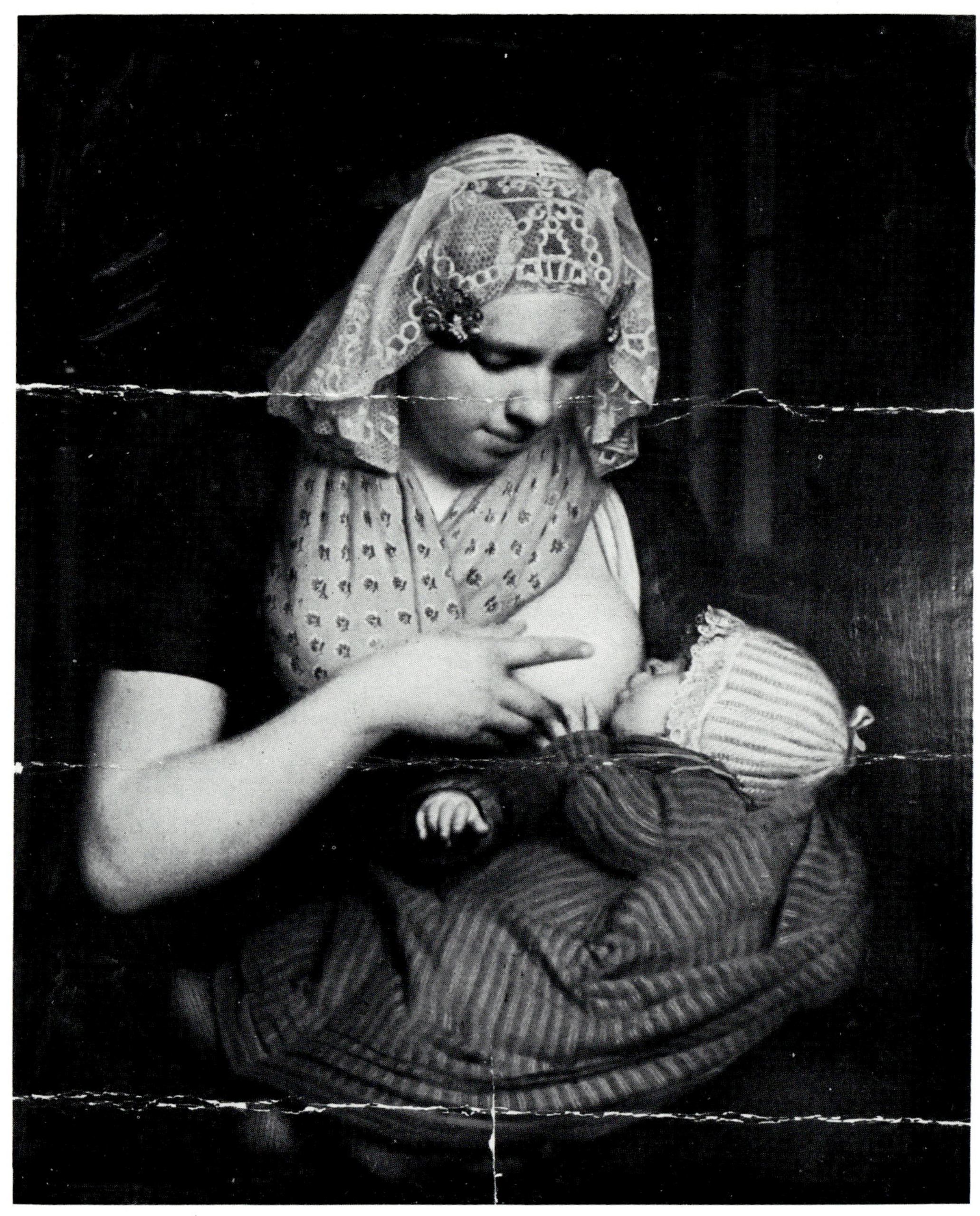

Willem Bartel van der Kooi (1768-1836) *was a young Friesian artist who combined politics with painting portraits and genre scenes. His work is rare. This painting was sold at Mak van Waay in 1953 and the photograph, in spite of damage, shows the simple insight and fine technique of a distinguished artist.* Photograph courtesy of Mak van Waay, Amsterdam.

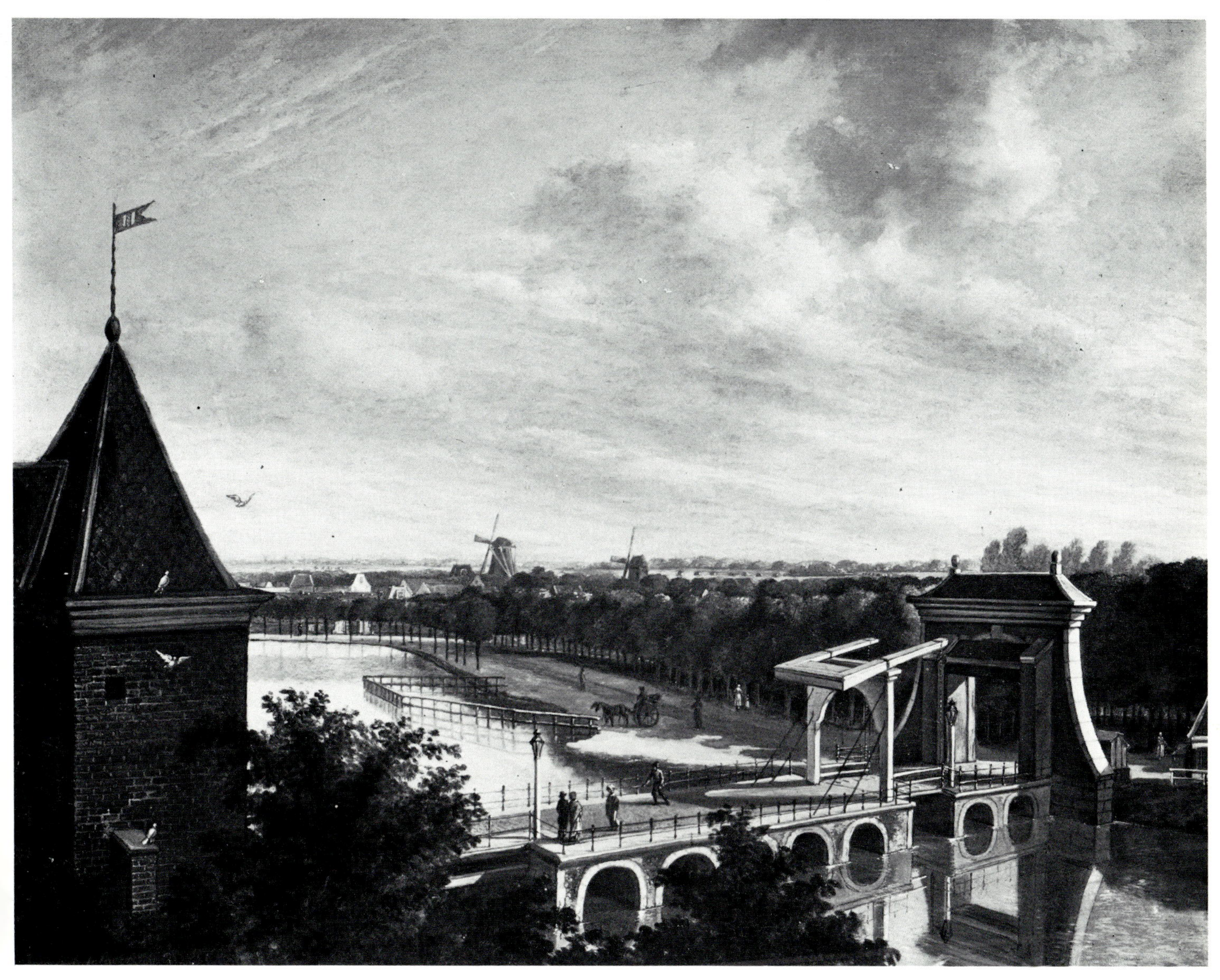

Johannes Jelgerhuis Rienkz (1770-1836) *here uses an unusual perspective to give us an intimate view of the Leiderspoort of Amsterdam (36.5 x 45cms.).* Photograph courtesy of the Rijksmuseum, Amsterdam.

genre-painters, were Wybrandt Hendriks (1744-1831) and Adriaan de Lelie (1755-1820), both of whom have left interiors which, while lacking all the concentration of light, all the fine atmosphere in which, in the old masters, the figures move so naturally and freely, still have something that connects them with the older pictures. Hendriks, an Amsterdammer by birth, painted landscapes, portraits, corporation- and family-pieces and still-life pictures of game and flowers. His *Woman reading,* in Teyler's Museum, bears a distant resemblance to a Metsu. He is more original in his portrait of *Notary Kolme and his Clerk,* whom he painted in their own environment, at full-length, but in small dimensions. This little piece, which has nothing in common with the seventeenth century, hangs at the Rijksmuseum beside a genre-painting by Quinckhard.

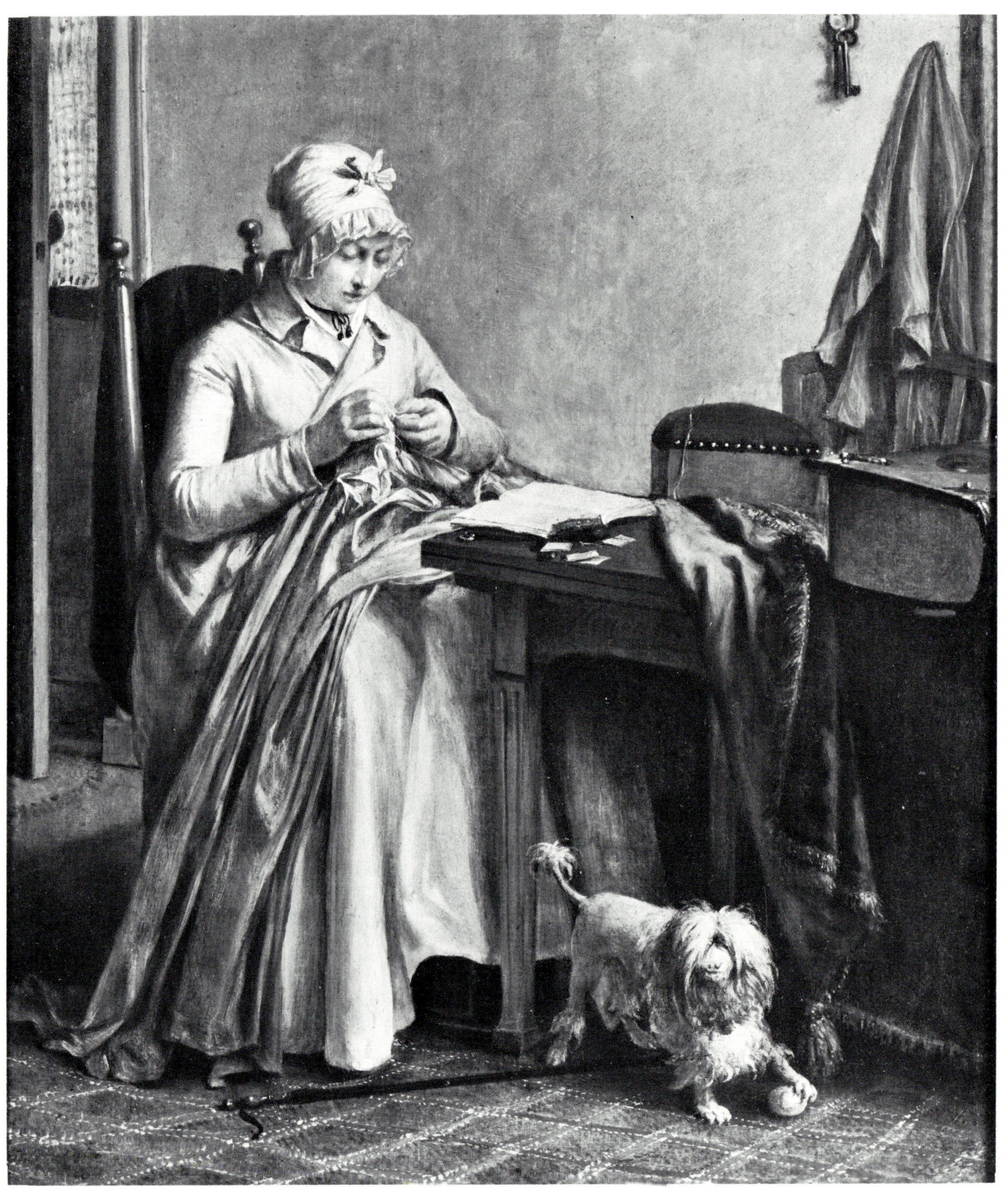

Wybrandt Hendriks (1744-1831) *is shown to good advantage as a genre painter in this small panel of a woman sewing. (34.4 x 29.3 cms.).* Photograph courtesy of the Rijksmuseum, Amsterdam.

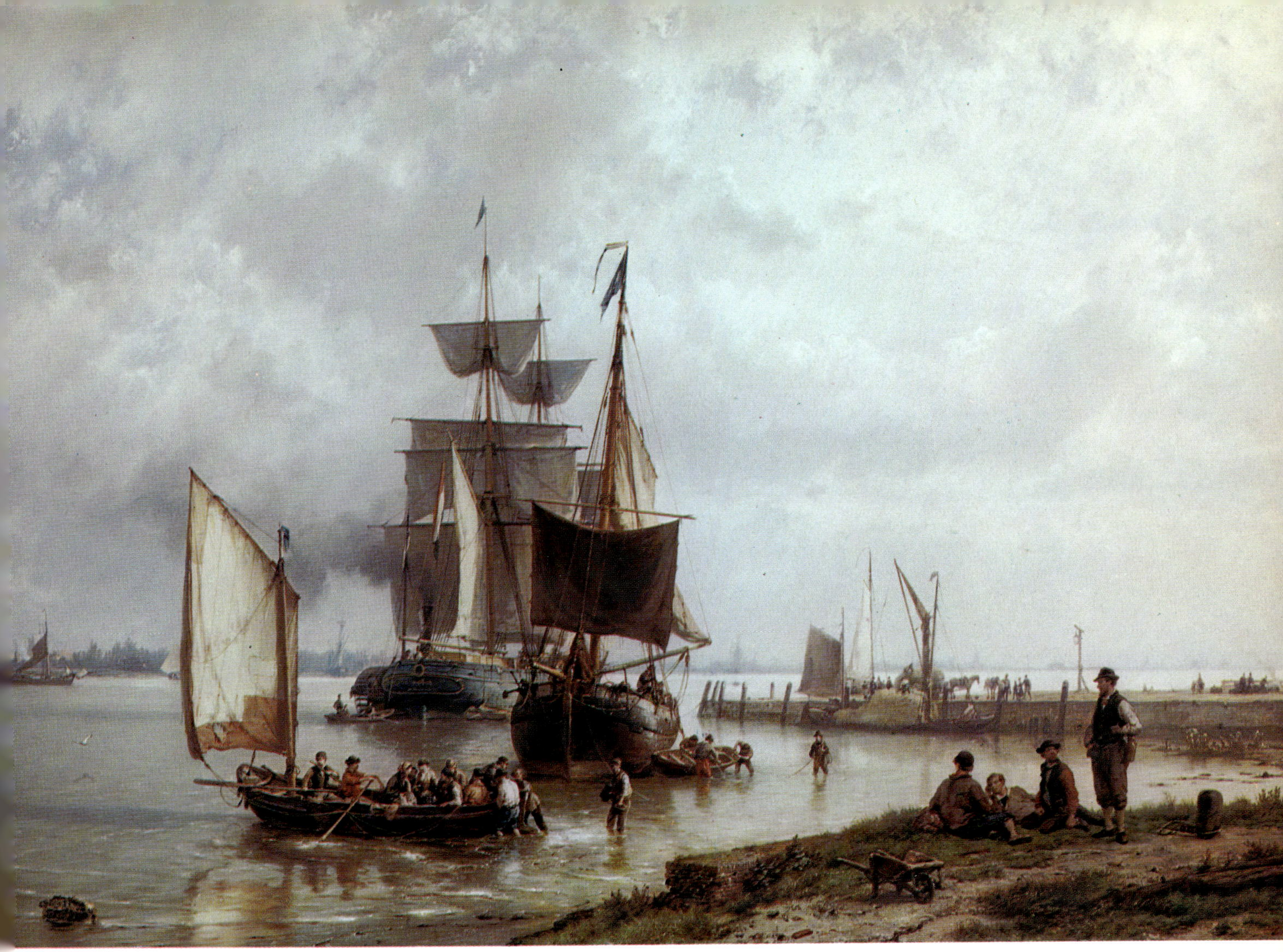

Hermanus Koekkoek (1815-1882). *"A harbour scene with shipping." (31 x 45ins.).* Photograph courtesy of Richard Green.

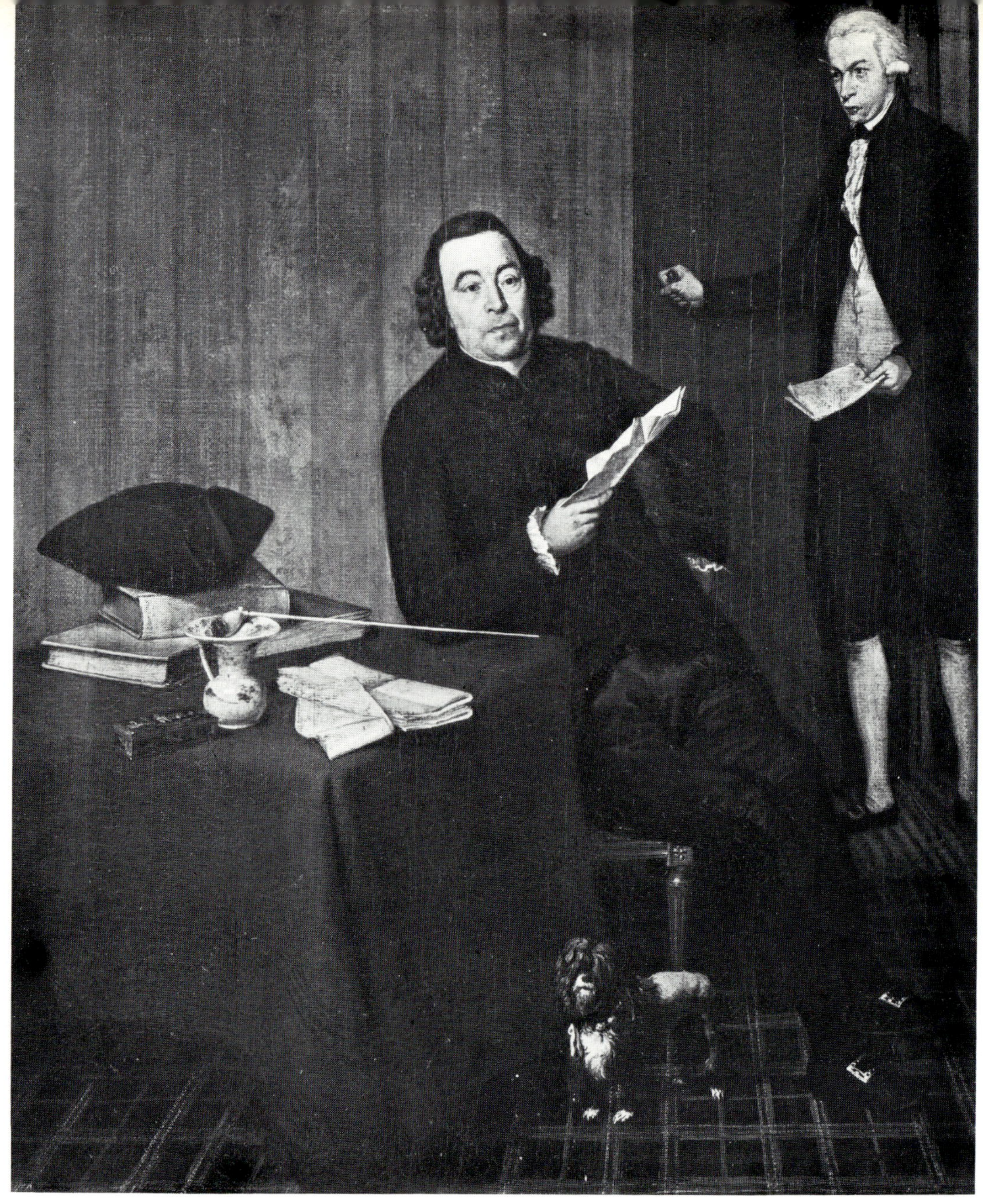

Wybrandt Hendriks (1744-1831) *was noted both for his landscapes and interiors. This interior "Notary Köhne and his clerk" is a piece of simple realism in small dimensions. (63 x 51 cms.).* Photograph courtesy of the Rijksmuseum, Amsterdam.

It is blacker in tone, but surpasses it in originality and distinction. To judge by the prices fetched by his works after his death, his views of towns, or rather streets, were esteemed more highly than his interiors. The reason may, however, be due to topographical considerations. Hendriks was, for more than thirty years, steward of Teyler's Institute and superintendent of the collection of pictures attached to it.

Although Adriaan de Lelie was, in many respects, far behind Hendriks, he was a deserving painter of interiors. He was born at Tilburg, studied at Antwerp and Düsseldorf and settled in Amsterdam, where he painted mainly interiors, portraits and family and corporation-pieces. His works are to be found in the principal collections and were also valued and sought after by foreigners. The Fodor Museum has a *Cook* by him which, although somewhat empty and rather flat and narrow in the face, is, like the *Woman making Cakes* in the Rijksmuseum, a well-painted, well-composed picture.

Chapter V

The Forerunners of the Hague School

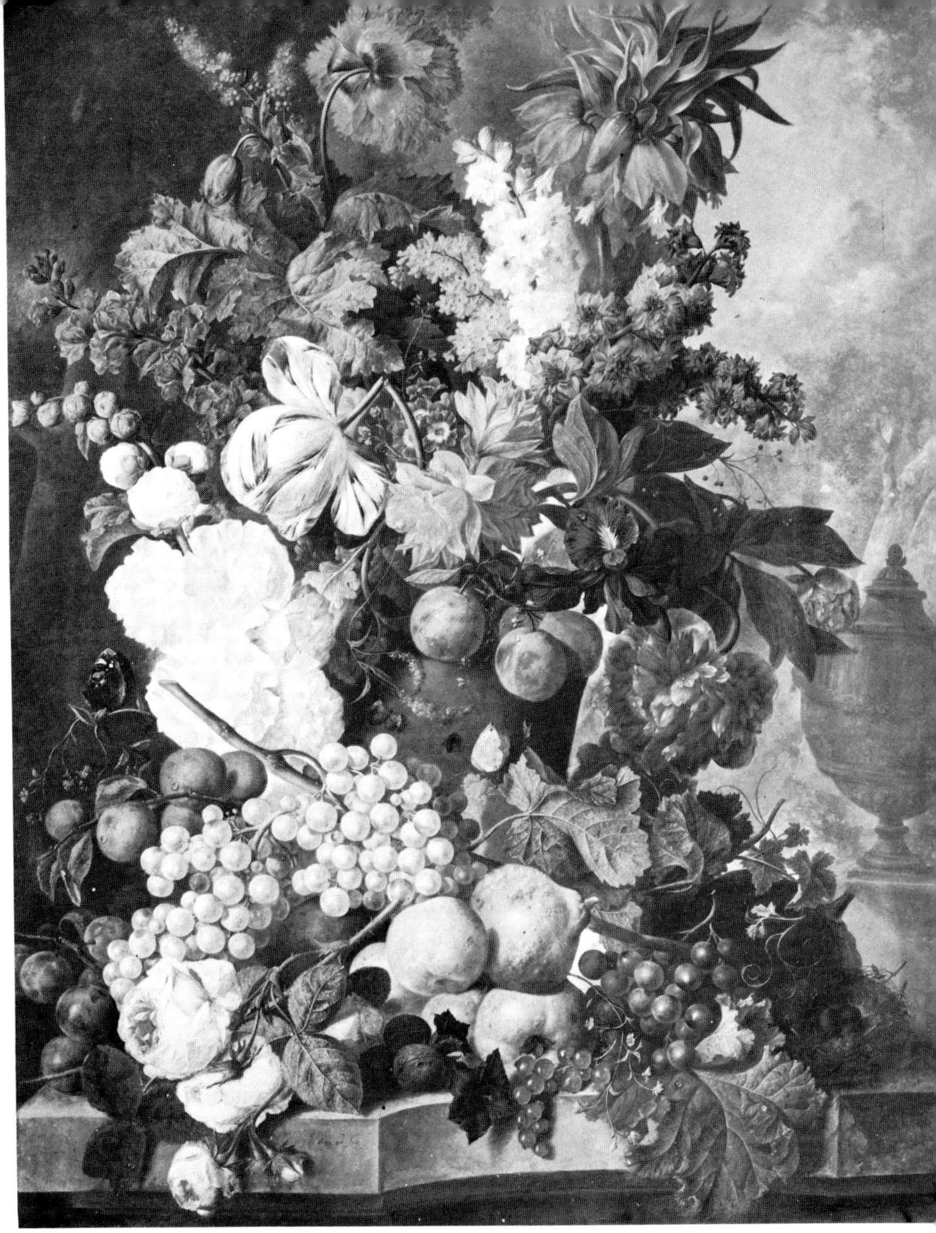

Jan van Os (1744-1808), *the father of a tribe of painters, now tends to be looked on as an "Old Master" although he lived into the 19th century. His still lives of flowers and fruit, usually orgies of highly decorative vegetation like this one, are highly sought after. (37¾ x 28¼ins. on panel).* **Photograph courtesy of Christie, Manson and Woods.**

The Van Os family of painters, of whom Jan, the oldest (1744-1808), his son Georgius Johannes Jacobus (1782-1861), the flower-painter, and the latter's brother Pieter Gerardus (1776-1839), the cattle-painter, were the best known, can boast of good qualities in spite of the fact that each of its members now counts mainly as a master of later generations. In addition to the above, there were Pieter Frederik (1808-1892), a son of the last-named, and Margaretha (1780-1862), a sister of the same Pieter Gerardus, completing a painting family of five that covers the period between 1744 and 1862, over a century in all. The father, Jan van Os, was a painter of flowers, but was far surpassed by his son and pupil, who, in some respects, may be called an excellent flower-painter. His pictures of still-life and flowers were much sought

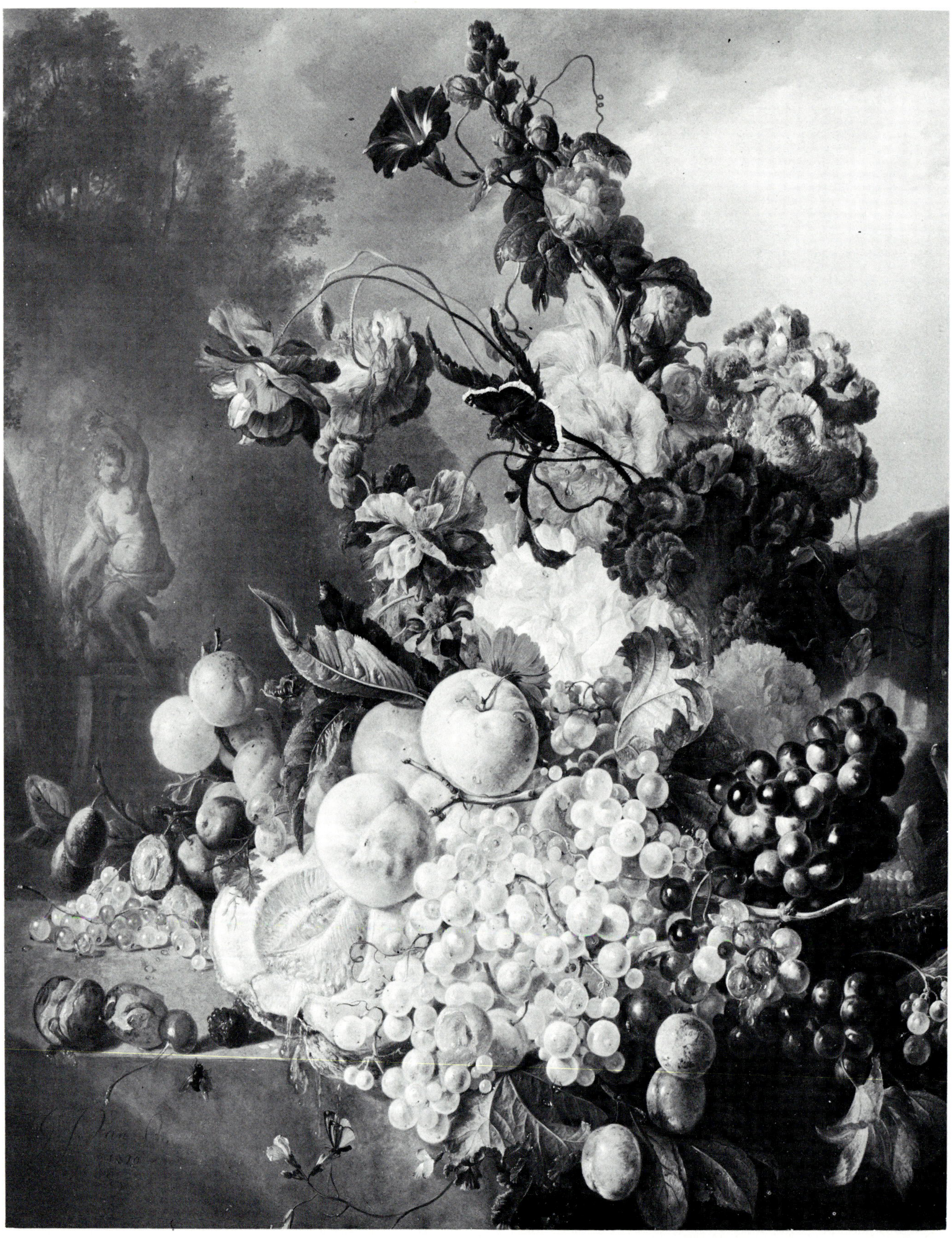

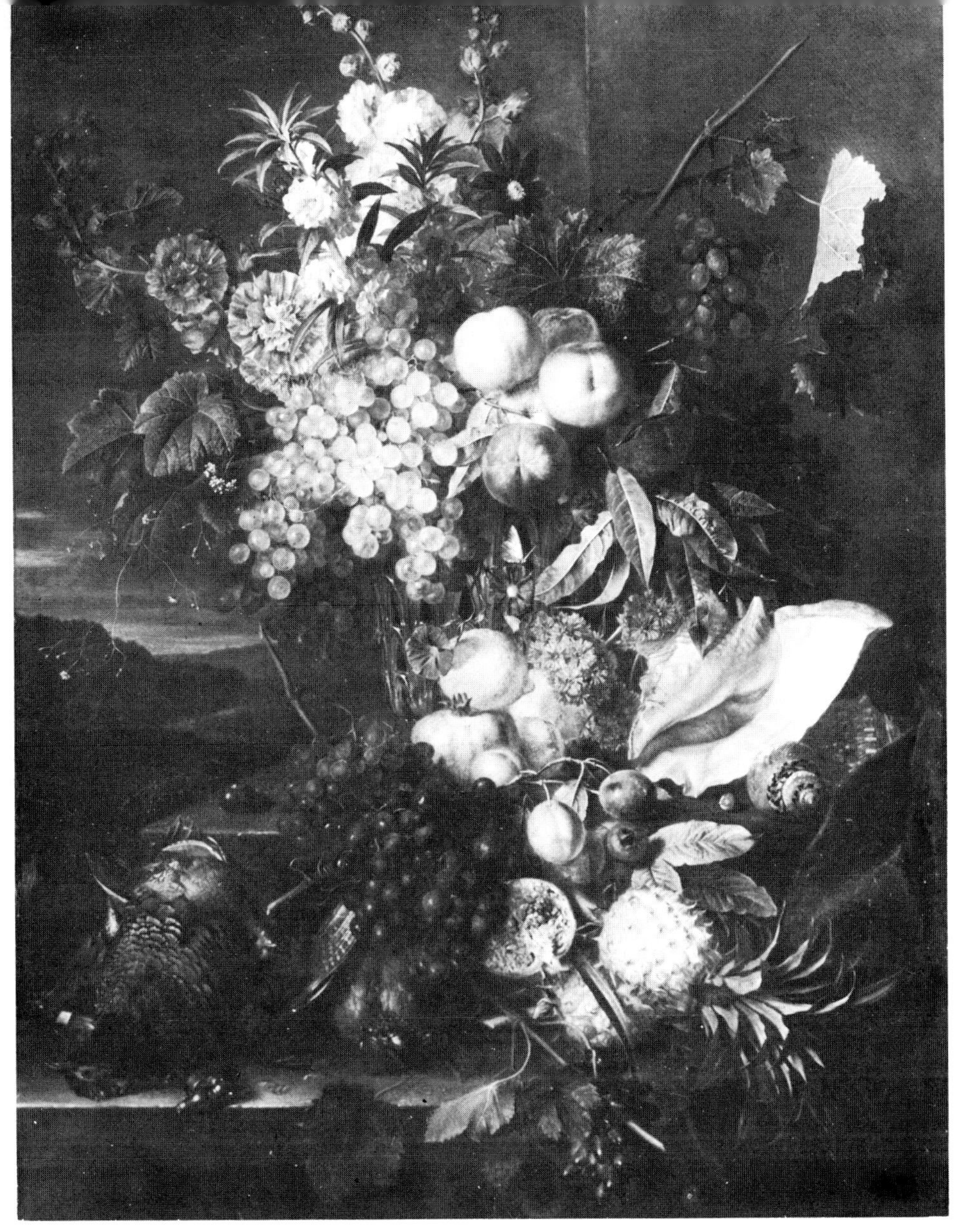

Above and left: **Georgius Johannes Jacobus van Os (1782-1861)** *followed in his father's footsteps as a flower painter and has been considered the greater of the two artists. These two examples measure 30½ x 24¾ inches and 111 x 115 cms. respectively, that on the right being dated 1815.* Photographs courtesy of Richard Green and Mak Van Waay, Amsterdam.

after and one of them fetched 5,650 guilders at auction in 1845. His brother, Pieter Gerardus, also made a name for himself. He painted in the manner of Potter and, though he received his earliest lessons from his father, he formed himself, by industrious copying, upon his illustrious model. His incidents of the Siege of Naarden, in which he took part as a volunteer, are more important than the ordinary historical pieces of his time; and there is something spontaneous in his *Cossack Outpost* which almost recalls Breitner in the unity between the landscape and the group of soldiers. His chief pupils are Wouterus Verschuur (1812-1874), Simon van den Berg (1812-1891), who left some cabinet-pieces not devoid of feeling, Guillaume Anne van der Brugghen (1811-1891), a fine dog-painter, whose studies remind one of Maris, and Jan van Ravenzwaay (1789-1869), who continued his master's ideas, while Pieter Frederik, his son, became the valued

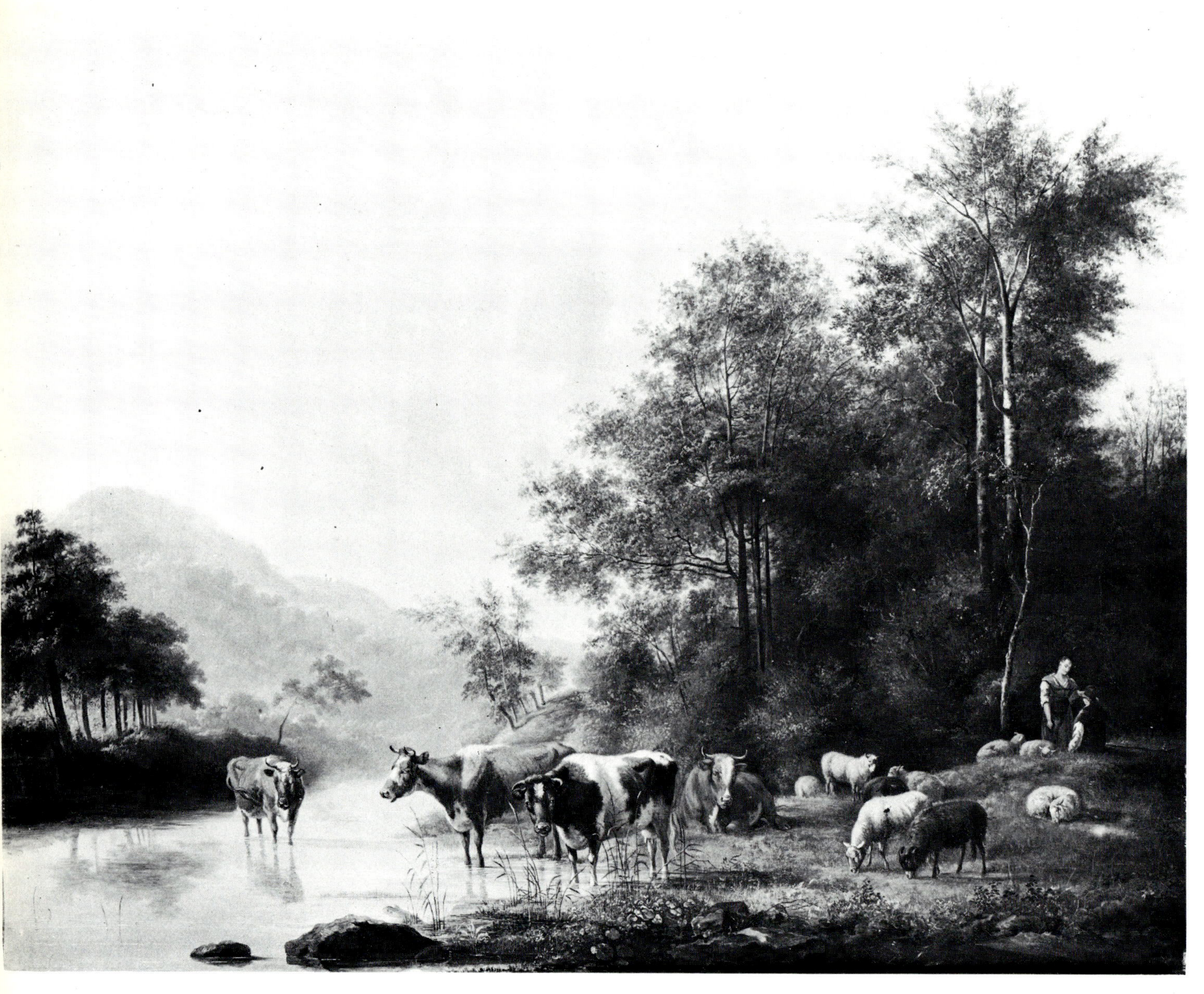

Above: **Pieter Gerhardus van Os** (1776-1839) *was a devoted follower of the 17th century cattle painter Paul Potter. This painting demonstrates how closely and successfully he emulated his master. (71 x 88cms.).* Photograph courtesy of Mak van Waay, Amsterdam.

Right: **Jan van Ravenzwaay** (1789-1869) *was a pupil of P.G. van Os. The relaxed brushwork of this small view of a Dutch fishing village at dusk looks forward to the Hague School. (7½ x 11½ins.).* Photograph courtesy of Sotheby & Co.

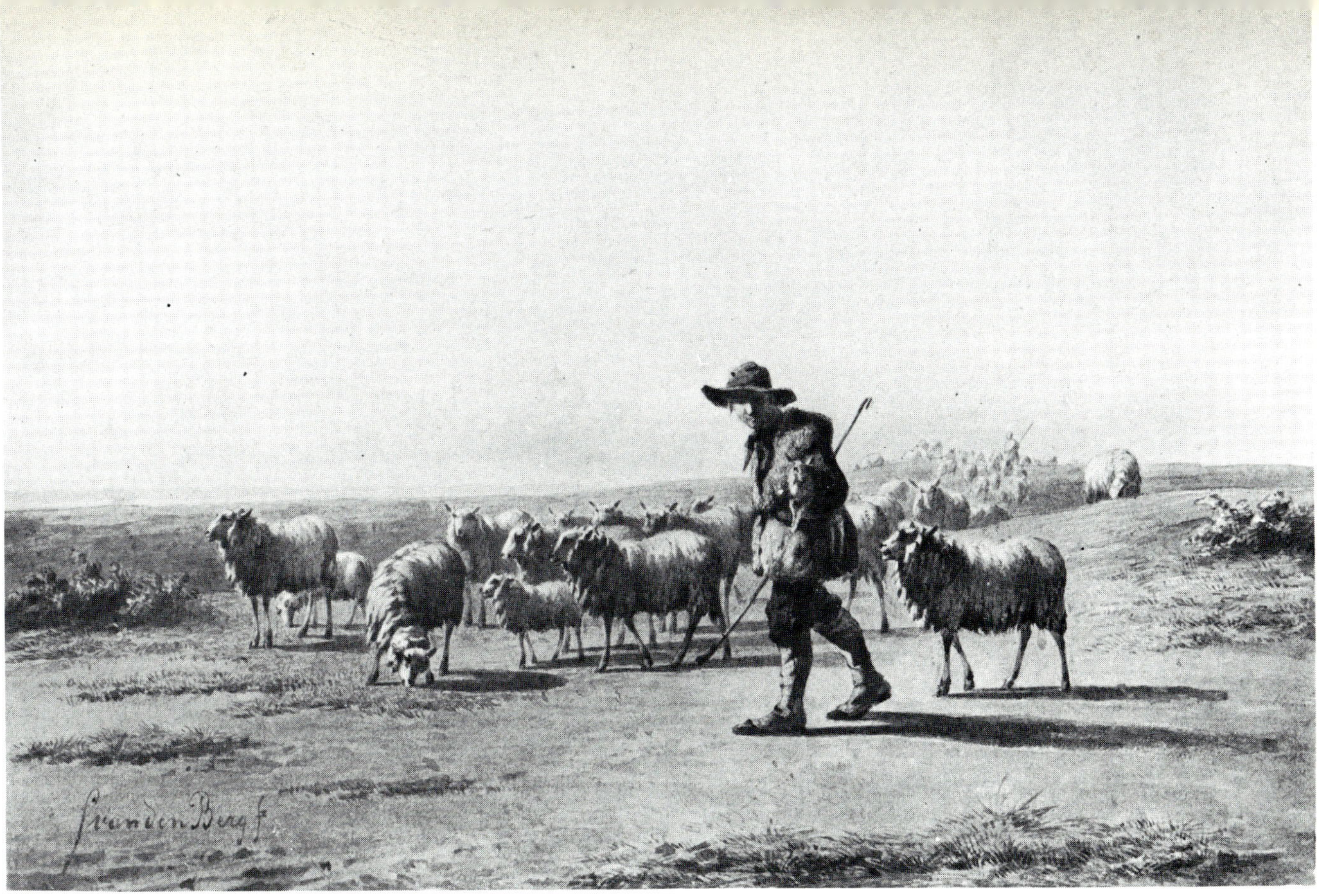

Simon van den Berg (1812-1891) *was a pupil of P.G. van Os, whose influence can be traced in this watercolour. He worked at the Hague and became Director of the Royal Museum. (20½ and 29cms.).* Photograph courtesy of Mak van Waay, Amsterdam.

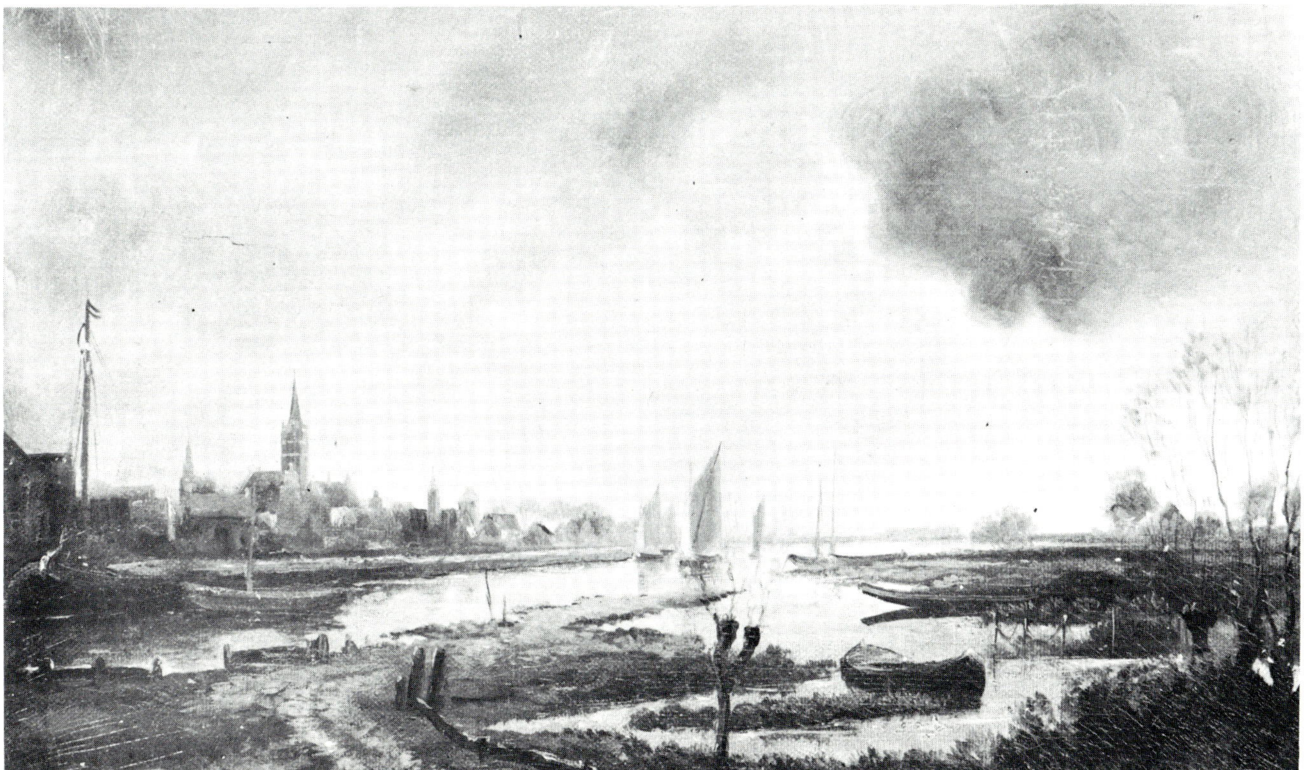

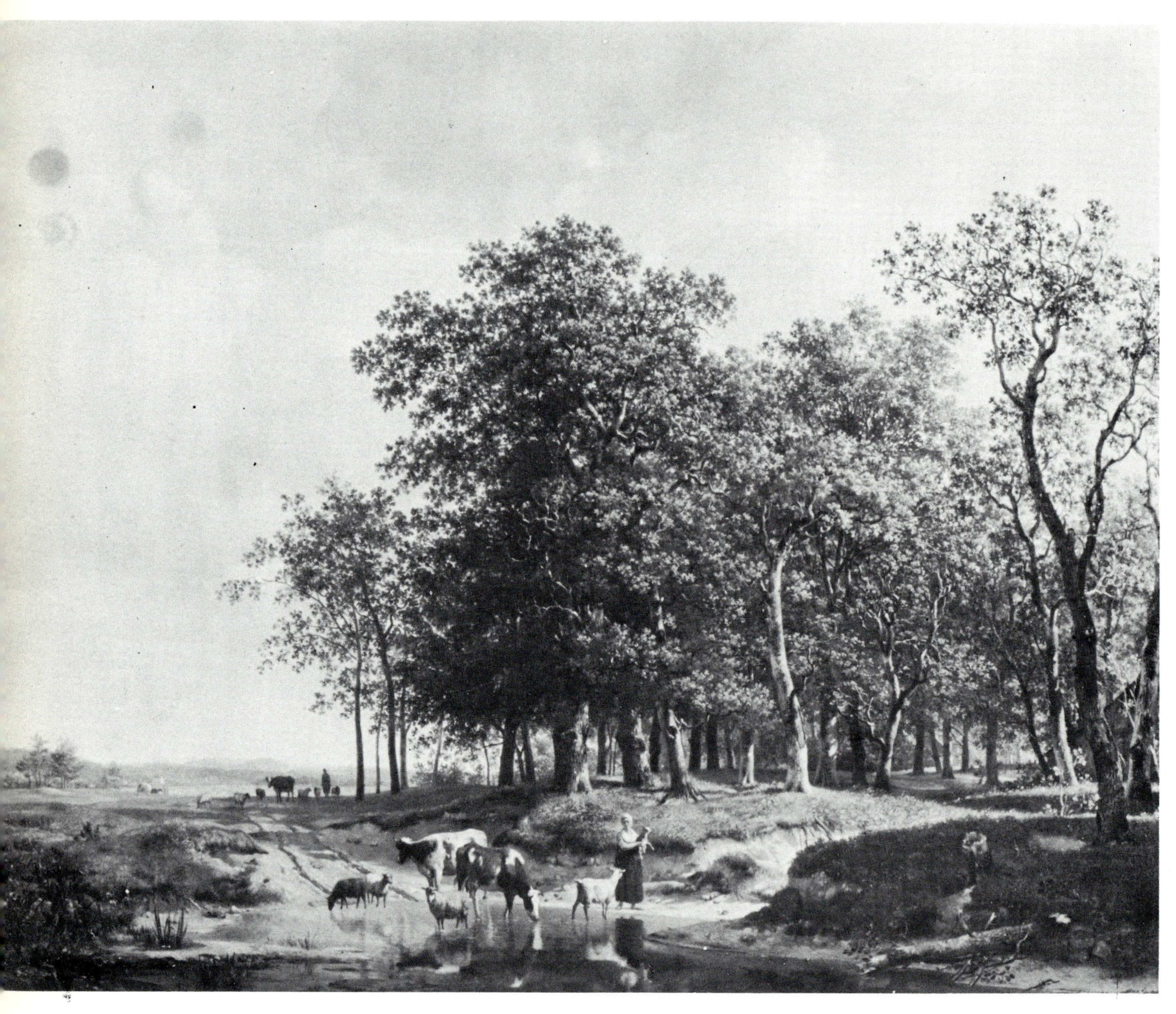

Hendrik /van de Sande Bakhuijzen (1795-1860) *was another gifted exponent of landscape with cattle and sheep and had many pupils. This examples is full of gentle rural peace. (62 x 78cms.).* Photograph courtesy of Mak van Waay, Amsterdam.

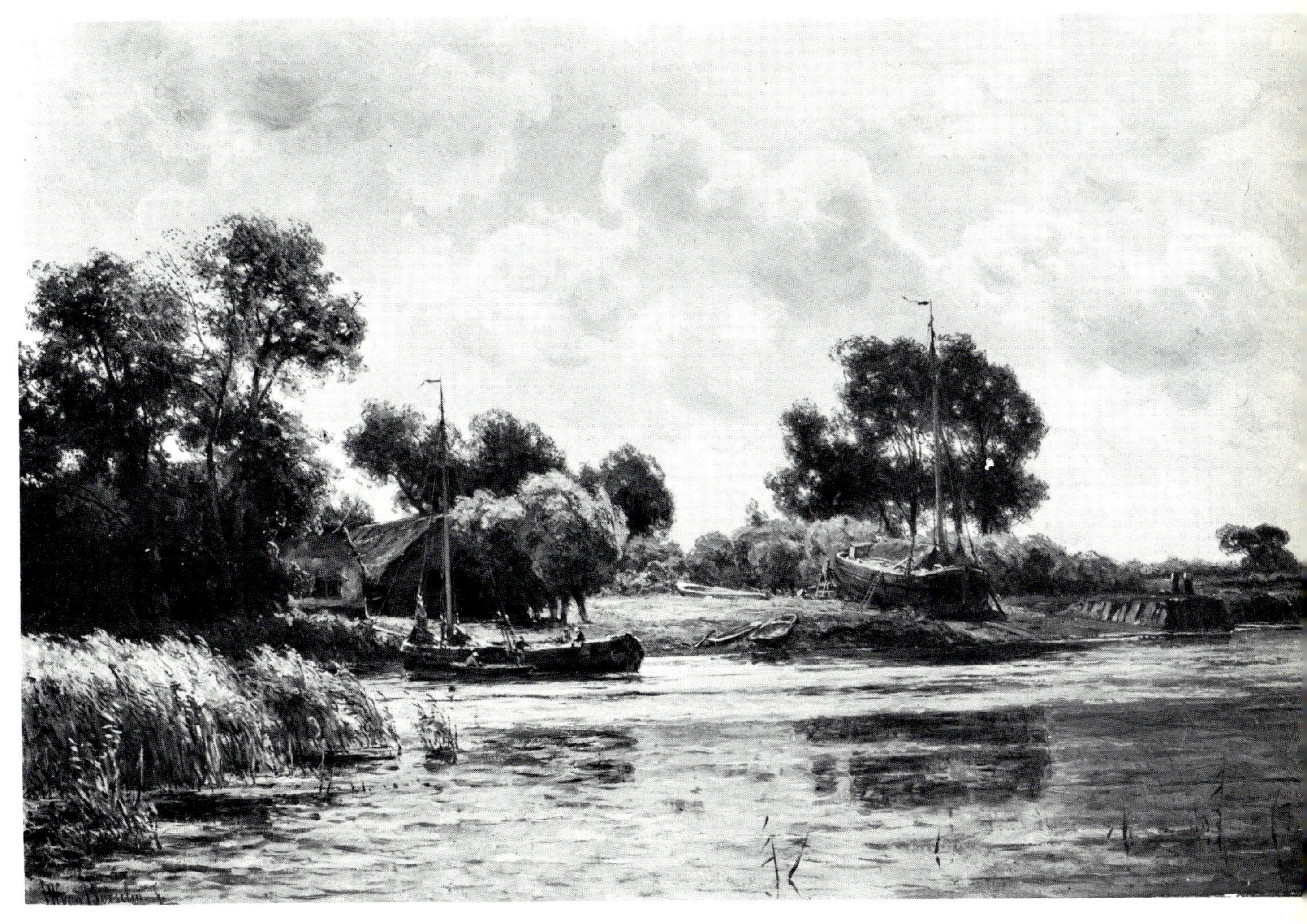

Jan Willem van Borselen (1825-1892) *a pupil of Bakhuijzen, was a master of the wind-swept landscape. The play of broken light proclaims him as a later generation than his teacher. (44 x 70cms.).* Photograph courtesy of Mak van Waay, Amsterdam.

master of Mauve, whose early work constantly betrays the influence of Van Os. As in the case of his more famous father, the arrangement of his pictures was inspired principally by Potter and not always by that painter's best side. He seemed to prefer to take the composition from the left – the spectator's left – of Paul Potter's *Young Bull* in the Mauritshuis, variations on which are continually found in Mauve's early drawings. In any case, though Van Os may have been deficient in pictorial instinct, it is pretty certain that both Mauve and his fellow-pupil, J.H.L. de Haas, must have learnt much from him in the anatomy of cows and sheep.

In this respect, perhaps Hendrik van de Sande Bakhuijzen showed better work. Born at the Hague in 1795, he was the pupil successively of S.A. Krausz (1760-1825), a Hague painter and a pupil of L. Defrance of Liège, of J.W. Pieneman and his pupil J. Heymans and of the Hague Sketching Club. He did not possess Kobell's gifts of agreeable and distinguished composition, but he was a good draughtsman and painted his pictures with simplicity. His landscapes are entirely free from mannerism and artificiality; and, if they contain no trace of feeling and as little merit of colour, at least we find not an atom of borrowed sensibility or borrowed colour in the pictures of this

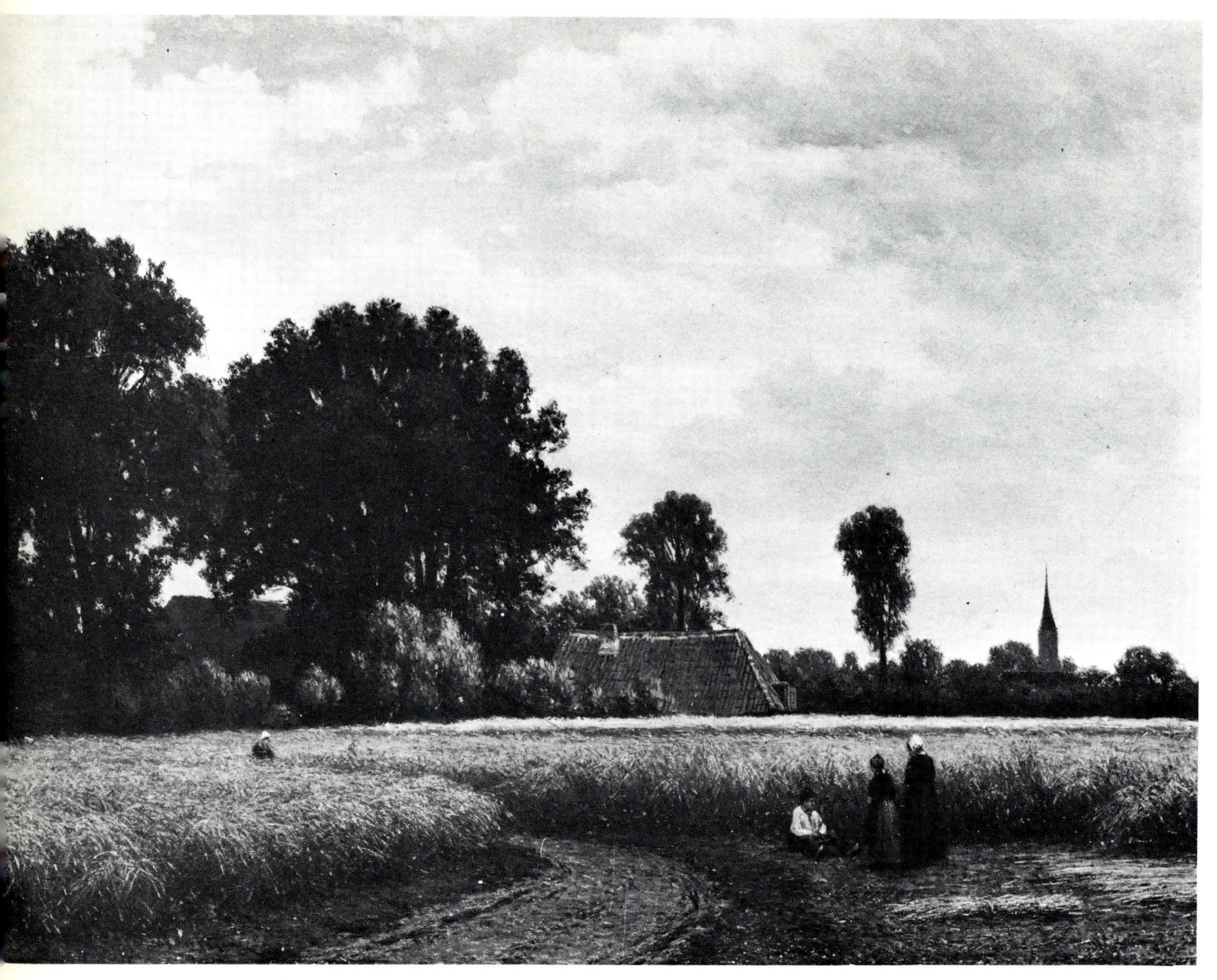

Jacob Jan van der Maaten (1820-1879) *was a noted landscapist and can be claimed as a forerunner of the Hague School as is shown by this sunlit "Cornfield" (35 x 44.5cms.).* Photograph courtesy of the Haags Gemeentemuseum.

honest landscape-painter. He had many pupils: Willem Roelofs, the pioneer, who first came from Barbizon to tell of the beauty of nature as seen through the painter's temperament; Jan Willem van Borselen, who loved to paint those blustering moments when the colourless side of the leaves is blown upwards by the wind and who produced excellently-painted and daintily-conceived little pictures on panels smaller than a man's hand; Jacob Jan van der Maaten (1820-1879), whose *Cornfield* in the Hague Museum shows that he was an attentive, if not an emotional painter; Christiaan Immerzeel, born in 1808, who painted romantic, but feeble moonlight scenes; Jan Frederik and Willem Anthonie van Deventer (1822-1886 and

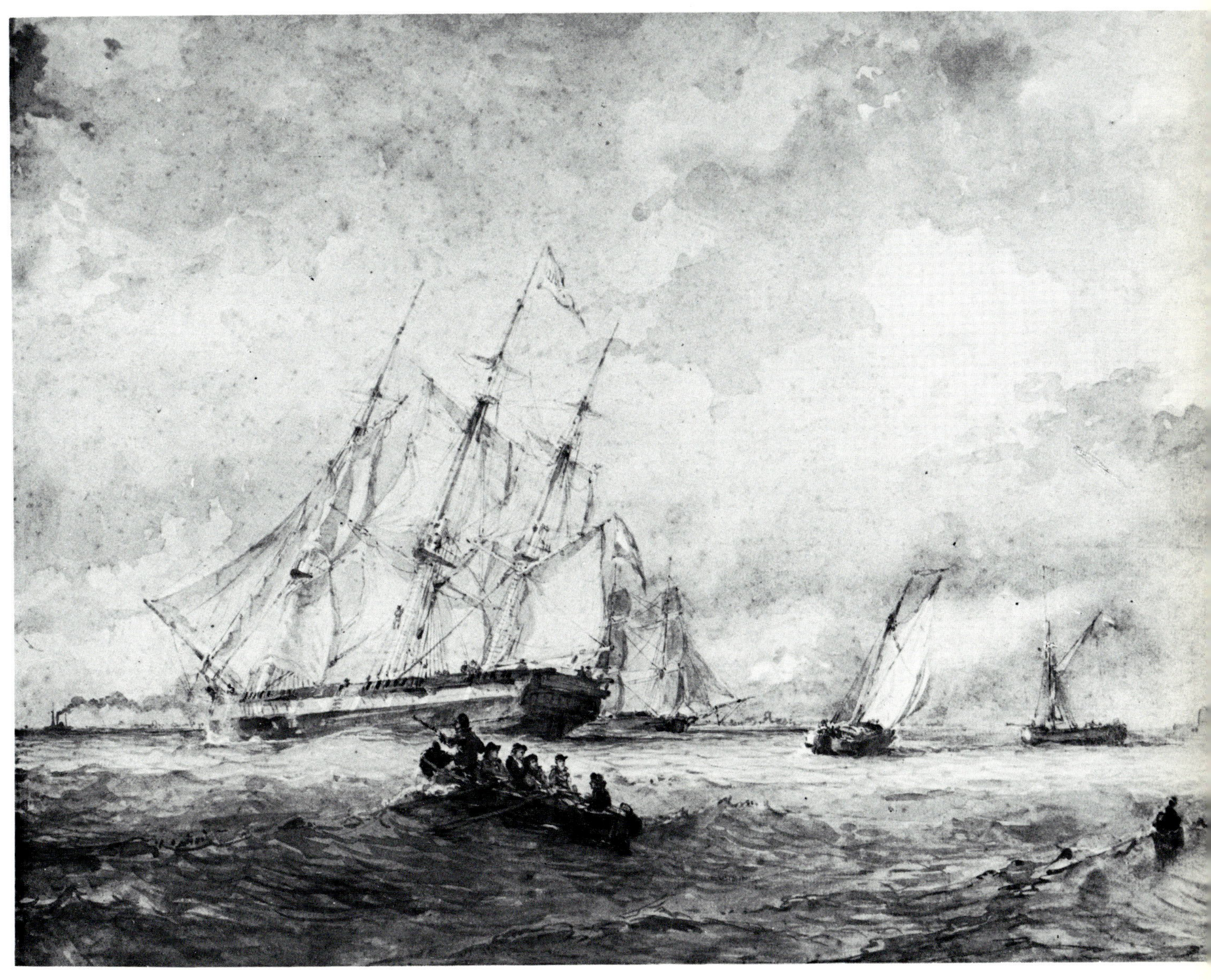

Willem Anthonie van Deventer (1824-1893) *was another of Bakhijzen's pupils and a specialist in sea and river views. This example shows him very much the master of his medium with a light impressionistic touch. (Watercolour 36½ x 47cms.).* Photograph courtesy of Mak van Waay, Amsterdam.

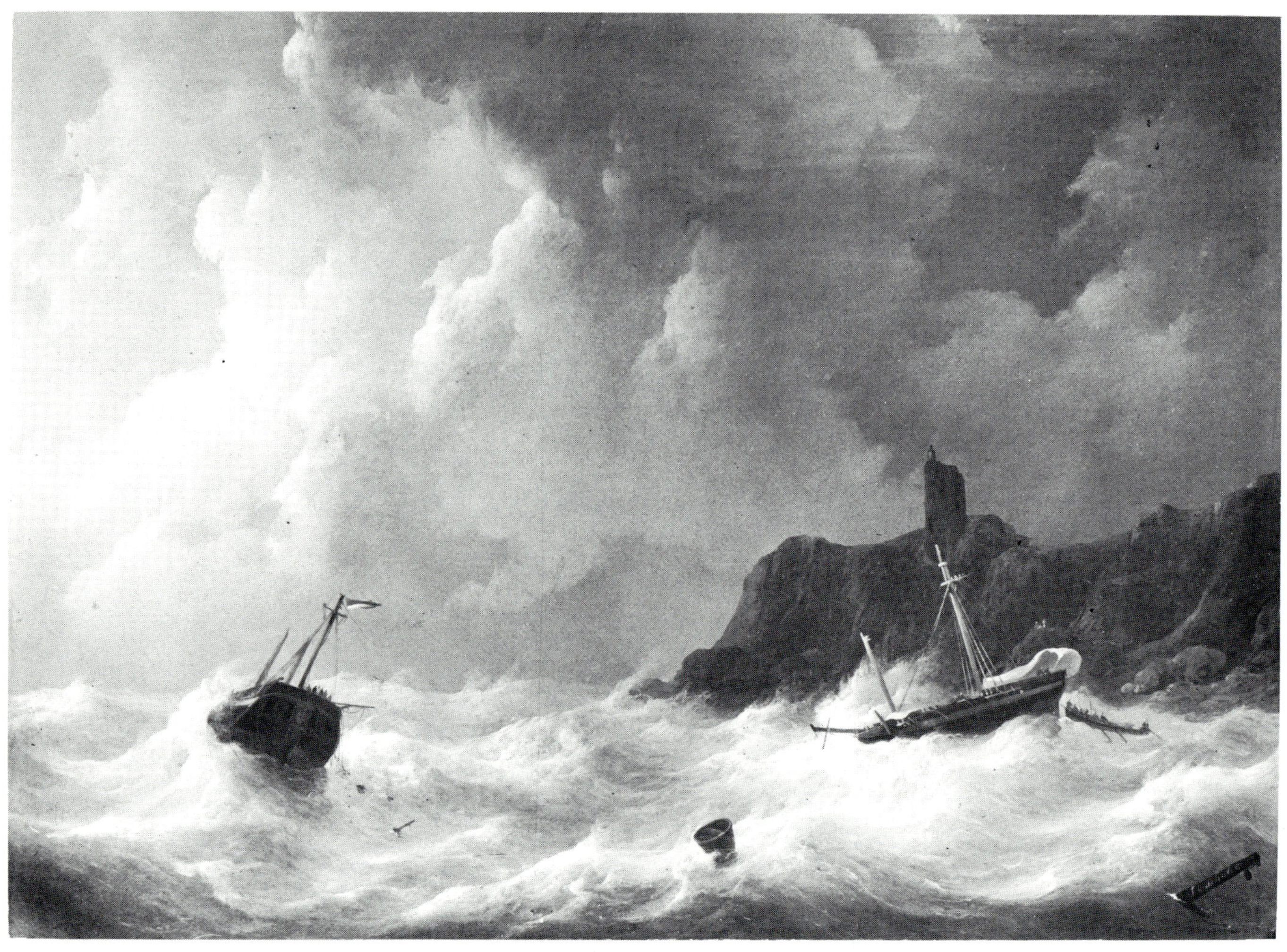

Johannes Christianus Schotel (1787-1838) *was famed for the accuracy with which he painted ships and their complex rigging. This stormy scene is still close to the 17th and 18th century masters in feel. (37½ x 51½cms.).* Photograph courtesy of Mak van Waay, Amsterdam.

1824-1893), of whom the first was a landscape-painter and the second a deserving painter of sea and river-views. Hendrik van de Sande Bakhuijzen died in 1860.

When we look at the sea-pieces of Johannes Christiaan Schotel (1787-1838) at the Rijksmuseum, we are inevitably reminded of the Pienemans and Krusemans. Any objects that have not to do with pure painting are perfect and those qualified to judge have said that his ships are equipped with so much technical accuracy and ride the waters so admirably that the most expert skipper could not improve upon them. Small wonder that he enjoyed the same esteem as the painters of *le grand art*. It is true that his skies were often out of harmony with the sea and appeared to be made of cardboard and that the water displayed more paint than transparency; still, he was a thoughtful painter, who cleverly supported the movement of his ships by the composition of the waves and knew how to put a picture together. These qualities appear particularly in his drawings, which surprise us agreeably with the untrammelled outlook, the firmness of the execution and the majestic effects which, seated in his boat and drawing direct from nature, he often succeeded in attaining. Here we see none of that antiquated soapy hardness or hard soapiness which clings to all his painted work however clever the latter may be. His first master was the Dordrecht candle-light painter Adriaan Meulemans (1763-1835) and he

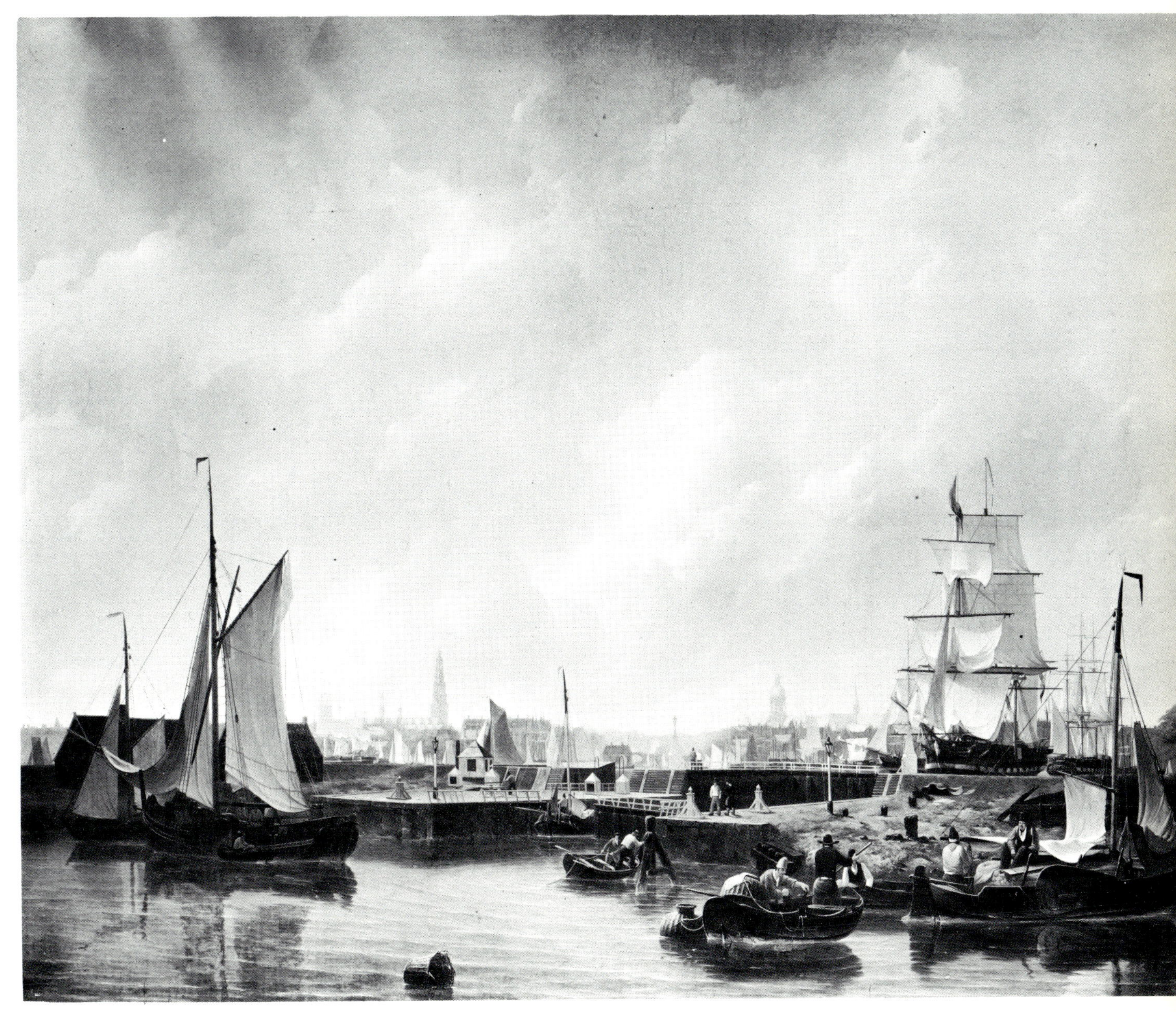

Petrus Johannes Schotel (1808-1865) *inherited his father's expertise in the accurate portrayal of every kind of ship and boat. This view of the Willemshuis is a sparkling masterpiece of the genre – still closer to the 18th century in mood than the 19th.* Photograph courtesy of the Rijksmuseum, Amsterdam.

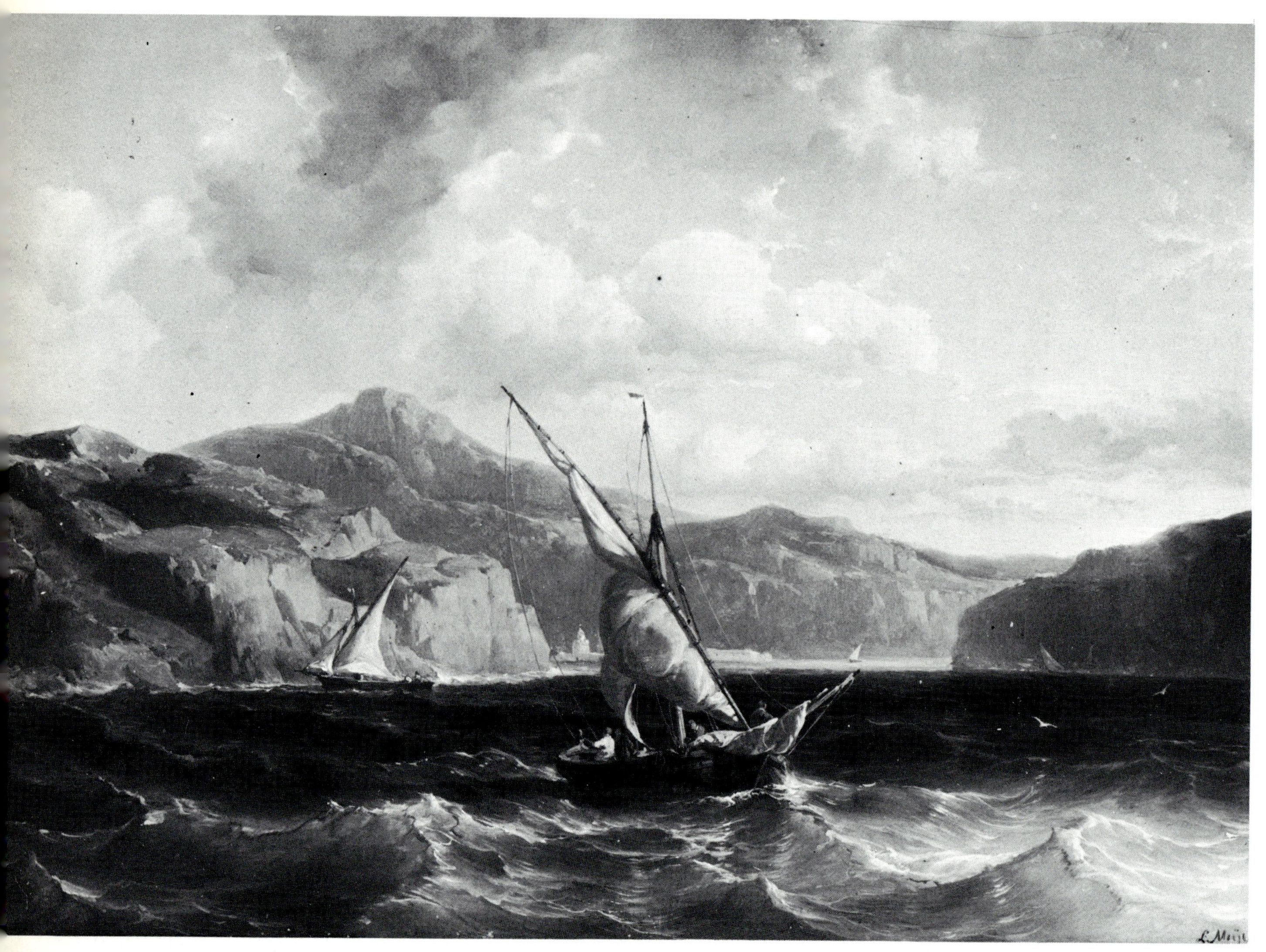

Above and right: **Johan Hendrik Louis Meijer (1809-1866)** *links two opposite poles of Dutch 19th century painting as the pupil of J.W. Pieneman and teacher of Jacob Maris. His early seascapes often included some historic event in emulation of the fashionable history school of Pieneman – Jacob Maris took a hand in some of his later canvases. The development of his style from old masterly precision towards impressionism is shown in these two pictures (38 x 57cms. and 9 x 12ins.).* Photographs courtesy of Mak van Waay, Amsterdam, and M. Newman Ltd.

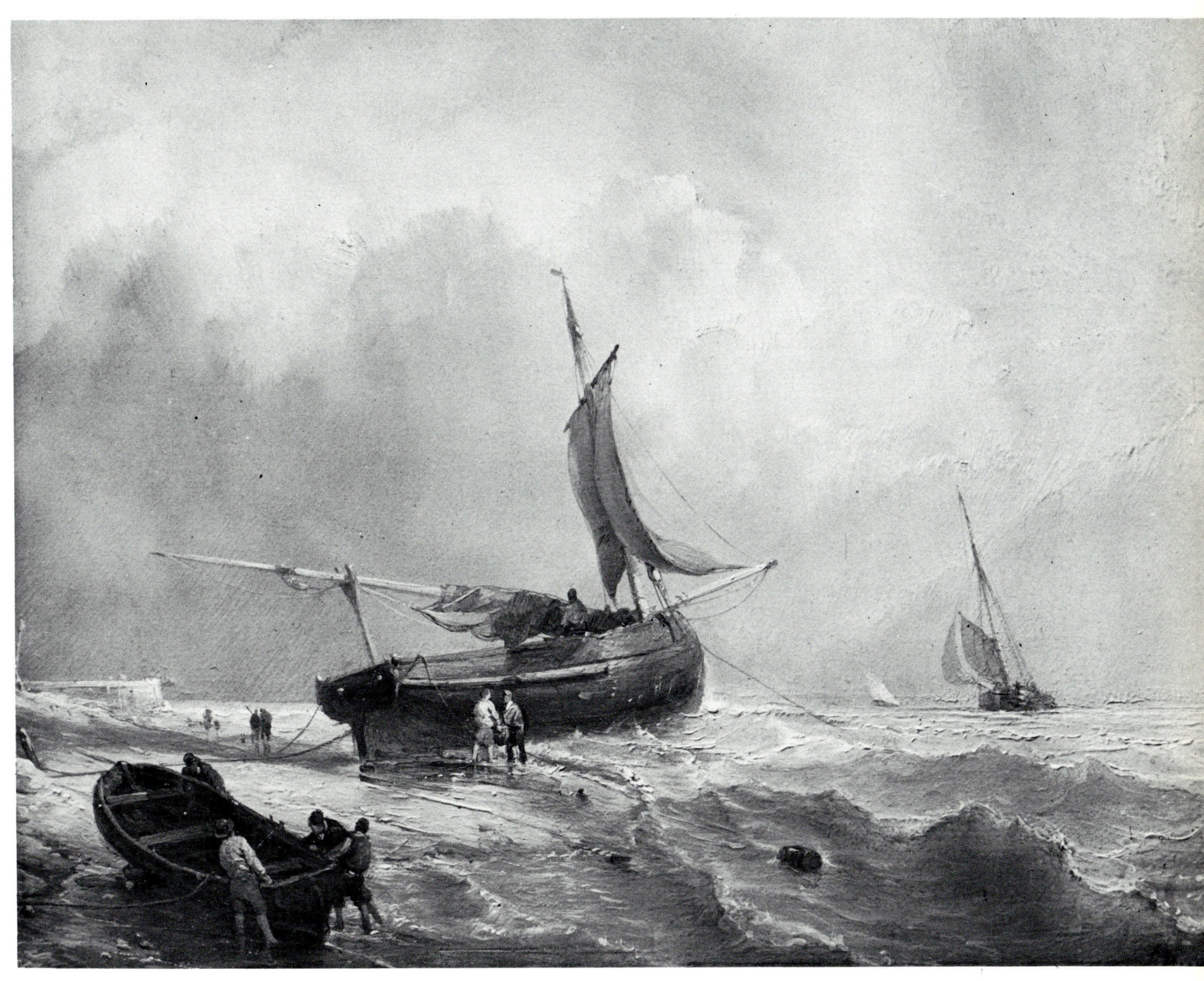

received his artistic training at the hands of Martinus Schouman (1770-1848), the best sea-painter of his time. His pictures often fetched considerable prices and his success descended, in a certain measure, to his son and pupil Petrus Johannes Schotel (1808-1865).

A sea-painter of the same school was Johan Hendrik Louis Meijer, who was born at Amsterdam in 1809, studied under Pieter Westenberg and, later, under J.W. Pieneman, lived for some years at Deventer, settled in Paris in 1841 and afterwards moved to the Hague, where he died in 1866. At the commencement of his career, he used to introduce history-painting into his sea-pieces, but seldom to such an extent as to interfere with his seeking for good effects of light. He was a very systematic and successful painter. Among his pupils he may be said to include Jacob Maris, who, however, really attended his studio rather to assist him with his sea-scapes, and, in any case, Matthijs Maris, although Meijer told the latter, when he came to his studio as a child of ten, that there was nothing that he could teach him, for Thijs knew everything.

Andreas Schelfhout formed himself as a landscape-painter upon Meijer's seascapes. He was born at the

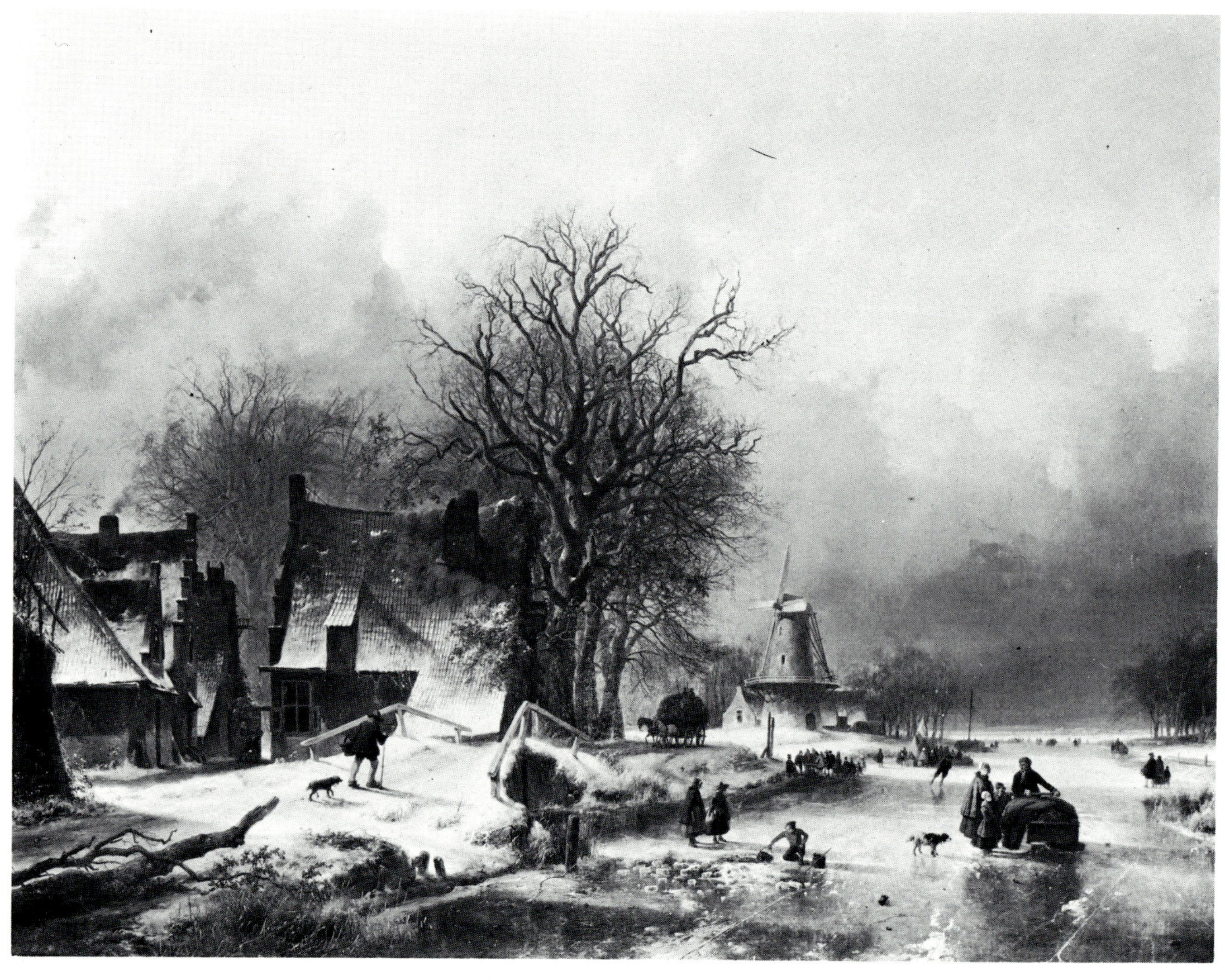

Andreas Schelfhout (1787-1870) *is particularly known for his winter landscapes. This one is dated 1839. (44 x 55ins.).* **Photograph courtesy of Christie, Manson and Woods.**

Hague in 1787 and worked until his twenty-fourth year in the shop of his father, who was a maker of picture-frames, devoting his spare hours to painting. A landscape which he exhibited in 1815 was seen to possess something out the ordinary and this was confirmed by a *Wintry View* exhibited a couple of years later. Some of his earlier land-scapes display a certain freshness of idea, nor should any painter generally be judged exclusively by the work of his later years. Schelfhout's first little pictures often impress us by the original colouring of their skies, by the reflection of those skies in the cold blue of the frozen water below, even though the smooth and unreal treatment lead us to entertain a not unmingled appreciation of his merits. He was an indefatigable worker, never wasting a moment, and achieved a certain reputation beyond the confines of his own country. As late as 1870, most collectors thought themselves fortunate to possess one of his ice-pieces. And his colouring – I am speaking of his best period – undoubtedly entitles him to take rank among the founders of the modern landscape school.

Schelfhout died at the Hague in 1870. His chief pupil was Jongkind, who for many years was unable

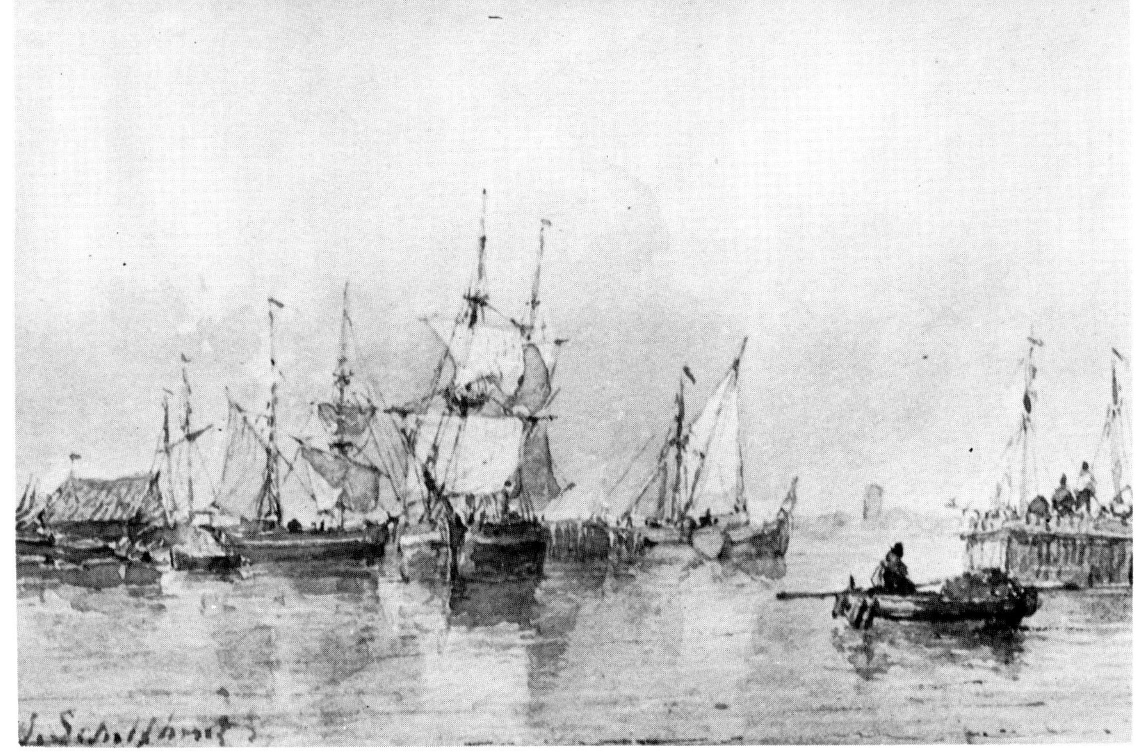

Andreas Schelfhout (1787-1870) *is placed by Marius among the founders of the "modern" landscape school. This small drawing (3¾ x 5½ins.) clearly demonstrates his influence on the much sought after marine drawings of his pupil Jongkind.* Photograph courtesy of M. Newman Ltd.

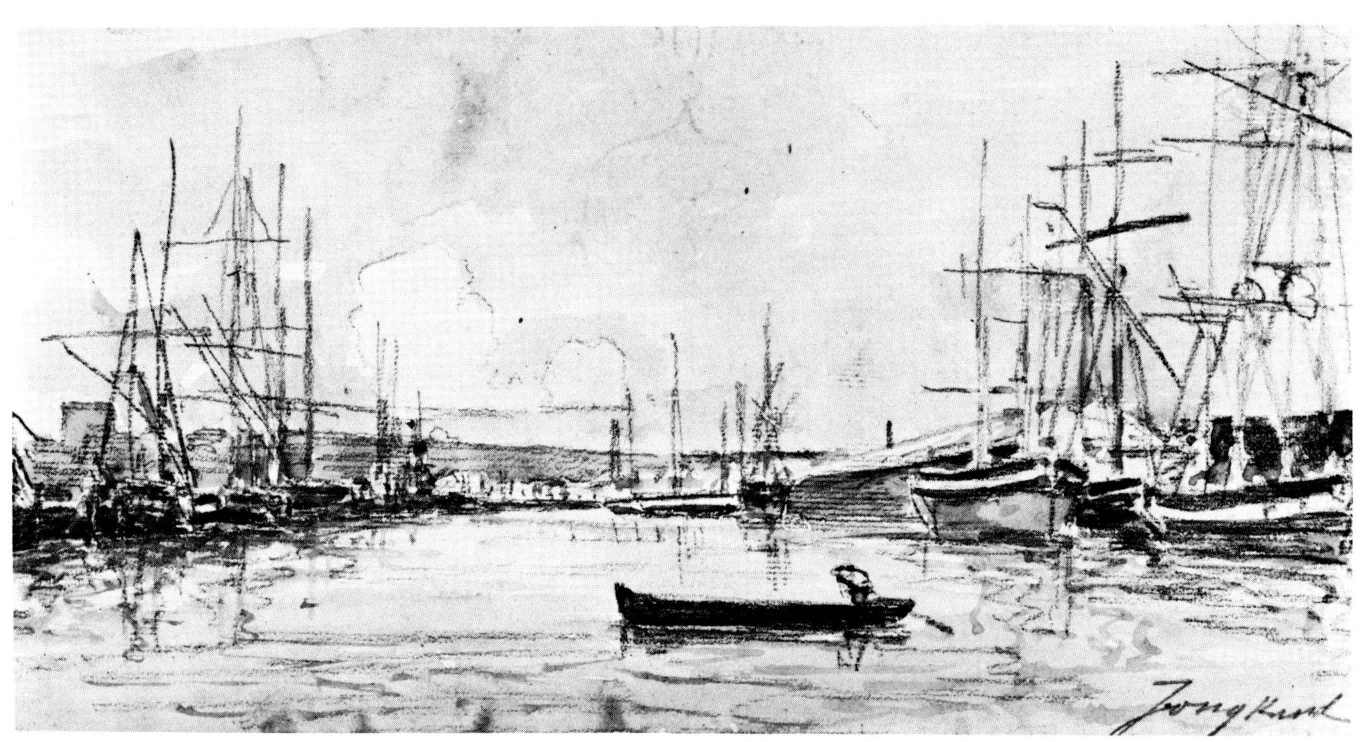

Here **Jongkind** *has sketched a similar scene. The close relationship of master and pupil as draughtsmen is demonstrated.* Collection Alain Delon. Photograph courtesy of Sotheby's.

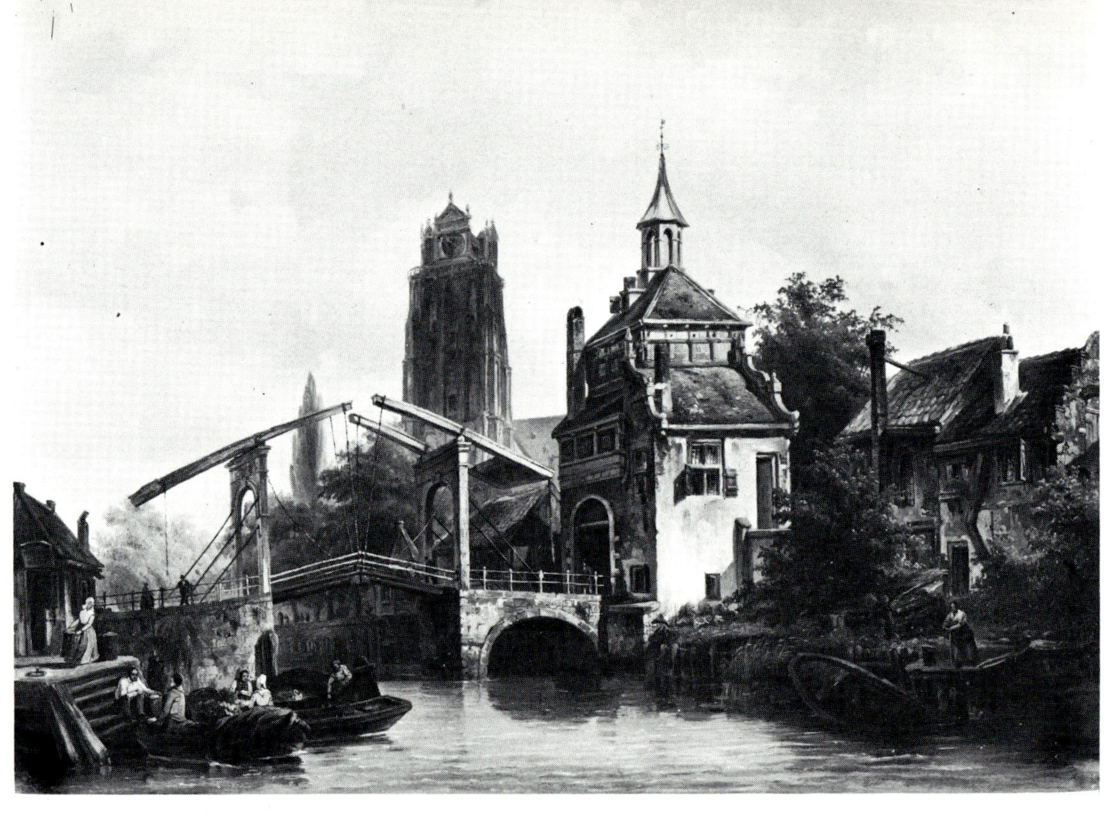

Above and Below: **Jan Bedijs Tom (1813-1894)** *learnt his fine technique from Schelfhout and continued to paint firmly in the landscape and townscape tradition of the Dutch Romantic School. The view of Haarlem with busy life on the canal measures 21 x 27ins. The landscape with sheep and cows measures 46 x 64½cms.* Photographs courtesy of Sotheby & Co., and Mak van Waay, Amsterdam.

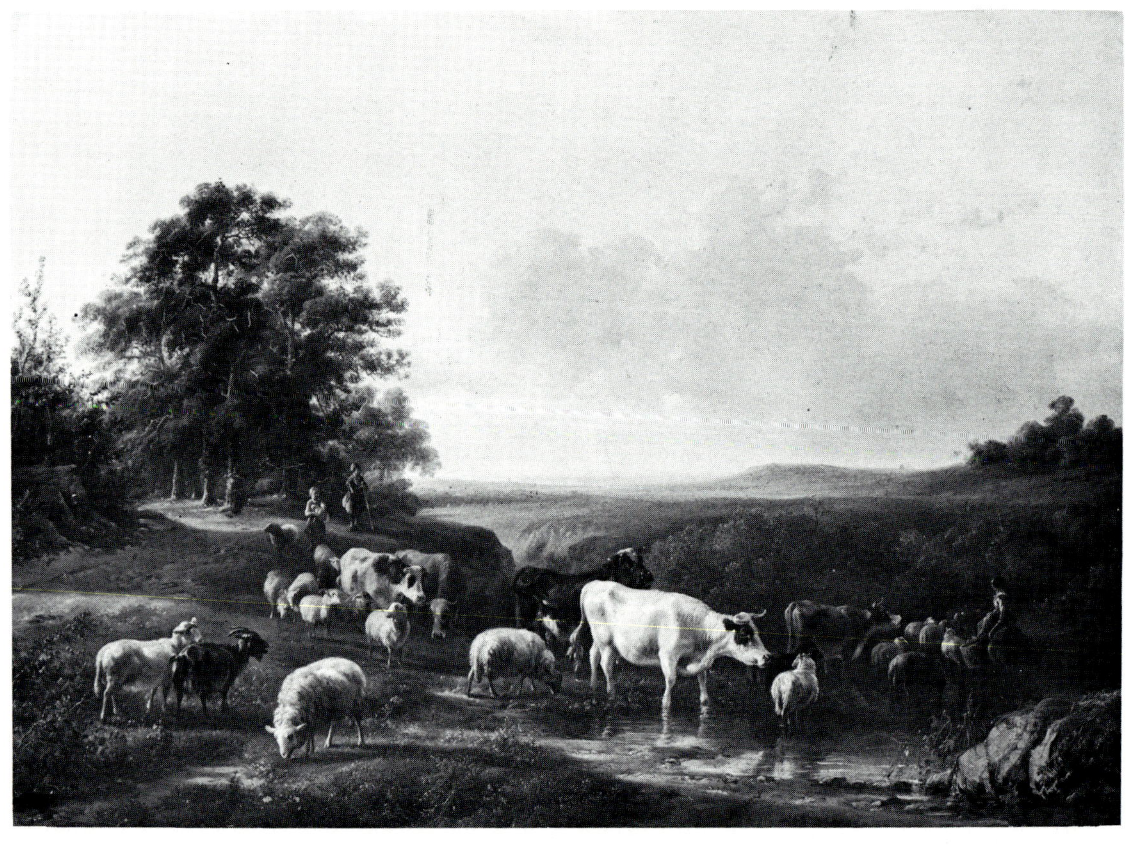

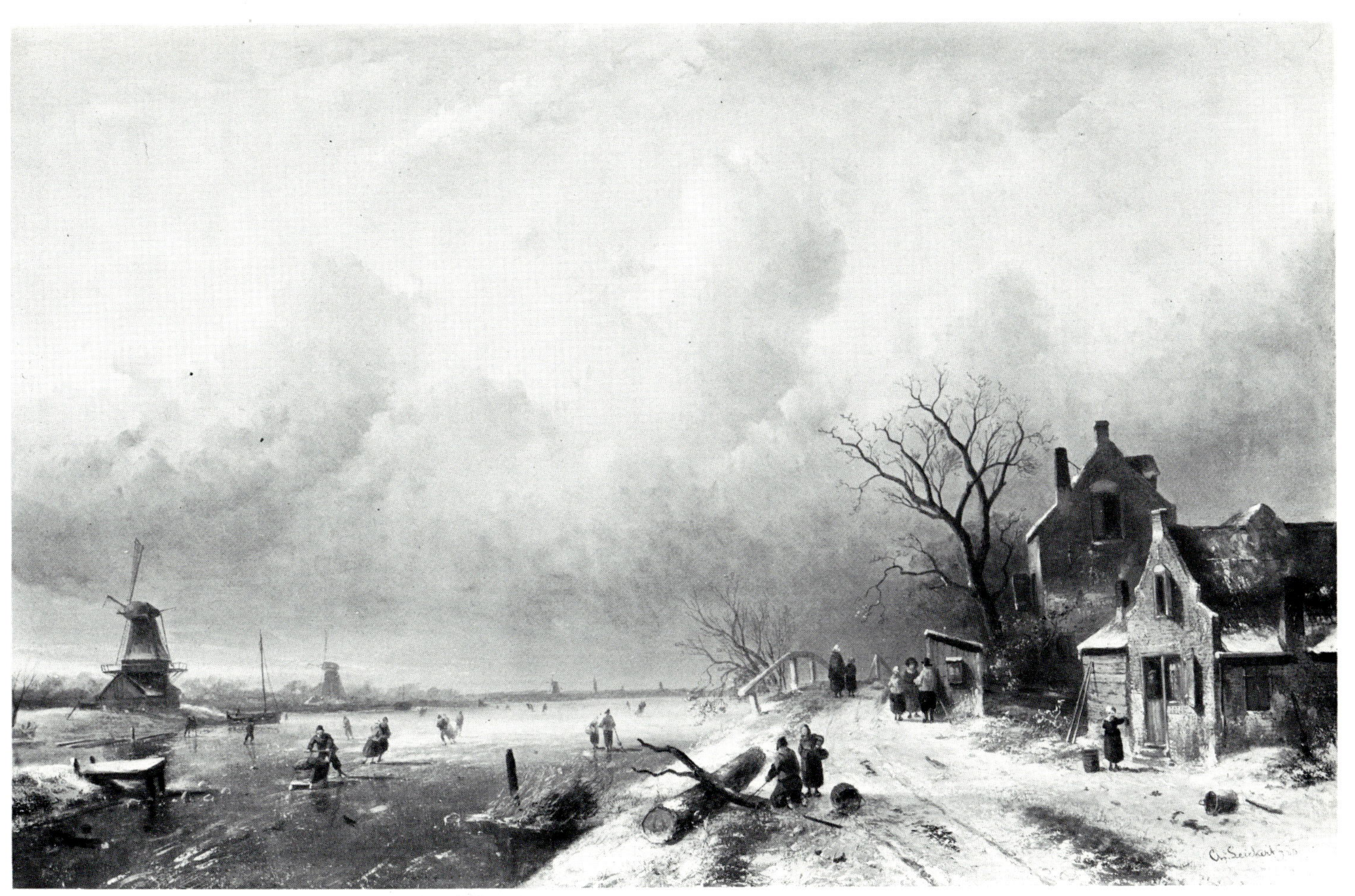

Charles Leickert (1816-1907). *With the current re-assessment of the Dutch Romantic Landscape School, Charles Leickert is emerging as a much more important figure than he was rated by Marius at the turn of the century. The fact that he lived to almost ninety explains his prolific* oeuvre *and the variations in style and quality among his pictures. He can be a traditional landscapist in the manner of his master Schelfhout, as above or he can paint sparkling effects of light with quick impressionistic brush strokes – an altogether more modern manner. At his best he is something of a Dutch version of Constable, a high point in a century exceptionally well supplied with landscape artists. He studied with both Nuyen and B.J. van Hove as well as Schelfhout.* Photograph courtesy of Richard Green.

to free himself from his master's method. He also taught Nuyen, whom I will mention below, Jan Bedijs Tom, the animal-painter, Charles Henri Joseph Leickert, born in 1816, who also painted under Nuyen, but never achieved any considerable distinction, and Dubourcq, a deserving Amsterdam landscape-painter.

Wijnand Jan Joseph Nuyen was born at the Hague in 1813. There have perhaps been few painters who roused such confident hopes in their fellow-artists as did Nuyen; few young artists – Nuyen died in 1839, in his twenty-seventh year – who were so greatly mourned for the sake both of their own personality and of their promising work; few who, at so young an age, wielded so great and so seductive an influence

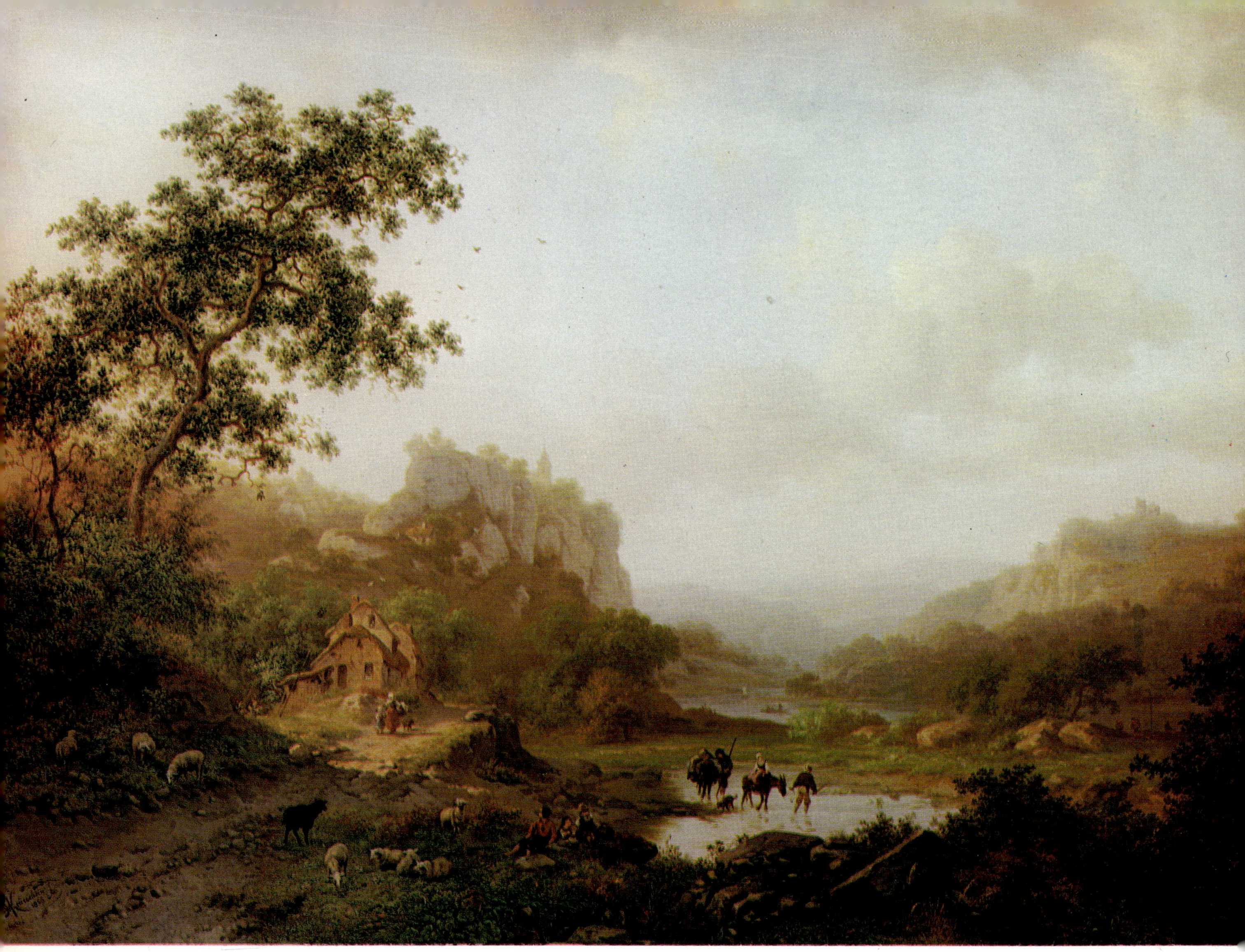

Frederik Marinus Kruseman (1816-1882). *"Mountainous river landscape with shepherd near a pool." Signed and dated 1866. (21½ x 29ins.).* Photograph courtesy of Richard Green.

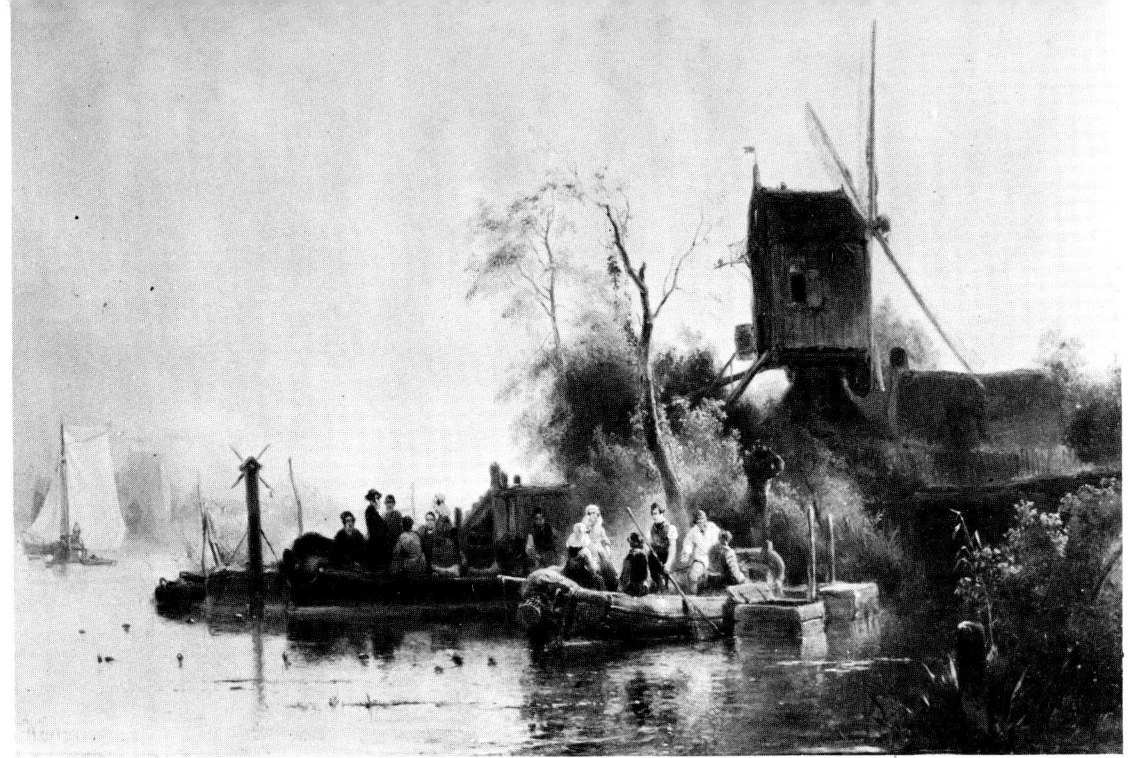

Above and Below: **Wijnand Jan Joseph Nuyen (1813-1839)** *was also a pupil of Schelfhout, as short-lived as Leickert was long. His clever figure painting looks forward to the gay realism of his illustrator pupil Rochussen. Though firmly grounded in the old landscape tradition, his passion for colour and light and, on occasion, original perspective mark him out as ahead of his time.* Photographs courtesy of Mak van Waay, Amsterdam.

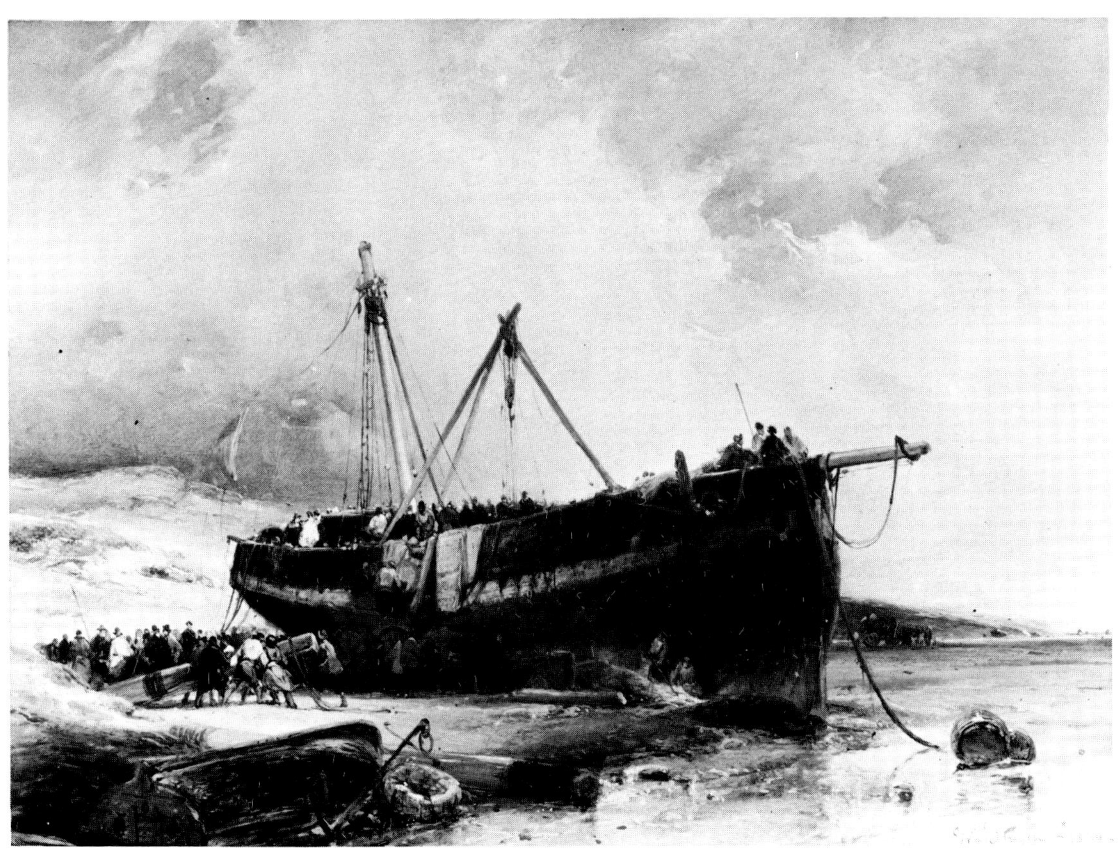

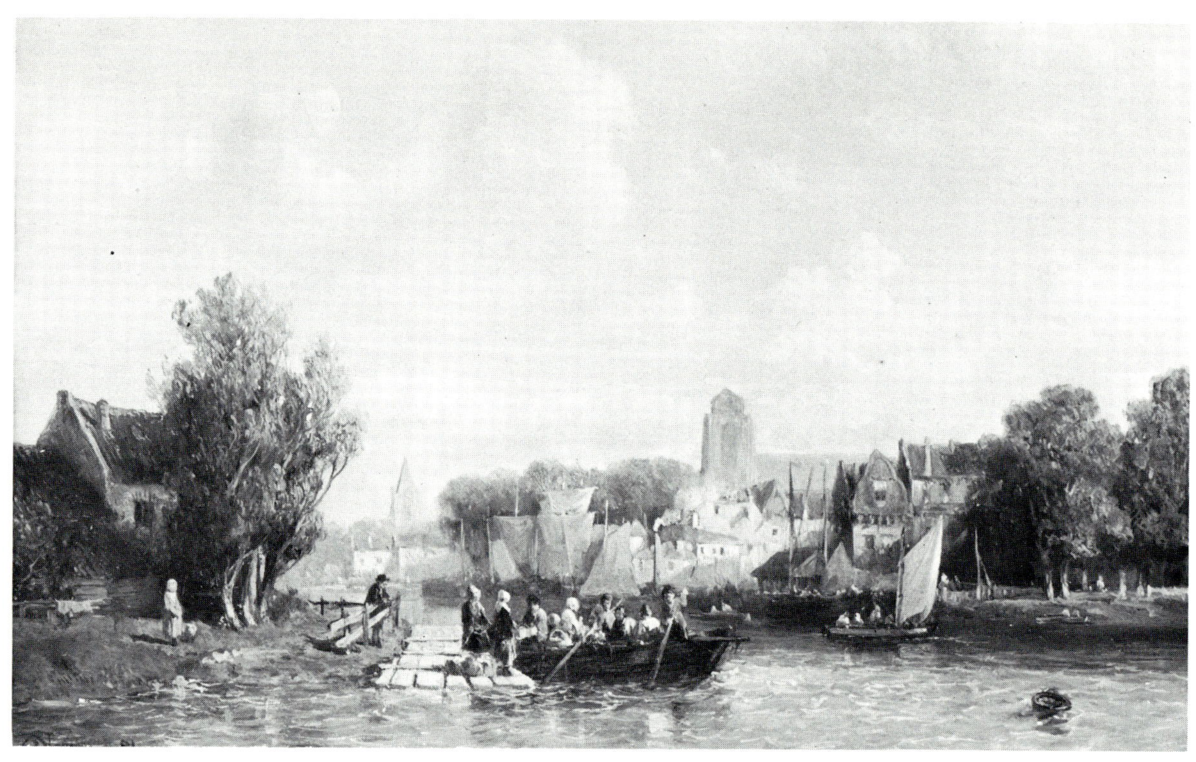

Above: **Samuel Leonardus Verveer (1813-1876)** *was a relatively traditional pupil of B.J. van Hove – though notably successful in his time. He exhibited in France, Germany, Belgium and America, winning a medal at Philadelphia in 1876.* Photograph courtesy of M. Newman Ltd.

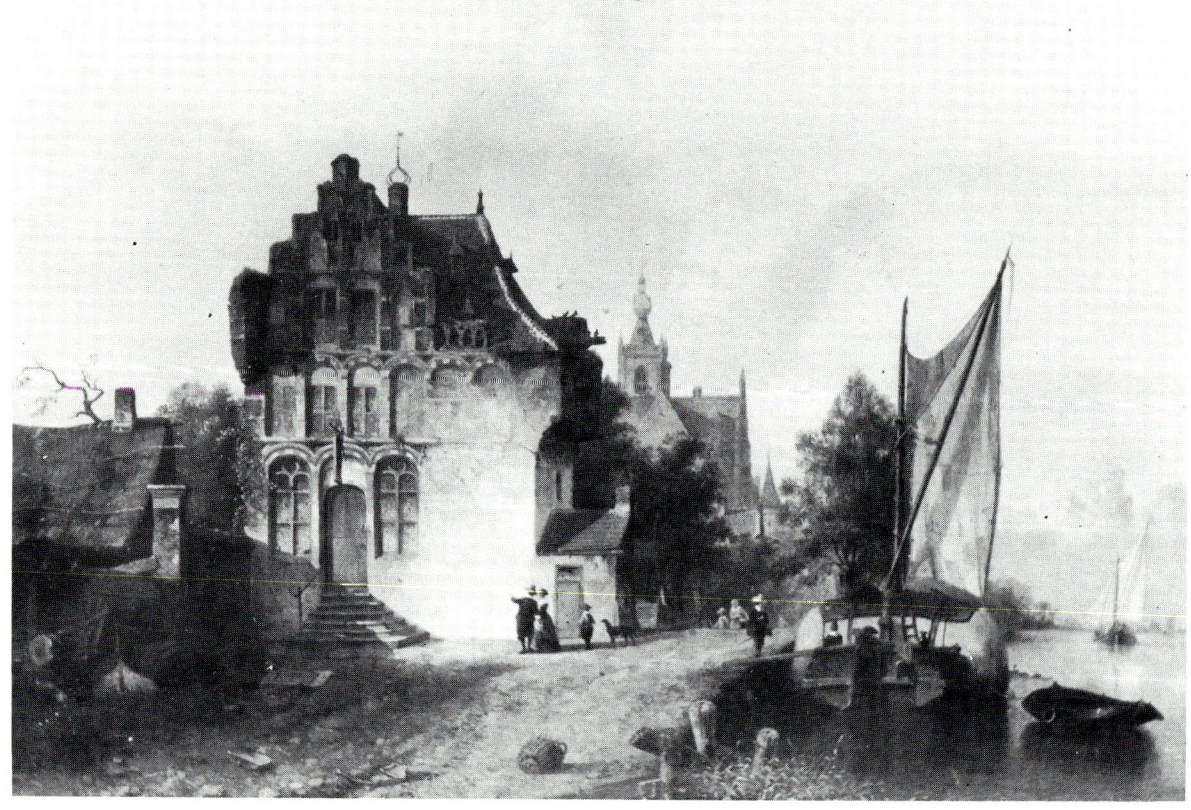

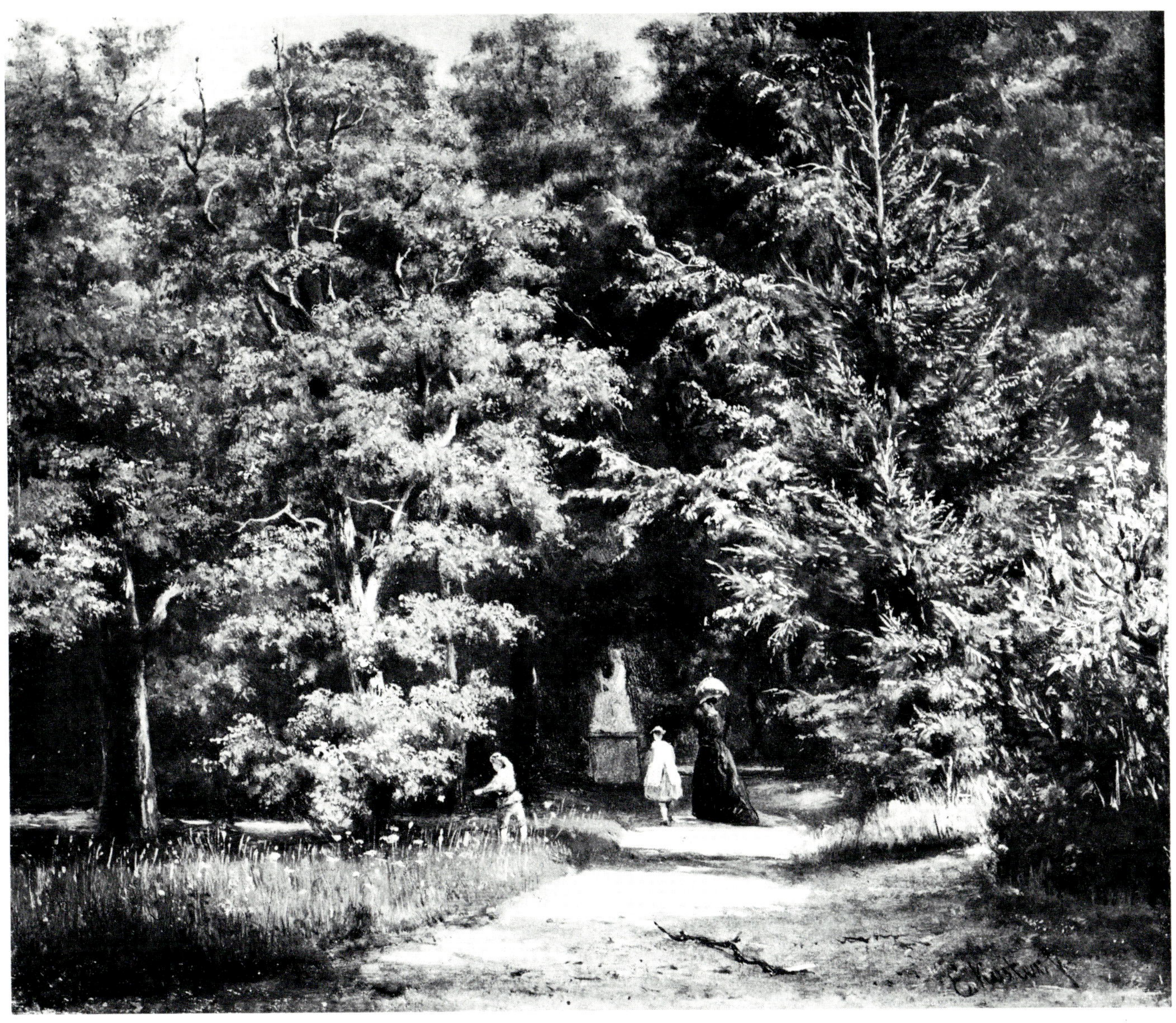

Left and above: **Everardus Koster** (1817-1892) *is best known for his river scenes, reflecting the influence of Waldorp and Nuyen, as in left (58 x 38ins.). But it is clear from the painting above that in the course of his very long life the century's revolutionary change of approach to landscape painting did not pass him by. This sunlit scene of figures in a park measures 34 x 41cms.* Photographs courtesy of Williams & Son and Mak van Waay, Amsterdam.

over their contemporaries. The young Catholic painter possessed more of the true artist's passion than his contemporaries: most of his pictures in spite of their treacly brown, display a yearning for colour, a search for the splendid, a groping after the romanticism of the middle ages that inspired all his work and induced others to follow in his footsteps.

He has left church-porches in which the persons streaming out of the edifice count not as separate figures, but as a connected group, lit up by a warm and life-giving sun. He also painted river-scenes in the style of his friend Waldorp, less pretty, perhaps, but also much less illustration-like. One of these river-scenes, known sometimes as *Le Coup de Canon,* is in the

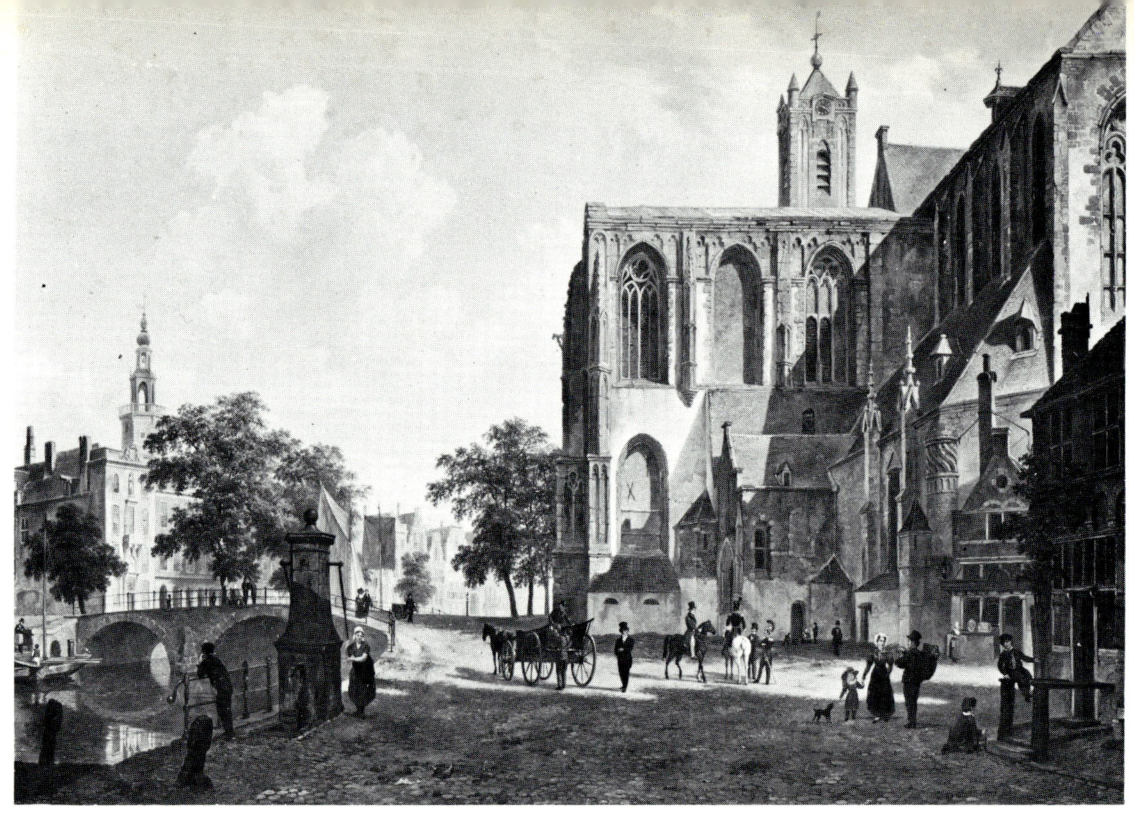

Above and Below: **Bartholomeus Johannes van Hove** (1790-1880) *made a speciality of church architecture, a fascination which he passed on to his pupil Bosboom. He was the teacher of many leading artists of the late century although his own work speaks essentially of the beginning rather than the end of the period. (56 x 76cms. dated 1829, and 17½ x 22ins.).* Photographs courtesy of Williams and Son, and Sotheby & Co.

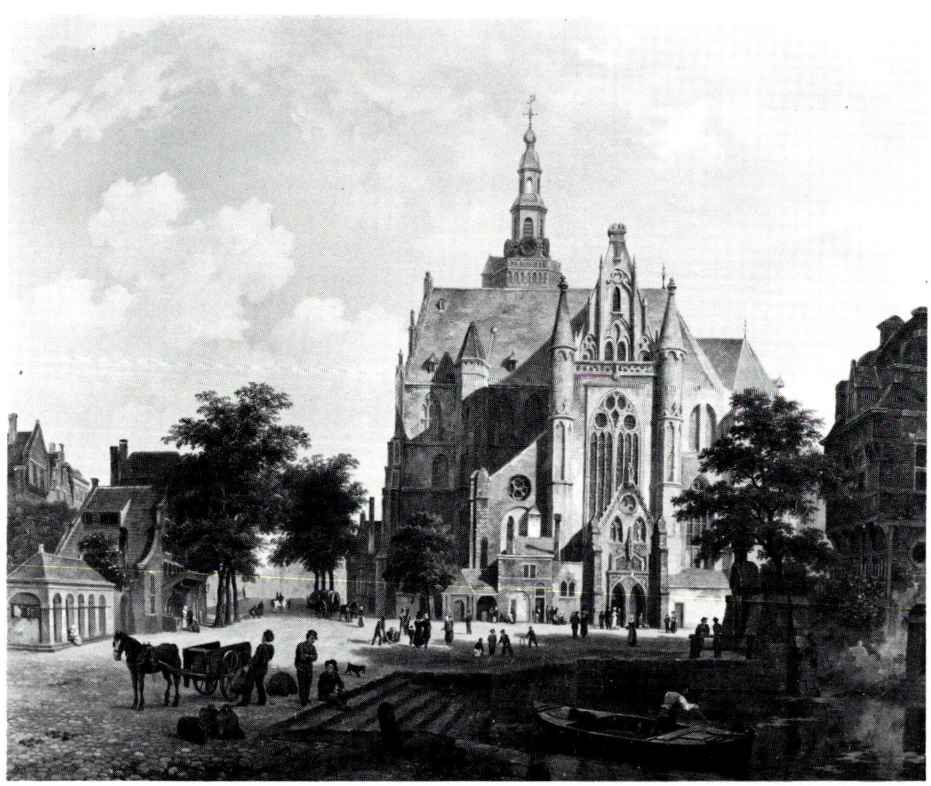

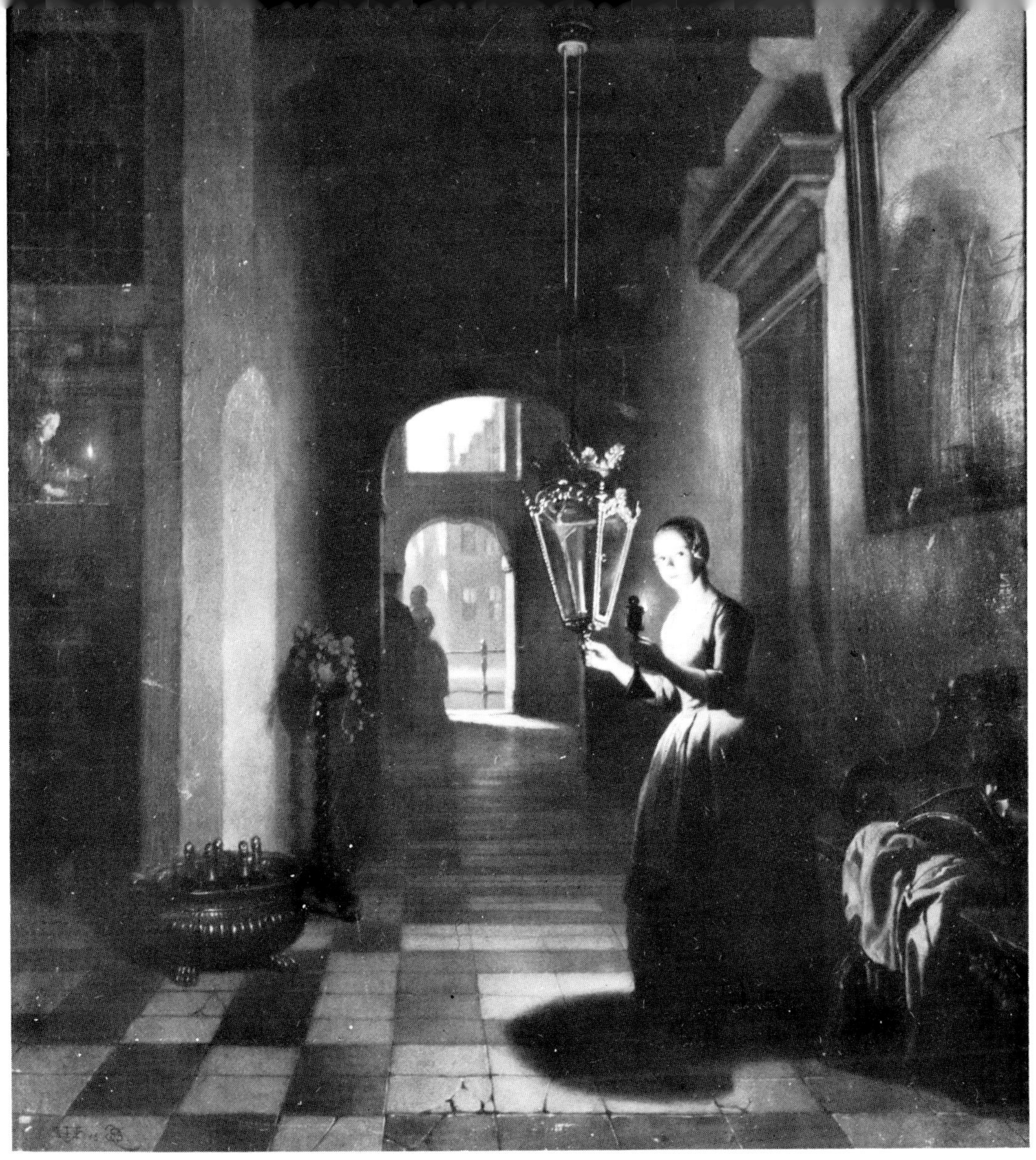

Hubertus van Hove (1814-1864) *seldom strayed from domestic vistas inspired by Pieter de Hooch. There are always two centres of light, one in the foreground, a window or candle (as in this example) and a distant doorway, into a sunlit street. The accessories of the interior are sometimes dressed up in 17th century style and sometimes in that of his own time. (24½ x 21¾ins.).* Photograph courtesy of Sotheby & Co.

Wallace collection in London. He also painted many admirable Gothic church-interiors.

His short life was one mighty effort, one incessant artistic enthusiasm, of a kind which had not been known in recent years. It seems surprising that he should have had Rochussen for a pupil, if we remember only the latter's illustrative talent. But many a little painting of Rochussen's shows a relationship with Nuyen – *minus* the brown sauce; and, when all is said, are not the wagon and horses in Nuyen's *Old Mill* in the Hague Museum typical and illustrative in the best sense?

Antonie Waldorp (1803-1866) was a pupil of Brechenheimer's, whom he helped in his scene-painting, and it was not until after his marriage, in his twenty-third year, with the sister of his fellow-pupil Bart van Hove, that he began to apply himself entirely to the practice of painting proper, executing various subjects: church-interiors, portraits and domestic interiors. When he reached the age of thirty-five, he confined himself more particularly to river-scenes, for which he had a great reputation in his time. He was a friend of Nuyen, with whom he took a journey to Germany and Belgium, and it is not improbable

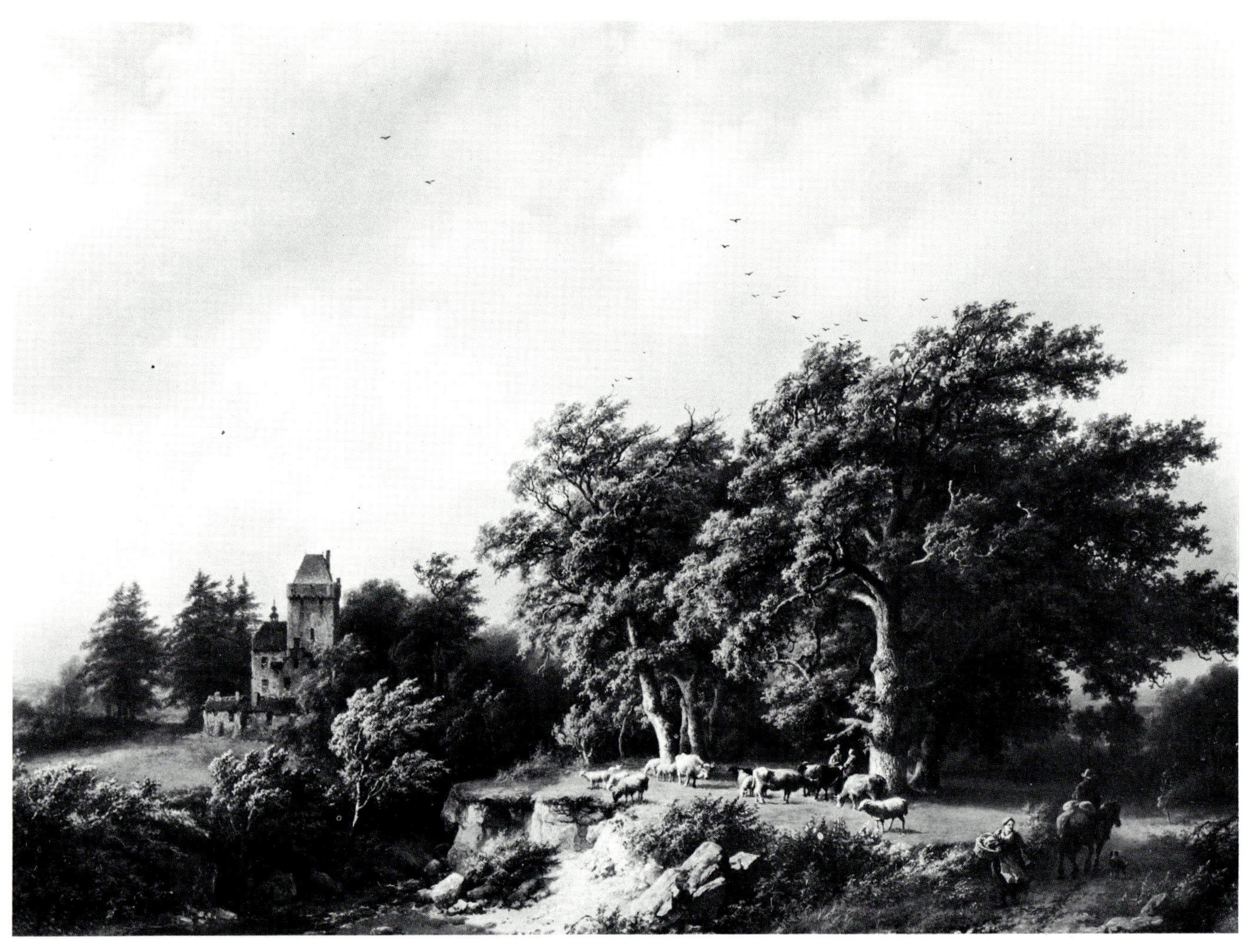

Above and Right: **Barend Cornelis Koekkoek (1803-1862)** *was the most highly regarded Dutch landscape painter of the mid-century. Marius records that his work was greatly valued and highly paid in Paris, Brussels and St. Petersburg. His trees are etched against luminous skies which Marius dismisses as suggesting "scene painting" – but are now loved as a quintessential part of Romanticism. His work in summer and winter vein is illustrated here, both leaning on the 17th century masters, but with their own originality. (27 x 20½ins. and 26¾ x 38½ins.).* Photographs courtesy of Williams & Son and Sotheby & Co.

that, although his young and more gifted friend was ten years his junior, Waldorp was nevertheless influenced by Nuyen in his choice of subjects and especially in their romantic conception. Although Waldorp's river-scenes are painted in too treacly a fashion to find much favour in our days, although their shadows show signs of affectation, we are bound, on the other hand, to recognize a certain freedom of treatment and a well-considered composition.

Of much greater importance than Schelfhout to nineteenth-century painting was the Hague scene-painter Bartholomeus Johannes van Hove (1790-1880), who may be described as the foundation upon which a whole generation of artists has built, either directly through himself or indirectly through his son and pupil Hubertus van Hove. There are little pictures of his, representing churches seen from the entrance to the choir, which anticipate his pupil Bosboom; and, while he displayed a certain grandeur in his acceptance of his art, although he is not to be compared with his pupil, he was an excellent instructor, who, following the good traditions, directed the art of painting into another and wider channel.

B.J. van Hove, like most scene-painters, was a Jack-of-all-trades. He painted a complete set of scenery for the theatre at Nijmegen, where the curtain is admired

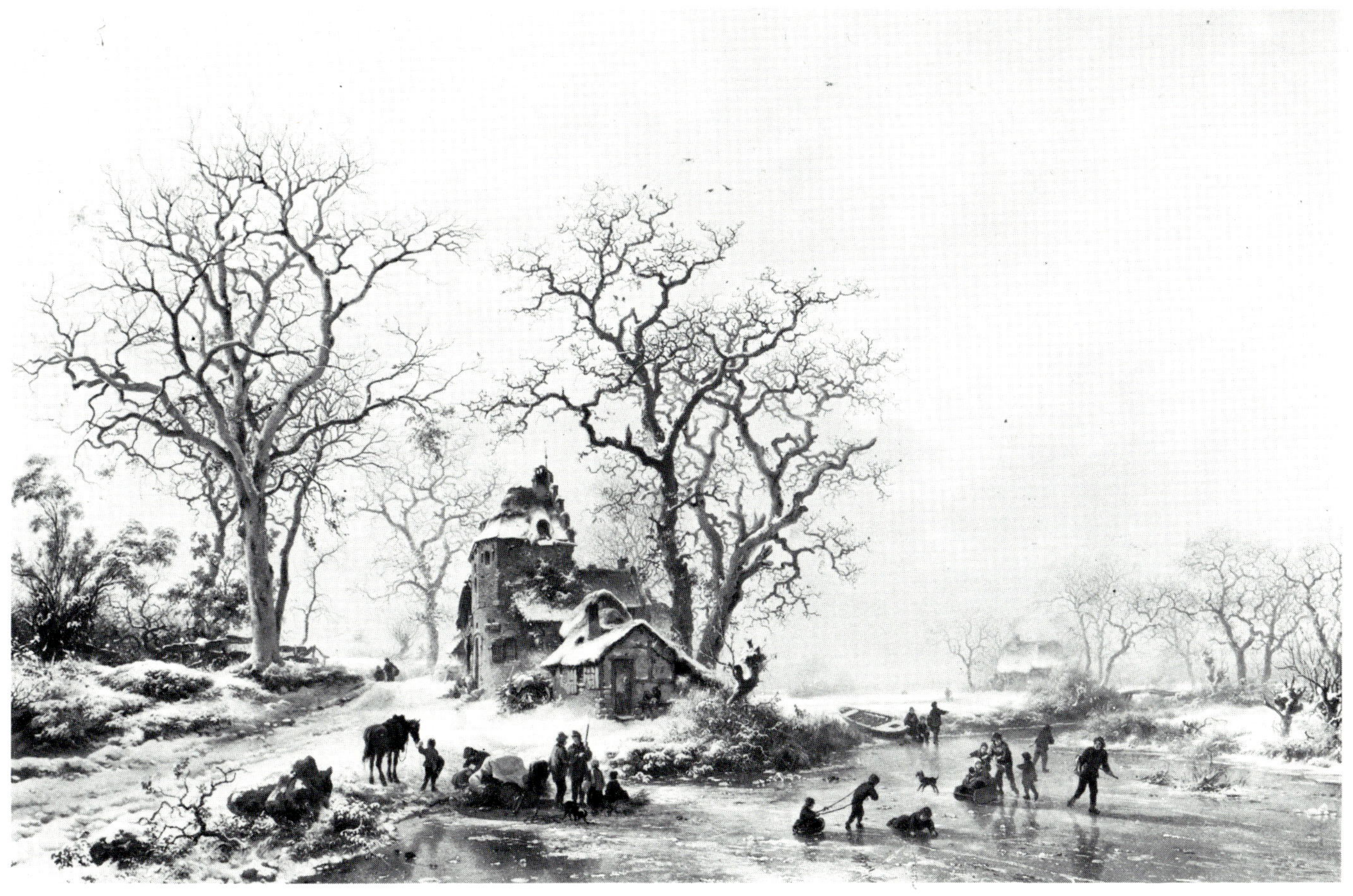

to this day; for the Hague he designed the side-scenes for *The Wreck of the Medusa,* which are considered his best stage work. In this his pupils assisted him and it is quite possible that, in so doing, they acquired that boldness and breadth in painting which they could never have learnt from Van Hove the painter of town-views. As a lad, he had begun with engraving; afterwards he worked under his father, who was a frame-maker and also did a little engraving, and through him he became acquainted with the scene-painter of the Hague Theatre, J.H.A.A. Breckenheimer, who trained him in his own art. Van Hove's little pictures, mostly town-views, were much valued in their time and, though there is no question of direct drawing and the colouring is feeble, yet, in the general conception of his subject, usually a piece of a large church, he undoubtedly proves himself a precursor of Bosboom. His seventieth birthday was splendidly celebrated at the theatre and by Pulchri Studio, the well-known artist's club, which presented him with an inscribed silver goblet. That uncommonly gifted singer, Mrs. Offermans-van Hove, pressed a crown of laurels on his silvered brow. He lived to be nearly ninety years old. His chief pupils were Bosboom, Sam Verveer, H.J. Weissenbruch, Everardus Koster (1817-1892), who painted river-scenes in the manner of Waldorp, but whose drawings of Gothic architecture rank higher, and his eldest son Hubertus.

Hubertus or Huib van Hove (1814-1864) was taught painting not only by his father, but also by Van de Sande Bakhuijzen and, though he constantly kept pace with Bosboom and painted churches in the latter's manner, he started as a landscape-painter. But the force of this none too forcible painter lay in neither of these two styles. His love of colour and bright light was best displayed in his so-called *doorkijkjes,* or domestic vistas, in the style of Pieter de Hooche, that is to say, views of outdoor light seen through an interior, a room or kitchen situated be-

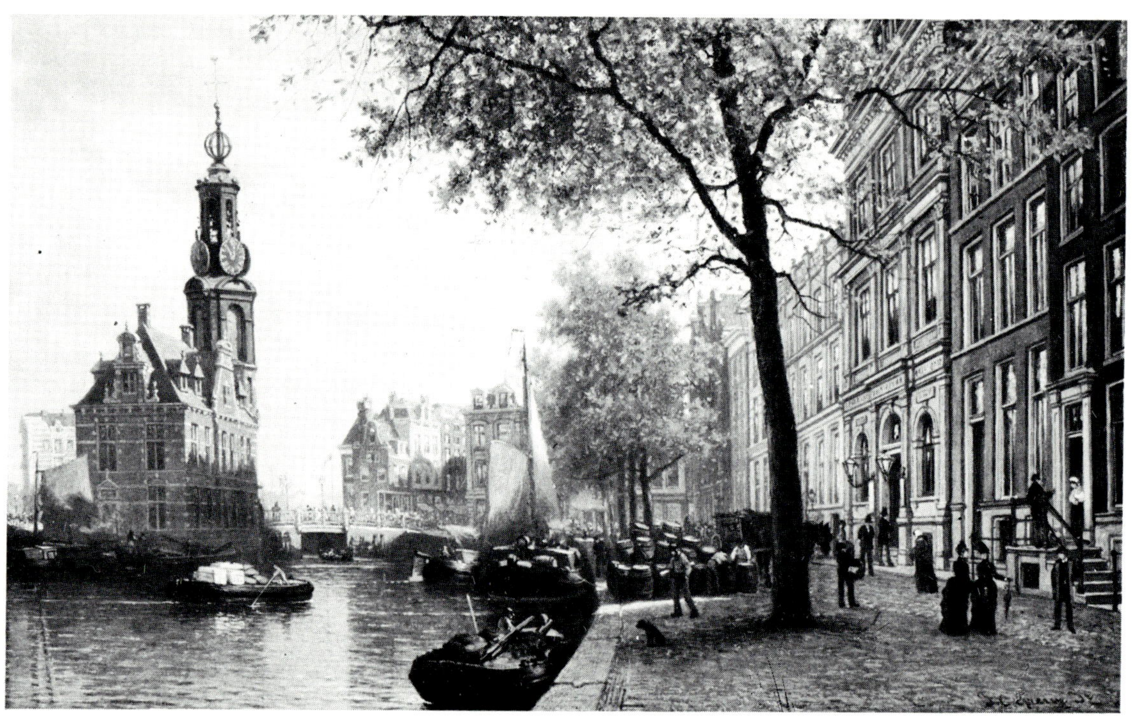

Johan Conrad Greive (1837-1891) *was a pupil of his uncle, P.F. Greive, the painter of old Dutch interiors, and made a name for himself with his river scenes and barges. This view though traditional in subject is more* fin de siècle *in style.* Photograph courtesy of Mak van Waay, Amsterdam.

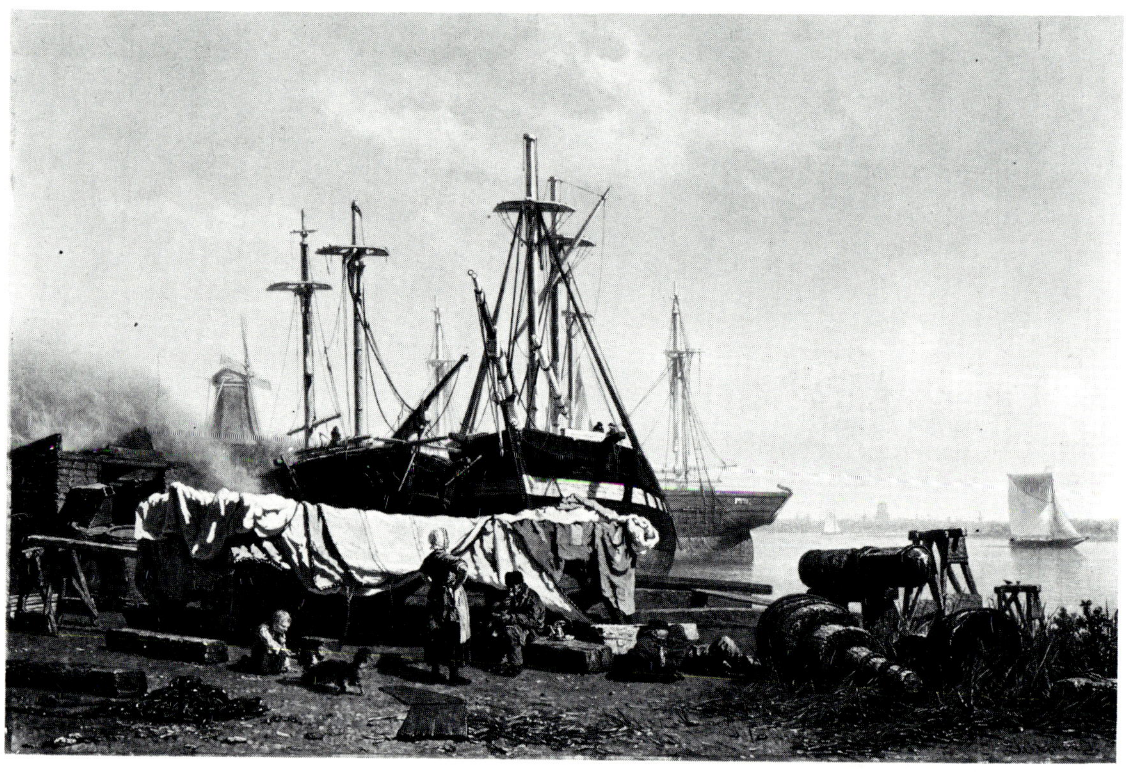

Here **Greive** *paints "The Break for Lunch" in a boat yard (78 x 119cms.).* Photograph courtesy of the Rijksmuseum, Amsterdam.

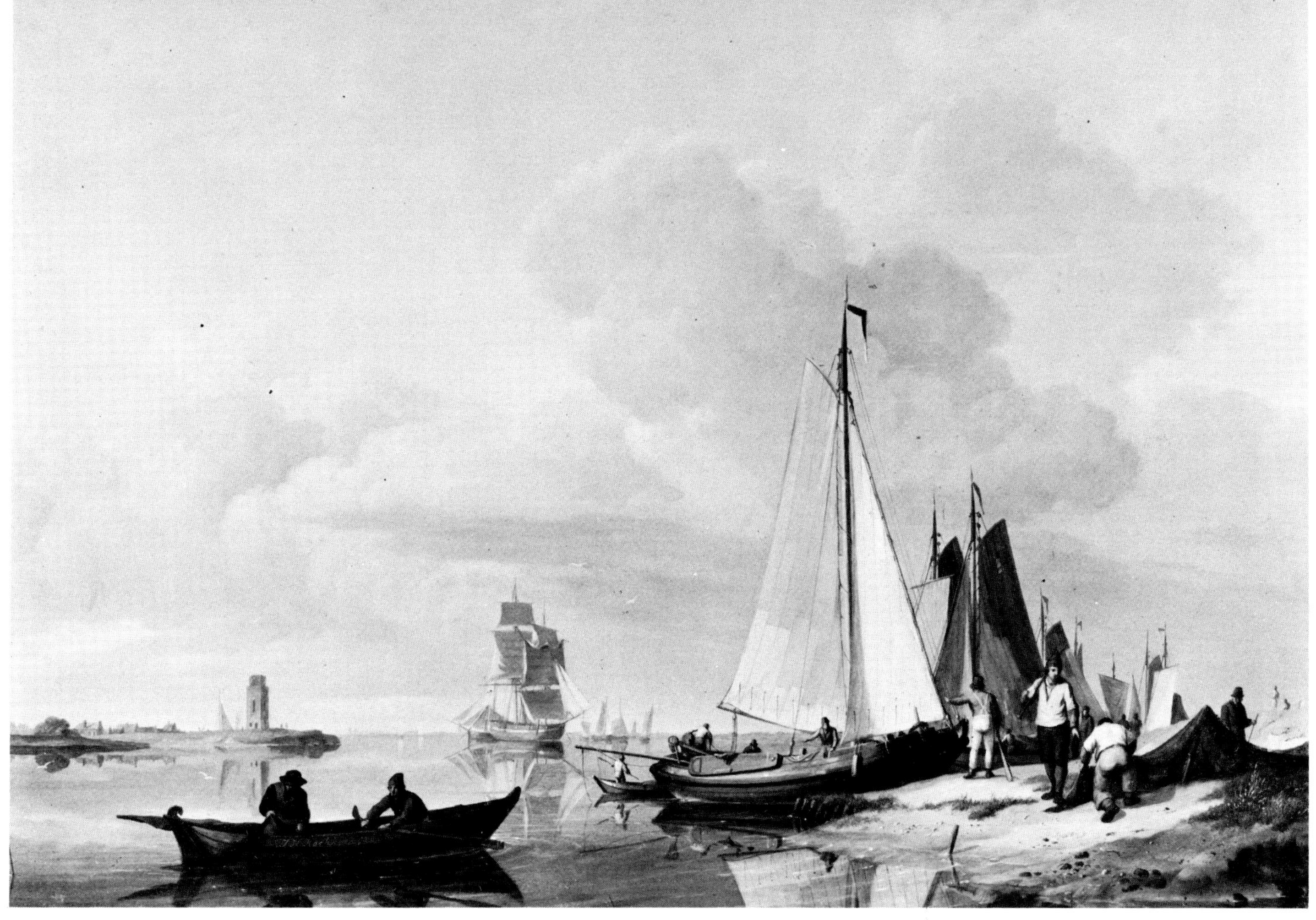

Johannes Hermanus Koekkoek (1778-1851) *was the father of Barend Cornelis and a line of distinguished painters. His gentle seascapes are closer to the 18th century in feel. (for Koekkoek family of painters, see addendum).* Photograph courtesy of Richard Green.

tween the street-door and an inner yard. Teyler's Museum possesses an excellent specimen in *The Knitter,* a picture which, although it lacks all the essence of his sublime model, is of a lively composition and shows an inclination for a stronger and fresher colouring than prevailed in Van Hove's day.

Among his pupils were Jacob Maris, Christoffel Bisschop, Stroebel, Maurits Leon (1838-1865), who died so young and whose *Interior of a Synagogue,* although not his best-known work, aroused great expectations at the time, and Hendricus Johannes Scheeres (1829-1864), who continued his master's teaching in his *Armourer* and *Linen-shop* and who enjoyed the appreciation of his brother-artists. He, also, died too young to establish his name.

A painter who rendered excellent service to Dutch art not only through his own performances, but also by his influence upon his pupils was Petrus Franciscus Greive, who was born in Amsterdam in 1811 and died in 1872. He was "a painter to the bottom of his heart," as his contemporaries used to call him, and was closely related to Huib van Hove in his love for Hooche-like interiors. But, whereas neither of them really had anything to speak of in common with Pieter de Hooche, Greive had not the command of light, shade and colour that was afterwards to distinguish the Hague painter. It is true that the enormous number of his lessons prevented him from quite coming into his own as a painter; and, moreover, he started in much less favourable circumstances than Huib van Hove. In the first place, his master, the feeble history-painter Christiaan Julius Lodewijk Portman (1799-1868), was not to be compared with B.J. van Hove either for his old-Dutch cabinet-pieces or for his composition and workmanship. And then the difference between his surroundings and those at the Hague amid which Bosboom, Huib van Hove's fellow-pupil, worked! Nevertheless, the Rijksmuseum possesses of this estimable artist, who was perhaps more of a draughtsman than a painter, an *Old-Dutch Serving-maid,* in a De Hooche

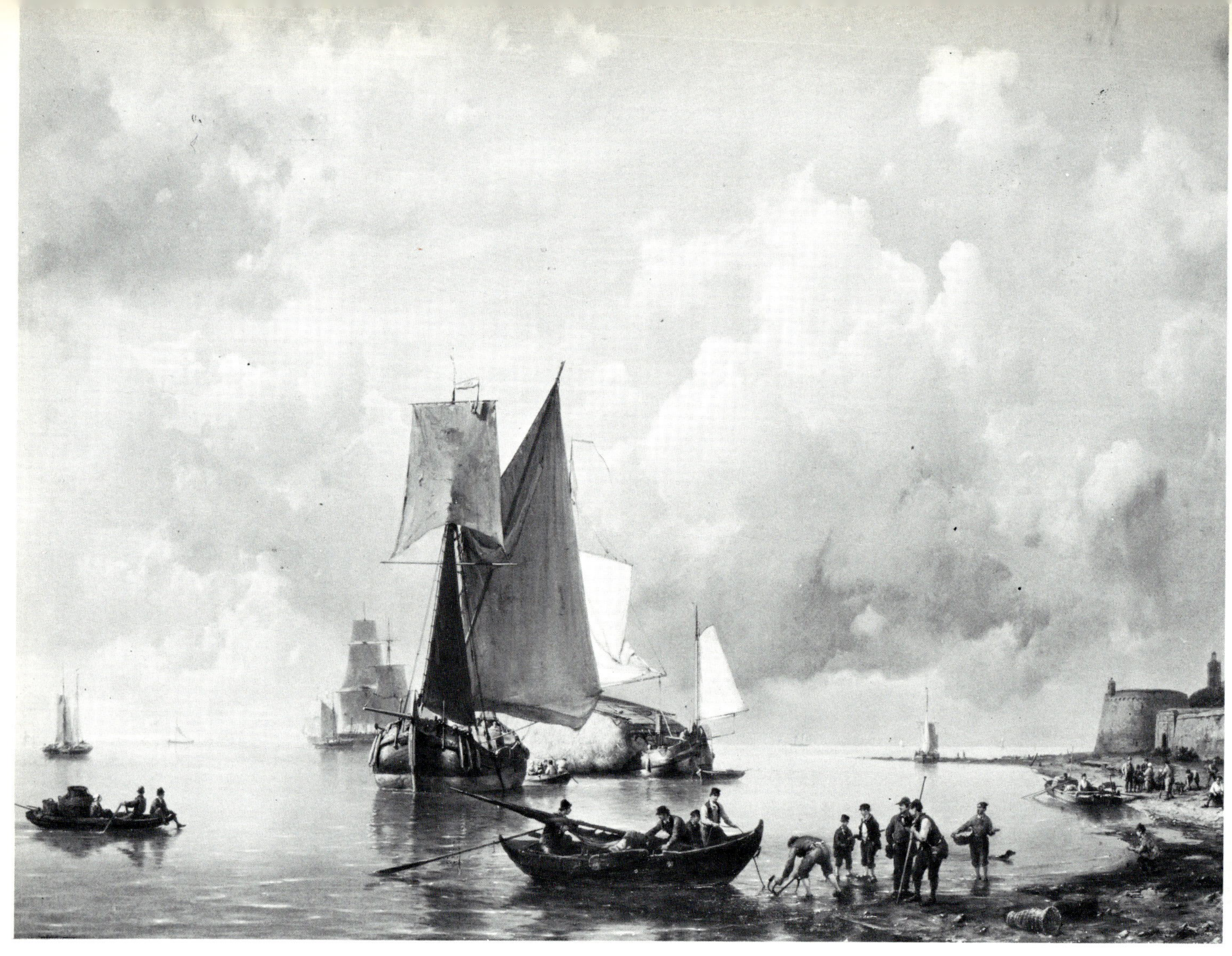

Hermanus Koekkoek (1815-1882) *was the youngest of Barend Cornelis' four artist brothers and the best known as a painter in his time. This picture dated 1862, a calm scene but full of busy action, is of the type most highly regarded today. (33 x 44ins.).* Photograph courtesy of Spenser, S.A.

setting, which lacks nothing except truth to life, while Teyler's Museum has a *Marken Interior* which contains more movement and which, as regards the subject, reminds one rather of Jozef Israëls' more romantic period.

Greive is of most importance to our own period through his pupil Allebé. He had many others, including Leon, whom I have already named, Diederik Franciscus Jamin (1838-1865), who died young and who, within the bounds of a limited talent, was full of promise, Hendrik Jacobus Scholten, born in 1824, who excelled in the depicting of satin and also painted from a more emotional point of view, in addition to his nephew, Johan Conrad Greive Jr. (1837-1891), who became known as a painter of river-scenes with barges and views on the IJ.

Barend Cornelis Koekkoek (1803-1862) was esteemed as highly as a landscape-painter in his time as Jacob Maris in ours. Although he is now antiquated and out of fashion, his value remains. And this is not without good reason. When hung between indifferent works by modern landscape-men, his work impresses the spectator by its power, by the firm and correct construction of the trees, by the broad, natural growth of the leaves and boughs, by the careful and elaborate reproduction of the wooded landscape, even though the representation be, as I have said, antiquated and somewhat cold. He seems to have based his method by turns upon Hobbema and Wijnands, but mainly upon the latter, while he lacked the simple distinction of his illustrious models, however excellent he may have been in the portrayal of heavy trees. His best pieces

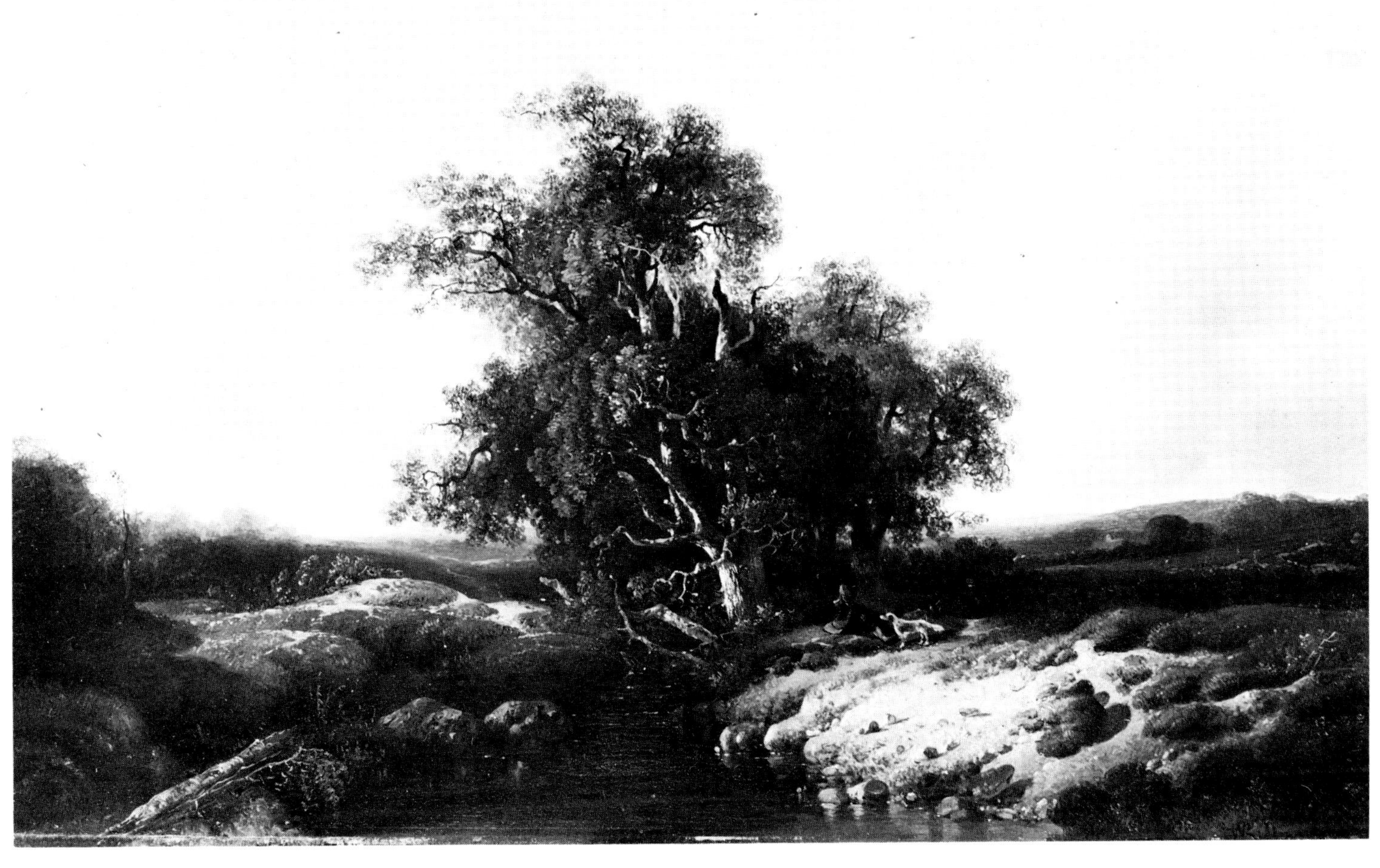

Johannes Wernardus Bilders (1811-1890), *though inescapably connected to the old Dutch landscape tradition, began to add new dimensions to it. He took "nature" as his master and fell under the influence of Delacroix. (42 x 60½cms.).* Photograph courtesy of Mak van Waay, Amsterdam.

are those which show but little of the open air, for the landscape fell more within his scope than the sky, which in his pictures often suggests scene-painting.

B.C. Koekkoek was a native of Middelburg; he was the eldest son of Johannes Hermanus Koekkoek (1778-1851), a well-known sea and river-painter, who, after learning his trade in a tapestry-factory, formed himself by studying from nature and afterwards brought up all his sons – he had four, of whom, after Barend, Hermanus was the best-known – as painters. Our Koekkoek did not confine himself to the landscape of his own country and found the scenes that best satisfied his taste in the Harz Mountains, the Rhine Provinces, Belgium and particularly, in Gelderland and the Cleves district. His work was greatly valued and highly paid in Paris, Brussels and St. Petersburg.

Johannes Wernardus Bilders (1811-1890) was born at Utrecht and took lessons from Jan Lodewijk Jonxis (1789-1867). In the phrase of that time, however, "nature," or, more correctly, "his own genius was his best master." After a course of travels in Germany, he settled down at Oosterbeek, which had not yet become a "park" of villas and "desirable residences." In 1854, he went to Amsterdam, where his friend N. Pieneman, Schwartze, who had already made his name, and their junior, Jozef Israëls, were living. Bilders had exhibited for the first time in 1840; Schwartze's first work was shown between 1845 and 1850; Israëls had exhibited his *Aaron* in Amsterdam in 1854, painted his romantic *By Mother's Grave* in 1856 and followed this up in

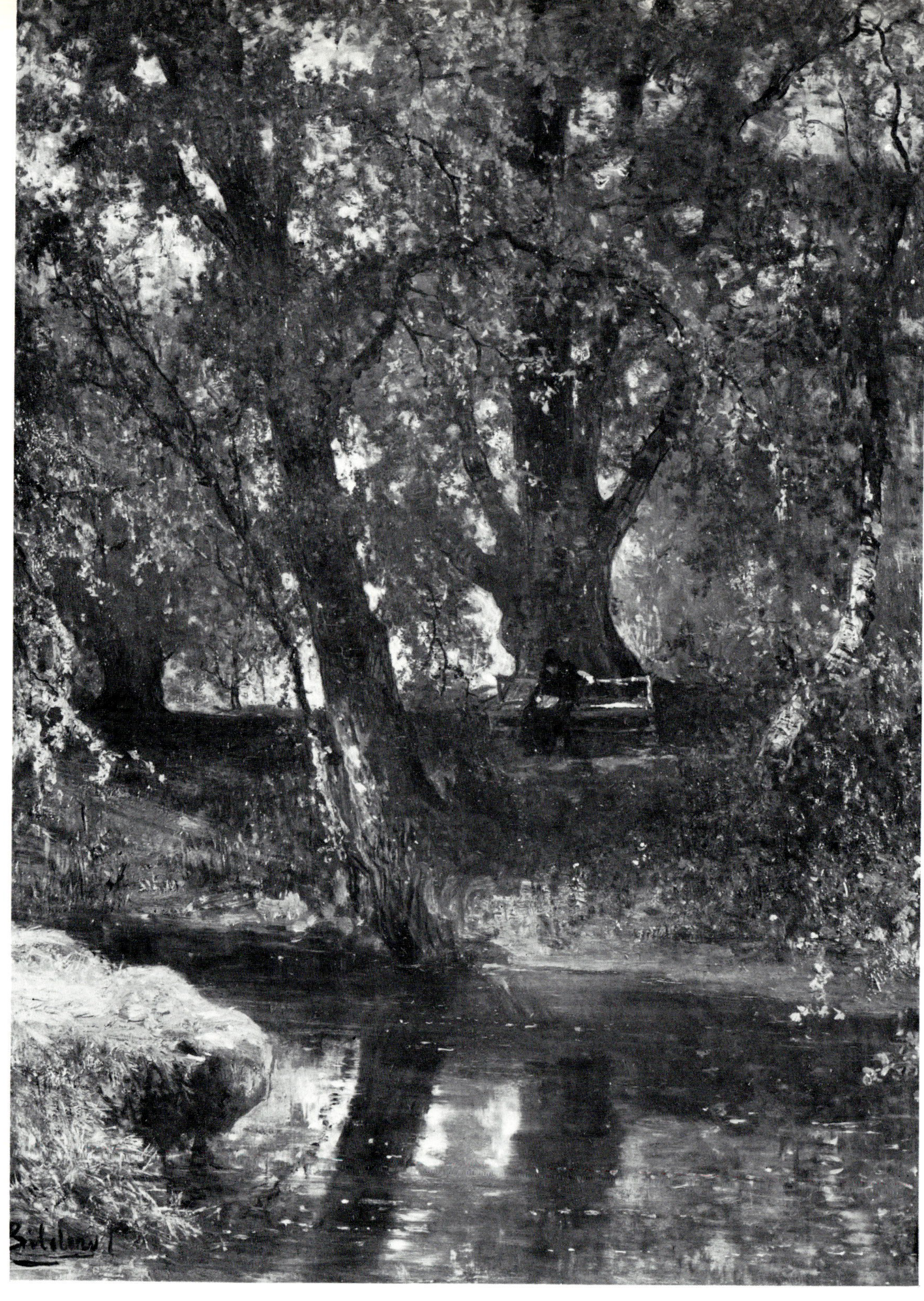

Here **Johannes Bilders** *paints the interior of a wood at Wosterbeek.* Photograph courtesy of Rijksmuseum Hendrik Willem Mesdag.

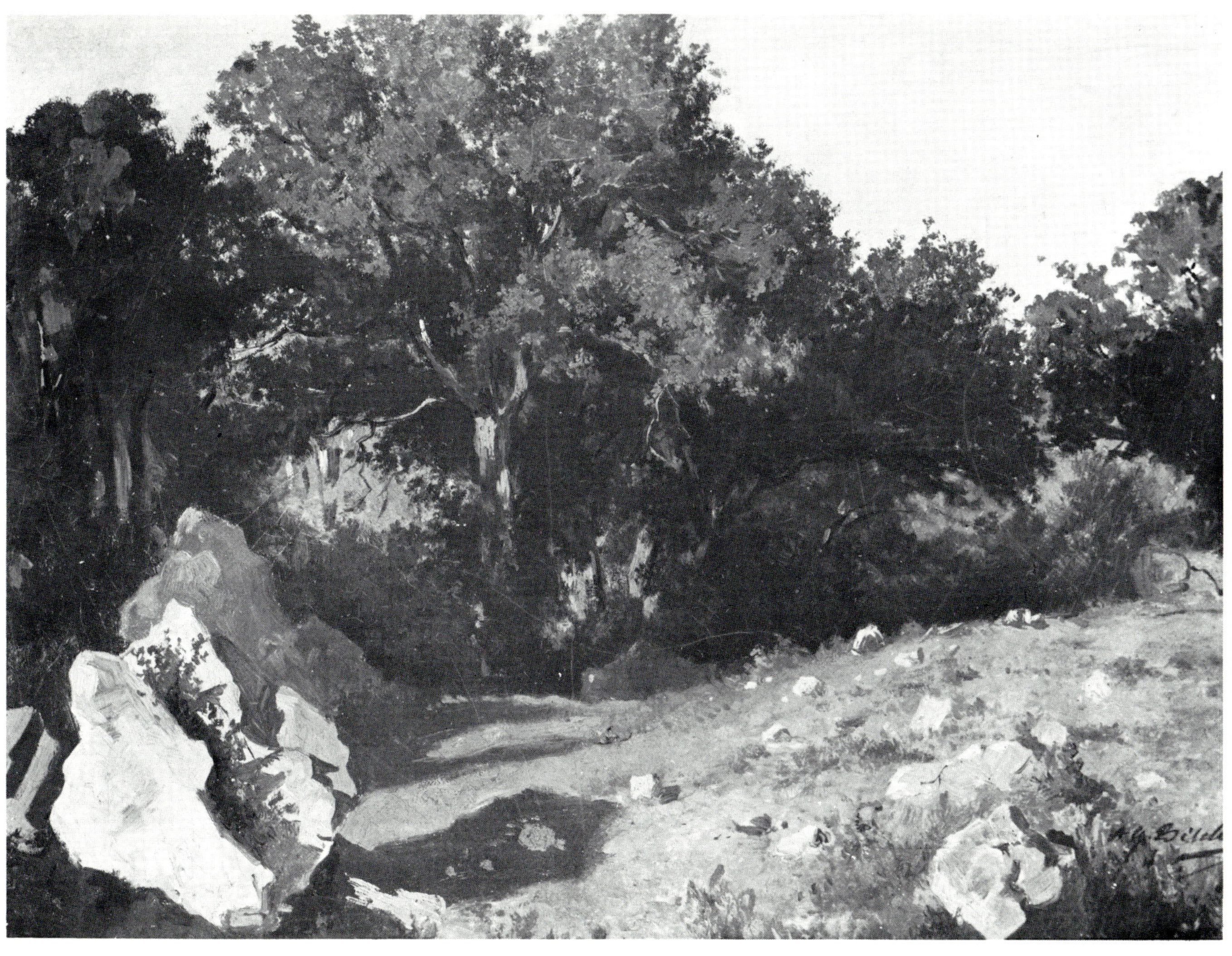

Albert Gerard Bilders (1838-1865) *was the first of the Hague school painters to discover the marvels of the French Barbizon masters and in his short life led the way that Mauve and the Maris brothers were to follow. This "Landscape near St. Ange" already shows the preoccupation with light which is the hallmark of late 19th century landscape. (33 x 44cms.).* Photograph courtesy of the Kröller-Müller Museum, Otterlo.

1858 with his well-known *Little Knitter* and, somewhat later, with that little master-piece of romanticism, *After the Storm.*

I doubt whether Bilders' great talent ever reached its full development. He stood alone, absolutely alone. The phlegmatic painters who were content slavishly to copy nature, the eminent painters of fields and cattle had little or nothing in common with him and the studies which were sold at the auction held in the studio of the late Mrs. Bilders-van Bosse, his second wife, prove that he felt a longing for more colour, that, directly or indirectly, he had experienced the influence of a Delacroix. At any rate, there were some among them which exhibited a great tendency towards modern methods with their sharp colour-scheme, into which no bitumen, no brown sauce entered to spoil the clearness of the impression conveyed.

As his pupils, I may name his son, Albert Gerard Bilders, who died young, and Miss Marie van Bosse, who afterwards became his wife. I will return both to the former, who proved himself a pioneer, if not by his painting, at least by recording his wishes and longings in the matter of the painters' art, and to the latter, who was a well-known landscape-painter.

Chapter VI

The Masters of the Cabinet Picture

David Bles was the foremost painter at the Hague when Jozef Israëls was feeling his way in Amsterdam, from 1854 to 1864, and when Bosboom, at the Hague, was following the road which he had seen clearly before him from the beginning. Israëls has described how honoured he felt when, as a promising painter, he was permitted to walk round an exhibition arm in arm with Bles and how lucky he thought himself to receive a word of approval from the great man, who, nevertheless, told him pretty frankly that he did not understand the so-called poetry in Israëls' painting and that, for the rest, he had never understood what poetry and painting had in common.

Nor was this to be expected from our rather cynical artist, with his humorous subjects borrowed, to a great extent, from *la vie galante.* He was a clever draughtsman and a good painter, who improved upon the soapy method of his time by means of cunning after-touches, smart strokes and powerful shadows and who placed his cleverly-conceived little figures freely and spaciously and yet in such a way that the action was concentrated and the point of his anecdote invariably realized. Still, he was in every respect the very opposite of an Israëls or a Bosboom, though he was artist enough to entertain a great respect for the work of the latter.

Born at the Hague in 1821, he first studied, for three years, under Cornelis Kruseman and afterwards worked in Paris in Robert Fleury's studio. At a very early age, he painted, under the influence of his first master and even more under that of the romanticism of his day, such genre-pieces as a *Savoyard Hurdy-gurdy Girl,* an *Hungarian Mousetrap-vendor,* or else he made offerings to history in the shape of a *Rubens and young Teniers* or a *Paul Potter taking his afternoon Walk,* until, after his return from Paris, at twenty-two, he found himself soon devoting his powers to those little anecdotal paintings which attained so widespread a fame both in his own country and abroad.

His subjects were taken from our middle-class moral life. He almost certainly created a special type of soubrette, with roguish, ogling brown eyes, tiny fingers and dainty, neatly-rounded figures. He began at a time when brunettes were in fashion, at a time when one half of the public went mad about the tear on the cheek of a Monica, while the other half, brought up on French literature, enjoyed the smallest suggestion of a *double entente.* It was also the time when collectors attached importance to a picture according to the number of pretty figures of women which it contained, the time when they would put their little paintings on the table before them in order to examine them at their ease, discuss the qualities and the expression and, magnifying glass in hand, smack their lips over the piquancy of the anecdote represented. It goes without saying that so-called miniature-painting was then in great favour; but the carefully-executed subjects, details and figures, the natural poses, lively presentation and warm colouring and, especially, the clever little lights and touches, so very conformable with the spirit of the subject, are all qualities which we can even now afford to appreciate.

And yet his sketches, heightened with sepia, often show something that attracts us still more. A swiftly-grasped movement, such as that of a girl pulling on her slipper with one finger, bending slightly aside, her shoulder thrust back in the doing of it; a flute-player; a soubrette hurrying past on her high heels; a fragile figure of a woman recovering after her confinement (in the completed picture, the young husband bends over her, while a healthy peasant-woman nurses the child): these are the figures in his sketches, which we find repeated in his favourite subjects, reproduced in a bright, life-like and natural style.

A time came, a time was bound to come when

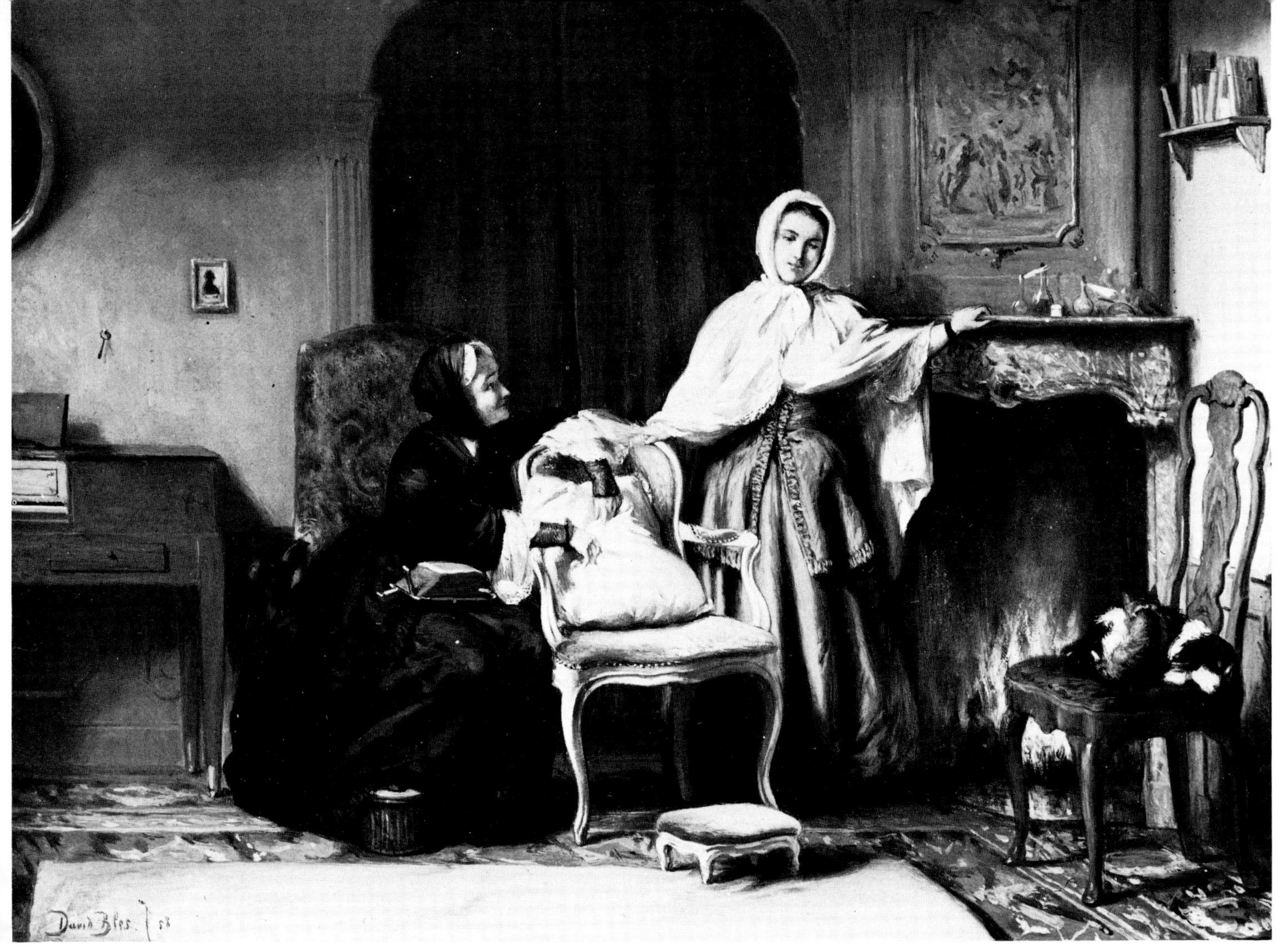

David Bles (1821-1899) *was the Hague's most honoured artist in the 1850's and 1860's. Pretty girls, cosy domestic scenes, humour, and a whisper of* double-entendre *fitted exactly with his middle-class patrons' taste. They were usually small in size – like this one which measures only 24½ x 31cms.* Photograph courtesy of Mak van Waay, Amsterdam.

people had had enough of these anecdotes, of these stories in paint, when they were no longer able to laugh at the ready-made gaiety of these pieces. This was the time when the masters of the Hague school offered their inner vision for our contemplation instead of an anecdote, when the depth of emotion of the Barbizon painters, the epic simplicity of Millet, the large view of nature of Daubigny, the more rugged greatness of Rousseau and the tortured Dupré, as contrasted with the classic Corot, made their influence felt. It was the time, too, when the Marises, with the magnificence of their conception of things against which Bles seemed so trivial, and with their purity and their wealth of colour, when Israëls, with the biblical grandeur of his interiors, Bosboom, with the sober stateliness of his churches, Mauve, with his simplicity, saw the world from a nobler standpoint and rendered in pure plastic form not so much external objects as the depth of their own feeling.

Time is just.

The pictorial qualities for which, at this or that time, a given painter has been valued remain the same. His good qualities are often thrust into the background, because of a change in the accepted formula; but, at each new turn of the road we catch a fresh glimpse of the former period, which is then weighed and frequently valued anew. But what can never be made good is the sorrow that must needs be felt by a painter who, after passing through years of triumph, is forgotten in his own lifetime. David Bles died in 1899, too early to witness the revolution which has

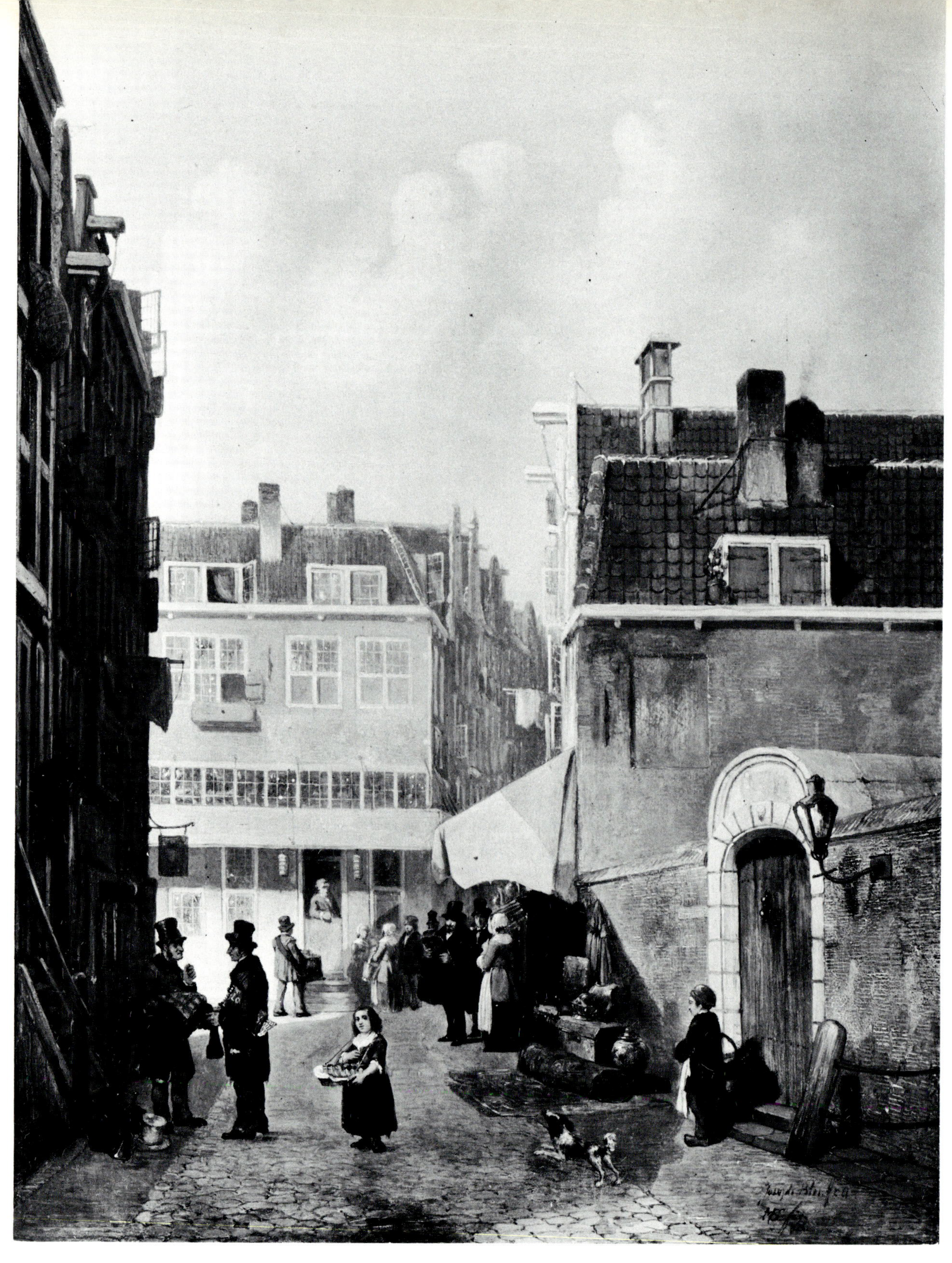

Joseph Bles (1825-1875). Photograph courtesy of MacConnal Mason.

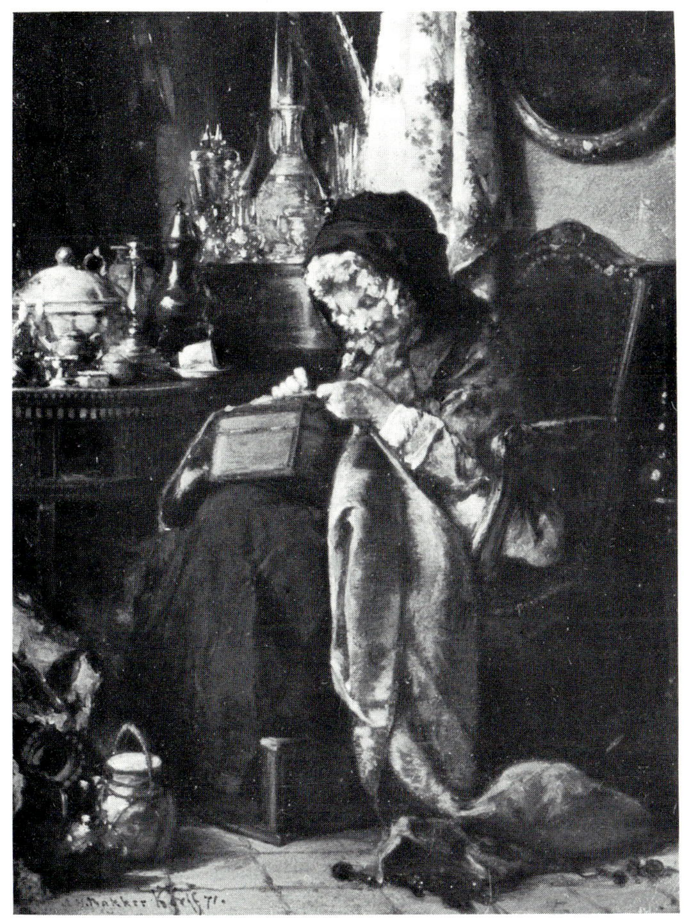

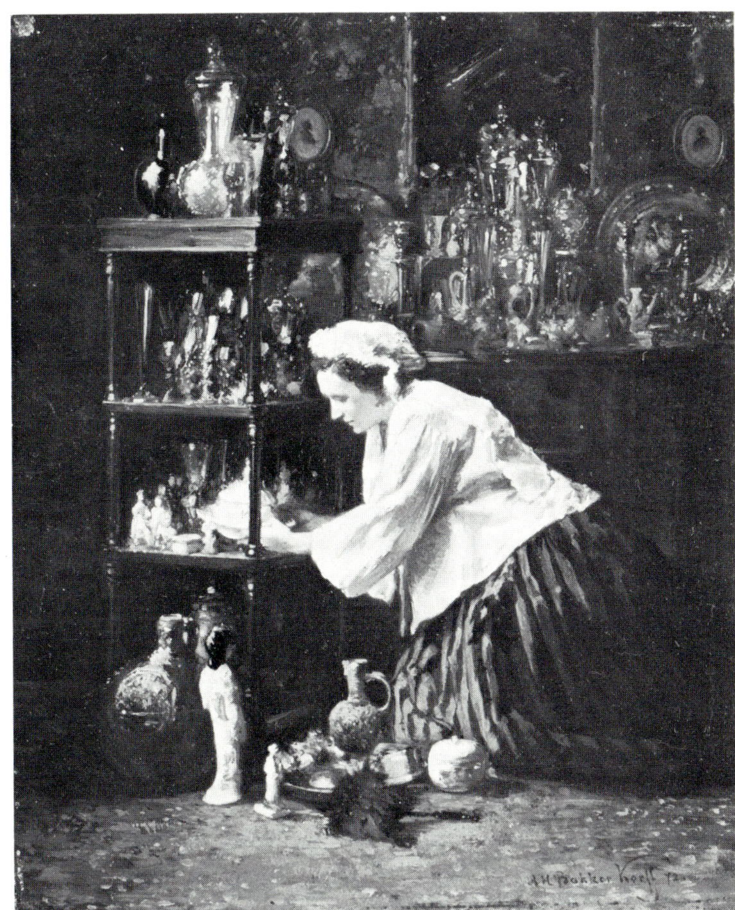

Alexander Hugo Bakker Korff (1824-1882) *combined his own form of psychological realism with the small cabinet picture format popular in the mid-century. Unromanticised old ladies in interiors painted with the loving eye of a still life painter are his usual themes. These are two good single-figure examples dated 1871 and 1872 respectively (3½ x 4½ ins. and 4¾ x 5½ ins.).* Photographs courtesy of Williams & Son.

once more enabled us to see what was good in the days before the coming of the great Hague men.

If we place David Bles side by side with Bakker Korff, the Leiden painter (and there is due reason for the comparison), we feel inclined to compare the subjects of the first with a spicy French farce and those of the other with a drawing-room play at a girls boarding-school, performed mainly for the sake of the "dressing-up" involved. David Bles's pictures are seldom complete without some allusion to *la vie galante* aforesaid, whereas Bakker Korff's afford a genial laugh at the affectation of the pompous and stately old spinsters, with their scent-bottles, bonbon-boxes and fiddle-faddles, continuing the greatness of their forefathers in the sumptuous decoration of their houses, chatting and enjoying themselves with friends who resemble them in every respect, waxing sentimental over a forgotten ballad, sitting rapt in admiration round a fine fuschia or a bowl of gold fish, talking scandal, arch, simple, but always with a suggestion of that same "dressing-up" and always seen with the eyes of a painter of still-life. It is in this that the value of these little panels lies. The Saxony soup-tureens, the lacquered Chinese urn-stands, the flounced skirts, the black silk aprons, the costly tea-services, the motley carpets, all reproduced with cunning touches of colour in a dignified, eighteenth-century living-room, the faces with the prominent noses, the little curls on the temples and all the coquettish gestures of the old belles who had been flirts in their day, the delicious effects of light, which Bakker Korff employed so sparingly, but to such good purpose, the firm painting and witty brushwork, with something of Meissonier in the drawing: all these cause him to rank perhaps a little higher than David Bles, even though the latter displays more variety in his subjects, more expression in his figures and more point in his anecdotes.

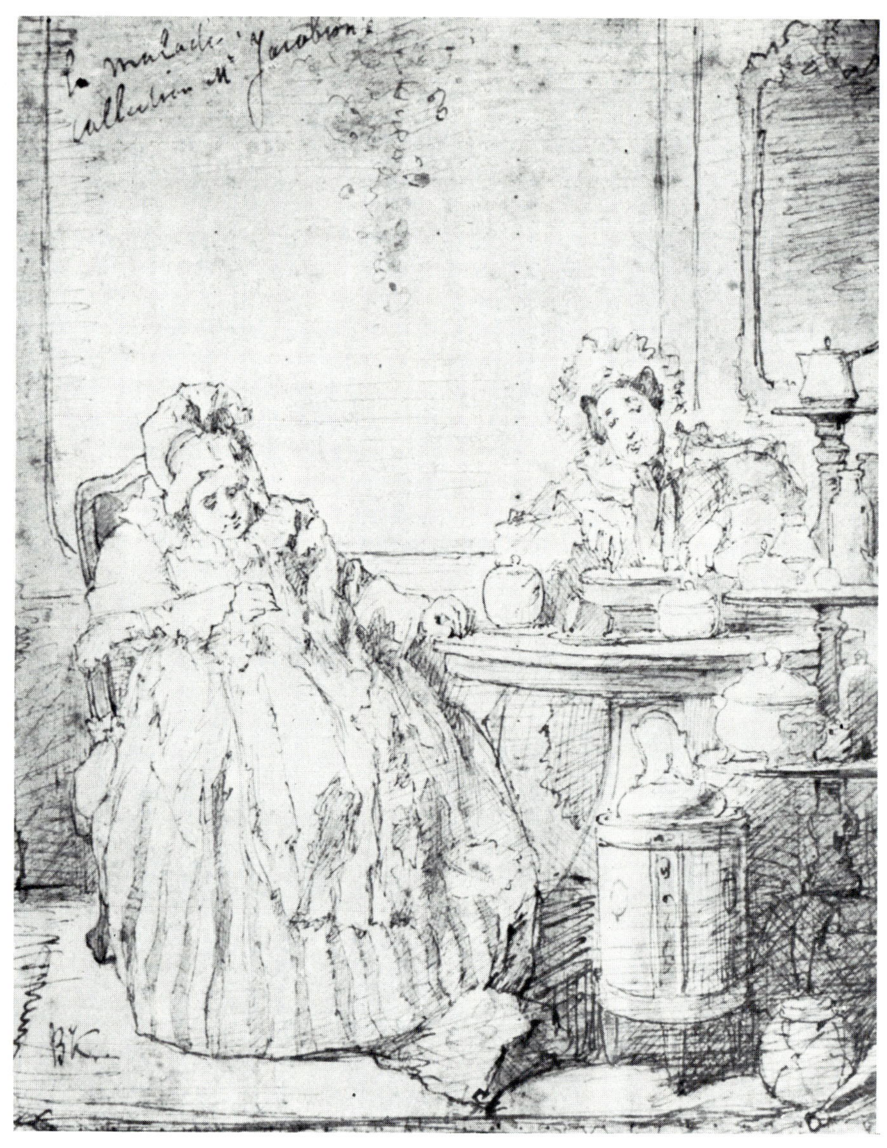

Bakker Korff's *sensitive reading of a particular aspect of female psychology comes out vividly in this pen and ink drawing entitled "La Malade" (13½ x 11cms.). One feels some sympathy with his unmarried sisters who sat for him and no doubt provided this special insight.* Photograph courtesy of Mak van Waay, Amsterdam.

Alexander Hugo Bakker Korff was born at the Hague in 1824, attended C. Kruseman's studio together with David Bles, H. ten Kate, Jan and Philip Koelman and Vintcent, took lessons under J.E.J. van den Berg at the Hague Academy and afterwards worked in the studio of Huib van Hove. His first pictures consisted of biblical and historical subjects: life-size figures, exacted by the classic painters in imitation of the antique statues, as though there were no salvation outside the giant cartoon. He excelled to better purpose in smaller compositions drawn with the pen, after the manner of Rethel and Flaxman. And, soon, driven to the painting of miniature-pieces either because of his near-sightedness or because of the taste of the day, we find him at Oegstgeest, far from all schools of art, taking up that genre-painting in which he was essentially himself and for which his unmarried sisters sat as voluntary models. Although

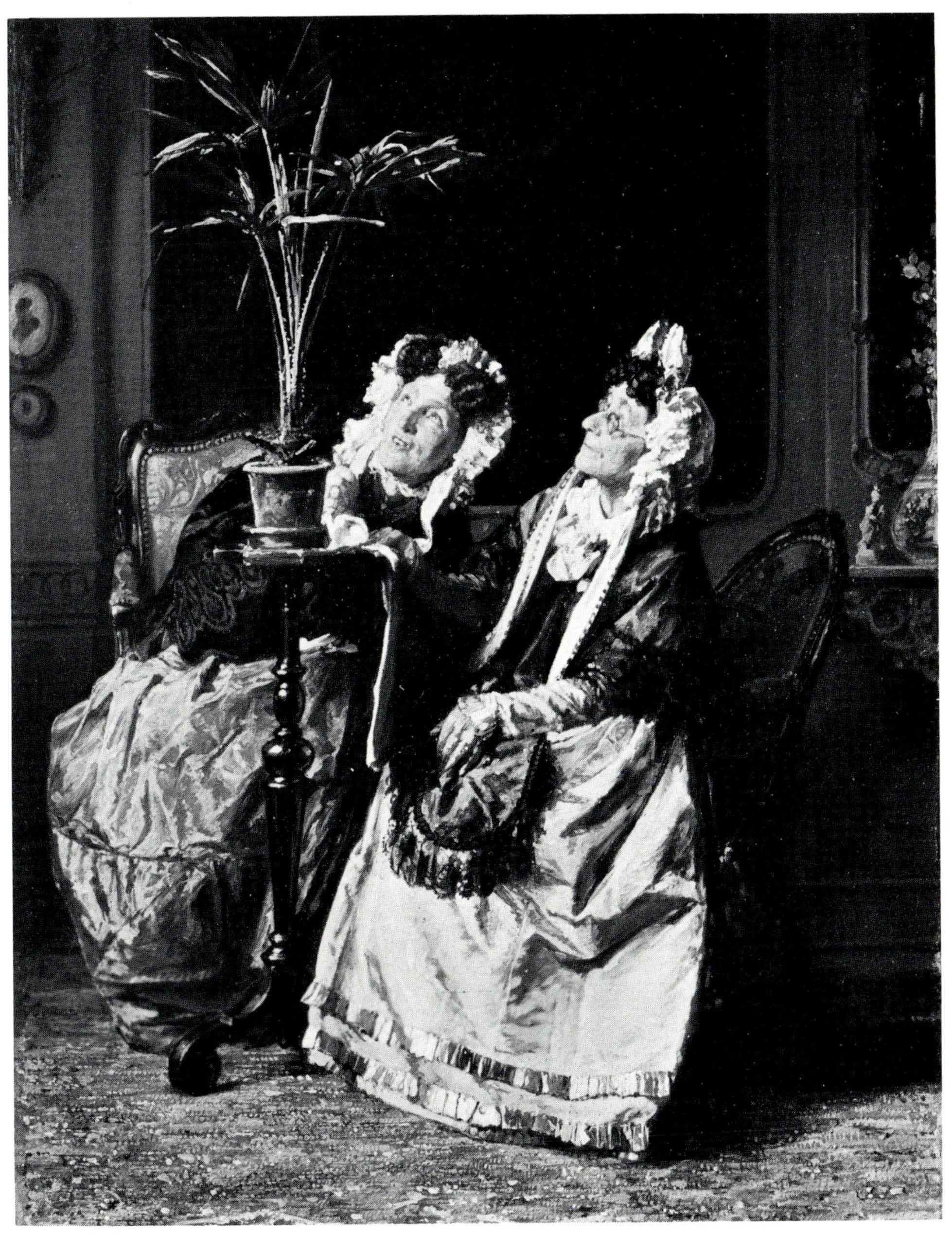

Another example of **Bakker Korff's** *favourite theme, this time entitled "Under the Palm". (17.5 x 14 cms.).* Photograph courtesy of the Rijksmuseum, Amsterdam.

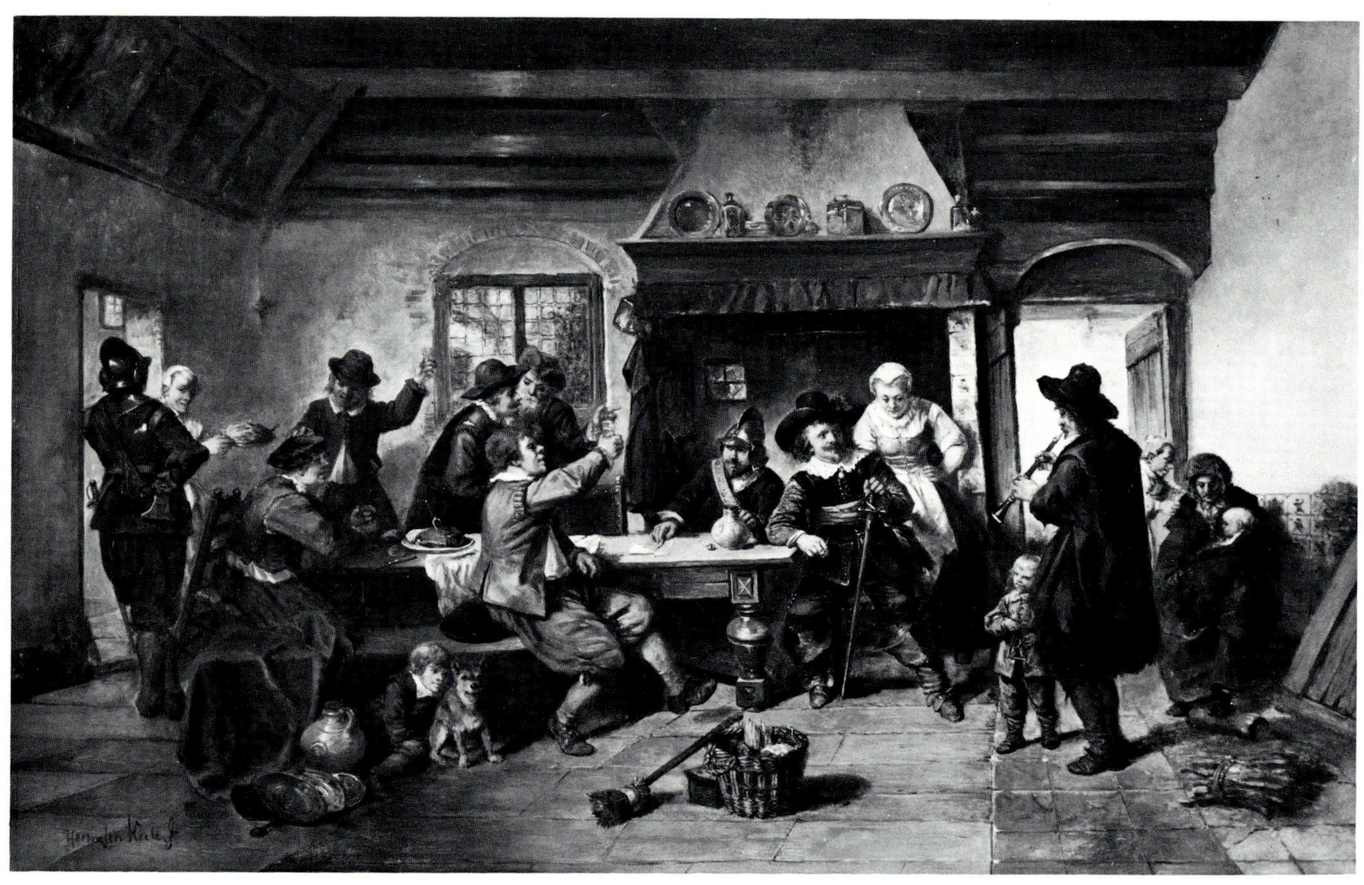

Herman Frederik Karel ten Kate (1822-1891) *was working at a time when Meissonier's cavaliers were all the rage. He has added an element of Teniers – his soldiers are constantly to be found in the tavern, as in this example. Marius records that his work was highly sought after in his lifetime. (22½ x 35ins.)* **Photograph courtesy of M. Newman Ltd.**

the pictures with many figures are more interesting, I prefer the single figures for the colour-scheme: it is more unconstrained and often contains more tone. I know a little piece in which a portly person of the middle-class, in pink cotton, is mending a calico coverlet. The woman in this bright pink contrasting with her black apron, with the many-coloured coverlet on her lap, against the elaborate background of an old-fashioned kitchen, or else a single delicate little figure, all in white against a rich background: these are the pictures that stand highest as specimens of his powers. He is also admirable in such pieces as *The Mischief-maker*, *The School for Scandal*, *The Fuschia*, while, of his larger works, *The Ballad* is perhaps best-known, because of the engraving. Less well-known is a still-life picture of fine glass seen against a mirror, a problem which seems hardly solvable, but which he was nevertheless able cleverly to decipher. Bakker Korff himself regarded this as his best work. He died in 1882 and, though his work too was disregarded for a time, it is now valued more highly than that of Bles. It is something that both escaped the soapy influence of Cornelis Kruseman.

As much cannot be said of Bakker Korff's pupil Herman Frederik Karel ten Kate (1822-1891). His pictures illustrative of the Eighty Years' War appear, at first sight, to be treated in lively fashion and a certain roughness of colour gives them a spurious air of strength. But, on reconsideration, everything about them – the colour, workmanship, the composition – becomes tedious and nothing remains but a considerable adroitness. His soldiers, clad in mail or jerkin, endowed with huge jack-boots, drinking, dicing, courting the wench at the inn, are all cut from one pattern

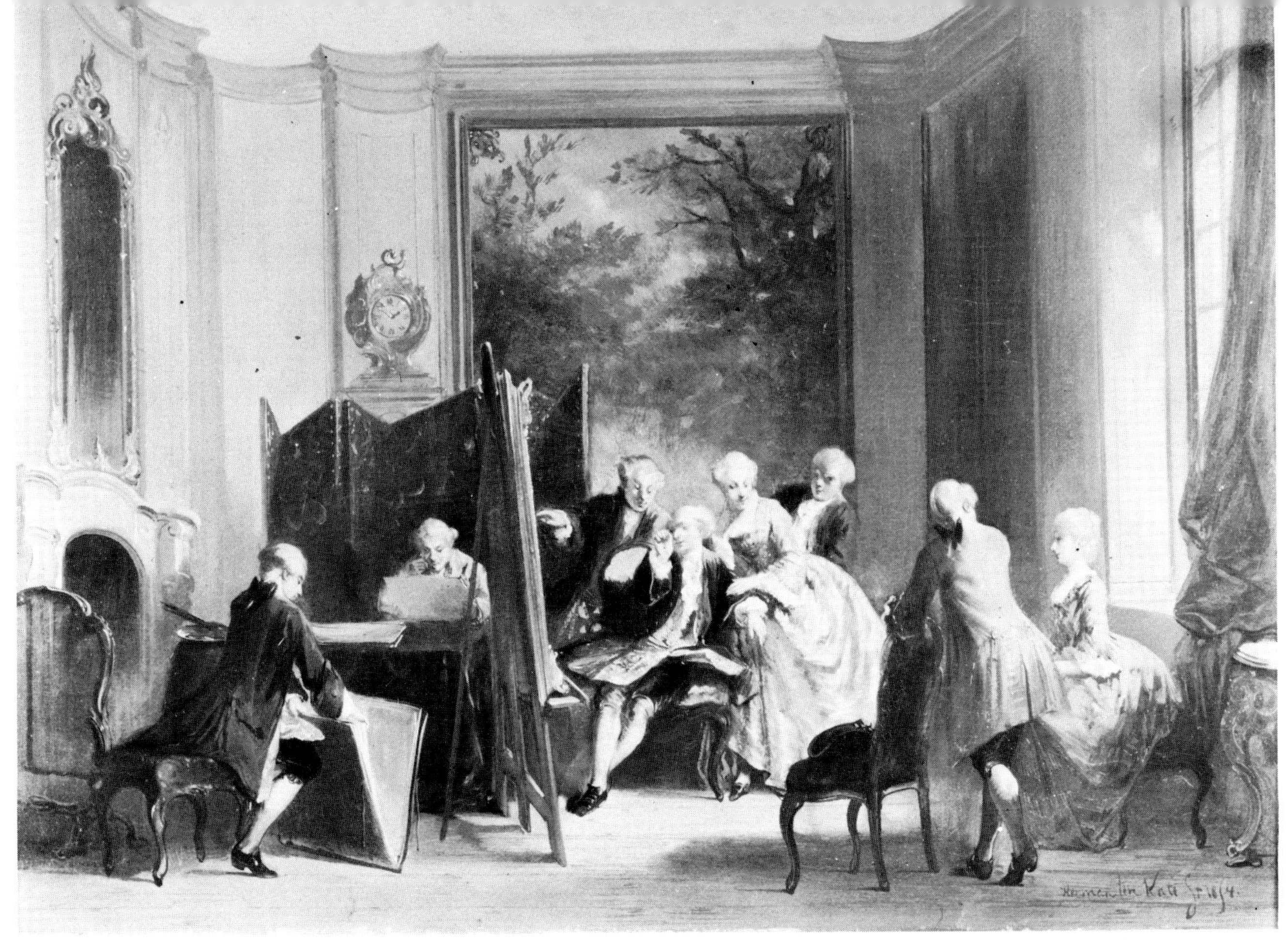

It is most unusual for **Herman ten Kate** *to wander from the 17th century into the 18th century. In this example, entitled "The Connoisseurs", he has made the transition with a light relaxed gaiety. (9¾ x 13¼ins.)* Photograph courtesy of Sotheby & Co.

and, though we know that their costumes are authentic, they remain stage characters in a stage scene. Herman ten Kate's was an affected method. He lacked the certainty of workmanship which give Bles's subjects their pictorial value. Nevertheless, his work was greatly sought after and he was personally highly respected.

Johan Mari ten Kate, born in 1831, his younger brother and pupil, borrowed his subjects from child-life; his work is often weak and, at the same time, a little exaggerated in the conception of it. Mari ten Kate's best work consists of the studies which he made at Marken with his brother Herman.

Allebé may be regarded as the fine painter who closes one period and introduces a new one. He belongs to the anecdotal painters in so far as his subjects are concerned, while the composition and the execution of his best works approach very near to the finest that we possess. It is owing to the distinguished quality of his talent that this artist, who, for some years, has practically ceased production, is rated perhaps even more highly in this twentieth century than when he was most constantly at work.

Allebé is a born painter of cabinet-pieces. These are well-considered compositions, often endowed with a touch of anecdote, at times romantic, but rarely sentimental. One would have to collect all his works together in order to trace any sort of gradual development. To judge from what we know – and this is constantly increasing in volume in proportion as our admiration increases of late years – he is one of those artists who confirm the rule that a man is either an artist or not. All that we do know is distinguished by a certain completeness. The subjects are interiors such as that with the little old Brabant woman winding up her clock, a more or less witch-like type which he repeated later and strengthened by adding one of those tortuous, stretching cats which often recur in his work. Would you see how a little picture such as this is painted? You can tell neither where it begins nor where it ends. Muther once said of Menzel that he added up with too many small figures. The same remark, differently applied, might be made regarding Allebé, were it not that every detail of the treatment

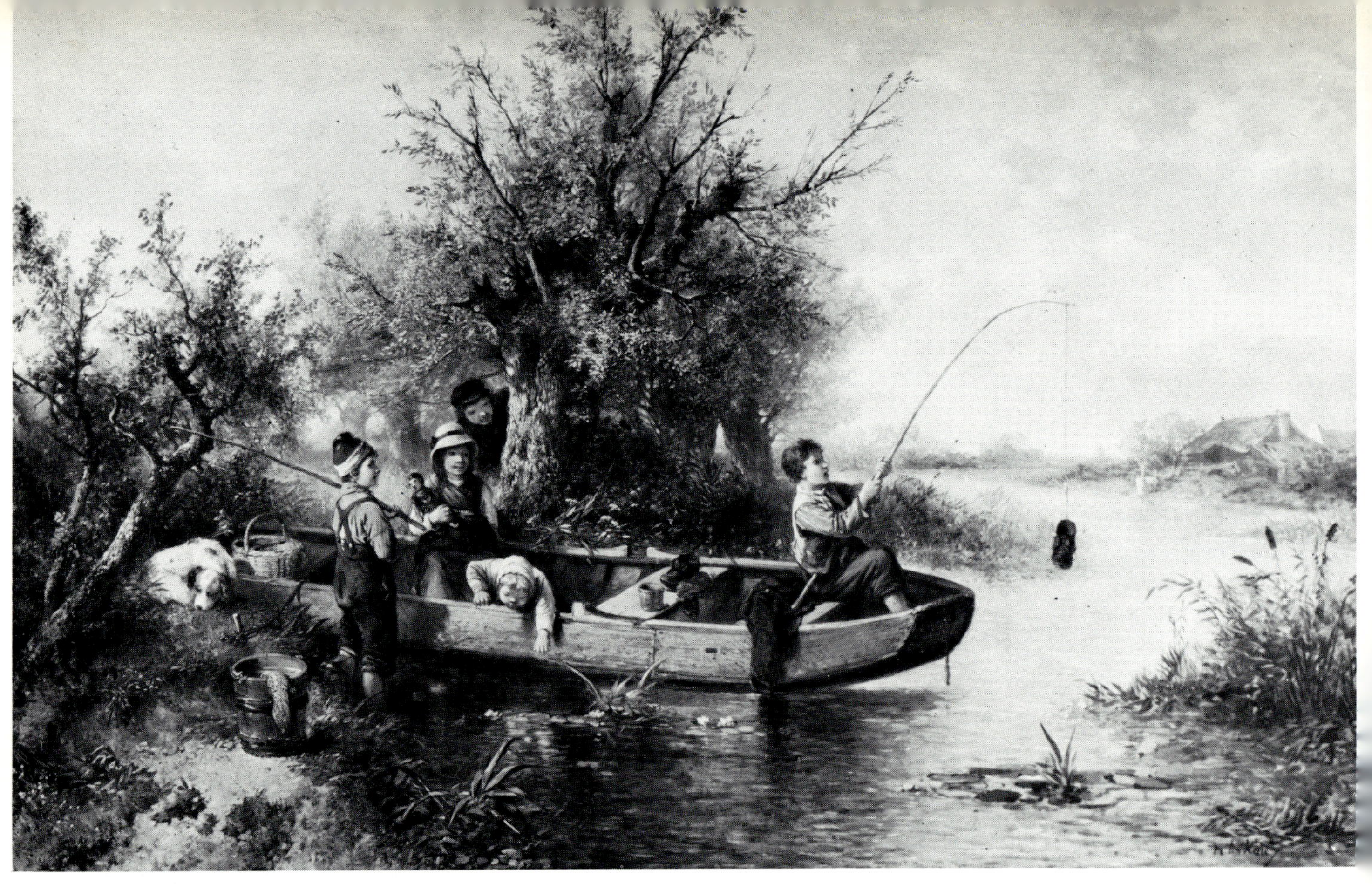

Johan Mari ten Kate (1831-1910) *was the younger brother and pupil of Herman. He constantly painted children at play as in this comical piece of fishing for a boot.* (24¾ x 39ins.) Photograph courtesy of M. Newman Ltd.

in his case is covered with so delicate a gloss, while all those tiny dots of colour are mingled so inextricably that it is hopeless to look for any weakness.

From the point of view of the effective distribution of light, *The Well-watched Child* at the Rijksmuseum stands highest of all Allebé's pictures. The subject is an old-fashioned farm-house, containing dwelling and stable in one. In the background is a cradle with a child, watched over by a placid cat, a cow and a number of yellow chickens, which trip close past the cradle: a deliciously homely and delightfully-painted slice of life, enlivened by the rays falling from the skylight upon the cradle and deepening all the colours in the foreground, so that the blue becomes bluer, the green real, mellow grass-green, and the scene of the cradle, the cat, the cow and the chickens, with a few objects around, placed in the full light, forms the centre of the picture.

Auguste Allebé was born in Amsterdam in 1838 and received his first lessons at the Academy. Later, he followed the course at the École Normale in Paris, where he learnt much of Mouilleron, the well-known lithographer, and it is perhaps to the latter's lessons that we owe those immaculate lithographic portraits of Allebé's, which are models of simple, unaffected draughtsmanship. Together with Jamin and Maurits Leon, he worked for two years in P.F. Greive's studio, subsequent to which came his *Early in Church,* formerly in the Van Lynden collection. In 1868, he went to Brussels and, on his return, in 1870, was appointed professor at the State Academy of Plastic Art, under De Poorter, whom he succeeded as director on the latter's death in 1880.

Many have regretted the fact that this fine painter, with his pronounced talent, should, after ten years of success and general appreciation, have abandoned his artistic career. Perhaps, at first, he flattered himself that he would be able to combine the two callings and allowed himself to be persuaded accordingly. But, even as he had been a conscientious painter, so now he became a careful and scrupulous teacher. The two were not to be combined and the artist was swallowed up in the professor. And, however much we may regret this from the point of view of our national art,

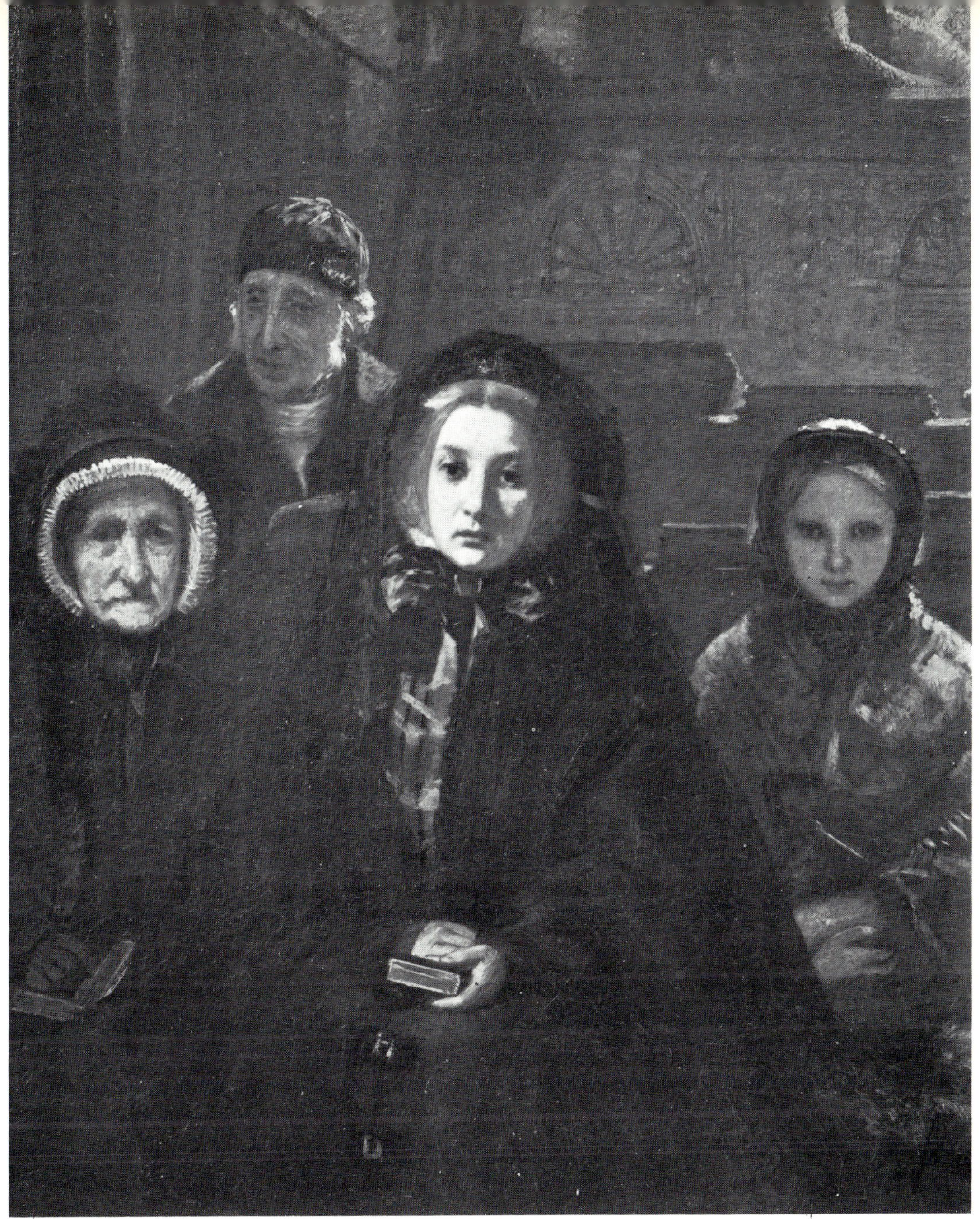

Through **Auguste Allebé (1838-1927)** *the clever small genre pieces, cabinet paintings, popular in the mid-century are linked to the new unromanticised genre of the Hague School. This small painting "Early Hour at Church" (43 x 34 cms.) is already closer to Isräels and the Marises than to David Bles. Allebé's influence was particularly important through his teaching. He was Director of the Rijks-Academie voor Beeldende Kunsten from 1880 to 1906.* Photograph courtesy of the Rijksmuseum, Amsterdam.

it is not for those who have enjoyed his teaching to complain: the excellent pupils whom he has formed bear witness, in many respects, to the culture that distinguished his teaching.

His years of study and his principal years of work, from 1860 to 1870 (although some of his best water-colours are dated after 1870), coincided with those of Matthijs, Jacob and Willem Maris and with the time when the masters of the Hague school, while preparing for the full flight which they were to take after 1870, had already produced some of their most finished work. It was a time rich in promise, strong in reserved force; for the Hague school it was the burgeoning of the buds, the beginning of a spring which was soon to burst into full blossom and become a luxurious summer of latter-day Dutch art.

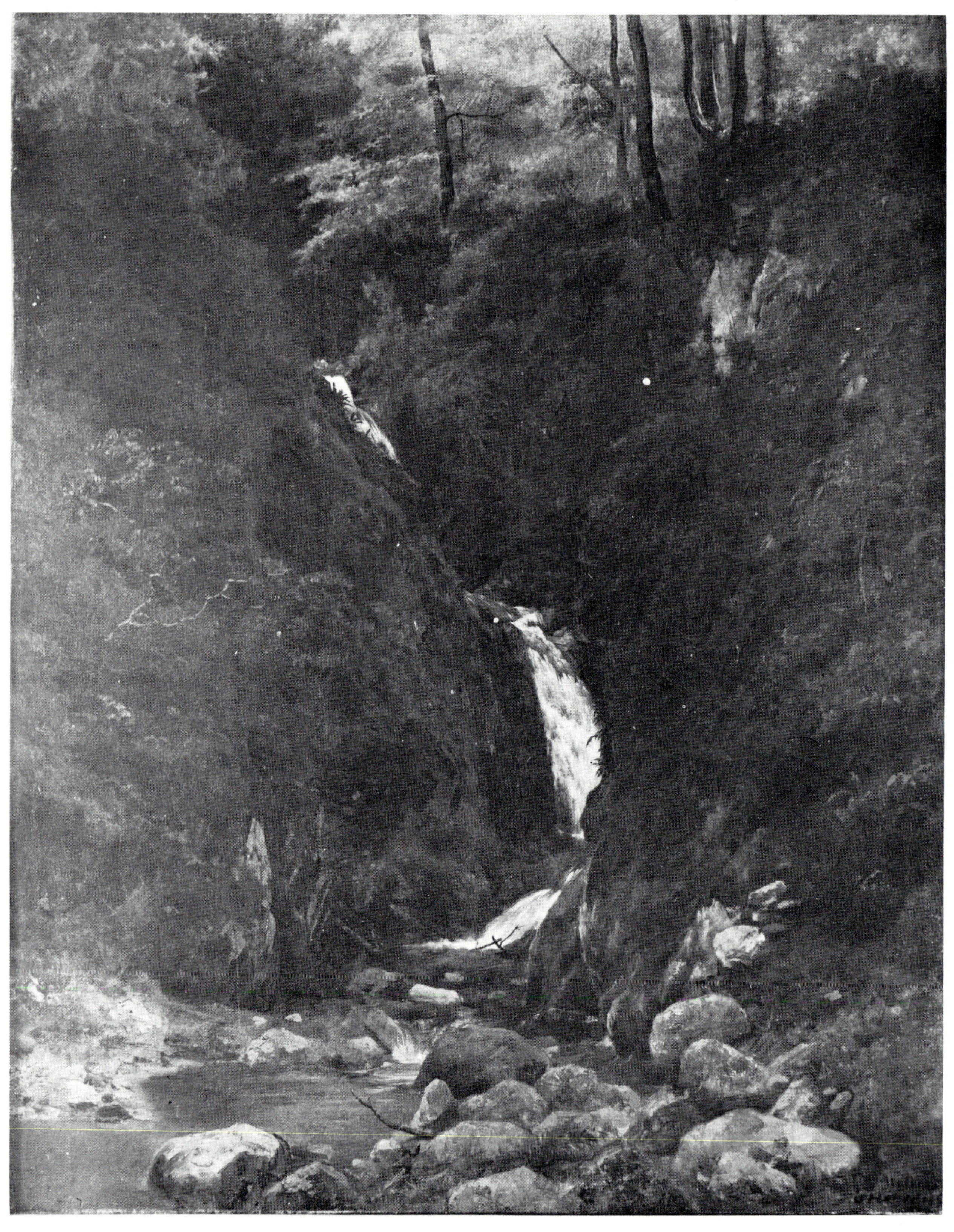

Louwrens Hanedoes (1822-1905) *modernises the landscape technique of his master B.C. Koekkoek in this view of a waterfall.* Photograph courtesy of Mak van Waay, Amsterdam.

Chapter VII

The Hague School - Introduction

If we look back upon the painters of whom I have written in the previous chapters, we behold a procession of teachers who displayed their talent to its fullest extent in their pupils. We find in Amsterdam J.W. Pieneman and J.A. Kruseman, who have the honour of having introduced Jozef Israëls to Dutch painting; B.J. van Hove, who gave us Bosboom, but also Weissenbruch – two painters who, despite the different forms of their art, and probably owing to the influence of their master, show so many traces of resemblance – and also his son Huib, who, in his turn, produced Jacob Maris, Bisschop and both David Bles and Bakker Korff; Schelfhout, who, in Jongkind and Weissenbruch, gave us the best that he had to give and, through his pupil Nuyen, prepared Rochussen for us; Samuel Verveer, who contributed to Jan Weissenbruch's artistic training; Louis Meijer, the pupil of J.W. Pieneman, who taught Matthijs Maris the rudiments of his art, and P.F. van Os, to whom Mauve and Roelofs owe much, while Roelofs, to a certain extent, formed Mesdag. We find H. van de Sande Bakhuijzen, who taught his son Julius and his daughter Gerardina, the flower-painter, and who was also the master of Weissenbruch and Ter Meulen; B.C. Koekkoek, who formed Hanedoes (b. 1822) and J.W. Bilders, the teacher of his own son Gerard (1838-1865); Gijsbertus Craeyvanger (b. 1810), the painter of town-views, who for a time had Albert Neuhuijs as his pupil, while Bisschop gave Blommers and Israëls art lessons which they turned to good account.

And in these names we see the whole glorious array of the masters of the Hague school. The Hague school! An approximate title invented by the Amsterdam painters of a younger generation. A name for which there would be no room in our little Holland, but for the fact that, in general, Amsterdam and the Hague differed so greatly in their methods of painting. A name that expresses the loftiest point reached by Dutch painting since the seventeenth century.

And yet, when Bosboom, in 1833 to 1834, painted his first town-view in his master's manner; when Israëls, in 1848, sent his first picture, a biblical subject, from Amsterdam to an exhibition at the Hague; when Rochussen, the oldest of them all, who did not begin to paint until 1836, exhibited his small pictures and Weissenbruch painted his Schelfhout-like landscapes; when, lastly, during all those years, Schelfhout and Koekkoek, the Pienemans and the Krusemans remained the great men and, of the work of all those who were afterwards to be known as the Hague masters, only that of Bosboom was distinguished by those same qualities for which he was to be admired all his life and long after; nay, even when a member of a younger generation, Jacob Maris, painted in oils or water-colour his now so highly valued genre-pieces and when, in 1863, Matthijs and Willem Maris raised a contest through their personal views at a Hague exhibition, a contest which Jacob was afterwards to wage in a more lasting fashion: even then there was no mention of a Hague school!

Matthijs Maris in his *Back Slum* and Willem in his *Landscape with Cattle* display a quality of colouring of which young Bilders, painting in the same style as Willem Maris, gave the formula, oddly enough, before it had actually come into existence. Their colours are worked up into a tonality out of which the light draws the forms to the foreground whereas, before their time, the sky was generally no more than a piece of scene-painting, against which each form was traced out separately and positively. In 1860 (Willem Maris was then sixteen), Bilders wrote to Mr. Knepplehout:

"I am looking for a tone which we call coloured grey, that is a combination of all colours, however strong, harmonized in such a way that they give the impression of a warm and fragrant grey."

And again:

"To preserve the sense of the grey even in the most powerful green is amazingly difficult and whoever

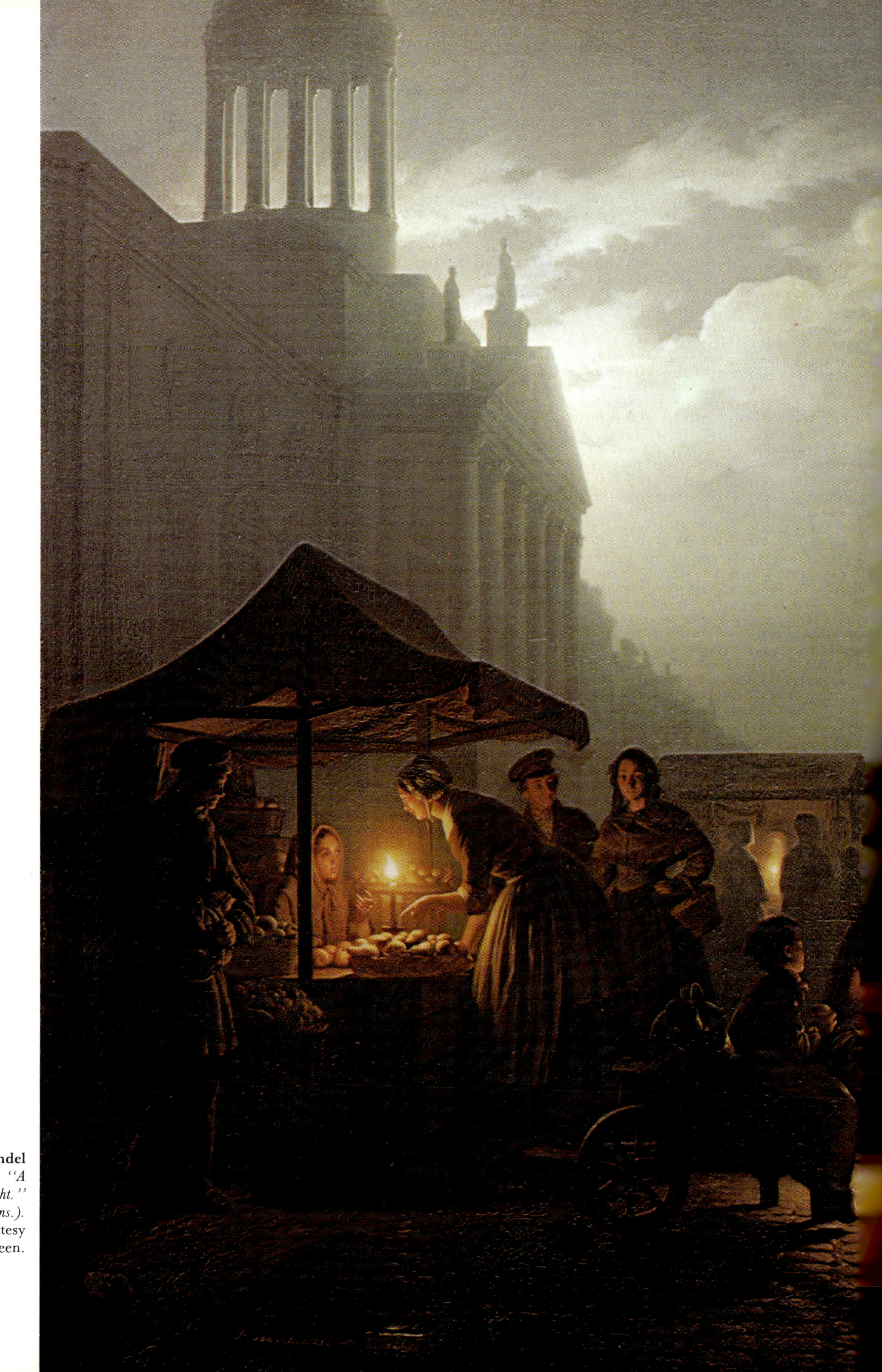

Petrus van Schendel (1806-1870). *"A street market at night."* *(35½ x 47½ ins.).* Photograph courtesy of Richard Green.

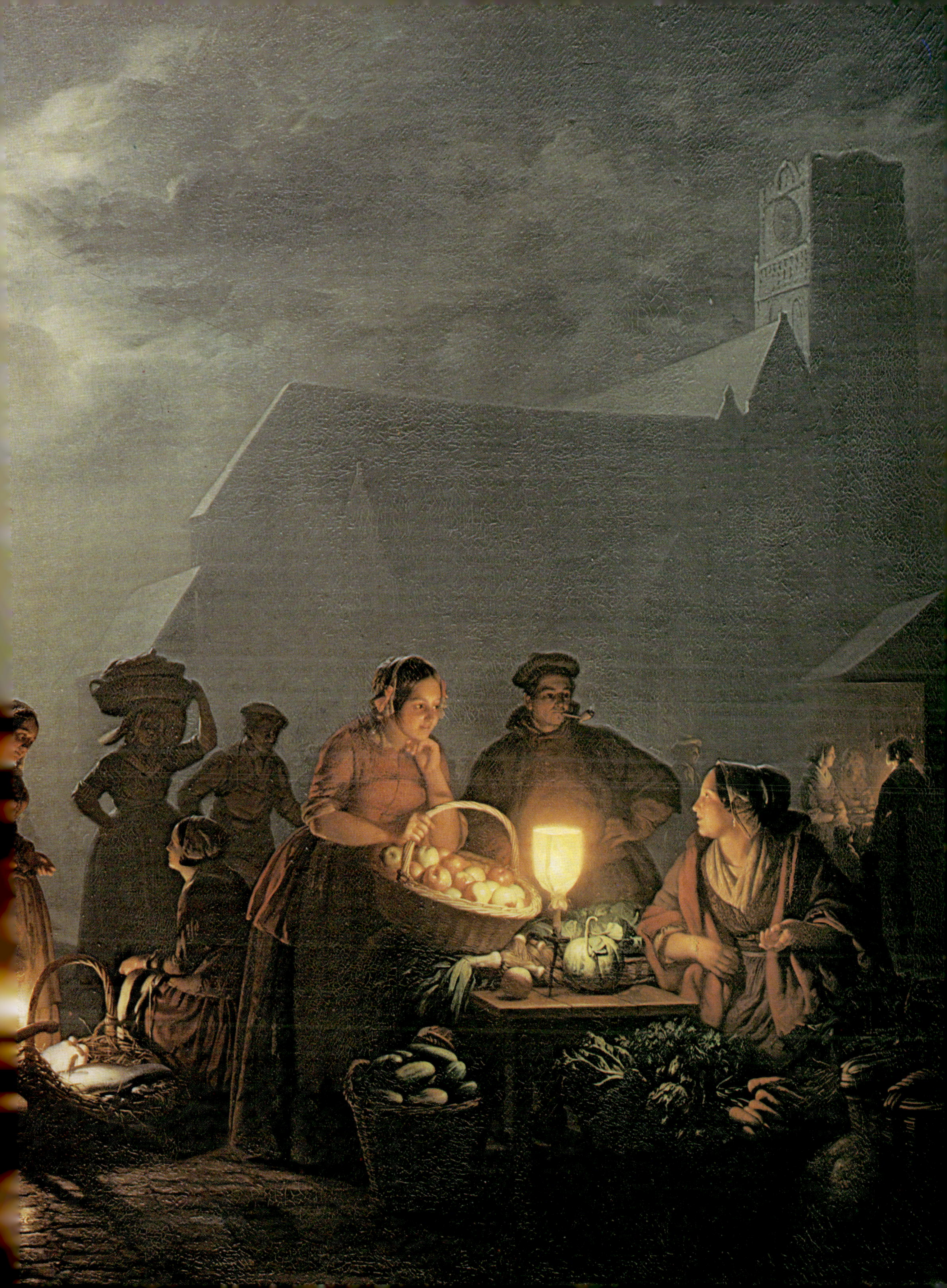

discovers it will be a happy mortal."

Later he wrote:

"It is not my aim and object to paint a cow for the cow's sake or a tree for the tree's, but by means of the whole to reproduce an impression which nature sometimes gives."

And, although he was not given time (he died at twenty-six) to attain in his work that symphonic result which a riper generation achieved, he did, in his little landscape in the Rijksmuseum, come near to finding the grey for which he was seeking and he showed that he did not paint the cow for the cow's sake. In the same year, 1860, in which he voiced his longing for a warm grey, he received the revelation of what painting can be, a revelation which the painters who came after him received in the same measure:

"I have seen pictures," he wrote, speaking of Brussels, "of which I had never dreamed and in which I found all that my heart desires, all that I nearly always miss in the Dutch painters. Troyon, Courbet, Diaz, Dupré, Robert Fleury have made a great impression on me. I am a good Frenchman, therefore; but, as Simon van den Berg says, it is just because I am a good Frenchman that I am a good Dutchman, since the great Frenchmen of today and the great Dutchmen of the past have much in common. Unity, restfulness, earnestness and, above all, an inexplicable intimacy with nature are what struck me most in these pictures. There were certainly also a few good Dutch pieces, but, generally speaking, when you place them next to the great Parisians, they lack that mellowness, that quality which, so to speak, resembles the deep tones of an organ. And yet this luxurious manner came originally from Holland, from our steaming, fat-coloured Holland! They were courageous pictures; there was a heart and a soul in them".

Probably this is the place once more to show how these so-called Barbizon painters, who were so entirely un-French in all their being, could be developed in France, in Paris; how an accumulation of foreign methods in England kindled the spark which ignited, in that country, a flourishing renascence of Italian and Dutch painting and, in so doing, transferred the art of absolute painting to modern times.

The English people are characterized in opposition to the foreigner mainly in their practical sense. This quality has, from an early date (and perhaps by way of reaction), prompted the English to cultivate all that is beautiful and has produced that series of poets of whom they are so justly proud, while their wealth has always enabled them to supply the lack of native art of painting by inviting to their country successive famous painters from abroad, of whom Holbein and Van Dijck are the chief. They have done more since the days of Charles II, they have never ceased buying pictures from the continent: Italian and especially Venetian masters; and, with an evident preference, Dutch masters. No country has collected with greater perspicacity than England; no people have so thoroughly realised the value of Dutch landscape, for which reason, perhaps, it has been said that, after the Japanese, no people are more devoted to what is nowadays called "nature" than the English.

This was bound to have an effect; and, eventually, from all these important painters and paintings arose the great English portrait-school of Reynolds and Gainsborough, based on Rembrandt and the Venetian masters and especially on Van Dijck. And, as the aristocratic life of the English was spent mainly at their country-seats and as these portrait-painters, with Gainsborough in particular, painted the portraits of the women of their time with unparalleled elegance against the backgrounds of their parks, the natural result was that, together with the portrait, the love of the landscape must lead to the painting of landscape for its own sake. And so it happened that, from the stately parks of his portraits, from the rustic village in which he was born, Gainsborough derived the first modern landscape based upon Rubens, but gently modulated, full of style and great. For, though he may afterwards have painted landscapes illuminated by his admiration for Cuyp, though he may occasionally remind us of Watteau and sometimes presage Corot, he was the first painter who, in the Netherlands manner, rendered the English landscape in the English style and thus became the harbinger of a renascence of the Dutch school of landscape-painting.

The question has also been asked by the English whether Van Dijck was not, in his turn, influenced by England, a question which, to judge by his English portraits, seems very possible, the more so as their particular qualities are those which we find most frequently repeated in the later English school. For, however much both Van Dijck, who was Gainsborough's exemplar, and Rubens inspired Gainsborough's landscapes, however Dutch Constable showed himself to be, to whatever degree these two reproduced their English landscape in the pure pictorial form of our seventeenth-century masters, there is no trace of plagiarism, no question of copying: their art,

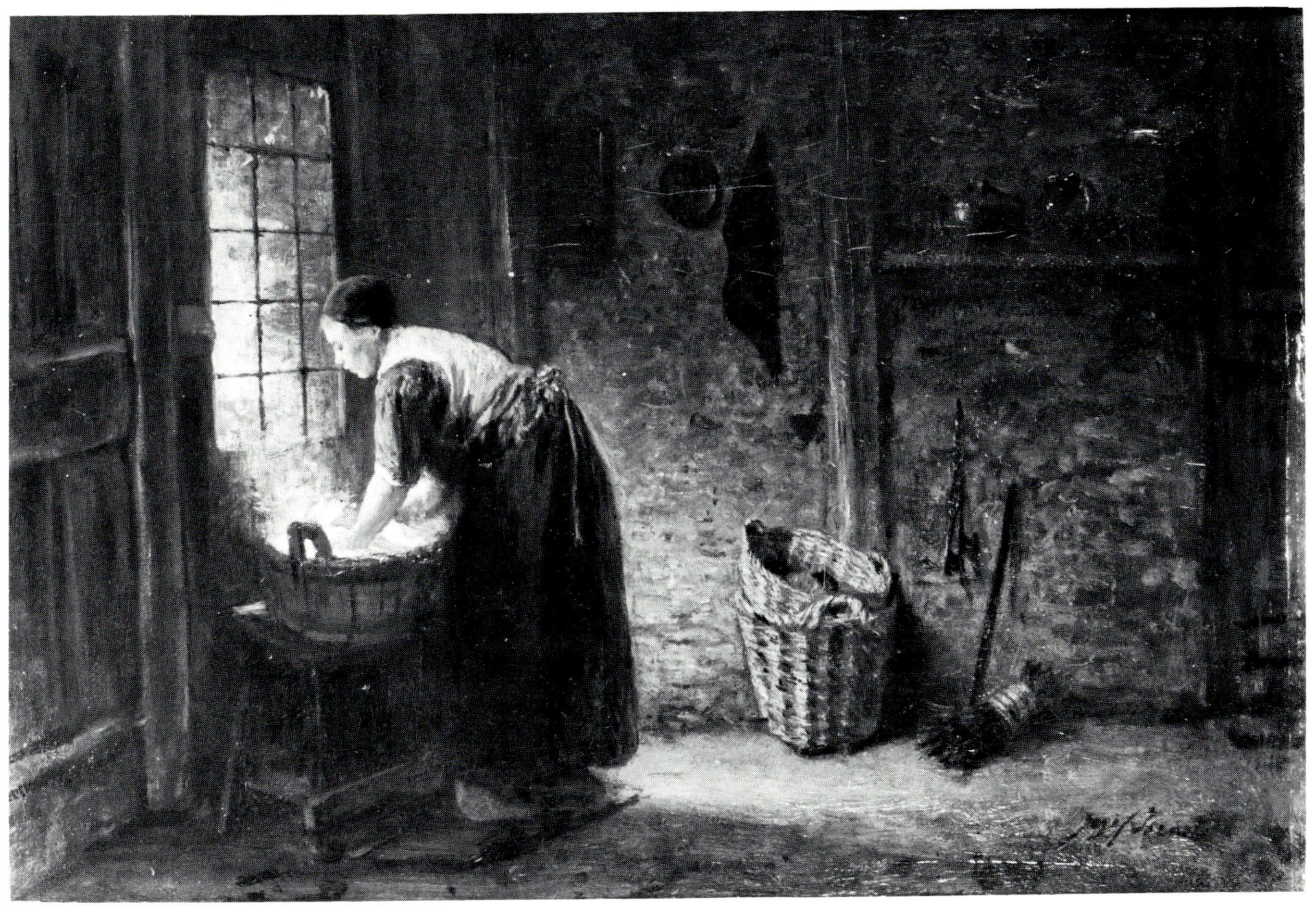

Jozef Israëls (1824-1911). *The peasant genre of Josef Israëls is only loosely linked to his Dutch forerunners. It is closer to Millet and the Barbizon School. This washday scene has lost the pretty romanticism of earlier times. (14¾ x 21½ins.)* Photograph courtesy of Sotheby & Co.

like that of Bonington, was purely English. And it was this art which was as a revelation to the French landscape painters, whose works, exhibited in Brussels and Paris, in their turn gave the Dutchmen an understanding of their own being and a clearer insight which, at first, perhaps, with a suggestion of borrowed riches, led them back at length into their own domain.

It is easy to overestimate an influence. For, although the art of painting, colour and the sense of a powerful movement can be taught and learned, it is not often that a foreign tradition leads to great display of strength. And the style built up from the classic Dutch landscapes has passed away in both England and France and survives in Holland alone of all the countries where it was introduced. Holland alone perpetuated it in its purity, stripped of all foreign adornments. And, although numbers of Germans, Swedes and Englishmen set out for the Forest of Fontainebleau to catch something of the spirit of the Barbizon masters and sat by the edge of the ponds at Ville-d'Avray, seeking for the genius of Corot, or came to Holland to study the old and new landscape-painters, the essence of the national art of the country remained as foreign to them as the land itself and the race.

The Hague masters did not at once achieve their complicated solutions of light, their breadth of view, their masterliness of touch.

The genesis of our art follows the same law at all times. Every painter, every school of painting passes through that which is symptomatic of the whole art of painting: stiffness and precision at first, breadth and width in the fuller expansion, more open in the measure as it commands more and occupies a freer position towards the technical power of representation. Is not the progress of Rembrandt, from the naive and compact little portraits of his early years to the *Syndics of the Cloth-hall* and after, on a line with the development of Bosboom, Israëls and the Maris

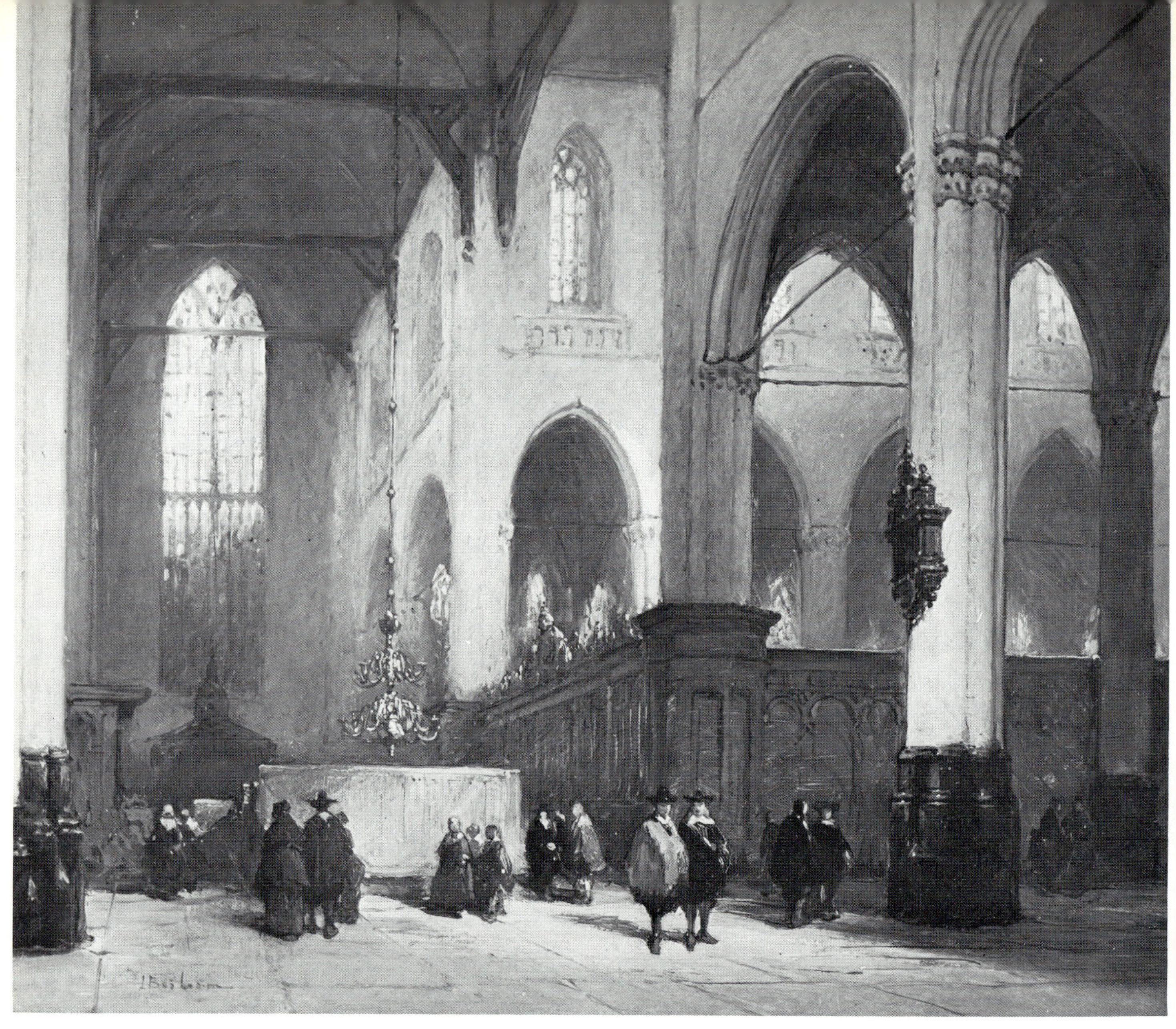

Above and right: **Johannes Bosboom (1817-1891)** *was the master of the church interior; occasionally his paintings stray inside a synagogue. The dominant influence on his work was that of Rembrandt. Working both in watercolour and oils he succeeded in transferring the face impressionism of the former into his oil paintings, as both these examples show. (10¼ x 12¼ins. and 44 x 35½cms.).* Photographs courtesy of M. Newman Ltd. and Mak van Waay, Amsterdam.

brothers? An immensity of talent and work were needed to bring our school of painting out of its latent power to the rich aftermath which it produced.

In the first half of the nineteenth century, almost all our cities – Amsterdam, the Hague, Rotterdam, Utrecht, Leeuwarden, Dordrecht, Delft – had their own painters. In 1870, the Hague, like Paris, became a centre to which all the painters flocked. Nor was this due to accident. The Hague, thirty years ago, was surrounded on every side by nature in all her fulness: to the south and east lay the endless, luxuriant meadows, with the distant horizon, absorbing every colour, unchanged since Potter's days: to the north and west, the delicious low-lying dunes and rich dune-valleys, with the great North Sea, which communicates its pale-grey atmosphere to the greater part of the Hague, and the long Scheveningen beach, with its active fishing life, all under that same silvery sky. Here, surely, if anywhere, the grey of which Gerard Bilders had dreamt was to find its realization.

To a certain extent, the Hague of 1870 to 1890 may be best compared with fifteenth-century Bruges. Even as the skilled painters of all the northern countries gathered at Bruges, so, in 1870 to 1871, did the

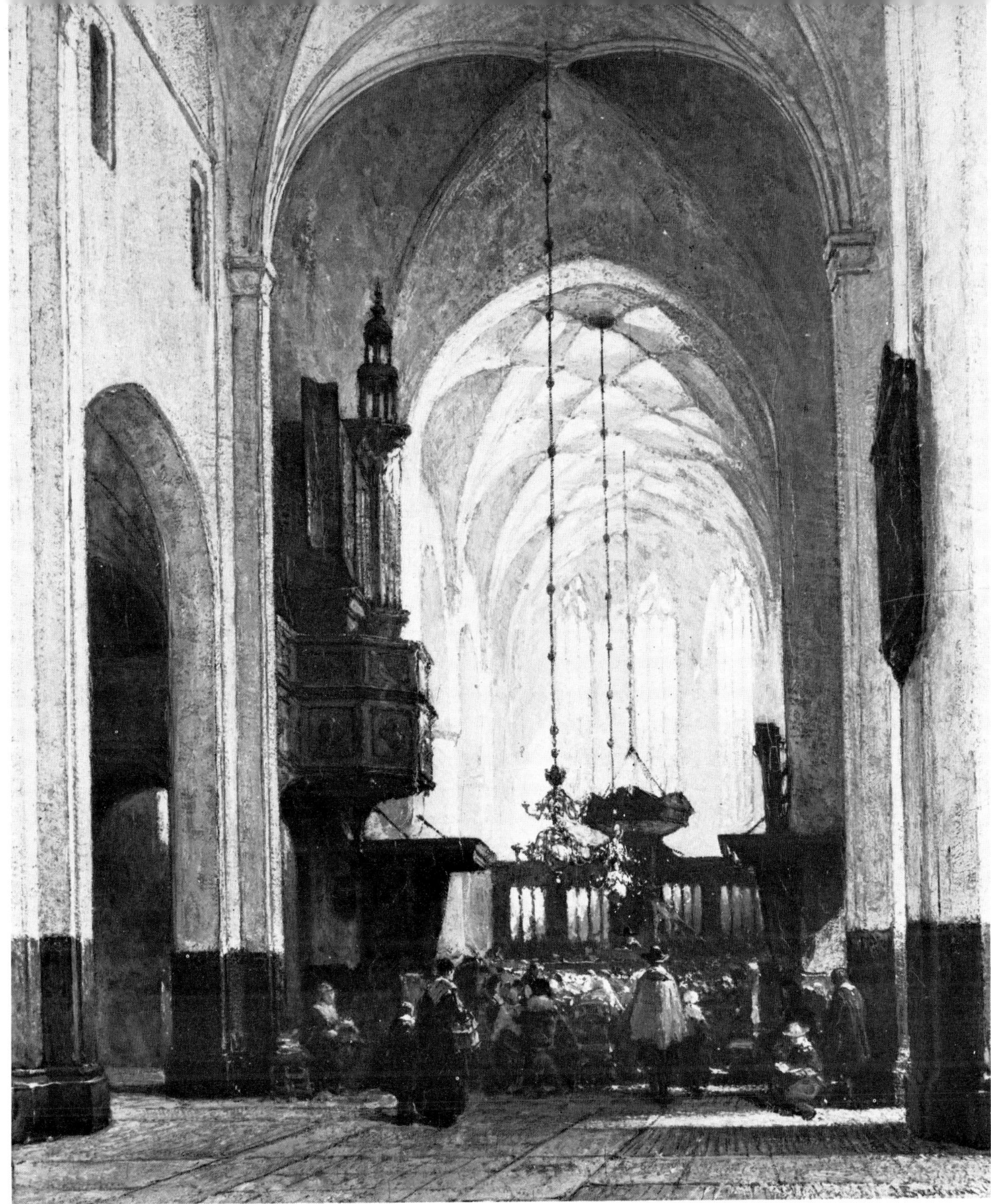

skilled painters of these later days come to settle at the Hague, attracted by the sea and the landscape, by the painters already residing there and, as at Bruges, by more material advantages, which consisted not, as at Bruges, in the presence of wealthy merchants, but in the recent establishment of the Maison Goupil, which in Paris, under Vincent van Gogh, had so strenuously supported the younger Dutch painters.

Israëls came to the Hague in 1869, from Amsterdam, as "a made man," although his greatest and most philosophical works were yet to come; Mesdag came in the same year, after achieving his first successes in Brussels; Mauve arrived in 1870, Weissenbruch was a native of the Hague; Bisschop, the Frisian, was living there as a young painter; Jacob Maris returned to the Hague in 1871, after the Paris Commune, and Artz a few years later. Albert and Jozef Neuhuys moved to the Hague from Utrecht in 1875; Gabriël from Brussels in 1884; Roelofs a little later; Breitner about 1880; and Tholen, Toorop and others joined the rest in 1886. When the first of these painters came to the Hague in 1869 or 1870, they found Bles there, as well

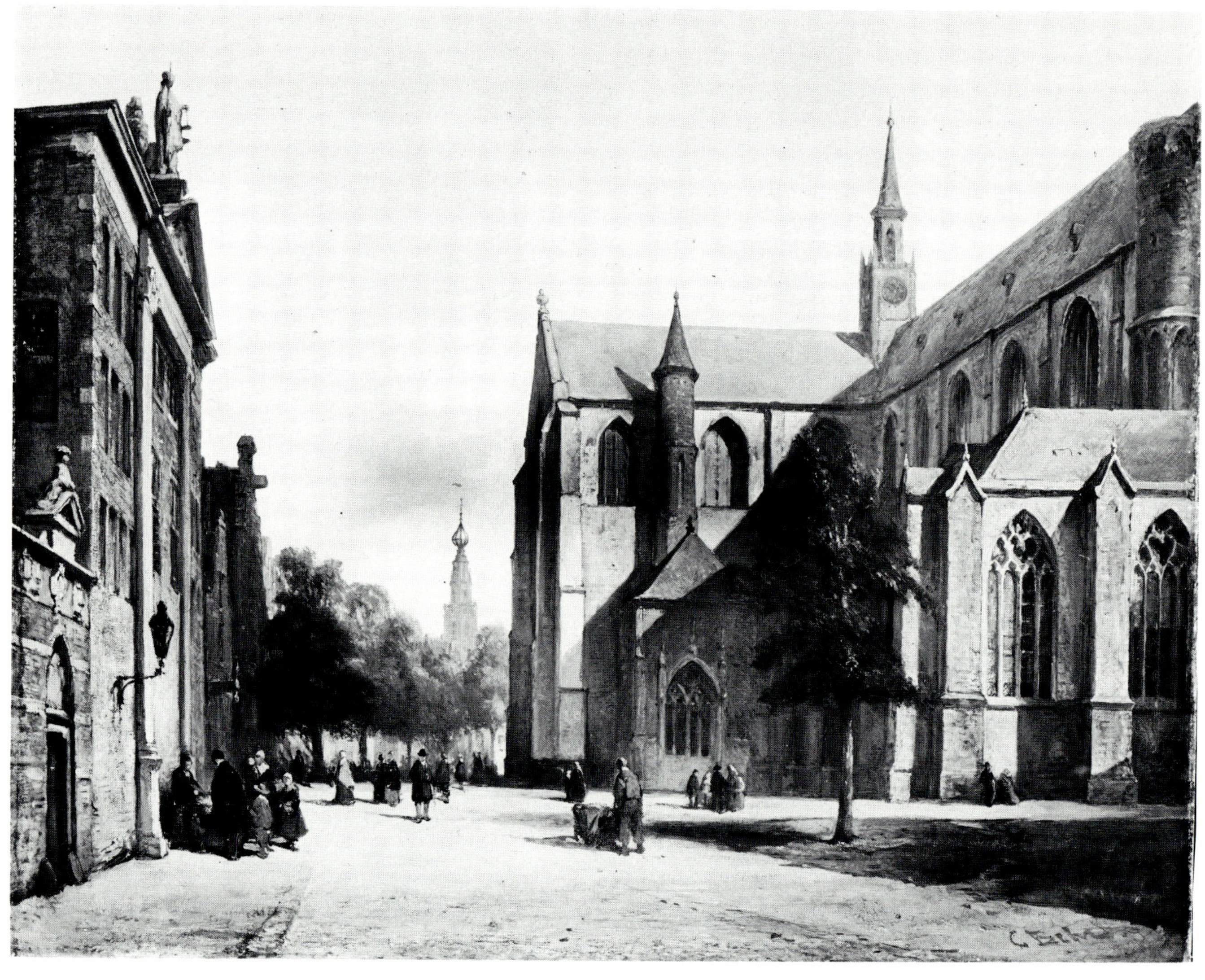

This Dutch townscape is the combined work of **Johannes Bosboom (1817-1891)** *and* **Carel Jacobus Behr (1812-1895)** *– the figures being Bosboom's contribution. Both artists were pupils of B.J. van Hove and it seems likely that this painting dates from their student years. The composition, dominated by the appealing architectural complex of the old church, is very much in their master's manner* *(see page 81).* *(68 x 86cms.).* Photograph courtesy of Mak van Waay, Amsterdam.

as Samuel and Elchanon Verveer and such painters as Tom, Destrée, the Van Deventers, Van Everdingen, Nakken, Stroebel and Hanedoes and also Bosboom, in the full vigour of his powers, and Willem Maris, who had pursued his own road as calmly as Bosboom himself.

The nucleus of the Hague school consists of Bosboom, Israëls, Matthijs and Willem Maris and Mauve. It is true that Matthijs Maris' Dutch period proper occurs before 1870 and that, in this case, the painter would be outside the circle of the school; but I have purposely, for practical reasons, drawn this circle pretty wide and, moreover, the more we come to know this painter's early work, the more we realize his great significance for his contemporaries, from 1860 to 1868, and the great influence which he exercised upon those who were to follow him in this school.

Bosboom was the master continuously from 1833, the year in which he first exhibited, to 1891, the year of his death. He may have been influenced by the Romanticists and, in particular, by Nuyen; later,

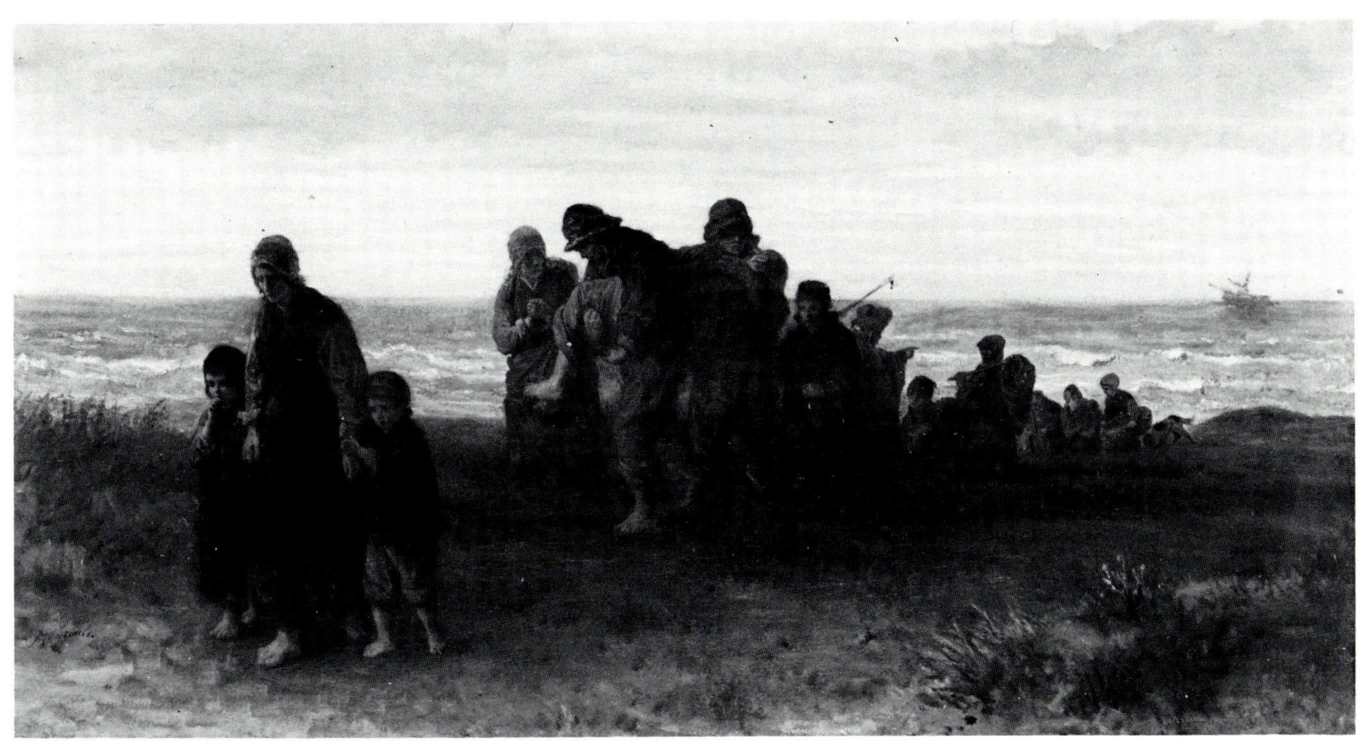

It was at Zandvoort in the 1840's that **Josef Israëls (1824-1911)** *discovered his true metier in painting the simple lives of the local fisherfolk. Here the local people are bringing the victims of a shipwreck in from the sea (17¾ x 34ins.). It is hard to believe that he was trained by Kruseman and the history painters – and was still working in that vein in 1856.* Photograph courtesy of Sotheby & Co.

he may have striven after heavier effects in his admiration for Rembrandt; after 1870, he may have allowed himself to be seduced by the modern breath of a budding impressionism (and this was incontestably the case): all this does not detract from the fact that, from the start, he remained himself, and was recognized for his gifts of heart and hand.

And the artist who influenced him more than any other was Rembrandt. The influence is seen in the motives of his *Synagogue at Amsterdam* and his *Treves Cathedral,* heavy and monumental in the second, glowing with rich effects of colour and light in the first. These are the pictures which brought him into general consideration about 1870, for the sake of the grandeur of their conception and their poetic mood, although a later generation prefers the simpler and more open drawings illumined by a less direct Rembrandt light, because they perhaps come even nearer to the essence of the master whom he held so high.

These drawings date to 1863, a year of adversity for Bosboom, of an adversity rich in consequences. In this year – incredible though it may seem, when we contemplate the well-balanced work of this classic painter – he was smitten, not for the first time, with an attack of melancholy and with so great a feeling of impotence that he wished that he might never have to paint again. He recovered his equilibrium at the country-seat of Jonkheer van Rappard, with whom he and his wife, the well-known novelist, went to stay. Van Rappard acted as his Mæcenas and bought all the drawings which he produced, while urging him not to confine himself to church-interiors. The hospitality and liberty which Bosboom enjoyed enabled him to wander peacefully between Utrecht and Loosdrecht, where he was struck by the massive build both of isolated trees and of the great farm-houses whose intimacy, whose ample construction he so well succeeded in reproducing. In later years, the number of his water-colours began to exceed that of his oil-paintings considerably. And, after 1891, the year of his death, portfolios came to light crammed with drawings, sketches and scrawls, by the hundred, which suggested great art even where the paper was barely touched, as in the sketch of the great church at

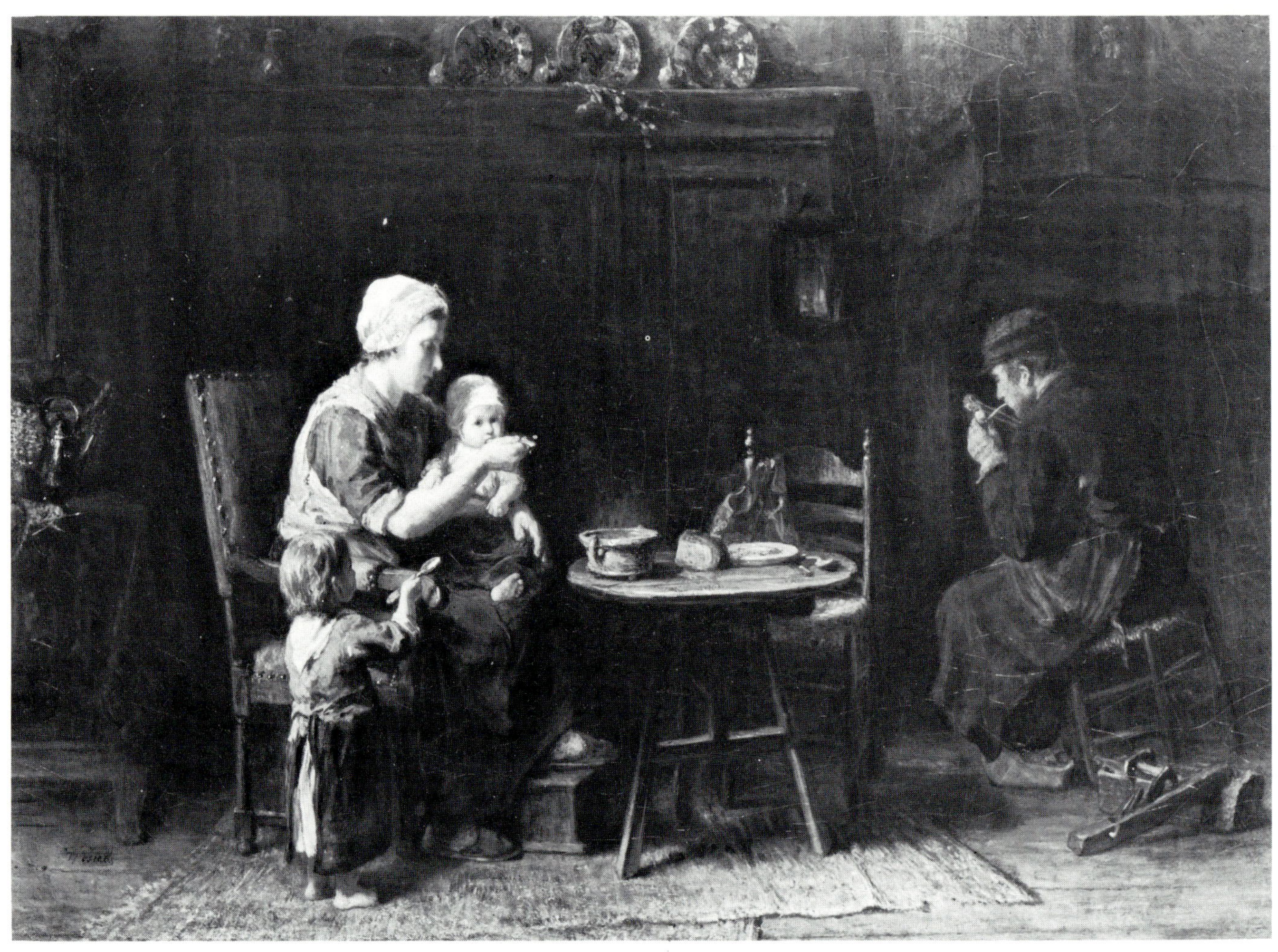

Above and right: **Israëls** *lovingly entered into the domestic life of his fisherfolk. The depiction of simple family life as in these two paintings was a powerful influence on the genre painting of his successors. (36¼ x 51ins. and 38 x 53ins.). The second painting "Pancake Day" was previously in the collection of Sir Kenneth Clark.* Photographs courtesy of Sotheby & Co. and M. Newman Ltd.

Alkmaar, in the cloister-stairs, in lightly-washed chalk-drawings, and made the same revelation to the more modern that his more solid work had made to an earlier generation.

And Bosboom's water-colours! Compared with the analytical water-colour art of Allebé, how great is his power to solve the most intricate difficulties by the simplest means, in his stately church-interiors, in his cloistered corridors, in his sacristies, as in his suites of apartments or his drawings of the Hofje van Neiuwkoop, the old home of Pulchri Studio. It is inconceivably simple; and, even if one stood behind him, following those little drawings, the simple movements of his hand, the brush flowing, dragging or serving as a drawing-pen, the fixing of a few details in those fluent, colourless spaces until everything is there, light and shade, the full, absorbed tone, the bright lights and, above all, a great, simple truthfulness: even then it appears to us a mysterious movement of the fingers, under which – O wonder! – that pure plastic art comes into being and gives its value to Bosboom's slightest sketch.

This great artist, who used to declare that he had known no other master than Rembrandt, adopted all that we most admire in Rembrandt's etchings: the stately design, the noble line, springing straight from the heart, the generous riot of his lines, the spacious gestures which have been handed down to us in his least scrawls, in his most ingenuous drawings or sketches in oils. But Bosboom did not inherit all his

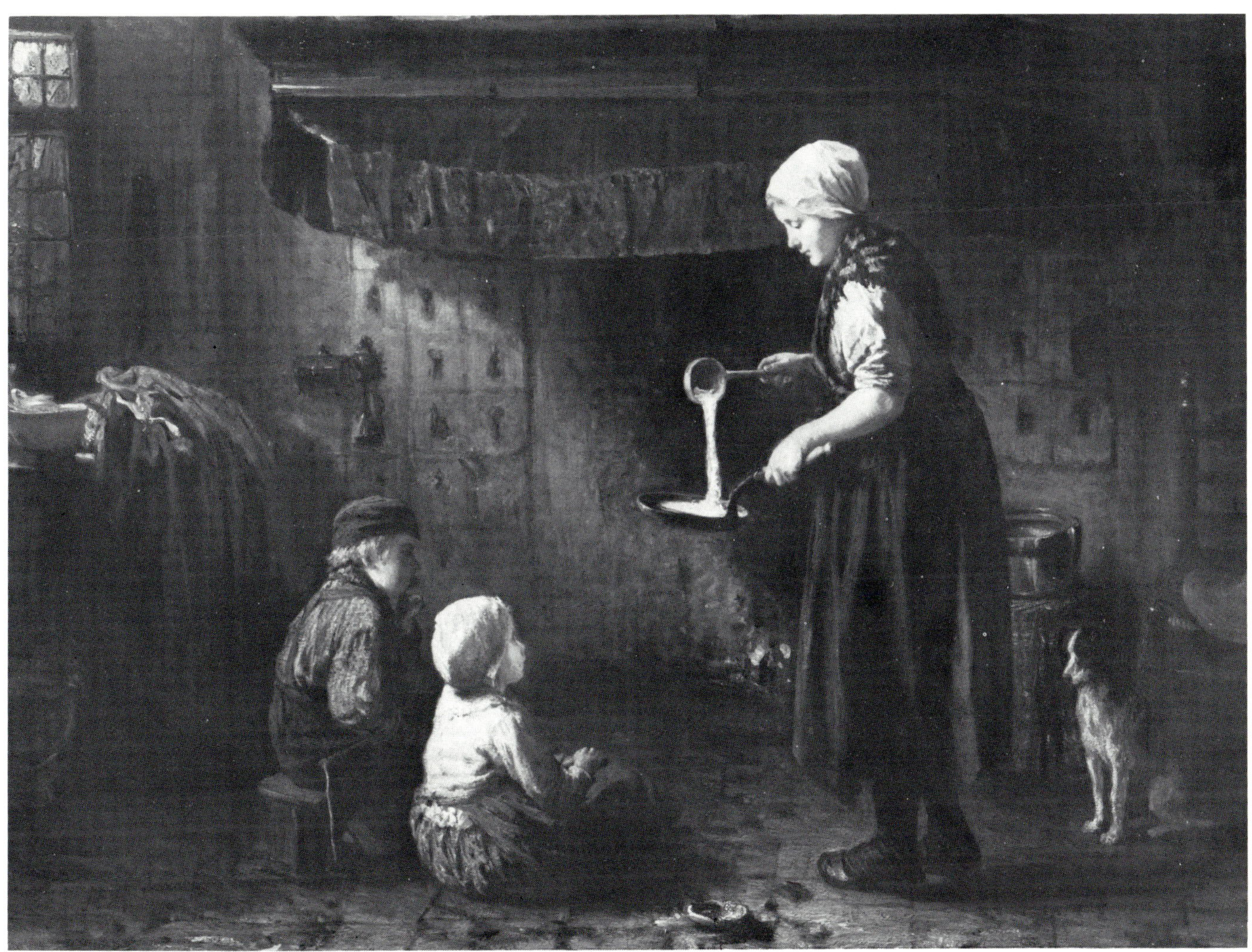

master's attributes. Rembrandt saw mankind: he was the seer who beheld the divine revealed in humanity; he saw men in their helplessness, their imperfection, in their awkward movements; he saw them poor, hideous or honourable; out of his rich life he saw them as they are: beautiful, because of that life; beautiful, because they live their piteous lives simply and manfully; great, because they are men and, therefore, of divine origin. He saw them with the eyes of the Bible: the halt and the lame, the blind, the Samaritans; he also saw the Pharisees. And it was this side of him that Bosboom was unable to touch, the side which none in these days was able to approach save Israëls alone.

Jozef Israëls sprang from a very different environment. Bosboom succeeded Van Hove, Schelfhout, Waldorp, Nuyen, the natural precursors of the Hague school, and saw his road lie straight and smooth before him. Israëls had not only to rid himself of the conventional conceptions of his masters, Pieneman and Kruseman, but also to shake himself free from Picot and Delaroche and his early admiration of Ary Scheffer.

Richard Muther fixes "the decisive year which led the stream of Dutch painting back into its old course" at 1857, "the very year when a new movement in Dutch literature was begun with Multatuli." Max Liebermann, in many respects a pupil of Israëls and, in any case, his brother in art, says:

"Israëls first realized himself at an age at which most painters have already produced their best work; and, had he had the misfortune to die at forty, Holland would have been unable to boast of one of her greatest sons."

He, therefore, fixes the date of the present Israëls at 1864. Jan Veth gives 1860 as the commencement of the Hague school; and, although there is truth in all

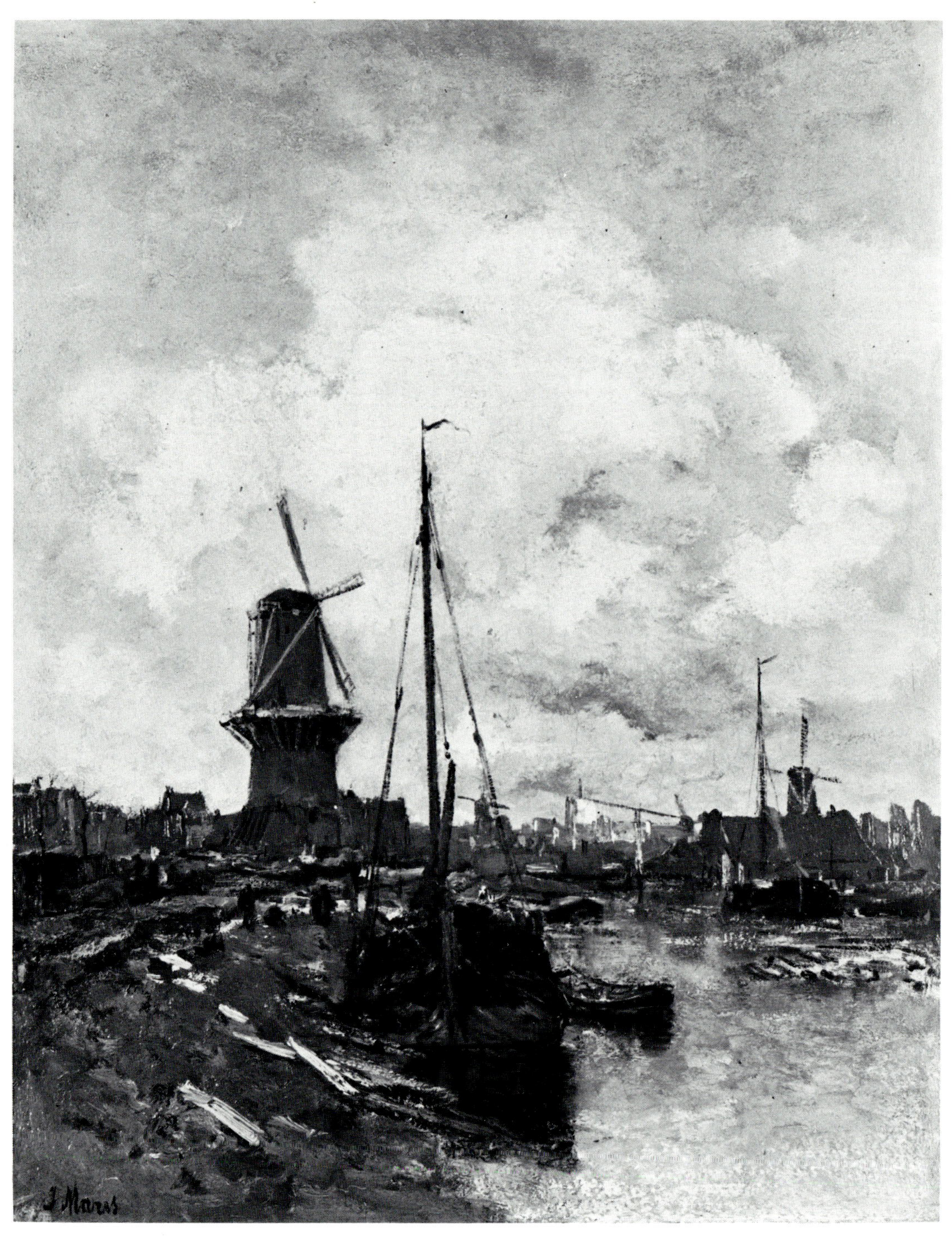

The windmills and the boats are familiar from earlier Dutch paintings, but this harbour scene by **Jacob Maris** (1837-1899) *opens a new era in Dutch marine and townscape painting. (19½ x 23ins.)* Photograph courtesy of Williams & Son.

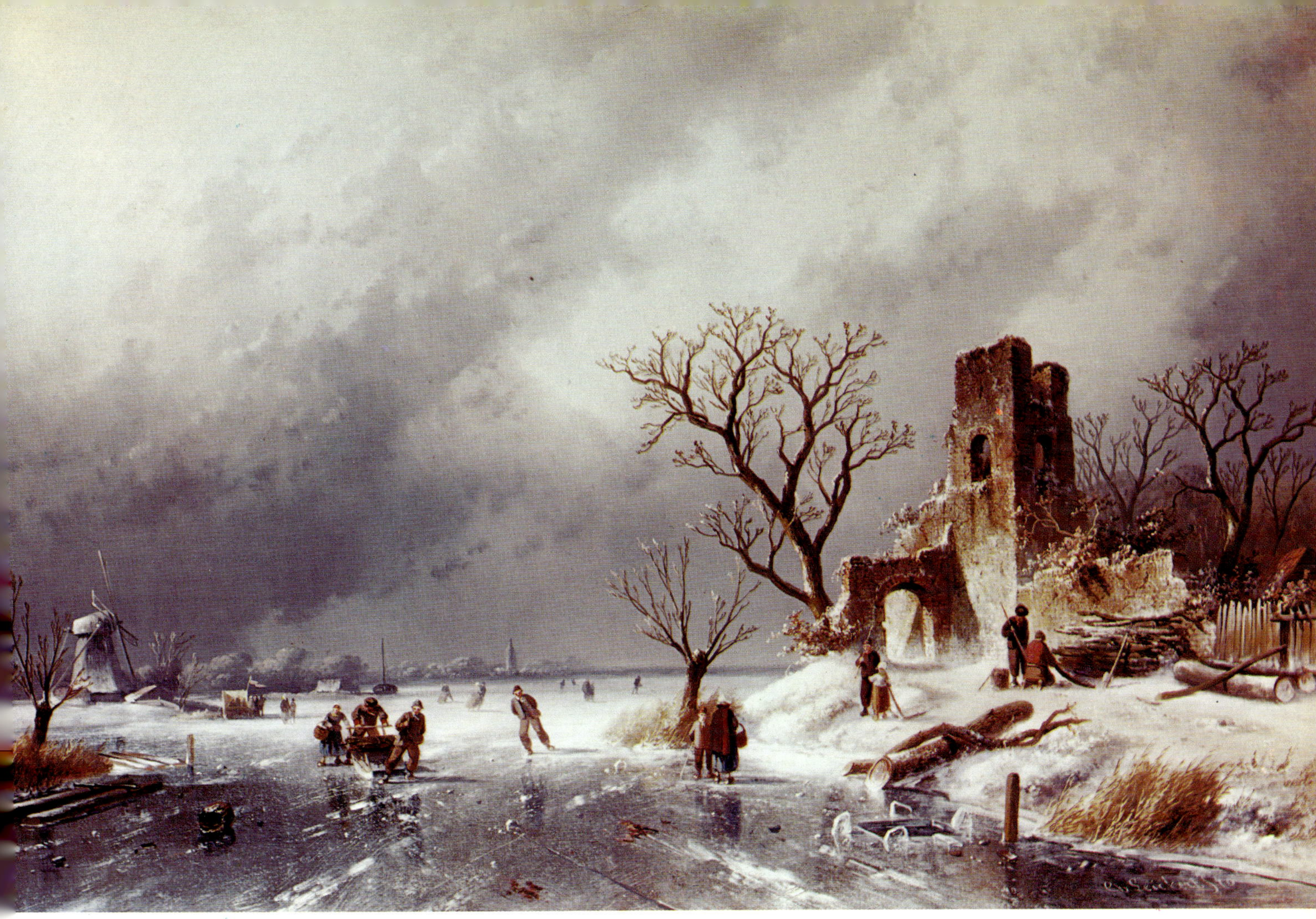

Charles Henri Joseph Leickert (1816-1907). *"Figures skating on a frozen river with ruins and town in the distance." Signed and dated 1870.* Photograph courtesy of Richard Green.

these views, I prefer to place the date at about 1870, the period when Israëls settled at the Hague, when Jacob Maris came home from Paris, when Mesdag and Mauve moved to the Hague and when Artz also came here for a time from Paris, to settle down definitely a couple of years later. For, if fate had decreed that such painters as Israëls, Jacob and Matthijs Maris, Willem Maris, Mauve, Mesdag and Weissenbruch should have ceased production about 1870 (as in the case of Allebé, Matthijs Maris's contemporary), there is no doubt that, in spite of the precious pieces which they bequeathed to us between 1860 and 1870, there would have been no question of a modern, of a Hague school of painting. They had, it is true, produced master-pieces which, to a certain extent, remained unsurpassed by their later and more matured works; but these mark the zenith of the art of 1830 to 1840 rather than an inspired and inspiring new birth. Only in Bosboom's sketches should we have perceived an unknown spirit, the announcement of an unfulfilled promise, while from the little pictures of the Thijs Maris of that time we should have seen that the seventeenth-century powers of Rembrandt and De Hooche were not entirely lost.

We can trace the general development by following Israëls' studies. Born at Groningen in 1824, he was brought up in the traditions of the old faith and was destined for the rabbinate. He seems to have been a promising lad, who was handy with his pencil, read the Talmud diligently, played the violin and wrote little poems. When he grew up, his father, who had a small business as a stock and share-dealer, required his services; and Israëls loves to tell how, as a boy, he used to go with his bag of notes and securities to the office of old Mr. Mesdag, where H.W. Mesdag was afterwards himself to sit on a high stool. About 1840, upon the persuasion of a Groningen Mæcenas, Mr. de Witte the lawyer, Israëls' father consented that he should go to Amsterdam to study under Kruseman and, for seven years, he worked in Kruseman's studio and followed Pieneman's classes at the Academy. But it was not to be expected that this lively, emotional, Jewish nature, brought up on the flowery, colourful narratives of the Old Testament, should rest content with the systematic methods, based as it were upon formal recipes, of his two painting-masters. He received his first great impression in 1855 from Ary Scheffer's *Gretchen at the Spinning-wheel,* then exhibiting in Amsterdam. He here found something different from the "calculated preciseness" that had been dinned into him and sentiment and poetry attracted him more than mere craftsman's skill. In the following year, he went to Paris and worked in the studio of Picot, a painter of the school of David. He returned in 1848, the year of the revolution; and it was clear that he had seen nothing in Paris of what was already brewing in the world of art, for, in that year, he exhibited in Amsterdam, where he had a studio in the Warmoes Straat, his *Aaron discovering the Corpses of his two Sons,* a biblical subject, in the style of his master, which met with as little success as his portrait of Madame Tagny, a Parisian actress at that time performing in Amsterdam. He continued, in spite of his inward leanings, to cling to tradition. Once, when he had painted the head of an old and ugly woman, Jan Kruseman told him that it was not right to paint ugly people, because this spoilt one's taste; and, although he proved later that out of old, crumpled faces he was able to create a beauty that was imperishable, he still hesitated between his master's and his own inclination to the extent of producing his *Reverie* in 1851, a violinist, *Adagio con espressione* (afterwards lithographed by Allebé), in 1852 and, in 1855, *The Prince of Orange for the first time opposing the orders of the King of Spain,* which was hung in the Paris Exhibition. Lastly, after he had found his province at Sandvoort and, in 1856, had painted that dramatic episode, taken from the fisherman's life, *By Mother's Grave,* he exhibited at the Hague a *Hannah vowing Samuel to the service of the altar.*

But the impression made upon him by the existence of the fisher-folk at Zandvoort was a lasting one. Israëls had gone to Zandvoort for his health and stayed in the house of a small shipwright, whose domestic life he shared; and here, far from studios, painters and the precepts of his masters, he began to observe for himself the daily routine of the fishermen's lives: their quiet movements, their natural, simple existence, with its sorrows and terrors and also its little joys, all unspoiled by social forms. In this environment, his eyes were opened to the beauty of real life, to the poetry of truth; and he came to see that there was a drama in life well worth depicting and yet far removed from the biblical, the historical and the heroic.

In 1856, he took a studio in Amsterdam, on the Rozengracht, in the house of a Mr. Helwig, whose portrait, now in the Rijksmuseum, shows how far Israëls' art had already advanced. In 1863, he married and settled on the Prinsengracht; but it was not until

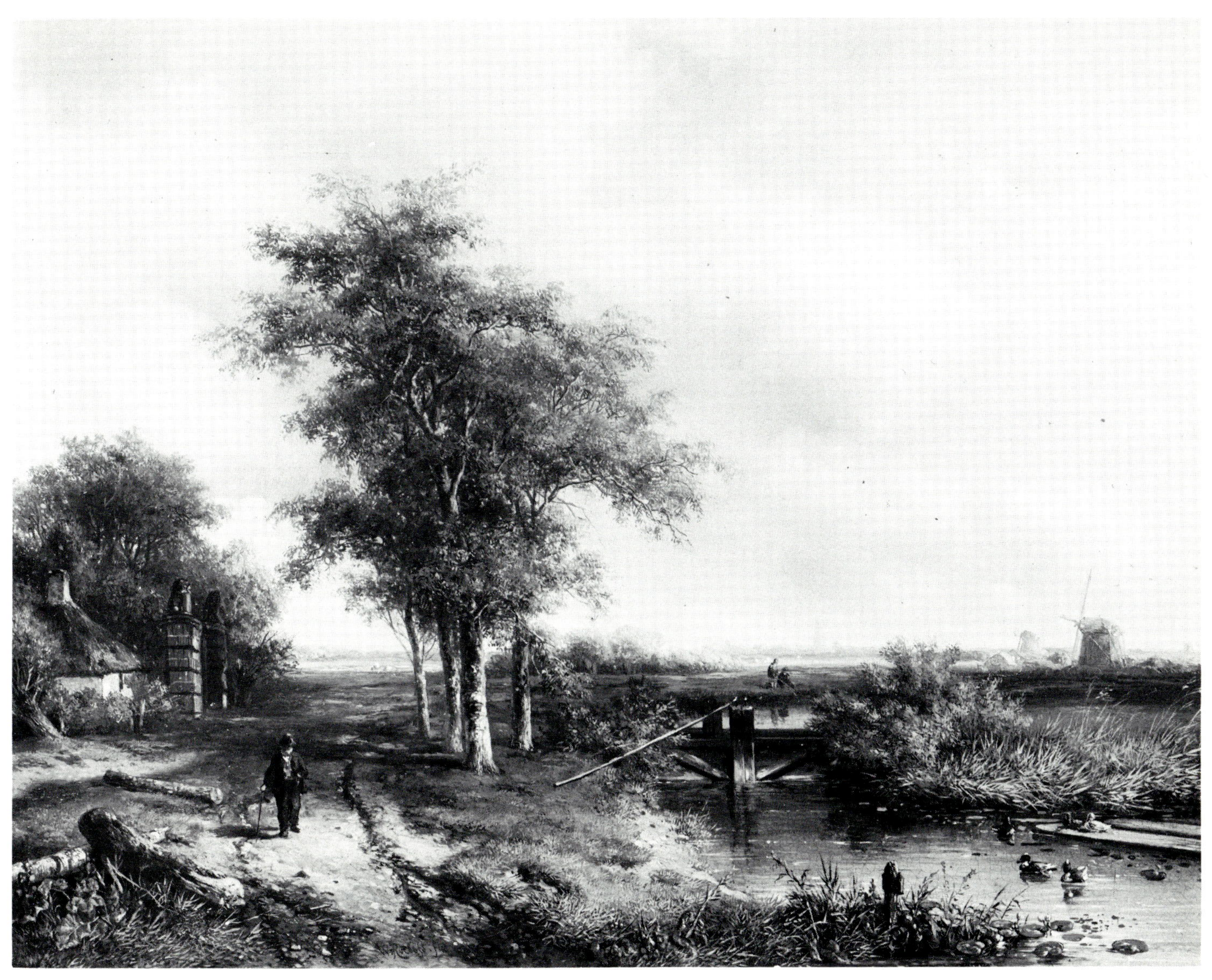

Willem Roelofs (1822-1897) *was a pupil of Van de Sande Bakhuijzen. This landscape painted in 1848 when he was only 26 shows him working in the popular Romantic vein of the time – with a quick sparkle to his brushwork which presages his simplified later work under the influence of the Barbizon School. (17 x 22ins.).* Photograph courtesy of Richard Green.

1869, the year in which he moved to the Hague, that he began to earn the title of head of the modern Dutch School which he has ever since retained. In this year, he began to paint that memorable series of interiors which, commencing as dramatic and romantic episodes, gradually expanded into more philosophical conceptions, wherein sometimes the family was exalted to the level of the patriarchal sense of the word. He not only painted his figures with extraordinary truth to nature, sitting at the frugal board, with all the dignity that characterizes the simple of heart, eating their dinners from the common dish, or folding their hands at grace before meat, or, in the case of the housewife, baking her cakes, or cooking food for the cattle, or sewing, or tending her child (this last was an inexhaustible source of subjects for the painter), but he knew how to make the surroundings, the atmosphere of those steaming fishermen's homes so tangible that the figures moved in it, breathed and lived their own unvarnished lives, at first amid a mass of symbolic details, afterward with the latter merely suggested to the spectator, while the

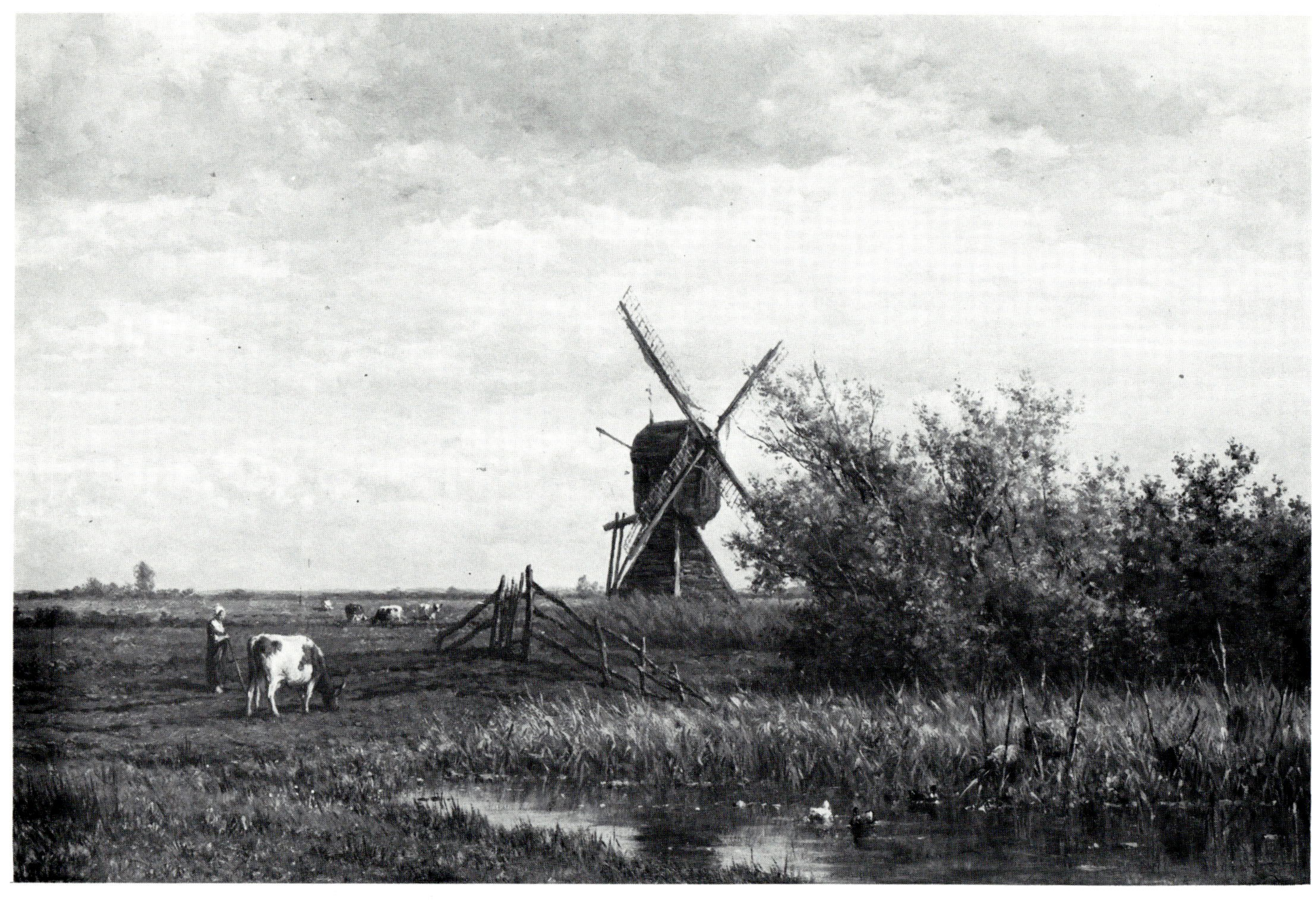

Above and right: **Roelofs (1822-1897)** *was the first major Dutch artist to fall under the spell of the French Barbizon School. Here he has re-imparted their simple realistic approach and applied it to the landscape of his own Holland. (28 x 17½ins. and 22 x 36cms.)* Photographs courtesy of Williams & Son and Mak van Waay.

whole of these small happenings was transferred to the wide domain of humanity.

How expressive are Israëls' hands! Van Dijck is said to have had a model with beautiful hands, whom he used for all his portraits of men. Here, the hands are the bearers of a sentiment, they serve to express the incident, they fill an important place in the painter's psychological powers of expression; they tell so soberly what they have to tell: they tell of the coldness of the hands which the shivering woman puts out to catch the last gleams of warmth of the dying peat-fire; they tell of impotent resignation when they lie squat and square on the knees of the figure in *Nothing more;* they tell of the spiritual weariness of *A Son of the Old People* as they hang limply between his knees; and they tell of ecstasy in the passion with which a harpist strives to draw tones from his classic instrument.

Israëls is, above all things, a psychologist, to whom no picture is complete without thought. He endeavours always to achieve the highest form of expression and never aims at rousing admiration by *la belle peinture.* But we must not imagine that, for this reason, he is any the less important as a painter. For it is not until we are penetrated with the fact that Israëls gropes rather than paints with his colours and brushes, that his pictures are born of hesitations and approximations rather than of regular painting: it is not until then that we come to be impressed by the mighty colour-schemes with which he has made tangible the atmosphere of a room, by solutions of light so subtle that everything concerts to draw the figure forward and to

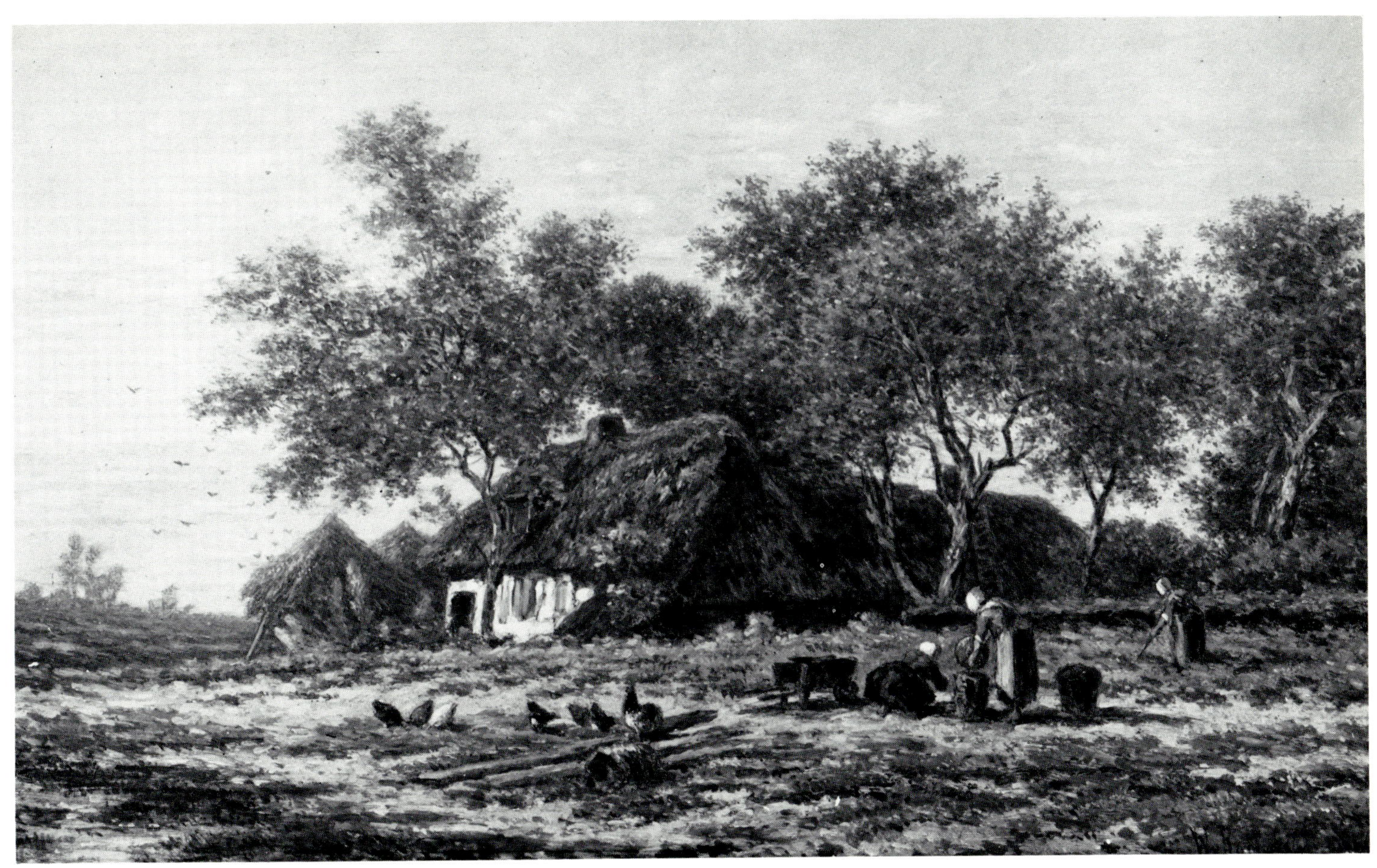

support it with light, colour and tone, so that the figure is firmly fixed in its environment, which nevertheless hangs quite freely around it; and we then see that Israëls is a painter who has a perfect command of the instrument which he himself has created, but seeks not so much to draw sweet tones from it as to turn it into the representation and symbol of life itself.

Nor, again, is anything less true than to say, as has lately been so often and so variously said, that Israëls painted his fisher subjects with an idea of raising the "fourth estate": this classification of estates is not mine. No proof is needed to show how great is the misconception. Israëls is far too much of a painter to be preoccupied with any such *Tendenz* intention. What attracted Israëls in the lives of the fishermen was the natural manner in which these unpolished people displayed their little joys, their sufferings, their fears, against the majestic background of the sea, the source of their livelihood and their affliction. A painter, he beheld in them picturesque figures in harmonious surroundings filled with atmosphere and with that incalculable light which is but seldom to be found in a solid, square interior fashioned of bricks and wood; he saw the children playing freely in the pools left behind by the retreating tide; he saw the mothers lulling their children to sleep; he saw death striking at the household; he saw the fishermen in touch with the sea. And his art is great even outside these subjects; and, without speaking of his portraits, which come so near to life, we admire the same breadth of view, the same expressiveness, the same poetry, whether he paints himself under the light of a lamp, or a harpist seated at her instrument, or a fashionable woman at her window, or a woman bathing. Even in his *Sexton,* that great pendant of the psychological interiors, that remarkable piece which, in its soberness, of all Israëls' mighty work perhaps approaches nearest to Rembrandt and, at the same time, is allied to the greatness of our little masters: even here there is not a vestige of what we may call *Tendenz.*

One who did not know Israëls and who judged him only by his works could readily picture him as a

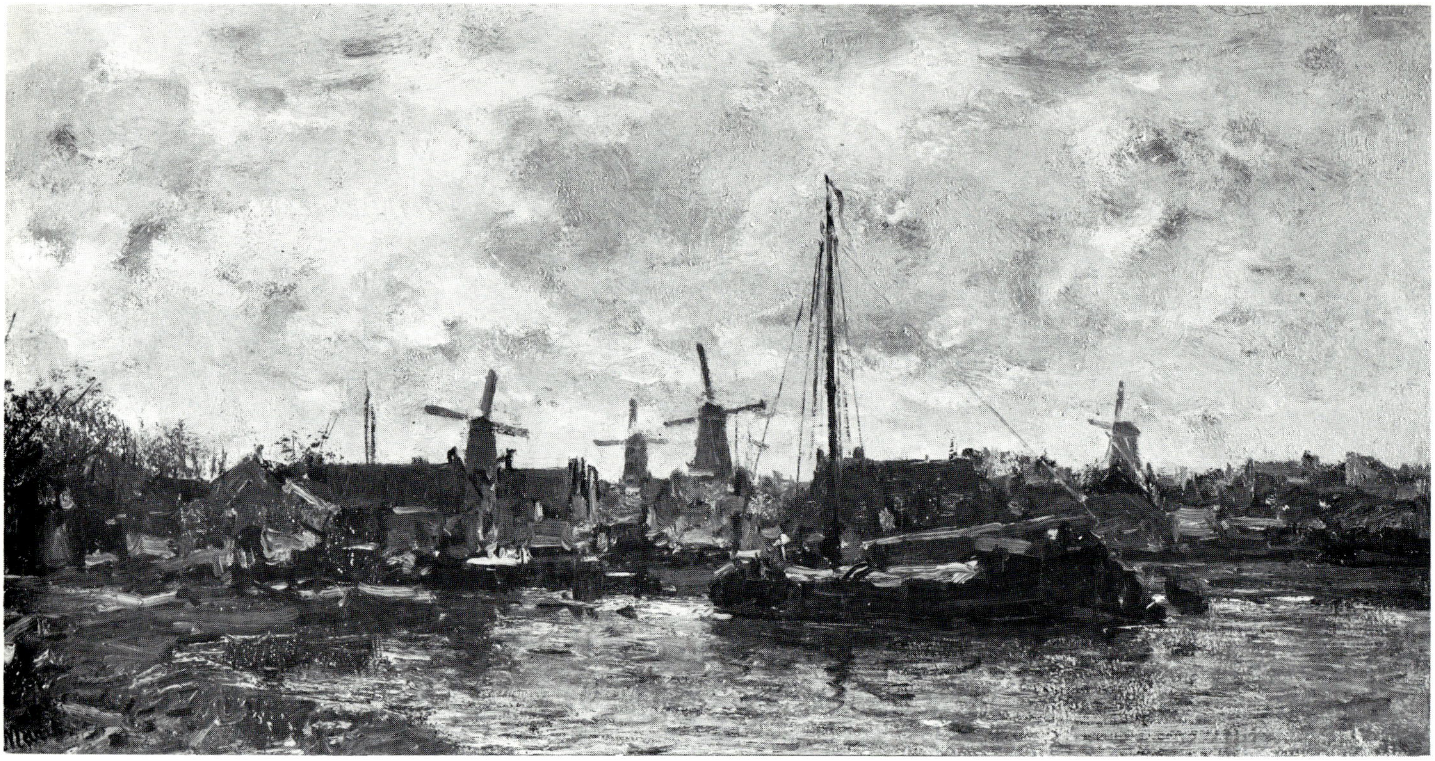

Jacob Maris (1837-1899) *was the leading landscapist of the Hague School and the eldest of the three Maris brothers who achieved fame with their painting. Here he carries the traditional Dutch waterside scene towards impressionism with a concentration on the effects of colour and light. (21¼ x 11ins.)* Photograph courtesy of Williams & Son.

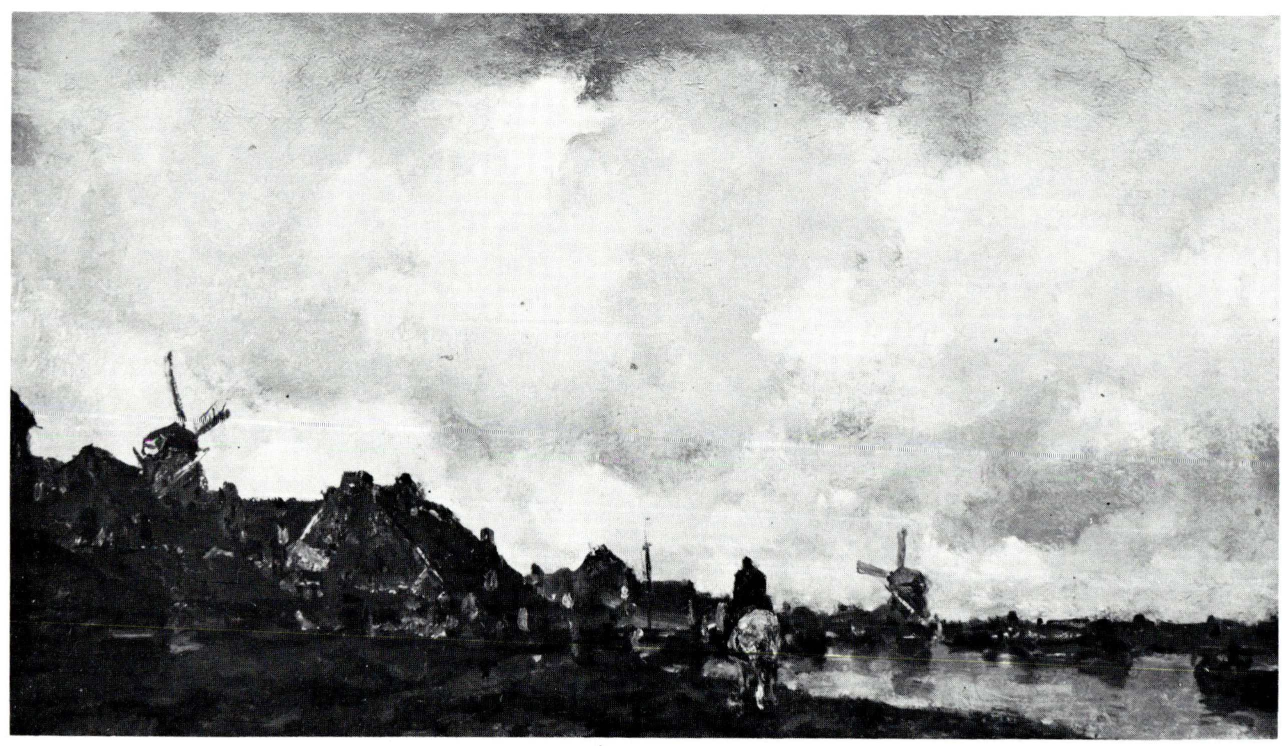

Here Jacob treats a waterside village in the stormy light of evening (48.5 x 78.5cms.) Photograph courtesy of the Dordrechts Museum.

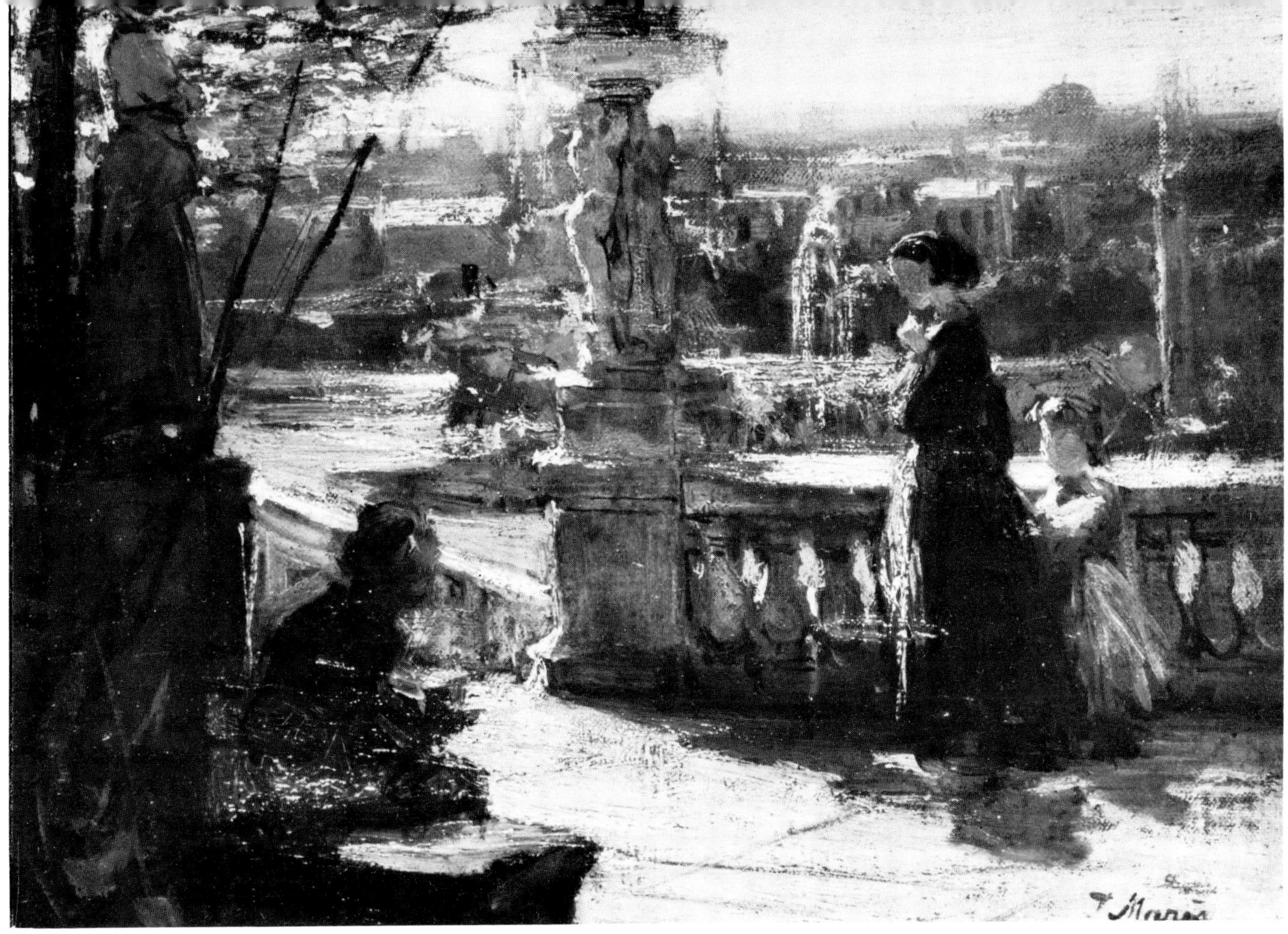

Jacob Maris *on his travels here applies his new-found impressionism to the ornamental Baroque steps of a park. (16½ x 22½cms.)* Photograph courtesy of Mak van Waay, Amsterdam.

melancholy man, burdened and bent with the suffering which he reproduces in his paintings. Nothing is farther from the truth. He sees the suffering; he penetrates into the loneliness, the poverty, the very being of forlorn humanity; he has the imagination necessary to exalt his single figures into types, to raise his episodes of the fisherman's life from the particular to the general. But he need no more be identified with the figures in his paintings than the novelist with those in his books. For, in his own being, he is a Jew, in whom the strength of the old race finds voice; a Jew to whom all philosophy is experience of life; in bone and marrow a son of the old people, not according to the letter, but according to the spirit, with a healthy dislike of all feeble sentiment.

Jozef Israëls is incontestably the head of the Dutch school of painting in so far that he, the powerful painter, the great psychologist, ranks with the most important artists of all countries, in so far, especially, that he has enriched our school with an art that observes the underlying essence of the things depicted. His influence, which at first related chiefly to his subjects, afterwards had the most far-reaching effects upon a much younger generation, owing to the purity of his psychology and his ever more and more magical powers of expression, while the delicate culture of his mind and his truly unsystematic philosophy made him the centre of a vast circle of admirers and friends.

On the other hand, Jacob Maris, thanks to his powerful palette, his masterly touch, his classical method, exercised a greater and a much more direct influence upon his contemporaries and the younger painters. This was not only through his work, but also through the force of his personality, which gathered all the younger painters around it, daily and incessantly, in evenings at which, in the intervals between the music, painting was discussed and all his words remembered and reported.

Eckermann tells, in his *Gespräche mit Goethe*, of the German painters in Rome, who, whenever there

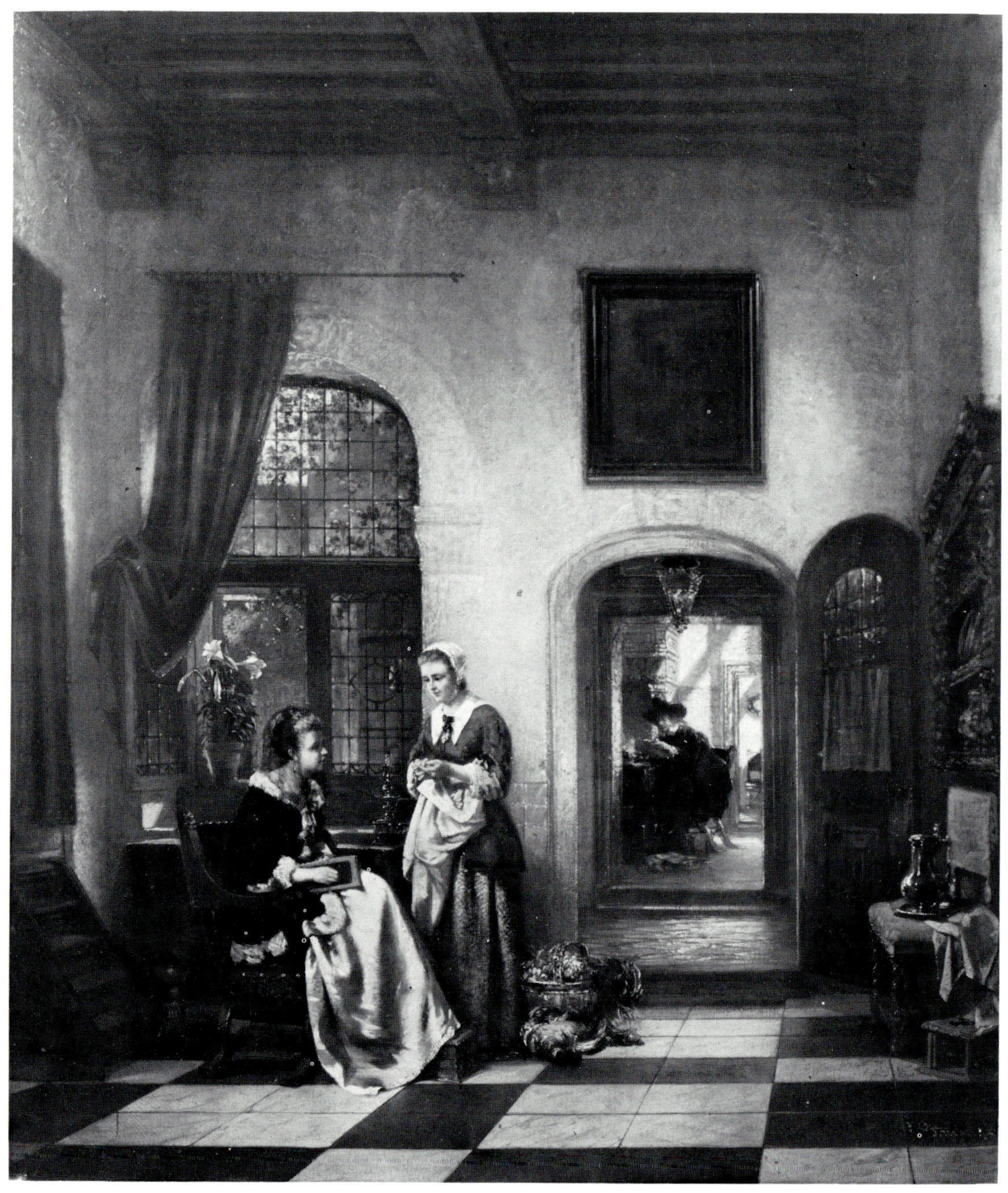

Above and right: **Johan Anthonie Balthazar Stroebel (1821-1905)** *was the teacher of Jacob Maris, and himself a pupil of Hubertus van Hove. In this Dutch interior (36½ x 31cms.) he is closely related to van Hove (see page 84). While the group of industrious burghers in their broad-brimmed hats (67½ x 82½cms.) has more than an echo of Rembrandt – whom he greatly admired. Both paintings show a lighter quicker brush stroke than van Hove which looks forward to the impressionistic revolution of Maris and the Hague School.* Photographs courtesy of Christie, Manson & Woods and Mak van Waay, Amsterdam.

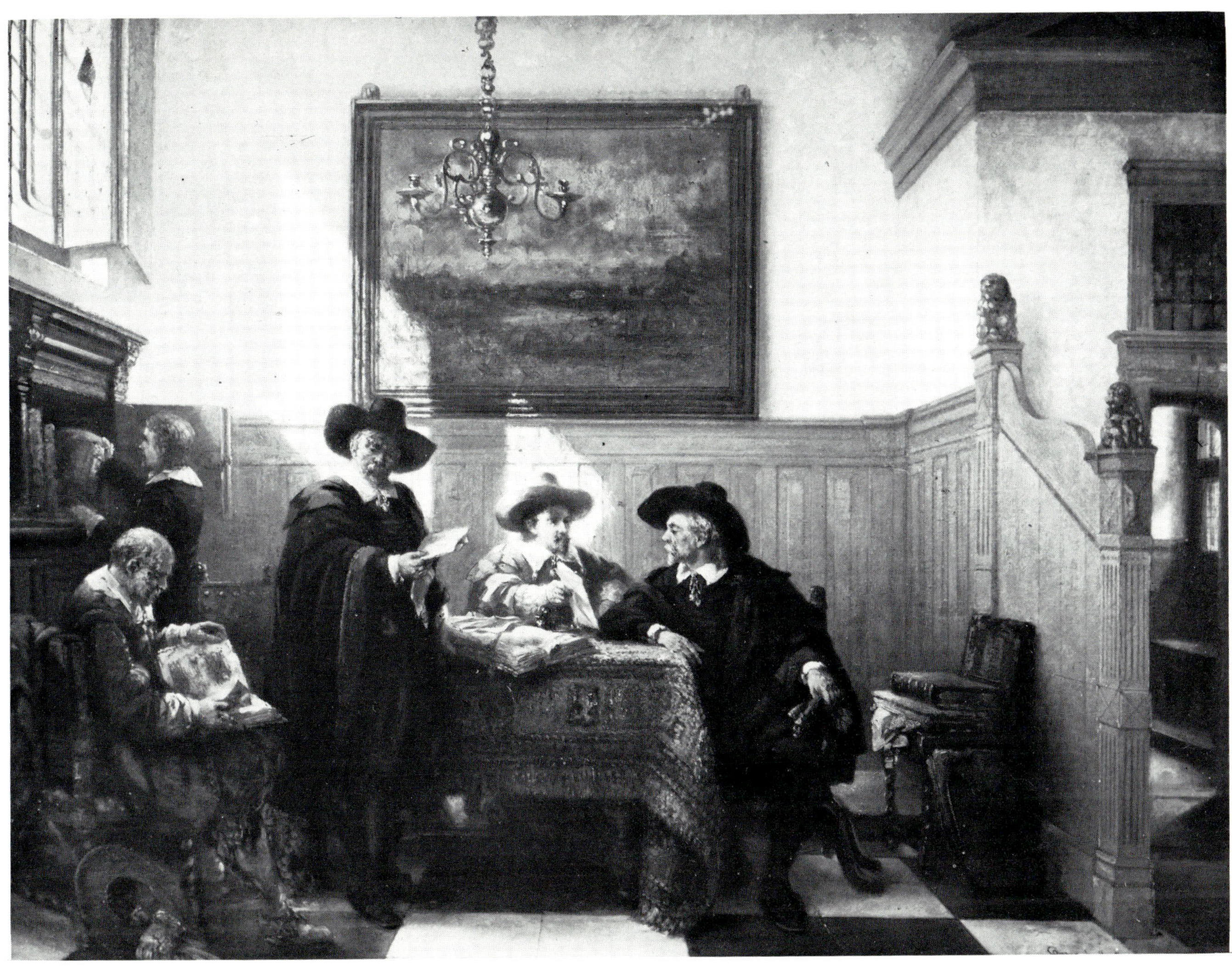

were enough of them collected in the *osteria,* came to loggerheads touching the respective merits of Michael Angelo and Raphael and, when the dispute was at its height, rushed off in two bodies to the Vatican, there to demonstrate in the presence of the paintings, and returned to the tavern to make friends over a bottle of wine and . . . to begin all over again on the morrow.

Even so men have quarrelled about other great artists: about Rembrandt and Velasquez; or, as they did and do to this day, about Jozef Israëls and Jacob Maris. Israëls was the first to give us, in the nineteenth century, life, living man in conflict with every phase of life, psychology, in short. Jacob Maris was the first to give us, in our day, colour, the joy of colour revealed in the gladness of Holland's skies and cities and fields, colour in light, colour in shade: he brought us master qualities of painting, the equilibrium between form and colour and the glory of light. All that he sought to achieve he achieved fully; he was in harmony with his conception; he was one with his art. This cannot always be said of Israëls. But Israëls aimed at something that lies outside the painter's art, something that may be described as metaphysical.

Although Bosboom stood first in the series of the Hague masters and Jozef Israëls was destined to represent Dutch painting, we must always look upon the three Marises, but especially Jacob and Willem, as the founders of the Hague School. There were great landscape-painters before them, including Hanedoes and Willem Roelofs (1822-1897), of whom both had, long before, felt the inspiring influence of the Barbizon painters and of whom the second had shown an early disposition as a colourist and the first, in his *Sunset,* in the Hague Museum, had proved that he realized

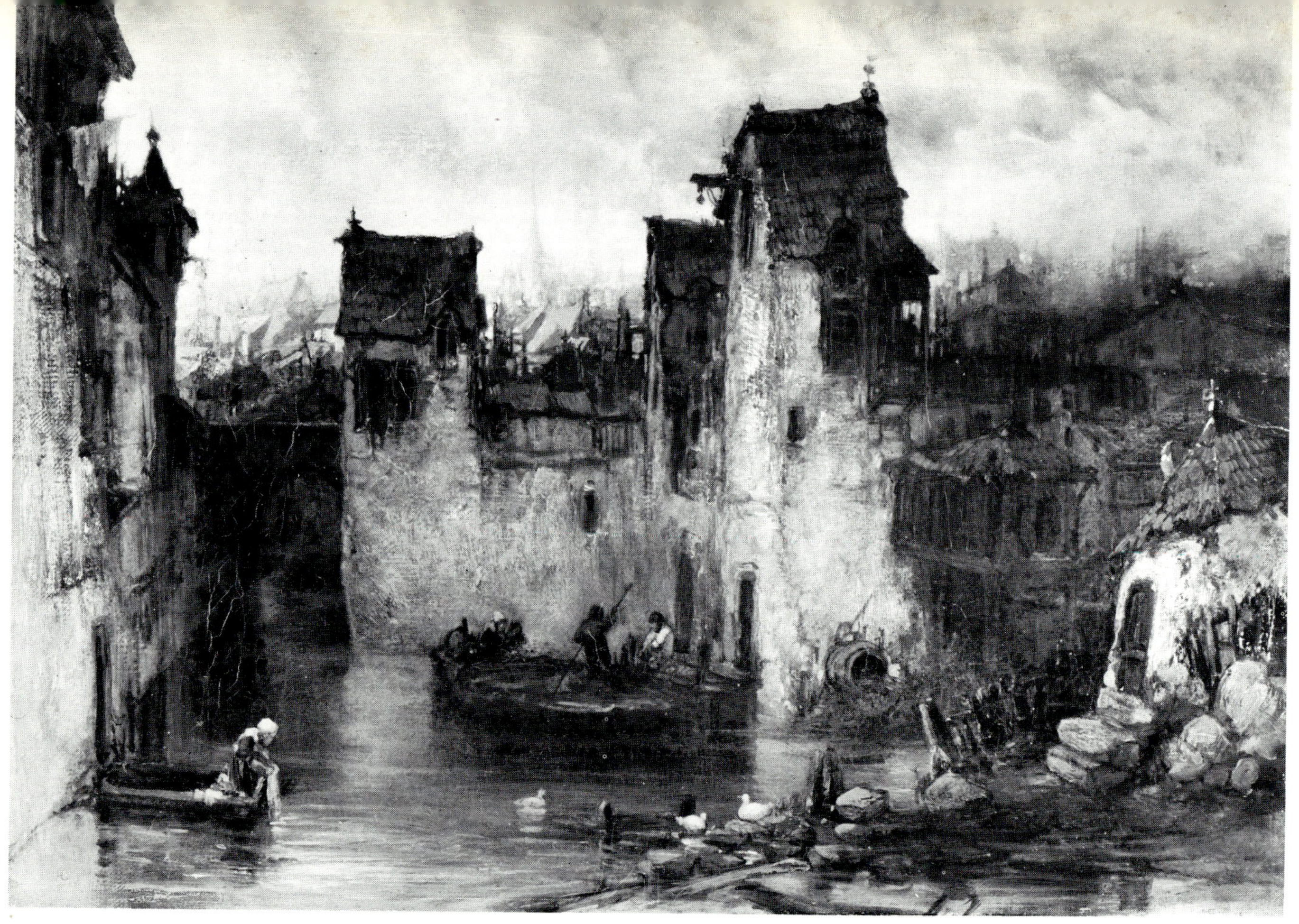

Jacob *and* **Matthijs Maris** *(1839-1917) studied and painted extensively together. Jacob freely admitted the debt he owed to his brilliant young brother. This townscape is the combined work of the two brothers, an exceptionally happy combination of Jacob's impressionism and Matthijs' visionary quality. (21½ x 15½ins.).* Photograph courtesy of Williams & Son.

how the sky gave life to the landscape, long before the Marises had learnt to know the French painters. But, though Roelofs, the Amsterdammer, drank with deep draughts of the wealth of colour which the Barbizon masters retained from the romantic period; though he was the precursor; though, at times, he was successful in his application of their colour-schemes; for all that, he never felt that the real being of their art was Dutch. And the result was that he saw the Dutch pastures, the fat fields, the great pools of water through their eyes, but did not, through them, come to realize and acknowledge the art of his country and his race. This does not do away with the fact that he was a strenuous painter, who often succeeded in reproducing the influence of wind and weather on the landscape.

When, in 1870, Jacob Maris made his appearance with his *Ferry-boat*, the difference became evident. To him had been revealed not so much the masters of Barbizon and their works, but the nature and essence of the lowlands of Holland. In the case of Roelofs, we behold a generous admiration and an admiring compliance; in that of Jaap Maris, an understanding, a revelation of his own country. And not one of them all (I am leaving Bosboom outside the question), about 1870, brought forth a work in which the traditions of our country and our people, the essence of our Dutch atmosphere, are so exquisitely understood and reproduced as in this *Ferry-boat* which, once and for all, marked the return to sheer painting.

He restored to the Netherlands, first of all, colour, which none of our nineteenth-century painters before him had displayed so purely. He also brought with him the art of painting, art in the sense in which the little masters of the seventeenth century understood it. For none of his works betrays Barbizon influences. No doubt, from the very beginning, he sought his way through formulas of every kind; no doubt, Matthijs Maris exercised a great, a very great influence upon him, but, starting with this first painting in which he

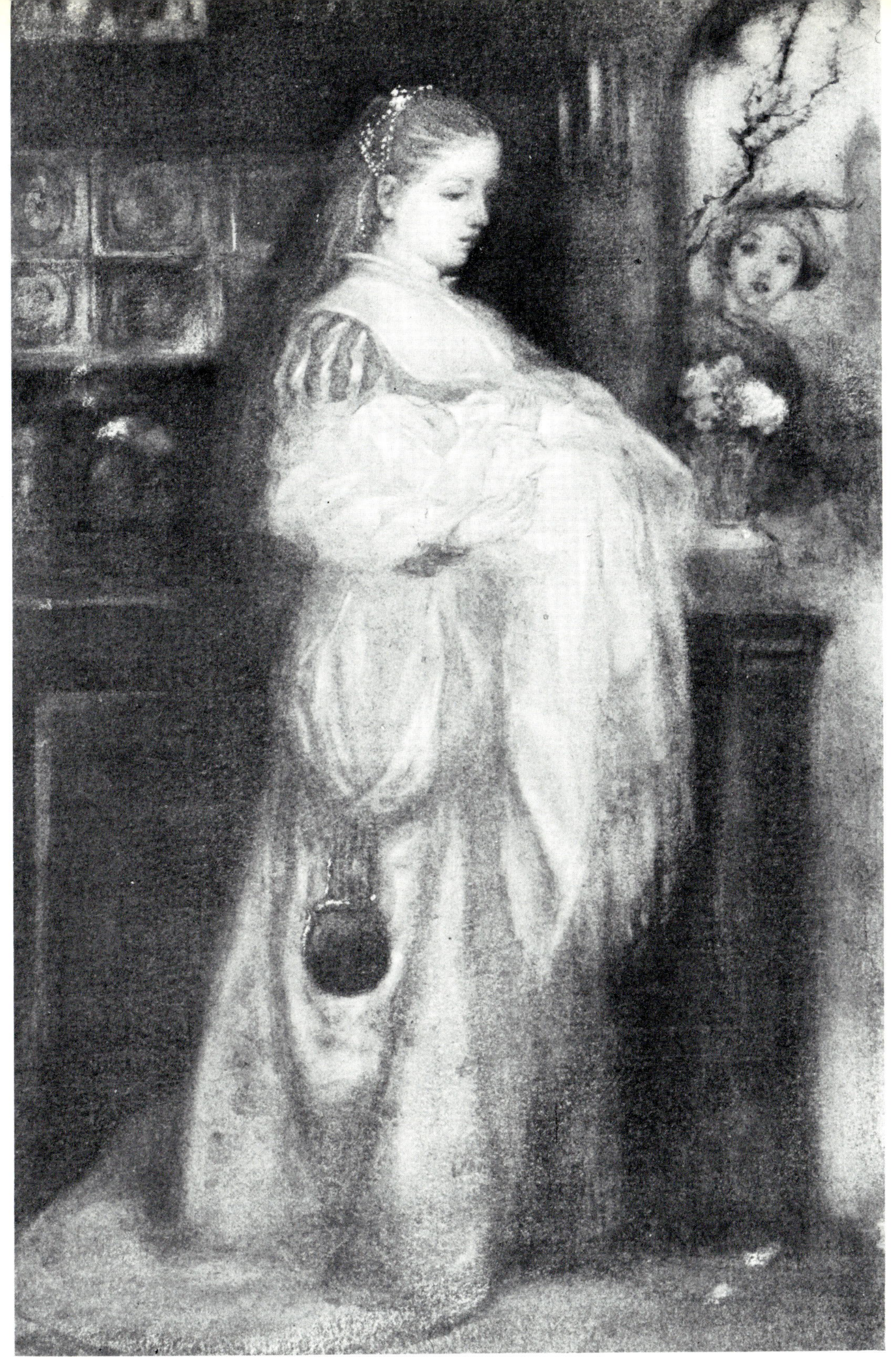

Matthijs Maris (1839-1917) *was a dreamer and instinctive artist of the highest order. While the Hague School was moving through Realism towards Impressionism he explored soft dream visions of the middle ages — as in this watercolour "The Infant Princess". (6½ x 10ins.)* Photograph courtesy of Williams & Son.

proved that he had seen his country, he was the real Dutchman: full of colour, lucid, great, above all, in those light skies in which Ruysdael and Vermeer of Delft before him so gloriously expressed their love of their country, firm of touch, sensitive in delineation, broad in expression, steadfast in workmanship and endowed with a colourful, but pure palette. The first of his town-views, smaller in dimensions than the later ones, more compact in composition, more pronounced in form, displays all the merits for which Jan Vermeer's *View of Delft,* the pearl of the Mauritshuis, is so dear to every Dutchman. All the merits? Maris gave us more but also gave us less, for, if the work of the modern master was more symphonic, he was not able to give that unfailing, self-contained representation which, when all is said, makes Vermeer so unapproachable. Still, the emotion in this apparently unemotional work is, as in that of the Delft master, of the purest order. His art is purely pictorial, his moods, his agitation, his admiration have their source in a rhythmical disposition which, seeing things in their own splendour, places them on view in the delicious colour-gradations of its own rich nature.

If we mention not only Vermeer, but also Rembrandt and Jacob Maris in one breath, we must remember that they who shout, "Rembrandt! Rembrandt!" the loudest, without being impressed by Jacob Maris' greatness, would certainly have belonged to those who, in Rembrandt's own day, most violently reviled him, or, for lack of understanding, denied him. And yet our delight, the nature of our emotion in the presence of Jaap Maris is less intense than in that of Rembrandt. It is the same insatiable feeling: the same sense of not being able to grasp so much that is grand and majestic and beautiful and instructive; the same growing admiration for the range, the wealth and the variety of the subjects, for the richness of the colour and the luxuriance of the treatment, for that noble structure and calm power of expression, for that same simplicity of heart, even though the later painter lacks the childlike faith that roused the visionary in Rembrandt. But all Jacob Maris' existence lies in the stately equilibrium, the glorious sense of measure which enable him to balance tall, burly windmills with huge banks of clouds, low-lying towns with the light of water and sky, smooth beaches with the rugged clouds in their grandeur, until, in a glorious equipoise, they set the very soul of the Dutch landscape before us

Has it ever happened before that one family has produced three sons, artists all three, all masters, all great in different manners? Three brothers, all entering upon life with the same ideal before their eyes, each moving along his own appointed road: Willem, the youngest, enamoured of the sunlight, the full sunlight as it lies spread in a golden glory over medes and meres or as, in the morning, it dispels the mists, absorbs the dew of the pastures and plays upon the moist twigs of the ditch-side willows; Matthijs, who turned his dreams into revelations with the reality of his memories; and Jacob, who, as it would appear, expressing himself more slowly and gropingly, prepared himself for the loftier flight which he was to take up, preceding his younger brothers, influenced by Thijs (especially in Paris) and caring for him, with his nature broad and great from the beginning: three brothers, all largely gifted, all three pure painters, who, from their childhood, felt the road that lay before them and who were painters at an age when most lads are still at school. This was how it came about that, from the beginning, they thought, felt and expressed themselves in paint, with never a literary tendency to disturb their intellectual power, concentrated wholly upon the logical execution of their painting: Jacob, who, discovered, in a certain sense, by his schoolmaster, began to study under Stroebel when he was twelve; Matthijs, who went to Louis Meijer at the same age; and Willem, who received no other direct tuition than that of his eldest brother and who worked untrammelled and uninfluenced from 1863 onwards. The three grew up in very fortunate circumstances, in a happy, simple household, of which the father, an Austrian on the paternal side, with Maresq for his name originally, was a compositor, earning twenty shillings a week and free from one-sided intellectual prejudices; simple, sensible people, who acknowledged their sons' talents and looked upon painting as a fine, a very fine profession and not as a luxury. Brought up under these conditions, the two elders were soon obliged to work for their livelihood and for the common good and they learnt their trade by copying old and modern pictures in water-colours, working for painters and studying under them: an artistic education in our old-Dutch manner.

Johan Anthonie Balthazar Stroebel, whose solid instruction Jacob Maris received, was born at the Hague in 1821 and was the pupil consecutively of B.J. and Hubertus van Hove. Like his second master, he was distinguished for his old-fashioned *doorkijkjes,* or domestic vistas, but expressed himself in warmer,

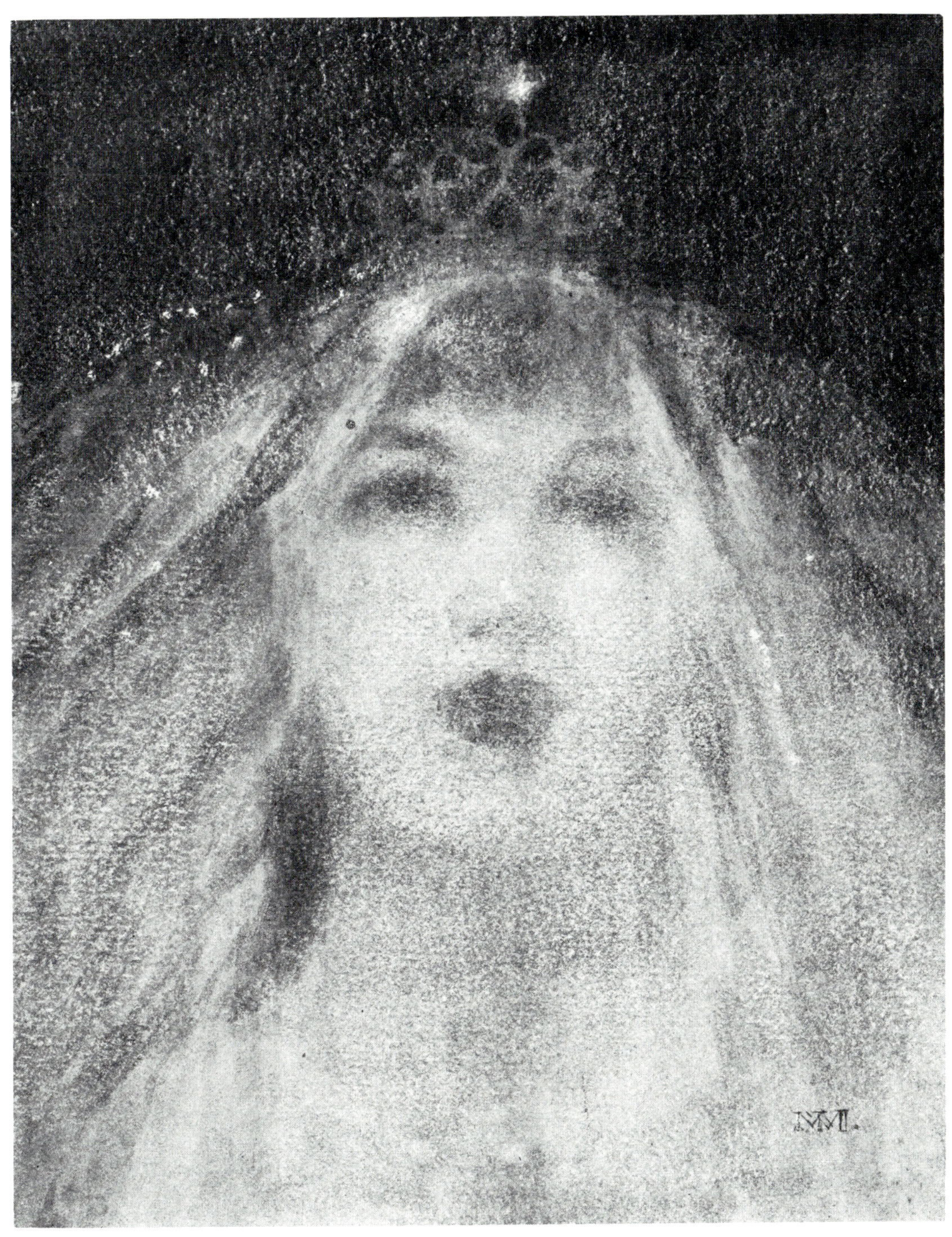

In his later years **Matthijs Maris** *followed the Symbolist road, drawing subjects from his own visions and dreams. His women "with something of the child and something of the Bacchante" exert a mysterious fascination as in this "Golden Aurelia". (watercolour 15 x 19cms.)* Photograph courtesy of Williams & Son.

sometimes a little fiery, but so-called Rembrandt tones. He made his pupil draw water-colours after still-life and also from models employed by himself, a method of instruction to which, in later years, he attached great importance.

A dealer in works of art, Mr. Weimar, found Jacob sitting one day with Matthijs on the Groenmarkt, where the first was making a drawing of the old Town-hall; and this meeting had as its result that the young painters (Jacob was then fourteen or fifteen years of age) came to work for him and, in particular, made water-colour copies of the pictures in his gallery, which contained the best products of Dutch and Belgian art. Weimar also introduced Jacob to the studio of the excellent Huib van Hove, which was then in the Hofje van Nieuwkoop, afterwards the first home of the Hague Artists' Club, best known by its motto of Pulchri Studio. In the evenings, Jacob visited the Hague Academy, as did Thijs, who, in his twelfth year, began to study under Louis Meijer. In 1853, he accompanied his master to Antwerp, where he visited the Academy from 1854 to 1856, Matthijs following him there in the latter year. After Antwerp, the brothers settled in the Hague, where Jacob made himself useful to the ailing Louis Meijer and also found time to work for himself. They were also for some time at Oosterbeek, where they met the elder and the younger Bilders, De Haas, Mauve and Gabriël and where the three brothers painted elaborate studies.

Jaap Maris felt his younger brother's influence most strongly after the trip which they undertook together to the Black Forest, thanks to a little fortune which they had earned by their copies of the *Frederick Henry* and *Amalia of Solms* in the House in the Wood, for which they received seven hundred guilders, or nearly sixty pounds apiece. The return journey was made over Cologne to Mannheim by boat, Heidelberg, Carlsruhe, Basel and Lausanne and back by Neuchâtel, Dijon, Fontainebleau and Paris. At Cologne, they found an exhibition in which the painters of the German romantic school, Moritz, Von Schwind, Kaulbach, Rethel and others confirmed to Matthijs all that he had learnt to surmise at Antwerp, while Jacob admired only the cartoons. In any case, although we find the subjects taken from this journey elaborated in a higher degree in Matthijs' work, we may take it that his ideas carried Jaap Maris with them for the Paris period, which followed soon after, gives the masterly *Marlotte,* that little pearl-grey French town painted in full detail against a hill, *The Cradle* and other pieces which, like his romantic church-interiors and *The Bird-cage,* we are disposed, at first sight, to ascribe to Thijs. The pictures are compactly painted and almost as elaborate as the younger brother's. Only, the difference here, too, is that Jacob was simpler and, from the first, inclined to look rather for the purely pictorial and that his work, therefore, did not possess that laboured quality which has from the beginning and always distinguished Thijs, if we except just one or two studies. He also underwent the influence of Hébert's studio, to which we owe a series of figures of Italian girls that had a quick success in Paris and in our own country. After his death, a number of fine, thoughtful little paintings were discovered, dating back to his Paris period; but it was not until he stood all alone in Holland that he became himself a pure painter of the old Dutch stock, powerful and delicate, distinguished and intimate at one and the same time.

Matthijs Maris' Dutch period really precedes the movement which was afterwards described as the Hague school. He never sought or hankered after what has been called impressionism; and it seemed rather as though he disregarded all other painters to follow only Pieter de Hooche, a perhaps unconscious endeavour which sometimes made him go in search of an even earlier method of painting: the early Flemings and Cranach.

As a lad of twelve, studying under Louis Meijer, he soon surprised him by the manner in which he had painted a boat with figures into a little sea-piece of Meijer's, a manner so excellent that his master admitted that he himself could not have done it so well and confessed that the picture was increased in value because of it. And we can safely say that his apprenticeship was devoted exclusively to self-realization. As Jacob Maris said of him:

"Thijs knew everything of himself; he was a genius."

The archives of the Hague Drawing Academy contain some drawings by Matthijs which are remarkably mature for a boy of fourteen or fifteen. One, a head of Christ with a crown of thorns and a naked breast, was drawn when Thijs was only thirteen and already shows wonderful qualities.

It may occasion surprise that the work of the Marises, who visited Fontainebleau and Paris as early as 1866, betrays so little of the influence of the Barbizon school. Although a few complete studies made by Thijs in the Forest of Fontainebleau show something of the luxuriant green, of the heavy tonality of this school, we can take the wonderfully perfect

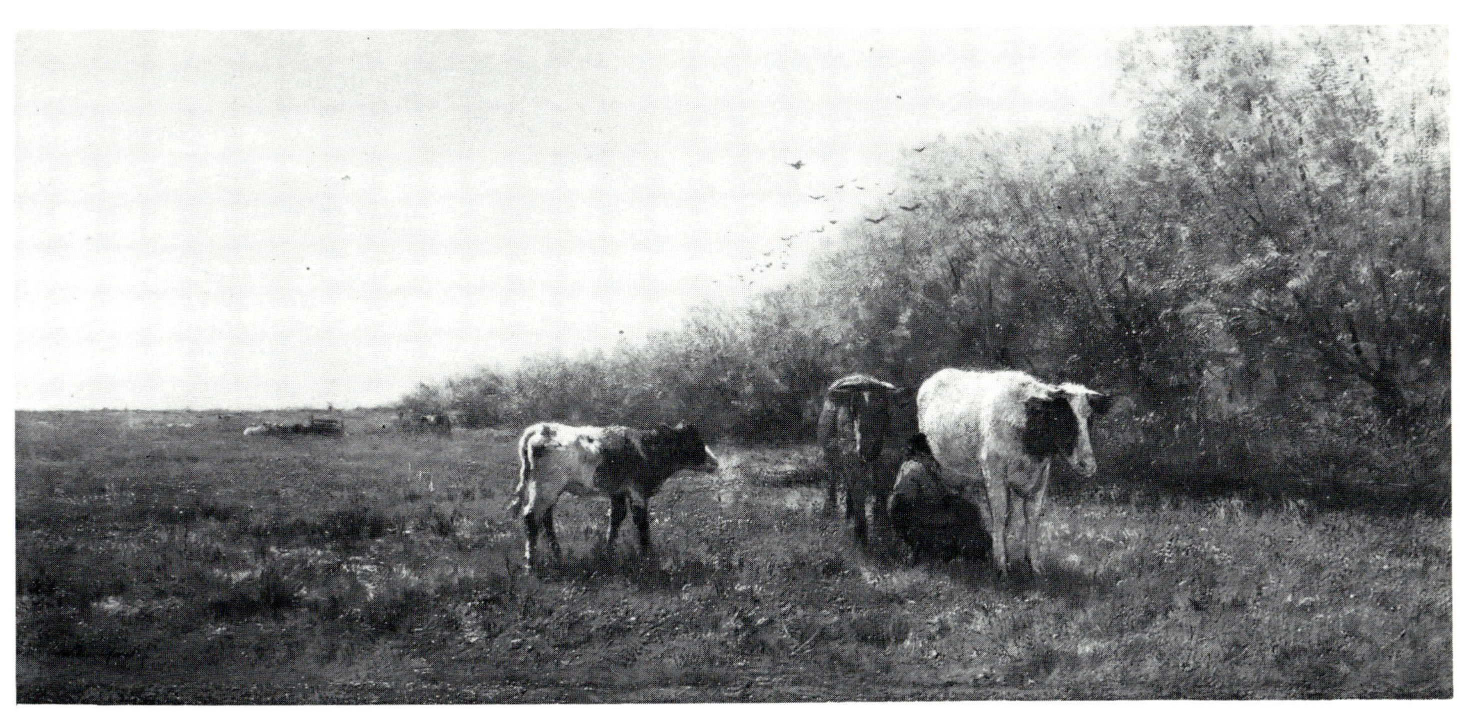

Above and below: **Willem Maris (1844-1910)** *was the youngest of the Maris brothers. Taught by Jacob he developed a similar impressionistic technique which he applied mainly to pastoral scenes in the Dutch countryside, full of glowing colour and light. These two views of a milk-maid and her cattle are typical examples. (The first 18¾ x 39½ins., the second 91 x 125cms.)* Photographs courtesy of M. Newman Ltd., and Mak van Waay, Amsterdam.

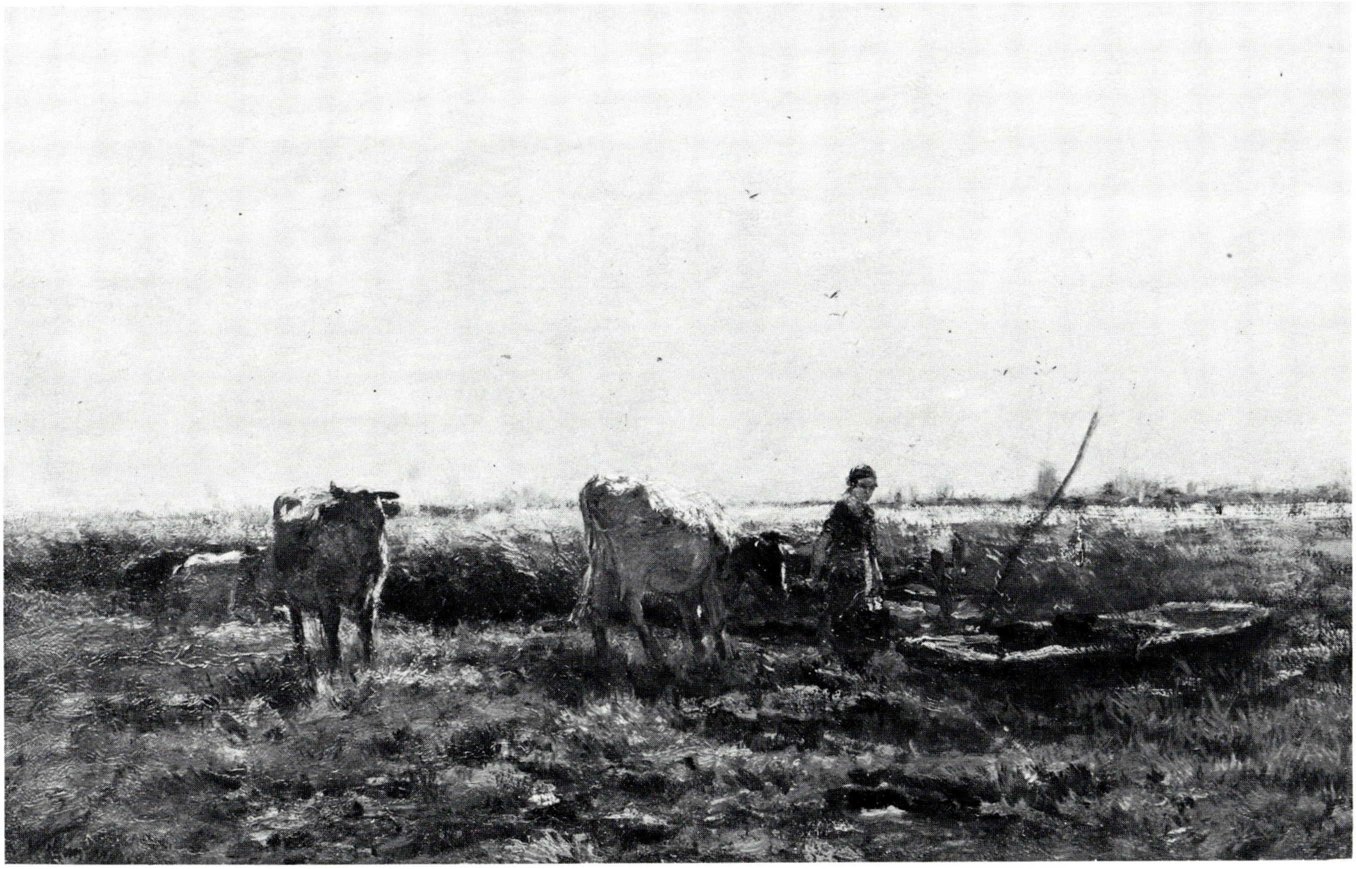

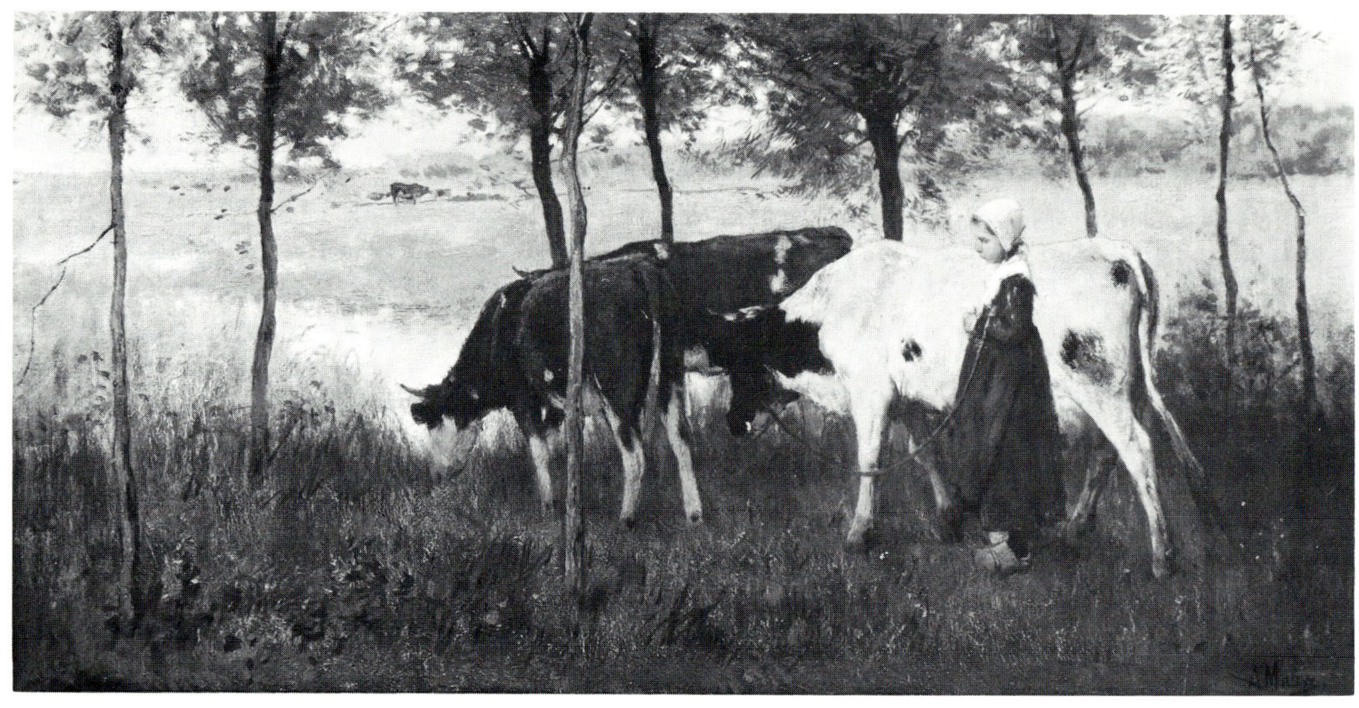

Above and right: **Anton Mauve (1838-1888)** *paints in his peasant scenes with a sturdy simplicity related to Millet whom he greatly admired. In the first of these pictures a young girl watches quietly over her cattle, (13¾ x 27½ins.) while in the second a sturdy peasant woman is working among her cabbages. (28 x 36½ins.) Both are caught with a quick realism.* Photographs courtesy of M. Newman Ltd., and Sotheby & Co.

little piece exhibited some time ago at the Biesing galleries at the Hague – a rustic bridge in a wood, with a couple of figures on it – and compare it quite as effectively with the angler in Isaäc van Ostade's etching; for, in point of fact, the drawing in this little piece is of a quite different order from that of the French painters of 1830. And again, if we take all the known work of Thijs Maris together – sketches, drawings, studies, elaborate paintings and academic studies – it would appear that the only work which betrays a trace of the broad, full tone of the French landscape-painters is the superb *Head of a Ram* in the Mesdag Museum. He is said to have been a boy still when he painted this admirable work; and, although this seems hardly credible, the fact remains that it stands alone, whether, as some think, it was painted in Paris or in our own country.

Undoubtedly the most perfect work of this earlier period is the famous *Souvenir d'Amsterdam.* It shows an extraordinary clearness and breadth of vision, combined with an unfailing touch, and the whole is permeated with a sentiment that seems to have its being in the essence of the capital rather than in the depths of the painter's soul. This view is the purest and most complete portrait that has ever been produced of Amsterdam; and there is not a painting in the world that can be quite compared with it, unless it be the perspective in Van Eyck's *Vierge au donateur* in the Louvre, which compels our admiration through the same accuracy of vision. True, Jacob Maris, in later years, painted views in the city of Amsterdam in which, in the inspiration of the moment, the touches seem almost more brilliant; he built up skies under whose movement the canals beneath appear small and low; constantly he took Amsterdam as a *Motif* with which he raised the harmony of light and colour and line, in rhythmic swellings, into a symphonic poem. Later again, Breitner set up the great town movement of Amsterdam, piece by piece, full of colour and full of life, against the old background of the canals or the Dam, with mighty and vigorous strokes. But neither has represented the imperishable type of the old trading-city, in all its complicated essence of restfulness and bustle, with such absolute completeness

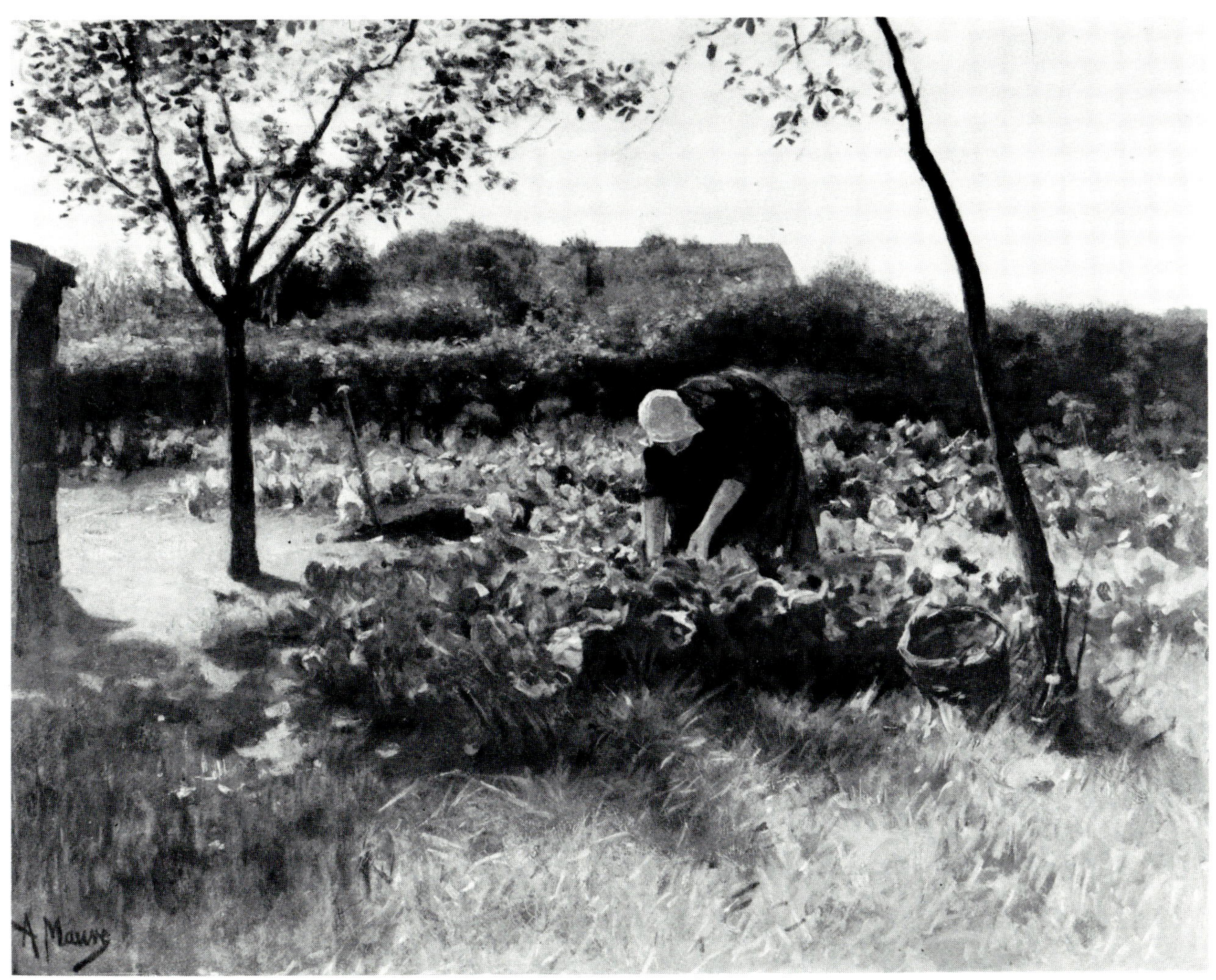

as Matthijs Maris.

Thijs Maris went to France in 1869 at the instigation of his mother, who did not know what to do with this unpractical son of hers who preferred to erase and hide his work rather than sell it. Jaap, who was always good to his brothers, had invited him to Paris, where he was living with his wife and child, and it was no great burden to him to receive the ascetic Thijs into his household.

The parting with his output continued to be the difficulty which Thijs was ever less and less able to surmount. Jaap has described how Thijs would work at the most exquisite things, until the time came when the picture could easily be finished in a day. Then he would upset the whole work and utterly refuse to be convinced of its excellence. He painted, for instance, a *Mother and Child* for which Mrs. Jacob Maris and her baby sat. This, according to Jacob, developed into one of his finest pictures, both as regards the faces and, in particular, the modelling of the child's little legs and feet. When it was almost finished, he began to paint it all over again, in a stiff, old-German fashion, and to make it look like a Cranach, with the result that all his work was wasted.

Nevertheless, Thijs produced some of his most charming pictures in Paris, such as, in 1870, his *View of a Town* and, in 1874, *The Butterflies,* that sunny page in his work: a little girl, in a blue frock, with a face lit up with an indescribable smile, not unlike those which curl the lips of Leonardo's women, her hair the colour of that old red gold of which Wagner speaks; this fairy-like, but positively-rendered child in an environment of Dutch sand-dunes, in which the sweetbriar grows around her and, a little further on,

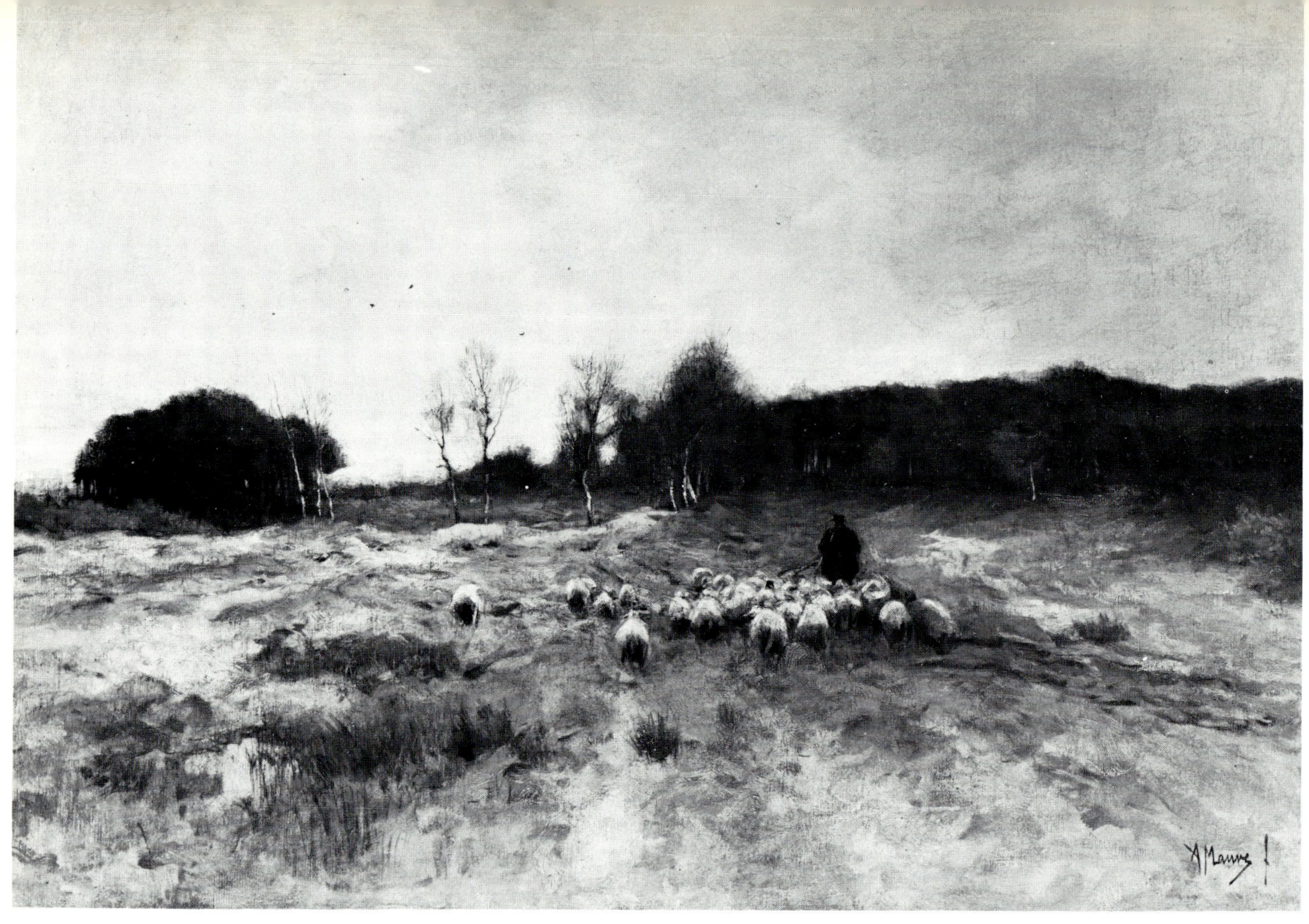

In this view of a shepherd and his sheep Mauve *has caught the scene in a cold, grey light. The light and the distant saplings are favourite features of his work. (23½ x 34½ins.)* Photograph courtesy of Williams & Son.

the sedge stands in rhythmical rows; and two butterflies, at which the child reaches with upraised hand, in the sultry summer sky. A little before this, he painted *The Woman baking Cakes,* that half-mediæval half-modern, French-Flemish kitchen interior, a pearl-grey master-piece that has its home in the Mesdag Museum; also the magnificent *Montmartre,* of which, as of *The Butterflies,* a second similar work is in existence; drawings of Gretchens, or, at least of the type which we call Gretchens; of churches with figures, sketches executed on his travels or from memories of them, such as the interesting Black Forest drawings, *The View of Lausanne,* the scarcely rivalled *Outskirts of a Town,* the *Three Mills;* memories also of Oosterbeek; and portraits, of which that of Artz the painter is a model of simplicity in the rendering of a face.

Amid all these works imbued with the peace of bygone centuries, in the midst of the thought which he devoted both to the conception of his subject and to its immaculate execution came the Commune, which coincided so entirely with his views, but in which, nevertheless, this Hamlet-like nature took part not of his own will, but because he was enrolled in the Municipal Guard and was therefore automatically transferred to the troops of the Commune.

After the Commune, Jacob Maris left Paris, leaving Thijs behind him. Although Matthijs worked and occasionally sold a picture (Goupil's bought his *Butterflies* for £50, which was not a bad price at the time, although the picture has since fetched forty times as much), he passed years of distress before, in 1877, he was discovered in a sorry plight by young Van Wisselingh, the son of the artistic art-dealer of the Hague, at whose suggestion he went to London.

There was a time when innocent sceptics had drawn

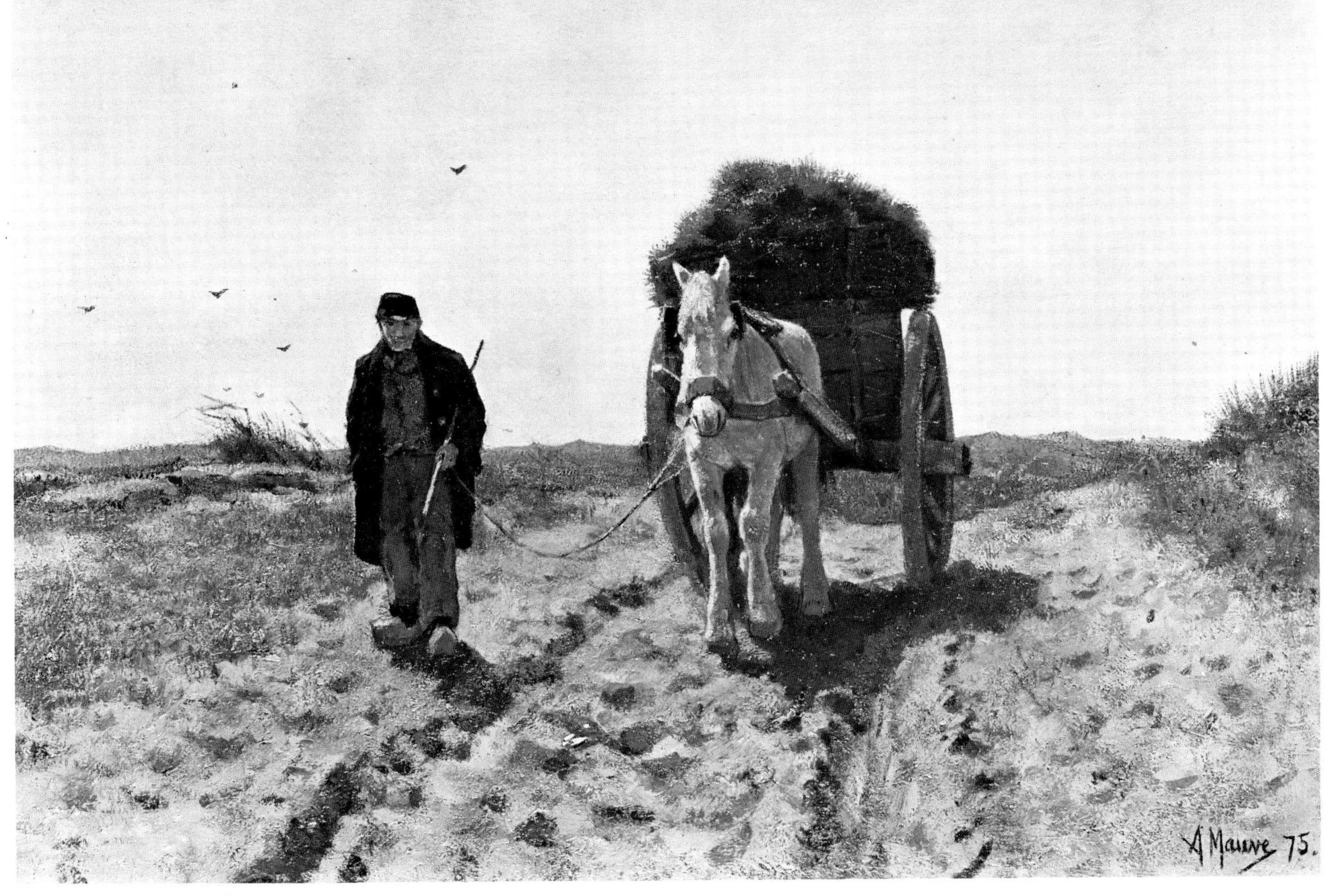

This painting of a peasant and his cart by **Mauve** *is dated 1875. Its short stubby brushstrokes and strong modelling is startlingly close to the work of Van Gogh's Dutch period. (82 x 55cms.)* Photograph courtesy of Williams & Son.

a line through his name. But, slowly and gradually, through works despatched by Van Wisselingh's London branch to Amsterdam, through auctions at which his early works came under the hammer and through select exhibitions, the wonderful personality became a living thing to us, the dreamer better known to us; his stately fancies roused new sensations; and, when the masters of the Hague school, in 1890, had already displayed the extent of their glorious talent, Matthijs Maris revealed himself in his full force, of past and present, as the noblest of our possessions. And this revelation concerned not only his sovereign imagination, but also his peerless knowledge and the perfection of his workmanship.

There came a time, in this English period of his, when Thijs Maris, who was, as the poet Swinburne has said of Blake, "beautifully unfit for walking in the way of any other man," was no longer content to paint things in their sheer being, as they were, when complete representation made way for imagination, for the dreams that haunted him, when his thoughts wandered aside in lonely musings that brought before his eyes forms which defied all positive knowledge, musings that summoned poetic figures which he endeavoured to grasp and to embody. And these figures were full of life: laughing with their perturbing smiles as in *The Butterflies;* more monumental in the etching of the woman with the distaff; fleeting joyfully towards the heyday of life like *The Bride;* figures of exquisite refinement as in *Primavera,* of a princess's fairy-tale as in *The Promenade* or in *The Lady of Shalott:* all with that intensity of life which thrills in its pure form, all with something of the exquisite longing for life of the Florence of Botticelli and Da Vinci . . . . His figures, monumental and child-like, constitute a type of woman of their own: they are women through and through, with something of the child and something of the bacchante, Juliet rather than Beatrice, living and full of life, rhythmical of shape and, at the same time, figures of light, with

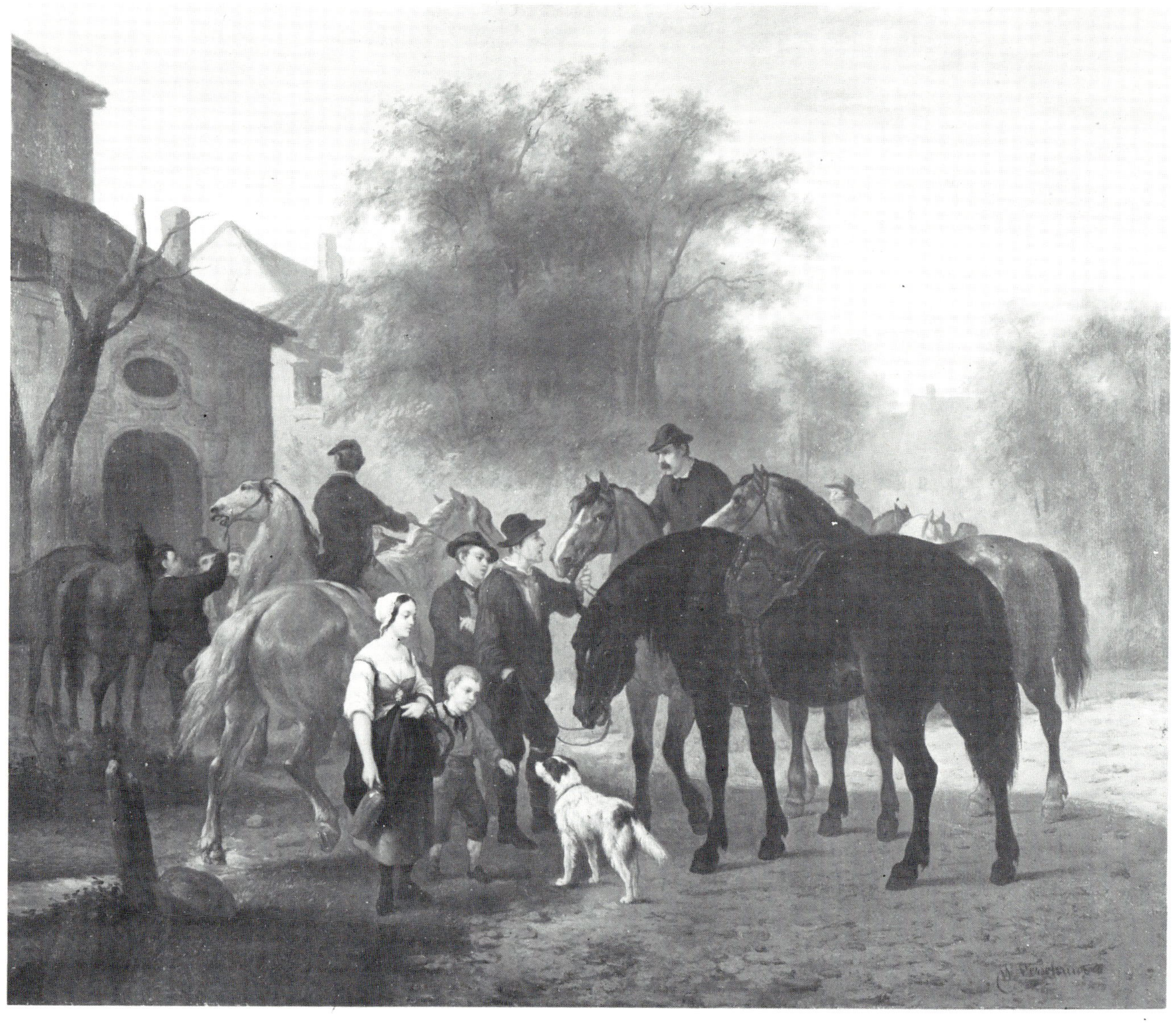

Above and right: **Wouterus Verschuur (1812-1874),** *the teacher of Anton Mauve, was a rustic painter of much more traditional stamp. His penchant for horses is well demonstrated by both these paintings. (The first 26 x 31½ins., the second 28 x 16½ins.).* Photographs courtesy of Christie, Manson & Woods and Williams & Son.

raised hands and sphinx-like smiles, a wonder in our day, a wonder of feminine charm and lastly, an exotic flower budding in a suburb of Puritan London, reversing Taine's theory of environment.

Outwardly considered, Willem Maris, the youngest of the brothers, has little or nothing in common with Matthijs, as regards either the technique or the conception of his subjects. Nevertheless, there are studies and also pictures of the Oosterbeek period in which all the three brothers show an inward similarity with one another; there are carefully-executed sketches in which we find a closer link between Willem and Thijs than between Willem and Jaap Maris. And, like Bosboom and Israëls, the three Marises all have something of the central point round which all Dutch art revolves: Rembrandt. In Willem Maris, this lies in the expression of the sunlight, in the broad, sketchy touch, in that pure impressionism of which Rembrandt, in his later period, appeared to be the originator.

Willem seems to have "arrived" at an early date,

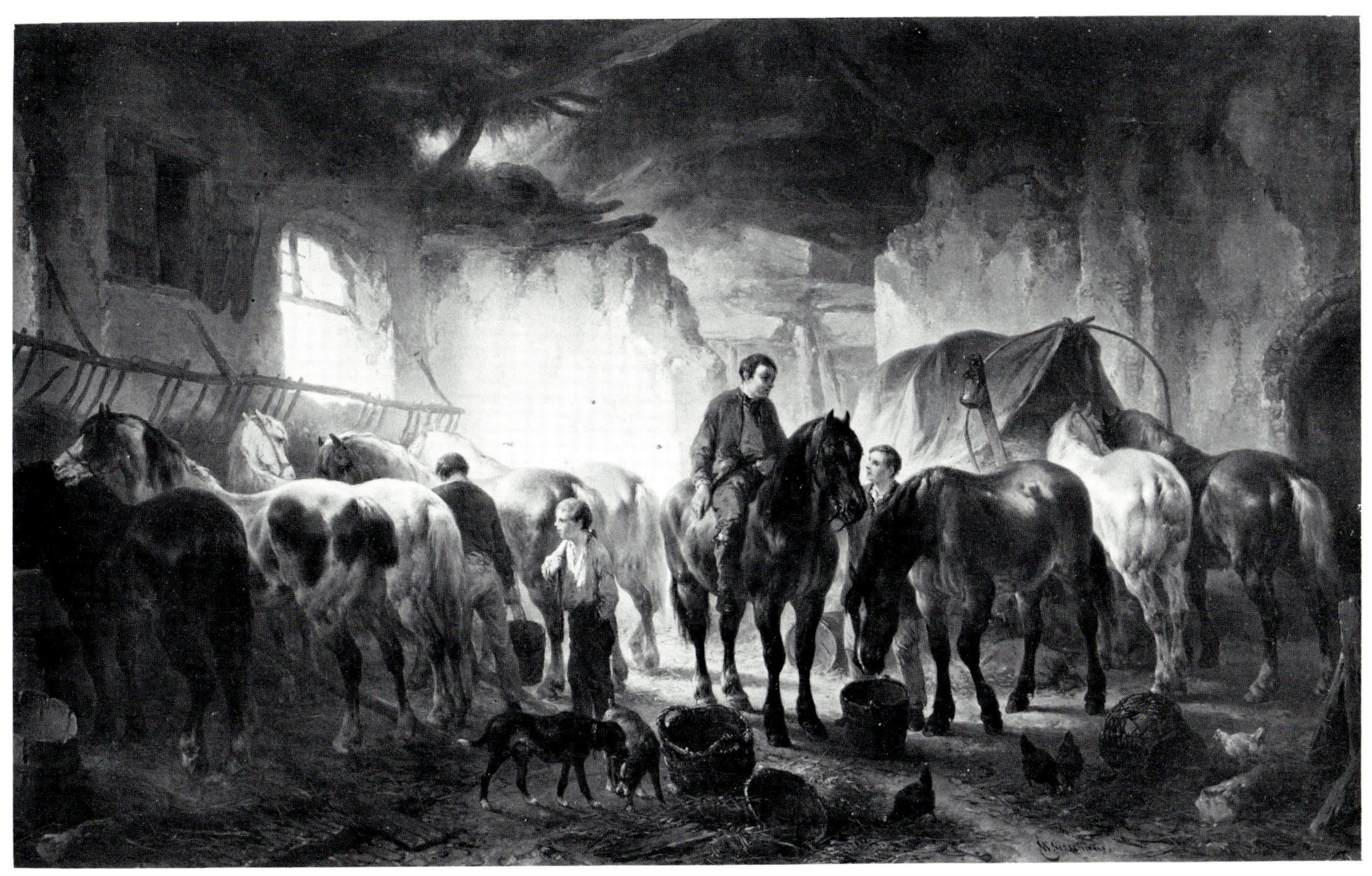

for we know, through Gerard Bilders, that the fame of his talent reached Amsterdam as early as 1863 through his two little pictures, *Cattle at a Pond* and *Young Calves at the Milk-pail,* which he sold for £12 each at the same Hague exhibition at which Thijs received £16 for his *Back Slum.* Willem Maris was then just nineteen. Mauve has told how, at Oosterbeek, a pale, delicate little lad came up to him and modestly asked leave to introduce himself and to accompany him, so that they might work together:

"At first," says Mauve, "I did not feel much inclined to agree, but I did not like to refuse the little fellow flatly, so we went off together. My companion did not suffer from loquacity; and, coming to a field with cows in it, I sat down to go on with a drawing which I had begun that morning. The little chap strolled around a bit and then settled down to work himself. We sat there for hours under the pollards, until I grew curious to see what the little fellow was at. He sat sketching with a bit of chalk; but, oh! I stood astounded. I seized him by the hand and stammered in my turn, 'My boy, what an artist you are! You stagger me! It's magnificent!' "

Even as with Jacob, so for Willem a painting has always been a material reproduction of a momentary aspect of nature. His glorious ditches with their waving reeds, with the gold-green duckweed, so full of rich colour, are the synthesis of a series of close observations of such a character that their expression, synchronizing with the painter's mood and with an impregnable truthfulness, presents a scene, simple in itself, so marvellously that we learn through it to see and admire nature. Willem Maris is the last of the great lyrical painters of our time. His sentiment is what it was in the glorious days of 1880 to 1890 and there is none to approach him in that artistry in which every point of view at once becomes lyrical.

Anton Mauve has not the depth of colour, nor the rich palette, nor the powerful and supple touch, nor the rhythmical line, nor the symphonic composition of the Marises. He does not wield the plastic powers of Jozef Israëls. And, compared with Millet, whose influence and personality held perhaps even greater sway over the painters of northern countries than over the Parisians, Mauve is so domestic, so unspeakably simple, that the two painters are not to be named in one breath. Millet – and herein lay his greatness – saw the peasants in the great biblical simplicity of their existence. His art is a sentimental art, full of style, representing the husbandmen with all the purity of form of the ancient Greeks. Mauve's relationship with Millet lies in the inward calmness with which they both set down the little actions of the simple labourers, without comment. But Millet's was a more far-searching formula, whereas Mauve's best works, his water-colour drawings, are more spontaneous. He followed the old painters, the Ostades and Esaias van de Velde, but he was more refined in his representation; he had a modernity that was all his own.

It is a sort of privilege to find, in the shop of a Paris art-dealer, one of these drawings of Mauve's surrounded by an environment of French boudoir art, an environment in which this drawing is even more full of surprises than an old Dutch painting in a foreign museum. It is pleasant to admire the unartificiality, the delicate truthfulness of it; to contemplate just that ditch, with the little white goat, among all those cold and clever things.

To this first period belong those masterly studies of calves on the dunes and in the fields, painted so firmly and broadly; those scenes on the sea-shore with donkeys, horses, fishing-boats drawn up on the beach, brown horses in the silky light of the Scheveningen sands; those delicate, grey roads; those water-ways with the sluggish barges; those admirable pictures of cows.

Compared with the Marises and Israëls, Mauve's pictures of the Laren period are sometimes dry and colourless and inferior both to his earlier work and to the watercolours which he produced at Oosterbeek or in the dunes. They have not the same power of colour or of workmanship as his earlier studies of cows, nor the attentiveness of his water-colours; they betray a certain weariness and hurry.

And yet, in his later drawings, he never entirely lost his touch, never neglected the delicacy of the representation. He painted the still, pearl-grey days of autumn and winter, when the sheep stand out warm against the withered green of the meadows and the labour in the fields is confined to ploughing and potato-digging; or when the snow lies untouched over the farms; or when there is thaw in the air and pale-yellow and lilac streaks appear above the sheep-fold. Or else he painted those exquisite days marked by neither sun nor wind, white days on which, as they say in Overijssel, "the weather stands listening": this is the atmosphere in which he preferred to place his figures.

Mauve was born at Zaandam in 1838 and died in 1888. He was taught at Haarlem by the animal-painter P.F. van Os and by Wouter Verschuur (1812-1874), the gifted but not powerful follower of Wouwerman. At Oosterbeek, he painted in the company, especially, of Bilders and, later, of the Marises, without whom he himself declared that he would never have become the personality which we recognize in him and value.

Among the talented and honest admirers of Mauve, the first place is occupied by François Pieter ter Meulen, born in 1843, who was intended for literature, but studied painting instead under H. van de Sande Bakhuijzen. He never possessed the purely pictorial point of view of his illustrious exemplar and his colouring, generally, is somewhat cold. Nevertheless, in his water-colour in the Mesdag Museum *A Drente Sheepfold by night,* the colour is brighter than we usually find in Ter Meulen.

Many other Dutch painters of similar current subjects have, with more or less success, followed the fluctuations of the American market, that degrading market which now, as in Mauve's day, asks one year for "Sheep going to pasture" and the next for "Sheep returning" and the year after for something else, much as the height and breadth of our hyacinths is laid down for us by the exigencies of Anglo-American taste. Mauve himself suffered from these conditions in a certain measure, as did all our leading painters. Jacob Maris would receive a commission for four pictures all of the same size, all four to contain white clouds; Jozef Israëls is asked for countless replicas of his works or else has orders for pictures with one or more figures, according to the sum to be expended on the purchase; Gabriël and Weissenbruch are asked for windmills to the exclusion of all else. Hence, the appearance of the American dollar would be unwelcome in the midst of our art, but for the fact that great painters commit these domestic crimes as it were with the left hand and that the reaction against this degrading toil gives birth to the purest works and to moments of inspiration. Only the weak succumb.

At a time when the nineteenth-century sea-painters, in imitation of Ludolph Bakhuijzen, composed their tempestuous seas as the history-painters composed

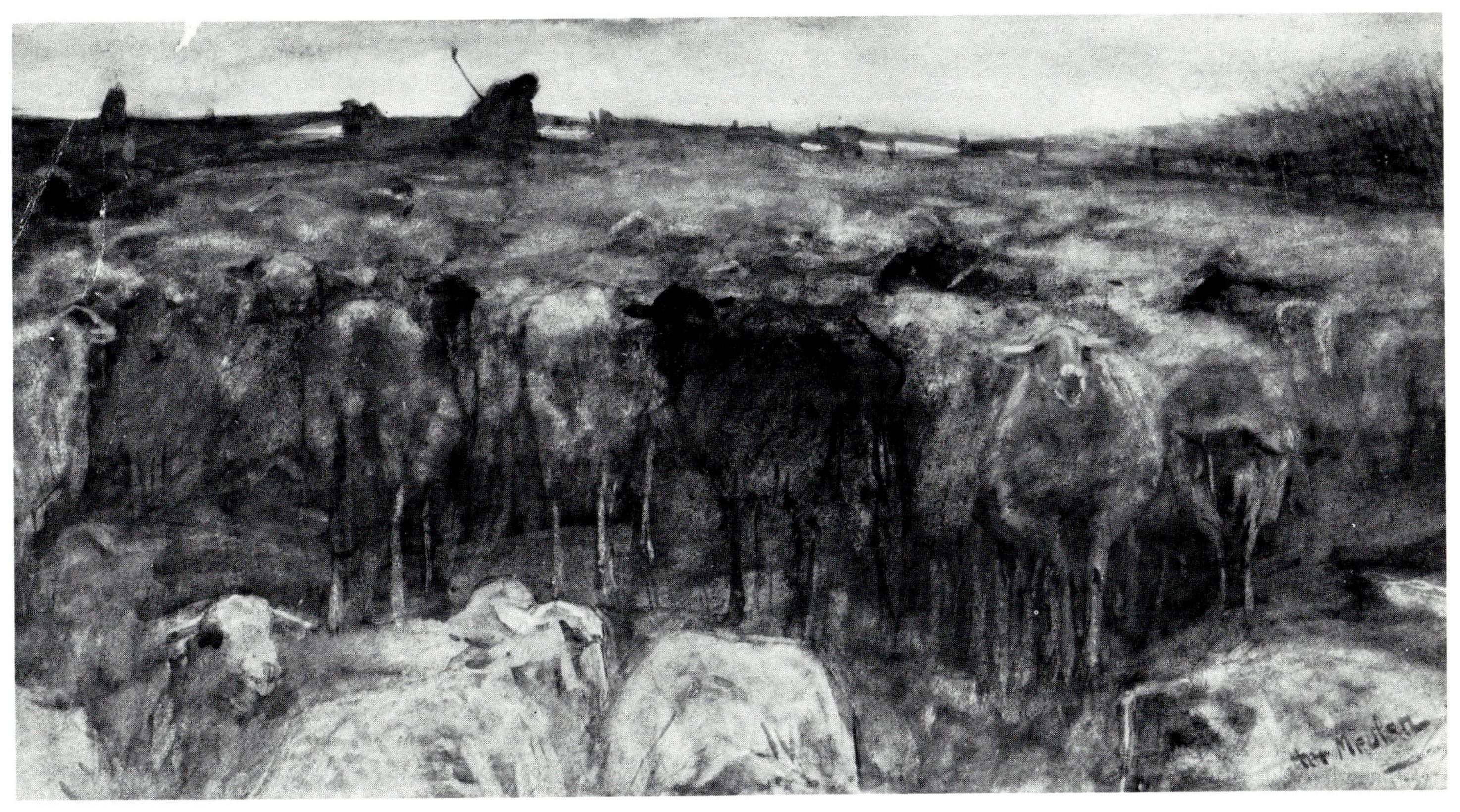

Francois Pieter ter Meulen (1843-1927) *shows himself a gifted follower of Mauve in this watercolour of a sheepfold. (14¼ x 27½ins.)* Photograph courtesy of the Mesdag Museum, the Hague.

their historical episodes; at a time when they threw a huge wave in the foreground in the shade the better to enhance the effect of light towards the horizon; at a time when they dramatized the sky and the waves in accordance with the horrors of the shipwreck depicted, Hendrik Willem Mesdag came, with his direct, realistic point of view, to surprise the world with the fact that the unbiased painting of the sea, straight from nature, was not only possible, but even so desirable that the aspects of the North Sea coast were now for the first time, in the nineteenth century, represented as they appeared daily before our eyes.

It does not often happen that one who has sat on a high stool in his father's office until his thirty-fifth year ends by becoming a painter, even though he may have sketched and painted in his spare moments. The greatest painters tried to dissuade Mesdag, who was born in 1831, from his plan. But a man like Mesdag is not so easily dissuaded; moreover, he was firmly supported by his wife, who herself afterwards became a deserving artist. For that matter, if all men followed the wise counsels lavished upon them in their youth, there would never have been a great man in the world. In any case, Mesdag, with his wife, went to Brussels in 1866. He there found his friend and kinsman Alma Tadema and also the Dutch landscape-painter Roelofs.

In the summer of 1868, Mesdag visited Norderney, not so much for the purpose of painting, as for relaxation and health. This visit was to be for him what the stay at Zandvoort was for Israëls. He brought back with him a series of studies so fresh and original that they decided his career for good and all. From an industrious pupil he had become an original painter. In the same year, he settled at the Hague, so as to be near Scheveningen, and, in 1870, he received the gold medal in Paris for a sea-piece. The fact that the French painters were readier than the Dutch to admit Mesdag's talent is doubtless due to this, that his simple, natural, artless realism seemed to them refreshing after their own affected academicism and the profundity of the Barbizon men, whom the Parisians had never understood.

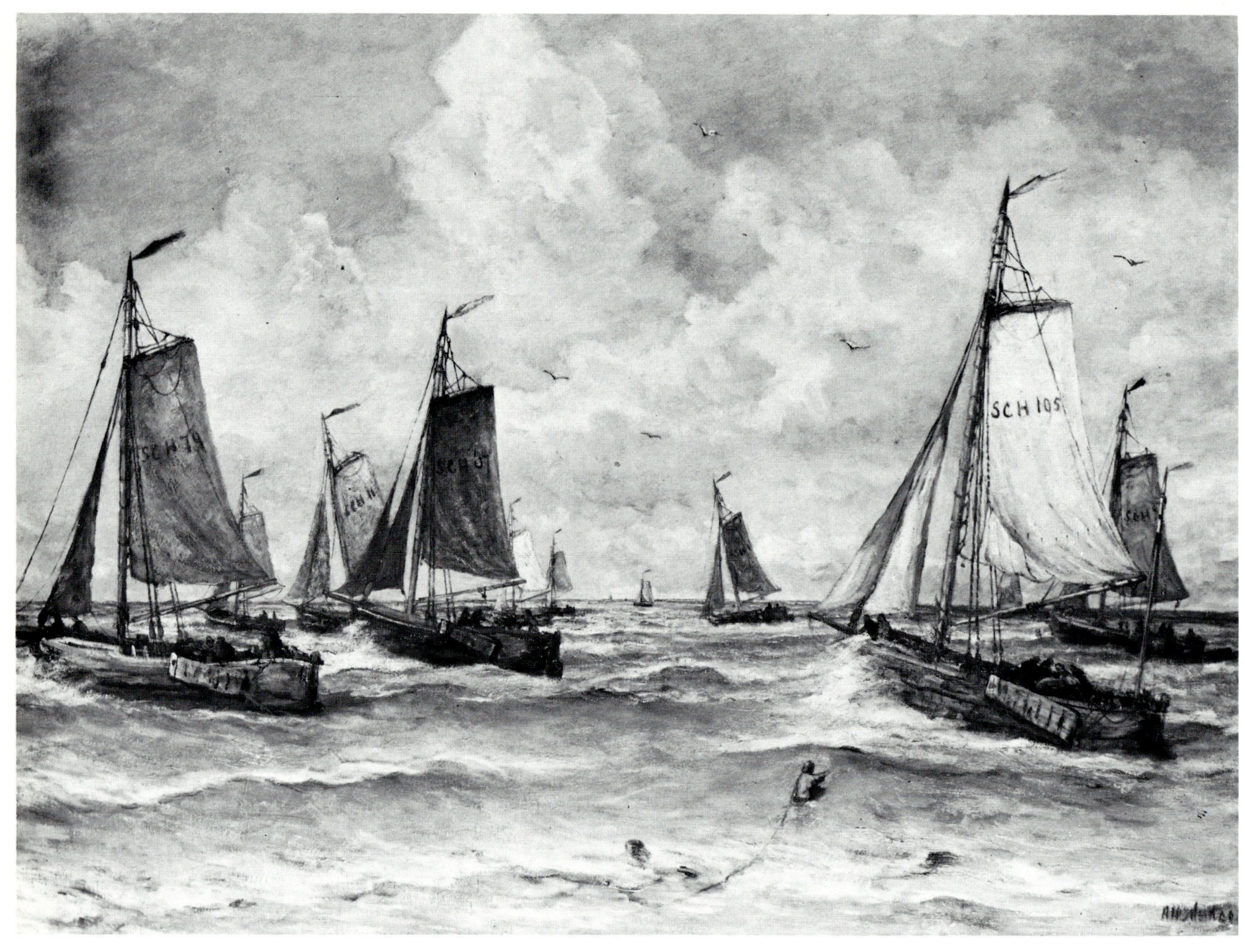

Above and right: **Hendrik Willem Mesdag (1831-1915)** *did not take seriously to painting until 1866. A visit to the sea at Norderney for his health changed his life and led to his seascapes painted with a simple realism new to Dutch art. In both these paintings he shows sailing boats outside Scheveningen on a tossing sea. (120 x 167cms., and 109½ x 79cms.)* Photographs courtesy of Mak van Waay, Amsterdam.

There is something so open in his work, so much frankness in his subjects and their treatment, such an utter absence of introspectiveness, that one could almost describe his pictures as decorative, although this is not wholly the case, for the painter loves above all things the broad whiteness of the open air and, if he does not always find unity in the light, it is there in the treatment, so that Mesdag's least scrawl possesses the allure which distinguishes his completed paintings wherever exhibited. This painter, ill-suited to spend his life on an office-stool, was not the one to sit patiently bending over the easel, plunged in the secrets of his craft; and we may here seek the reason why he did not achieve fame in the land of pure painting so early as in France.

Mesdag may be described as the transition between landscape-painters like the Marises and Hendrik Johannes Weissenbruch. In neither of the two artists is colour the impelling force of his art: form, rather, predominates. The white clouds in Weissenbruch's pictures are connected with the landscape through their outline; they counterbalance the mills, the houses and trees by their form rather than that they exist as the result of a logical connection of the light falling on the earth, as in the more symphonic compositions of Jacob Maris.

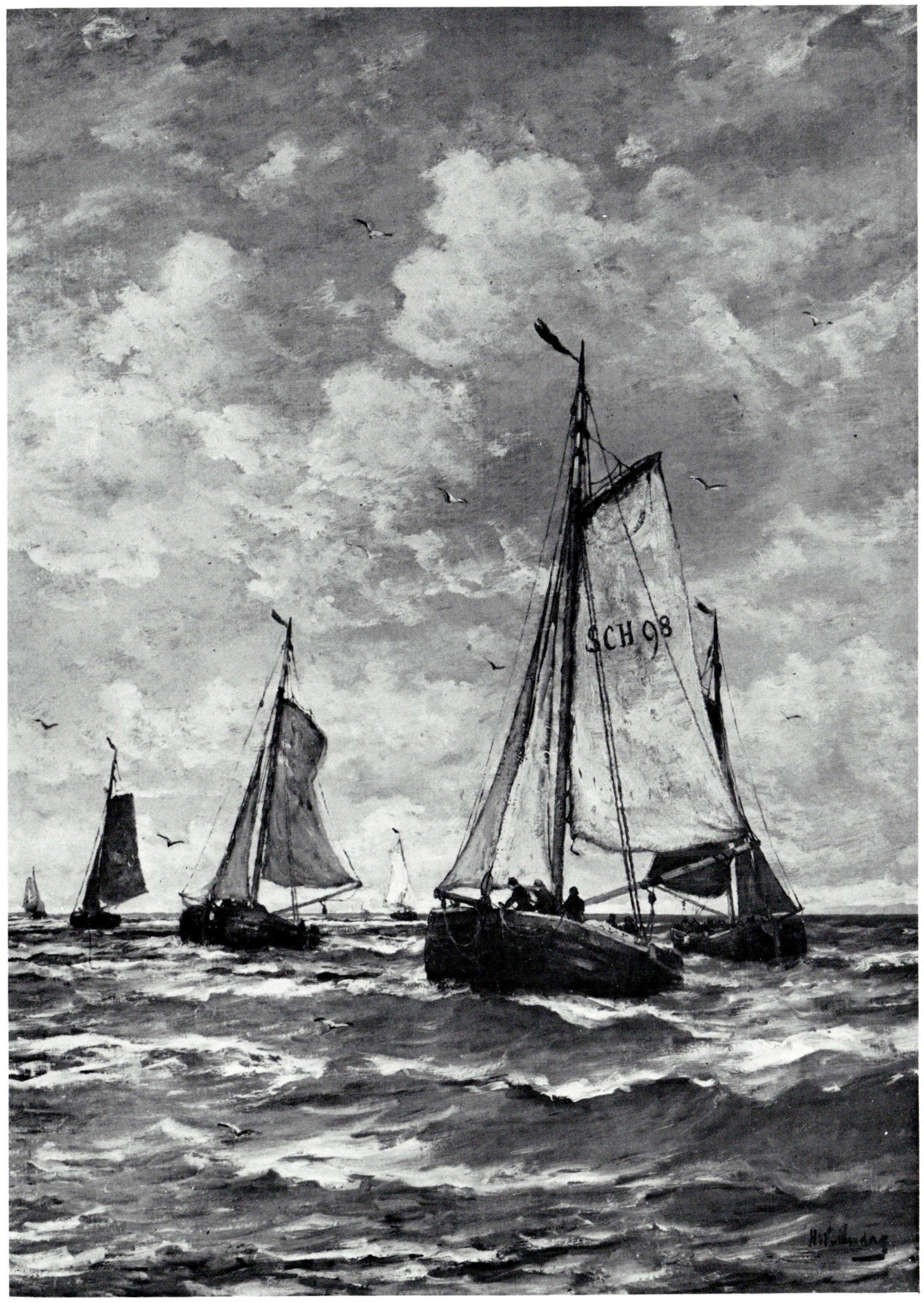
SCH 98

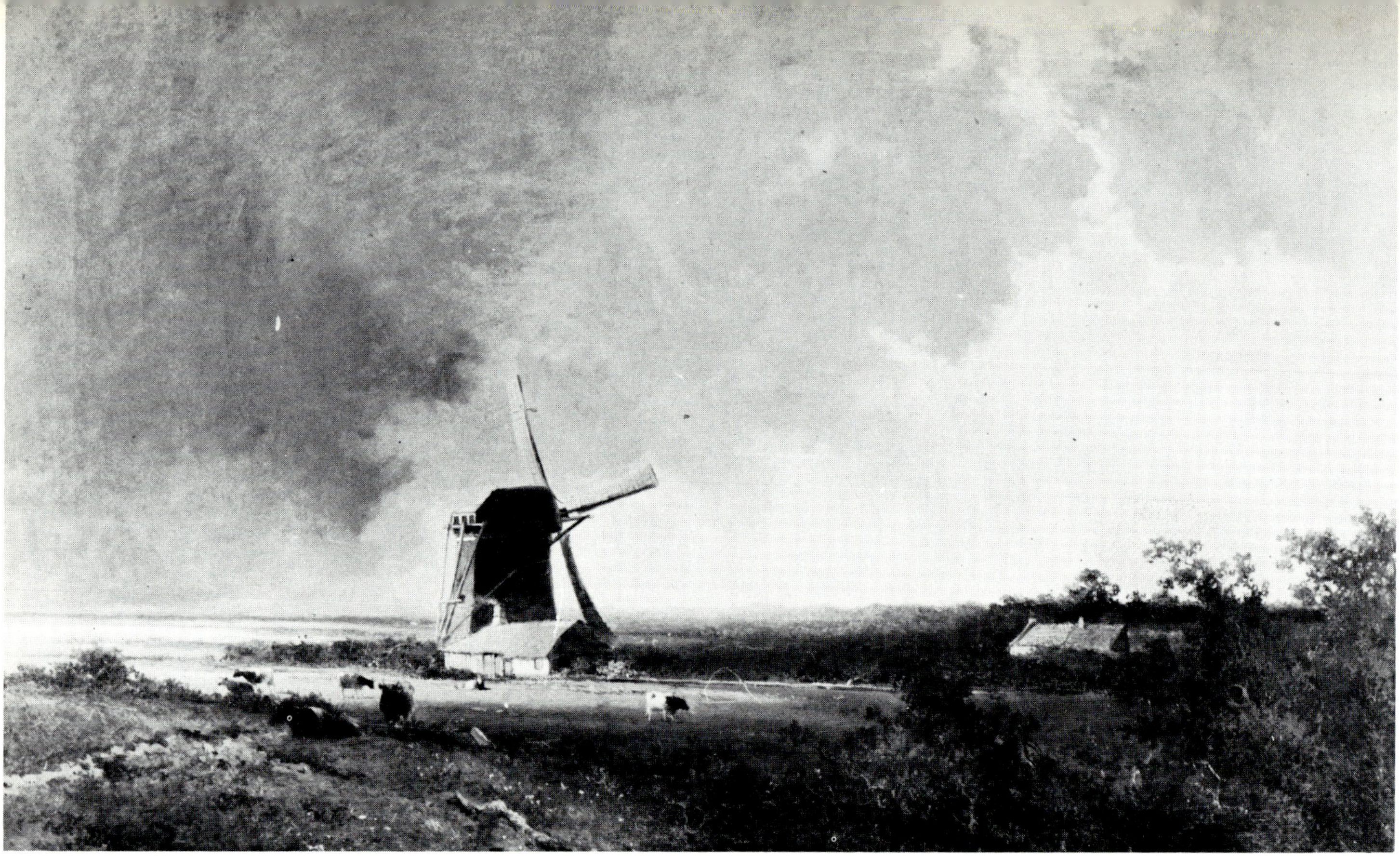

Above: **Hendrik Johannes Weissenbruch** (1824-1903), *not to be confused with his cousin Johannes, or Jan Weissenbruch, was artistically a bridge between traditional landscape painting and the Hague. This view near the Hague with an old windmill has an early feel. (65 x 100cms)* Photograph courtesy of Mak van Waay, Amsterdam.

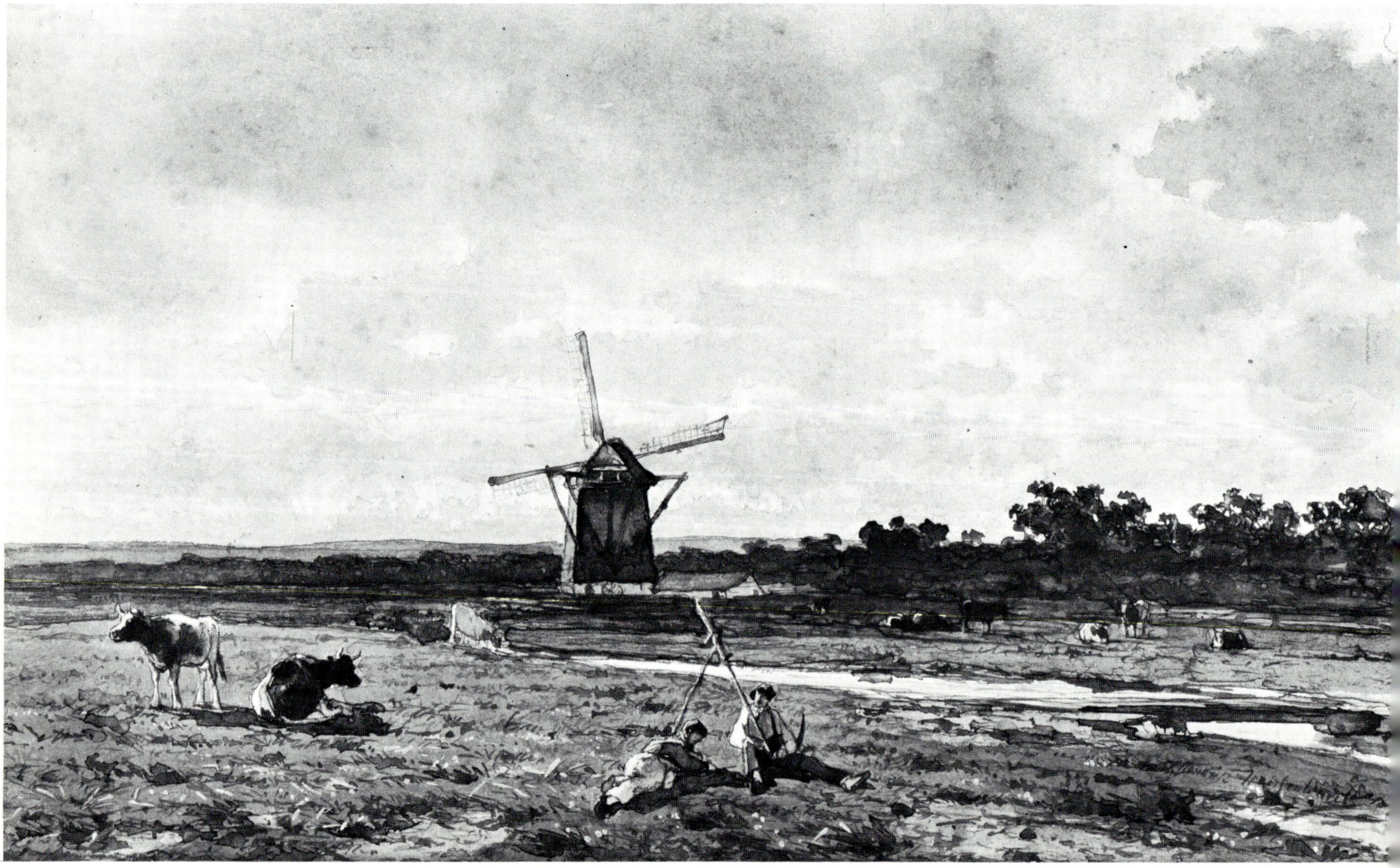

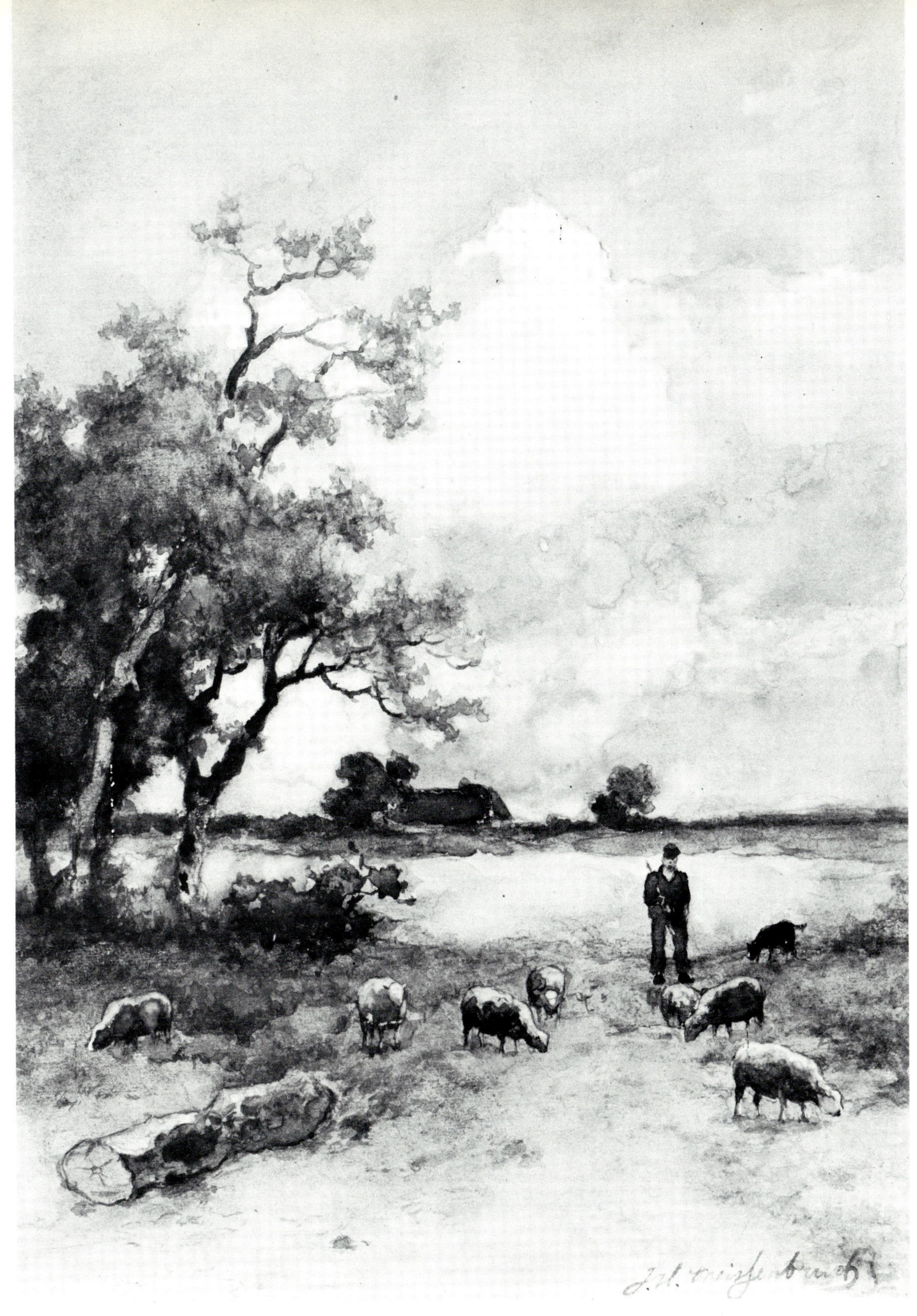

Above and left: In these two watercolours **Weissenbruch** *shows his debt to the Maris brothers in his simple unromanticised treatment. Marius comments that his watercolours "are about the finest in modern Dutch art". (8¼ x 14ins., and 15 and 10½ins.)* Photographs courtesy of Williams & Son.

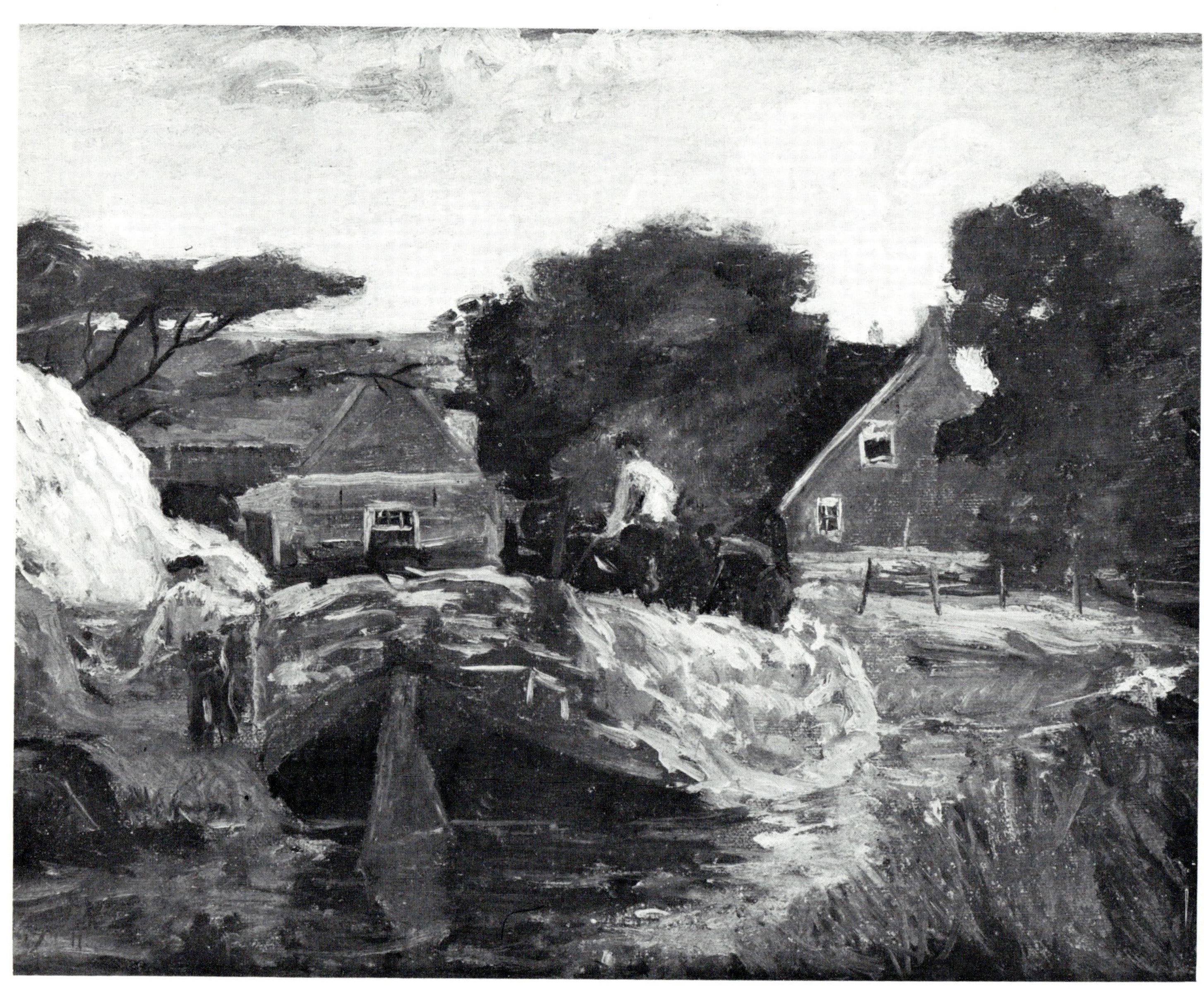

A farmyard scene by the Dutch-Frenchman **Victor Bauffe (1849-1921)**. Photograph courtesy of Mak van Waay, Amsterdam.

What matter if Weissenbruch, nicknamed the merry Weis, was not the man to sink into his own moods? All roads lead to Rome! He belonged to the real stamp of those landscape-painters who, starting betimes, receive quick impressions, ready subjects, nimbly-seized moments of the day. He was a passionate fisherman and, perhaps more than any other, caught the atmospheric influences on the marshy lands, the construction of the broad pools and waterways and dykes and polders, while his water-colour sketches are about the finest in modern Dutch art.

This artist did not receive the public recognition due to him until later in life. It is true that he had never to complain of lack of appreciation by the artists. And then his early pictures were so different: works with fine artistic qualities, better works perhaps than his later, somewhat too facile productions. Still, like most of the painters of his generation, Weissenbruch delivered his purest work after 1870. He was born at the Hague in 1824 and died in 1903. The Dutch Frenchman, Victor Bauffe, and De Bock were both pupils of his.

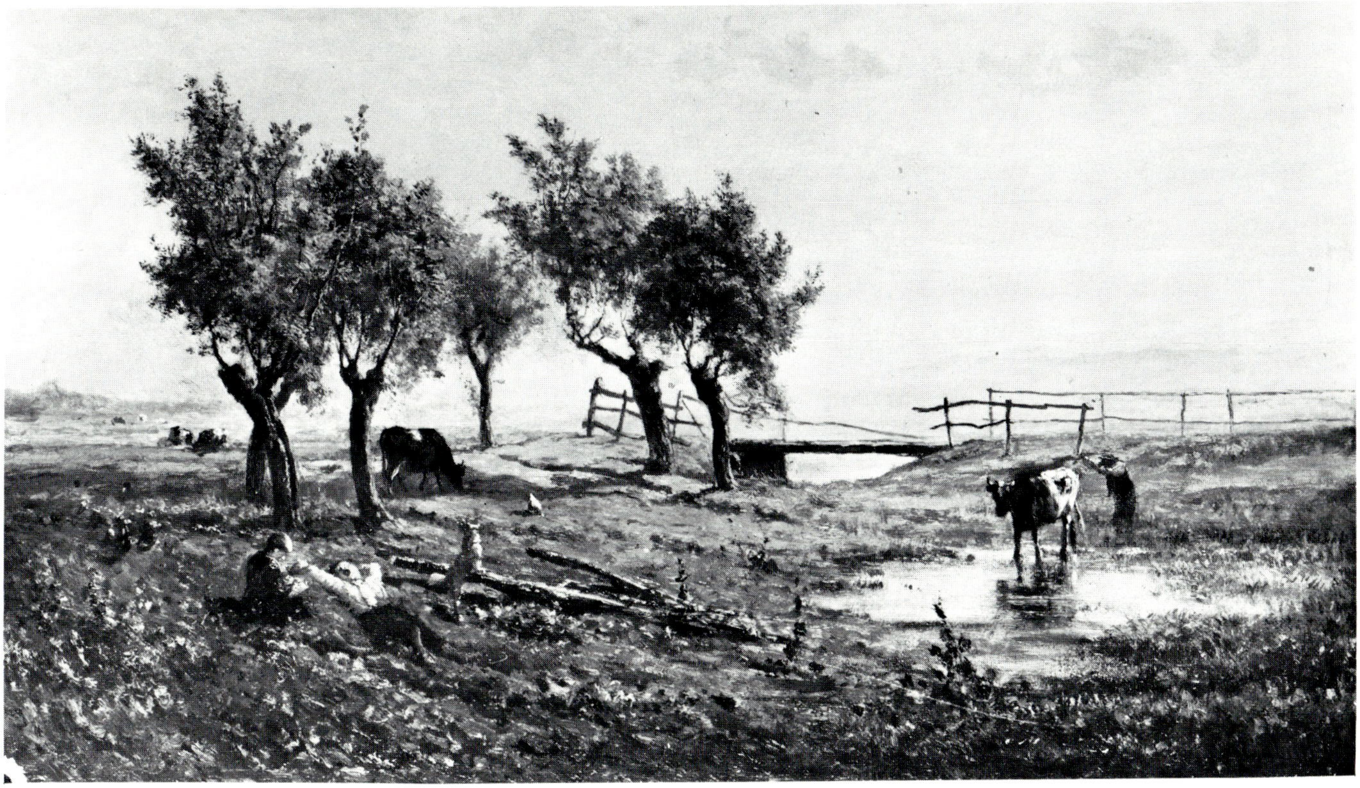

Above: **Paul Jozeph Constantin Gabriël (1828-1903)** *studied with B.C. Koekkoek at Cleves in addition to attending the Amsterdam Academy. He rejected the romantic tradition for a quiet simplicity as in this painting with its relaxed glimpse of willows, an old bridge, peasants and their cows. (19½ x 12ins.)* Photograph courtesy of Williams & Son.

Below: In this painting of "Peat Gatherers" **Gabriël** *has taken his love of simplicity even further, concentrating on the firm modelling of his boat, figures and distant windmill. (8 x 14ins.)* Photograph courtesy of M. Newman Ltd.

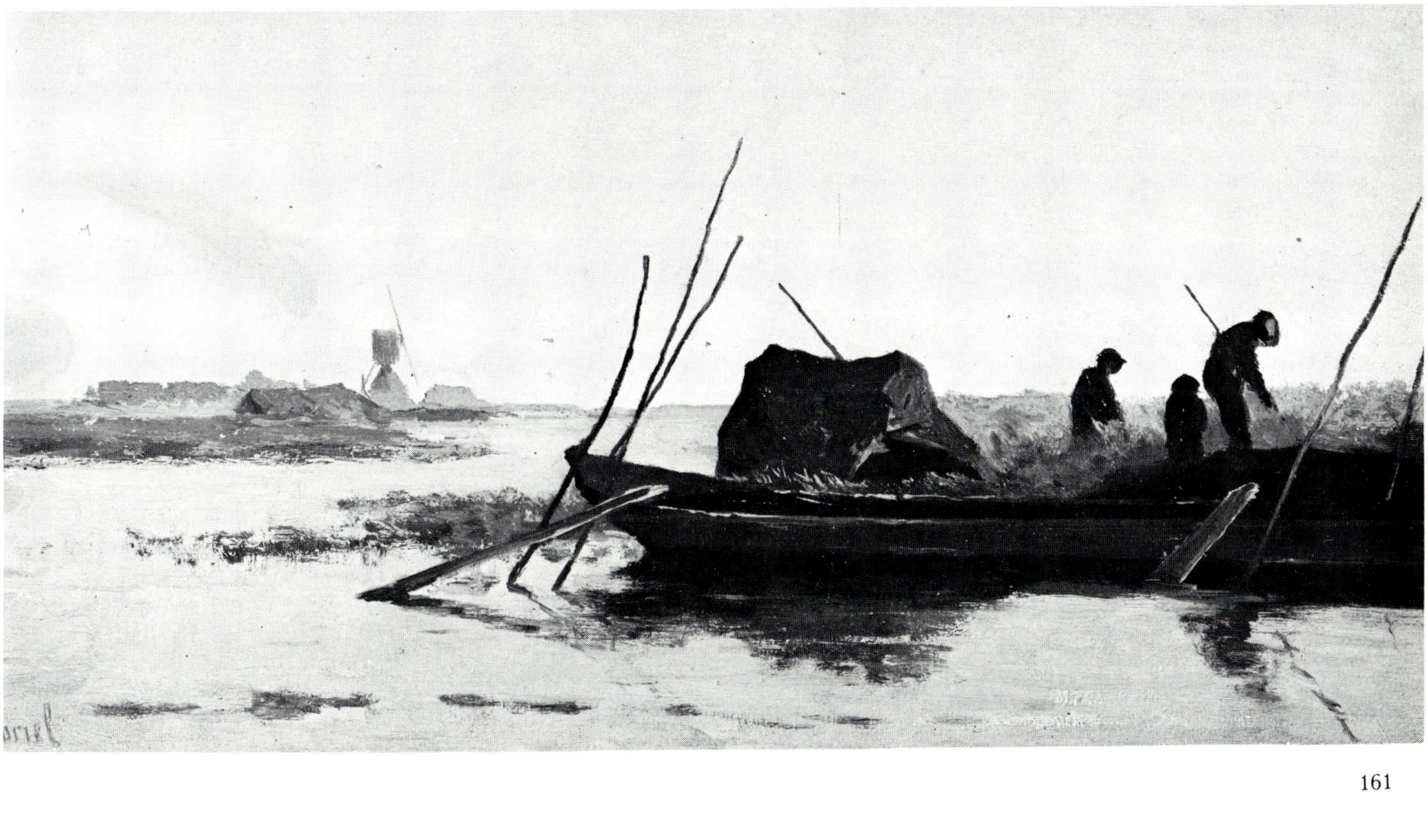

Although Paul Jozeph Constantin Gabriël was also impressed by the low clouds hanging over flat polders, this delicate painter never belonged to the real impressionists in manner and one might more justly describe as natural problems, scientifically solved, his polders, his canals with windmills, his expanses of water with eel-traps, with the light reflected in the water or influencing the land. For they are rendered with so much certainty, so much calmness and precision that they place the spectator in the presence of a fact that admits of no discussion. Speaking of these somewhat concrete landscapes, Gabriël used to say that he preferred subjects that did not contain much in themselves. And no simpler subjects could well be imagined: great splashes of water, which he selected in the bogs around Giethoorn, in which the only accident is a punt, an eel-trap or a duck-fence; canals cutting straight and square through the fields, with the tall windmill at the end; pools with a few willows; huts by the water-side. And all painted with the simplest means, clearly and thinly, with finely-chiselled outlines. Gabriël carried his painting so completely in his head that the setting down of it on canvas seemed to cost him no trouble and scarce a *repentir.* To make sure of his tone, he used to place the picture upside-down or sideways on his easel. He was one of the few Dutch painters whose delicate poetry was understood in Paris. Geffroy, writing of the Dutch exhibitors, rarely mentions any save Israël and Gabriël.

Gabriël was born in Amsterdam in 1828. He received his first tuition at the Amsterdam Academy and afterwards went to the landscape school set up by B.C. Koekkoek at Cleves. He lived for some time in Brussels and settled at the Hague in 1884, when the Hague school was at the height of its fame. He died in 1903. Gabriël's chief pupil is W.B. Tholen, who worked in his studio in Brussels.

Chapter VIII

Intermezzo

An attempt has been made in this volume to group the nineteenth-century painters. The Hague masters, in particular, have been collected under the heading of the Hague school, which, however, can hardly be made to include such painters as Jongkind, the Oyens brothers or Alma Tadema. And yet, even as Bisschop is essentially related to Tadema and, properly speaking has very little in common with the Hague school, so Jongkind is essentially related to this particular circle.

If we could lay side by side a beach-scene by Bosboom, one by Weissenbruch in the Mesdag Museum and one by Jongkind in the Hoogendijk collection, water-colours all three, we should be struck by the same sensitive sureness of construction, the same manner of design, the same treatment in each case. It is true that Bosboom and Weissenbruch were pupils of B.J. van Hove and that Weissenbruch and Jongkind were also pupils of Schelfhout.

Jongkind's art, like Bosboom's, was rooted in Schelfhout, the master whom he always held so high; and, like Bosboom again, Jongkind, with his water-colours, came near to the most modern feeling: to Monet, Pissarro and Sisley. Edmond de Goncourt constantly praises him; and, not long ago, the writer heard a modern Parisian artist tell how, at Durand-Ruel's, where a Jongkind was hanging among a number of Monets, Sisleys, Seurats and Maufras, he had said to Pissarro that all these things seemed feeble beside Jongkind, whereupon Pissarro replied:

"Yes, if he had not existed, none of us would have been here."

Despite his modernity, he was and remained a genuine Hollander. Year after year, he left Paris for the pools between Rotterdam and Dordrecht. He sketched his water-colours direct from nature and painted his pictures from them. When in 1891, the year of his death, his works were exhibited before the auction at the Hôtel Drouot, all Paris stood amazed not at the paintings, which were known to every connoisseur, but at the exquisite, fresh, spontaneous water-colour sketches.

Gustave Geffroy called him the inventor of the atmospheric shades, but, at the same time, admired in him the careful composition, the fine division into back- and foreground peculiar to the old Dutchmen. Despite the appreciation which he met with, things did not go well with him. He appears to have been content to earn his 3,000 francs a year, whereas his *Maas at Rotterdam* was sold, in 1892, for 28,000 francs and his *Canal at Brussels* for 17,000 francs, not to speak of the comparatively even higher prices fetched by his water-colours.

Johan Bartholt Jongkind was born in 1819 at Latdrop, near Ootmarsum, and died in 1891 at Côte-Saint-André, mourned by his Parisian colleagues for both personal and artistic reasons. Holland must admit that she did but little for this pure national painter. Boymans' Museum bought a *Moonlight Scene* of his and the dealers occasionally exhibit one of his precious little paintings or some of those water-colour drawings which roused so much admiration at the Hôtel Drouot after his death and won for him that unstinted recognition for which he yearned when living.

There is another painter, or rather there are two others who worked all their lives in a neighbouring country as real descendants of the seventeenth century, robust and delicate, artists and observers, painters of still-life and painters of manners, combining the palette of a Brouwer with a structure of line not unlike that of the classic Dégas, while either their own nature or their long residence in Brussels caused them to couple the copiousness of a Jordaens with Adriaan Brouwer's greater delicacy. The work of these two

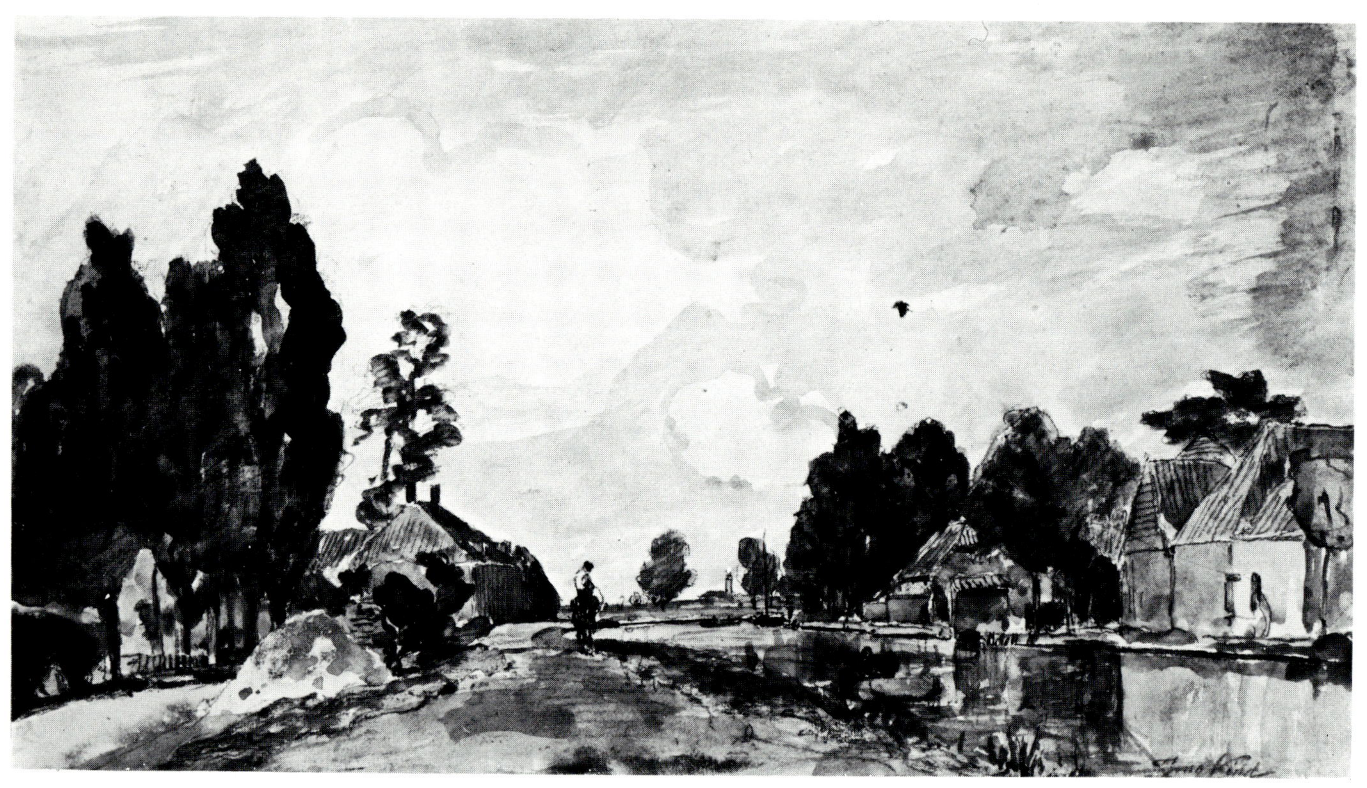

Above and right: **Johan Bartholt Jongkind (1819-1891)** *was more honoured in France than in Holland, a friend and inspiration to the Impressionists. He sketched his watercolours straight from nature and painted his pictures from them. The relationship between his watercolour and oil technique is illustrated by these two well watered landscapes. The watercolour above, is a Dutch scene (9 x 16ins.), the oil was painted at Bas Meudon.* Photographs courtesy of Sotheby & Co.

brothers, David and Pieter Oyens, has, in point of fact, little in common with our modern Dutch art; at any rate, their work has none of the sentiment or emotion displayed by this art, though they had a very correct sense of what we call "values". They selected the subjects of their pictures for the most part in their studio, where the brothers sat to each other by turns, sometimes with a third or fourth figure added. One of them is turning over a portfolio, or painting, or peering through his eye-lashes at the model, or arranging his palette while the model is getting ready to pose. They supplemented this with new attitudes or curious incidents, observed in a café, which they studied together, one of them the next day adopting the pose with a full sense of the situation. In this way, that witty little piece came into being in which a broad-backed man is holding an open newspaper before him, the paper forming a diagonal across the reader's outspread arms, and also *The Beer-drinkers,* which is so very old-Dutch – just a figure at a little table – and at the same time so modern, taken as it is from life. Sometimes we see more complicated little scenes, such as *Le Farceur,* who is amusing a couple of servant-girls.

The difference between David and Pieter is considerable. Pieter was the robuster of the two in his work, more *flamand* perhaps, whereas David's talent was more supple and pliant, his workmanship more delicate, his wit more abundant. Pieter was the sturdy worker who, producing with greater difficulty, brought forth good and solid work; David was the one who gave life to things.

These two real painters were born in 1842 (they were twins) of an important Amsterdam commercial family and it is surprising to see how little their birth hampered them and what thorough painters they were, reading little (except Dickens, whom they read from cover to cover): painters, no more and no less. They received their education in Brussels under Portails and in Amsterdam under P.F. Greive. Pieter died

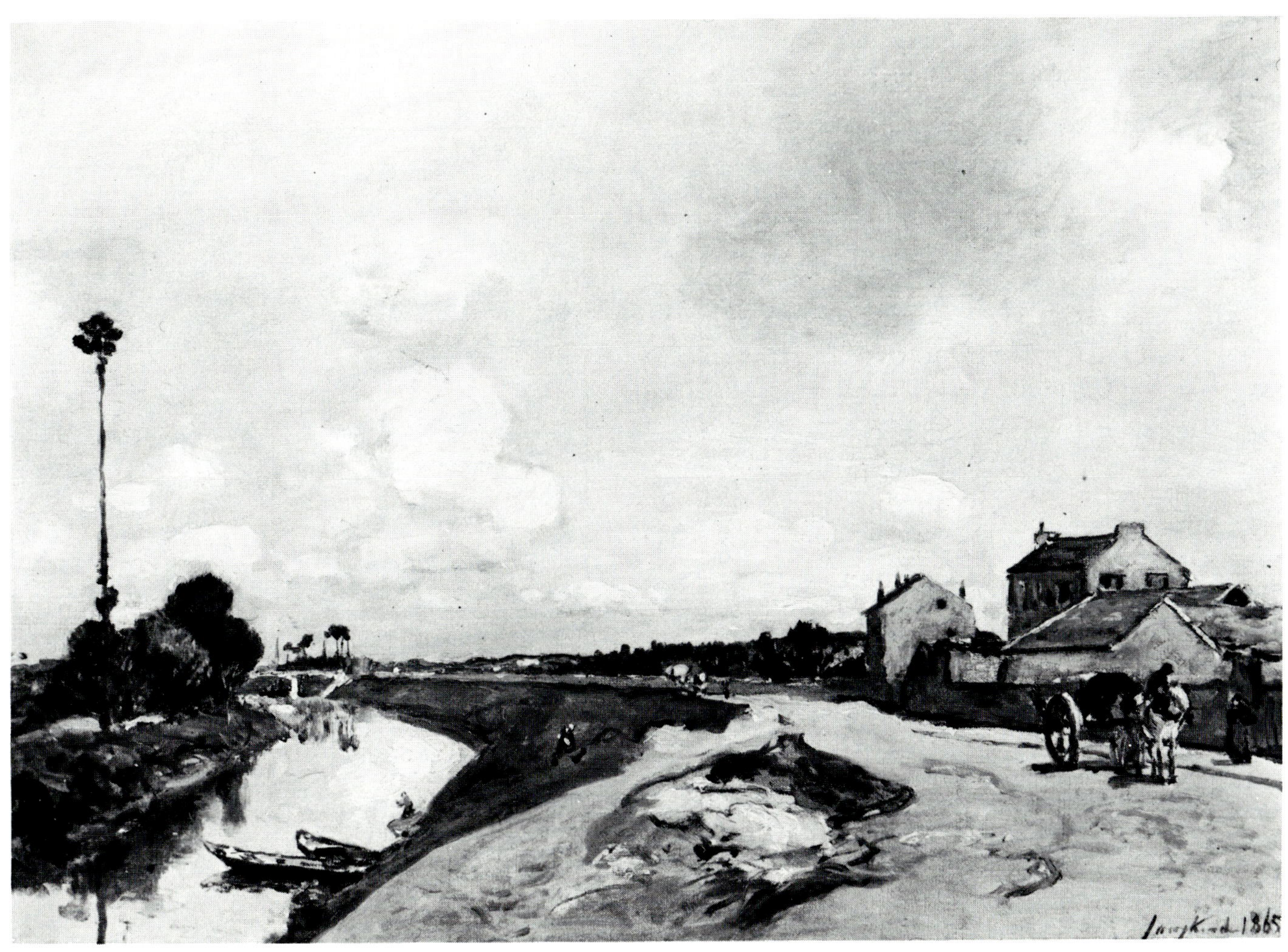

in 1894 and David eight years later.

Very different from the quiet life of these two artists is that of the Parisian Dutchman, Frédéric Henri Kaemmerer, who, born at the Hague in 1839, gradually freed himself from the culture of his native land and cleverly conquered a place of his own in the French art of the *Salon.* He excels in the reproduction of Directoire costume and has made a name by his *Wedding* and his *Baptism under the Directoire.* The photogravures of these paintings have been favourites even in Holland and the former has been reproduced as a living picture at wedding-feasts innumerable. We are compelled to admire the cleverness of his pretty figures, with their coquettish colouring, even though that cleverness lies entirely outside the frontiers of our own art of painting. Nevertheless, Kaemmerer, who has since painted *mondain* subjects for the Paris Gobelins factory, began by painting familiar Dutch topics. He exhibited a *Wood-cutters* in 1863 and also had a few subjects in common with his friend Artz.

In mentioning the English "Sir Lawrence," I run a danger of being accused of wishing to adorn the cap of Dutch painting with a foreign feather. It is true that Laurens Alma Tadema, born at Dronrijp in 1836, in accepting naturalization, fairly turned his back on his countrymen. But the early period of this painter's career is inseparable from the Leeuwarder Bisschop, while his first years of tutelage under Leys, whose art constituted a renascence of the old Dutchmen and Flemings, added to the fact that he was the master of Mesdag, cause Tadema to figure at least in part in the history of Dutch painting.

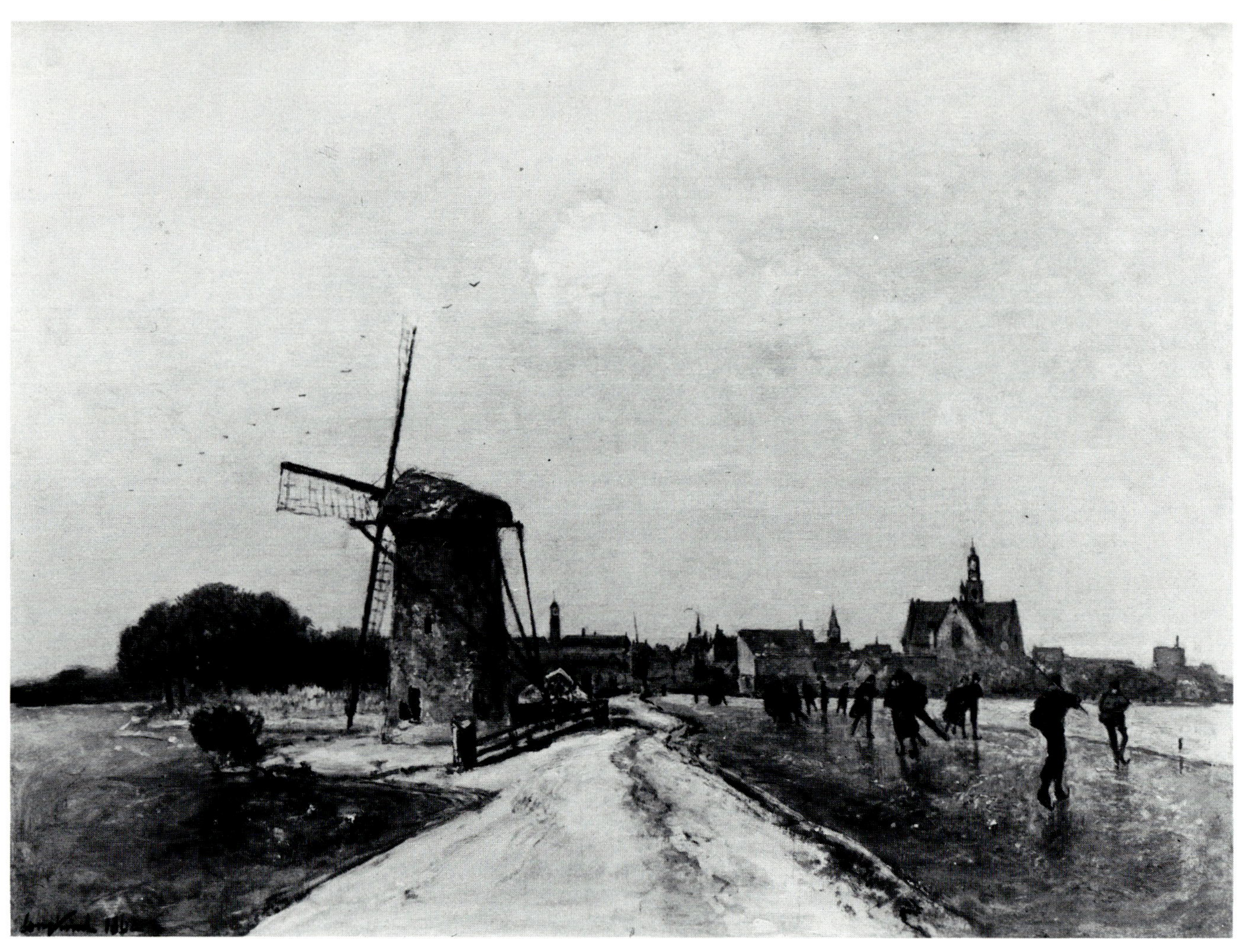

Jongkind's *"Patineurs à Maasluis" of 1862 demonstrates his debt to Schelfhout and the Dutch winter landscape tradition (16 x 21¾ins.).* Photograph courtesy of Sotheby's.

It is easy to see that Alma Tadema and Bisschop came from the same district. There are so many points of unison in their view of their art; both were wholly immersed in by-gone times, although Bisschop's Hinlopen is of very much more recent date than Tadema's Pompeii or Byzantium; while their minute rendering of antique objects with no other aim than to serve as a scene and setting for the figures makes them, however greatly they may differ from each other, stand side by side as against the Hague masters, their contemporaries. And there was reason enough for this in Friesland. When these two painters were young, many Leeuwarder women still wore their gorgeous costume, with its Eastern *cachet:* the free Frisians had not yet submitted to the shackles of Paris or London fashions. And, although, probably, as boys, they paid but little attention to this circumstance, the difference must have made all the greater impression upon them in their subsequent residence at Antwerp and the Hague. Add this fact, that Friesland contains not only a mass of Merovingian antiquities, distributed over the private houses as well the museums, but also many treasures of artistic craftmanship of the eighteenth century and earlier, so that the love of pretty things grew in these painters with their imagination and their memory. Again, the dallying with the past, the search for historical surroundings formed part of the time in which they both "arrived", although Tadema was a good deal younger than Bisschop.

Alma Tadema enjoyed the privilege not only of

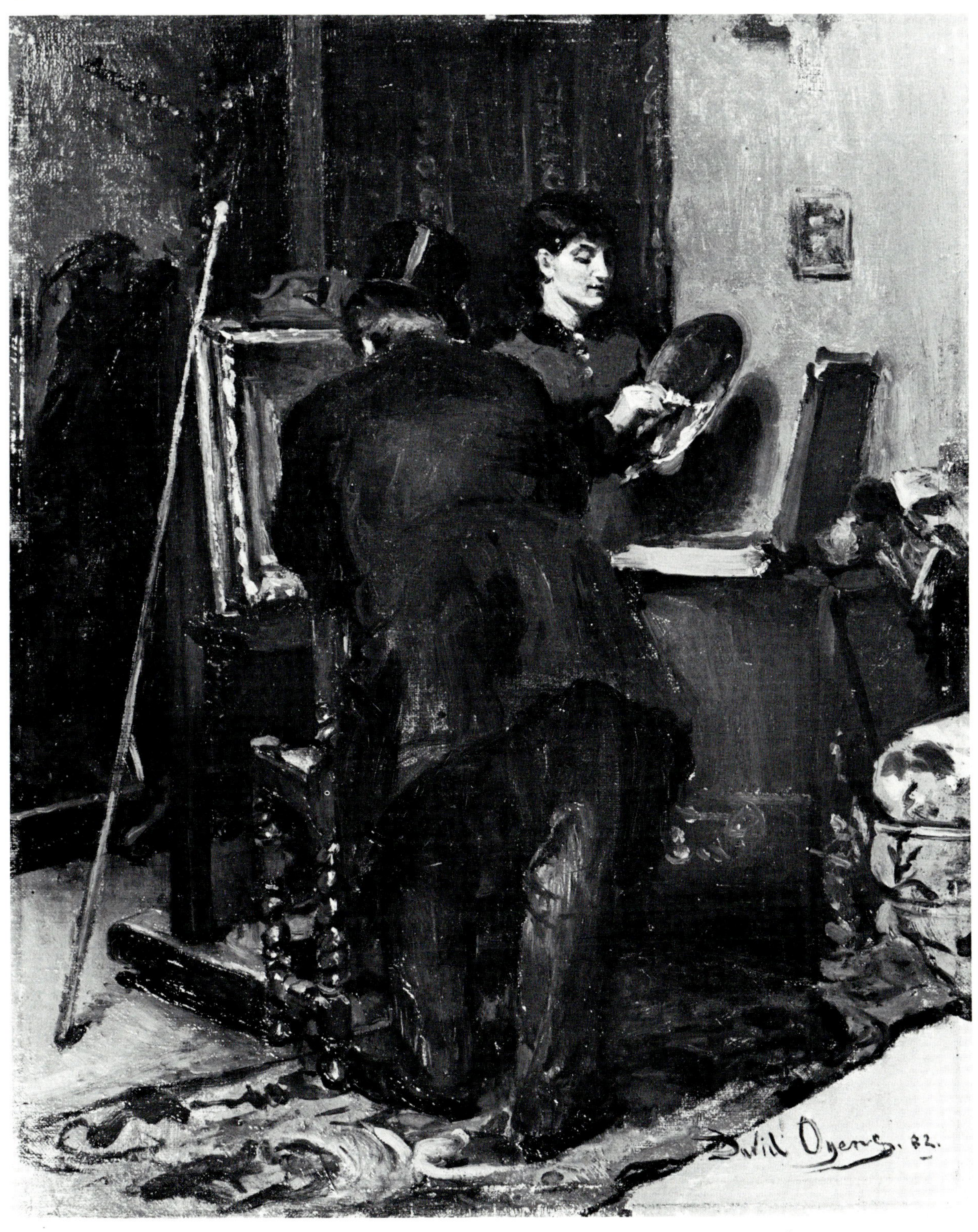

David Oyens (1842-1902) *and his twin* Pieter *painted constantly together with the result that their studio is a constantly repeated subject – each painting the other painting. Here we have David's view of the scene. His work, according to Marius, is characterized by more humour and a lighter, quicker touch than his brother. (32 x 26cms.)* Photograph courtesy of Mak van Waay, Amsterdam.

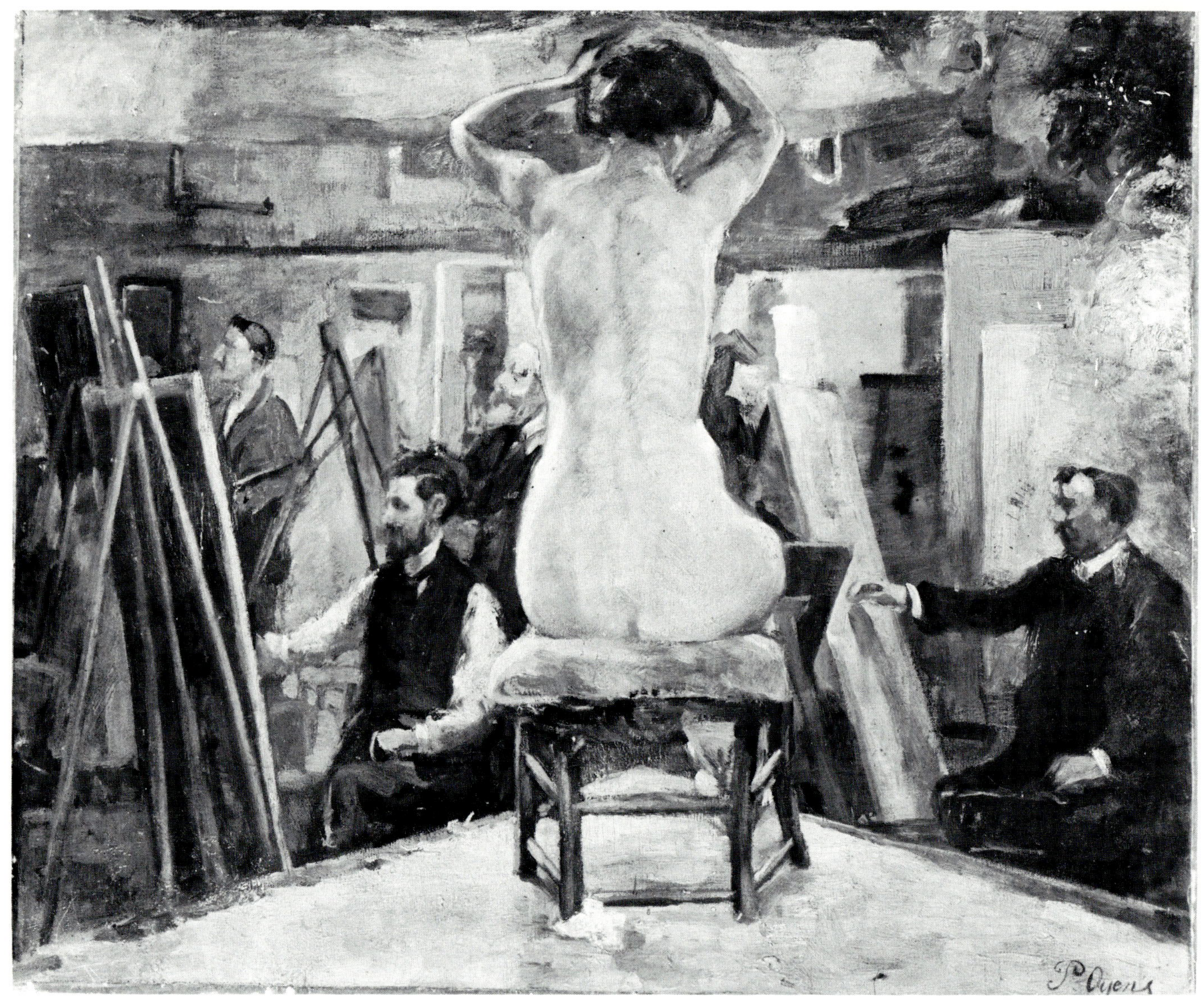

Pieter Oyens (1842-1894) *and his brother* **David** *constantly painted each other in their own studio. Here is a fine example of the studio theme by Pieter.* Photograph courtesy of Phillips, auctioneers.

having Leys for a master, but of assisting him, in 1859, with his frescoes for the Antwerp Town-hall, which at once introduced him to monumental painting. It is a pity that Tadema did not keep more to this trend, even as, from a Dutch point of view, it is to be regretted that he allowed himself to be diverted from his first artistic ideas, possibly by German influences.

I do not propose to trace the career of this well-known painter, who was a Frisian by birth, a Belgian by training, an archeologist by inclination; who, it is true, had Mesdag for a pupil, but finds his followers in London; and who has exercised no influence upon modern Dutch art and has remained uninfluenced by it. Not his manner of reproducing textures, nor his composition (and herein lies his chief force), nor his workmanship, nor his colouring, nor even his modelling or drawing is Dutch or ever has been Dutch. His art has always been decorative, even as our seventeenth-century art and that of the nineteenth-century Hague painters are, in their essence, concentrated. He has never been anything of a tonalist, not even in the more pictorial sketch of *Willem van Saeftinghen,* which,

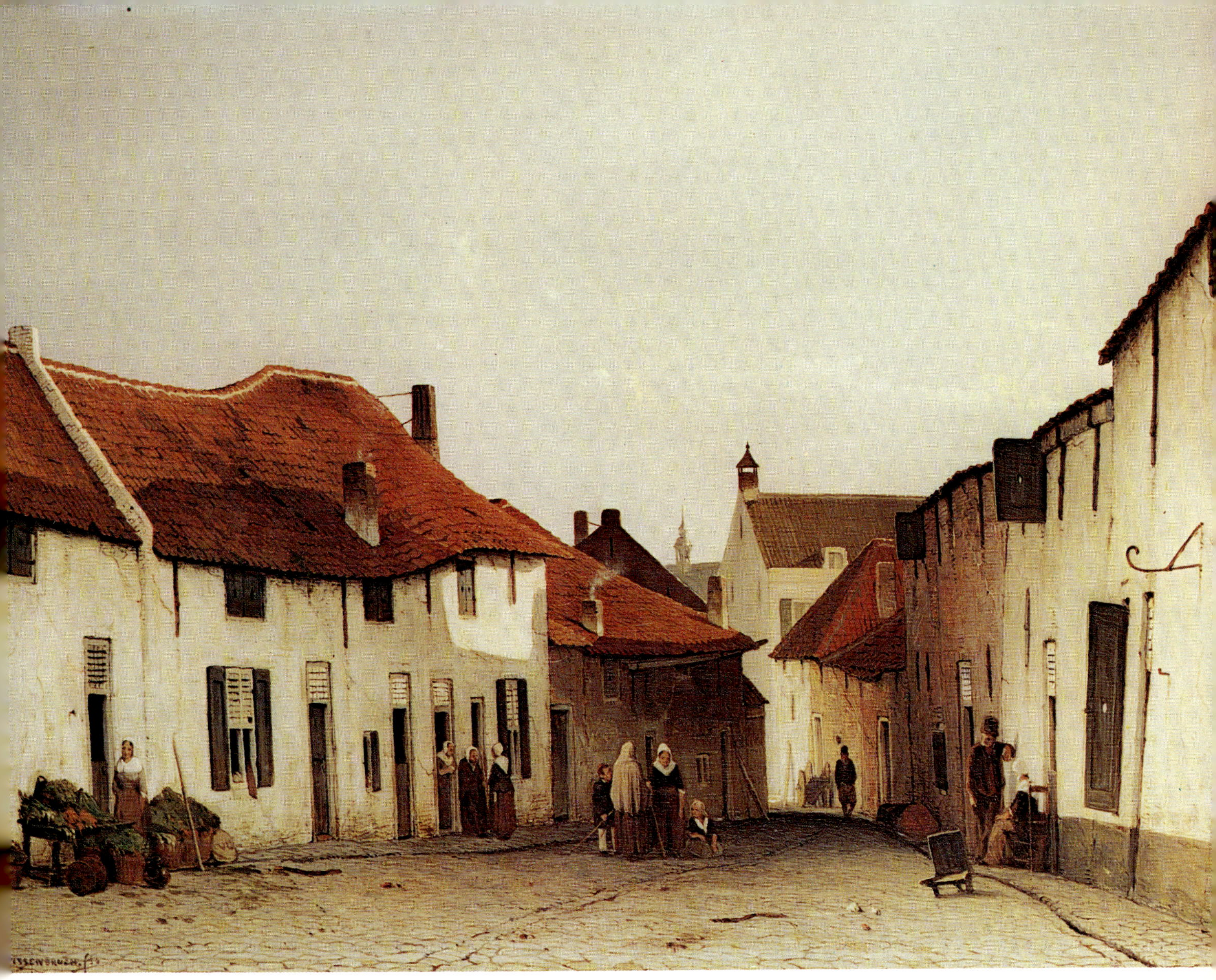

Johannes (Jan) Weissenbruch (1822-1880). *"Street scene."* Photograph courtesy of Mak van Waay, Amsterdam.

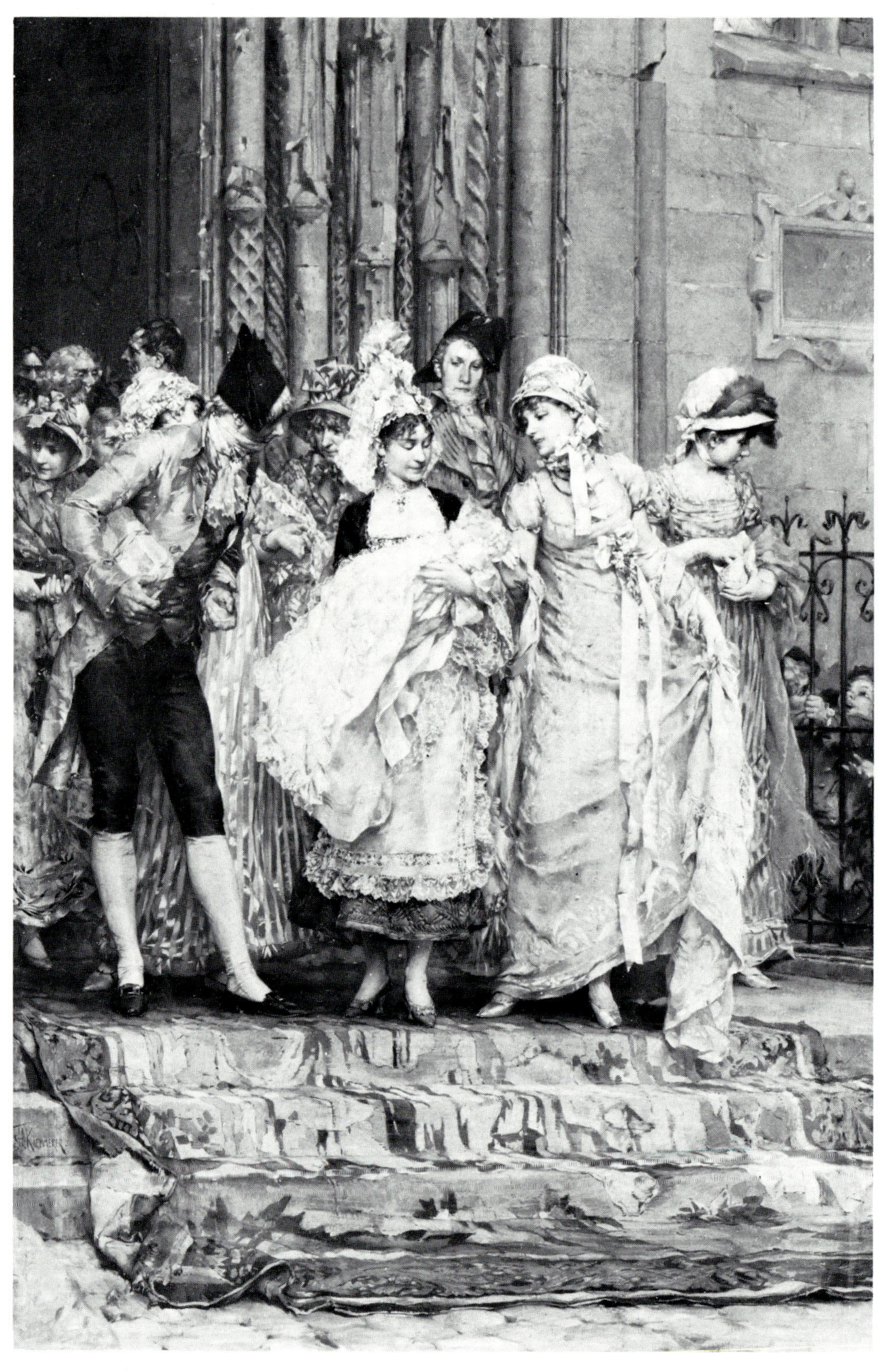

Frédéric Henri Kaemmerer (1839-1902), *while receiving his early training in Holland, settled in Paris and worked there for most of his life. His sprightly little scenes set in the Directoire period, such as this christening, were a success at the Salon, and greatly in demand among American collectors. (43 x 29½ins.).* Photograph courtesy of Christie, Manson & Wood.

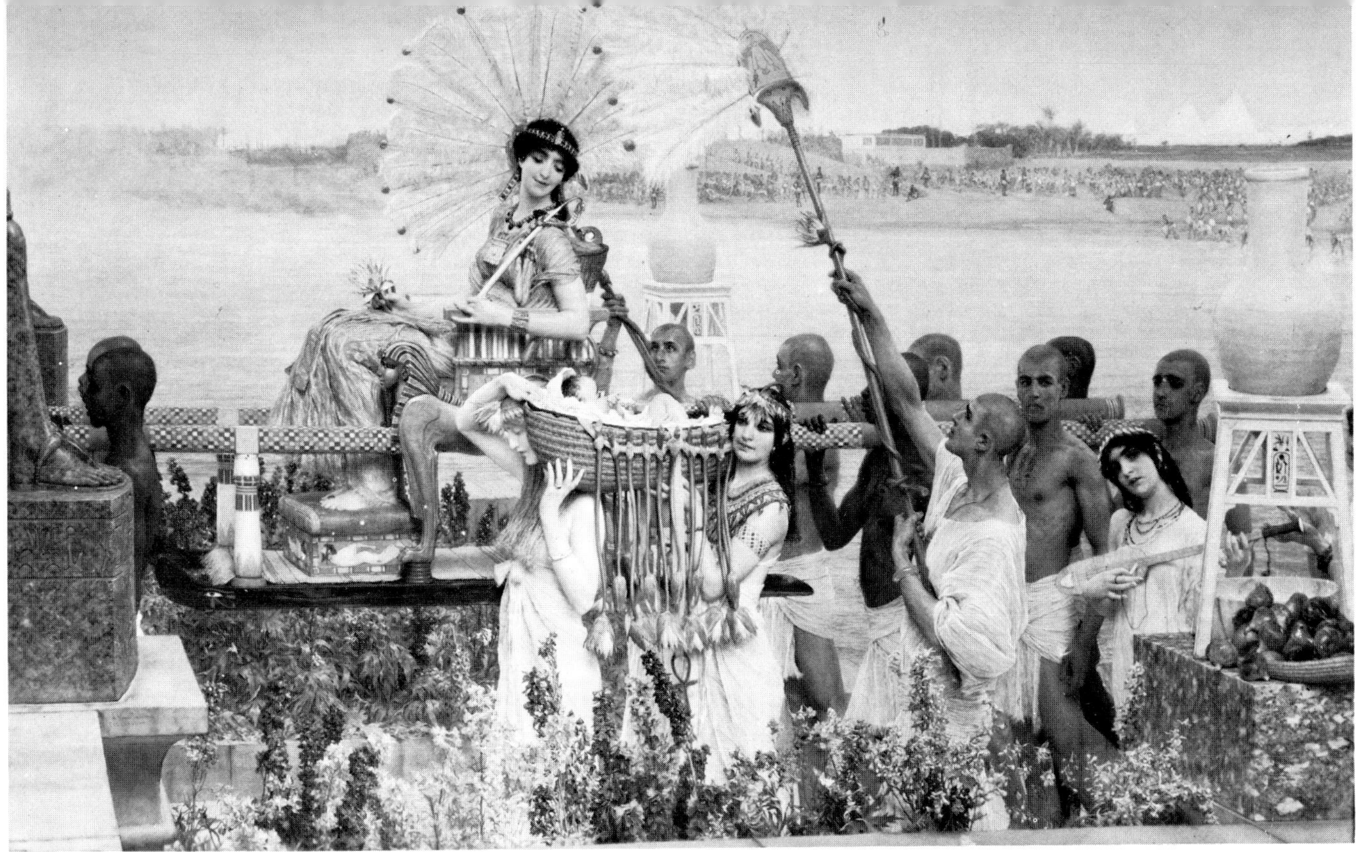

Laurens Alma Tadema (1836-1912), *or Sir Lawrence, was an anglicised Dutch artist with little or nothing in common with contemporary Dutch art. His training in Belgium under Baron Leys was the formative influence on his art, giving him that love of texture and still life detail well illustrated by this "Finding of Moses" (53 x 84ins.) His only Dutch pupil was Mesdag who adopted a style of painting at the opposite pole to his master.* Photograph courtesy of M. Newman Ltd.

after the manner of the great Leys, has something rather of the hot colouring of burnt glass. He has never envied anything in the modern Dutchmen, as, from the start, he saw colour prettily as colour and, in a cunning sequence of equivalents (see his *Prætextatus* in the Amsterdam Municipal Museum), set it down flat and smooth into a well-ordered colour-scheme, governed not so much by lines as by a monumental architecture amid whose forms the figures play their decorative parts. To imagine that Alma Tadema looked for colour only in the second place would lead to mistaken conclusions, for, although his art is not emotional, he does not belong to the literary painters and all his works, although decorative rather than purely pictorial, are "observed" from the painter's point of view. Nevertheless, superb as is the composition of his larger paintings, as in his *Vintage Festivals* and *Prætextatus;* unsurpassed as is the cleverness of his reproduction of marbles, of textile fabrics; beautiful as is the colouring of his smaller pieces, the quality in which he excels first and foremost is that in which all the figure-painters of all time have every excelled in England: the depicting of pretty Englishwomen in nicely-chosen attitudes.

Whether the great painters of the eighteenth century, in a more frivolous age, painted the charms of Lady Hamilton as a bacchante, or Rossetti imbued his English models with the passion of a Juliet or the sensual charm of a Venus Astarte, or Lord Leighton, following Ingres' example, gave them the impassivity of goddesses, or Alma Tadema, in his turn, paints Englishwomen as Pandora or Sappho or dancing at a vintage festival or reclining upon panther-skins, they remain, for all that with their fair, full faces, their phlegmatic movements, their studied attitudes, their invariable classic outlines, types of English beauty of their day. Here we have the lasting side of Alma Tadema's art. His archæological pictures may prove his originality and his sound acquaintance with bygone ages; but it is the beauty of his female types that gives them their value.

Chapter IX

The Hague School–Sequel

Albert Neuhuijs, Blommers and Artz followed the example of Israëls and infused new life into our art of *genre*-painting.

Neuhuijs belongs to the school of Israëls in his choice of subjects and to that of Jacob Maris in his colouring. He has shown himself a painter of feeling who is able to represent the calm workaday life of the people of Laren or Brabant in a natural and unforced manner: a woman tending her child, or preparing dinner, or watering flowers; an elder sister teaching a younger child to knit: all against the rich red of a cupboard, or a white wall, or a low dresser. Although his work of 1875 to 1885 possesses the solid merits of the cabinet-painters and will undoubtedly stand the test of time, he altered his methods afterwards to this extent, that he now paints in the houses themselves that form the back-ground of his subjects, thus giving a more spontaneous effect, although he misses the precious side of his earlier pieces. The studio gives him no ideas and so he goes off with his big canvases to those Laren interiors where, as he says, "nature herself places the colours in his hands and the movements and attitudes of the figures are there, in their natural environment." And, even if the picture, as such, suffers occasionally through the defective lighting of his work, we gain the natural little child-figures upon which, in the ripe tone of the whole picture, the sunny light falls that gilds a *profil perdu,* a downy neck, a head of yellow hair.

Albert Neuhuijs was born at Utrecht in 1844 and received his first instruction at the hands of Gijsbertus Craeyvanger, studying later at the Antwerp Academy. He began as a history-painter in the Antwerp manner and is said to have excelled at that time in the painting of satin. The portraits of women which he produced during this period were noted for their elegance. He did not begin to turn his attention to the painting of interiors until 1870 or later.

Bernardus Johannes Blommers, the youngest of this generation of painters, was born at the Hague in 1845. He is a pupil of Bisschop and of the Hague Academy, but he formed himself and his work has nothing in common with that of his master, nothing of Israëls and but little of Jacob Maris, whom he admires above all others. As against the tender conception of his subjects displayed by Neuhuijs, Blommers sees his fisher-folk from the glad and robust side. There is a great contrast between his sturdy children of the sea and Israëls' frail, pensive creations. Like most painters, he began by producing powerfully-drawn small figures, like that strong picture, *Maternal Joys,* at the Municipal Museum in Amsterdam: a cabinet-piece which possesses every quality save that of atmosphere. It belongs to the time when our painters felt more strongly bound to the old masters and to their model, the time when the trend towards wider harmonies, subtler analyses of colour, quicker solutions of light was still slumbering. However delicately treated and powerfully modelled, the young mother in this picture already shows that healthy side of his art which, afterwards, about 1882, found its most forcible expression in *The Fish-woman,* engaged in gutting fish, in the Hague Museum: a strong figure painted in deep red tones, against which the white of the fish lying on the red tiles in the foreground stands out as a delightful still-life, completing the warm browns and reds of this truly imposing work.

Next to or together with Hein Burgers, David Adolphe Constant Artz was undoubtedly Israëls' principal pupil. He first came into contact with Israëls at the evening-classes under Royer at the Amsterdam Academy, where he painted by day from

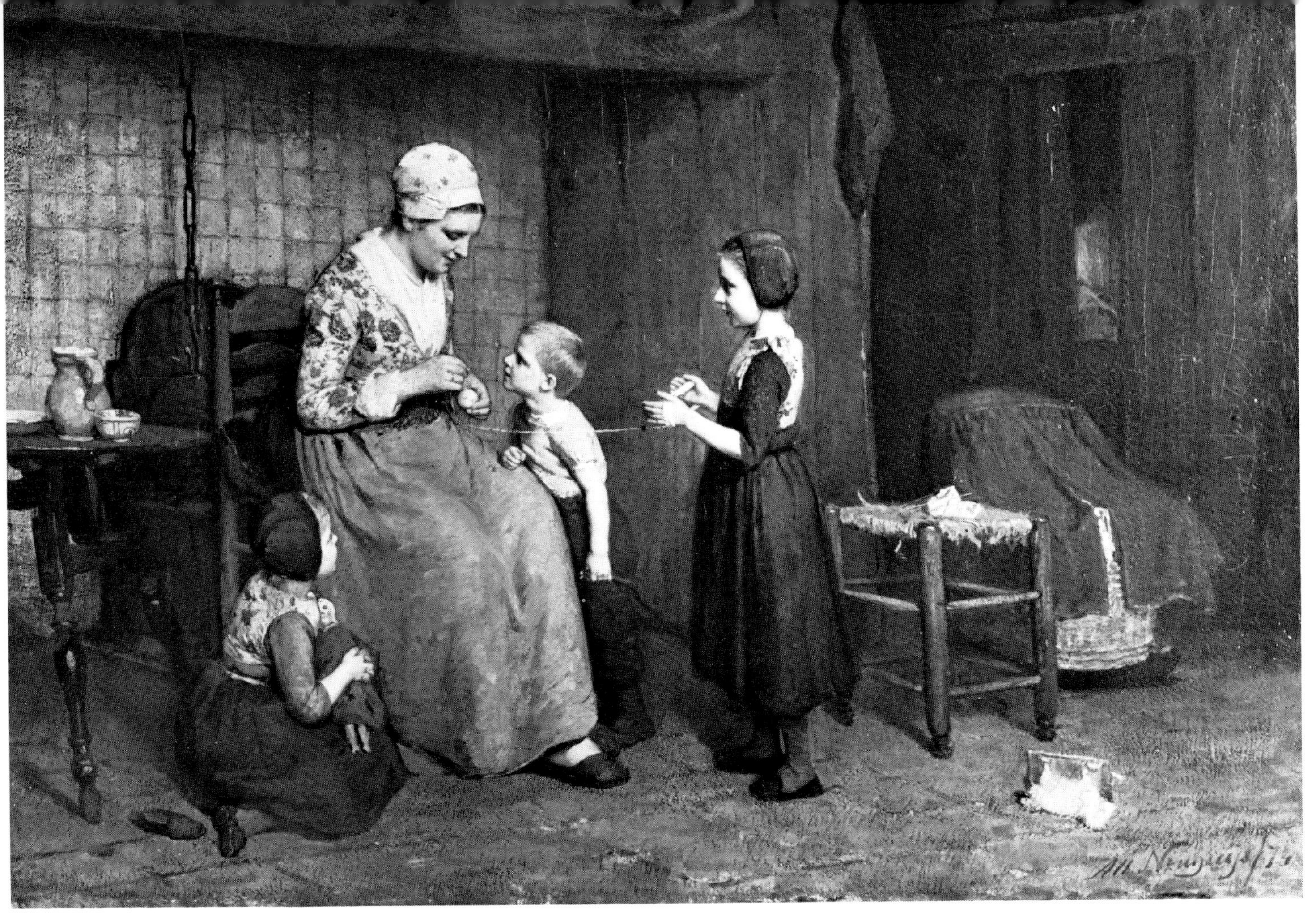

This **Neuhuijs** *interior is dated 1974. He still uses the attention to detail of older masters though the choice of peasant interior is very much of his time. (86 x 121cms.).* Photograph courtesy of Mak van Waay, Amsterdam.

the living model, under Egenberger. From that time, he worked with his master, whom he followed to Zandvoort. Afterwards, when he had selected his tendency, he resolved to go to Paris, where he became very intimate with Jacob and Matthijs Maris (who painted the well-known portrait of Artz) and with Kaemmerer.

If we compare Artz, Israëls' pupil, with his master, we are struck by the absence of those mystic qualities which the latter's later works reveal and which Artz admired so whole-heartedly and lacked quite consciously in his own work. In a picture such as *Mourning,* despite the fine expression of sorrow, despite the fine sentiment that places the sobbing woman bending forward against the rosy, utterly unconscious child, we are struck by the fact that this sorrow does not, as it would have done were the picture painted by Israëls, permeate the whole figure, the fall of the folds of the woman's dress, the fall of the light, every detail of the apartment, which would have been dramatized as it were in and through the human tragedy; we see that Artz is more positive and more practical, that he prefers to follow his model, to give his attention to each object and that, from this point of view, the folds of that dress are beautifully painted, beautiful too and seventeenth-century those squat little baby-shoes on that empty floor, a detail upon which Jan Steen could not have improved.

Properly speaking, Artz was one of the first realists in our country. Loving nature, he carefully followed her in his models and, especially in his studies painted from nature, showed a very complete, correct and delicate sense of the pale tonalities of beach and dunes. He was particularly happy in his open-air pictures, in which his work showed a great charm. The studies, again, for his most famous picture, *The*

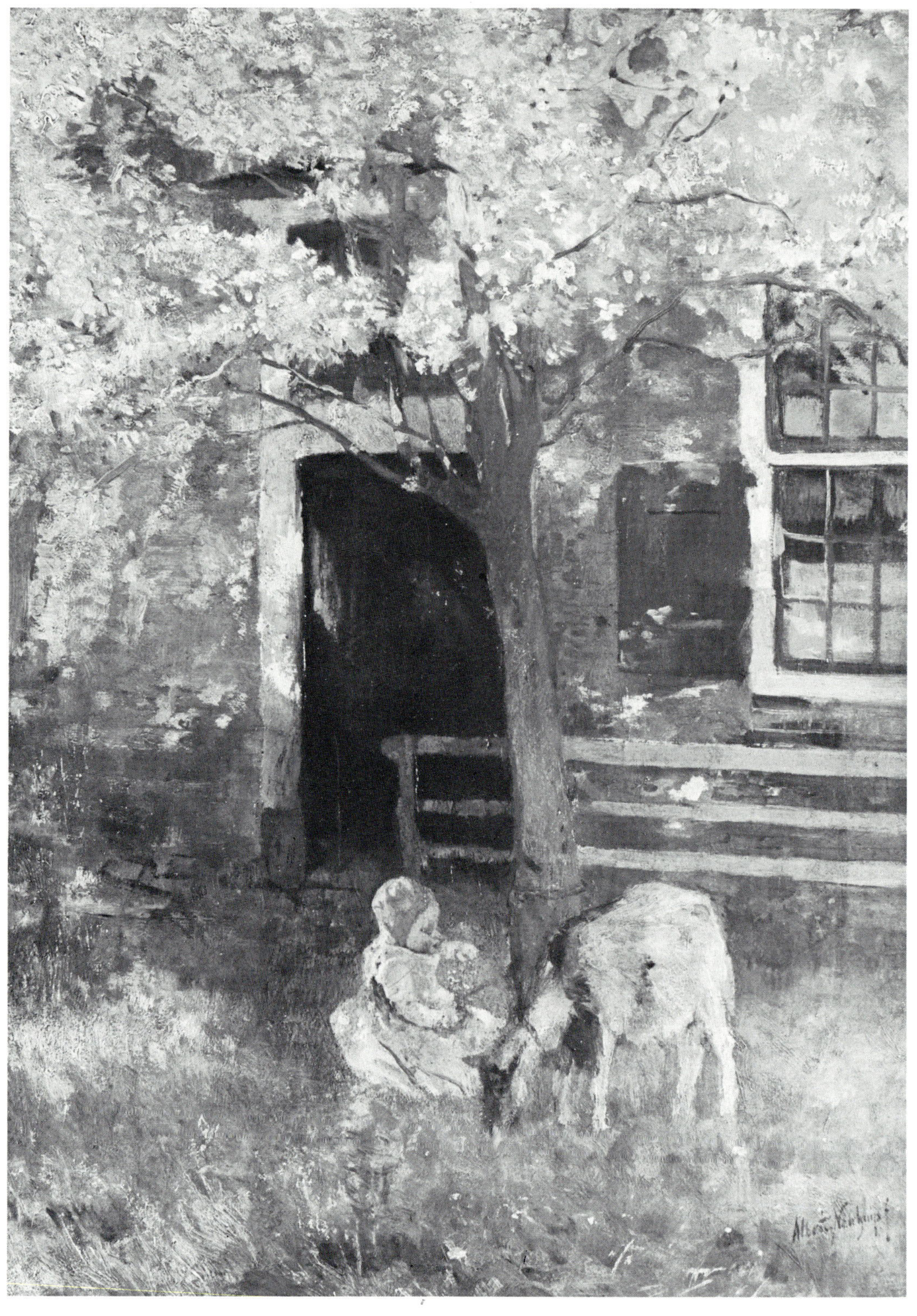

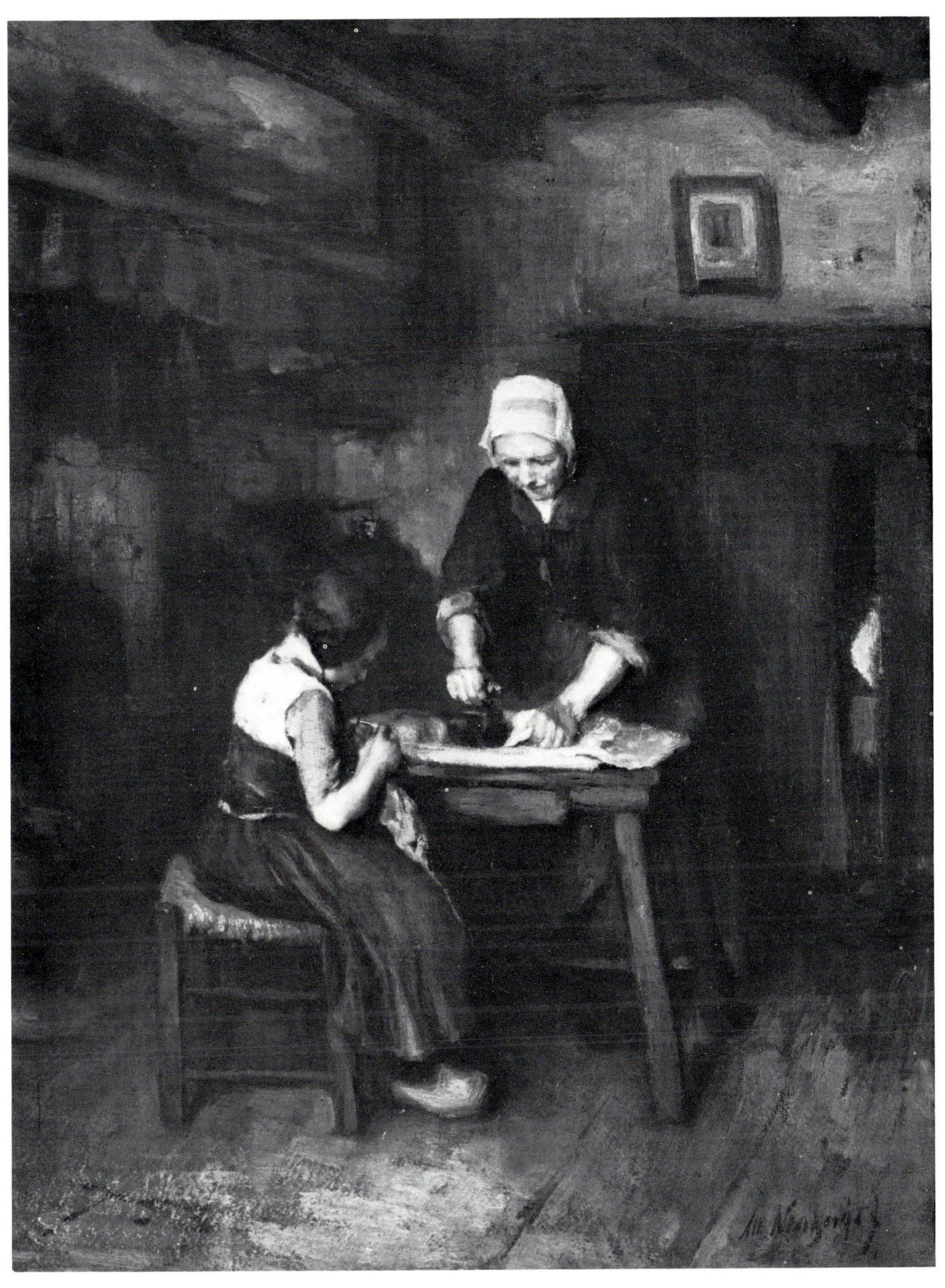

Above and left: **Johan Albert Neuhuijs (1844-1914)** *started out as a history painter but found his true vocation in realist genre scenes depicting the peasants of Laren or Brabant. Mothers and children were his speciality as in this little outdoor scene where a baby shares the garden with a goat (85 x 65cms.) or, more typical, this interior with the mother ironing while her daughter sews (50 x 40cms.). Marius says that he followed Israëls in his subjects and Jacob Maris in his colour.* Photographs courtesy of Mak van Waay, Amsterdam.

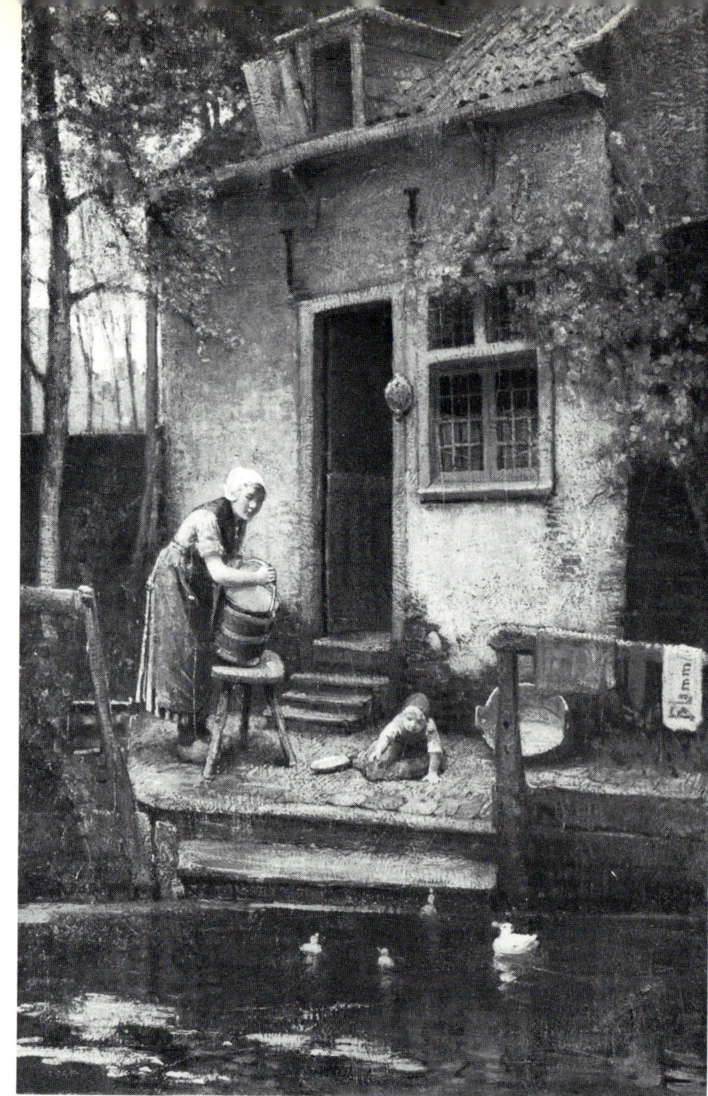

Right and below: **Bernardus Johannes Blommers (1845-1914)** *escaped from his father's profession as printmaker with the encouragement of Jacob Maris and was taken up by Israëls. He followed Israëls in taking fisherfolk almost exclusively as his subjects, but both this painting and watercolour demonstrate his much more robust and earthy approach to these people. (Painting 73 x 47cms., watercolour 23 x 39½cms.).* Photographs courtesy of Mak van Waay, Amsterdam.

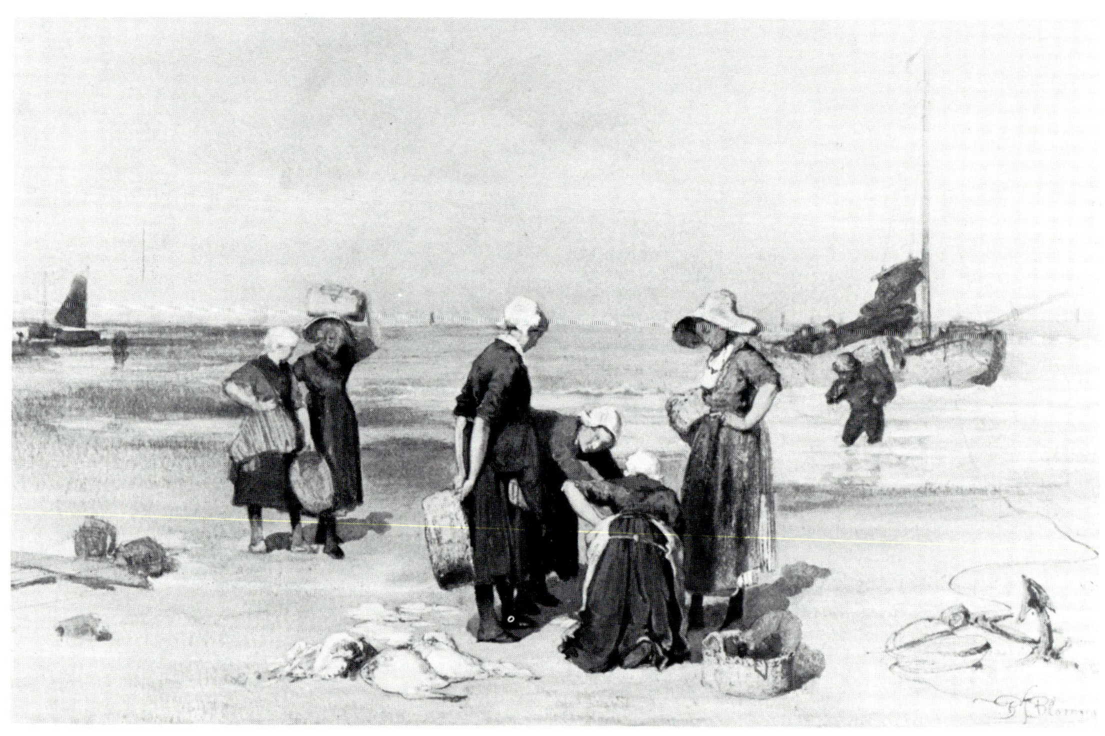

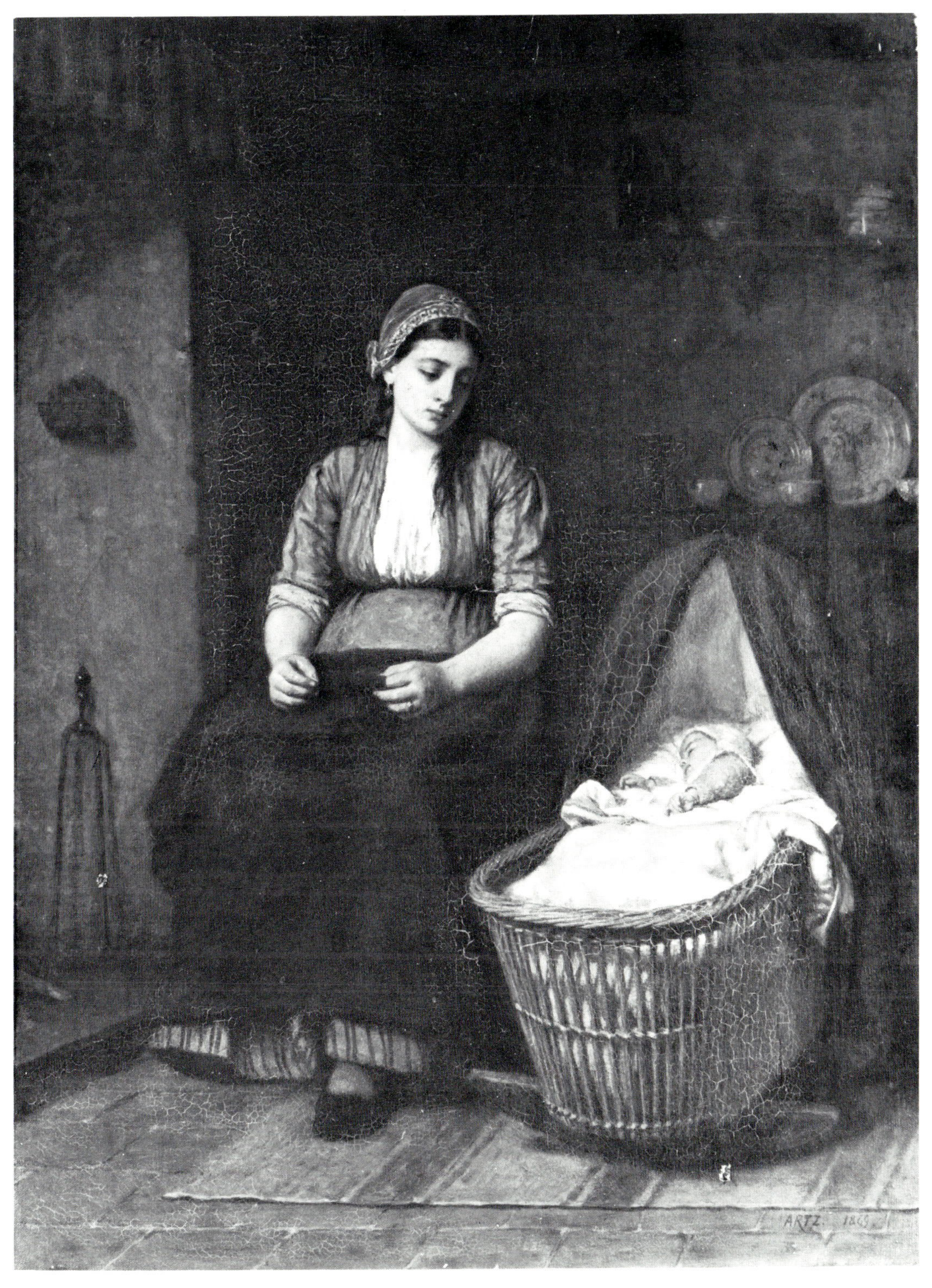

David Adolphe Constant Artz (1837-1890) *was Israëls' principal pupil. This painting, "Minding the Baby", is closely related to his master in subject but is a much simpler piece of genre painting than Israëls' psychological and atmospheric work.* Photograph courtesy of Sotheby & Co.

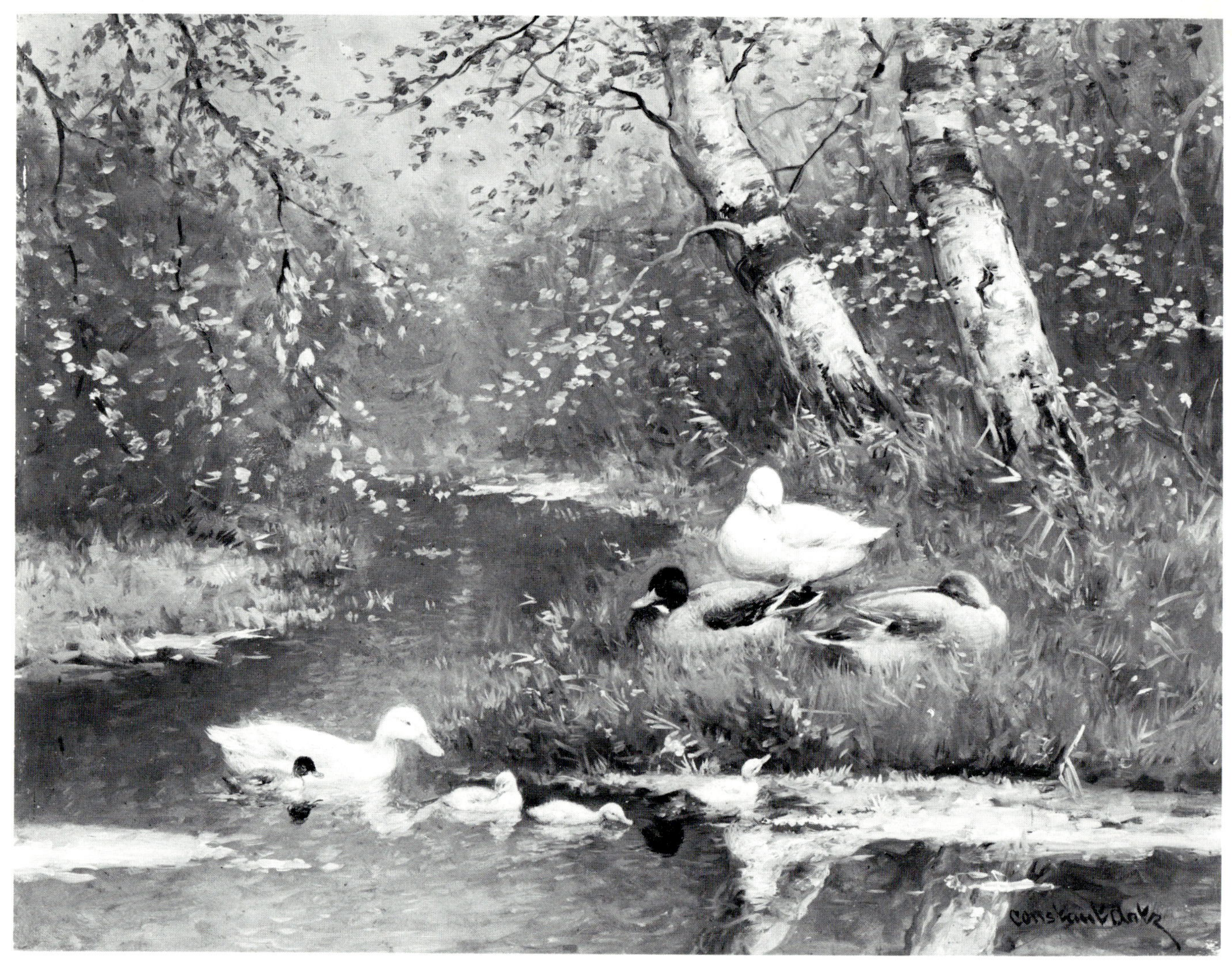

Artz *developed a penchant for open air cameos - with a duck frequently featured - in which he shows his powers as a realist painter.* Photograph courtesy of MacConnal Mason.

Refectory of the Katwijk Almshouse, belong to the best and the most original that we possess in this respect. Artz was born in 1837 and died at the Hague in 1890.

In addition to Hein Burgers (1834-1899), Jozef Israëls' only actual pupil, who, it is true, adopted mainly the somewhat morbid side of his intrinsically sound and healthy master, but who left some delicately painted little pictures, Valkenburg, the painter of interiors, was a faithful and capable follower of Israëls. Hendrik Valkenburg (1826-1896) was a painter who was prevented by circumstances until he had almost attained his fiftieth year from devoting himself, free of all school-lessons, to an art to which he had felt attracted all his life and in which he eventually succeeded in making a respectable name, in the style of Israëls. He painted farm-house interiors, honestly and simply rendered, mostly of those enormous Twente kitchens, simply and truthfully and well and unpretentiously drawn. Valkenburg once related, before falling under the charm of Mauve in his Laren period, that Israëls had said to him that, in every tone and every shadow, a colour should retain its own principle, so that blue remained blue, red red and so on. The

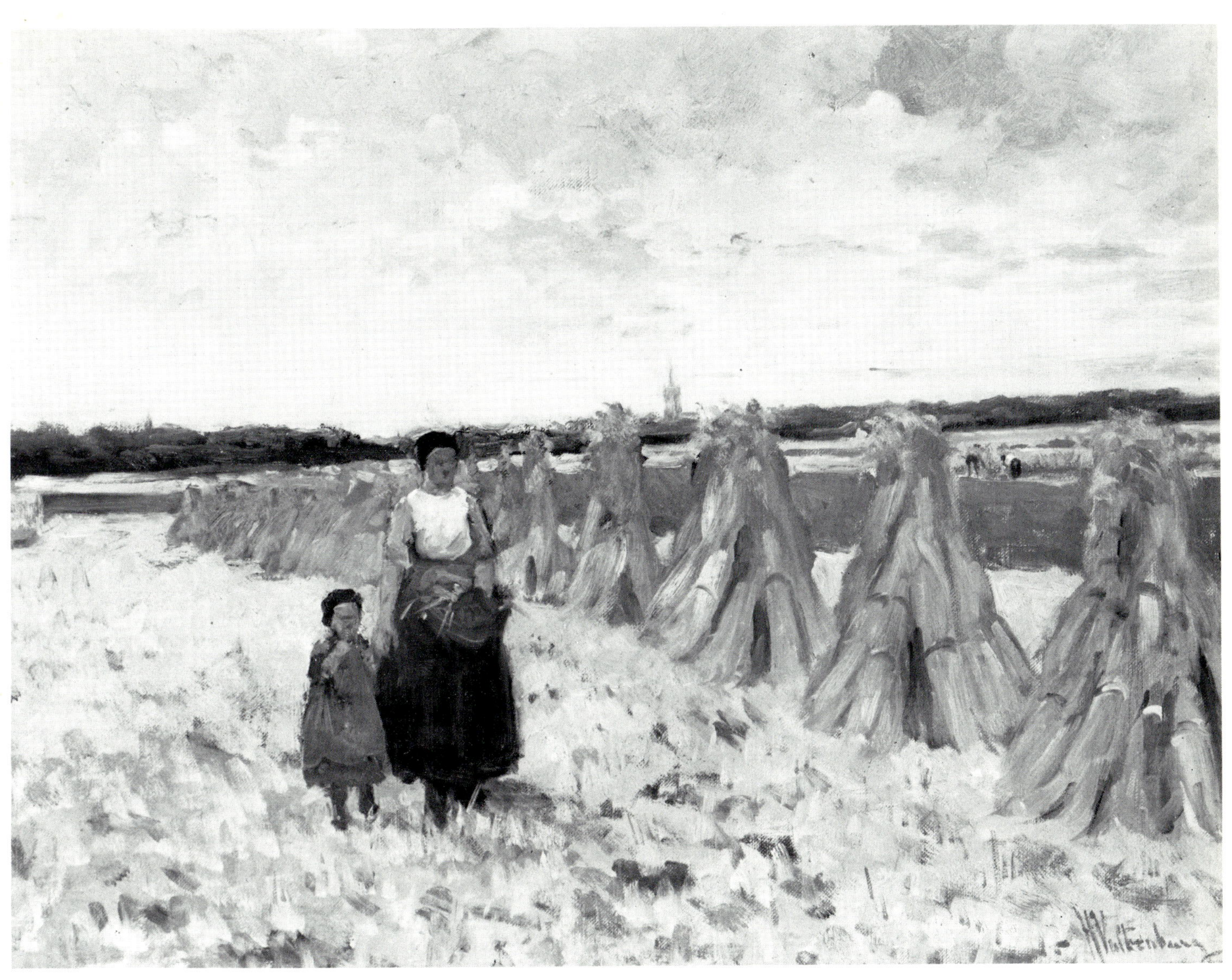

Hendrik Valkenburg (1826-1896) *took to painting late in life but made a notable reputation among the Hague School of painters with his country scenes like this "Mother and child in the harvest" scene.* Photograph courtesy of the Rijksmuseum Hendrik Willem Mesdag, the Hague.

Hague master, the inscrutable painter of luminous browns, had long abandoned this principle for a less narrow solution of light, for a freer analysis of space; but Valkenburg held fast to it and we must admit that it constitutes his strength. For that matter, at Laren too and especially in his little kitchen-gardens this painter showed great merit.

Though Bisschop's conception of the interior is not related in respect of artlessness and not at all in that of the joy of life with the pictures of the old "little masters," neither was his conception that of Israëls or of Jacob Maris. It is true that he gave a portrait of the old Hinlopen life, a *peinture des mœurs* of the old popular life in Friesland, of everyday happenings in the household, but he failed to expand it into something generally human. Nor did he aim at doing so; for, whereas Jozef Israëls looks upon things only as a means to increase the expression for his model, Bisschop was above all a painter of still-life, to whom the figures were necessary attributes to give life to the

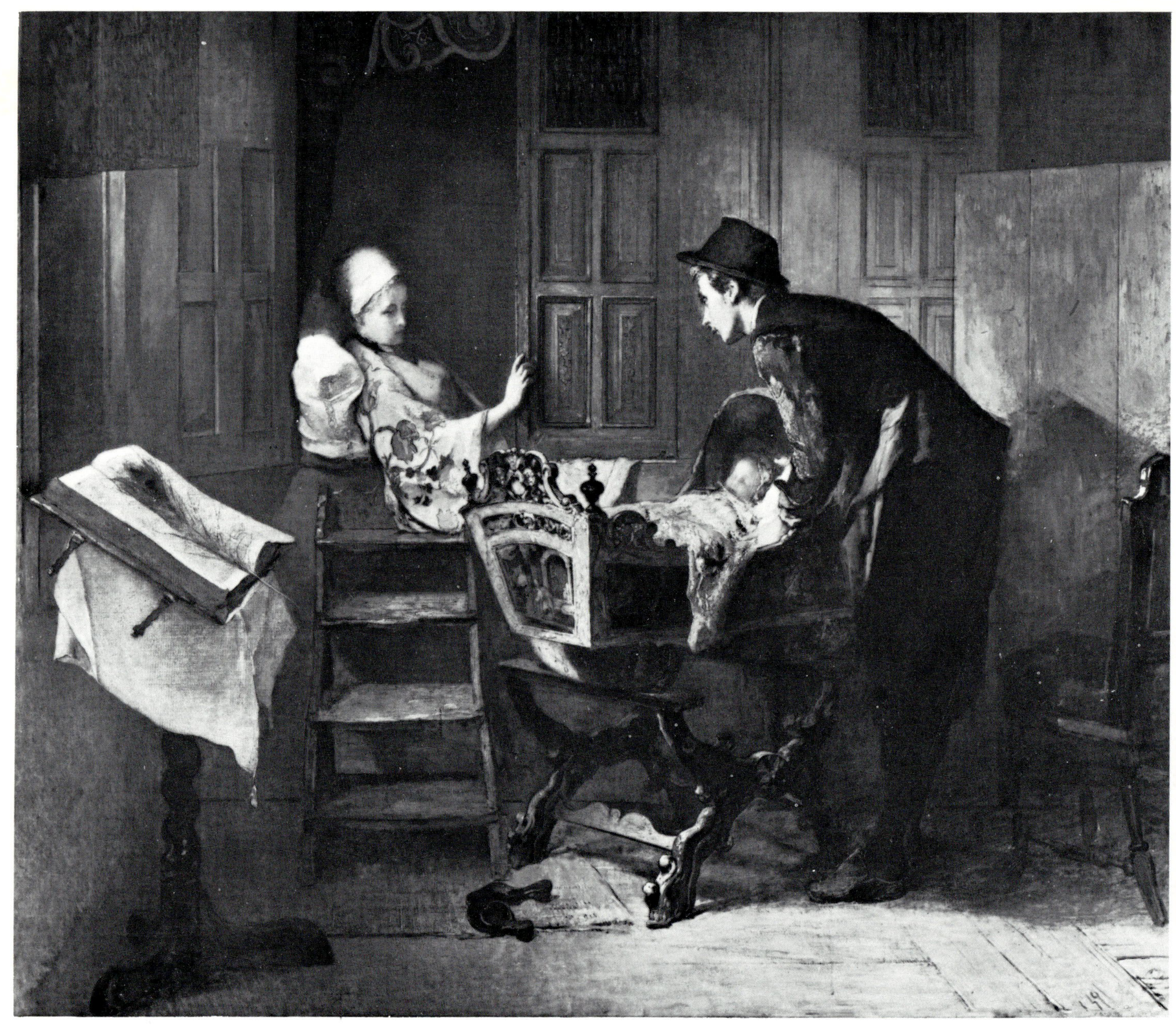

Christoffel Bisschop (1828-1904) *was profoundly influenced by the Hague School, though of an older generation. He retains the emphasis on decorative composition and still life detail of his master, Hubertus van Hove. This scene of young parents with their firstborn has a narrative charm seldom echoed in the later realists. (123 x 153cms.).* Photograph courtesy of Mak van Waay, Amsterdam.

precious objects of a past age and to justify their use. Nevertheless, I know pictures of Bisschop's in which the figures form the main feature, such as those young women standing before a mirror or reading at a writing-table; and in *The Mennonite Supper at Hinlopen* figures and still-life are very happily combined.

Christoffel Bisschop was born at Leeuwarden in 1828. In 1846, after receiving an elementary education in his native town, he went to Delft to work under Schmidt, then in the zenith of his fame. After Schmidt's death, Bisschop studied under Huib van Hove. From 1852 to 1855, the year in which he settled at the Hague, he worked in the studio of Le Comte and Charles Gleyre, formerly the Atelier Delaroche,

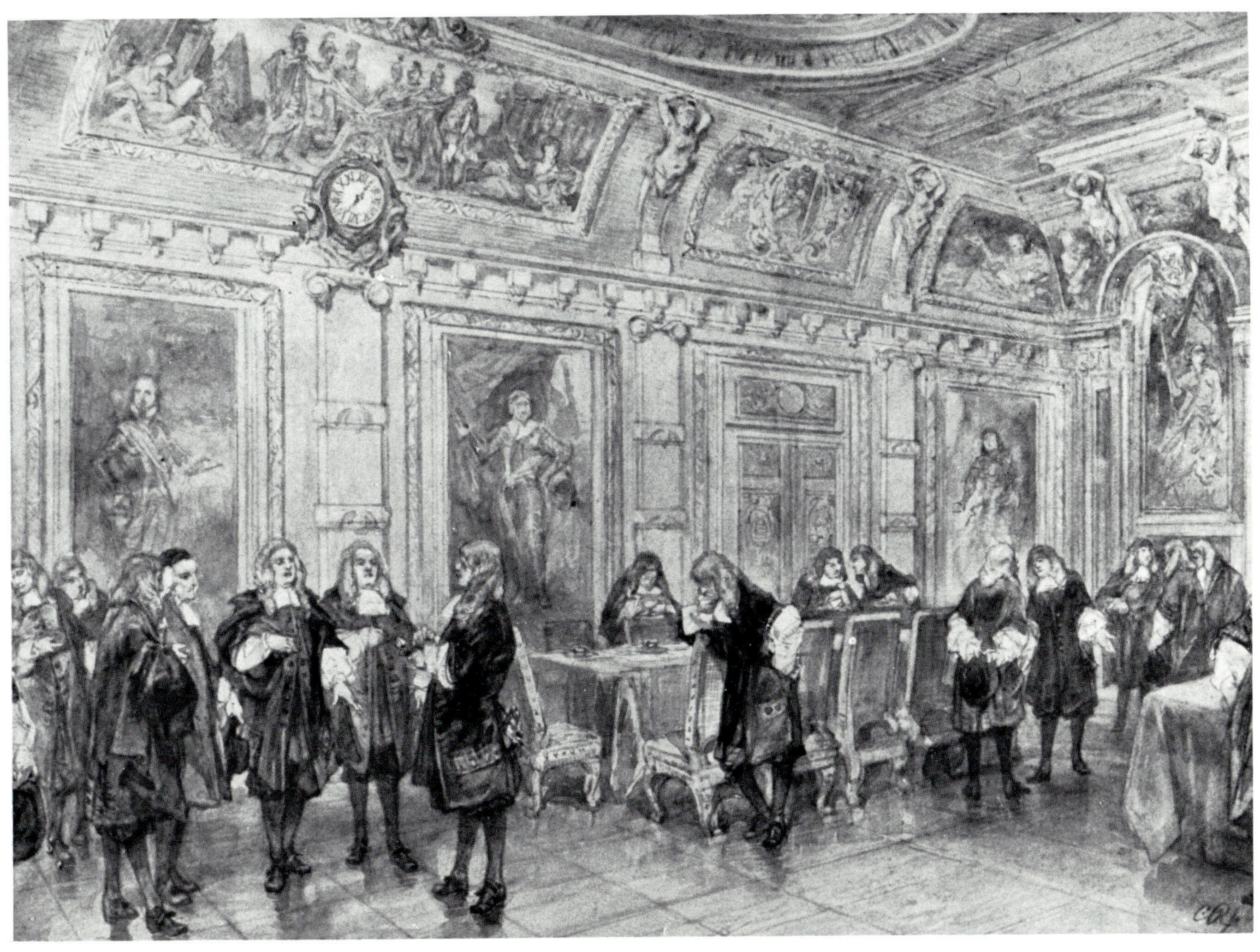

Charles Rochussen (1814-1894) *was the leading Dutch illustrator of his time. In this sepia drawing he has looked back to the busy but grandiose affairs of diplomats in the 17th century. (22½ x 31cms.).* Photograph courtesy of Mak van Waay, Amsterdam.

in Paris. He made a considerable name. The house which he occupied with his wife, an Irish lady by birth, in the woods between the Hague and Scheveningen, was arranged as an old Frisian dwelling-house and might be looked upon as a museum of domestic art. He died recently, in 1904.

The art of painting in water-colours underwent great changes in the hands of the Hague masters. A water-colour ceased to be either the compact picture in oils which an earlier generation had produced or the pencil, chalk or pen-and-ink drawing, lightly washed with colour, of the old masters. In the hands of our impressionists, water-colour painting, like oil-painting, became an emotional art, an harmonious whole, until, with the aid of this thinner medium, our Dutch impressionism went further, arrived at subtler results and attained a more general modernity than the more classic oil-paintings.

Long before the institution of the exhibitions of the famous Hague Sketching Club, the views held by the Pulchri Studio Society at the Hague and Felix Meritis and Arti et Amicitiæ in Amsterdam had given occasion for the display of water-colours. At first, these took place only in the evenings. For a time, they were attended regularly by Queen Sophie and Prince Henry of the Netherlands and by the Duke of Saxe-Weimar and his daughter. The general public continued reactionary in matters of art and I can remember the

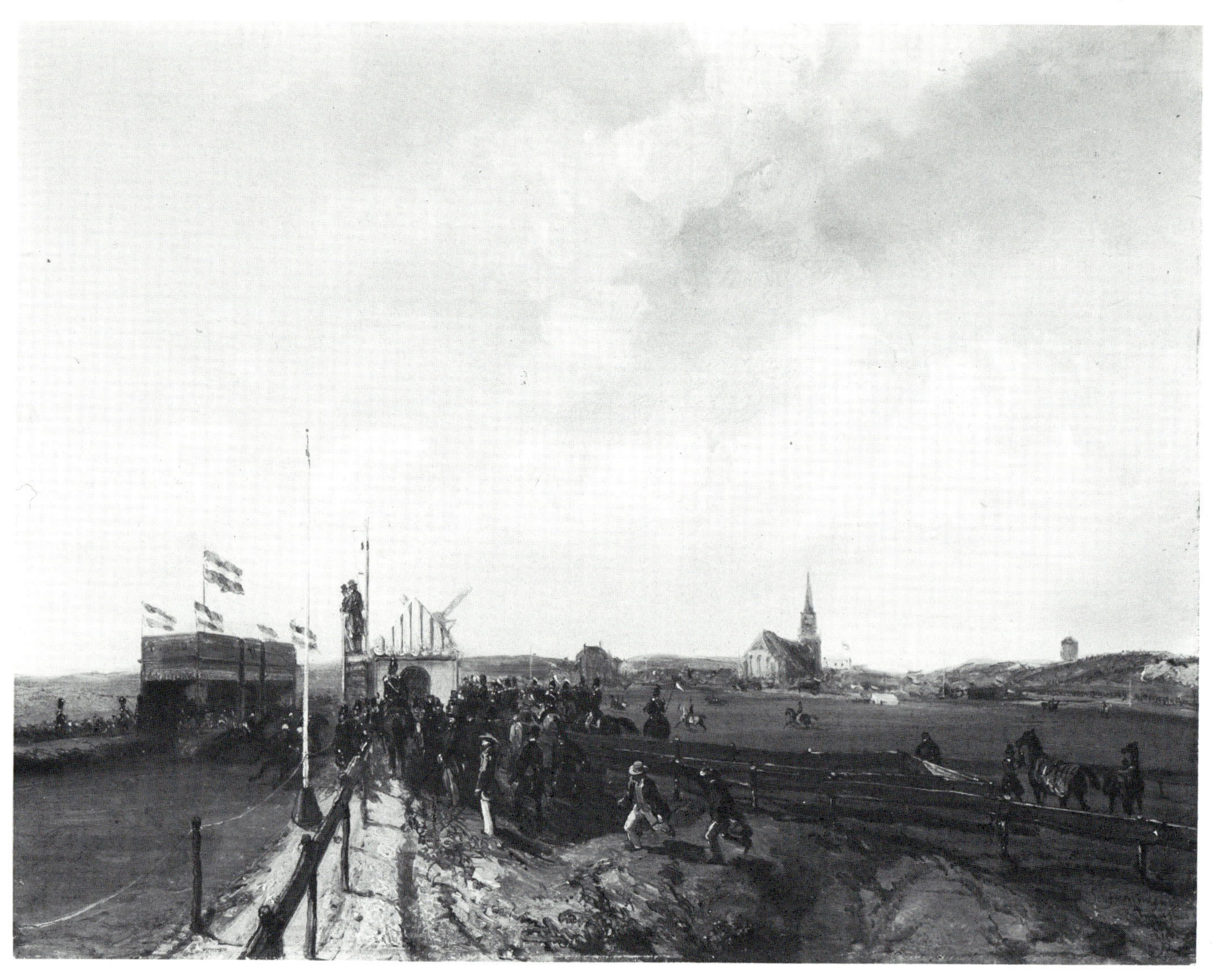

Rochussen *here uses a free and sparkling style to depict the races at Scheveningen.(31½ x 42cms.).* Photograph courtesy of the Rijksmuseum, Amsterdam.

speeches delivered about 1880 on the subject of Jacob Maris' delicious water-colour drawings, speeches embodying gruesome anticipations concerning the future of an art in which sketches, as Maris' drawings were called, were exhibited as completed works. And this was at a time when Jaap Maris had long been acknowledged as a master, a title which was denied him by the older generation of Hague painters for many a long day.

The original members of the Hague Water-colour Society were Van de Sande Bakhuijzen, Miss van de Sande Bakhuijzen, Bisschop, Mrs. Bisschop-Swift, Bles, Blommers, Bosboom, Henkes, Israëls, Jacob and Willem Maris, Mauve, Mesdag, Sadée and Pieter Stortenbeker. These were immediately joined by Artz, Duchattel, Nakken, Albert Neuhuijs, C.S. Stortenbeker, E. Verveer and Weissenbruch, as ordinary members; while Alma Tadema in London, Allebé and J.W.

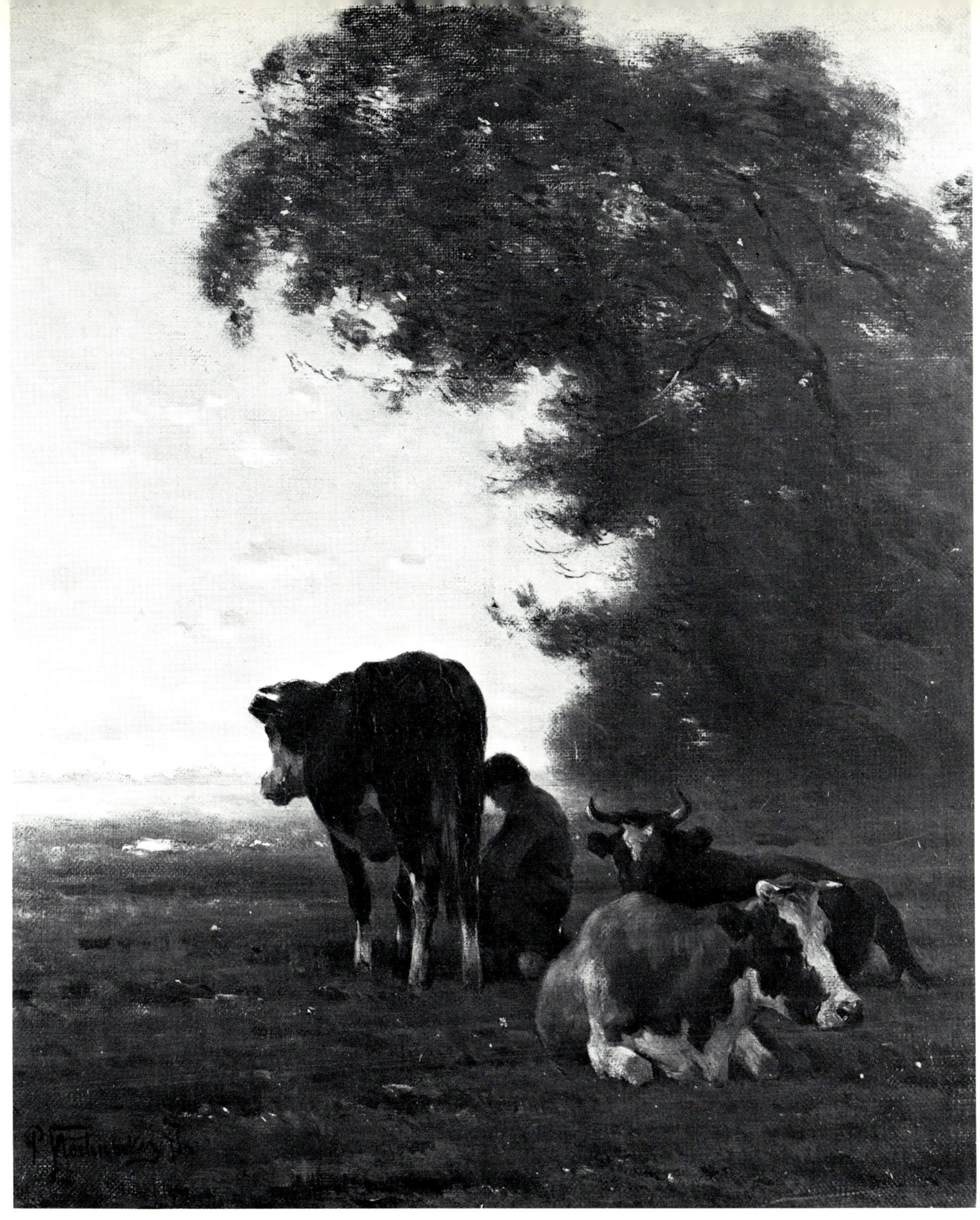

Pieter Stortenbeker (1828-1898), *the animal painter, here sets his cows in a Corot-esque evening landscape.* Photograph courtesy of the Stedelijk Museum, Amsterdam.

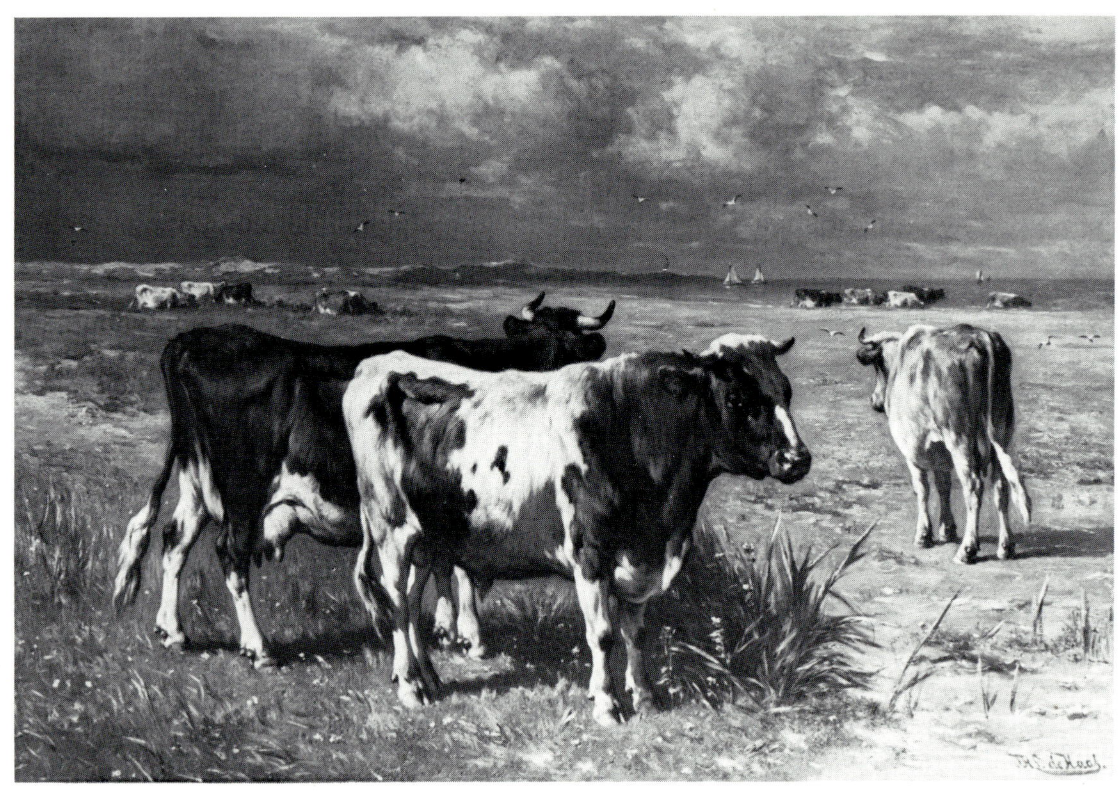

Above and below: **Johannes Hubertus Leonardus de Haas (1832-1908)** *studied with P.F. Van Os and became a sought after Hague School artist. The first group of sturdy cows are painted with impressionistic realism (73 x 98½cms.). In the second he has effectively used a strong light to achieve an almost architectural modelling. (12½ x 16½ins.).* Photographs courtesy of Mak van Waay, Amsterdam, and M. Newman Ltd.

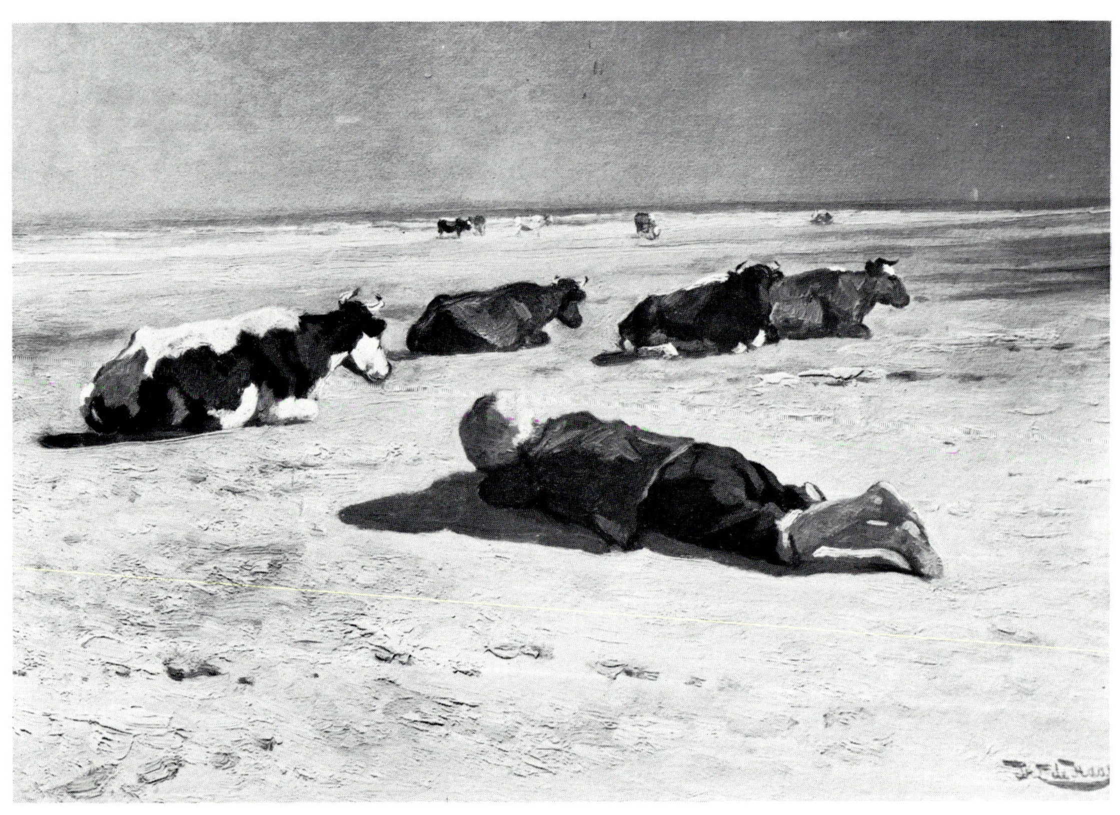

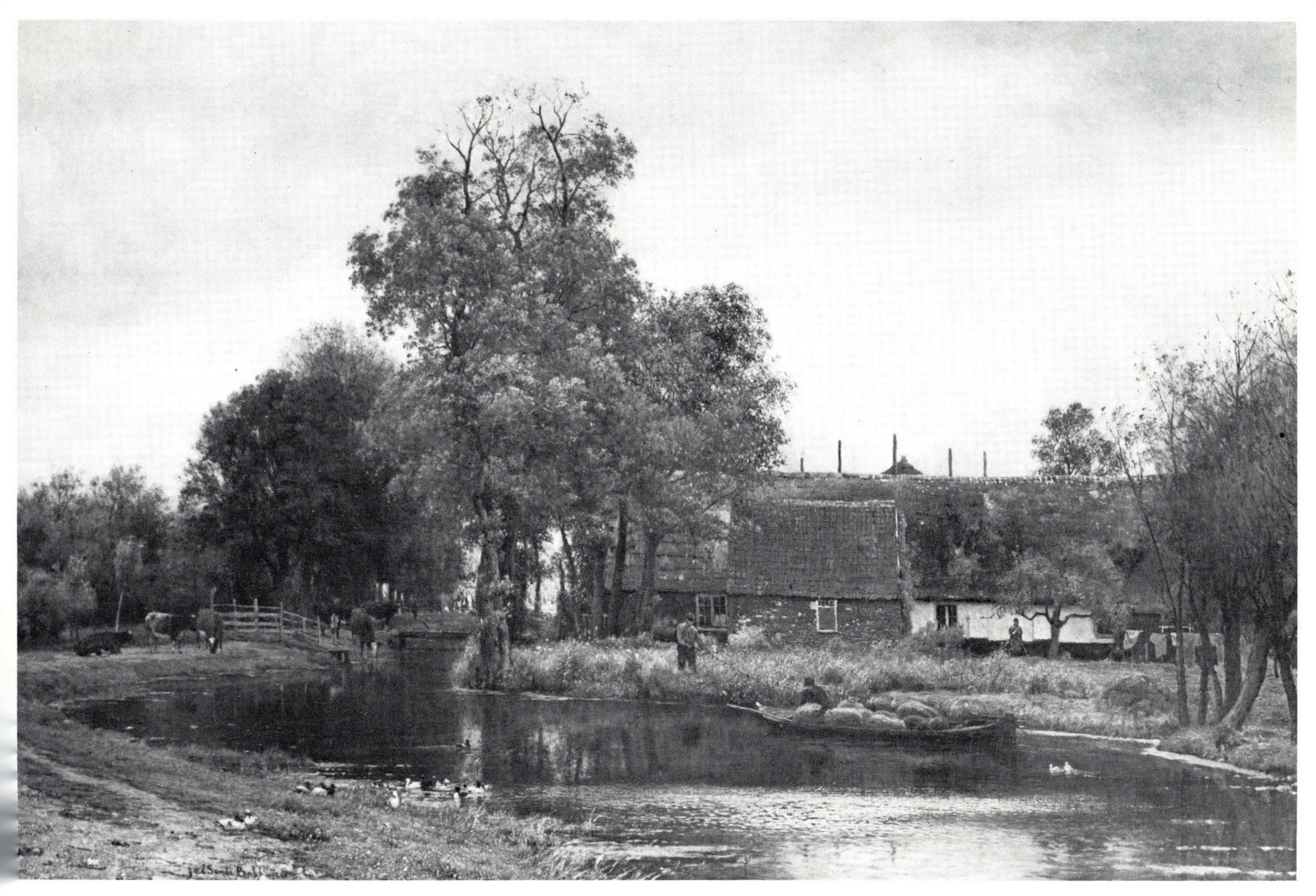

Julius Jacobus van de Sande Bakhuijzen (1835-1925) *was the son and pupil of Hendrik (see page 69). He painted some fine landscapes of which this view of cottages across the water is a nice example. It is dated 1872. (65½ x 103cms.).* Photograph courtesy of Mak van Waay, Amsterdam.

Bilders in Amsterdam, David and Pieter Oyens, the Famars Testas, Gabriël and Roelofs in Brussels, Rochussen in Amsterdam and a few Belgians, including Emile Wouters, and many Italians, including, at a later date, Segantini, took part in the famous August exhibitions as honorary members.

First, in chronological order, among the minor artists of the Hague school is Charles Rochussen, born at Rotterdam in 1815, who was looked upon, in the latter half of the nineteenth century, as the only illustrative talent of importance among us. Teyler's Museum at Haarlem has a *Hunting Party,* painted in 1857, a scene filled with lords and ladies on horseback on a hilly heath in Gelderland, which, for observation, delicate drawing and happy colouring, is quite excellent of its kind. The Fodor Museum in Amsterdam possesses similar little pieces and also a *Dog-cart,* which is cleverly drawn and admirably painted. Rochussen died in 1894. It is a pity that this painter of very considerable talent and originality was eventually merged, as it were, in the draughtsman and illustrator; and yet he was the only illustrator of any importance that our country has produced.

Elchanon Verveer (1826-1900), like Israëls, Artz and Blommers, took his subjects from amid the life of the fishermen on the sea-coast.

Pieter Stortenbeker (1828-1898), the animal painter, may be said to have surpassed both his

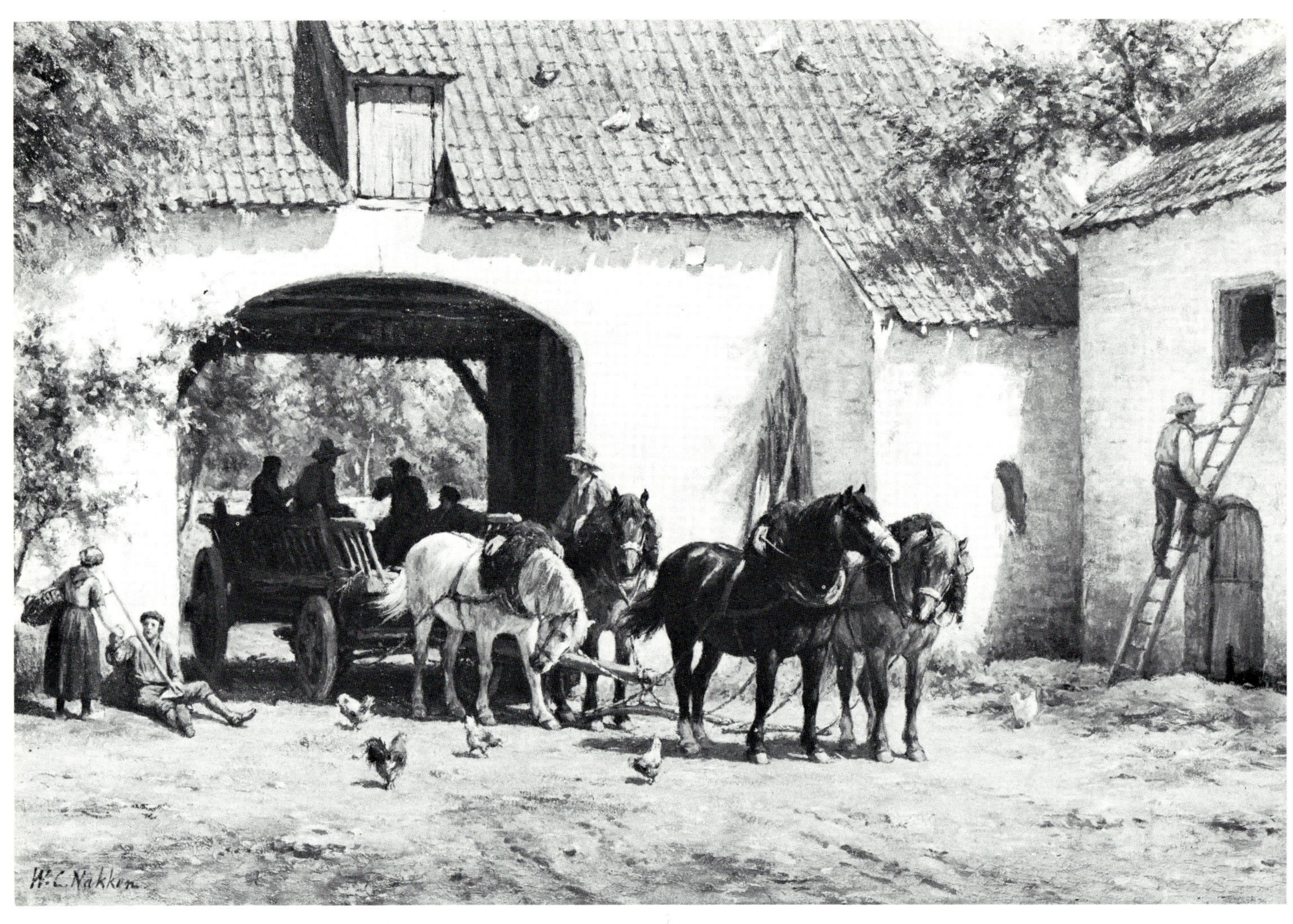

Willem Carel Nakken (1835-1926) *had a lively way with country life, in which he usually succeeded in placing a good number of horses, as in this farmyard scene. (54 x 82cms.).* Photograph courtesy of Mak van Waay, Amsterdam.

masters, H. van de Sande Bakhuijzen and J.B. Tom.

Johannes Hubertus Leonardus de Haas, the Guelder artist, born in 1832, had the same master as Mauve. He moved to Brussels at an early age and, though he there learnt to make a perhaps superfluous use of white paint, he nevertheless displays, in his *Early Morning* at the Rijksmuseum, a great power of form and a strenuous search after atmosphere.

Julius Jacobus van de Sande Bakhuijzen, born in 1835, a pupil of his father's, is a moderately good landscape-painter who has found his level more particularly in forest-views.

Willem Carel Nakken, born in 1835, a pupil of Dona's, has some very good paintings with horses scattered through various museums.

Paulus van der Velden, born in 1837 at Rotterdam, is a full blooded painter of interiors.

Philip Sadée, born at the Hague in 1837, is a painter not without importance.

Jozef Hendrikus Neuhuijs (1841-1889), an elder brother of Albert Neuhuijs, displayed a very delicate and sensitive talent.

Gerke Henkes, born at Delftshaven in 1844, enjoyed a not undeserved success at a time when anecdotal painting was more generally appreciated than now.

Pieter ter Meulen, born in 1843, a pupil of H. van

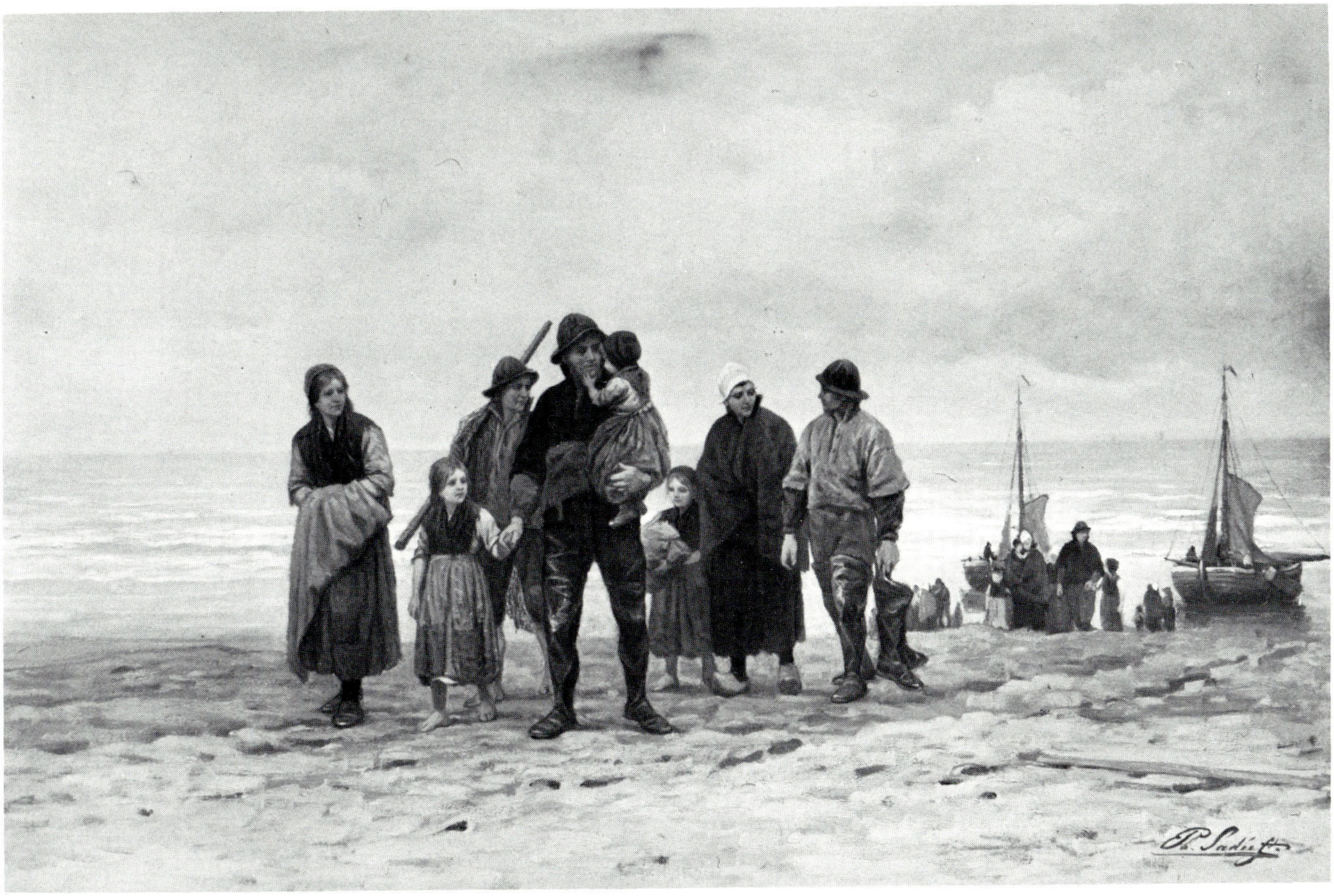

Above and below: **Philip Sadée's (1837-1904)** *debt to Israëls is made more than apparent in the first of these paintings. The composition virtually repeats the painting by Israëls reproduced on page 111 (28 x 39½cms.). In the second scene he has found a more individual and robust realism (55 x 31ins.).* Photographs courtesy of M. Newman Ltd., and Williams & Son.

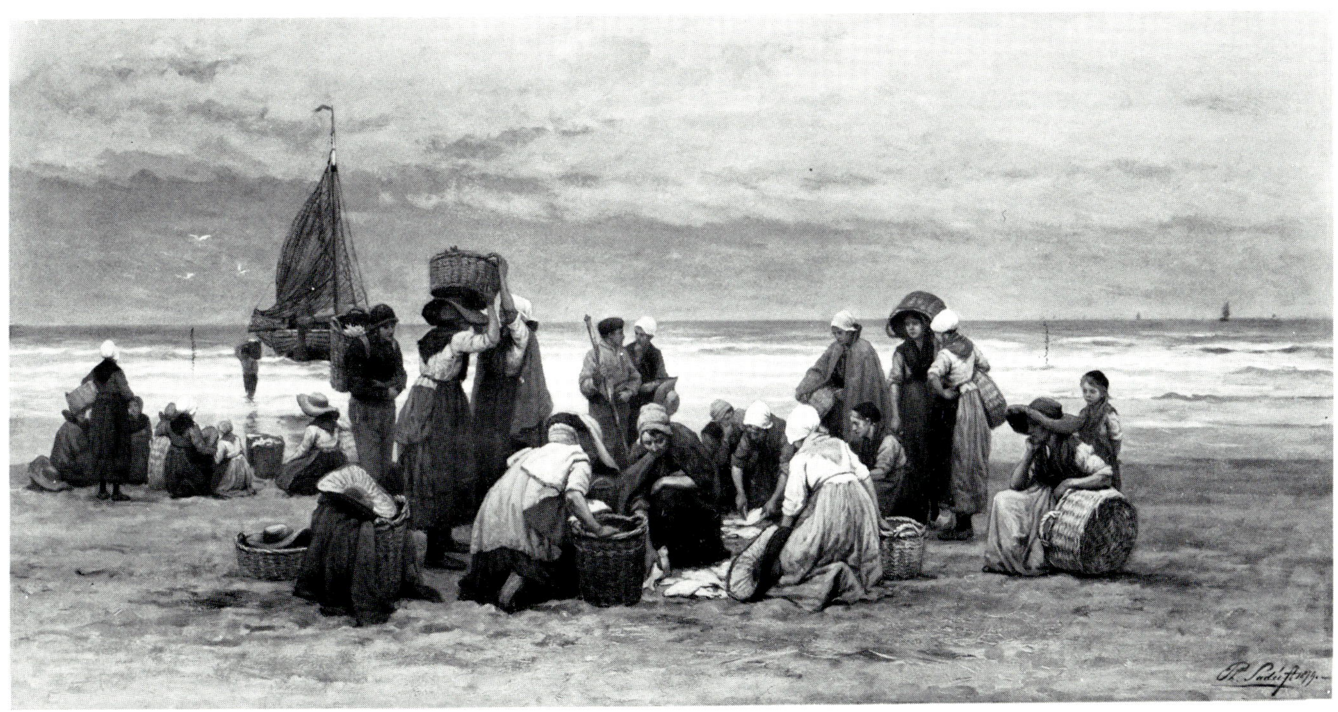

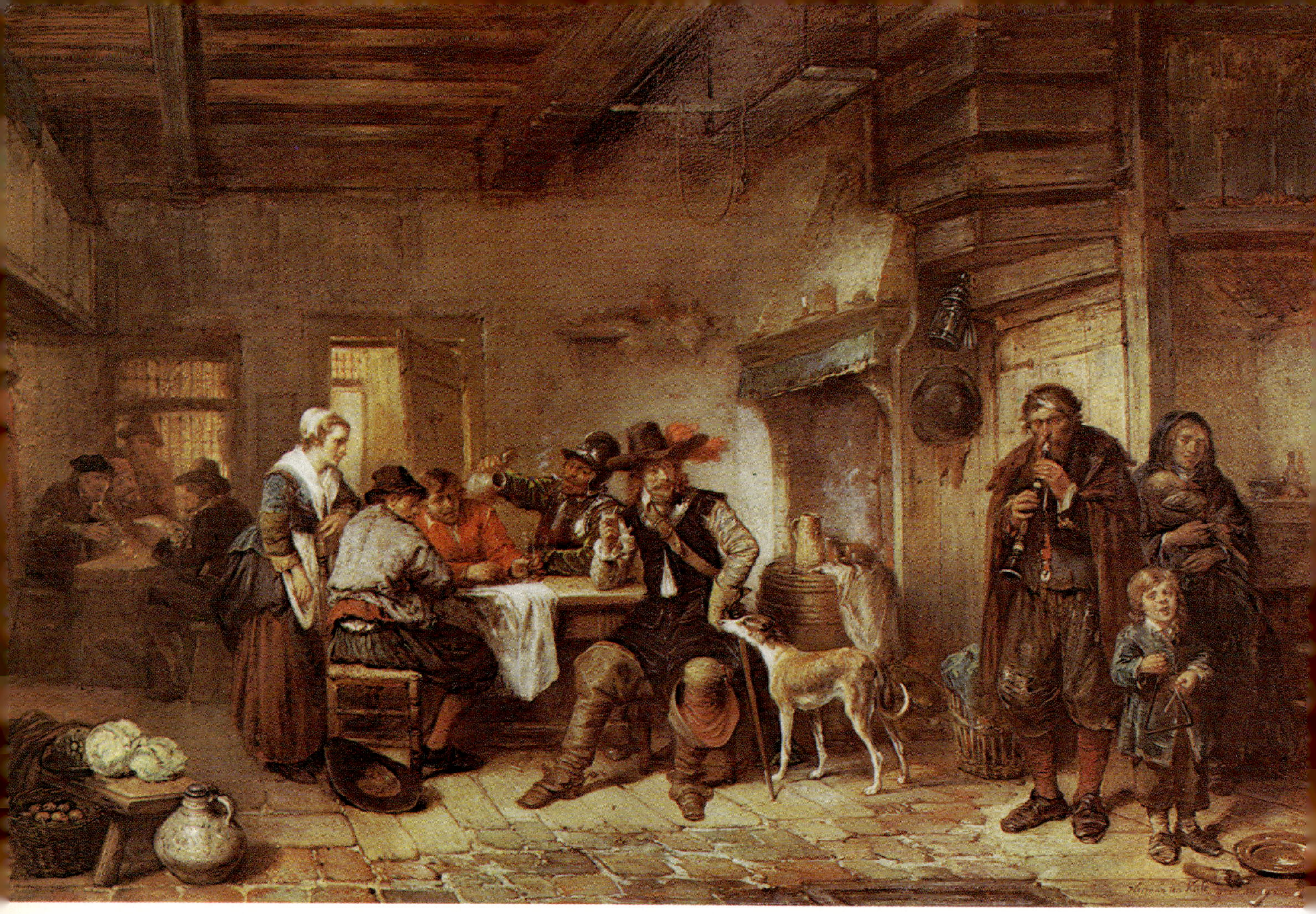

Herman Frederik Karel ten Kate (1822-1891). *"Itinerant musicians."* Photograph courtesy of Williams and Son.

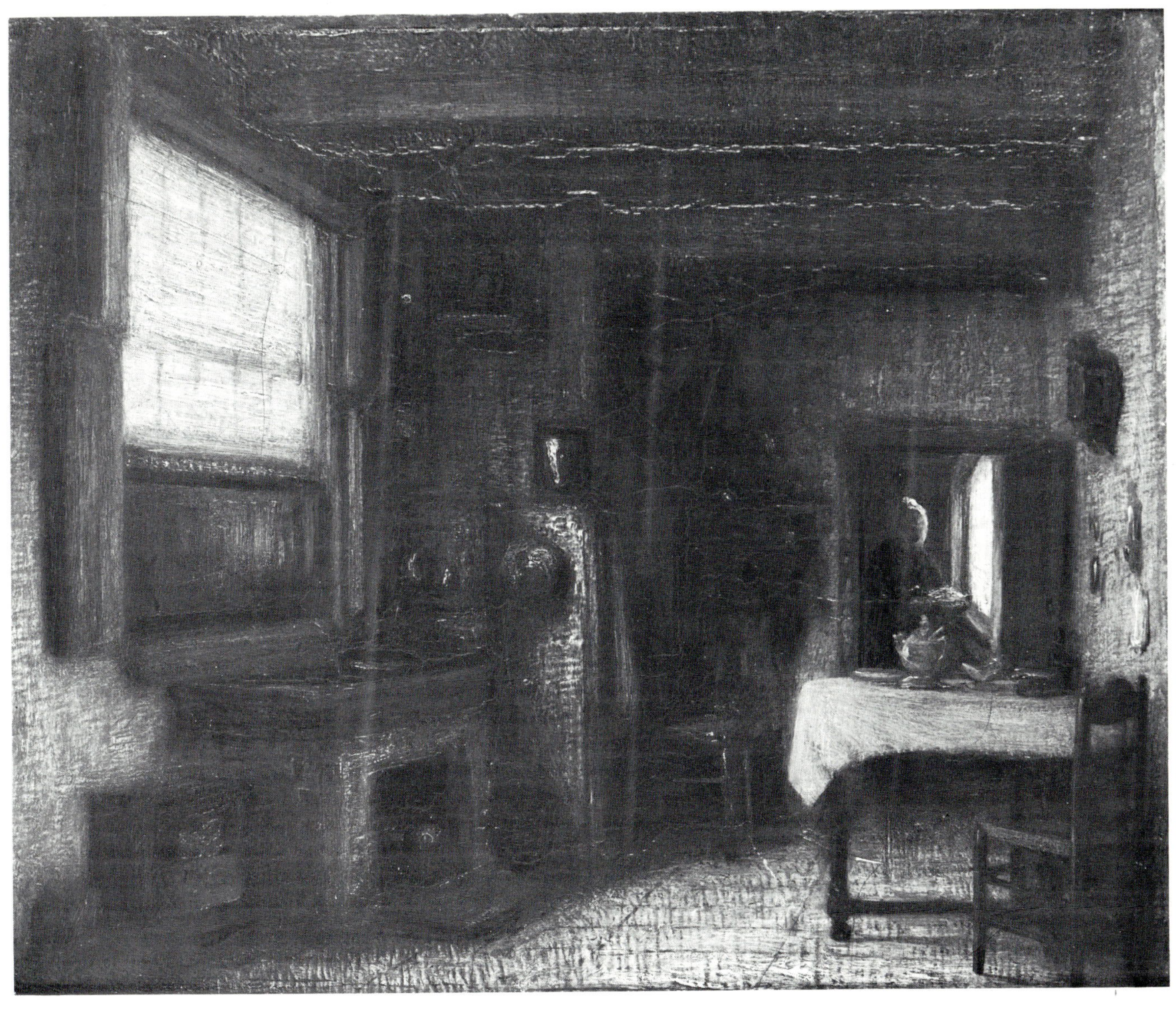

A simple interior by **Gerke Henkes (1844-1927).** Photograph courtesy of Mak van Waay, Amsterdam.

de Sande Bakhuijzen, although lacking Mauve's fulness of tone, is one of the most honest followers of that great painter.

Far above any of these stood Eduard Alphonse Victor Auguste van der Meer (1846-1899). Although he was not a painter of wide scope, he possessed the merit of portraying well and faithfully the polderlands reclaimed by Weissenbruch and Gabriël. If he were not at the same time such a pure painter, one might call him the topographer of the pools of South Holland, for none of them all was able so simply and succinctly as he to write upon the smooth surface of those pools, whether in autumn or winter, the little accidents pertaining to it: the thin reeds, a boat or a belt of underwood. His work may be somewhat too even and this is probably due to the fact that he was deaf and dumb, which caused him to turn his thoughts too much upon himself; but, on the other hand, his sense of still nature became all the greater.

A few women painters belong to his period. Henriette Ronner-Knip, born in Amsterdam in 1821, a pupil of her father, J.A. Knip (1777-1847), was

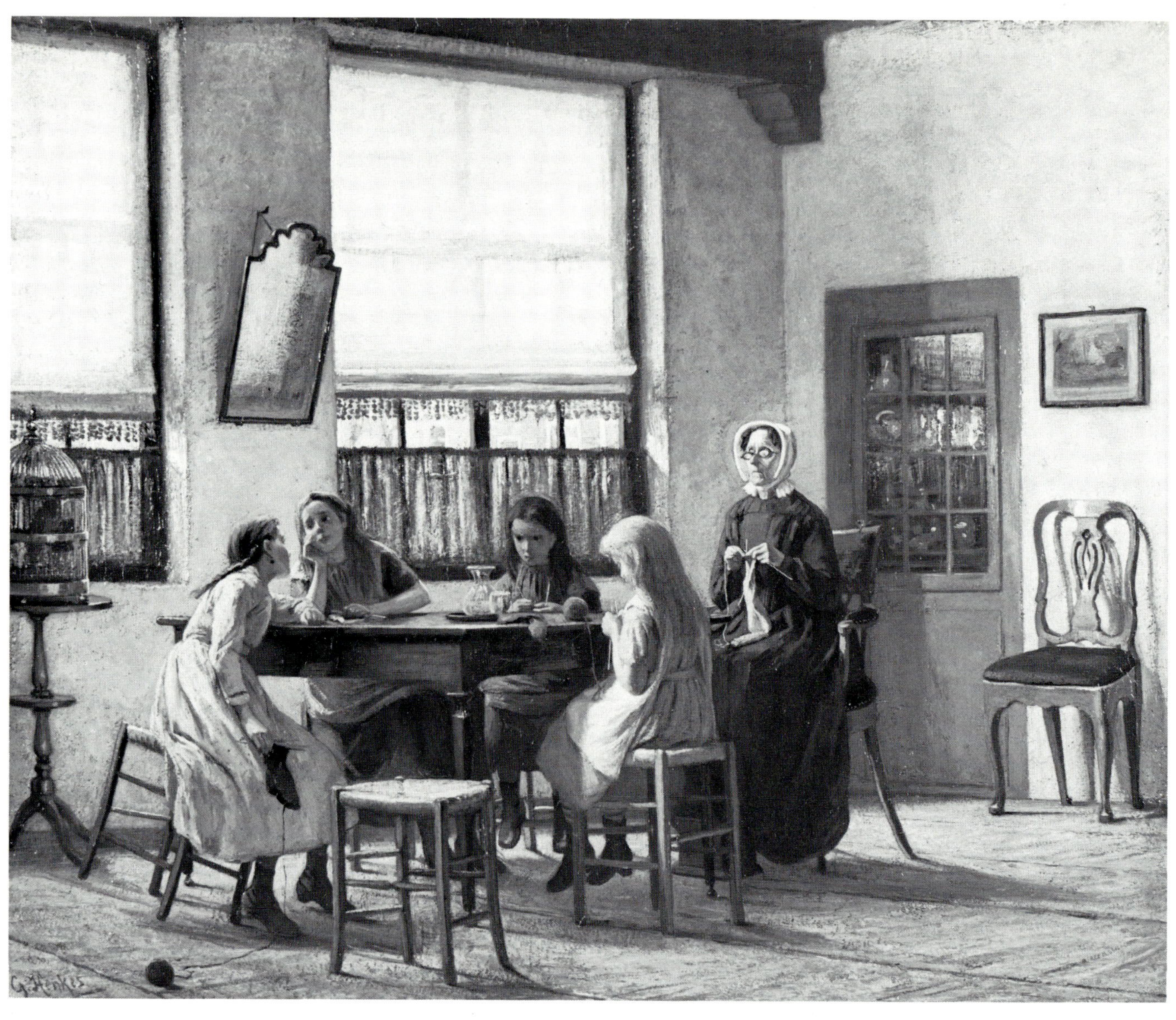

Henkes *continued to use an anecdotal strain in his paintings as in this work entitled "Learning to knit".* Photograph courtesy of the Rijksmuseum Hendrik Willem, Mesdag, The Hague.

doubtless the most popular woman painter of her time. From the first, she applied herself to the painting of animals, of dogs and especially cats; and she owes her name to the natural movements which she knew how to give to her pet cats and kittens.

Maria Philippine Bilders-van Bosse (1837-1900) proved herself a ready pupil of painters such as Bosboom, Van de Sande Bakhuijzen and especially, J.W. Bilders, who subsequently became her husband. She had a very simple feeling for landscape-painting.

Sina Mesdag-van Houten, born at Groningen in 1834, married H.W. Mesdag and began to paint at the Hague. She received her first instruction (her real education came to her from the French painters whose works Mesdag had collected), as far as regards drawing, from D'Arnaud Gerkens and she declares

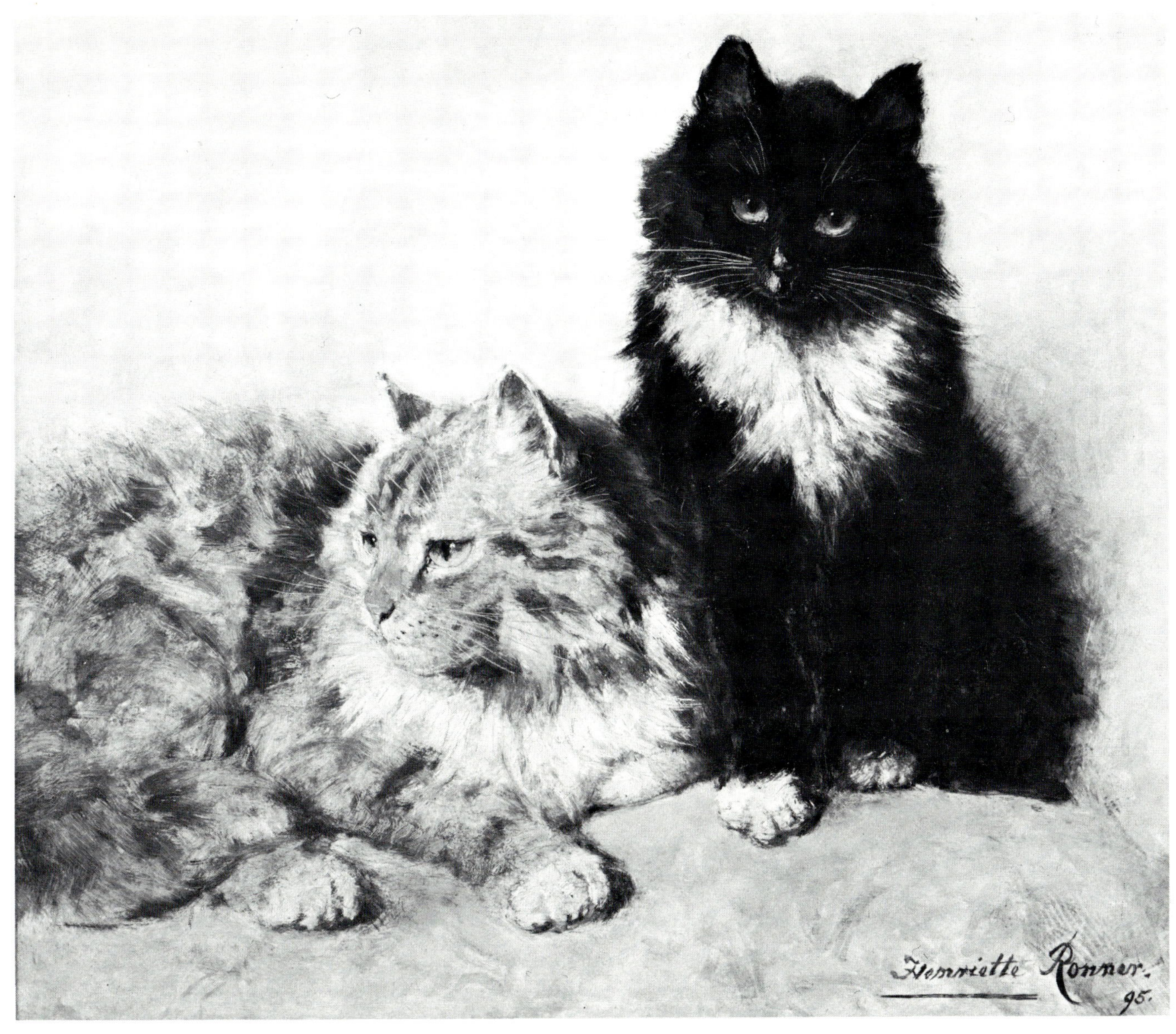

Henriette Ronner-Knip (1821-1909) *was the most popular Dutch woman painter of her time. She was an animal painter, but it was with cats that most of her paintings dealt. These two pussies painted in 1895, were exhibited in Glasgow in 1897. (15¼ x 18½ins.).* Photograph courtesy of M. Newman Ltd.

that she also learnt much from a talented woman painter, Harriet Lindo. Mrs. Mesdag has proved herself to be an artist of emotional power, able to set before us in the grand manner the spacious solitude, the startling loneliness and abandonment of our heaths and dunes.

Margaretha Vogel-Roosenboom (1843-1896), granddaughter of Schelfhout and wife of Johannes Gijsbert Vogel (born in 1828), the landscape-painter, and Gerardina Jacoba van de Sande Bakhuijzen (1826-1895) represented the female element at the Hague exhibitions and made a fair name for themselves with their flowers and fruit. Technically, the latter was the superior of the two; but the former had more artistic feeling, in so far that she selected her own arrangement of colour.

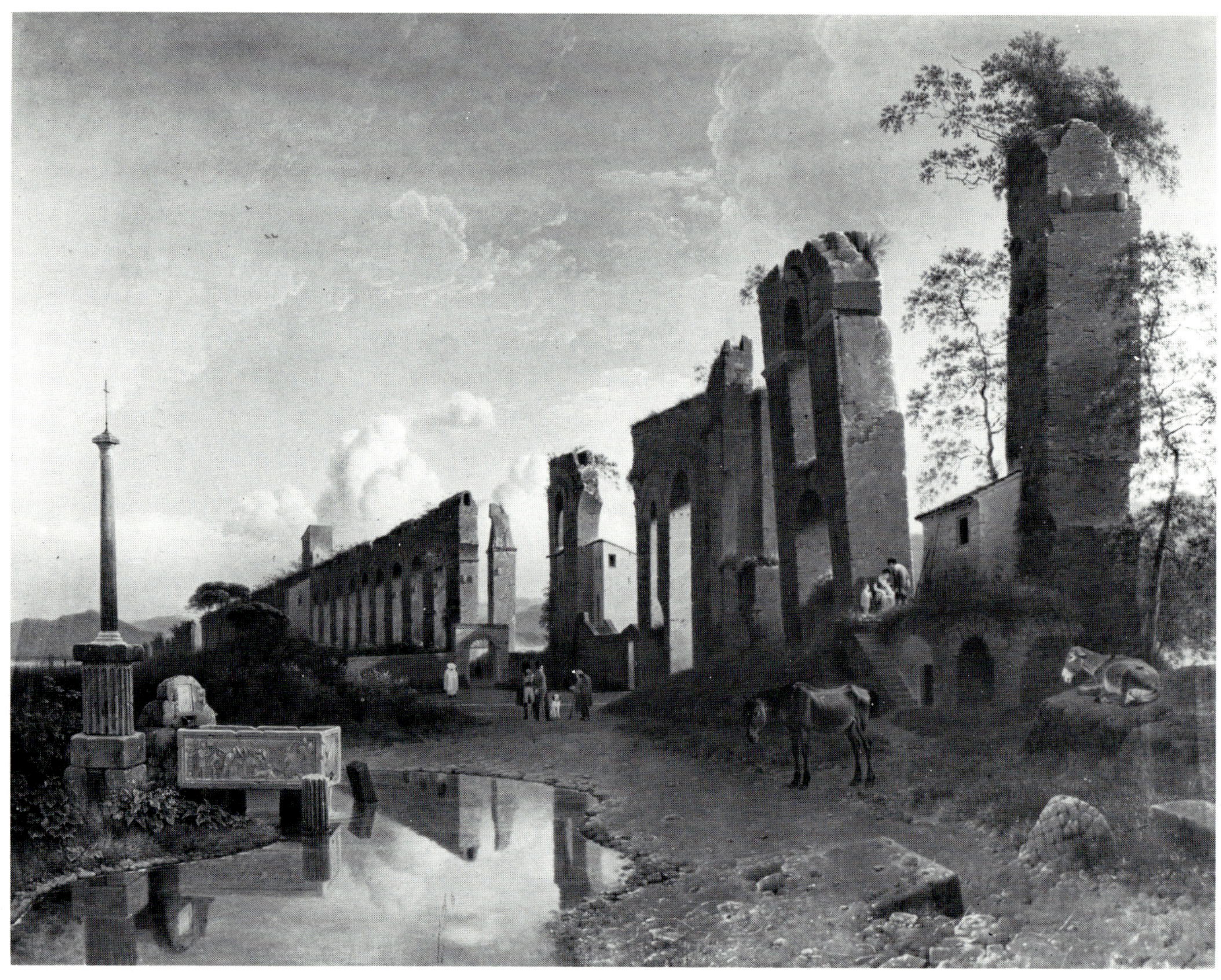

Joseph August Knip (1777-1847) *was Henriette's father. Seven years in Paris divided him from the Dutch landscape tradition. This satin-smooth Italian view dates from a visit to Rome in 1819 – he went blind in 1832. (69 x 90cms.).* Photograph courtesy of Mak van Waay, Amsterdam.

Neither of them possessed the solid talent of their senior, Maria Vos, born in 1824 and a pupil of Petrus Kiers, whose painting partook rather of the old Dutch excellence. She is represented in Boymans' Museum by a picture of still-life which goes to show that she is unsurpassed by any woman painter of this style in our country.

J.B. Tom's mantle may be said to have descended upon Johannes Martinus Vrolijk (1845-1894), an unemotional but serious painter of fields and cattle. Vrolijk was a pupil of Pieter Stortenbeker, distinguished himself by his own etchings and managed the Pulchri Studio press, which produced Jacob Maris' *Mill* and so many other famous etchings.

Richard Bisschop, born at Leeuwarden in 1849, is a cultured painter of church-interiors, which he executes with great thoroughness and completeness. Occasionally, in his water-colour drawings of Catholic churches, in the twilight of the columns seen against the candle-light and the faint light from outside, he shows his relationship with Israëls; while, on the other hand, his painting reveals the influence of his uncle and master, Christoffel Bisschop.

Marinus Boks (1849-1885) was an immediate pupil of Mauve's and a pure landscape-painter. In the few pictures of his short life known to us, he has said

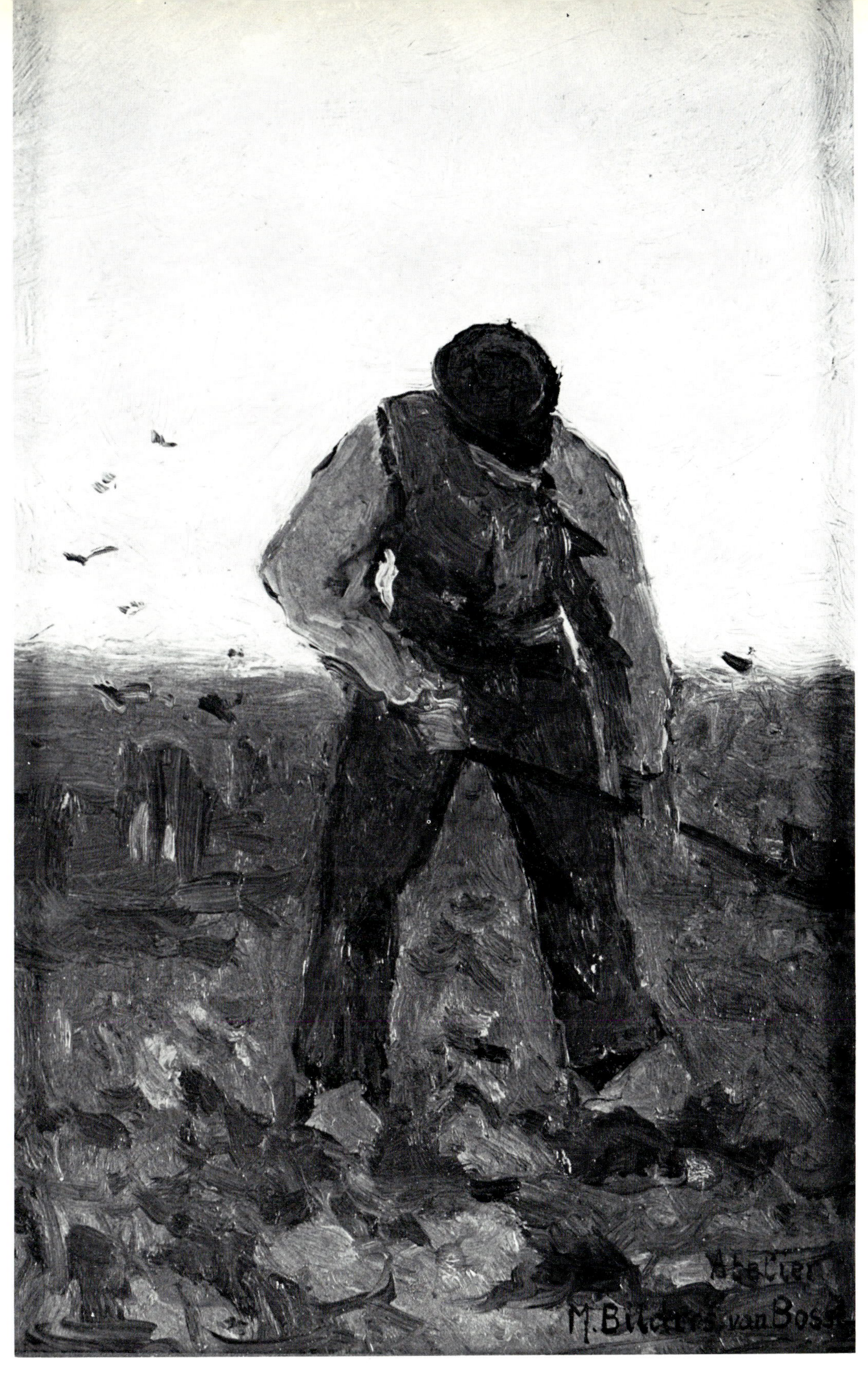

Maria Philippine Bilders-Van Bosse (1837-1900) *is true to the Hague School tradition in this simple painting of a peasant digging.* Photograph courtesy of Mak van Waay, Amsterdam.

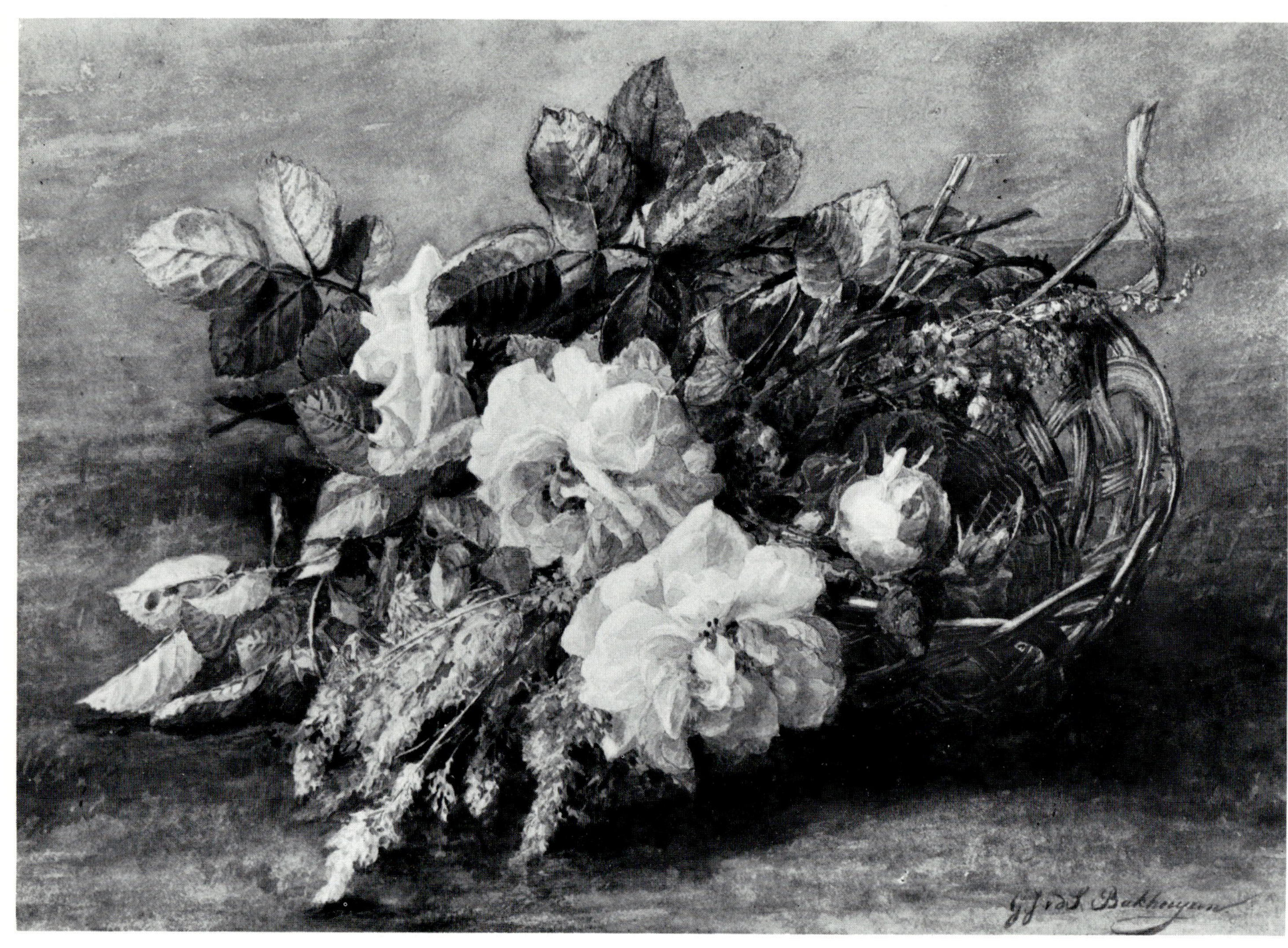

Gerardina Jacoba van der Sande Bakhuijzen (1826-1895) *exhibited with the Hague School of artists but specialised with still lives of flowers and fruit, of which this is an example.* Photograph courtesy of Rijksmuseum Hendrik Willem Mesdag, the Hague.

something about the dunes that none had said before him. Yet it is not possible to judge with certainty, because, during his illness, Jacob Maris often completed his unfinished pictures for him with his own powerful hand.

Lodewijk Frederik Hendrik (known as Louis) Apol, born at the Hague in 1850, was a pupil of the Hague Academy, of Johannes Franciscus Hoppenbrouwers (1819-1866) and of P. Stortenbeker. He is a skilful painter, who achieved the full measure of his talent at an early age, making a name, when only twenty-five, with a snow-piece, *A January Day,* now in the Amsterdam Municipal Museum.

A more powerful figure is Theophile de Bock, born at the Hague in 1851. Although he was a pupil of Van Borselen and Weissenbruch, he began by painting important landscapes, inspired by Corot, and afterwards passed over to Jacob Maris, with whose palette, as it were, he painted some quiet pools, conceived in a virile manner. He displays his talent not only in his earlier pictures, but also and more especially in his chalk drawings relieved with a touch of colour. Here he shows both strength and delicacy and also his later originality, without a certain clumsiness which spoils

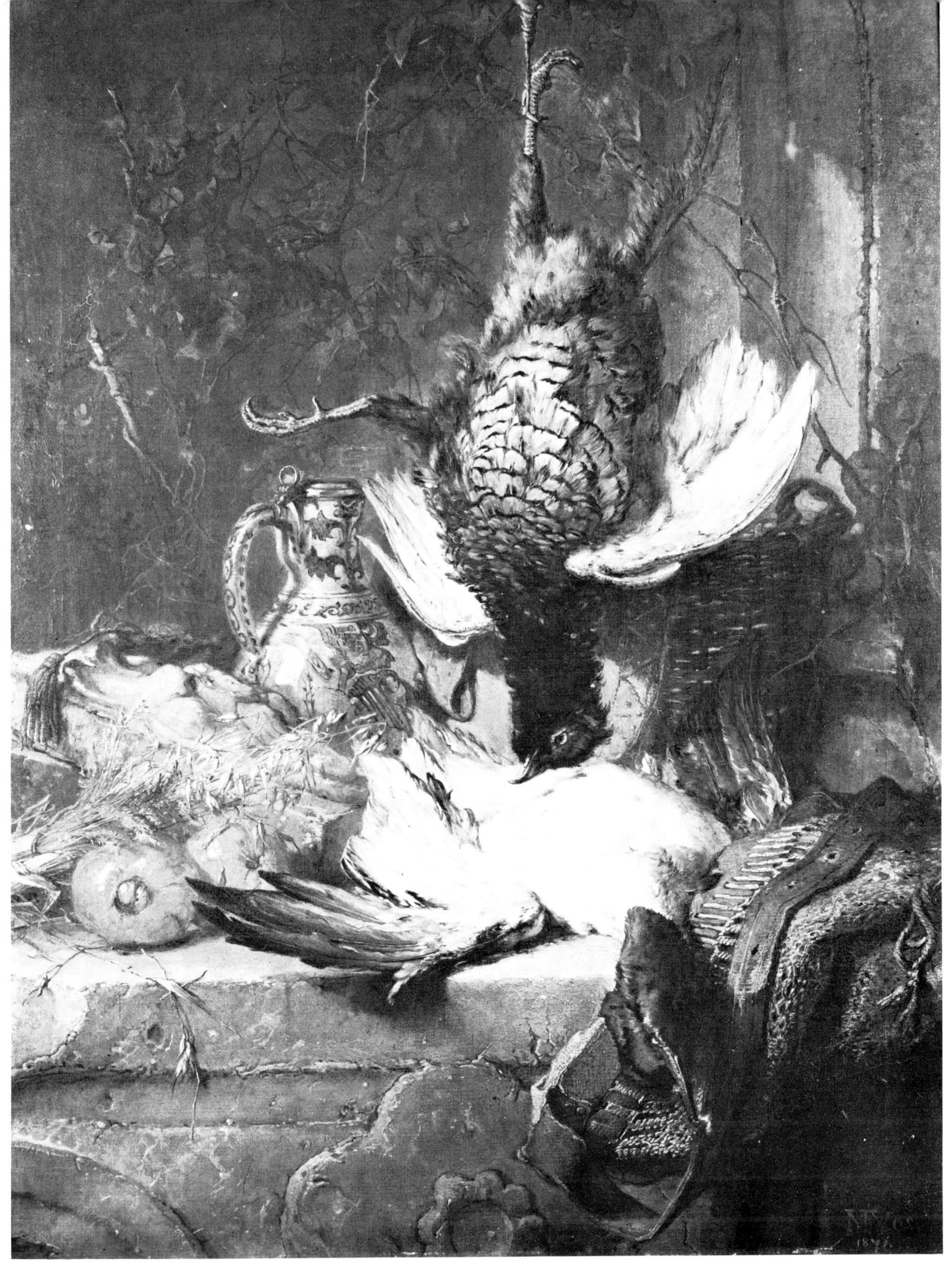

Maria Vos (1824-1906) *was a leading still life painter. She added a modern twist to the old Dutch tradition as in this still life of game and sporting equipment on an old stone ledge. (100 x 75cms.).* Photograph courtesy of Mak van Waay, Amsterdam.

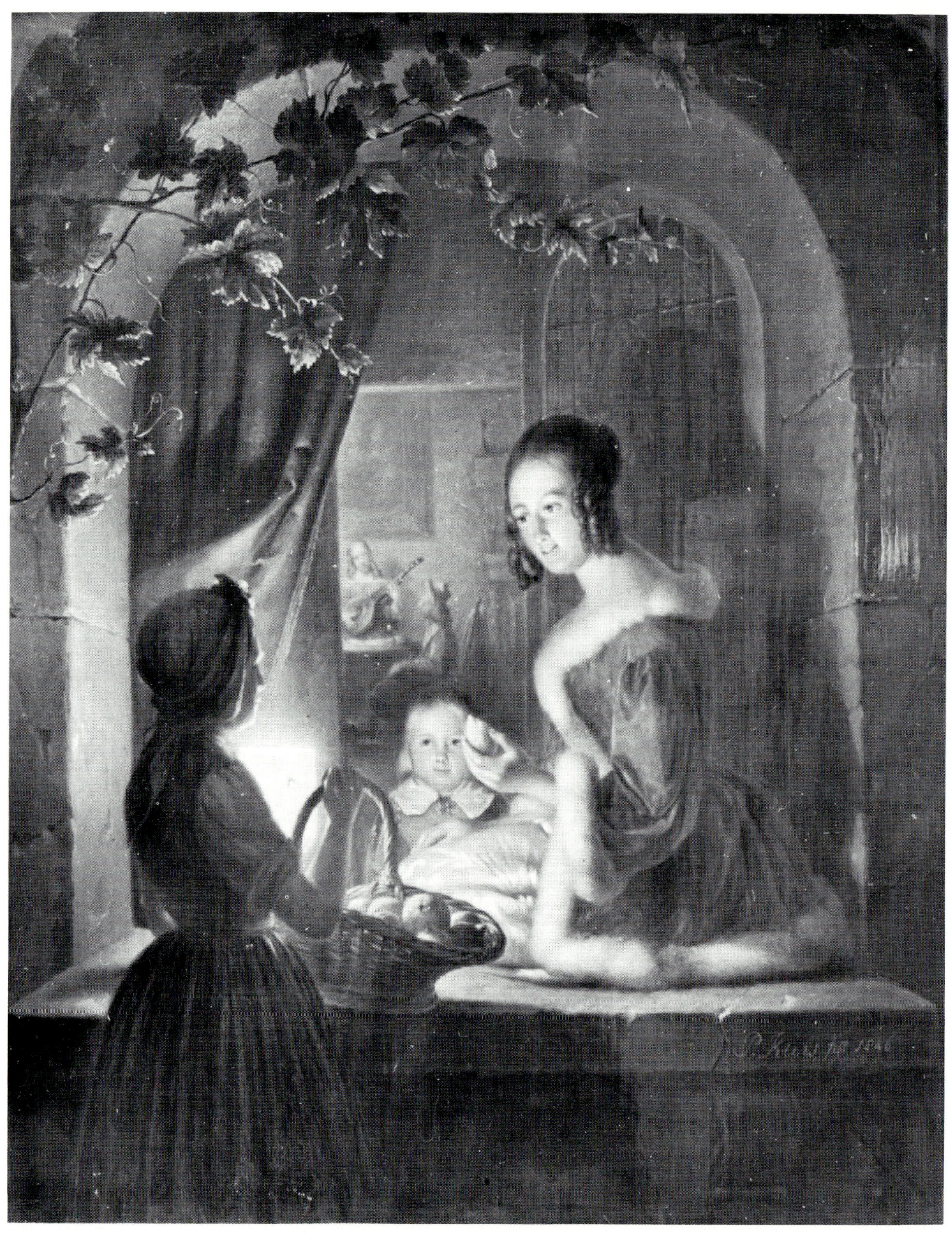

Petrus Kiers (1807-1875), *the teacher of Maria Vos, was an expert in the perennially popular genre of candlelit scenes. This one is dated 1846.* Photograph courtesy of Mak van Waay, Amsterdam.

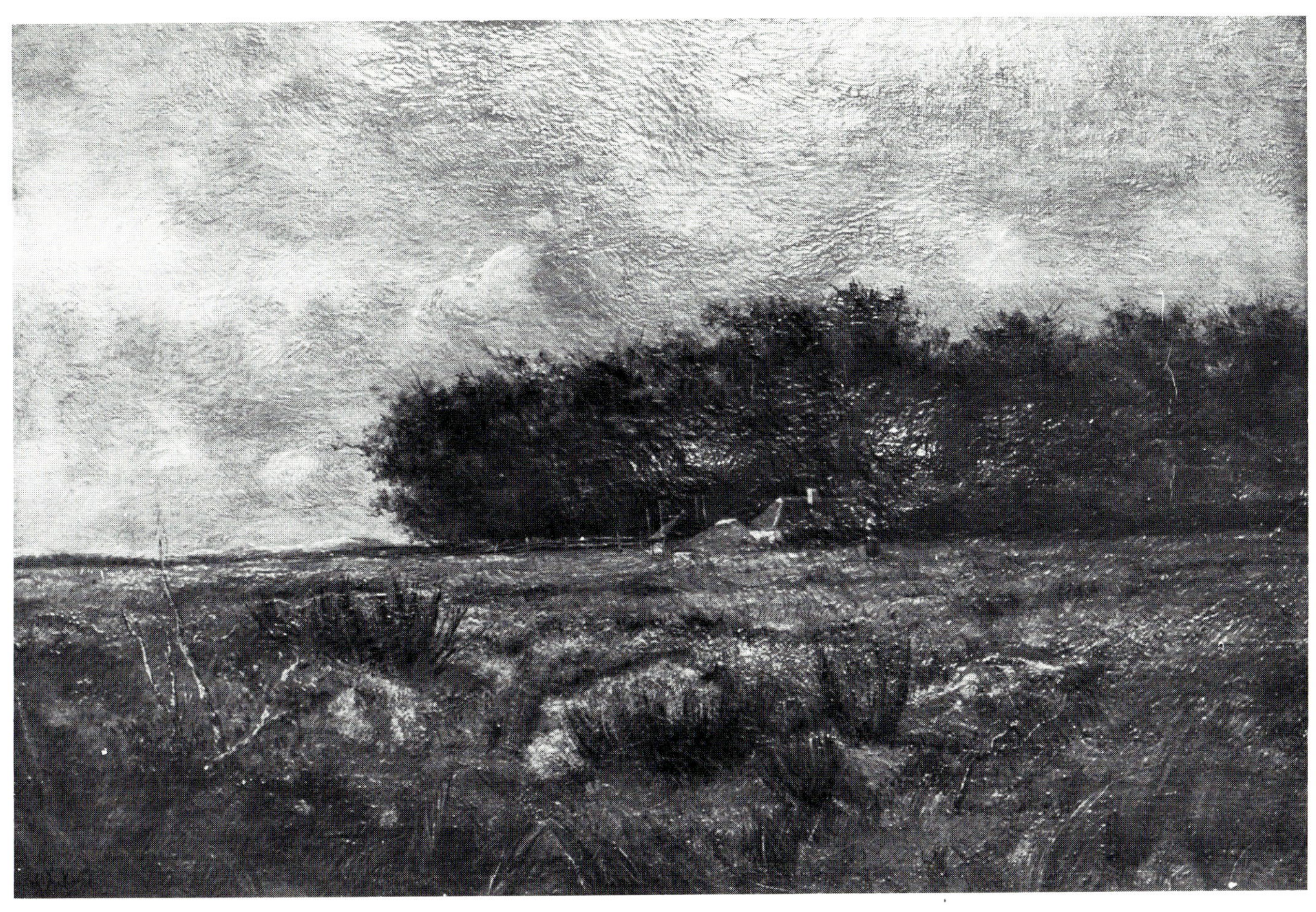

Marinus Boks (1849-1885) *was a pupil of Mauve. This "Dunes Landscape" is typical of the genre which earned him contemporary fame. (31 x 45½cms.).* Photograph courtesy of the Kröller-Müller Museum, Otterlo.

the harmony of his boldly-constructed landscapes.

Johannes Christiaan Karel Klinkenberg, born at the Hague in 1852, is a painter of town-views, an illusive limner of bright sunlight on house-fronts, quite as topographical as Springer, but less colourful, less studied in his composition, painting the old buildings and squares and canals of our country cleverly and unemotionally, in a manner that is always reminiscent of his master, Christoffel Bisschop. Klinkenberg is a painter of whom one might have expected that he would have taken the excellent Jan Weissenbruch, with his fine, sound workmanship, for his guide in a style which, separately considered, has been produced by no later artist with the same amount of truth and value. However, he found himself and worked out his ideas, which, if they do not fall within the domain of pure painting, are, in any case, popular.

George Poggenbeek (1853-1903), the Amsterdam representative of this generation following immediately upon the great Hague masters, has more than any other reproduced the sense of this school in his distinguished conception of our landscape with meadows and cattle, which has been painted in so many various ways. To the delicacy of Mauve he added the luxurious green which Willem Maris gives us in his "duck" motives; and, though he lacks the passion of the latter and the simplicity of the former, he commands a daintiness of line, of a more or less decorative quality, by which he atones in distinction of composition for his shortcomings in power.

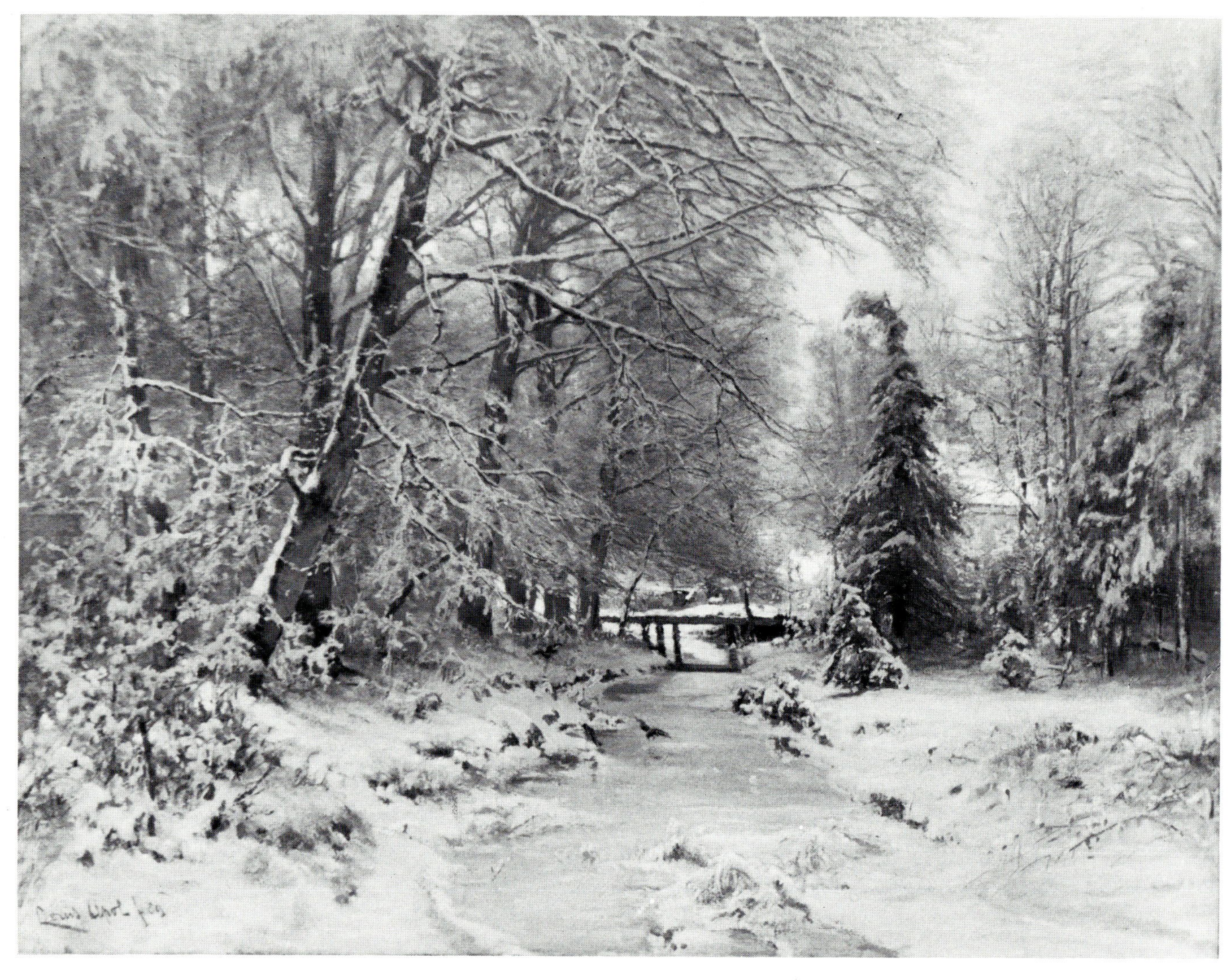

Louis Apol (1850-1936) *was a successful landscapist. This winter scene is dated 1889. (52 x 40ins.).* Photograph courtesy of Williams & Son.

Poggenbeek was destined for commerce; his intercourse with that talented and short-lived painter, Hamrath, made him take to drawing and painting when he was nineteen. He received his instruction from Z.H. Velthuizen, a painter who was not much heard of in his day, but who formed a number of pupils. He also learnt much from his connection with Bastert, with whom he lived for seven years at Breukelen. He also painted in Normandy and Brittany: fresh, bright town-views drawn with a quick sense of French nature.

Nicolaas Bastert, born at Marseveen in 1854, is a pure landscape-painter, a pupil of the Antwerp and Amsterdam Academies and of Marinus Heyl. He formed himself more especially at the Hague, under the influence of the clarity of Mauve and the Marises, and has produced good work in a strong and restful manner: views on the Vecht, subjects taken from the Amsterdam water-ways, also old castles. He excels particularly in views of rivers and other waters.

Fredericus Jacobus van Rossum Duchattel, born at Leiden in 1856, attained fame as a painter, both at home and abroad, thanks to the natural facility of his talent, for he had no other masters than the painters

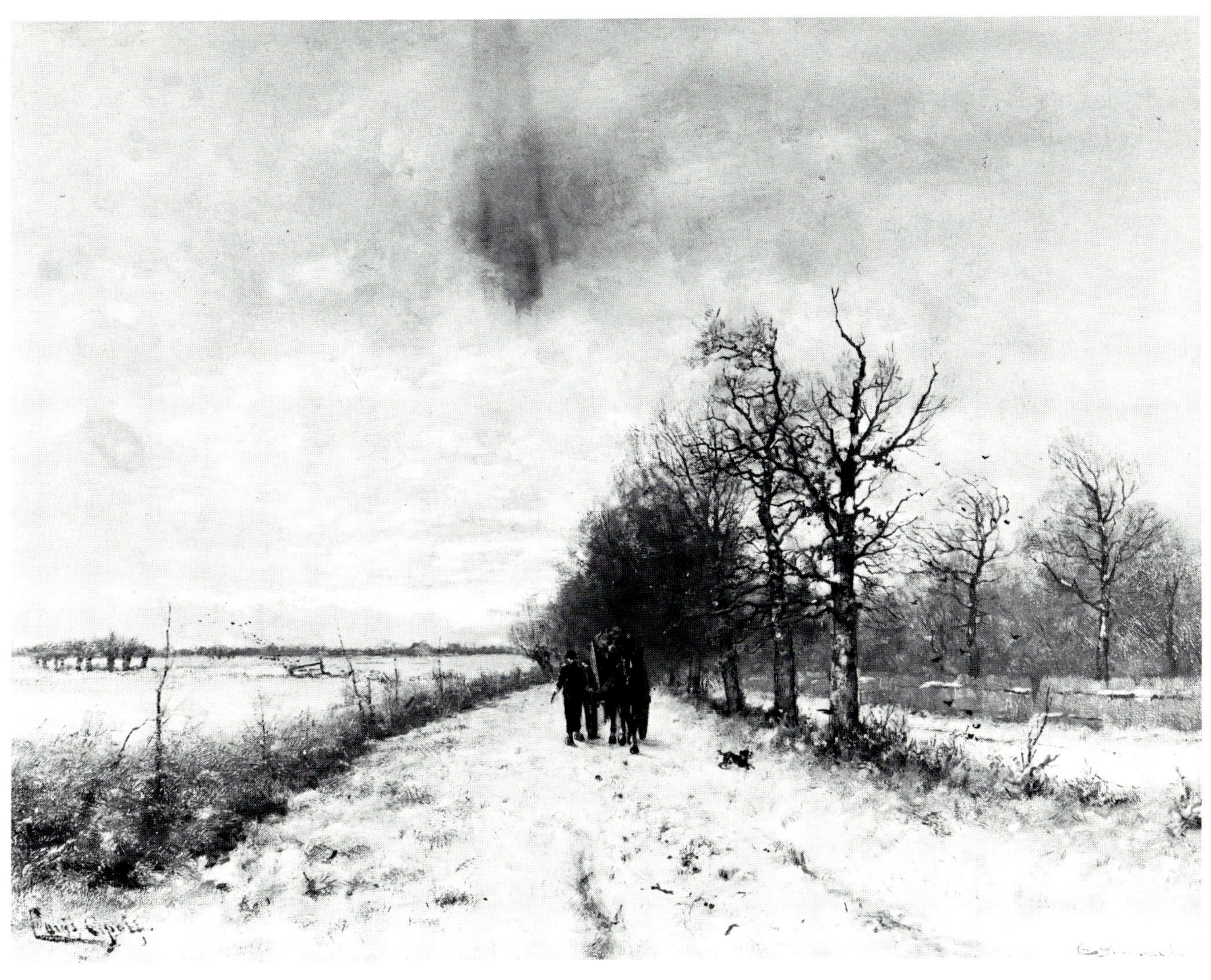

In this winter landscape **Louis Apol** *has collaborated with Cornelis Springer. It is to Springer that we owe the figures. (23¾ x 31¾ins.).* Photograph courtesy of M. Newman Ltd.

and paintings he observed around him. He was known in particular for those Vecht views which Bastert rendered in a more pictorial fashion. He possesses a dexterity in painting with water-colour which would, I verily believe, enable him to set down a view of the Vecht on a brown-paper coffee-bag as easily as on a sheet of Whatman drawing paper. From the beginning, this sort of water, with country-villas, summer-houses and barges along its banks, formed his favourite subject.

Jacobus Simon Hendrik Kever, born in Amsterdam in 1854, is a pupil of P.F. Greive, but soon began to follow in the footsteps of Albert Neuhuijs. He appears to belong to those painters who, endowed with a good palette and an easy method of painting, require another's formula in order to be able to express themselves. And often our Amsterdam Kever paints excellent Neuhuijs pictures, notable for good workmanship and a fine composition.

Tony Lodewijk George Offermans, born in 1854 at the Hague, paints shop-interiors, somewhat in the style of the Hague school with an admixture of the earlier Mesker, well-painted pieces which have a merit of their own, thanks to the capital workmanship and the faithful rendering of the types represented. He is a pupil of Blommers and, indirectly, of Artz; and, what

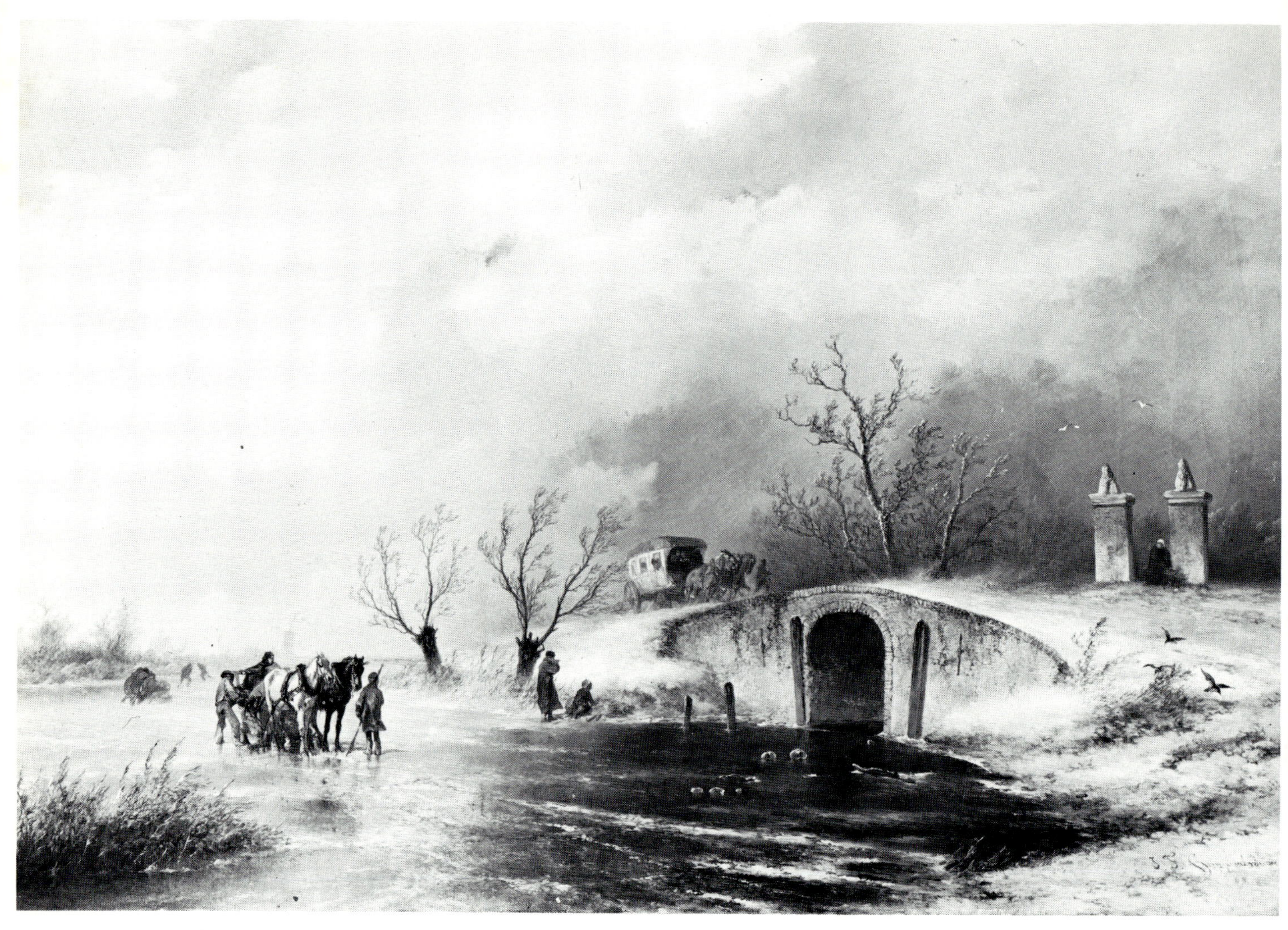

Johannes Franciscus Hoppenbrouwers (1819-1866) *taught Louis Apol. He was himself a pupil of Schelfhout whose work is recalled by this winter landscape. The figures in this painting are by Charles Rochussen. (60 x 90cms.).* Photograph courtesy of Mak van Waay, Amsterdam.

is more, he is the son of our greatest lyrical singer, Mrs. S. Offermans-van Hove, who came of a family that has always produced painters and musicians.

The portrait-painters of this period were Thérèse Schwartze, born in Amsterdam in 1851, and Pieter de Josselin de Jong, born at St. Oedenrode in 1861. Strictly speaking, neither of them belongs to the Hague school; but they accompany this earlier period, as it were, as its official portrait-painters and must needs be reckoned with it, although they have been surpassed in power of expression by a later generation. Thérèse Schwartze is not only the most widely-known Dutch woman painter of the last thirty years, or even of the whole of the nineteenth century, but she is to be credited with the fact that, at a time when portrait-painting, notwithstanding a few master-strokes of Jozef Israëls, had practically fallen into decadence, she honoured her father's tradition as a free art, not devoid of fantasy. She is a born painter, whose fluent modelling seems to be something quite her own, and, although draughtsmanship is not her strong point, although her faces could not withstand the criticism

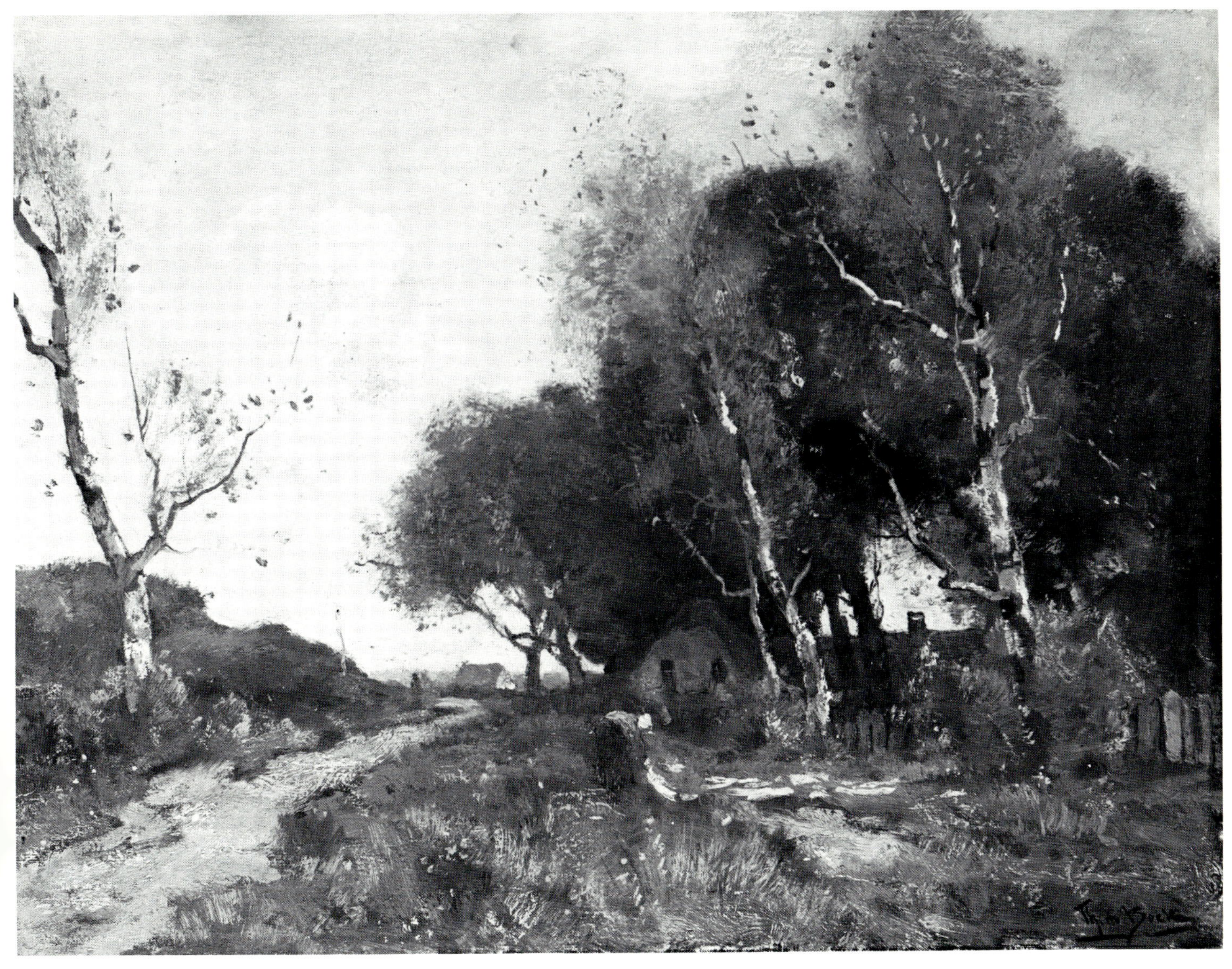

Théophile de Bock (1851-1904) *actually worked at Barbizon. His debt to Corot is clearly visible in this landscape. The silver birches with their light ration of leaves is a very Corot-esque feature, though the sturdier brushwork is essentially Dutch. (47 x 65cms.).* Photograph courtesy of Mak van Waay, Amsterdam.

of an academic expert, although – true woman that she is – she occasionally enlarges the eyes, reduces the mouths, refines the finger-tips of her sitters, she has sometimes produced portraits, swiftly seized in a few days' sittings, of such great excellence that we come to know the originals better through them. Of this first period, the portraits of Mr. Frederick Muller and of Mr. Toewater, the advocate, are doubtless the most powerful. The whole construction of the first, the head, shaded by a soft black hat with a broad brim, lighted with Rembrandt effects, brisk in colour, excellent in attitude, square and stately, points to the quickness of comprehension which is one of this painter's foremost qualities.

Thérèse Schwartze is a woman and her womanly intuition led her to woman's domain and to the use of a material in which womanly intuition rather than practical knowledge points the way. She began to

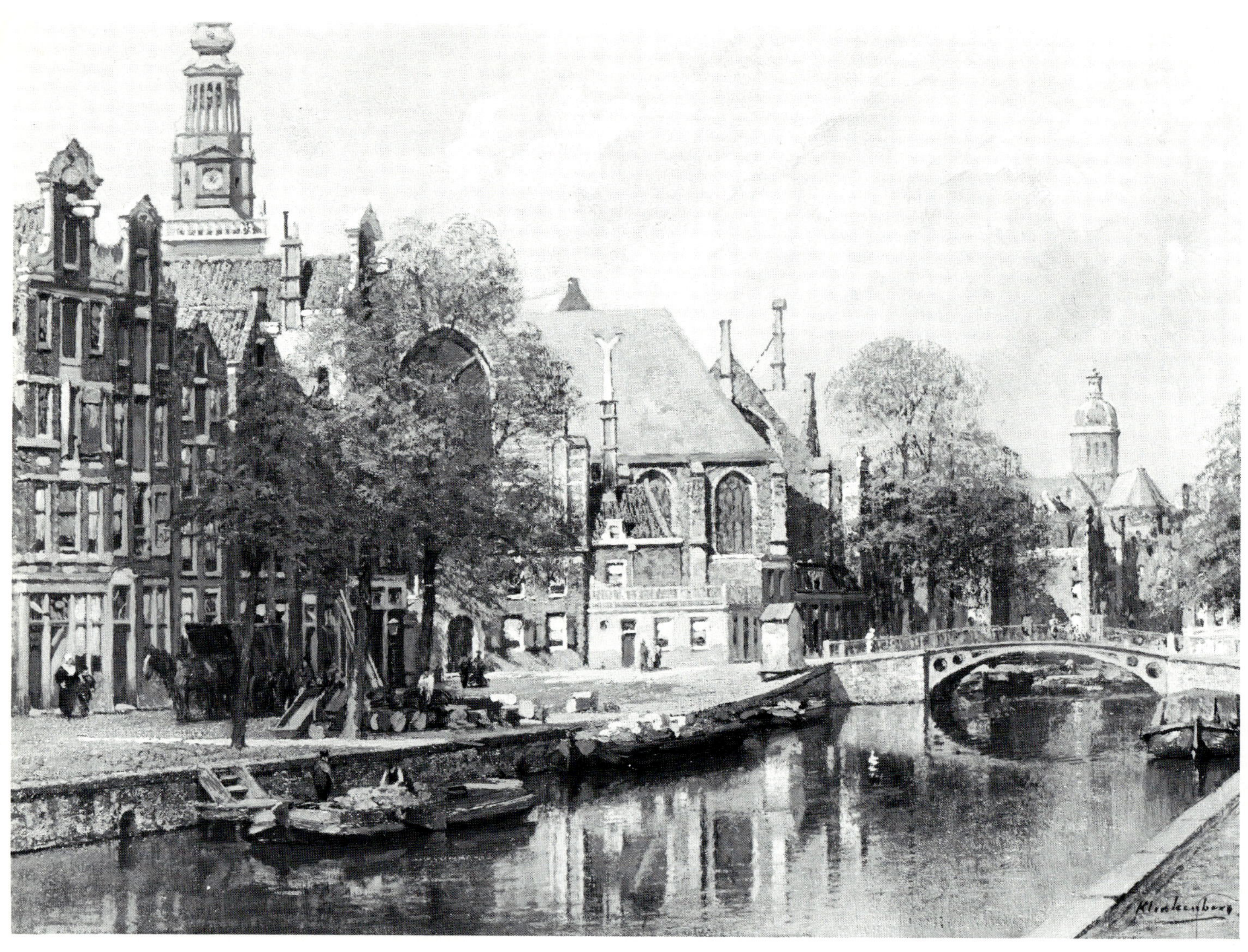

Above: **Johannes Christiaan Karel Klinkenberg (1852-1924)** *painted traditional town views with a more modern impressionistic brushwork and bright palette. This canal scene is set in Amsterdam with the Oude Zijck Ackterburgwal and the Oude Kerk. (15 x 20½ins.).* Photograph courtesy of Richard Green.

Right: **Cornelis Springer (1817-1891)** *was a leading exponent of the traditional townscape, relatively unmoved by the experiments that were going on round him. These two street scenes show his debt to his teacher Karsen. (12¼ x 16½ins. and 13⅜ x 16½ins.).* Photographs courtesy of Sotheby & Co

produce pastel portraits in 1885 and soon achieved technical perfection, particularly in the modelling of the face, which is more natural and simple, at least in so far as regards the portraits of women, in this medium than in oils. And, whereas, before, she was reproached with being able to paint only men's portraits, that is to say character-portraits, since this period she has shown, in a series of charming portraits of women and children, that pastel is a very beautiful medium in which to make the fleeting, evanescent, pale qualities of a woman's face tell against the brilliancy of the white silks or muslins in which she prefers to array her sitters. Of these portraits, perhaps that of the Baroness Michiels van Verduijnen is, as regards both composition and exquisiteness of colouring, the most elegant, the most *mondain* portrait painted of late in our country, while the likeness has not suffered through the well-thought-out arrangement of the picture.

De Josselin de Jong received his first lessons from

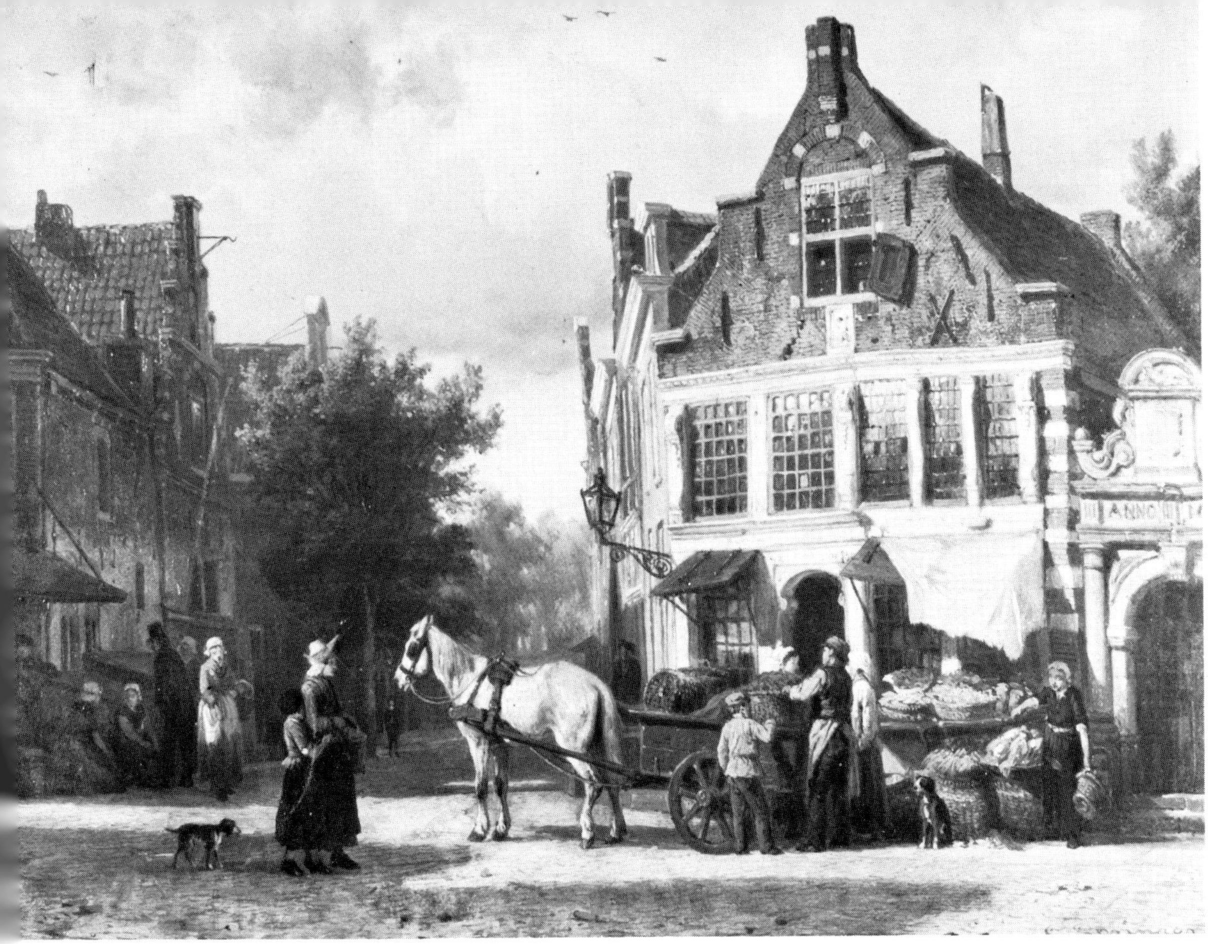

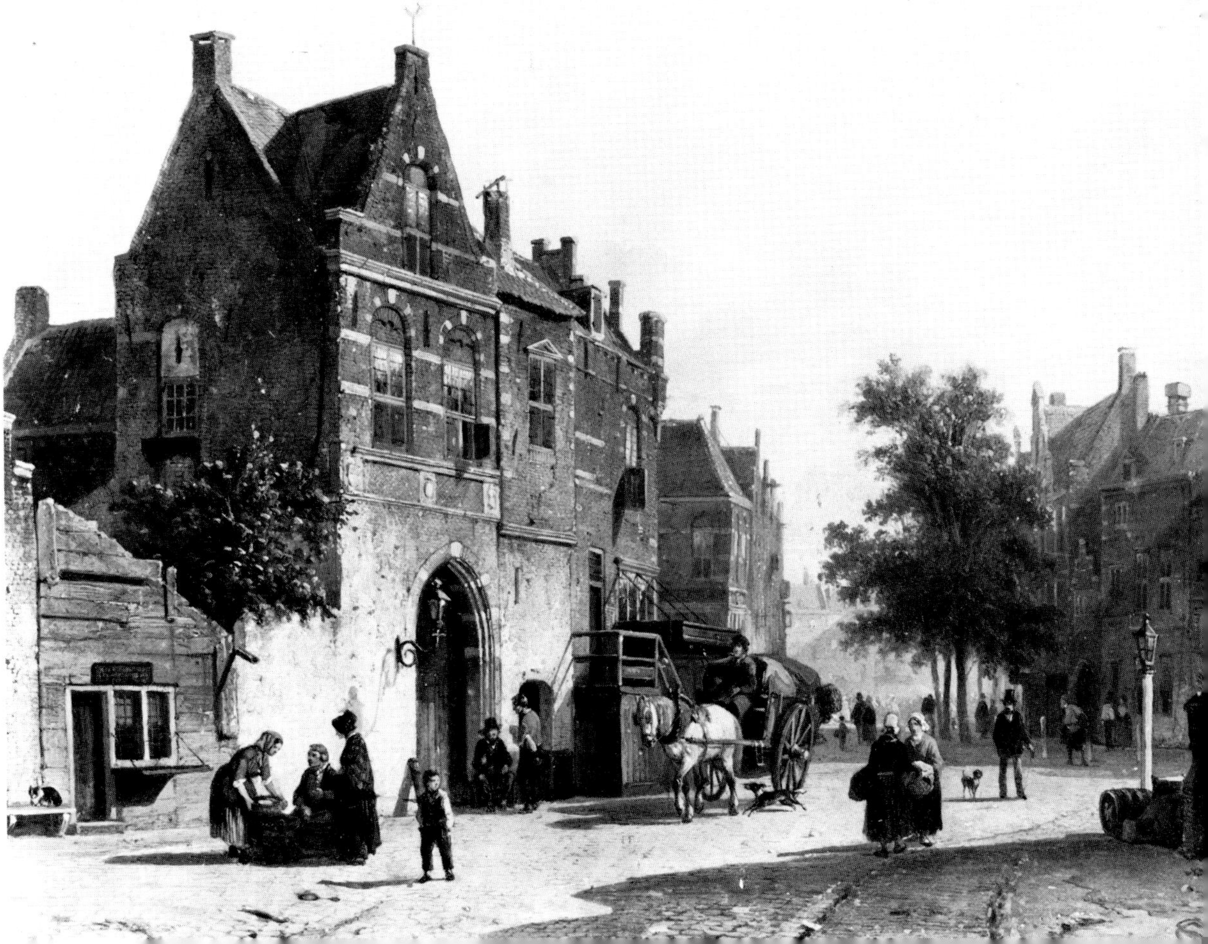

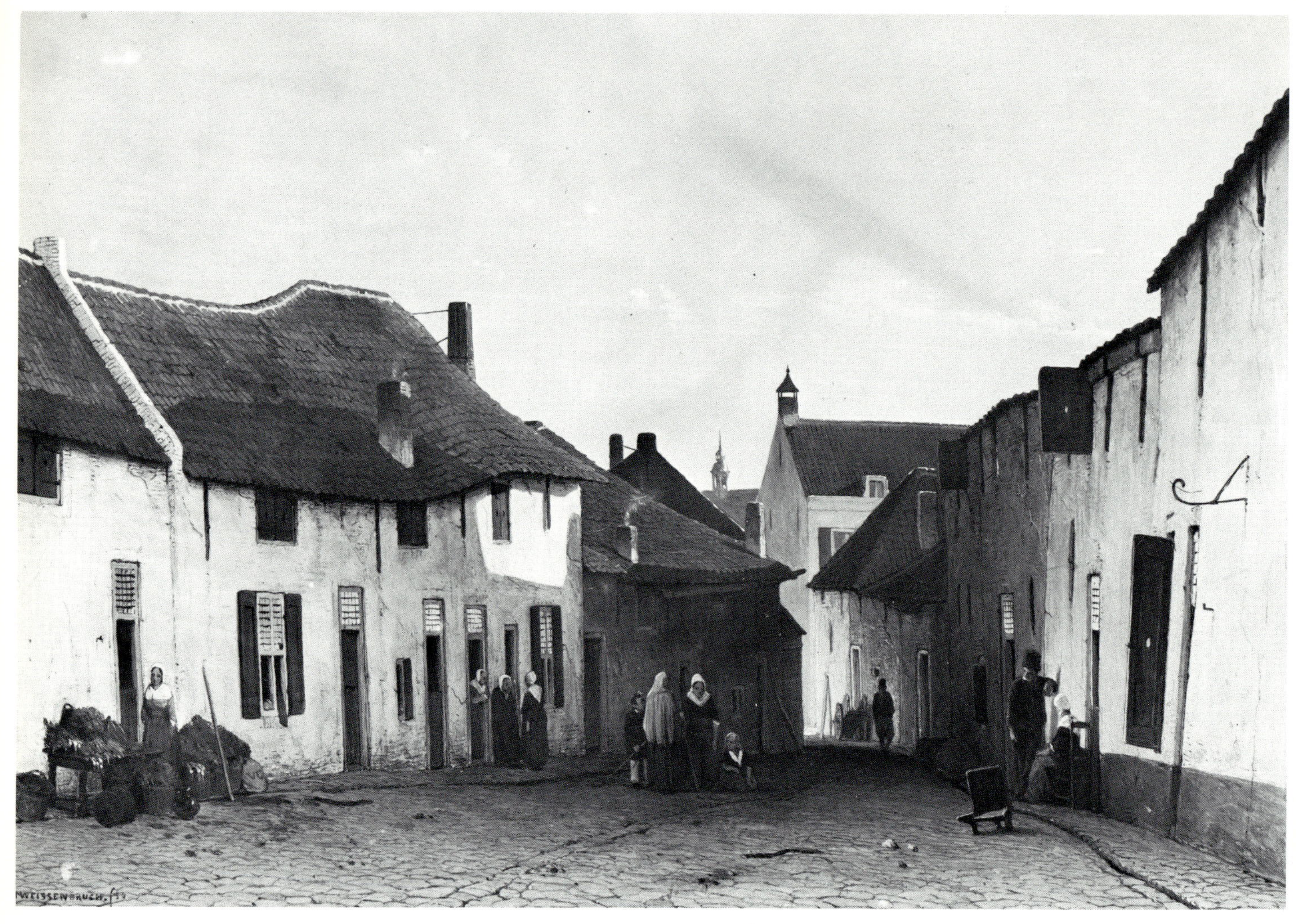

Above: Another variation on the townscape approach of the time is to be found in the work of **Johannes (or Jan) Weissenbruch (1822-1880).** *Here he uses a strong sunlight to model his village street. (39½ x 53½ins.).* Photograph courtesy of Mak van Waay, Amsterdam.

Below right: **Nicolaas Bastert (1854-1939)** *studied in Amsterdam and Antwerp but developed a pure landscape technique all his own. His particular penchant for waterways and old buildings is shown to advantage in this painting. (83 x 147cms.).* Photograph courtesy of Mak van Waay, Amsterdam.

P.M. Slager, at 's-Hertogenbosch; afterwards he frequented the Antwerp Academy and completed his education in Rome. His training, like Therèse Schwartze's, was quite foreign to the ideas existing at the Hague. And he excels rather as an academic draughtsman than as a powerful painter, so that it would appear as if the building up of a head or the outline of a hand never cost him the slightest trouble. We do not find in his work the little defects which mark that of Miss Schwartze, nor, for that matter, her charm. He has painted a series of portraits, honest, free from exaggeration and soberly observed, which amply satisfy the general requirements. He has also painted horses ploughing, water-colours that often display great power and are original by reason of the stiff lines of the agricultural slopes of Limburg, a very happy subject, to which he afterwards added glimpses of the life of the foundries, which give occasion for forcible illustration-work rather than for a well-considered harmonious whole, although we are bound to

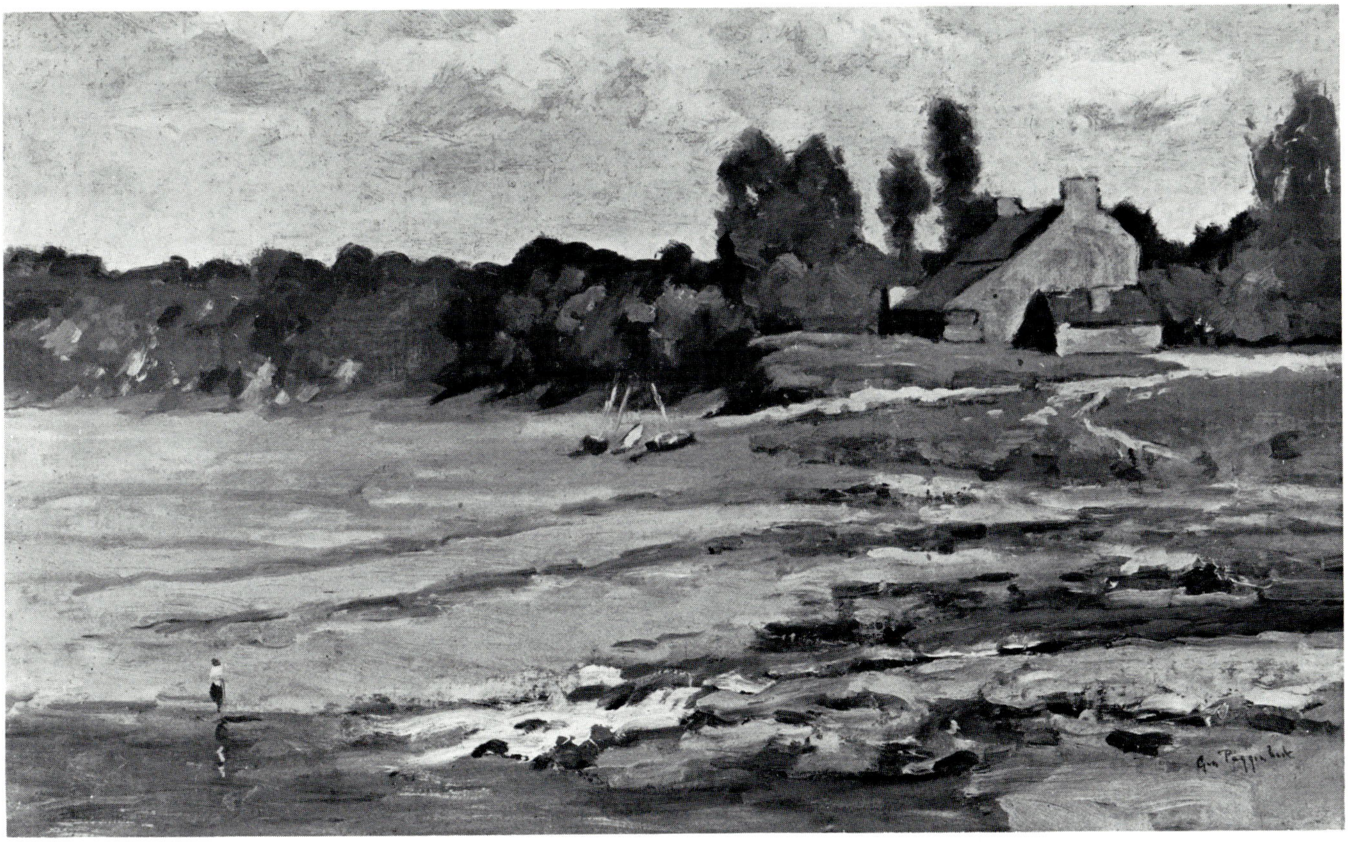

Above: **George Poggenbeek (1853-1903)** *was an Amsterdam landscapist who adopted the new style of the Hague masters. Here he has painted a simple coastal landscape. (33 x 50cms.).* Photograph courtesy of Mak van Waay, Amsterdam.

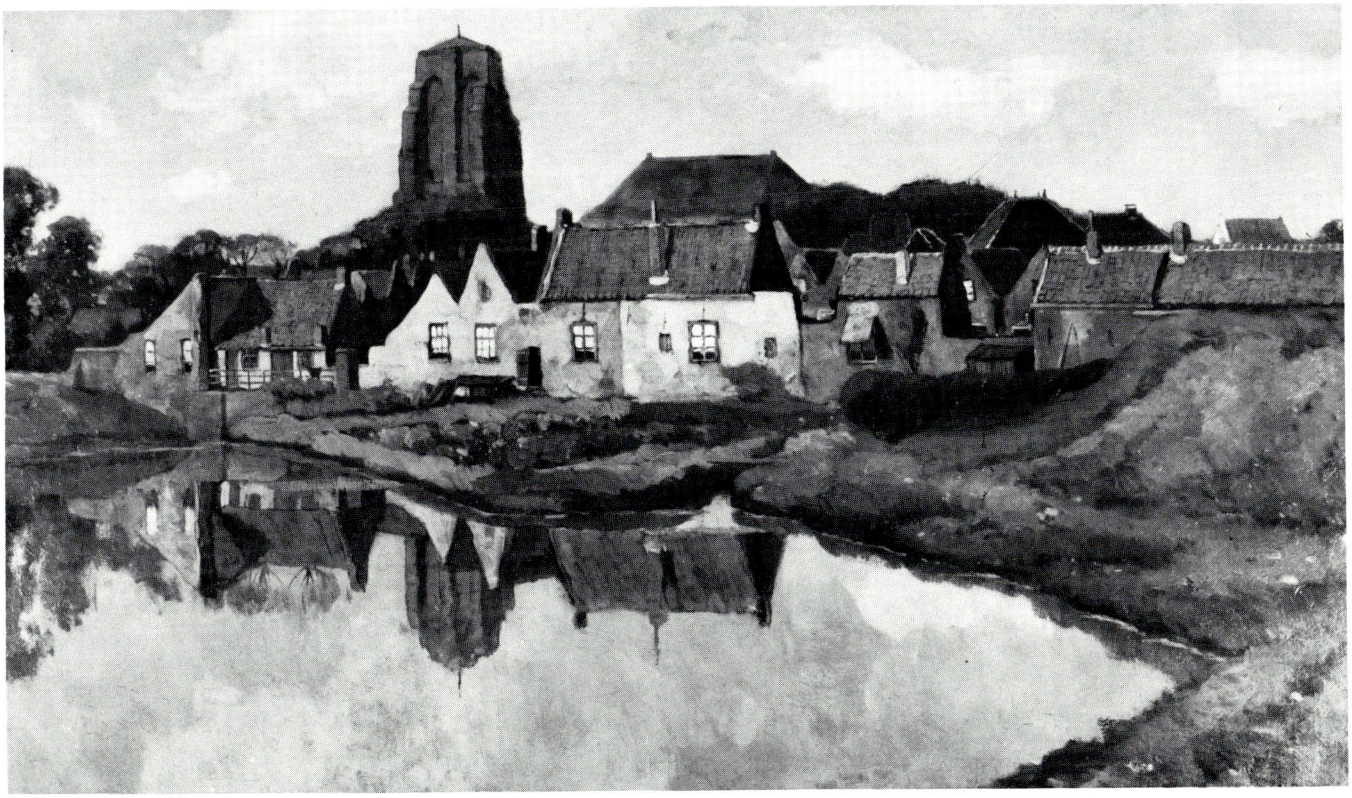

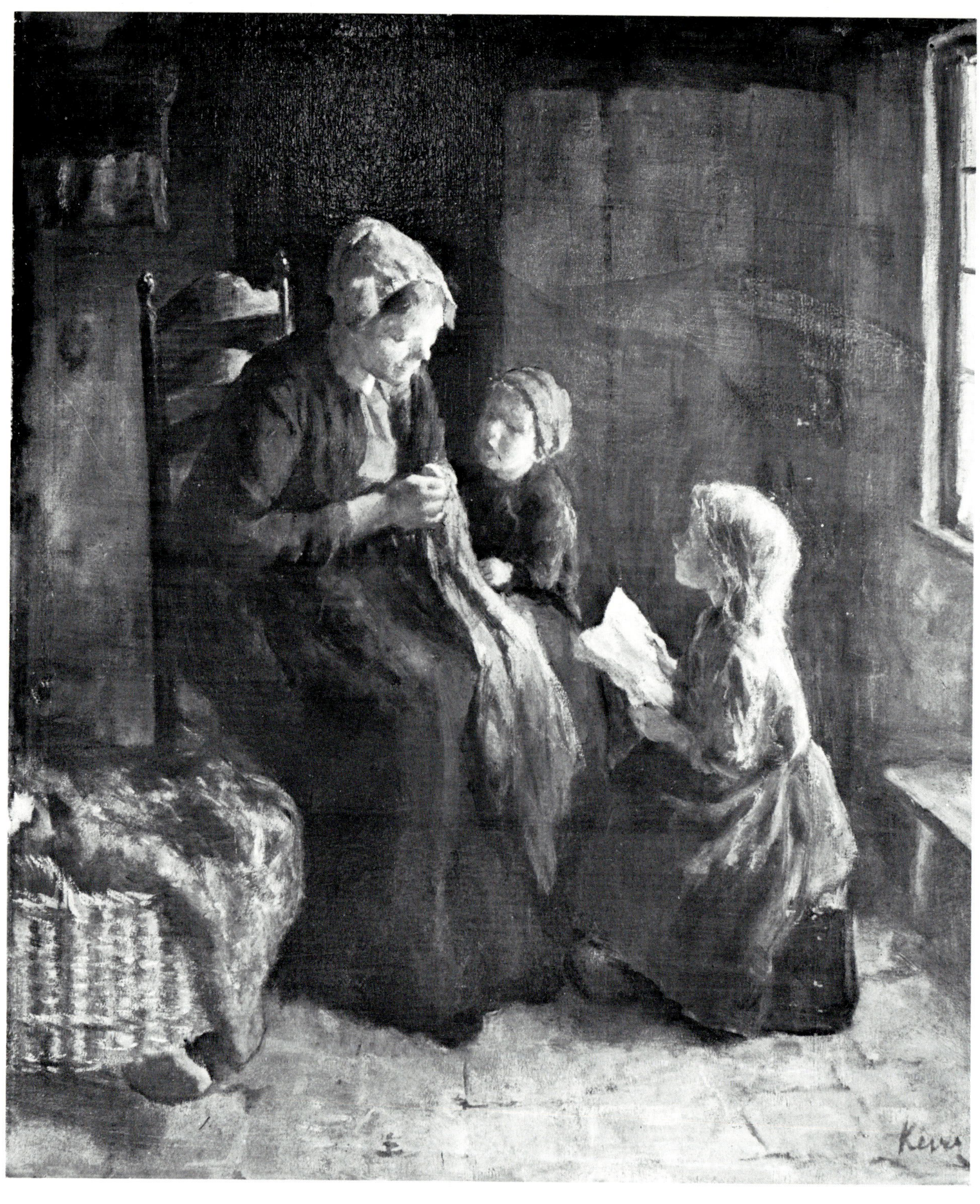

Jacobus Simon Hendrik Kever (1854-1922) *is described by Marius as painting "excellent Neuhuijs pictures". This interior with a mother and her two children is closely related to Albert Neuhuijs though the choice of subject can be traced back to Israëls, the father of the genre' (54 x 46cms.).* Photograph courtesy of Mak van Waay, Amsterdam.

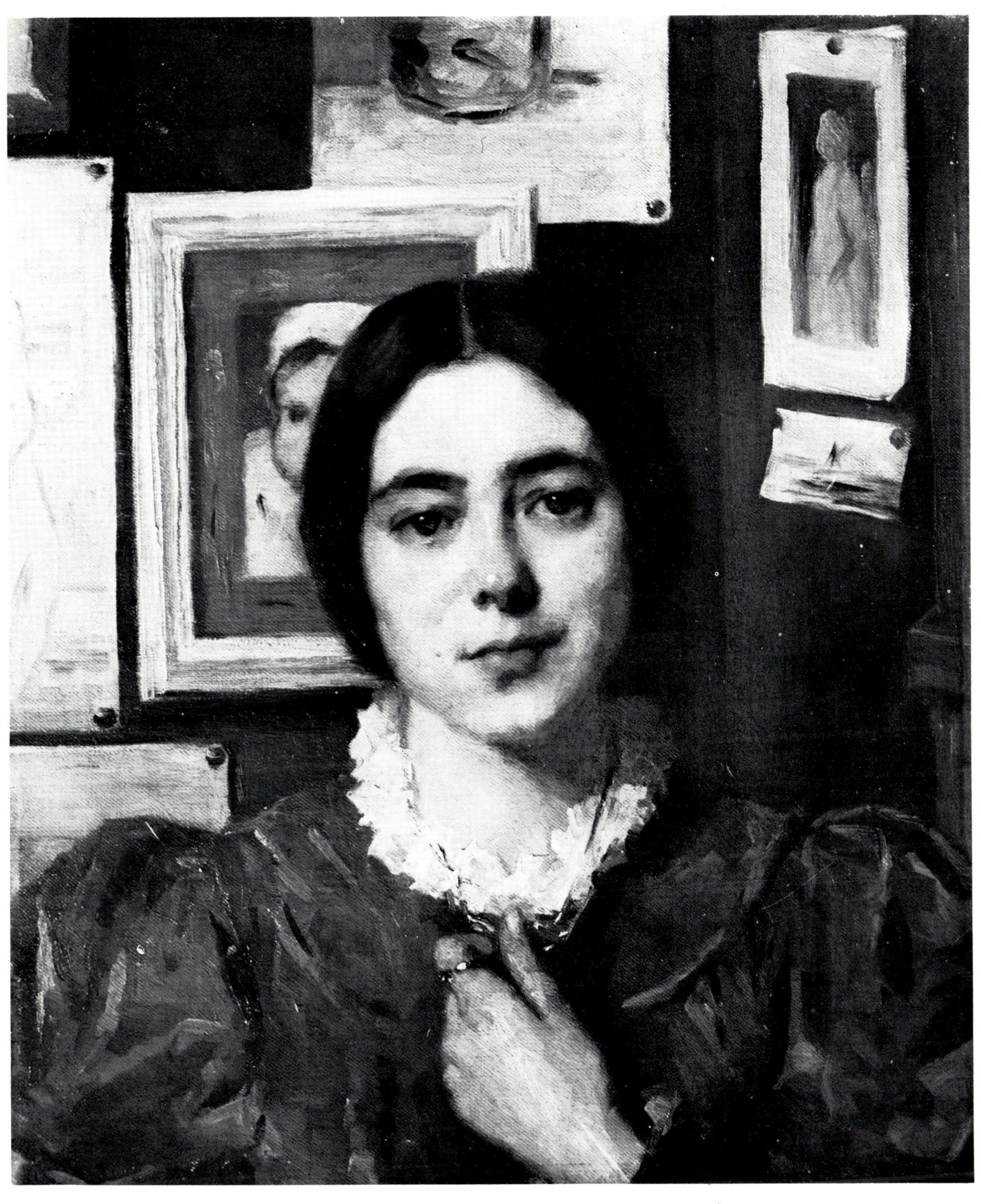

Thérèse Schwartze (1851-1918), *the daughter of a renowned portraitist, equalled her father's fame in the last twenty years of the century. Here she has caught the head of a young girl with fluent, impressionistic brushwork.* Photograph courtesy of the Stedelijk Museum, Amsterdam.

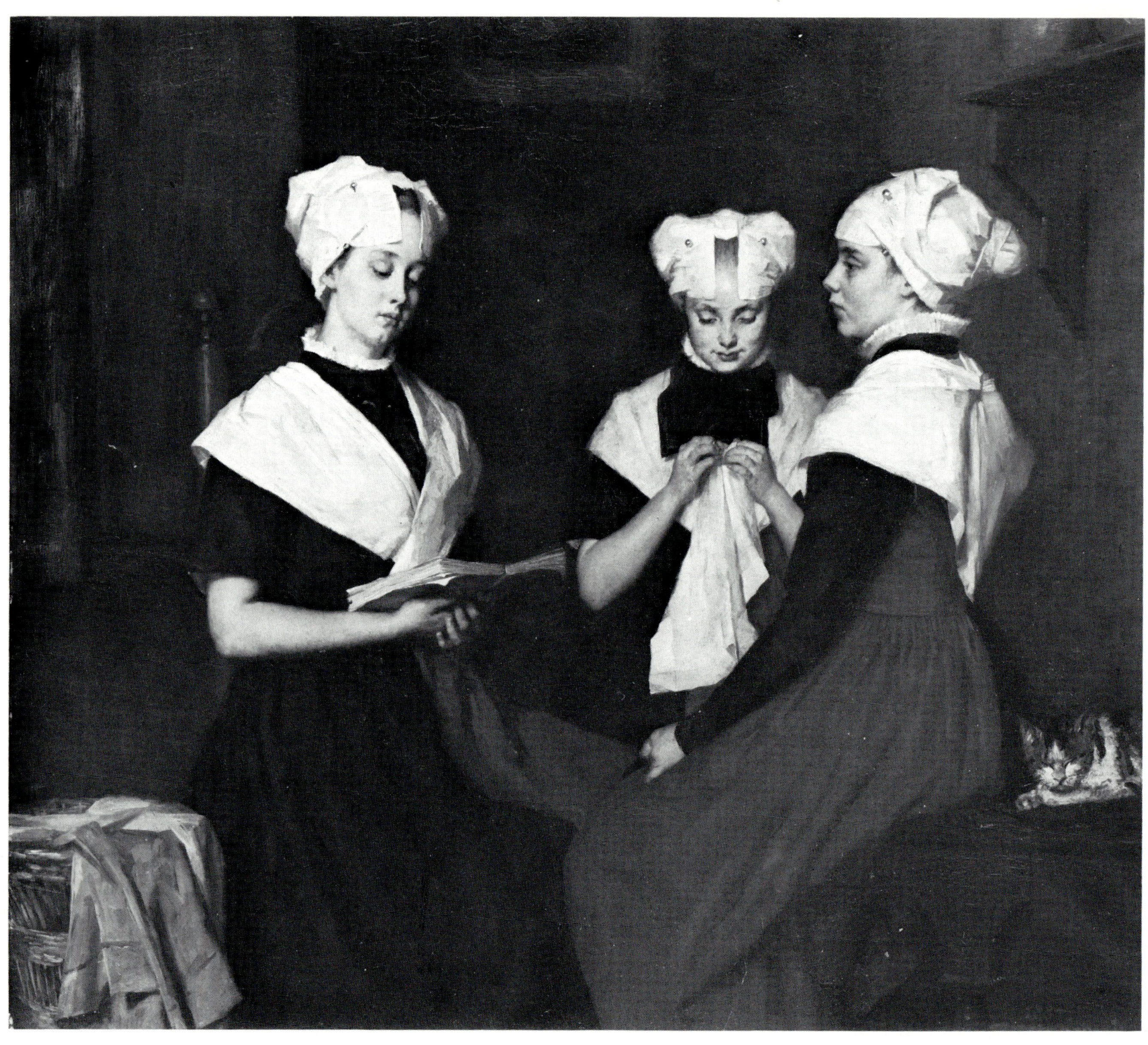

This painting of three girls at the Amsterdam orphan house was painted by **Thérèse Schwartze** *in 1885.* Photograph courtesy of the Rijksmuseum, Amsterdam.

admire his powers as a draughtsman when he represents his puddlers at work.

When we think of the Hague masters to whom this school owes its name, we realize that, sad though the fact may be, they too are subject to the universal law that the things of this earth do not endure. The first blow fell in February 1888, when Mauve died while the Hague painters were at the height of their productiveness. In the midst of his work, in the full flower of his life, he was snatched away, unexpectedly, from among that host of powerful masters. Bosboom died in 1891, Artz in 1890, Jacob Maris in 1899, Weissenbruch, Gabriël and Poggenbeek early in the twentieth century. The death of Jacob Maris in August 1899 was a blow from which the Hague school was never to recover. He had been a tower of strength to his juniors, a constant assistance, a helping hand; and his loss was irreparable.

Chapter X

The Younger Masters of the Hague School

All who followed the older masters of the Hague school based their methods upon them at the start and in this sense, therefore, followed in their footsteps. But the more powerful figures in this second generation, as soon as they were able to dispense with the crutch of the older men, struck out lines of their own. Their names are Bauer, Breitner, Isaäc Israëls, Van der Maarel, Kamerlingh Onnes, Suze Robertson, Tholen, Verster and De Zwart.

George Hendrick Breitner, born at Rotterdam in 1857, was the oldest and also the most vigorous of his contemporaries. He was a pupil of Willem Maris, whose broad smooth touch he applied, together with the colour-schemes of Jaap Maris, to a more passionate colouring in his charges of cavalry, in his artillery seen in profile against the sky-line, powerfully built up, with the long foreground represented clearly and evenly in forcible tonalities. He is, above all, the painter of movement, whose artistic bent inclined him towards the depicting of the bewildering bustle of military life: mounted artillery-men displaying their outlines against the smooth sky, or galloping down the dunes, full of screaming yellow and blacks, of horses and of the bright, white sand; or a shoeing-smith; or a halt by a Brabant homestead, one of those moments in the manœuvres which he would attend sketch-book in hand. Afterwards, it drove him to paint the huge complication of the trams starting from the Dam at Amsterdam, with all its noisy life and bustle of motley pedestrians and passengers and vehicles, or else of overburdened coal-wains, standing out high and huge against the petty life of a still canal. These town-views are pieces of a magnificent naturalism, of a passion that contains none of the spacious quietude in which Jacob Maris sees the town lying under the fleeting clouds, none of the latter's melodious harmonies, none of his symphonic view of nature, but rather a modern instrumentation, in which the brasses prevail. For Breitner is essentially a modern painter, who, coming from the restful Hague, must needs have been impressed with the great movement of a capital city; a passionate painter for whom it was reserved to reproduce in large and mighty and truthful strokes the monumental greatness of the old town and also its modern street-life, with the dissonance of the shrill street-lamps, the brightly-lighted shops, glaring through the peace of the evening, shining fiercely upon the passers-by, turning the wet asphalt into a mirror in which the figures are lengthened in an unreal fashion.

But for us who acknowledged Breitner from the beginning it was finer than all this to watch him on the drawing evenings at Pulchri Studio, in the little sketching-room, with the tobacco-smoke floating up to the ceiling and obscuring the model. There he sat fixing a water-colour, holding the drawing-block between his ankles, dripping the paint from his brush according to its true values. And in a moment there would come into being the white of an apron, the blue of a soldier's uniform, amid the admiration of those who stood gathered round this perfect virtuoso in colour.

This was in the Hague time of his period of storm and stress, when he painted as and because he must. I remember later an occasion at the short-lived, but uncommonly distinguished art-club on the Keizersgracht in Amsterdam, how Lord Leighton's *Phryne* compelled our admiration by the magnificent soundness of its qualities and how we were in the same moment impressed by a brilliant colour-sketch of Breitner's, a woman in yellow with a withered tulip in her hand, painted entirely with an eye to beauty. It

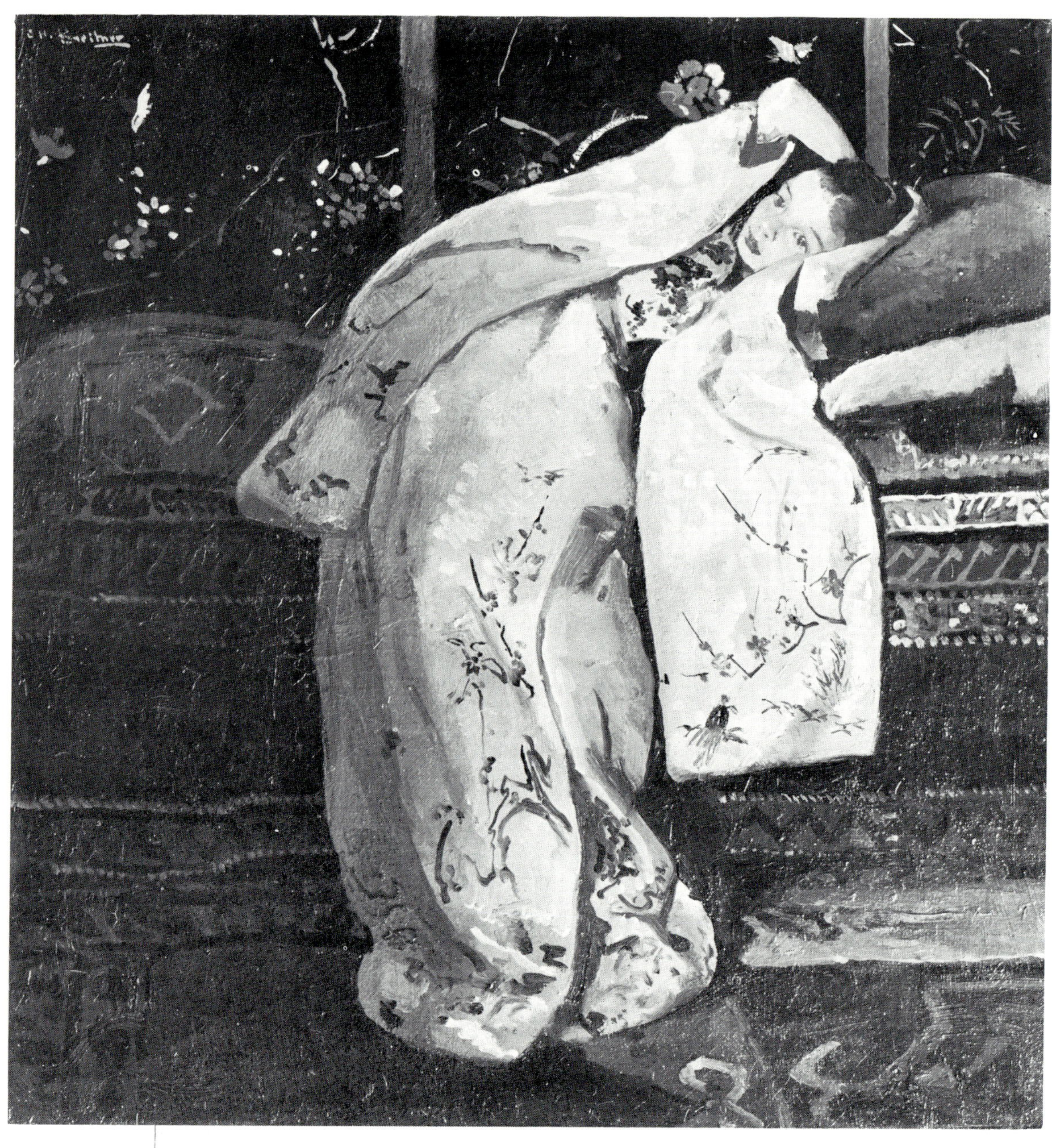

George Hendrik Breitner (1857-1923) *was a pupil of Willem Maris but very much a painter of a later generation. He has been called Holland's leading Impressionist. Here he follows the Parisians in his fascination with Japanese design. (59 x 57cms.).* Photograph courtesy of the Rijksmuseum, Amsterdam.

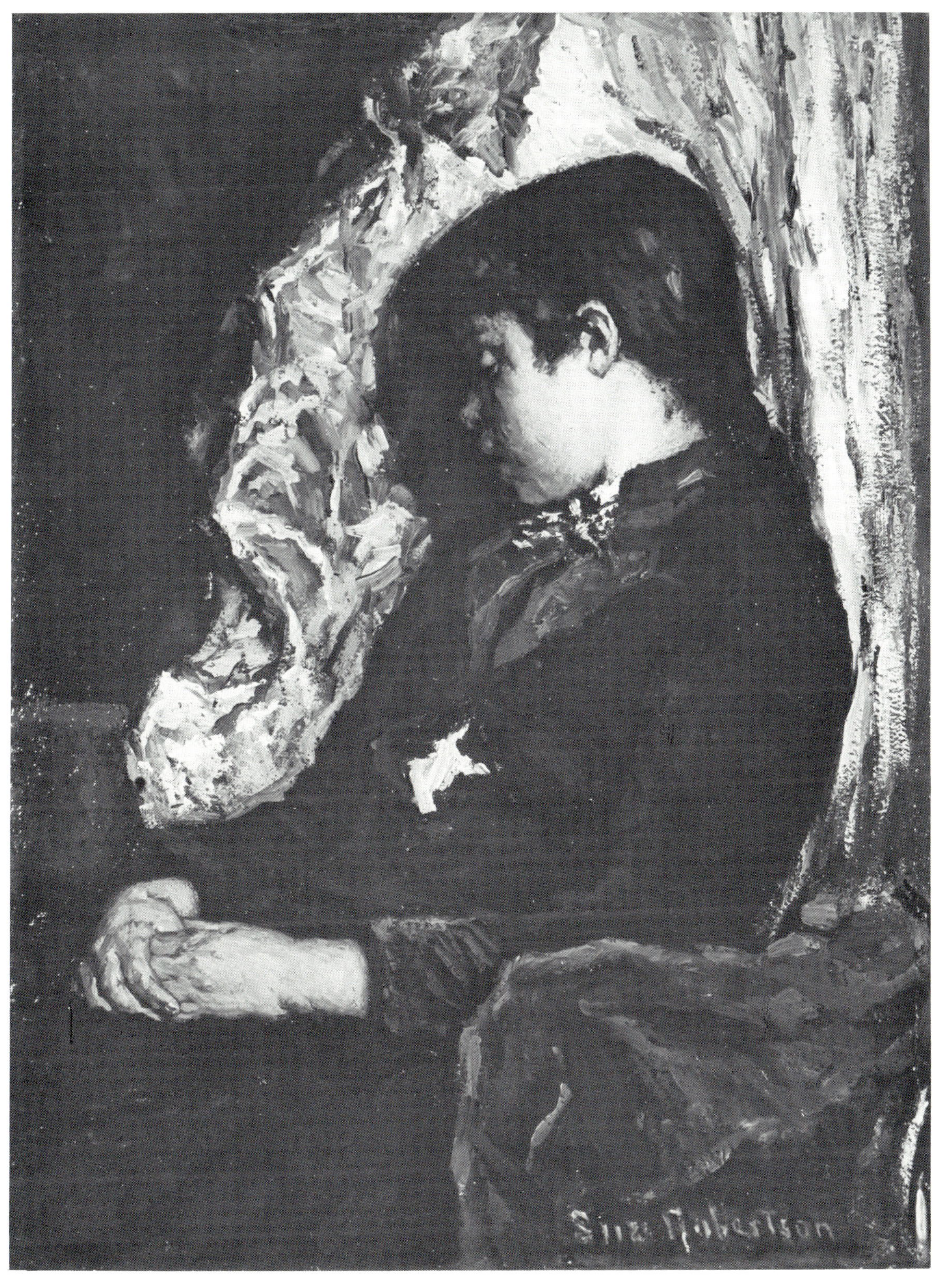

Suze Bisschop-Robertson (1855-1922) *painted with a rich palette which shows to best advantage in her figure studies. Marius praises highly this "little dark figure of a girl seen against a yellow silk background". (80 x 60cms.).* Photograph courtesy of Mak van Waay, Amsterdam.

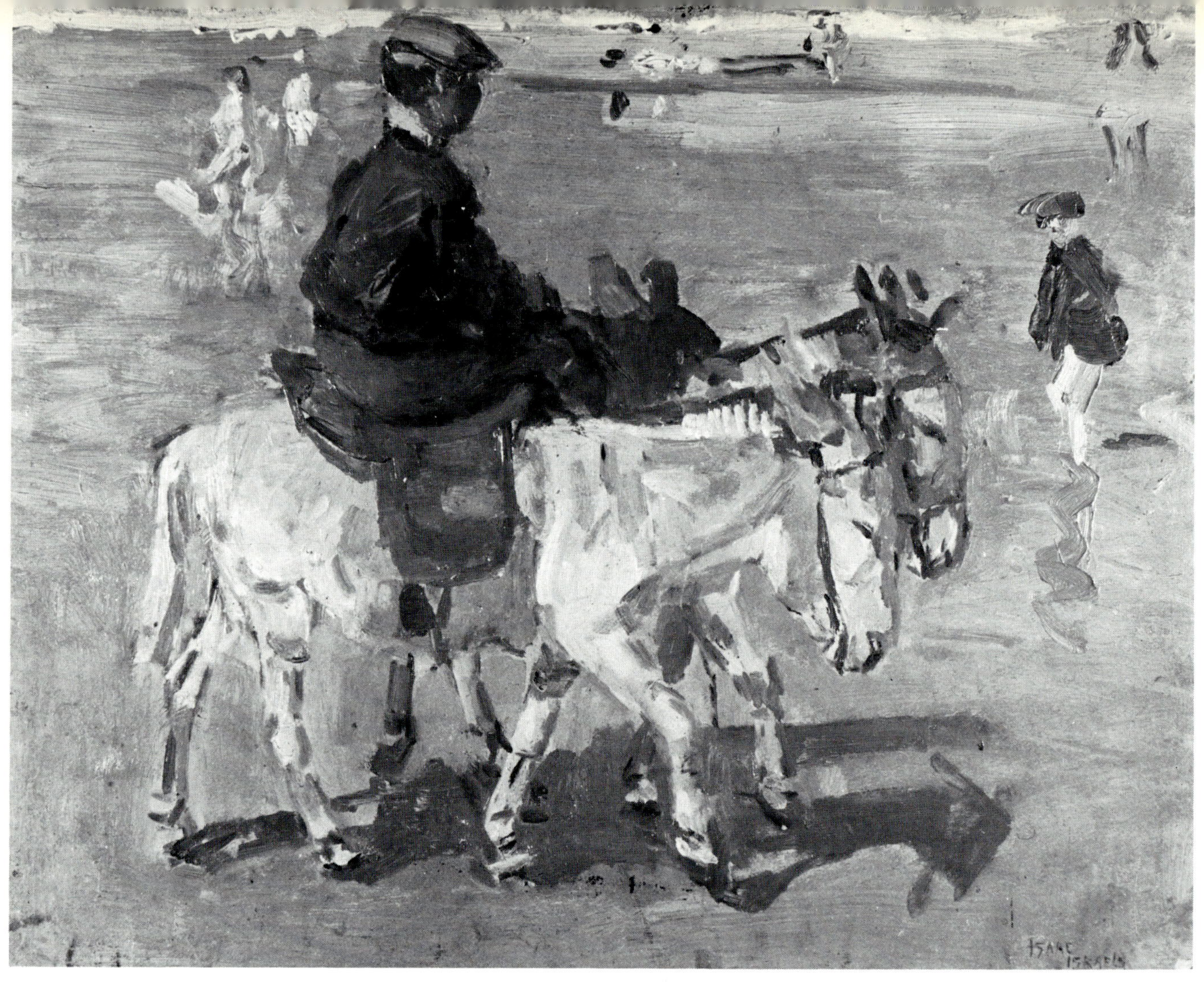

Above and right: **Isaac Israëls (1865-1934)** *was the son of Jozef and one of Holland's leading Impressionists. He seized on little moments in ordinary life and rendered them with swift colour and charm. In one of these paintings he has given us a glimpse of the beach at Scheveningen (48½ x 59½cms.), in the other a father with his children in Amsterdam's Osterpark. (39 x 59cms.).* Photographs courtesy of Mak van Waay, Amsterdam.

was thus that Frans Hals painted his master-pieces: *The Laughing Cavalier,* the corporation-pieces at Haarlem; thus that Rembrandt painted *The Lesson in Anatomy:* not thinking of the public, disregarding commercial values, from sheer love of beauty, following nature's promptings alone. And it was thus that Breitner, who, in the matter of his tones is himself an old master, painted that woman with the black cat, painted those portraits of himself in that warm, yellow tone, painted those firm, yet delicate, living flowers, painted those powerful Amsterdam studies from the naked model.

Although his artistic training was very different from that of Jacob Maris, Breitner never ceased seeking for means to overcome his defects of form. And, notwithstanding the effective hints which he received from that fine horse-painter, Rochussen; notwithstanding the fact that he passed an examination in intermediate drawing (he used to say that, if you stood in the Veenestraat pelting people with potatoes, nine out of every ten men hit would have one of those certificates in his pocket: nevertheless, his own enabled him to give a course of lessons at Leiden, where, among others, Floris Verster was his pupil); notwithstanding his having painted for twelve months in the studio of Willem Maris, who then lived at Oud-

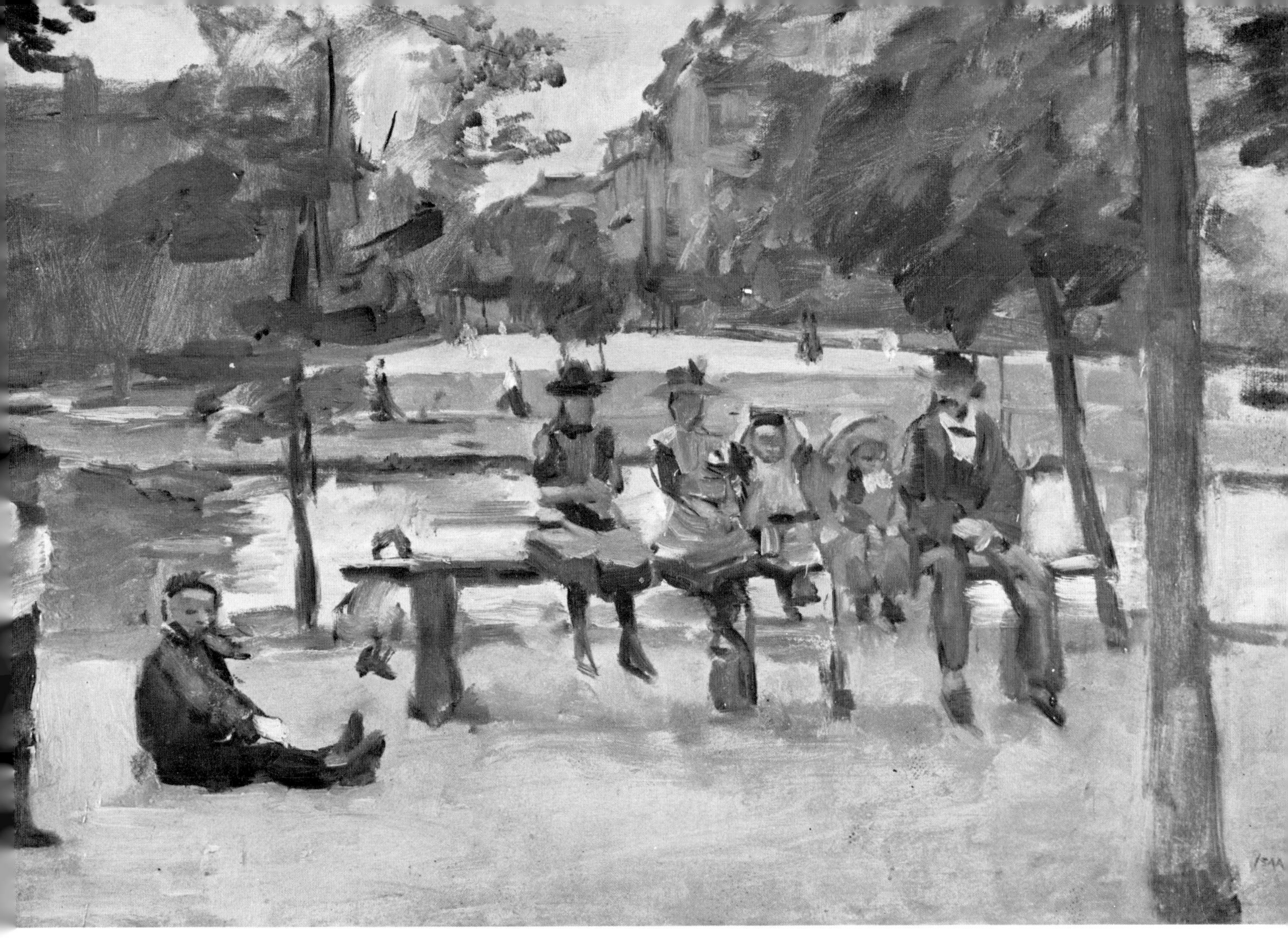

Rozenburg; nay, even after he had already made an absolute name for himself among the younger and even among some of the older painters of his time, he resolved to go for two years to the Amsterdam Academy, to learn drawing under Allebé. I know not in how far he here found what he had come to seek; but one thing is certain: he saw Amsterdam, was smitten with its strenuous life, became the great painter of the great city and never returned to the more contemplative Hague.

If Breitner, in his later paintings of moorlands on the bright outskirts of Amsterdam, was obliged to subordinate his rich tonalities to a more open technique of line, Suze Robertson, on the other hand, born at the Hague in 1855, although more closely related to him at the start, was able not only to retain, but even to increase the wealth of her palette. Nearly all the painters of the Hague school lost the intensity of their colour in the search for light in a wider aspect. She, who can hardly be called a landscape-painter, except in her little views of Noordwijk, of which she only borrows the form to employ it as a subject for her colourful temperament, has made splendid studies of figures in her studio, worked up occasionally to something very complete, as in the little dark figure of a girl seen against a yellow silk background, a subject which, thanks to its heavy modelling and its heavy tone, became a quite exceptional and independent artistic utterance. Combined with great technical qualities, she has displayed this wealth of ripe tones both in oils and in water-colours, a feeling for colour that is visionary rather than realistic. Her models do not command the gloriously outspoken veracity of Breitner's: they approach more nearly Rembrandt's conception; and I doubt whether Suze Robertson has ever admired any Rembrandt more than the *Suzanna* in the Mauritshuis, seen through her own rich temperament.

She is of the same age as Breitner; but, although born at the Hague, she hails by origin from Rotterdam, the great commercial city on the Maas. Like Breitner, she began by passing her examination for intermediate education at the Hague Academy and, like him, began by giving lessons. Her circumstances compelled her to remain first for six years at the secondary girls' school at Rotterdam and for one year in a private intermediate school in Amsterdam.

If Thérèse Schwartze may be described as the most famous Dutch female painter of her time, Suze Robertson is undoubtedly the greater artist, perhaps the only woman of our day whose femininity betrays itself in her art not as weakness but as strength. In 1892, she married Richard Bisschop, the painter of church-interiors.

It is a remarkable fact that Isaäc Israëls, who, born at the Hague in 1865, grew up as much as or even more than Breitner in the florescence of the Hague school, never really belonged to it. For, when he began, he was first attracted by soldiers (I do not know if this was in imitation of Breitner) and painted them according to his own ideas, in small, compact, daintily-drawn pictures, independently of his father's work and very cleverly for so young a painter. At the same time, he produced some very delicately-painted little portraits of women, including one with a park for its background, without troubling about any considerations of *plein-air.* Still, these portraits were noticed only by a few in a time of broad brushwork in portrait-painting and it was the scenes of military life that made his name at a comparatively early age. His picture of colonial troops on the bridge at Rotterdam had a success in Paris.

How be brought himself to fling away what he had achieved before he had found a new pair of shoes to fit him I do not know; but one thing is certain, that the Amsterdam Academy, Amsterdam life, the influence of the literary movement that circled round the *Nieuwe Gids,* that this half-literary, half-pictorial, but in any case wholly intellectual life was well-adapted to change his point of view. In Paris, he would have belonged to that array of immense draughtsmen who reproduce the life of the boulevards with so much sadness, but also with so much refinement of form. With us, he also became a *peintre de mœurs;* but through it all, in spite of himself, there gleamed the impressionism of the Hague school. He began by making chalk-drawings, straight from nature: canals with figures, streets seen from some well-placed window; and in these very first drawings everything had disappeared that one used to admire in him: they were clever scrawls and scribbles, snapshots that presented an interesting glimpse of Amsterdam, without supplying anything new, unless we except *The Kalverstraat.* The first important production was *The Dancing-house,* an interior showing a stifling atmosphere, where, in a thick haze, sailors stare at women spinning round, a sickening episode, crudely and inexorably outspoken, like a scene from Zola, while in that perturbing painting, *Women smoking,* he displayed types that belong to the most naturalistic pages of our nineteenth-century art.

We must not look in these works nor in any others of his later period for the harmony of the great Hague men his masters, nor for their colouring, their sheer beauty, their charm of workmanship, their well-balanced composition. Nor again must we look to find in him a subject developed into a complete picture. What Isaäc Israëls aims at is to seize the moment, the movement, the street types, the street life forming part of the streets, of the town. He is essentially one of the younger men, endowed with more sensitive nerves and less balance than the Hague men, a son of his time, a son too of Jozef Israëls the psychologist.

No more honest artist exists; and, like that virtuoso of the brush, Manet, he might have said, in the catalogue of his first exhibition:

"Come here to see not complete, but upright work."

He sacrifices nothing to commercial values; one knows of no concession made by this restless worker; he adds nothing conventional, nothing acquired by knowledge or experience to his work. The faces are characterized with a stroke or two; the figures and the whole episode are reproduced with a genuine realism which is never touched up in the studio or elaborated into an imposing colour-scheme. His work is one long array of human documents, unique in our country for their unvarnished truthfulness. Nevertheless, in quite recent years, he has produced works which show that he is adopting a more synthetic manner of seeing and a more monumental, though always life-like mode of expression.

Pure landscape-painting is represented in this generation by De Zwart and Tholen. Willem Bastiaan Tholen, born in 1860, was, like Voerman, denied the privilege of being born at the Hague or, rather, of growing up there amid the riot of beauty to which the work of the great masters contributed daily. Both of them were natives of Kampen and received their

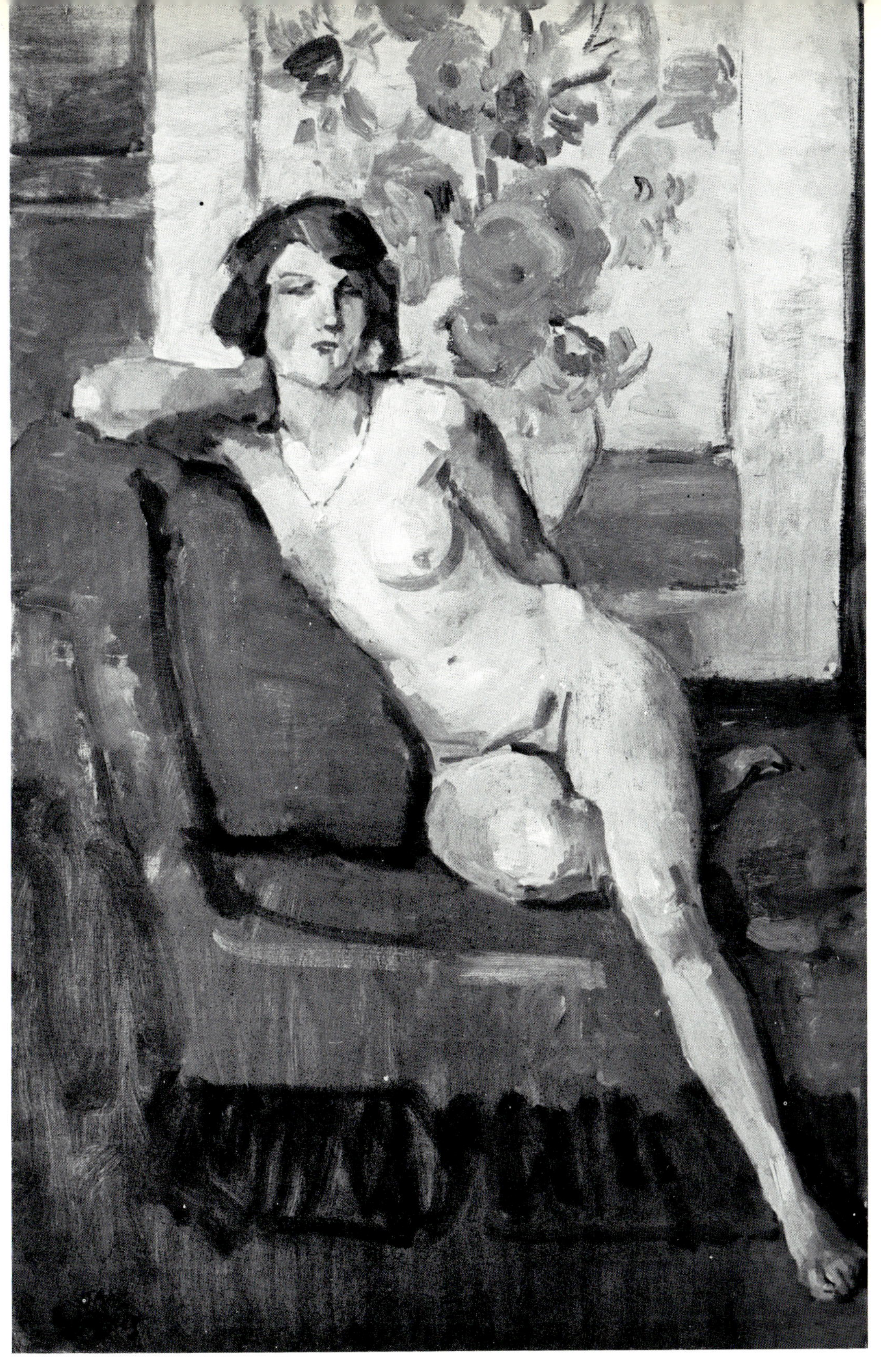

This nude study by **Isaac Israëls** *ties him interestingly into his time. On the wall behind the model is a still life of sunflowers by Vincent van Gogh. (94½ x 59½cms.).* Photograph courtesy of Mak van Waay, Amsterdam.

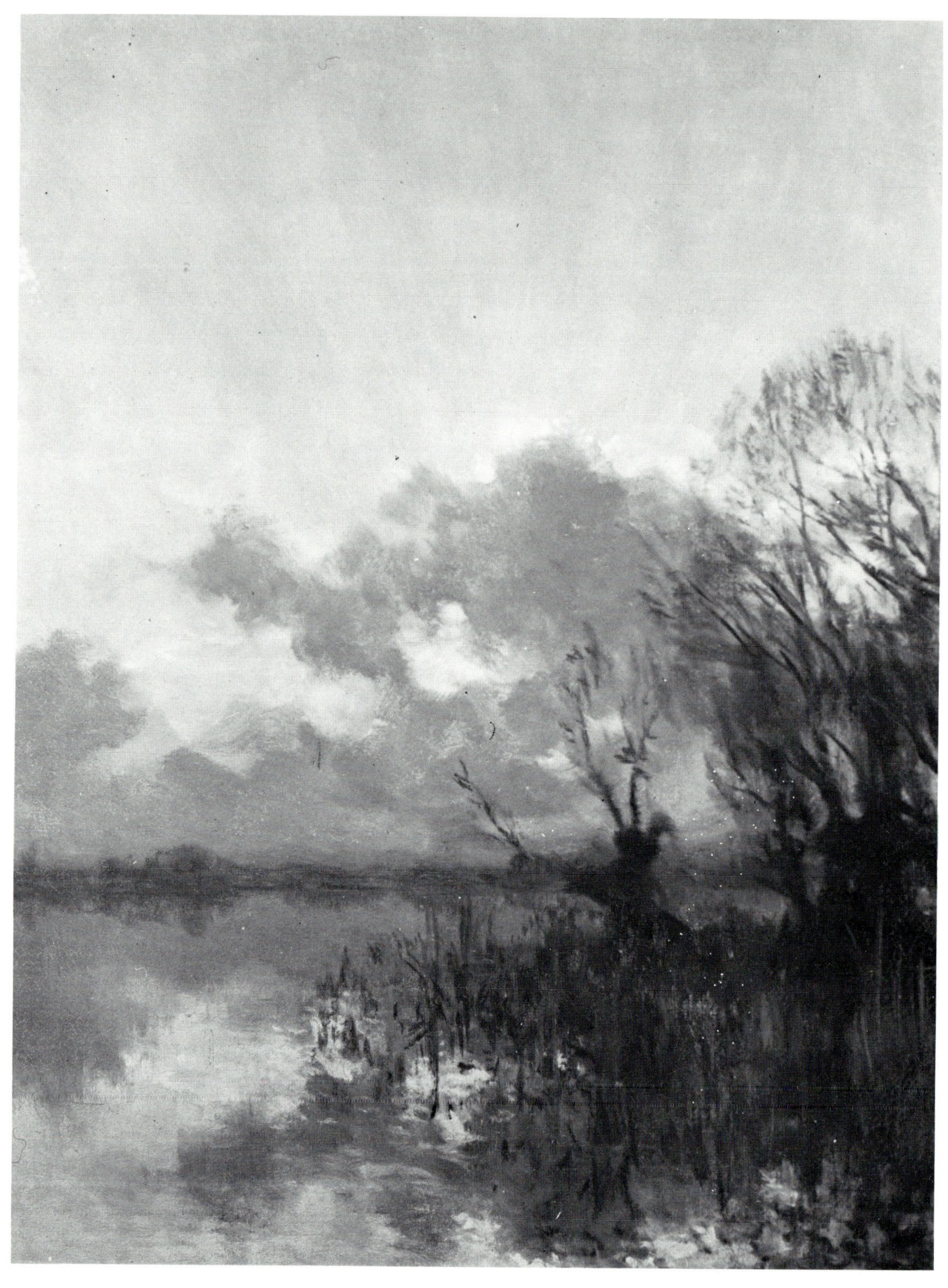

Willem Bastiaan Tholen (1860-1931) *was primarily a landscape artist. He studied under Gabriël and owes a strong debt to the Hague though himself belonging to a younger generation. Water and waterways are a constant theme as in this stormy little view. (54 x 43cms.).* Photograph courtesy of Mak van Waay, Amsterdam.

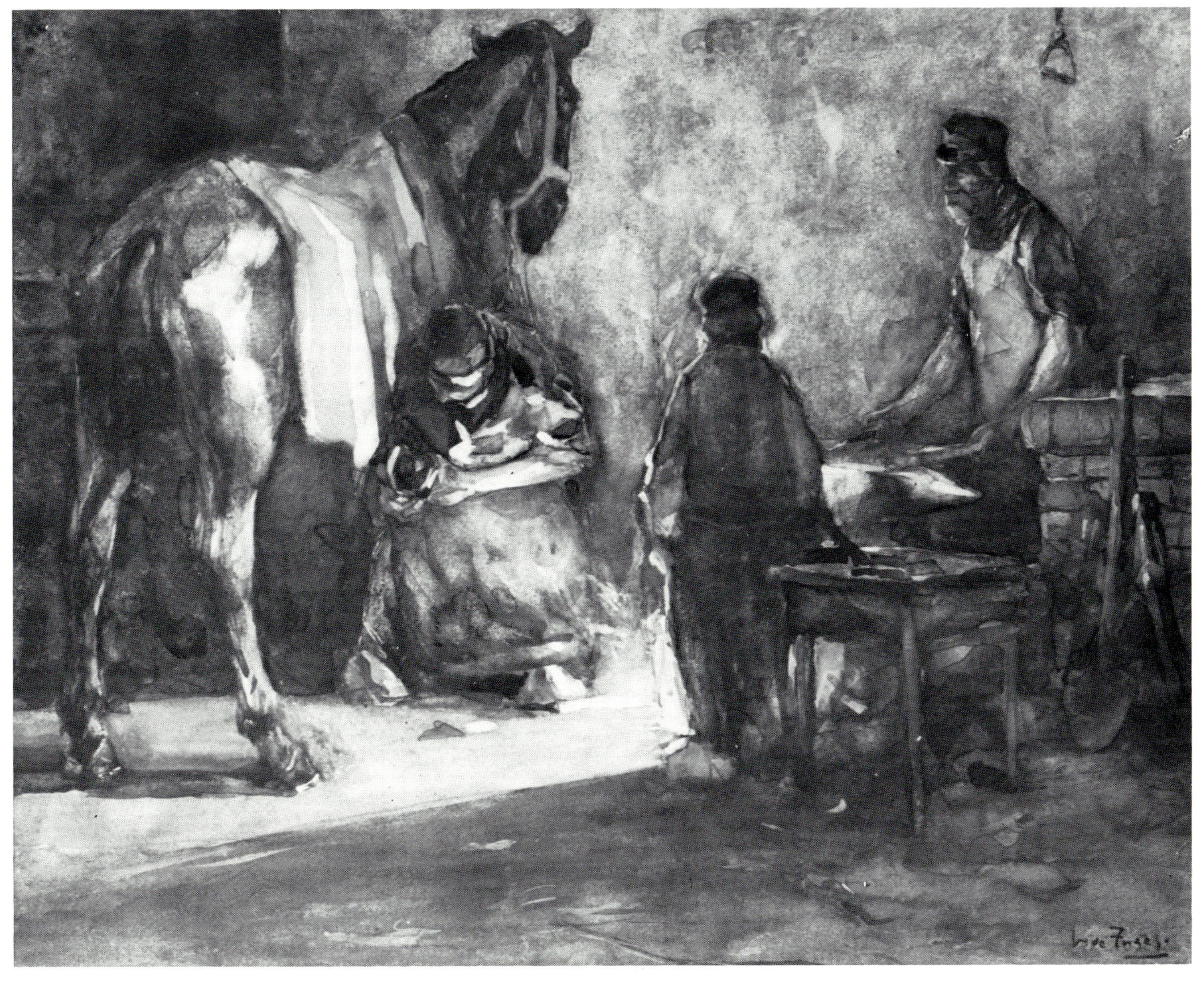

Willem de Zwart (1862-1931) *trained in the Hague and with Jacob Maris. This watercolour of a blacksmith at work still shows the influence of the Hague masters. (35 x 44cms.).* Photograph courtesy of Mak van Waay, Amsterdam.

education first under Hein, the landscape-painter, who was not able to instil much life into his pupils, and later under J.O. Belmer, the painter and drawing-master, who, newly-arrived at Kampen, encouraged his pupils, prepared them for the Amsterdam Academy and reconciled their parents to the idea of bringing up their sons to an artistic career. At the Hague and even in Amsterdam, it is easy to become a painter, almost too easy, in fact. But in the smaller towns, which possess no academies, no animated art-life, no picture-galleries, we cannot show sufficient appreciation of a painter who, compelled by circumstances to accept a position as local drawing-master, displays a true love of his art and devotion to his pupils. Tholen never fails to admit that, without this guidance, he would never have become the man he is. All his later masters might have been different; but he would have been nowhere without Belmer. After the Academy, he took Gabriël, then still in Brussels, as his master. This choice is an early characteristic of the practical painter that Tholen has since become.

Practical, sure of himself, learning in the midst of his admiring commerce with the Hague masters, Tholen made an early name with a couple of water-colours of

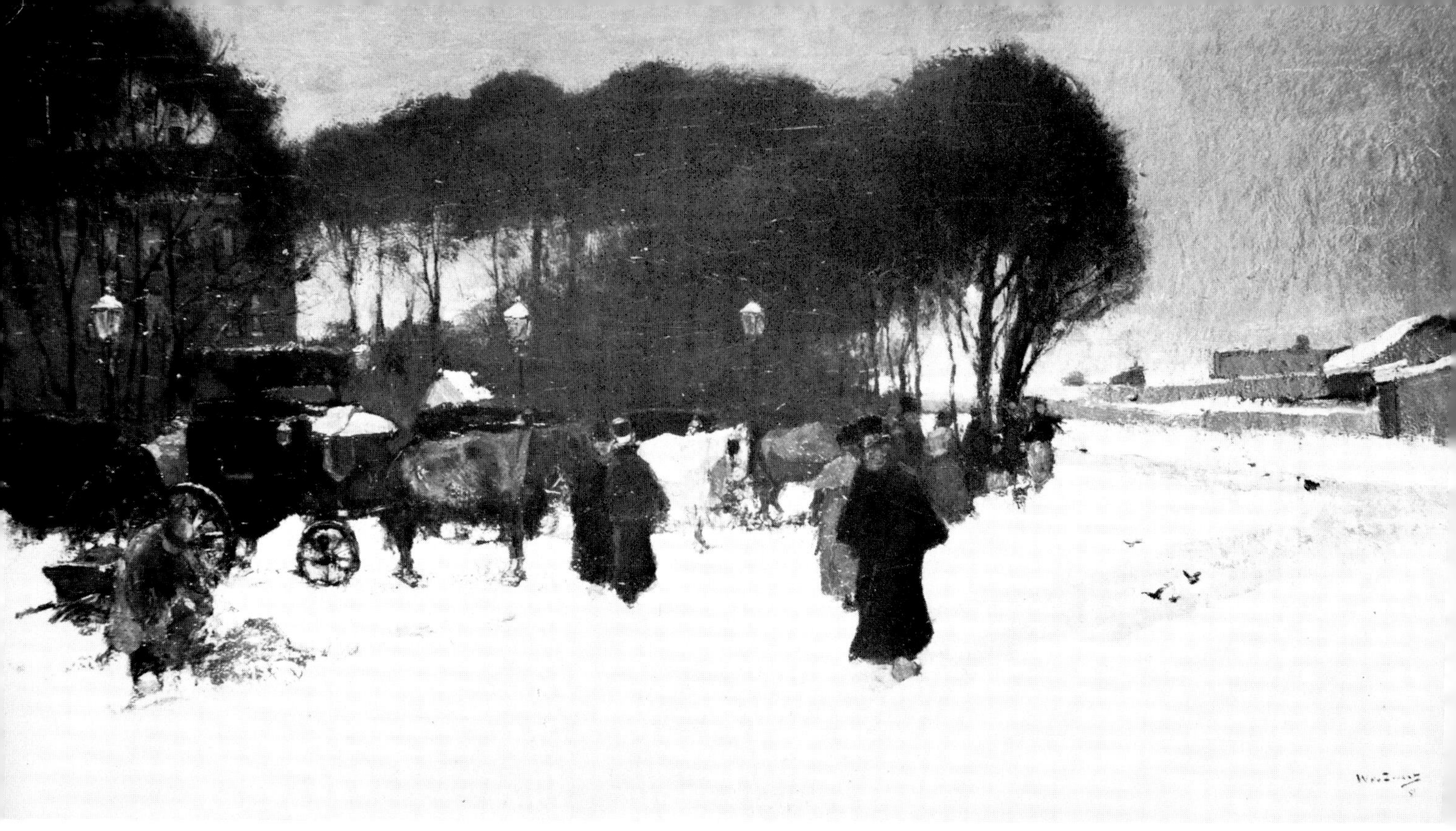

Here **de Zwart** *paints his favourite carriages in a snow decked street.* Photograph courtesy of Mak van Waay, Amsterdam.

the children's playground in the Scheveningen Woods. Later, at an exhibition of the Dutch Drawing Association, he showed the interior of a dairy, in which the reflections of the brass milk-pails, the white walls and a touch of blue were carried to a pitch of uncommon purity. Perhaps even more elaborate was *The Butcher's Shop,* an admirable interior with a vista, which, thanks both to the execution and the water-colour treatment, gained the admiration of all painters, young and old masters alike. A country-house in a labyrinth of bushes and bracken, green-houses, a toll-house, Scheveningen streets, the Scheveningen canal may be numbered among his most precious water-colours.

Tholen's work shows no trace of an endeavour in any other direction than the picturesque. From the first, he proves himself a sound and powerful landscape painter, whose streets and landscapes, with their boldness of construction and brightness of tone and firmness of line and colouring, tell all that they have to tell, without ever degenerating into illustrations. He is one of those painters who dare to be themselves, who place strength above feeble sentimentality, who do not consider our Dutch art of landscape-painting to be bound to any one formula and who do not object if they are called cold because of their cool expression of a fact, for the reason that they are convinced that strength and not weakness is their motive power. Years passed in which his work was sent straight to England, so that we but rarely saw anything of it. At present, his subjects are taken to a great extent from the Zuider Zee or rivers. And, if a change be perceptible in his work, this is in consequence of the reflections in which a painter often indulges at about his fortieth year, the age when we throw off the influences received from without and recover our own natures.

Tholen's nature is not an expansive one and therefore his merits as a painter are not always equally obvious. And, in the ever-growing admiration for a more fixed art, for the older men, he, with the best of the younger masters, stands alone.

Willem de Zwart, who is before all a colourist, was born at the Hague in 1862. He was a pupil of the Hague Academy and, what is more, he is, in point of fact, the only direct pupil of Jacob Maris. The influence is seen in his "Sand-pits" of about 1885 to 1890. Mellow, firmly painted, bright and full of tone, these sand-pits, lying in the yellow dunes under the grey skies, reflected in a canal, enlivened by the movement of sand-boats and navvies, belong to the best that he has yet painted. At that time, he was living at the Hague in the Beeklaan, a favourite quarter with artists, lying between the dunes on the one side and the fat fields, canals and farmsteads on the other. Here he would also surprise us with his figures of women, full of the breath of life, like Breitner's women, like Jacob Maris' portrait of his sister, like Terburgh's women, although less refined. And, above all, he was the first to turn into a sheer feast of colour the bright squares of the town, with the gleaming black panels of the passing carriages, pieces filled with rich tones, thoroughly intelligent performances which, nevertheless, did not go beyond the just demands of landscape-painting.

A turning-point arrived in his career too. This was when the Hague ceased to be the artistic centre, when Breitner and Isaäc Israëls were settled in Amsterdam, when Bauer went to Bussum and when De Zwart himself had gone to Hilversum. Was this for private reasons, or to enter the environment of the younger Amsterdammers, or from the longing for the country, for solitude, that drove the strongest to seclusion? One thing is certain, that De Zwart had his work cut out for him to recover his "form". He drew in chalks, he etched, he painted, until, a few years ago, he again began to produce paintings which attracted notice through the robust, not always harmonious colouring, through the powerful draughtsmanship which he displayed in somewhat Old-Dutch subjects, such as a *Poultry-market,* a water-colour, or in bright-coloured little interiors, or in pictures of slums. From that time, he has shown comparatively little connection with his master or with the traditions of the Hague school.

The talented colourist Johannes Evert Akkeringa, born in the isle of Banka in 1861, though not a pupil of De Zwart's, belongs to his school. He studied at the Hague and Rotterdam Academies and has produced supply-painted little pieces – figures, dunes, flower-gardens – real little cabinet-pieces, which are greatly valued and yet are modern, like something lying half-way between De Zwart and the earlier Rochussen. He has this in common with all the younger painters of the Hague school, that he has not yet said his last word.

Van der Maarel is a colourist of a different type

Johannes Evert Akkeringa (1861-1942) *belongs with de Zwart to the younger generation of the Hague. In this watercolour he shows the fishermen's wives of Scheveningen mending the nets. (34 x 60cms.).* Photograph courtesy of Mak van Waay, Amsterdam.

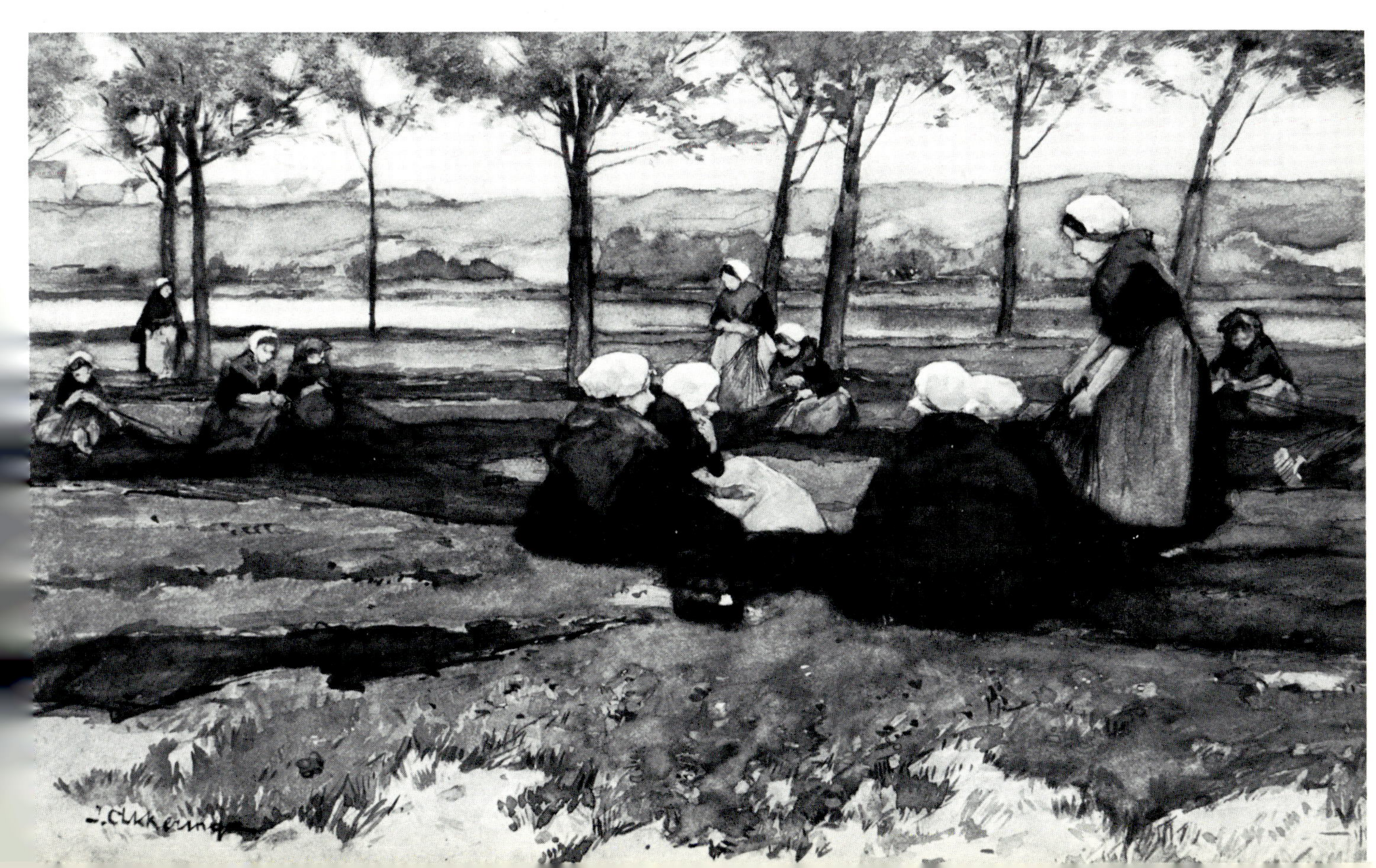

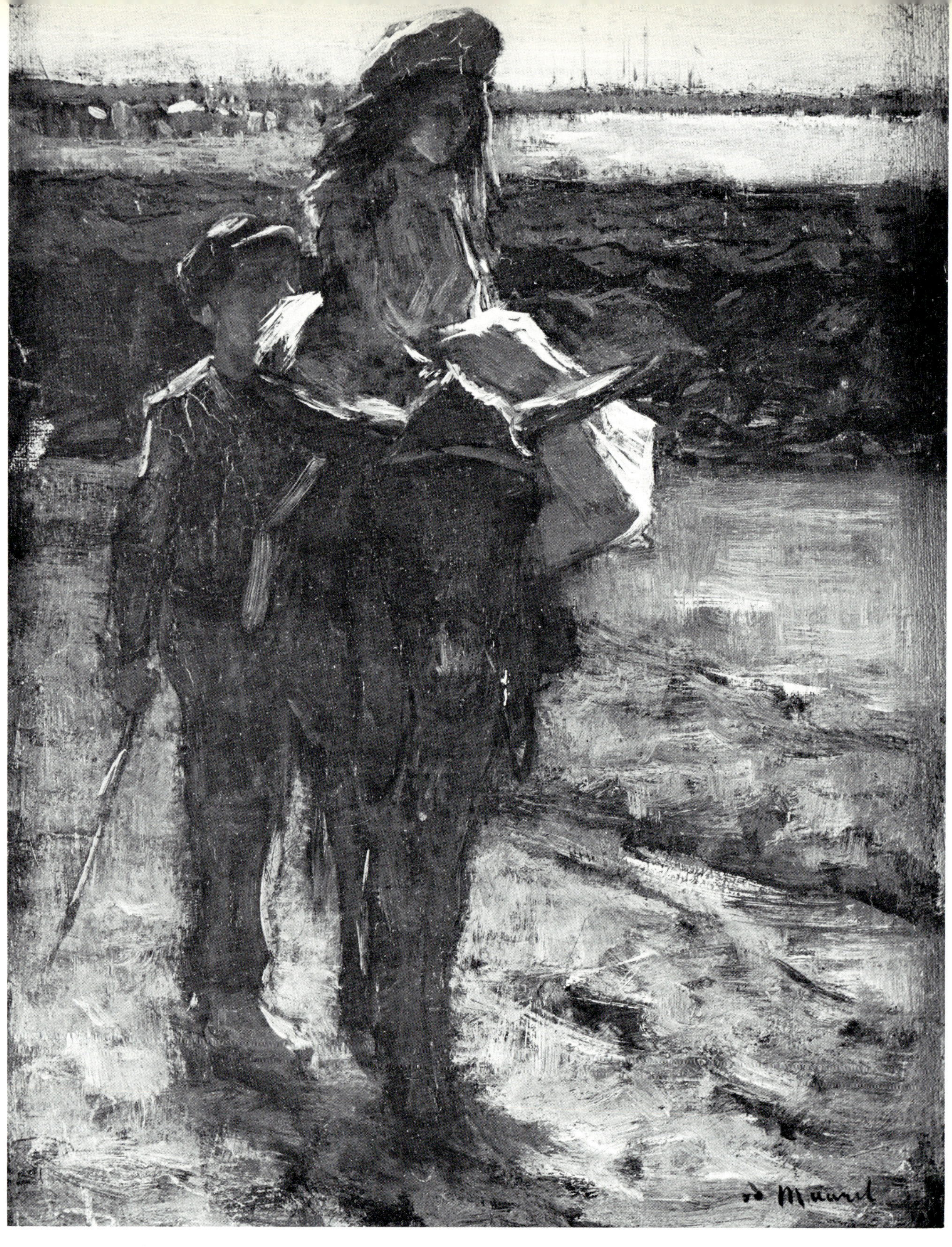

Marius van der Maarel (1857-1921) *looked on every painting as a problem in colour. This donkey ride on the strand is a subject that attracted many of his contemporaries.* Photograph courtesy of Mak van Waay, Amsterdam.

Willem Anthonie van Deventer (1824-1893). *"A sunlit estuary with figures working on boats." Signed and dated 1852. (25 x 32½ ins.).* Photograph courtesy of Richard Green.

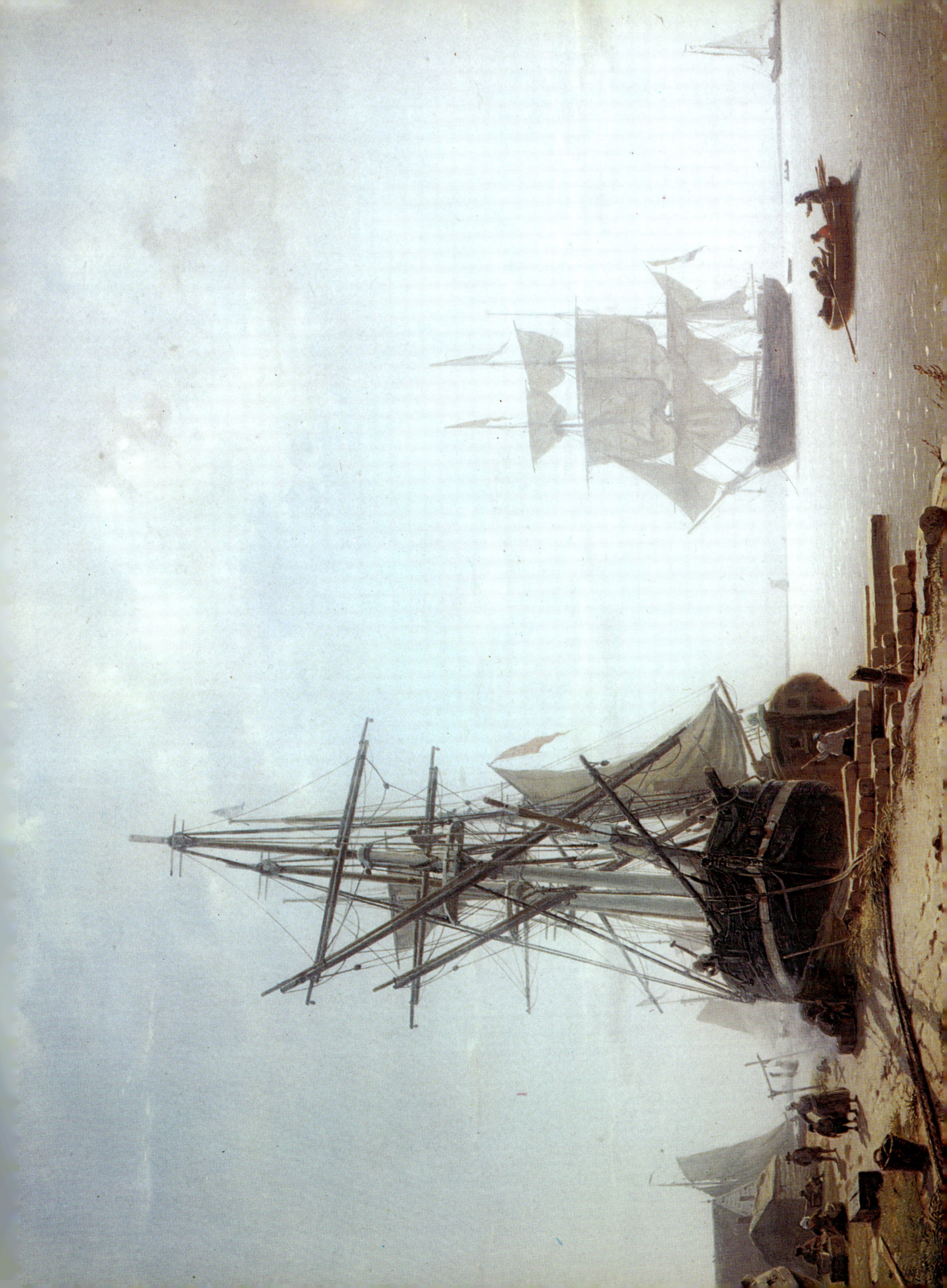

from either Breitner or Mrs. Bisschop-Robertson. Verster, in his colour period, and Voerman, in his early flower-pieces, both had something in common with him; nevertheless, Van der Maarel's aspirations in the matter of form and colour find a different expression. In reality, he is more nearly related to the Venetian masters, with their passionate love of colour, than to the Dutch. I remember, many years ago, seeing a figure of a little Italian girl by Van der Maarel, leaning against the stone balustrade of a Paris bridge, with a grey sky just broken up by harmonious orange. The purity of the red in the little figure and the charm of colour in the sky at once attracted the attention of the younger men, whereas some of the older painters did not think it worth while to make so much fuss of a bit of sky like that, which anyone might have painted in a happy moment.

Van der Maarel is, in fact, before all a painter of portraits; at least, he has produced his most important work in this direction. Yet he must not be regarded as a professed portrait-painter; for the demands of this branch of art are not, in his case, confined to a more or less simply-painted counterfeit presentment nor to that penetration into character which leads to psychological portraiture. For him, a portrait, even as a still-life piece or a landscape, is a piece of temperamental art, a problem in colour, so much so that he is unable to start upon his portrait, has no inclination to do so, before all the conditions of tonality in the face of his model and in the environment selected by him are such that they respond in a measure to the painter's own sense of colour.

Marius van der Maarel was born in 1857 at the Hague and began by attending the Hague Academy. Afterwards, he became a pupil of Willem Maris. Thanks to the distinction that marked his efforts, to the taste and refinement of his art, he was, in his earlier years, a leader of many. Bauer, in his richly-painted pieces of fashionable life, Verster and several others underwent the influence of this painter who had been fully formed at an early age. The superior colour-arrangements of Anna Adelaida Abrahams (born in 1849), the still-life painter, may be regarded as belonging to his school, while, as a direct pupil of his later period, we can reckon Frederik Salberg (born in 1876), who, up to the present, follows his master's ideas in figures and flowers.

Floris Henric Verster, born in Leiden in 1861, is rather difficult to understand. No sooner do we think that we have caught the intention of this pure artist than he changes his formula; and, when we penetrate this, he comes up with a work so directly opposed to the last that we are constrained forthwith to change our second conception for a third. Vermeer of Delft was called the sphinx of our seventeenth-century painting. I do not wish to suggest a direct analogy; but it must be admitted that Floris Verster is our latter-day sphinx, who, refusing to allow his riddles to be solved, poses a new riddle with each new picture.

In 1887, he produces a work representing two plucked fowls on a newspaper, painted in cool, firm tones of an original order, yet closely related to De Zwart and Jacob Maris: a master-piece, this drawing. Next, with mellower pigments and in deeper tones, he paints hollyhocks, with something of the passionate enthusiasm of Breitner. Then he changes his colour-scheme for more cruel tones in red and purple anemones, in pale-violet chrysanthemums, blood-red tulips, deep red and yellow roses and amaranth phlox, colours that suggest passages of Berlioz' *Faust.* Again, after turning over so many new leaves, he produces his gourds, his eucalyptus, his flowering branch in a Japanese vase, executed in childish detail with a wax-pencil: powerful, this, but suggestive of a woman picking out a flower on a tapestry; beautiful, but so coldly beautiful. Then, suddenly deserting his spontaneous landscapes, he builds you up his houses and streets and churches carefully, brick by brick. What next? Yet all these different phases are the work of one man, spring from the temperament and the sense of colour of one artist, intelligent always, a fine and true painter in his first, turbulent painter in his second period and, in all, a distinguished master of the technical side of his art, who has undoubtedly not yet shown us his last formula and is keeping many exquisite surprises in store for us.

Menso Kamerlingh Onnes, born in 1860, is first and foremost a flower painter, though he has also painted portraits. He, in his turn, has enlarged the technique of water-colour. Herein lies his strength. He is like a conjuror with his water-colours, with his solutions of colour, his fluent colours, in which he is able to produce his flowers with diaphanous delicacy. None of our artists is able to juggle with technique in the way that he does. And, although technique is far from being everything and his work often springs rather from a sort of cleverness than from an endeavour to represent what he sees or feels, yet he has given us, for instance, a drawing of quinces on a white plate, in a simple arrangement of yellow-green, white and a touch

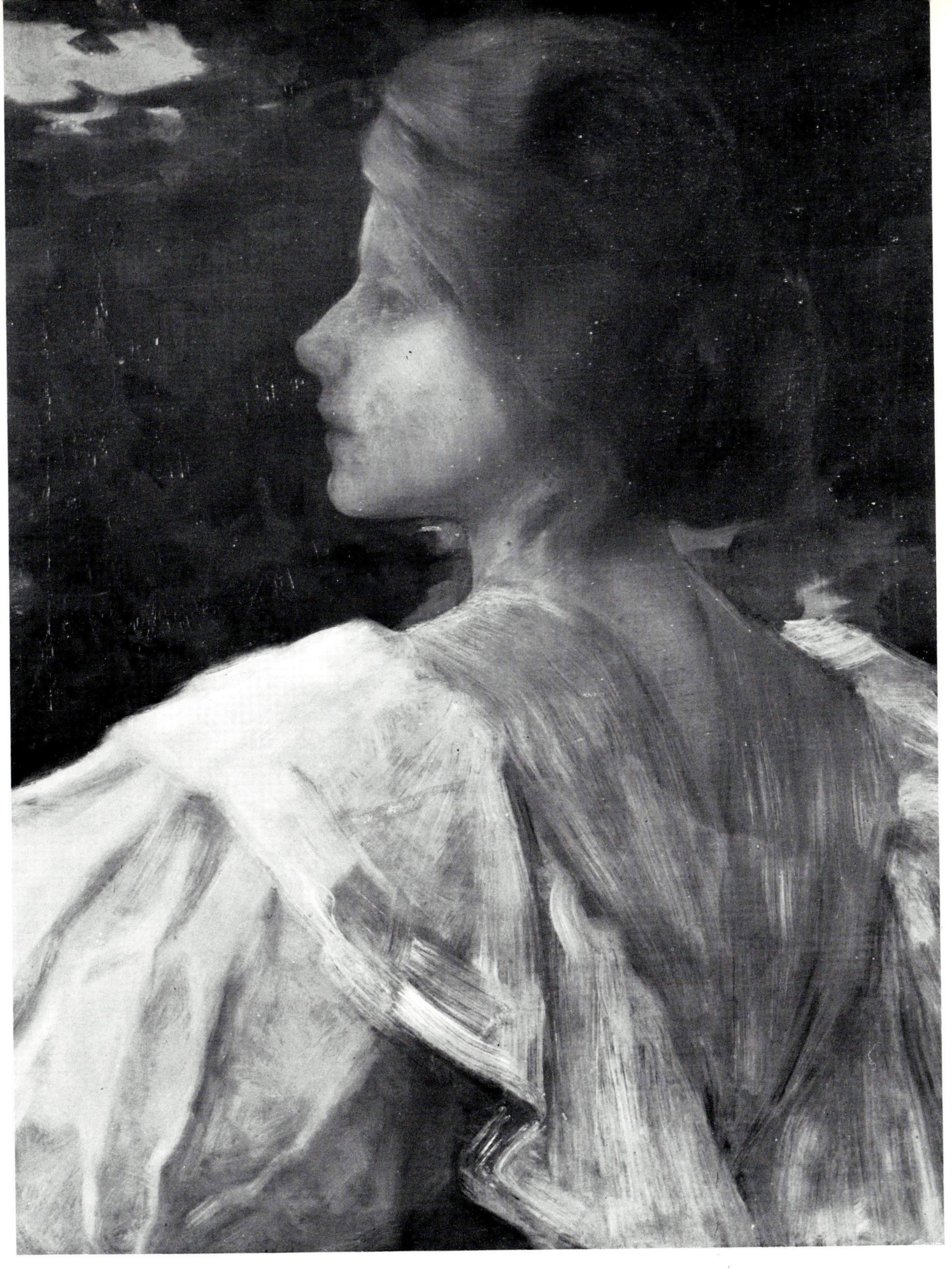

Van der Maarel *excelled as a portrait painter but, as is shown by this example, never sacrifices the pictorial element in the work in favour of a conventional likeness.* Photograph courtesy of Rijksmuseum Hendrik Willem Mesdag, the Hague.

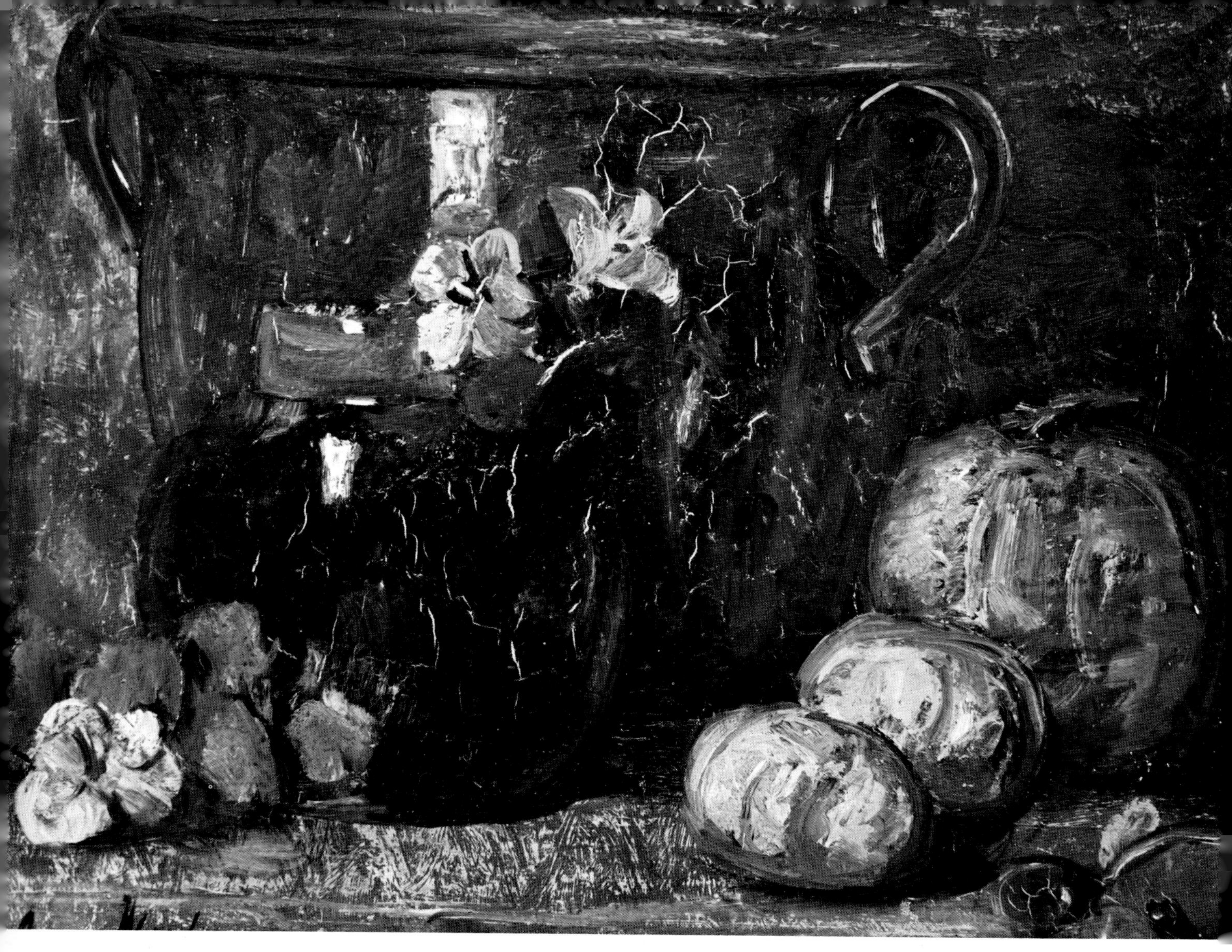

Anna Adelaïda Abrahams (1849-1930) *specialised in still lives of which this is an example. As a colourist she belongs to the school of Van der Maarel.* Photograph courtesy of the Rijksmuseum Hendrik Willem Mesdag, the Hague.

of black, that has seldom been surpassed as a pure reproduction in water-colour.

Mari Alexander Jacques Bauer was born at the Hague in 1867. He was a pupil of the Hague Academy, but received his real training at the hands of Jozef Israëls' friend Salomon van Witsen (born in 1833), a painter who produced but little and whose knowledge and impartial judgment rank higher than his painting. From his earliest days at Pulchri Studio, Bauer seems to have held the "muddy ditch" style in abhorrence; for what we know of him consists of glimpses of a music hall, or an elegantly painted piece taken from a suburban restaurant. He was much talked about, but worked little. When, on his return from his first visit to Constantinople in 1888, he brought back with him a view of a town in chalks and water-colours, this was considered really inadequate for one of whom so much had been heard. True, the foreground had something of the dry treatment of his rare Pulchri-Studio sketches; but, at the same time, the composition of the many cupolaed city, seen in the distance against a yellow sky, was full of suggestion, both as regards

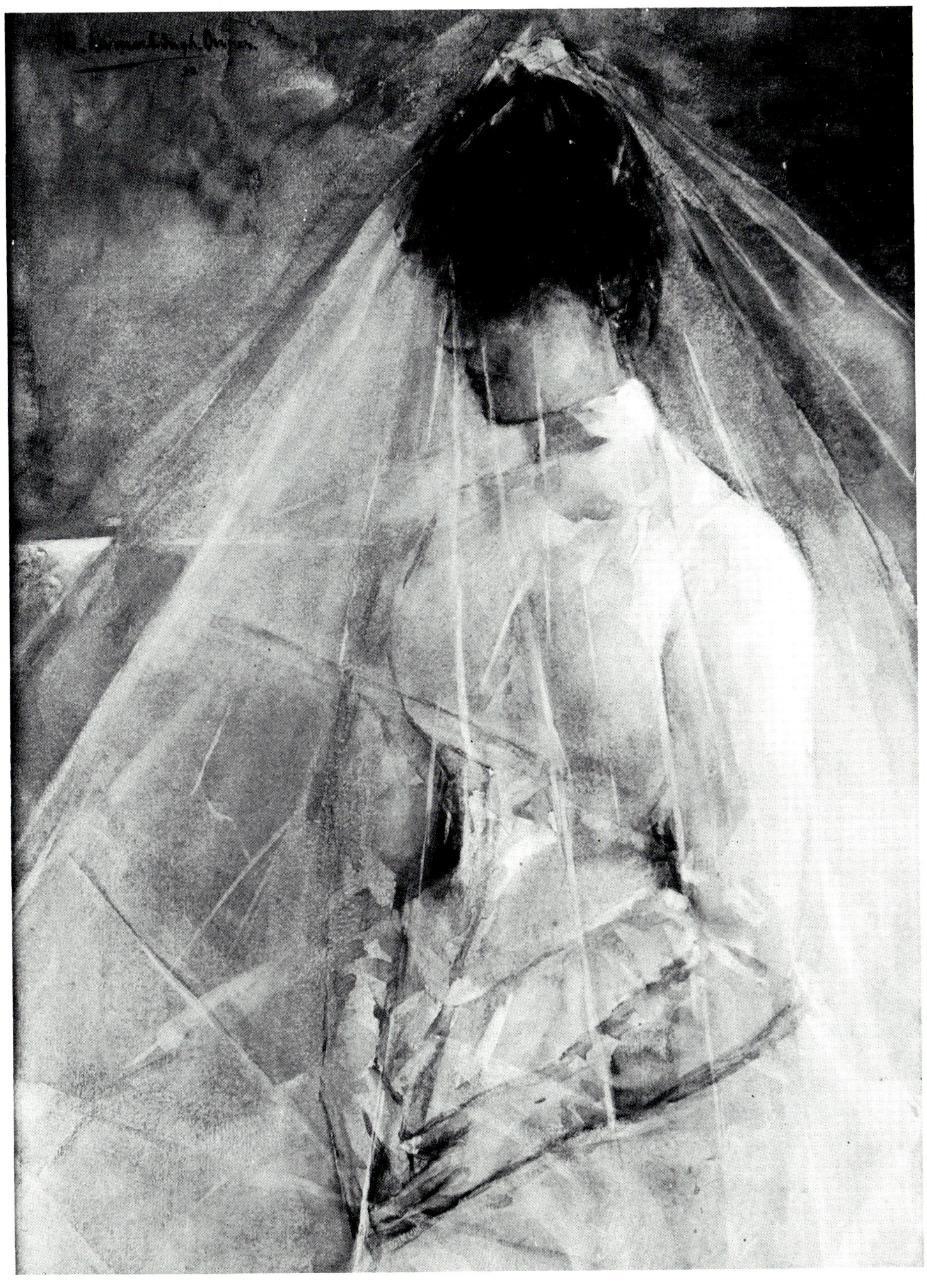

Menso Kamerlingh Onnes (1860-1925) *creates this diaphanous bridal veil in pure watercolour.* Photograph courtesy of Mak van Waay, Amsterdam.

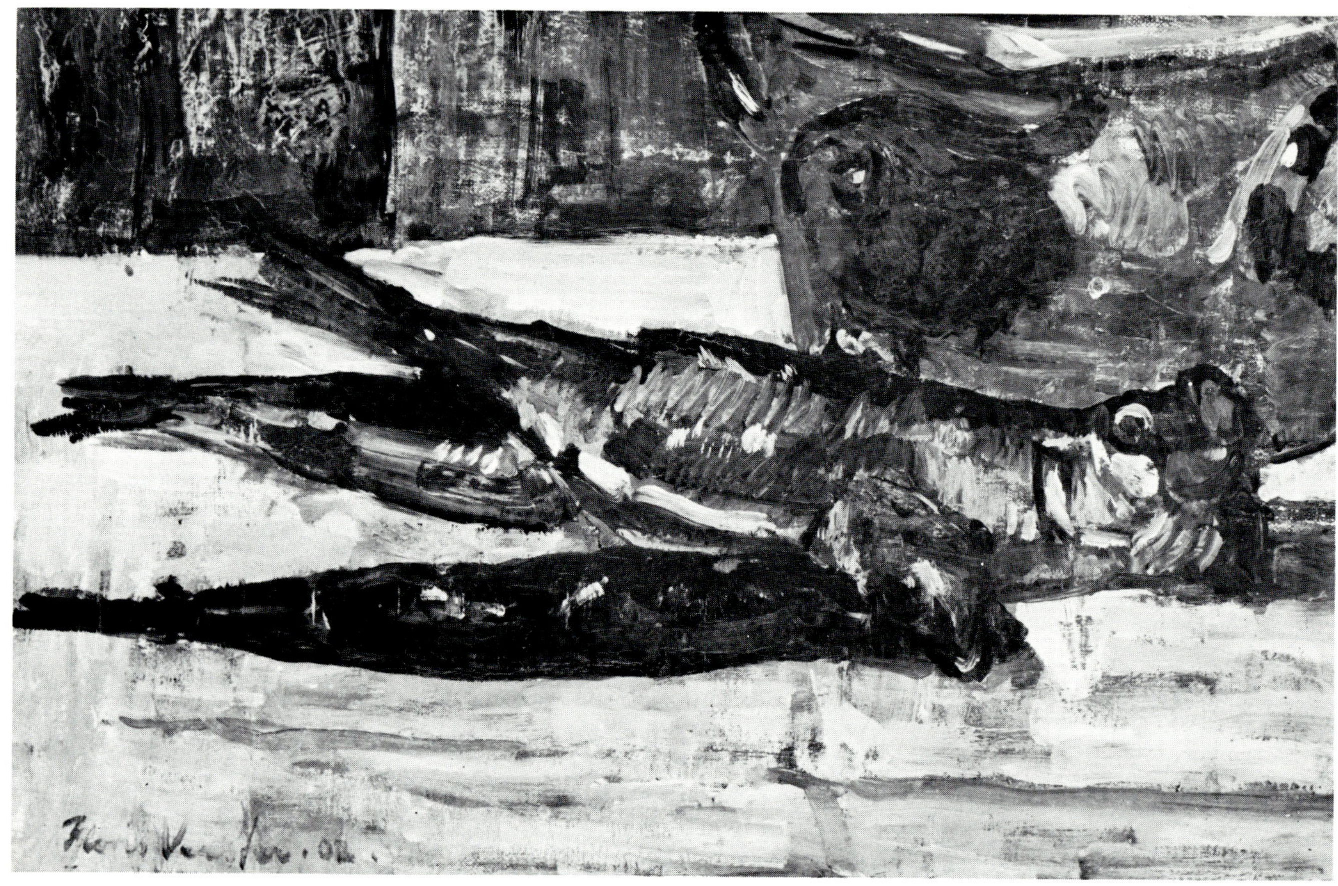

Floris Henric Verster (1861-1927) *was primarily a still life painter and a pupil of Breitner. Here he gives us a group of fish on table (24 x 38cms.).* Photograph courtesy of Mak van Waay, Amsterdam.

form and, especially, in the matter of the conception, which caused an oriental city to spring up on the horizon in all the haziness of a Dutch town.

Bauer, who had little in common with the Hague painters, sought to find a common standard abroad; and, despite the great difference, despite the eastern subjects amid which Bauer, the Hague man, prefers to move, despite the fact that he is more of a glorious imaginer than a mighty painter, we can look upon him as springing from the Hague school. For not only does he display Rembrandt's manner in his etchings, not only is the influence of Bosboom's drawings very evident in his work, but he has "seen" and reproduced the East after the manner of a painter of the Hague school, of one who has grown up under its masters.

Certainly, no one can expect of an occidental that he should see the East with the fatalistic impassiveness reflected in the art of that region. Nor can one expect that everyone who visits the East should contemplate it with the same eyes. In how many different ways has not our simple, methodical Holland been viewed by foreigners? I have heard of travellers who have disliked Egypt because the Sahara does not differ greatly in appearance from our dunes, while the dust provides an equivalent for the atmosphere of our country; whereas others will never cease dilating upon the glaring white of the sunlight on white walls, upon the light blue shadows under the motionless blue of the sky, a view which shows that not everyone shares Bauer's acceptance of the East. It is true that to many northern natures the East is often a sentiment rather than a fact, a longing for mother earth, a craving for miracles, for the land of the Bible, a dream of Paradise. And, if we are convinced that all art proceeds rather from self-recognition, then it follows that intuitive natures are able to feel and see the East, without ever having been there. Delacroix for many years produced his scenes of the East, full of the colours which we

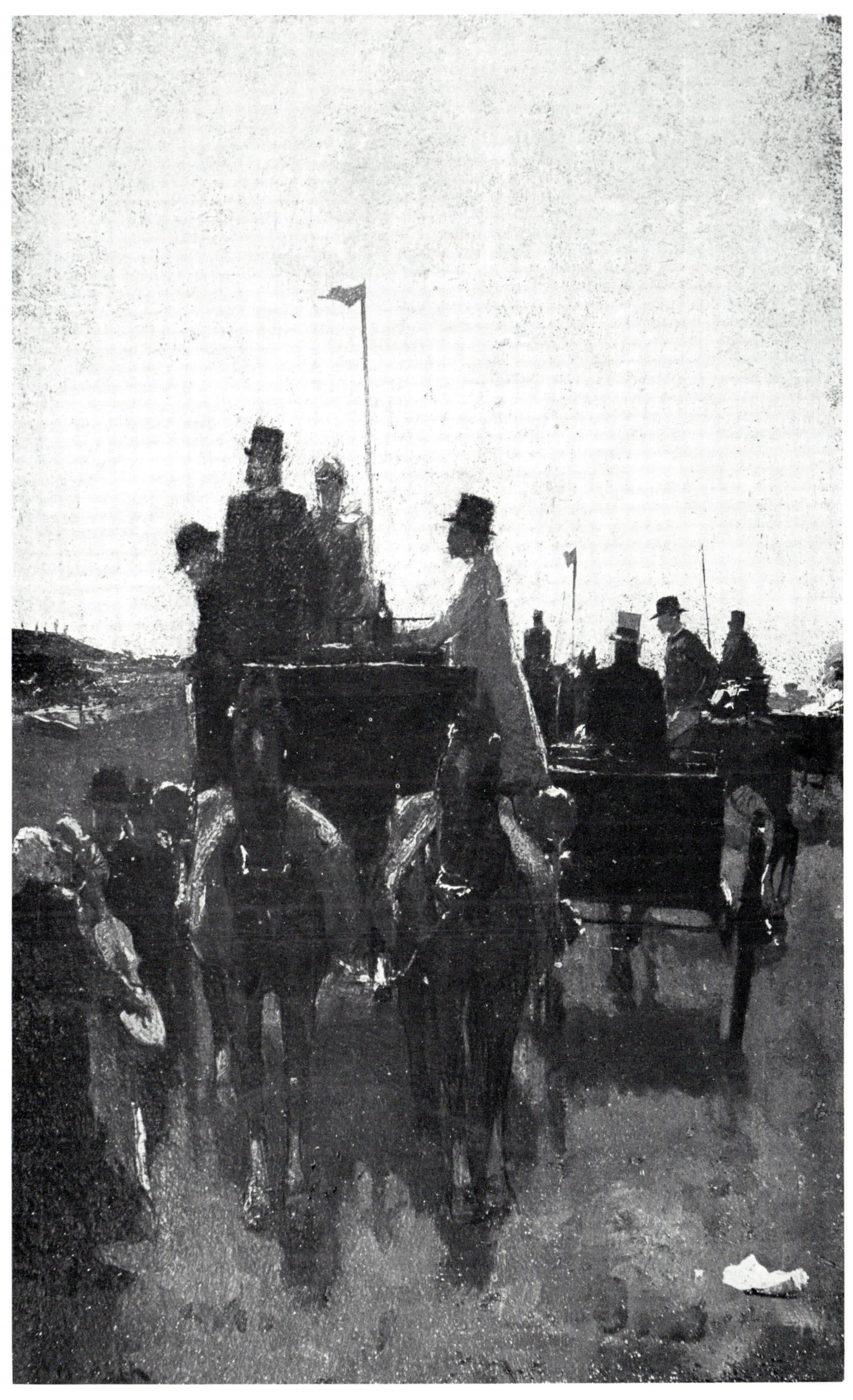

Left: **Mari Alexander Jacques Bauer (1867-1932)** *was a younger adherent of the Hague School. He combined Oriental scenes with little glimpses of everyday life in Holland. This race course scene has echoes of Degas.* Photograph courtesy of the Kröller-Müller Museum, Otterlo.

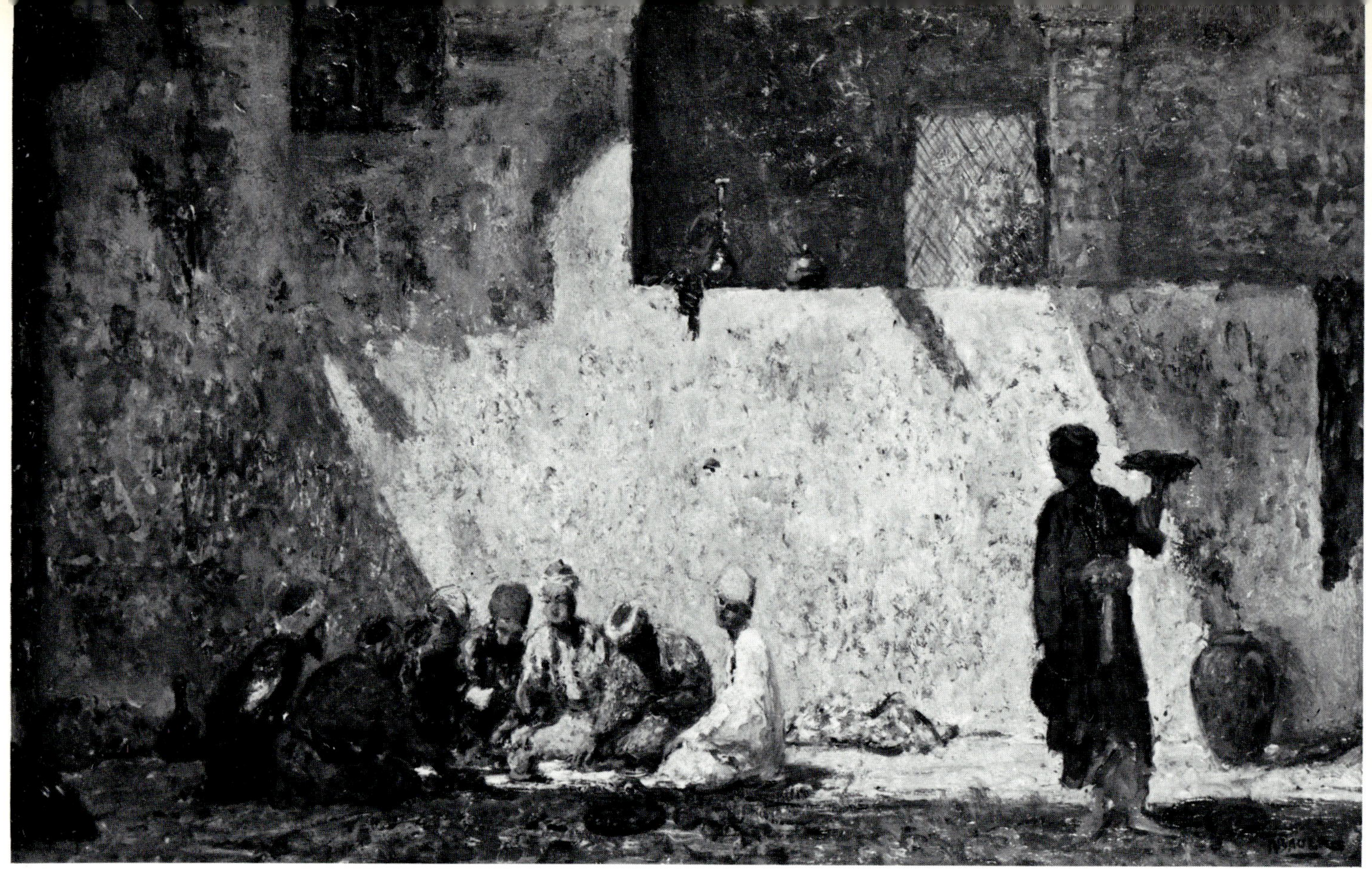

Mari Bauer *was trained by S. van Witsen at the Hague but travelled extensively in the East and made his name with his eastern pictures. Here he gives a brightly lit eastern interior peacefully observed in the Hague school tradition. (37 x 61cms.).* Photograph courtesy of Mak van Waay, Amsterdam.

associate with that world, from studies of the local colour brought home to him by a friend. And, while it is true that the dream is often fairer than the reality, yet there must also be artists, impressionable natures, who, going to the East full of expectations, but free from prejudices, have gazed upon the land with admiring eyes and returned overflowing with impressions.

I would include Bauer among the latter. It was about 1889 that he produced a swarm of etchings, studies, impressions, drawings, little paintings, a medley of bright green, hard pink, Indian yellow and Persian blue; scrawls of colour from which emerges a street, a troop of cavalry, a procession; or else an undecipherable harmony of grey-white, blue-white, rose-white, brilliant colours in subdued tones, whence arises Stamboul with its bright cupolas, like a flock of sheep rounding themselves against a pale copper sky; or, again, the caravans, biblical in their primeval surroundings, marching or halting, camels, riders, loads: one of them stands silhouetted against a town merged in twilight.

In later years, he saw Egypt: his realistic *Sphinx* dates from this time; it is faithfully drawn, spaciously observed. In 1896, he travelled through British India, delighting in the monumental character of the country, in the symbolism of the buildings, of the cities reflected in the Ganges. Bauer is said to have always dreamt of illustrating the *Arabian Nights* in their entirety. He could not do so in a livelier, more real, more fantastic way than he has already done in the colours which he makes us feel in his etchings.

Chapter XI

The Reaction of the Younger Painters of Amsterdam

A crisis came.

There were many who did not see it. Many refused to see it. Others, who did, almost refused to believe – so great was their instinctive hatred of the new that were to supplant the old ideals; and yet they were bound to accept it, because this new form of artistic utterance forced itself upon us with an undeniable cleverness, with strength and conviction, with an overwhelming importance. The formula adopted by the new men was not intimate, was not "pretty", did not capitvate the eye, rarely betrayed a mood of some sort. What they sought for was a more decorative composition; what they wanted was a more concrete form; what they longed for and found was line, outline, a reaction that must necessarily follow upon a form of art that dissolved its lines in atmosphere, subjected colour to the influence of light and regarded a line merely as the division between two pieces of colour. It was the reaction by virtue of which an art of outlines was as inevitably bound to succeed an art of mere brushwork as the conventional music of Beethoven was succeeded by Wagner's more outspoken phrases.

And so it came about that a race of painters arose between 1885 and 1890, formed at the Amsterdam Academy under the guidance of the conscientious Allebé, who impressed a whole generation of younger men with the stamp of his culture. The men of this race or generation soon showed that they were determined to seek a road for themselves, each according to his own nature, rather than follow feebly in the footsteps of the Hague masters whom they all so greatly admired. Most of them were figure-painters, either from personal inclination or because of their training.

The reaction of these painters, known as the reaction of 1880, moves within a period of ten years. Their names are Van Looy, Van der Valk, Voerman, Haverman, Derkinderen, Toorop, Witsen, Karsen and Veth. If we wish to sum up the endeavours of these artists in a formula, it may be expressed as a mistrust of any sort of impressionism, of any passion or painter's enthusiasm, a mistrust sprung from a reaction against the inane and feeble imitators of the Hague school, against the impressionism which Gerard Bilders went so far as to think that he could see in the imitations of the Barbizon school, and, consequently, as a conscious striving after form, pronounced line and purity of colour.

Jan Pieter Veth was born at Dordrecht in 1864. As a child he used to draw historical subjects, perhaps in consequence of the spirit prevailing in his father's house, where Potgieter was much read; perhaps also through the influence of Ary Scheffer. He went to the Amsterdam Academy in 1880 and exhibited portraits of his sisters in 1884 and 1885. These and his other painted portraits, including those of Dr. de Vrij and of Mr. Lebret in the Dordrecht Museum, are clever works and show power of colour analysis. They belong to an early transition-period which soon made room for portraits aiming more exclusively at the reproduction of expression and character and were often inlaid and paint-drawn rather than painted in the strict sense of the word. The same reasons that led to the great development of his critical powers caused him also to adopt a critical method of painting, that is to say, to portray heads showing character, to seek for the causes that bring lines and wrinkles into a face, to enter into the minds of his sitters. It goes without saying that his method was most successful when applied to eminent men who had distinguished themselves in any sphere of activity.

In 1892, the portraits of well-known contemporaries published in the *Amsterdamsch Weekblad* attracted

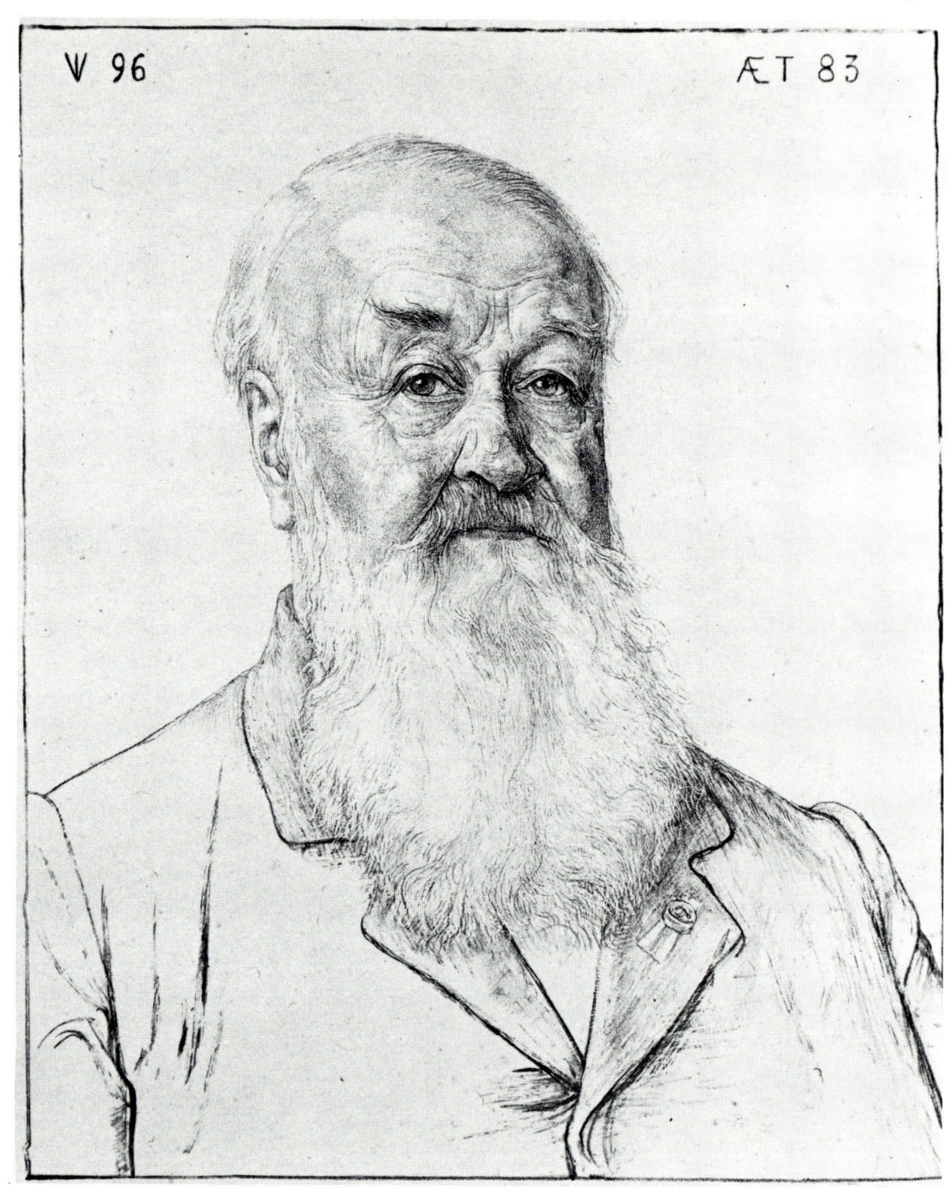

Jan Pieter Veth (1864-1925) *was essentially a draughtsman, even when he added colour to his work. His portraits proved, according to Marius, that "photography had again been beaten by drawing pure and simple" as in this depiction of Dr. J.E. de Vrij (25 x 20cms.).* Photograph courtesy of the Dordrechts Museum.

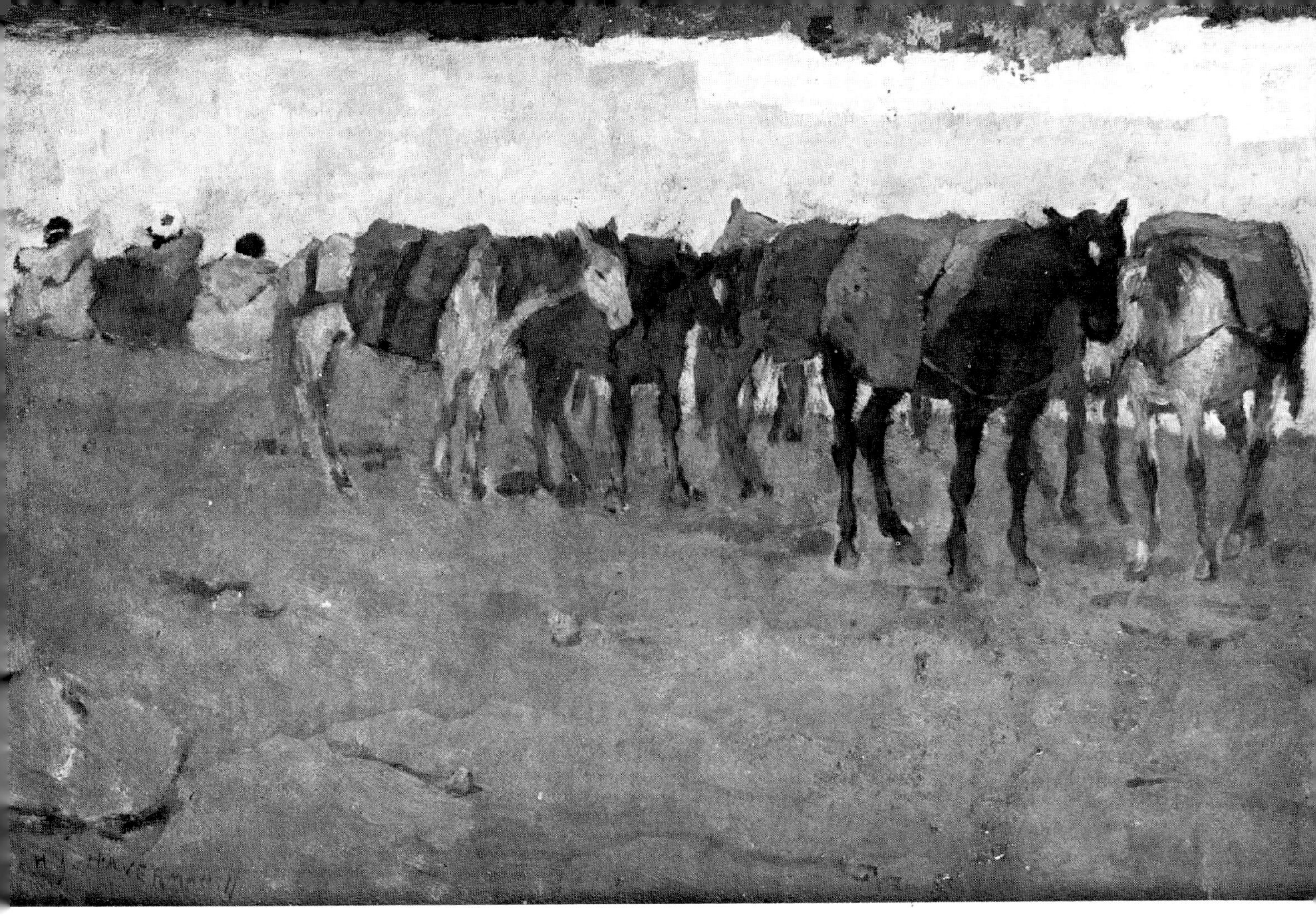

Hendrik Johan Haverman (1857-1928) *presumably painted this simple view of Tangier during his 1890 visit.* Photograph courtesy of Mak van Waay, Amsterdam.

general attention. They were lithographs by Veth, the painter, who was just becoming known at the Hague, but who had already made a definite name for himself in Amsterdam through the personal note of his portraits. One of this series, the little portrait of Jacob Maris sitting as his easel, was a revelation not only as a likeness of the painter, whose head, in full-face, reminds one of Jupiter, while, viewed in profile, the round forehead and the peculiar blue eyes show something at once refined and childlike, but also on account of the manner in which, after many years, photography had again been beaten by drawing pure and simple. Not all were executed in the same way: some were in outline, others elaborately drawn, others again set down in the old-Dutch fashion. Some were rather exaggerated and looked a little forced when seen beside Allebé's simple and complete little portraits. But still they were so characteristic, they showed such perfect grasp of the nature of the model (as in the portraits of Louis Couperus and of Dr. Frederik van Eeden) and they were so much admired by the Hague men that, later on, they often detracted from the appreciation that would otherwise have been evoked by his painted portraits. It is a remarkable thing that this painter, who so greatly admires Jozef Israëls, the brothers Maris, Bosboom and Mauve, should have deliberately turned aside from any of the magnificence or display which they showed in their work. He was like an ascetic, who knows how to value the pleasures of life and yet rejects them.

These psychological portraits, in which character-analysis is so clearly visible, must, necessarily, often be more attractive to the philosophical spectator than to the sheer painter, who, moreover, frequently considers that portraiture does not come within the scope of pure art. Nevertheless, Veth has proved himself a master in this series of portraits, not only by his search for the intellectual qualities of the sitter, but

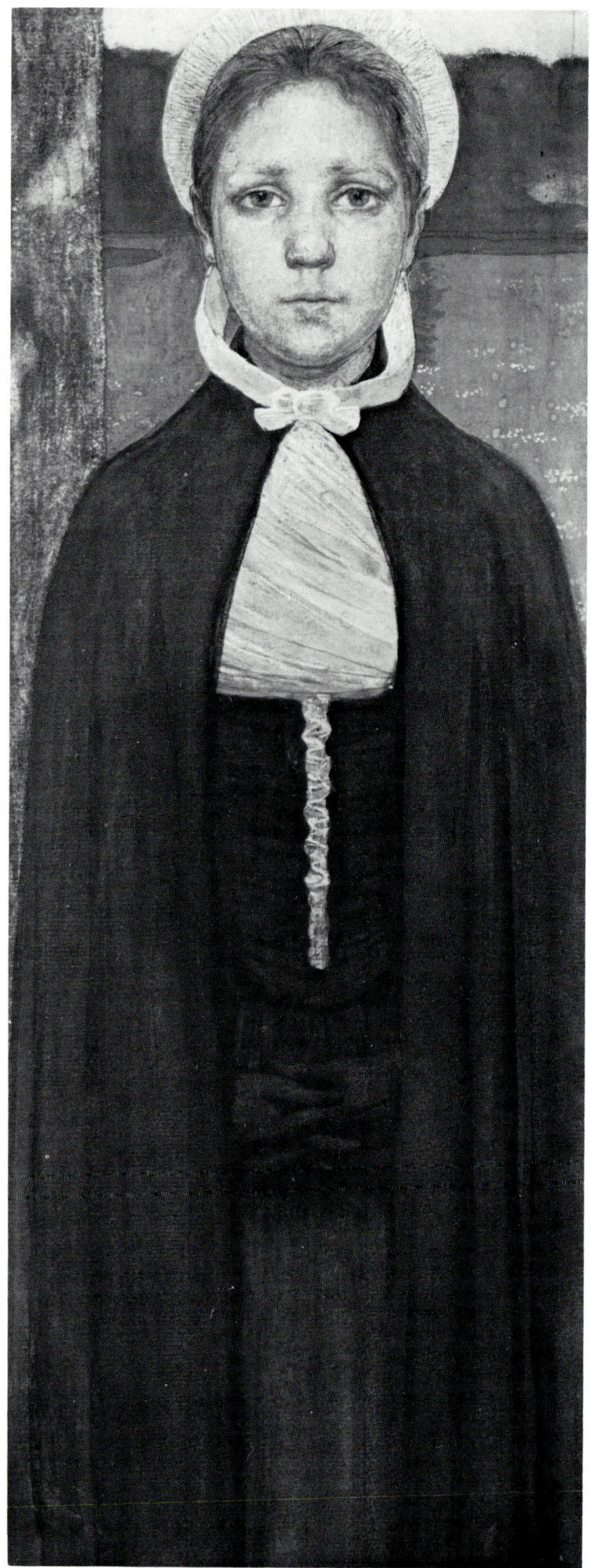

by his systematic construction of the portraits, in which good modelling of the head, minute and careful drawing, expression and will-power are evident. We must needs make our choice and it is difficult in our day to reconcile one of these complete representations of character with a portrait painted with a free brush. At the same time, we must remember that Veth is still young and it is quite possible that he may wish to acquire in his painted work something of that quality which he so greatly admires in the masters of the Hague school.

One of Veth's pupils is Miss Johanna Cornelia Hermana (Nelly) Bodenheim, who was born in Amsterdam in 1874. She made her first appearance in 1896, in the *Kroniek,* with a coloured lithograph, a sort of illustration to a well-known folk-song, in which she recalled the middle-ages in fresh and simple colours, without pomp or display, but with the same candour as the song itself; and I can only hope that she will not forsake this style altogether in favour of her clever and amusing illustrations to our national nursery-rhymes.

Miss Walburga Wilhelmina (Wally) Moes, born in Amsterdam in 1856, the painter of Laren interiors, although a pupil of Allebé and Richard Burnier, deliberately chose Veth as her leader, both in the modelling of the features as in general style, with the result that the expression of her women and mothers often acquires something very sensitive. Dutchwoman though she be, her talent often leans towards the German, inasmuch as her work is painted for the sake of the expression of the subject rather than for the sake of the general effect or of the colour.

In this respect, she resembles Louise Eugénie Steffens (1841-1865), a Catholic painter who died very young, not, however, before producing a few excellent pictures, convent-scenes or *genre*-pieces, all more or less German in sentiment.

Hendrik Johan Haverman was born in Amsterdam in 1857. He entered the Academy in that city in 1878 and, two years later, began to attend the Antwerp

Haverman *has used a linear simplicity in this painting of "The Orphan".* Photograph courtesy of the Rijksmuseum Hendrik Willem Mesdag, the Hague.

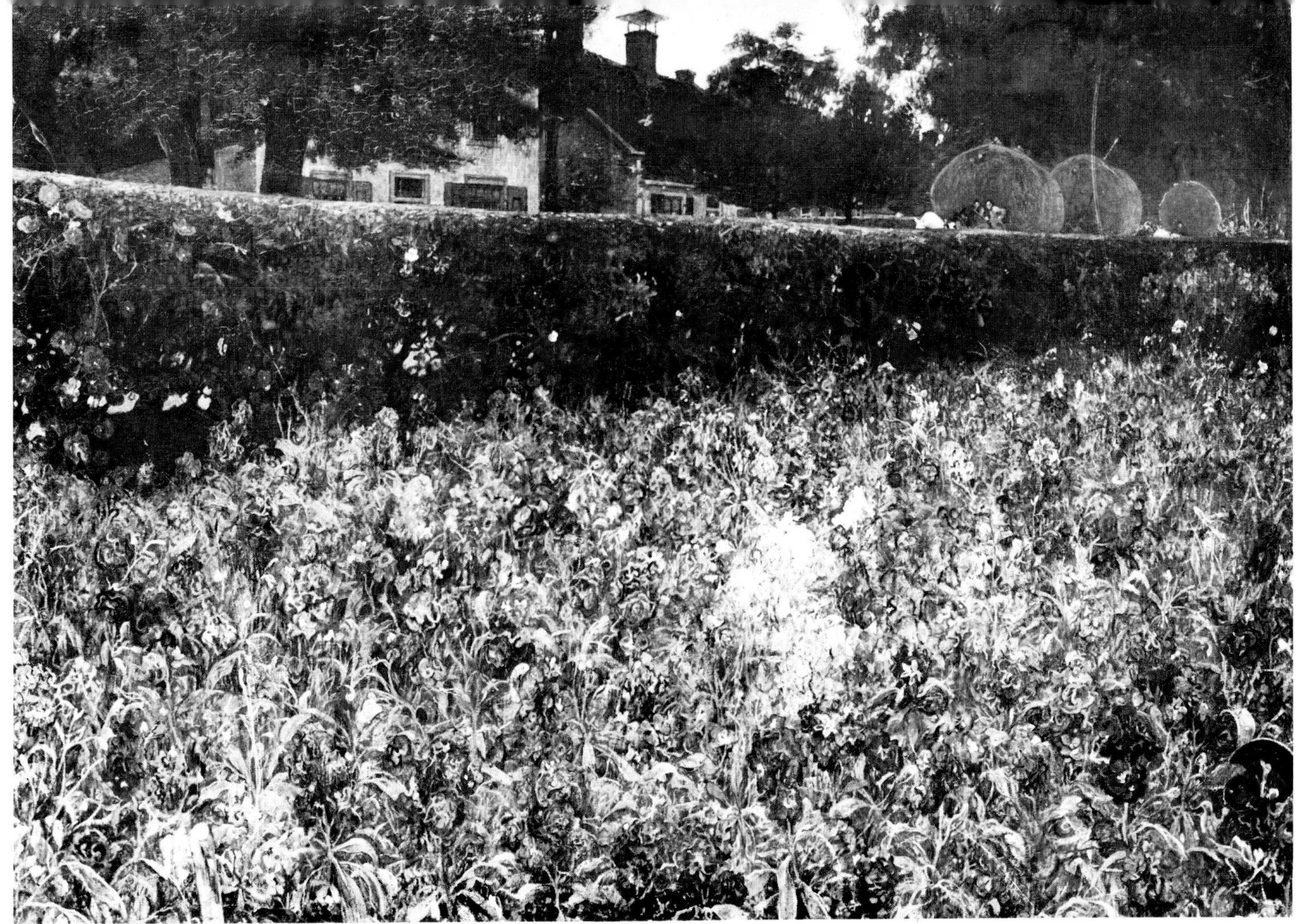

Jacobus van Looy (1855-1930) *was an author-artist renowned for his descriptive prose. In "Summer wealth – July" he describes in paint the overflowing richness of a summer field.* Photograph courtesy of the Stedelijk Museum, Amsterdam.

Academy under Verlat. Afterwards, he worked for a time in Brussels, where he admired Henri de Brakeleer and Stevens and was impressed by the powerful tradition of Jordaens, and then, not feeling certain of his own strength, returned to Amsterdam, to work under Allebé, from whom he received private lessons at the Academy. He painted mainly from the nude; and, although as early as 1880 he had sent a town-scene for exhibition from Antwerp, he made his first real start with figure-painting. To judge by *The Flight,* which he presented to the collection of modern pictures in the Amsterdam Municipal Museum, his style at that time was dry and his draughtsmanship correct rather than lifelike; yet this was a good foundation, upon which he worked at a much later date and more nearly approached the reality and beauty of the nude. He had learned a great deal at the different art-schools; but, like nearly all who have passed through a complete academic training, he had to drudge long before he was able to achieve anything of importance and before he discovered the formula which was to reveal him to himself.

He returned from a trip to Spain, Tangiers and Algiers, in 1890, with a number of studies and small paintings, remarkable for striking realism, well painted and broadly-conceived. In 1892, he made in wash, on a small scale, a full-length portrait-study of an uncommonly fat female figure, which he exhibited at Arti in 1893. The happy thought of reproducing the stoutness of this large sitter, who is wearing a tea-gown, of expressing the exact truth and yet producing an harmonious whole by means of careful colouring attracted the attention of the younger men. It is this frankness, this representation of a person not as what

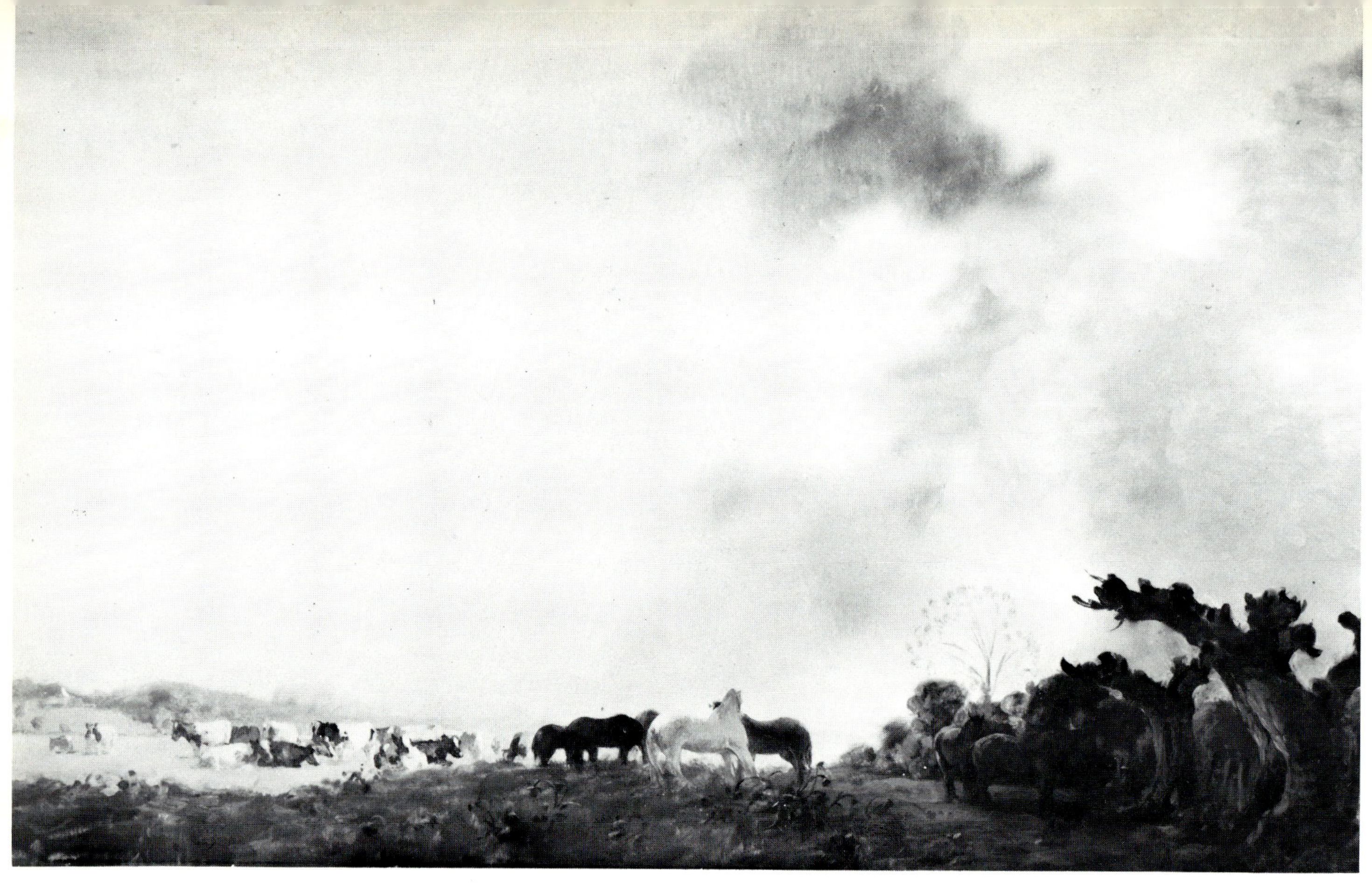

Jan Voerman (1857-1941) *developed a dream quality in his landscapes, with inspiration drawn from Toorop, as in this example peopled with horses and cattle. (38 x 63cms.).* Photograph courtesy of Mak van Waay, Amsterdam.

he should be, but as what he is, as himself, as what even his friends do not know him to be, it is this revelation of personality which distinguishes Haverman even as, in another sense, it makes Veth remarkable.

Other important portraits followed – Dr. van Delden, Dr. Birnie, Richard Bisschop, the artist's wife – until, in 1897, Haverman began to draw portraits of "celebrities of the day" for the then newly started (and now no longer existing) monthly, *Woord en Beeld.* And, although wood-cuts rarely do justice to an artist – and it is to this day to be regretted that he did not himself prepare the lithographs for the press – still it is the original drawings for these reproductions that have made him a permanent name.

If I were to compare the two most successful portrait-painters of late days, Haverman and Veth, I should say that, in the drawn portrait, Haverman's powers are more virile, the focussing of the features on the whole more sure and the likeness often sharper, whereas Veth, who searches rather for the mind of his sitter, draws out not so much his strength as his gentleness and goodness. That there are exceptions goes without saying: Veth's portrait of Dr. Kuyper, the late premier, and Haverman's *Portrait of Mrs. S.* are cases in point.

Anton Derkinderen was born at 's-Hertongenbosch in 1859 and grew up under the majestic shadow of its cathedral, where both he and his father sang in the choir. It was, therefore, by no accident that he was the first in our country to dream of monumental art, the first to achieve success in it. Moreover, his father was a goldsmith; and in his father's workshop he admired the monstrances and ciboria which were sent there for repair. He was brought up at the State training-school for school-teachers at the Bosch, where instruction was given in the arts of music and drawing, and he afterwards continued to receive drawing-lessons from J.P. Stracké, the sculptor, who was the director of the Royal School of Arts and Crafts in the Brabant capital. In 1880, he entered the Amsterdam Academy.

Imbued with the Catholic spirit, he went to Brussels in 1882 to work in the Royal Academy under Portaels. While there, he received his first commission,

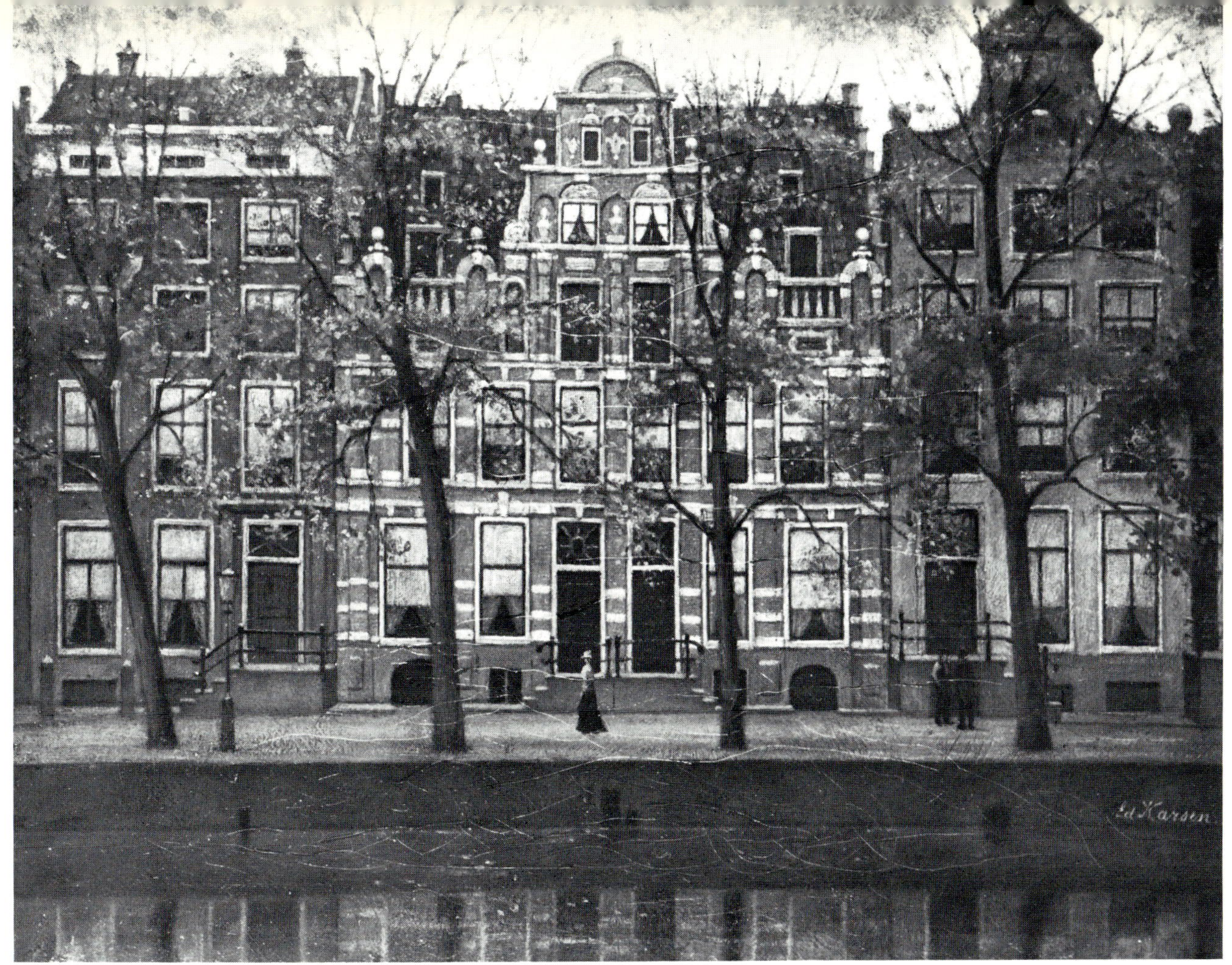

Eduard Karsen (1860-1941) *painted melancholy canal scenes, with quiet old houses mirrored in the water. Here the scene is Amsterdam (34½ x 54½cms.).* Photograph courtesy of Mak van Waay, Amsterdam.

to paint a religious and commemorative fresco for the church of the Amsterdam Béguignage: *The Procession of the Miraculous Blessed Sacrament as held in Amsterdam up to the sixteenth century.* Never was ecclesiastical painting executed in a more pious and joyful mood, more pervaded with the spirit of the *Te Deum,* as personified in this procession bearing the Blessed Sacrament along the shore of the IJ, with the shipping of the commercial capital for its background.

Nevertheless, the painting was not approved of and was indeed refused by the church. If Derkinderen had remained within the circle in which he spent his childhood and his first youth, if he had never known and admired the pictures of Puvis de Chavannes, if, above all, he had retained his early admiration of the services of the Catholic Church, his ideas would have been conceived in the spirit rather than according to the letter of Puvis de Chavannes and he would have understood that the works of Puvis, with his conception of colour, would have been as much out of place in a Roman Catholic church as a Fra Angelico in a Pantheon. Even though the church in the Béguignage were whitewashed in the style of the Reformation, a picture of this description has to serve for devotional purposes: its colours must harmonize with the stained glass and the brilliant vestments; it must keep its form and colour in the twilight of the columns and in the pale candle-light. And then too the young painter might gradually have developed into an artist who would have helped to raise the Catholic Church out of the slough of chromo-lithography into which she had sunk. This pale-golden painting, as it now stands, owes its origin almost entirely to a Germanic feeling and gives an exquisite representation of the religious life of the time, as seen through modern eyes that are themselves yearning to believe.

The paintings at the Bosch, which rank at the present moment as Derkinderen's finest works, owe their origin not so much to the wishes of his fellow-townsmen as to the initiative of a few amateurs. The dignity and distinction with which the artist, following the old chronicles, has, on the first wall, depicted the founding of the city in pure architectural forms make this work the master-piece of a transition-period, a master-piece in which the great lines of history are imbued with the spirit of the building of the city until they form an harmonious and truly monumental whole. The second painting, representing the construction of the interior of the cathedral, has more logical quality if regarded as a fresco, inasmuch as the whole design is on one plane. Yet it cannot be denied that the somewhat Byzantine character of the subject robs this work of that pious simplicity which makes the two earlier paintings so attractive.

Among the different forces and ideals of this age, Jacobus van Looy occupies a place apart. Born at Haarlem in 1855, he is a true artist, whose pictures, in spite of their strong brushwork, have nothing in common with those of Breitner or Isaäc Israëls. Van Looy first made his name as a writer of stately prose, in which he describes external things in such a way that they stand out, as it were, in the full glare of everyday life, a prose which becomes purely plastic in the hands of this painter in words, even as it is purely lyrical in those of Lodewijk van Deyssel. Those who know his prose know the subjects of his pictures. Both are the outcome of his impressions and are as closely related as are Rossetti's pictures to his sonnets.

He was one of the first in our country to make a study of the daily life of the streets. Take, for example, his *Peepshow;* or a barrel-organ, in a back slum, with a group of fat Jewesses and street-girls

Pieter Meiners (1857-1903) *followed a gentle impressionist vein as in this "Evening landscape with a Barn". (15½ x 20½cms).* Photograph courtesy of Kröller-Müller Museum, Otterlo.

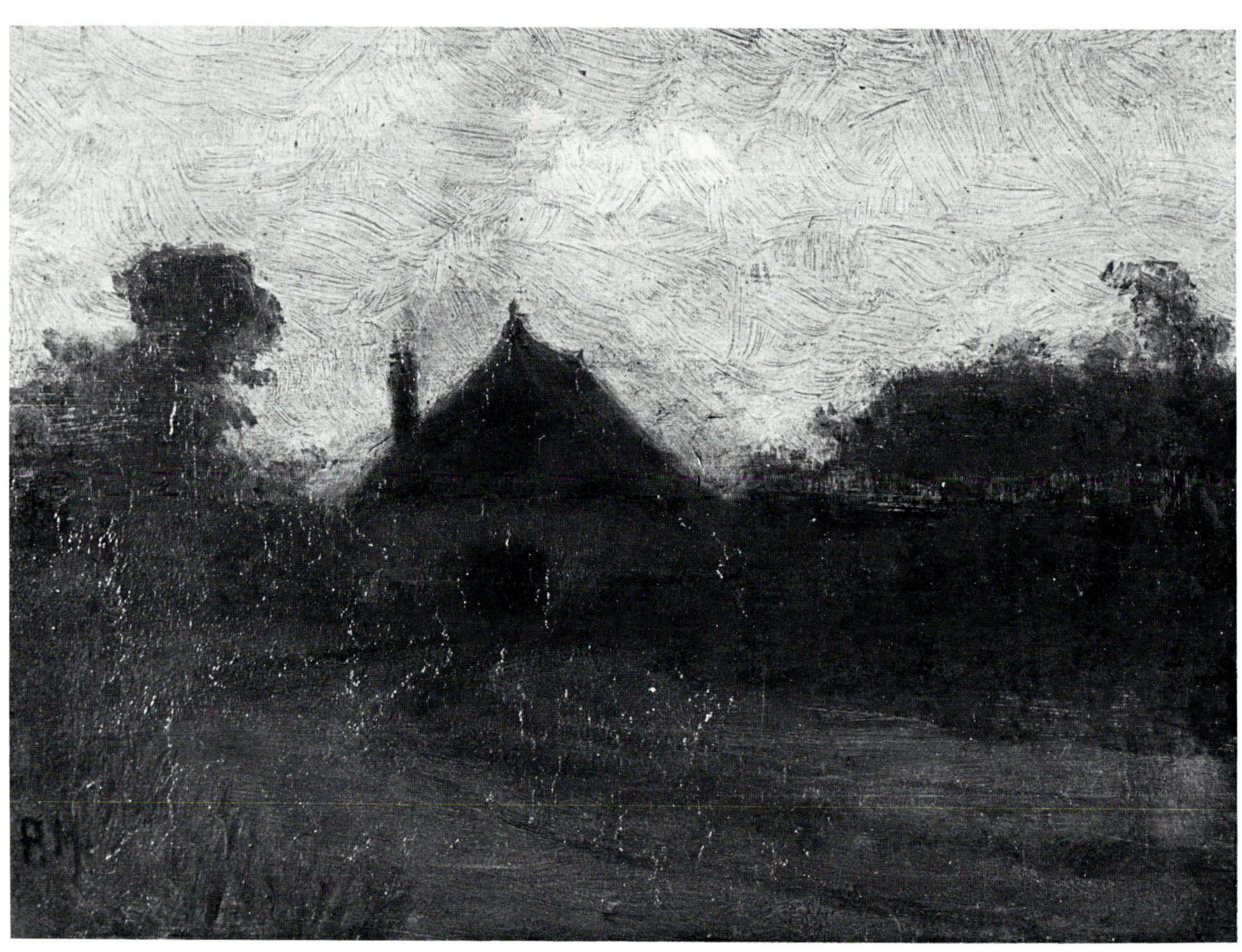

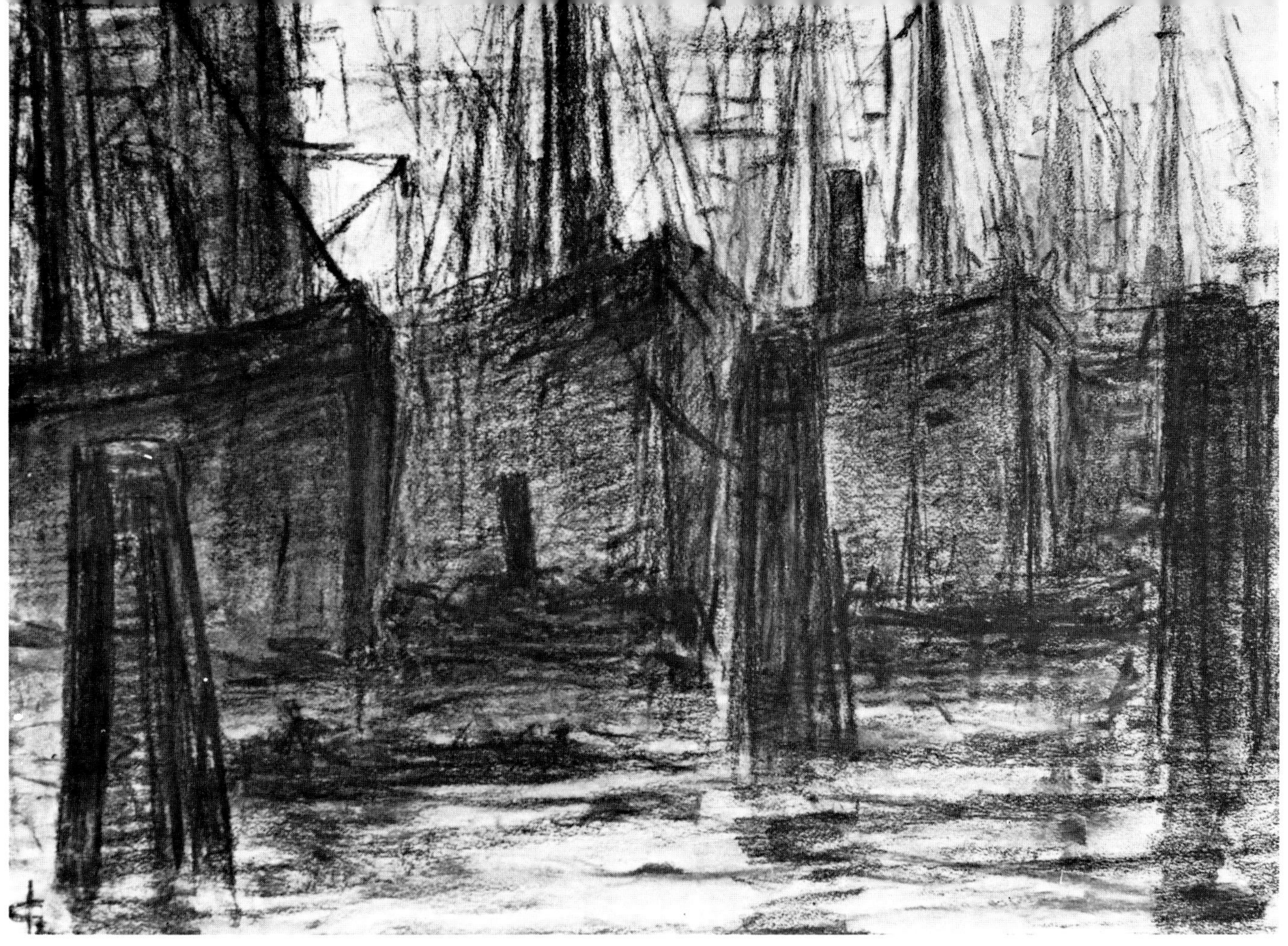

Jonkheer Carel Nicolaas Storm van 's-Gravesande (1841-1924) *was primarily a graphic artist. Here he has drawn a corner of the harbour at Hamburg.* Photograph courtesy of the Rijksmuseum Hendrik Willem Mesdag, the Hague.

dancing to its strains, amid effects of light that remind the spectator of *The Night Watch.* His colouring is often unreal and betrays a search after colour in the studio; but the action is taken from everyday life and seen with the eyes of an artist.

He was brought up for a carriage-painter, studied under Poorter and Allebé at the Academy and was subject to no other influences. His greatness is due to the power of his painting, but as an artist in words he is greater still: the prose of his *Spain* has perhaps never been surpassed in our literature. Who shall fathom the complex nature of this positive and strenuous painter-author?

Jan Voerman, born at Kampen in 1857, is, after Van Looy, the oldest of this younger generation. His first work, produced and exhibited in 1882, was a *genre*-painting of Jews, painted in the heavy manner of the Amsterdam school, a cleverly executed study. But his native preference was for landscape and nature: in 1883, he began to paint impressionist town-scenes and flowers; in 1889, he settled at Hattem and produced those pure water-colours of violets or azaleas in coloured ginger-jars, exquisitely drawn, full and dainty in form, which were to be seen at the exhibitions of the Sketching Club and of which an example now hangs in the Mesdag collection. Voerman was an impressionist and nothing more in those days, although he was already beginning to feel that he would need a different formula to express his own nature. By degrees he grew to understand that the work of the Dutch painters was not pure enough in colour; and he was struck with this fact more especially by observing the contrast between the works of Maris and Toorop and those of all the other artists at an exhibition held at Arti in 1891 or 1892. He had not visited an exhibition for years. It now became evident to him that he must alter his methods; and from that day he began to paint everything with pure colours and to mix as little as possible.

This simplicity, which the works of Maris and Toorop made manifest to him, expressed itself in his productions in a very different way. His *Irises,* shown at the Utrecht Exhibition of 1892, revealed a purity of colour, a beauty of form which, for the first time, perhaps, rendered the firmness of the petals with justice and already exceeded the efforts of a Jaap Maris. And afterwards, both in the exquisite lines and colouring of his La France roses in a crystal bowl and in his later landscapes, all painted in a kind of wash-colour, his style (perhaps against his own will) approached Toorop's more nearly than that of Jacob Maris, to which, in point of fact, Voerman's method but rarely showed any resemblance.

Eduard Karsen, born in Amsterdam in 1860, should no more than Voerman be said to belong to the Hague school. If he did, it could be objected that his treatment of his pigments is not supple, his manner uninspiring, his view of things narrow, that his colour would be more properly described as negative, that his work is lifeless, while the melancholy which it breathes is not such as music can give us; and yet, despite all this, there are few who, like Karsen, understand the charm of still-life, few who so well know how to reproduce the dark side of nature, that contracted side which tends so greatly to sadden sensitive characters. This is the spirit in which he renders those silent North-Holland farmhouses, lying in their heavy masses on the wide fields, or those small low houses by the side of the canals, lonely and still, mirrored in the water as though waiting for the coming of the night.

To the names of these artists must be added that

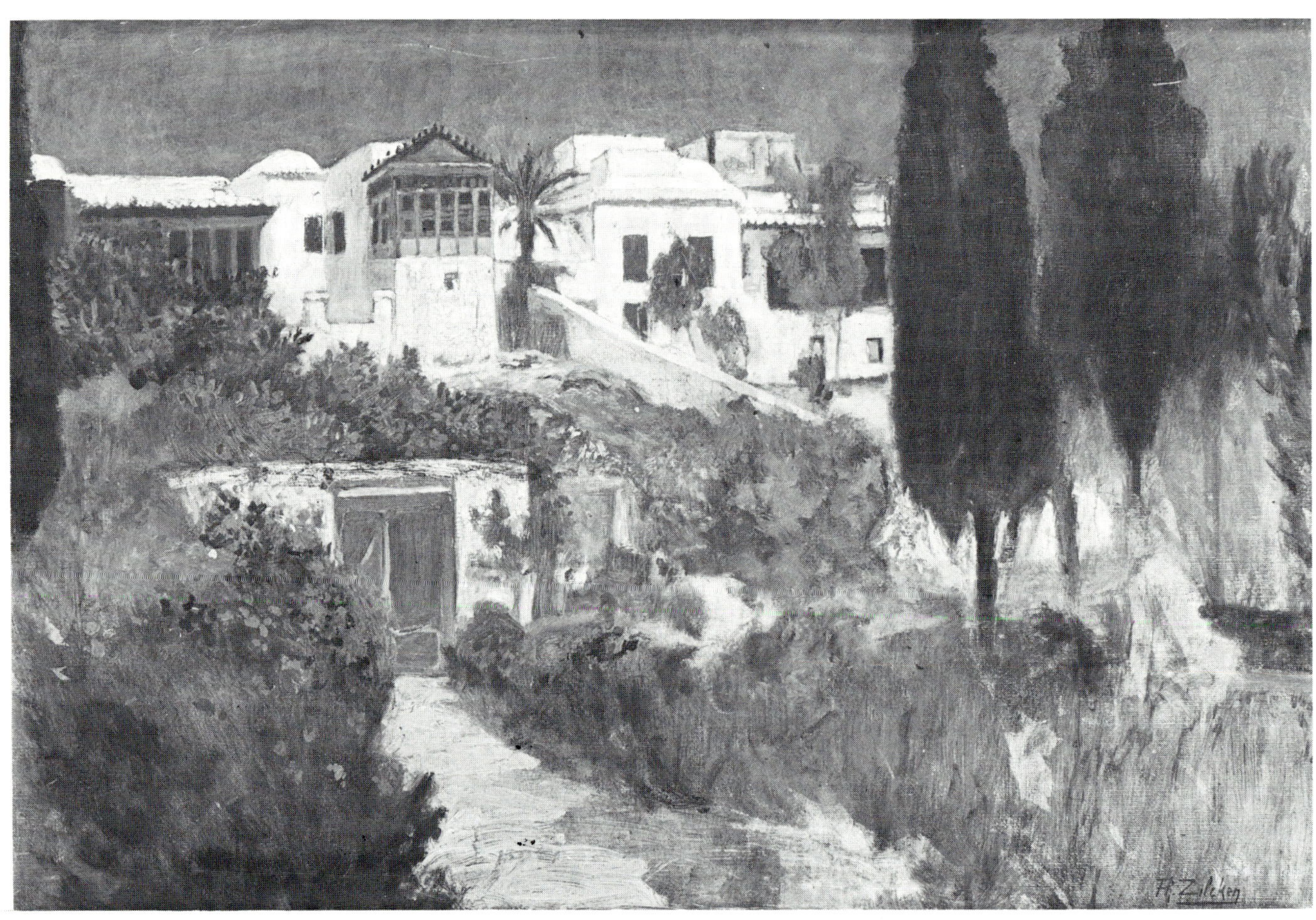

Philippe Zilcken (1857-1930) *adopts an impressionist technique for this Mediterranean view.* Photograph courtesy of Mak van Waay, Amsterdam.

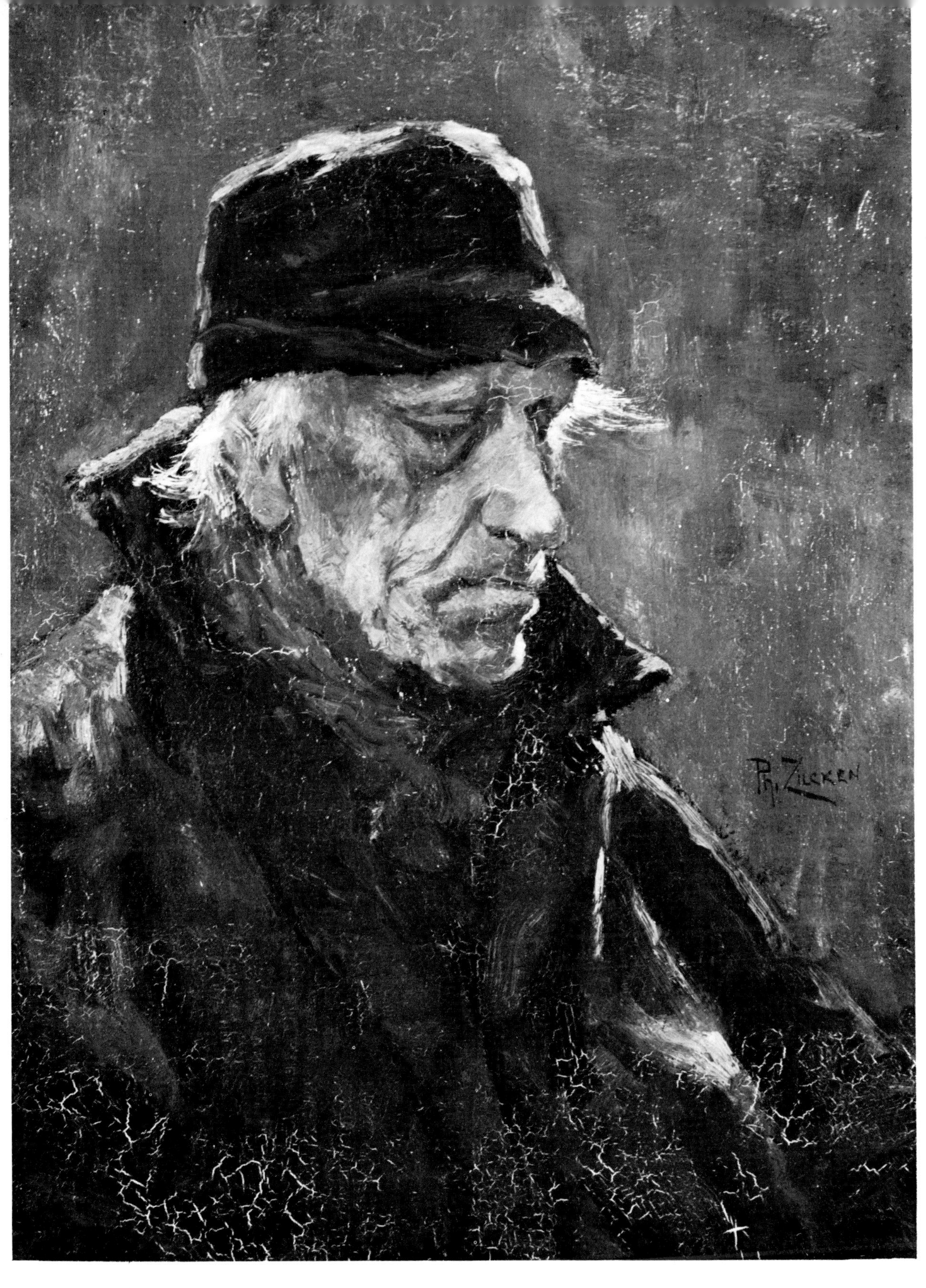

Here **Zilcken** *echoes the earlier Hague Masters with "An Old Fisherman of Scheveningen".* Photograph courtesy of the Rijksmuseum Hendrik Willem Mesdag, the Hague.

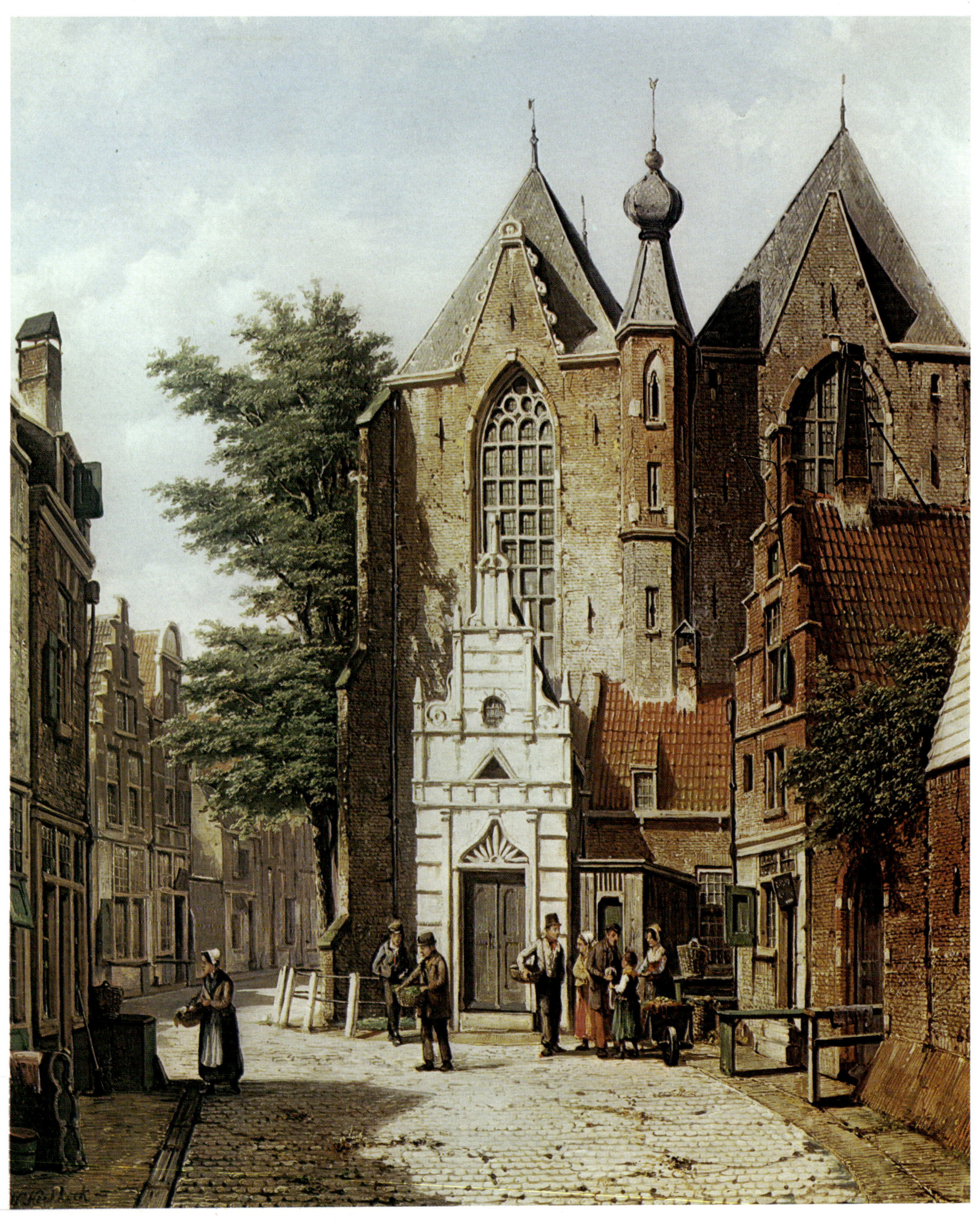

Willem Koekkoek (1839-1895). *"Street scene with figures near the entrance of The Westerkerk of St. Gommarus in Enkhuizen." (27¼ x 23ins.).* Photograph courtesy of Richard Green.

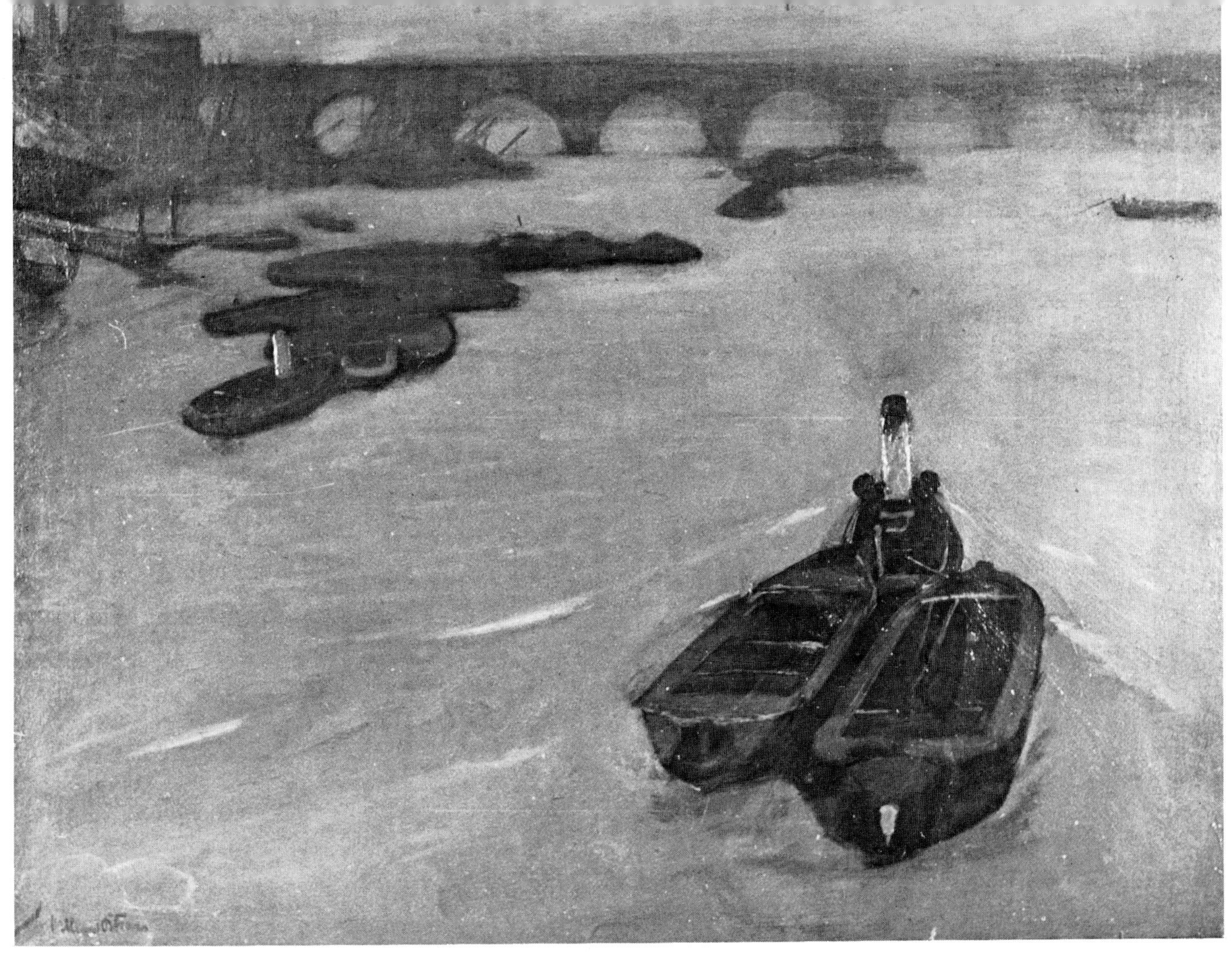

Willem Witsen (1860-1923) *established his first fame with his London etchings. In this "View of the Thames, London" he treats the same subject in oils. (79 x 100cms.).* Photograph courtesy of the Kröller-Müller Museum, Otterlo.

of Pieter Meiners, who was born at Oosterbeek in 1857 and died in 1903. He had an impressionable talent, though he made no great name for himself and left but few works behind him. He was a pupil of his father (himself a comparatively unknown painter) and also of the Amsterdam Academy, which he left with a pronounced feeling for form, softened by the supple touch of the Hague Masters. He produced carefully-observed pictures of still-life, notable for their silky tone, their inoffensive composition, their light shadow, their striking technique. His work was peculiarly placid and seemed never to have cost its author an effort. His talent was not great, but he had the good taste to make no endeavour to force it in any way.

In 1885, the younger men founded the Netherlands Etching Club, with Jan Veth for their president. This promotion of the arts of drawing, etching, lithography, of black-and-white work generally, to an honourable position was to the later generation all that the Sketching Club of twenty years before had been to the Hague men. The result was that the etchings of the Hague masters, of Israëls, Jacob and Matthijs Maris, Mauve, now saw the light of day; that the crayon-sketches of these masters were rescued from studio corners; and that, above all, graphic art once more began to enjoy the consideration of the art-loving public.

True, we had two professional etchers, one of whom, Jonkheer Carel Nicolaas Storm van 's-Gravesande, born at Breda in 1841, a pupil of Roelofs and of Félicien Rops, had, long before this club came into existence, made himself a name at home and abroad by a set of distinguished etchings, nearly all of

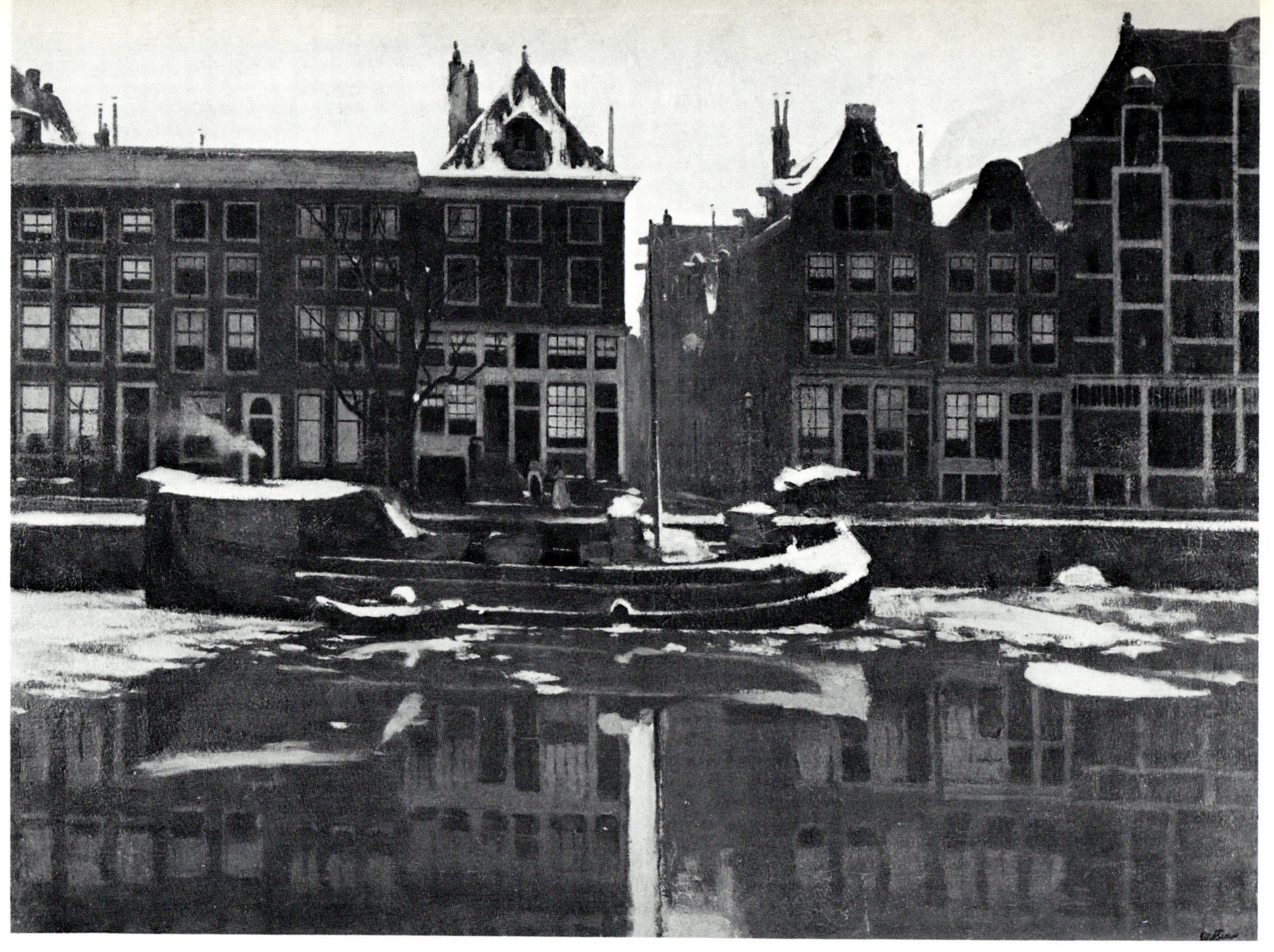

Witsen *stands between Klinkenberg and Breitner in this view of Amsterdam.* Photograph courtesy of the Stedelijk Museum, Amsterdam.

them of Dutch river-scenes. The other was Philippe Zilcken, born at the Hague in 1857, a pupil of Mauve and, like Jonkheer Storm, a painter, but, first of all, an etcher. His etchings after Thijs Maris' *A Baptism in the Black Forest* and Alfred Stevens' *La Bête au Bon Dieu* are triumphs in their way. His original etchings include a number of well-known profiles in dry-point.

When the Etching Club was founded, Willem Witsen, born in 1860, at once established his reputation as a great etcher by his series of open-air figures in the manner of Millet or Mauve. And, in spite of his water-colours and oil-paintings – his London bridges, his Millet figures standing out distinctly marked against the evening sky, his characteristic old Amsterdam houses – Witsen, like Bauer, is an etcher first and foremost and builds up his paintings and especially his water-colour drawings from subjects seen with an etcher's eye, with the same firm hand, the same preference for the massy, the same distaste for detail, the same powerful line and the same pure sense of values. Nevertheless, his pictures lack the compactness, the charming effects of light and shade which he succeeded in giving to his monumental London etchings produced between 1888 and 1891.

Witsen also lapses occasionally, as a painter, into the style in which the last word has been spoken by Breitner and this is not the style in which one would prefer to see him work; but I am inclined to think that this will prove to belong to a transition-period, for a man who has been able to produce such master-pieces as the London etchings and water-colours must needs have at his beck both ideas and powers which he will set forth for our admiration in his own good time.

Chapter XII

The New Formula

Johannes Theodoor (commonly known as Jan) Toorop was born in 1858 at Poerweredjo in Java and was the first to bring from France to Holland, *via* Brussels, the so-called Neo-impressionism of the "Vingtistes." Although in Amsterdam he belonged to the generation described in the preceding chapter, he received his real education amid the great movement of the young Belgians and may be said to have introduced a new phase into Dutch art. In 1889, he arranged, at the Amsterdam panorama, an exhibition of the XX, in which he showed his *Broek in Waterland* and his *Twylight Idyll,* two pieces painted in broken colour under the Vingtiste influence. The exhibition contained much that was interesting and much that was beautiful, but failed to make any general impression.

Whatever Toorop may have produced before this exhibition – and he had already made himself known by some drawings of London poverty of astonishing realism – it is certain that his work now struck out an absolutely new line and presented a new aspect of Dutch meadows, of the North-Sea coast and of the motives to be found in the lives of the fisher-folk. This was brought out in his *Broek in Waterland,* a picture in which the sober lines of a North-Holland pastureland were approached for the first time, intersected with rectilinear ditches, broken only by a few stumpy pollard-willows. It is a view entirely without artificial embellishment, without any search for the harmonious in those fields, where the setting sun filled the ditches with orange light, clashing crudely with the dark green of the meadows and the pale sky. There was no question here of beauty or ugliness: it was the brutal reality, powerfully grasped and strongly expressed.

This picture owed its origin to a trip to North Holland taken while Toorop was living in Brussels with the Belgian poet Emile Verhaeren. It was only when seen in this way, as it were with a foreign eye, that the sheer plainness of these meadows and ditches could have been observed and rendered in so ruthless and literal a fashion.

The Wave, the most important work of the first portion of Toorop's residence at Katwijk, is a wonderfully clever and elaborate analysis of the sea, a very feast of movement and colour, a mosaic of variegated tints, with the blue of the sky reflected in the bottle-green wave, the yellow of the fishermen's oilskins, the endless facets of the rippling waters. This work, although not painted in broken colour, already shows a tendency towards a more decorative style of composition.

A third important picture was *Melancholy,* represented by the figure of a woman of Katsijk-Binnen leaning against the doorpost of her house, with quiet eyes set in a pale oval, a slender little figure and narrow sleeves, appearing mediævally small against the breadth of the endless extent of her petticoats. She stares into the twilight; round her is the little garden with sunflowers and low railings, which look strange in the failing light. The predominant tone of the picture is the dark blue of her apron. To my mind, this *Melancholy,* so distinguished in its conception, so suggestive in its mood, is Toorop's most interesting work in this direction. Later, his ideas became much more intricate and metaphysical; but in no other work have idea and form, or rather mood and form been more perfectly blended and the result charms at the same time both the eye and the mind.

Thanks to an unusually complex ancestry, Toorop inherited the characteristics of the native East-Indian, the Norseman and the Hollander. Richard Muther, after describing the curious impression which Toorop's work made upon the Viennese public, goes on to

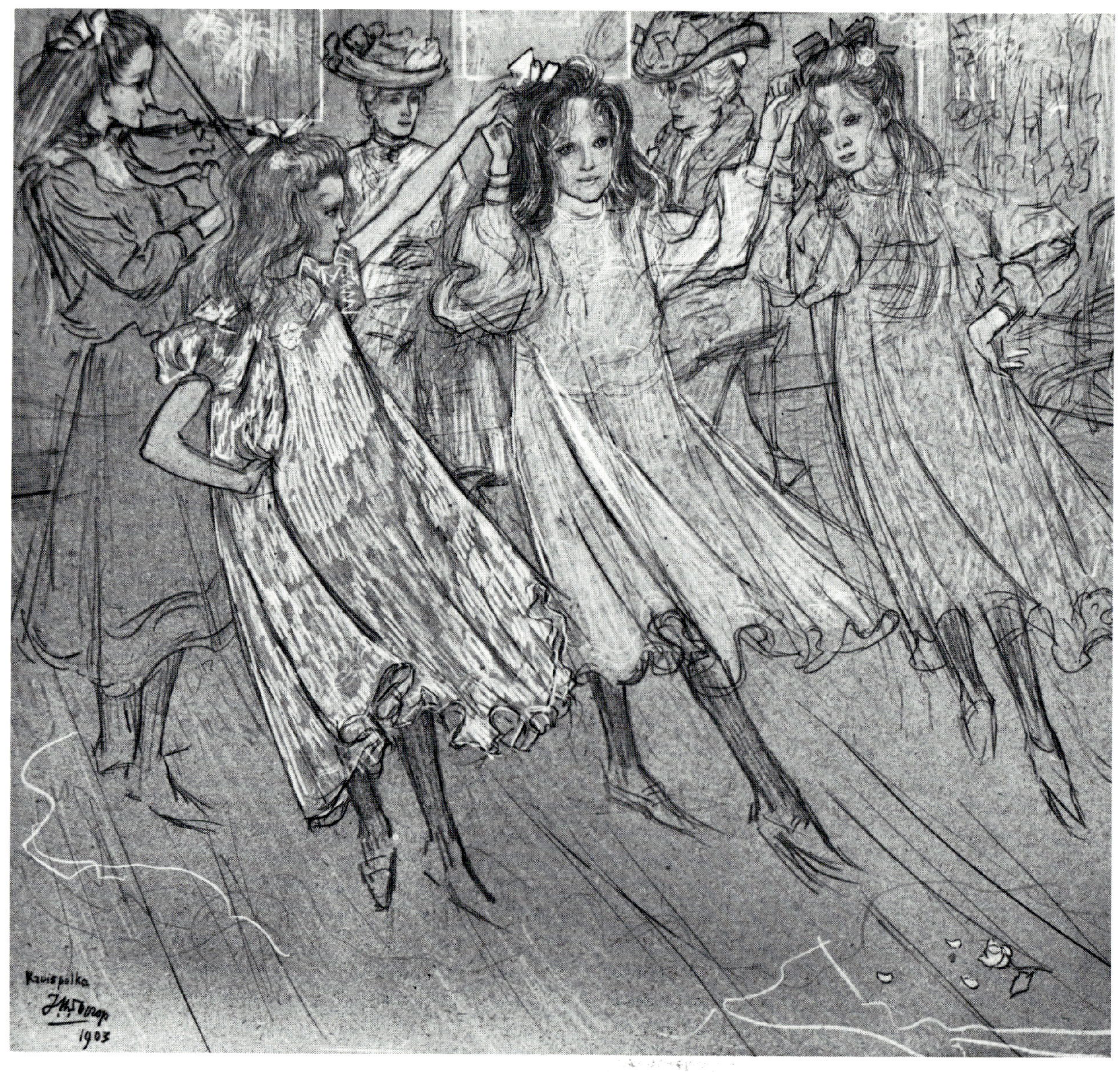

Johannes Theodor (Jan) Toorop (1858-1928) *is now hailed as Holland's greatest Symbolist painter. This "Dancing Lesson" of 1903 shows his expressive linear power. (62 x 67cms.).* Photograph courtesy of Mak van Waay, Amsterdam.

prophesy that at some future time he will be known as the Giotto of his day. I do not greatly care to anticipate the verdict of posterity and prefer to say that Giotto, the shepherd, who evolved his first vision of life with charcoal on the walls of the sheepcote, transferred the art of painting from the hierarchical forms of the Byzantines to the living being, whereas Toorop, in depicting nature, makes his human beings the exponents of his ideas. But what Toorop has indeed succeeded in expressing, at an earlier period and to a greater extent than our literature – and this, no doubt, is what Dr. Muther meant by his comparison – is the scepticism of our time, the decline of established religious belief, the search after new dogmas.

His mystic symbolism is popular in the best sense of the word. In his *Three Brides,* he represents the three aspects of womanhood, personifies the senses of sound and smell: the characteristics of the three women clash against one another in round and angular lines; sound is indicated by threads in a linear design resembling that of a great orchestra, richly and magnificently filled. Now sound had already been personified by Blake; and good and evil in Gothic art and even earlier. But the difference in Toorop lies in the obvious strength of his technique, a rare gift, which enables him almost to represent, set down and fix the abstract, daintily and delicately in his portraits of children, powerfully and nervously in his symbolic and robustly in his realistic works.

The work of Vincent van Gogh fell like a meteor into the plains of our national art in the winter of 1892, two years after the painter's death. A meteor in very truth! Here was no question of gradual, technical, artistic development, that had been followed out year by year. That which first greeted our eyes was the most passionate, desperate and impulsive work, the technical part of which, as it then appeared, before time had matured it, seemed beyond the power of the painter's art. It was the evidence of the artist's struggle with his medium, of his struggle with nature; it was the act of despair of a fanatic; it was the revelation of a visionary.

It was no easy matter for work like that of Van Gogh to find acceptance in an artistic environment such as ours, based upon a culture which we owe to the seventeenth century. The pictures selected for exhibition out of the plenitude which he had left behind him, unframed for the most part, unbridled utterances of artistic passion, swept over the white peace of our artistic effort like a seething lava, bubbling up from depths which only a few were able to understand or to admire.

Van Gogh's work represents not so much a creed as a man-to-man struggle; his colour is not the result of a well thought-out scheme, but is an effort rather to grasp the light, to hold it fast, to suggest colour in light without the use of brown or bitumen. And, as it was his chief object to render life, to express what he saw rather than to produce an harmonious painting, he strove to fling his impressions, as it were, upon his canvas in one breath; for, as he wrote, "*faire et refaire un sujet sur la même toile ou sur plusieurs toiles revient en somme au même sérieux.*" And his painting and drawing alike revealed the same mingling of conscious and unconscious knowledge.

Van Gogh was a born fanatic, a reformer and prophet preaching in the streets of London, an idealist travelling to the mines in the Borinage to carry to the slaves of the mine the gospel which Jesus once carried to the poor fishermen of the Sea of Galilee, a man in the full sense of the word, endowed with the temperament of a fanatic, in whom the balance is never at rest, a prophet by virtue of his belief in his own powers, a prophet also in the artistic sense through his belief in life and colour, a zealot in so far as he endeavoured to propagate the theories of the "Luministes" with all the force that fanaticism lends; but he had not the nature which can long endure a doubt as to its powers. And, notwithstanding the many moments of happiness which he owed to his art, despite the fact that the inspired hours in his short life as a painter were almost uninterrupted and leaving his more rustic Dutch period out of the question, he does in a way suggest the painter in the Japanese cartoon, who lies felled to the ground by his own work. His imaginative drawings and landscapes were the nightmares of a man who was bound to perish in the greatness of his own longings; they were nightmares of light and colour, flooded with the full glare of glistening sunlight, glittering with transparent greens, with sulphurous yellows, with startling violets; sultry atmospheric effects, more alarming at times than the visions of an Odilon Redon.

Many roads lead to Rome. Art is not bound to a few stated formulas; and the only question is whether Van Gogh, in a given subject, has expressed what he desired. This no one will deny. And, whether we see him move amid more attractive surroundings, such as summery parks, avenues of chestnut-trees in bloom, where the sun casts motley patches upon the ground and upon children at play, or the olive-groves of the South, "where the sun burns into the ground like sulphur"; whether he paints those glowing portraits or those works which we call the illustrations for Zola's novels: this much is certain that, in every case, he largely enriches our sphere of thought and our perceptive faculties.

And his flower-studies too! Who, in our country, has ever painted flowers as he did, so true to nature, so real, so actually lifelike?

"Vincent's flowers look like people," said Pissarro.

And Emile Bernard said:

"Vincent's flowers look like princesses."

To us they are real flowers in their distinction, their form, their bloom, their colour, simple and broad, just as they blossom in a Whitsun meadow before a child's delighted eyes.

Vincent van Gogh was born in 1853 at Groot Zundert, in North Brabant. He was the son of a clergyman and was brought up to be a dealer in works of art, in which trade his uncle Vincent was of great assistance to the younger Dutchmen, first at the

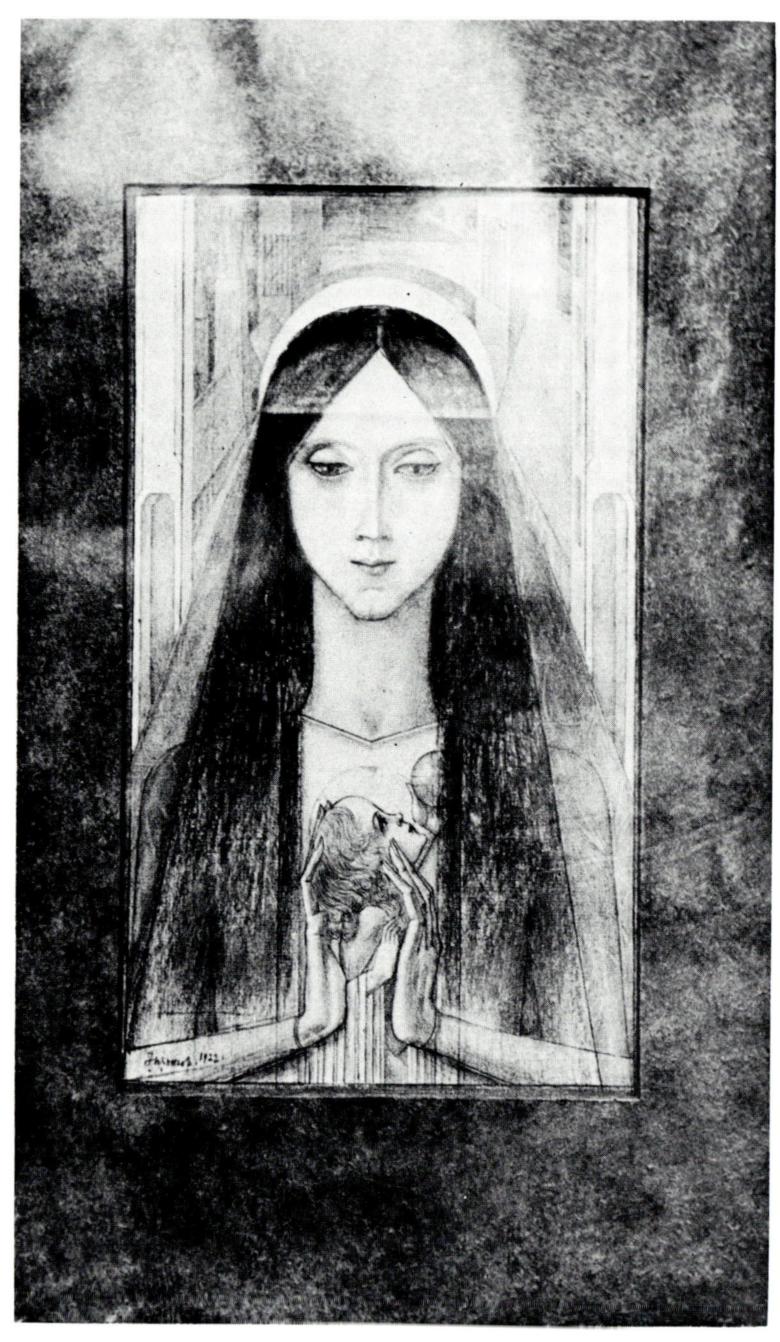

Above and right: These drawings date from Toorop's *later years, more than a decade after Marius was writing. He has developed a more simplified symbolic design.* Photographs courtesy of the Piccadilly Gallery.

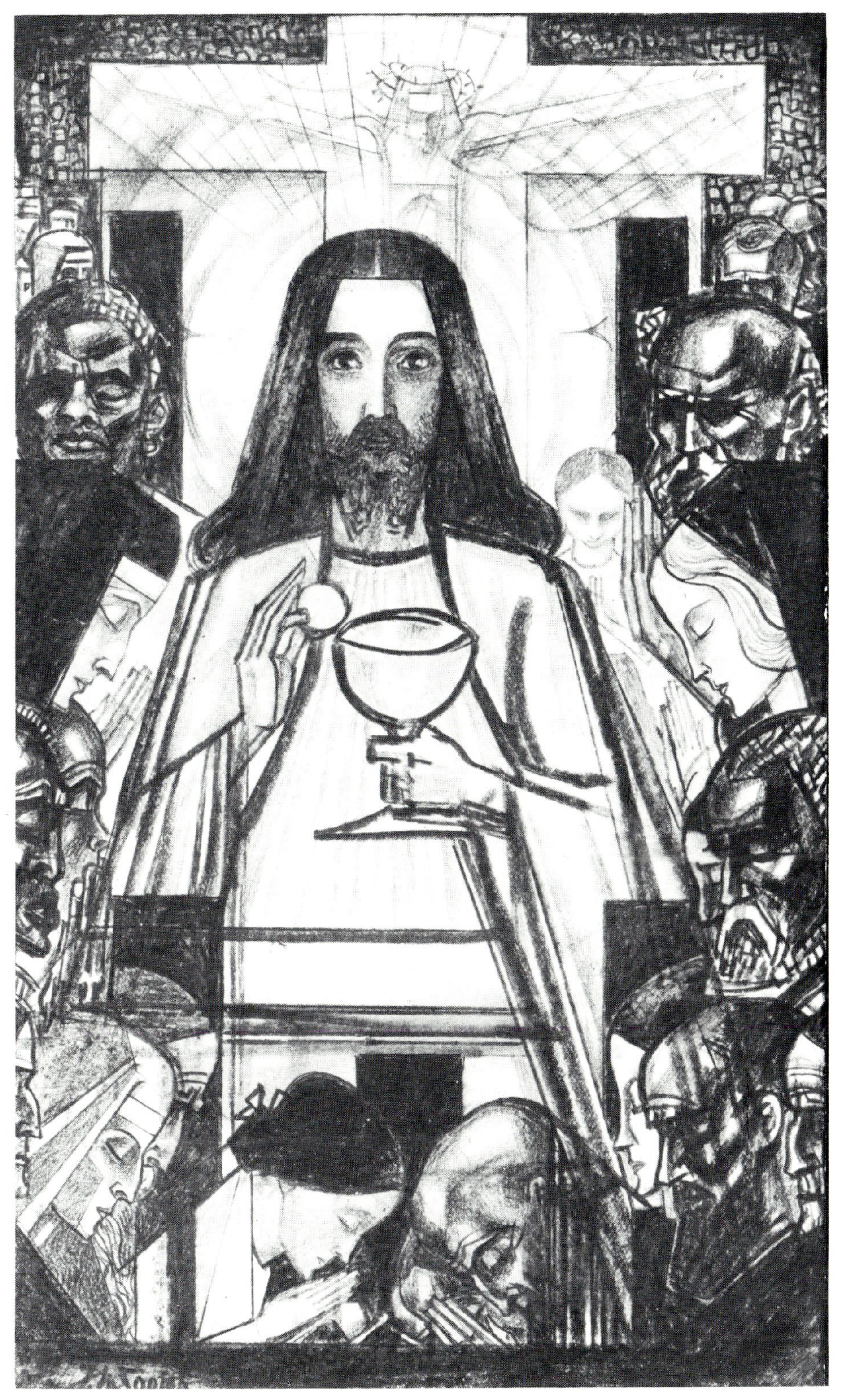

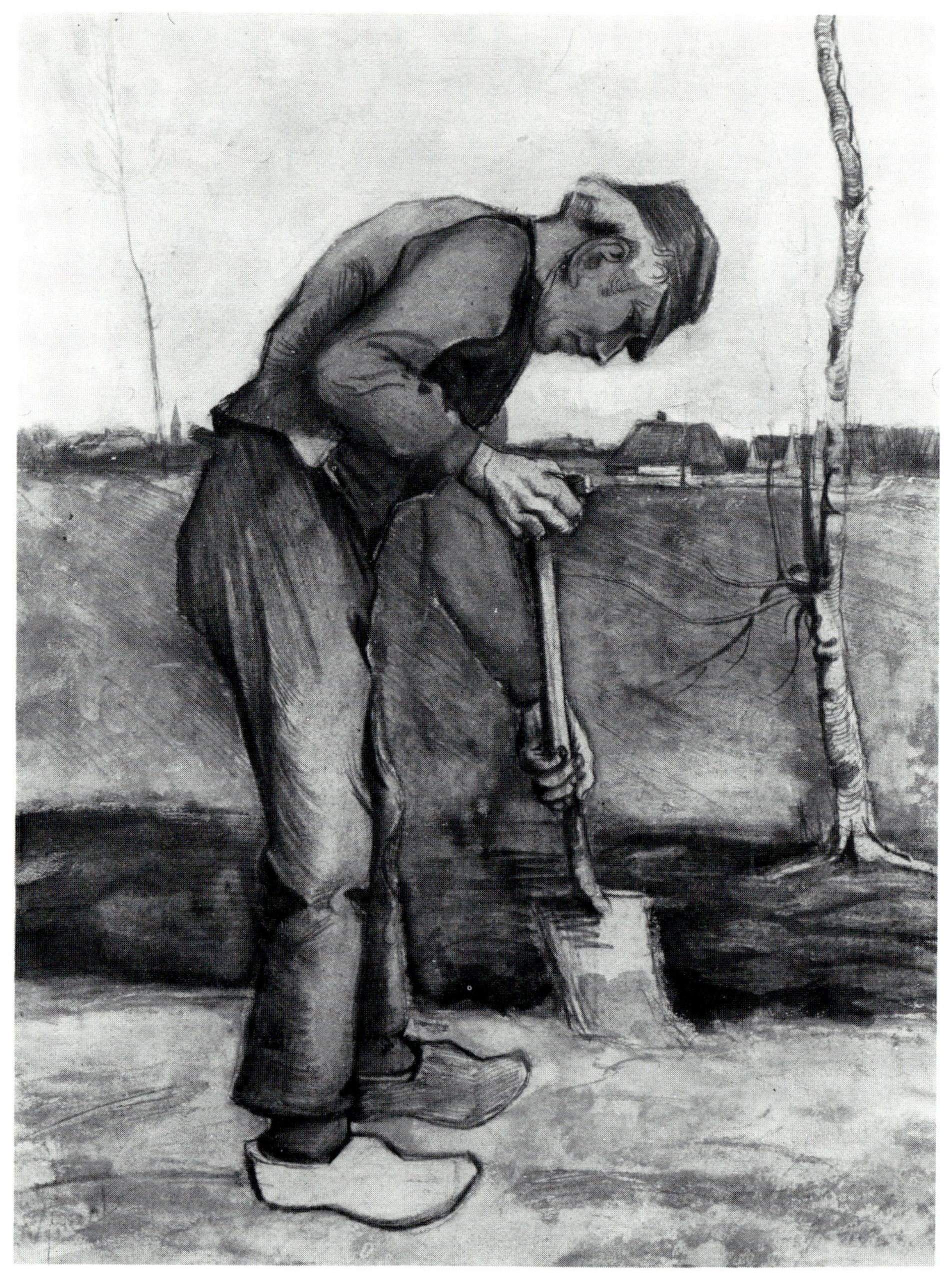

This drawing of a peasant digging by **Vincent Van Gogh (1853-1890)** *predates his arrival in Paris and reflects the influence of the peasant painters of the Hague School.* Photograph courtesy of Sotheby & Co.

Hague and afterwards in the firm of Goupil in Paris. His brother too, Theodoor van Gogh, who was also at Goupil's, afterwards helped the artists of Vincent's movement to the best of his power. After Vincent had worked for some time at Goupil's at the Hague, in London and Paris, he grew dissatisfied and left the business, in 1876, in order to go to London as a teacher. He returned to Holland, worked for a short time for a bookseller at Dordrecht and then went to Amsterdam to prepare for his theological studies. Here again he found the road too long: he threw up the university and went to Brussels and, thence, to the Borinage, to become a gospel-preacher among the miners. This environment influenced him more than any other: at any rate, it made him take to drawing.

It is true that, in a letter from London, he had sent home a couple of rather childish, yet well-

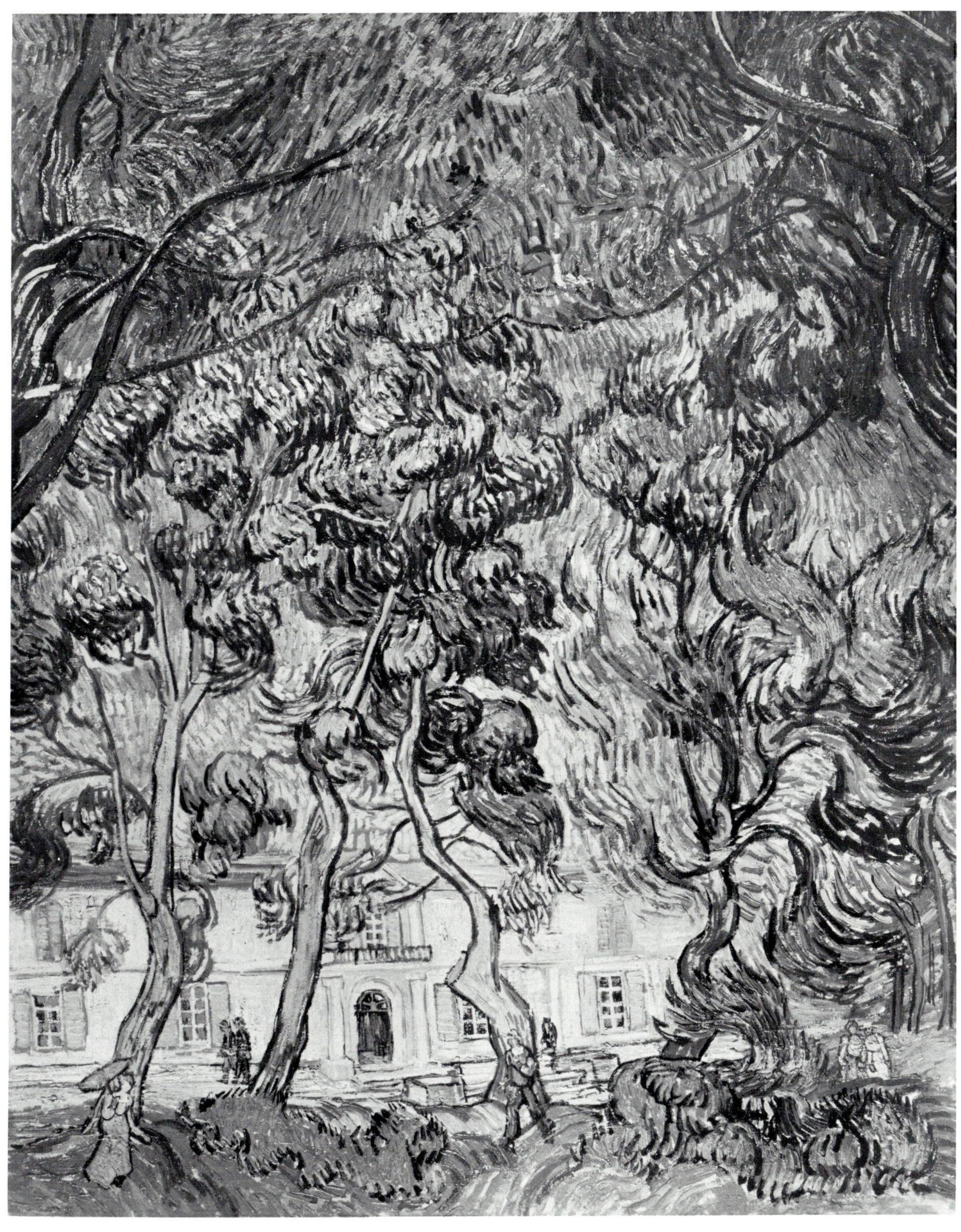

Van Gogh's *later style "fell like a meteor into the plains of our national art in the winter of 1892" according to Marius. This painting of "L'Hôpital de St. Paul à St. Rémy" dates from 1889, the year before Van Gogh's death.* Photograph courtesy of Sotheby & Co.

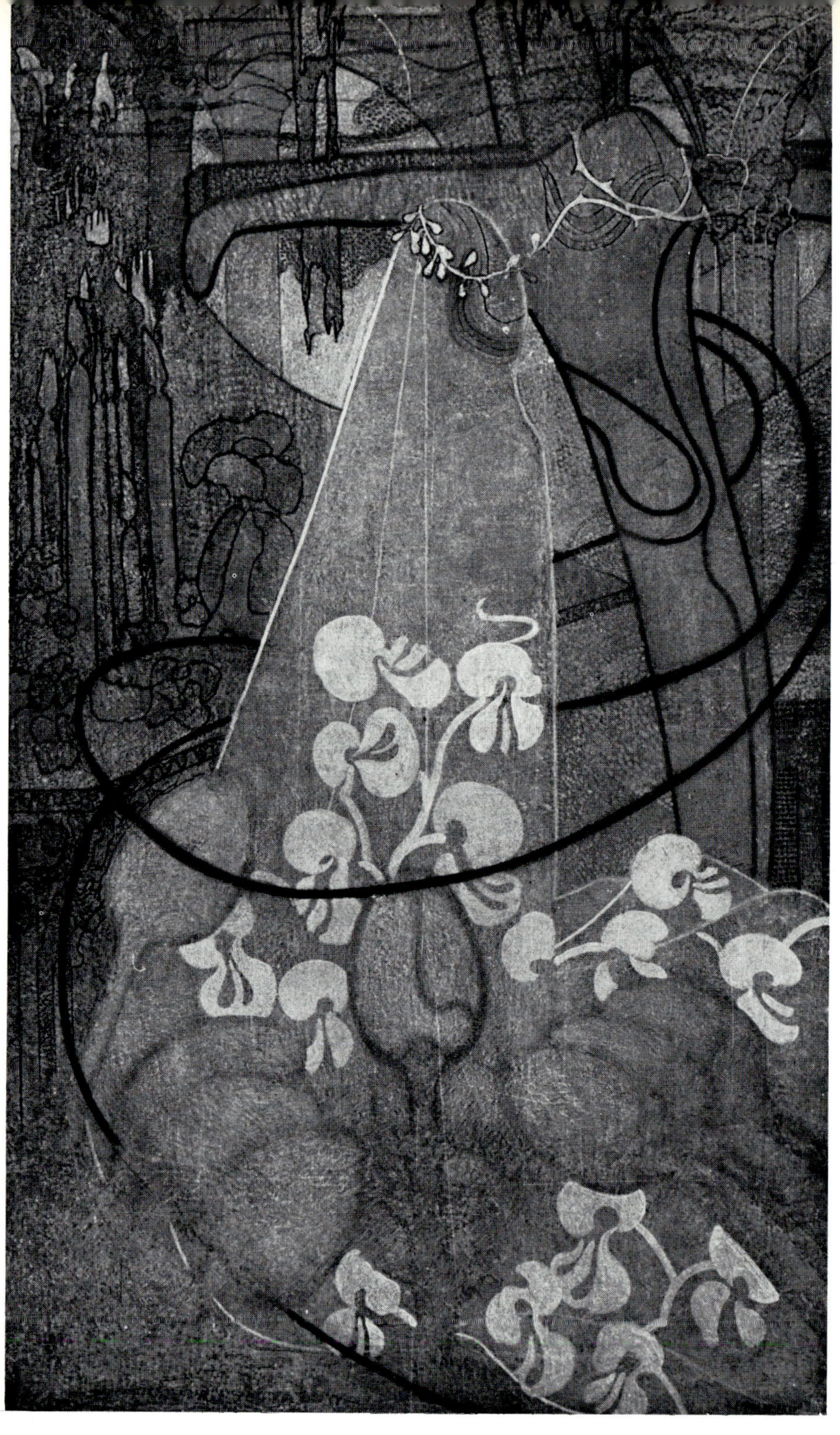

observed little drawings, but these could hardly give an inkling of his talent and, moreover, they stood alone, for, as a child, Vincent, although scribbling and even modelling, like most children, had shown no particular inclination for drawing and his relations were not aware that, before his visit to London, he had ever produced anything worth mentioning. This is also apparent from the excitement displayed by Theo, who, delighted at hearing that Vincent was sketching in the Borinage, exclaimed:

"Now you shall see something! Vincent has taken to drawing: that means a second Rembrandt!"

No sooner had he begun to draw than he suddenly left for Brussels, where he worked zealously at draughtsmanship. But he did not stay long, for, in 1881, he returned to his father's house at Etten and,

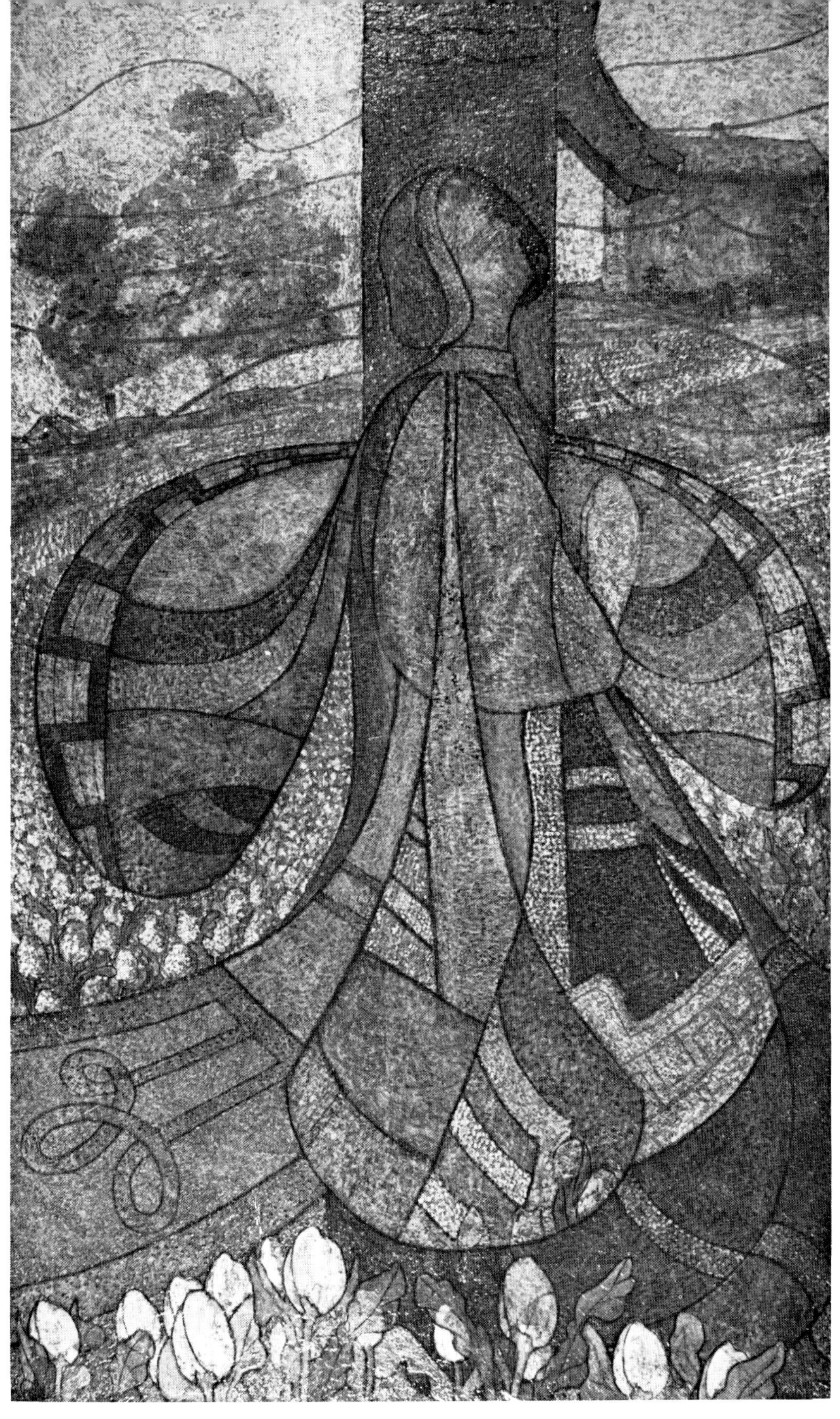

Above and left: **Thorn Prikker (1868-1932)** *has given us two important symbolist works in "The Bride" (146 x 58cms.) and the "Madonna among the Tulips" (146 x 86cms.).* Photograph courtesy of the Kröller-Müller Museum, Otterlo.

towards the end of that year, went to the Hague, where he received occasional advice from Mauve. He worked at the Hague until the summer of 1883 and, after a stay in Drente, went back to his parents, who were now living at Nuenen. In 1885, he went to Antwerp, spent a few months at the academy and, in the spring of 1886, arrived in Paris, where he was strongly influenced by the movement of Monet, Pissarro and Gauguin and himself exercised an influence upon that movement. He next left for the South, went to Arles, later to San Remy and, lastly, to Anvers-sur-Oise, where he died in the summer of 1890.

After his death, his friend Émile Bernard published, in the *Mercure de France,* a number of letters addressed to him by Vincent and later, some fragments of letters to his brother Theo van Gogh, which were supplied by the latter's widow. These letters, continued in a Flemish monthly, *Van Nu en Straks* – although we know only fragments in which he writes of his work and art (how long must we wait before the letters are published in full?) – give us an insight into Theo's devotion for his brother, which made him hold the trade of a dealer in works of art as sacred as a religious belief and made him suffer perhaps even more than Vincent himself at the delay in the acknowledgment of the new artistic formula. And they reveal all Vincent's theories and ideals, his goodness, his moods, variable as the mercury in a thermometer, his personality as a man and an artist, young, gay, unsuspecting, indefatigable: untiring, too, in spite of his lack of physical strength. As early as 1882, he wrote:

"My hands have become too white for my taste. People like myself have no right to be ill."

Most of the letters date from the last period, especially at Arles, the period of the longing to see and grasp all things. They are letters in which, between the cries of despair, gleam his indestructible ideals, hesitations, confessions, shrill contrasts, woven on the golden threads of his dreams, on the golden threads of his love for his brother Theo. Full of this admiring love, he writes that Theo is as great a painter, as great an artist through his selling of pictures, because, by each sale, he enables the artist to produce more pictures:

"Si un peintre se ruine le caractère en travaillant dur à la peinture, qui le rend stérile pour bien d'autres choses (vie de famille etc.), si conséquemment il peint non seulement avec de la couleur, mais avec de l'abnégation et du renoncement de soi et le cœur brisé, ton travail à toi non seulement ne t'est pas payé non plus, mais te coûte exactement comme à ce peintre l'effacement de ta personalité, moitié volontairement, moitie fortuitement. Ceci pour te dire que, si tu fais de la peinture indirectement, tu es plus productif que par exemple, moi."

Or again – and what artist endeavouring to make his own way has not a hundred times exclaimed the same? – he cries:

"Si l'on peignait comme Bouguerau, alors on pourrait espérer de gagner!"

Great regret was felt among his friends at his death:

"He felt everything, *ce pauvre Vincent,* he felt too much," said old Tanguy, the simple artists' colourman, the friend of all young painters and of Vincent too, who was always ready to accept pictures or studies instead of payment for his colours. And he was right: Vincent van Gogh felt too intensely to endure passively the greatness of nature, too deeply to work without hurrying, without swerving and with that composure which characterizes the majority of Dutchmen. Judge Vincent's work as we may, one thing is certain, that he, in whom perhaps more than in any other of our painters bubbled the passionate life of the last end of the century, afforded in his work the last great sensation which the art of the nineteenth century was to present to the Netherlands.

In 1891, the Hague Art Club was founded, in which Toorop and Vincent van Gogh were honoured as masters. Their followers included Thorn Prikker, born at the Hague in 1868, the painter who practised symbolism for a short time and who exhibited his dignified *Heads of the Apostles* at one of the club's shows, but who subsequently devoted himself exclusively to the applied arts.

Another exhibitor was Pieter Cornelis de Moor, born at Rotterdam in 1866, a pupil of Jan Striening, of the Antwerp Academy and of Benjamin Constant, whose little flower-decked *Bride* showed great promise at the time. He afterwards followed the modern French draughtsmen, to a certain extent, in his choice of subjects, but continued his method of symbolic treatment. He has often succeeded in showing what symbolists exactly desire to express, as for example in his *Princesse de Lamballe.*

Then there was Theodoor van Hoytema, born at Rotterdam in 1863, the facile draughtsman of ornithological subjects, which he introduced as illustrations in coloured picture-books with a great feeling for design and effect and afterwards lithographed

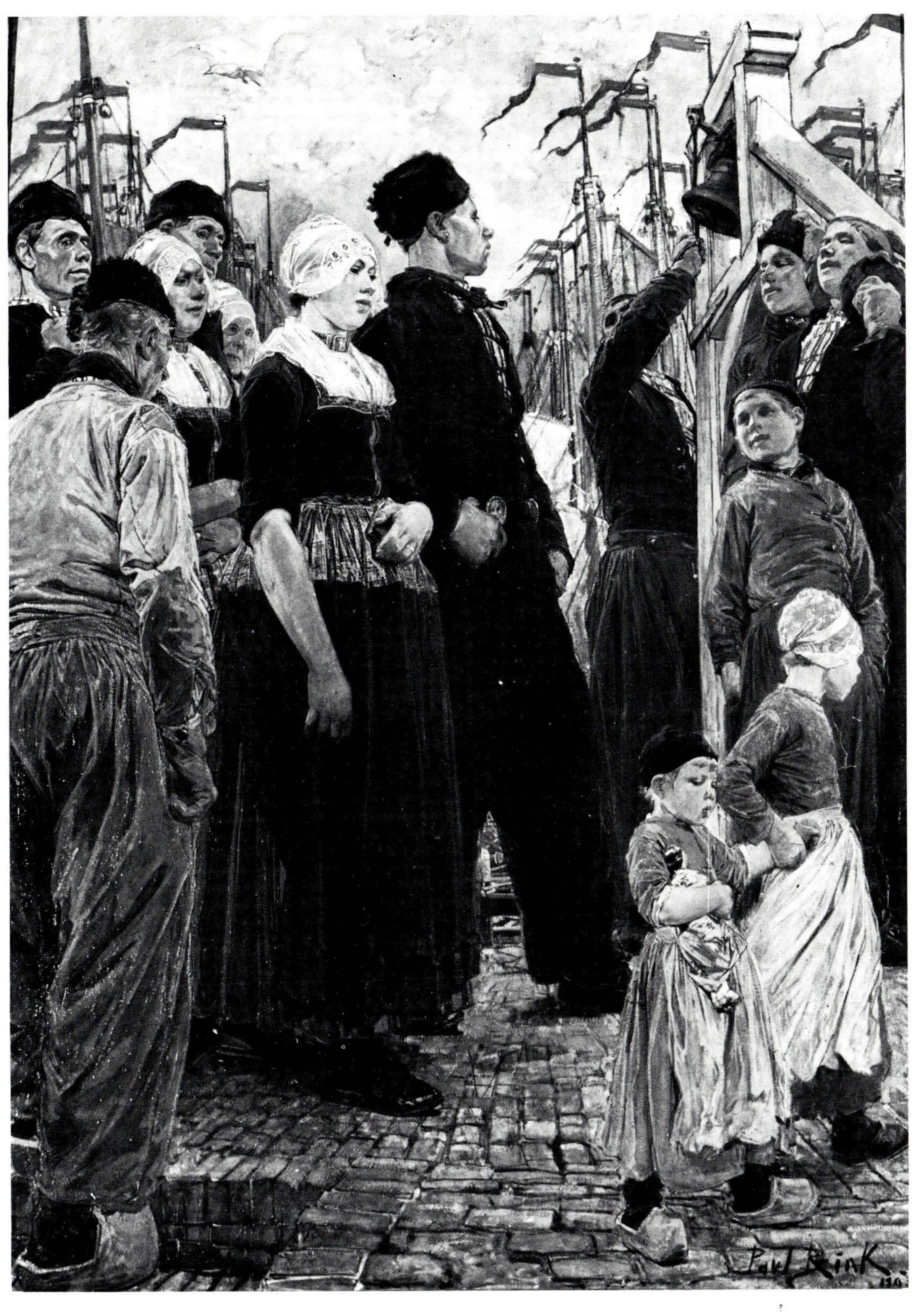

Paul Rink (1861-1903) *made his name depicting the daily life of Volendam, an opportunity to fill the canvas with colourful "types".* Photograph courtesy of the Stedelijk Museum, Amsterdam.

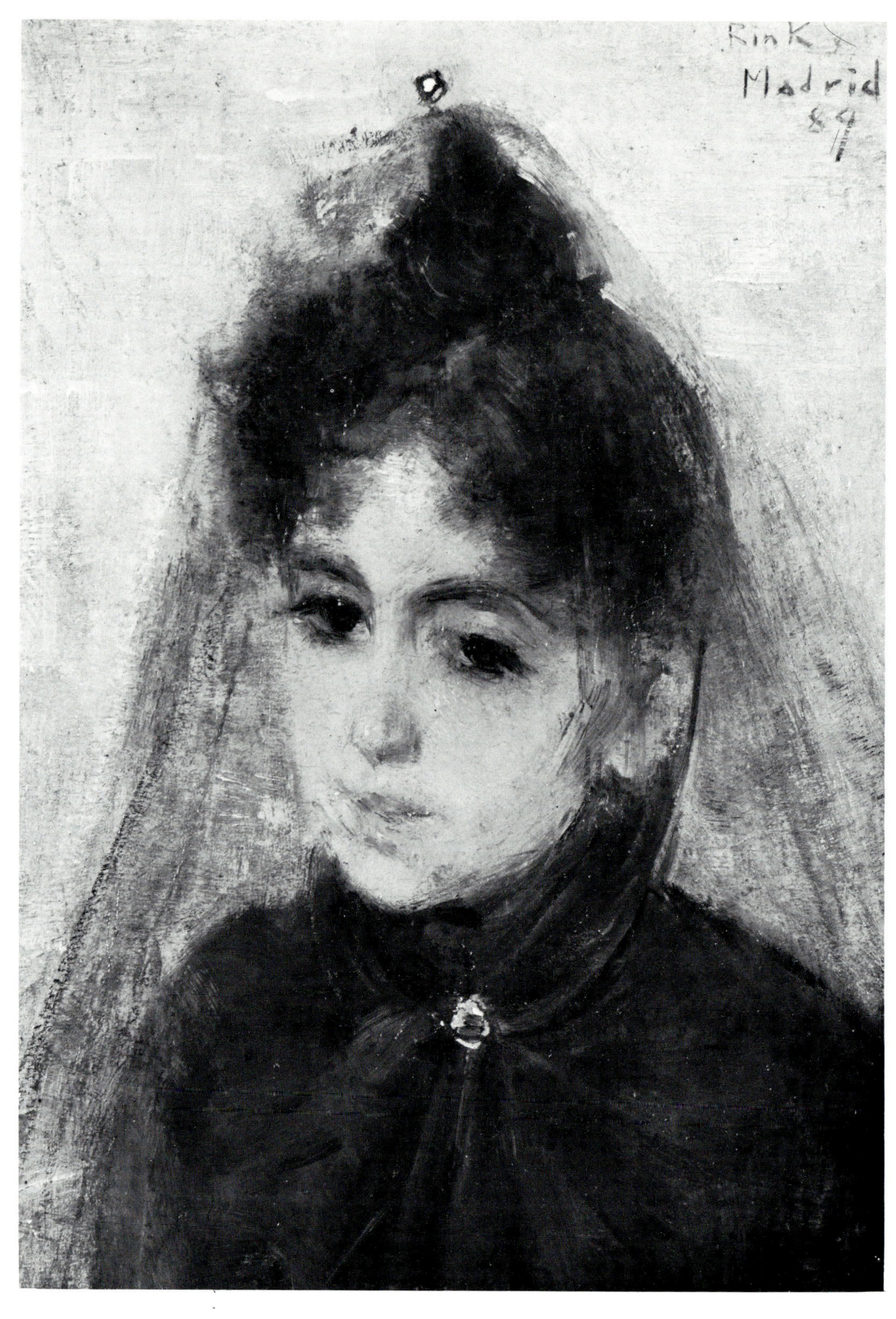

With this "Study of a Head", **Rink** *turns his hand to a Spanish beauty.* Photograph courtesy of the Rijksmuseum Hendrik Willem Mesdag, the Hague.

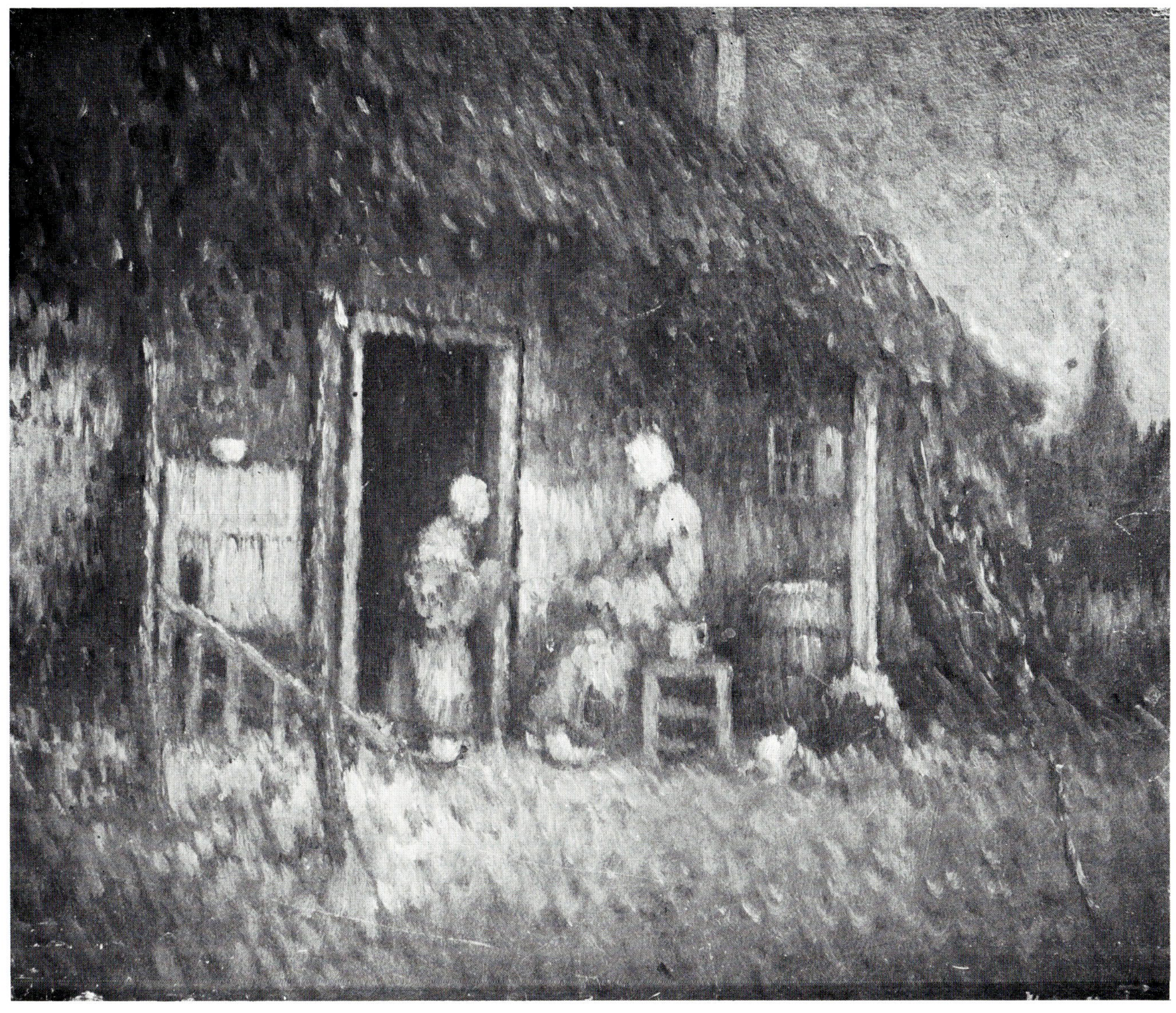

Henri Van Daalhoff (1867-1953) *uses short sharp brush strokes to build up this exterior of a peasant cottage.* Photograph courtesy of Mak van Waay, Amsterdam.

with style and taste.

Paul Rink (1861-1903) exhibited here: he, like Toorop, began by employing the colour-arrangement of the Belgians and brought back a number of bright and pretty studies and pictures from Tangiers, painted in this manner; he afterwards executed the mural decorations of the Hague Art Club, but made his name more generally known by his coloured sketches of Volendam types, often too fluently painted.

And I must also mention Edgard Willem Koning, born in 1869, who, with his *Nurses and Children,* was the first to show that a mural painting can be taken straight from life.

Simon Moulijn, born at Rotterdam in 1866, is one of those modern younger men who, like Thorn Prikker and, in certain respects, Hoytema, arriving early at a crisis, learn to think sooner than to paint, one of those who are influenced by many movements before they have acquired positive knowledge. The first conscious influence was imparted by the modern Frenchmen and especially by Toorop and Vincent van Gogh. Moulijn too wished to play his part in the new art which was to give so much that was beautiful to the end of the century, but which, at that time, as the painter him-

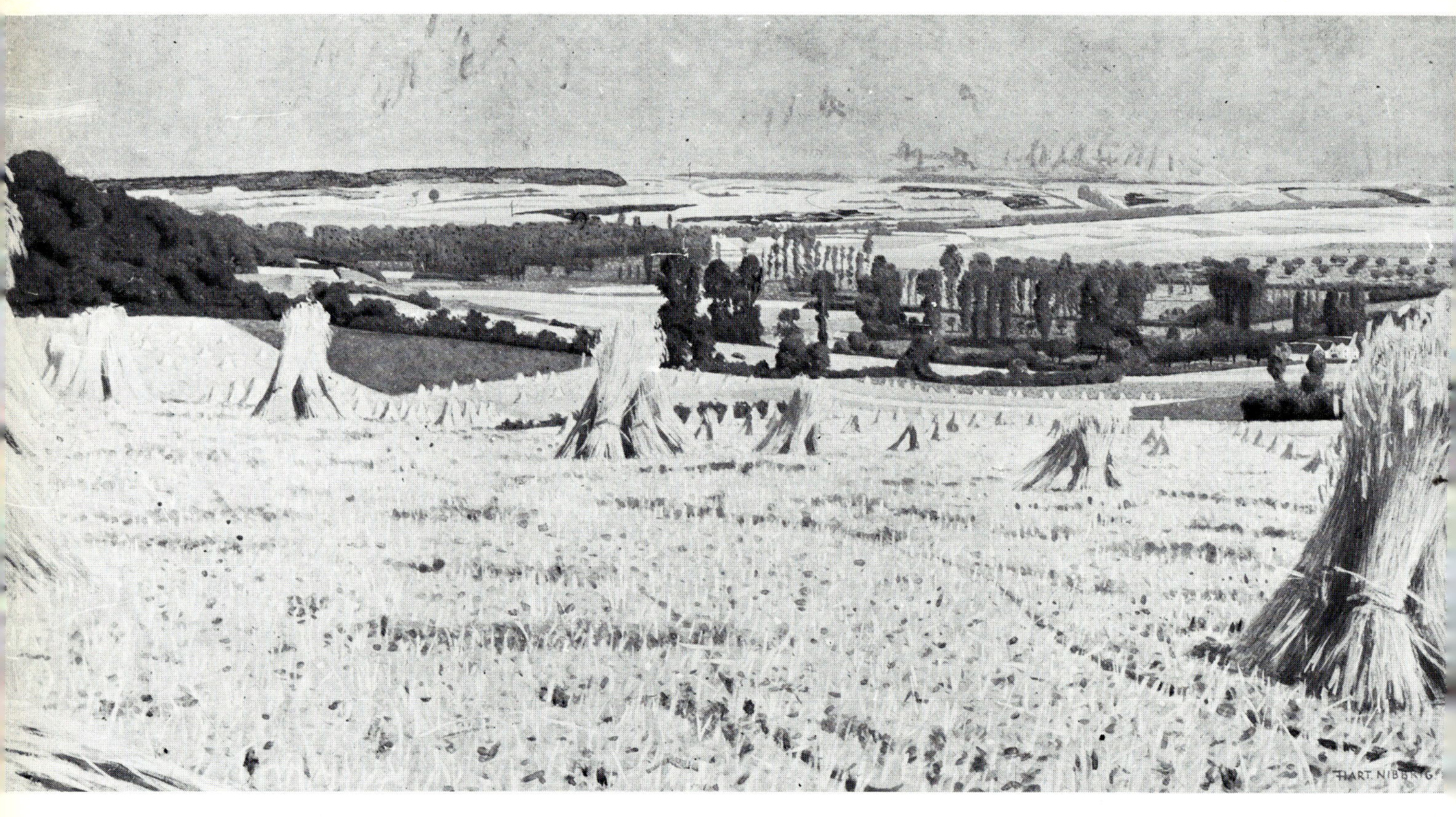

Ferdinand Hart Nibbrig (1866-1915) *adopted an Impressionist approach, painting in pure un-mixed colours. Here he depicts corn-fields in South Limburg under a hot sun.* Photograph courtesy of the Stedelijk Museum, Amsterdam.

self admits, gave rise to anomalous work. His first attempts at painting were attempts and nothing more; and, although he is now busy mastering the difficulties of the craft, he is of significance to us only as the lithographer, the draughtsman of peaceful little spots of nature, little hidden homesteads, which he represents in a refined and contemplative mood.

I must not omit the name of Henri van Daalhoff, born at Leiden in 1867, the painter of stories and fairy-tales. He is a sensitive, but not a powerful artist and is likely to make himself eventually a permanent reputation as an illustrator.

In that branch of landscape-painting in which form and lines were sought after not so much for the sake of mood or emotion as for their own sake, in that search for purity which the increasing admiration for it had aroused, I must first mention Maurits Willem van der Valk, born in Amsterdam in 1857, the amiable theorist who, at an early date, cherished the desire to make of a water-colour a pure water-colour, of an etching an etching, light and transparent, and nothing more. He learnt to see the lines in a landscape at Anvers-sur-Oise; adapted his knowledge to Dutch scenery; and, with something almost Japanese in his arrangement of mass and line, now seeks colour in flat tones.

To his group belongs Ferdinand Hart Nibbrig, born in Amsterdam in 1866, a pupil of Allebé's, who began by painting in the style of Neuhuijs. When he saw the tulip-fields at Bennebroek in all their luminous beauty of colour, he came to the conviction that colour should be rendered more as colour and light as light; and thus, as if of his own initiative, he arrived at the discovery which the great Frenchmen and Vincent and Toorop had made before him, a discovery which is of scientific origin, namely the juxtaposition of un-mixed colours in small proportions, without the intervening medium of brown or ochre, so that light becomes lighter and both light and shade more full of colour. Hart Nibbrig, who is especially to be praised for the honesty with which he sets down fields of grass and corn and buckwheat under a blazing sun, lacks something of the passion and enthusiasm necessary to make so systematic a proceeding express all

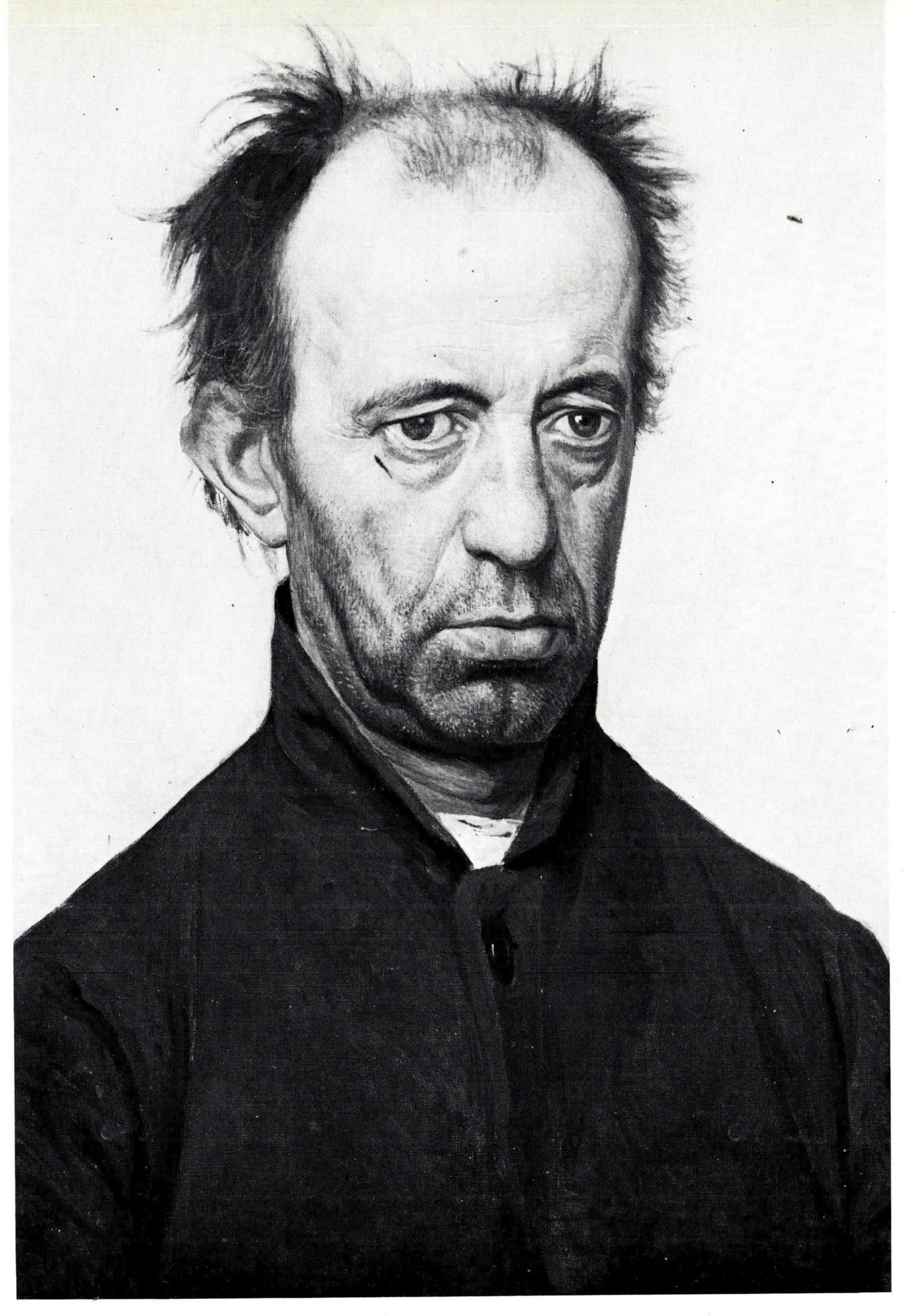

Hart Nibbrig *adopts a harsh realism in this painting of "The Vagabond".* Photograph courtesy of the Stedelijk Museum, Amsterdam.

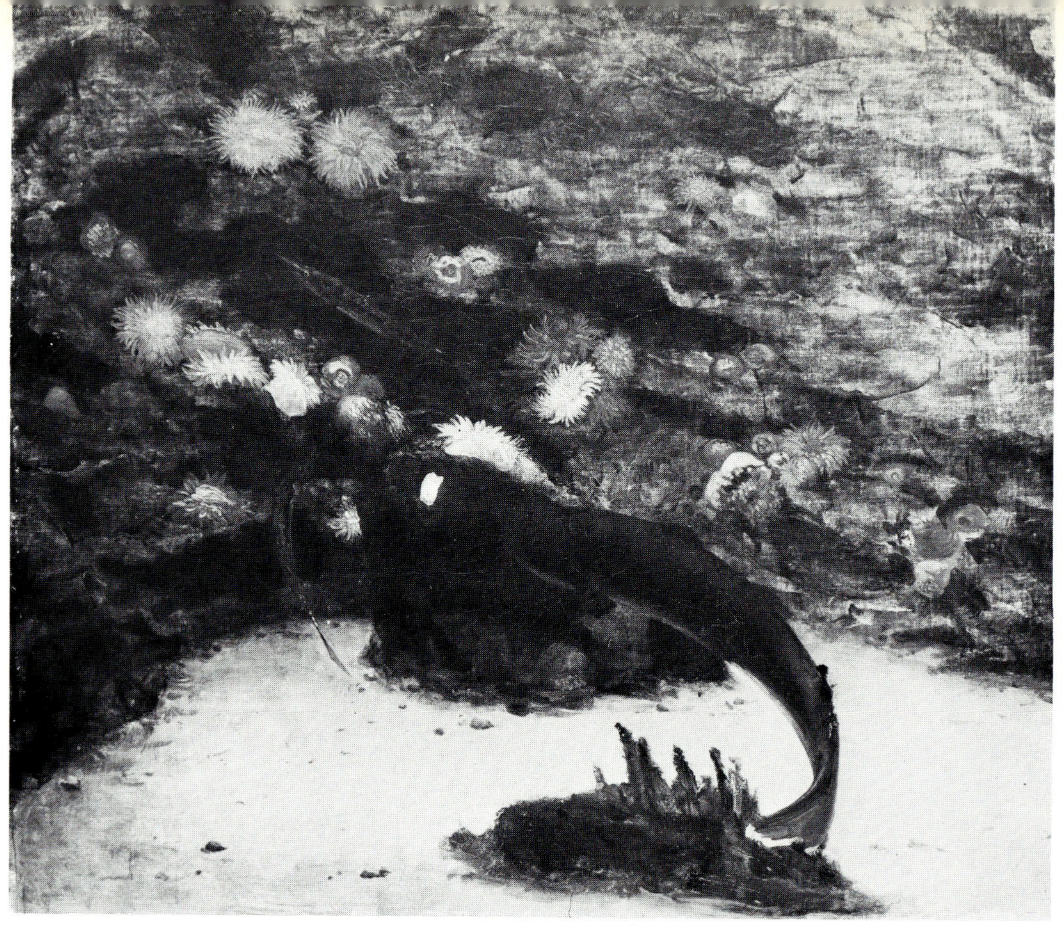

Gerrit Willem Dijsselhof (1866-1924) *found inspiration in East Indian art and applied it to underwater scenes, as with this fish swimming among sea anemones. (48½ x 45cms.).* Photograph courtesy of Mak van Waay, Amsterdam.

his feelings. The result is that, clever and consistent as his work may be, it does not wholly reach the spectator.

More harmonious is the work of Derk Wiggers, born at Amersfoort in 1866, the painter who, above all, sought for purity of form in the more broken and undulating Guelder landscape. His is an important and distinguished linear scheme, which he occasionally exaggerates, perhaps, but by menas of which he succeeds in rendering a few divine moments of nature. Such are *The Little Church at Heelsum, Bentheim Castle* and other panoramic drawings, in which the cool twilight sky hangs tense behind the hilly landscape.

Towards the end of the nineteenth century, the attention of many of these younger men was diverted in the direction of the applied arts, which some of them have enriched with exceedingly important works. I will mention only Carel Lion Cachet, born in 1864, and Theodoor Nieuwenhuis, born in 1866, who do not come within the scope of this book, and Gerrit Willem Dijsselhof, born at Zwollerskappel in 1866, who was the first in our country to achieve something exceedingly beautiful on a basis of East-Indian art. He is the only one who has produced decorative water-colour drawings that were not epicene because, in the colour – that of the *sarongs* of the native states of Java – a shrill and spontaneous blue, and on a ground of fine yellow, he has succeeded in introducing in the most decorative fashion all manner of small animals: silvery sticklebacks, drawn in a masterly way, Mediterranean crayfish, with their curious forms, or the motley sea-anemones, all worked up into a decorative, self-contained and absolutely harmonious whole.

In quite recent years, our young painters have been once more attracted by Paris, especially by that great draughtsman Steinlen, and also, though in a lesser degree, by the modern English and German illustrators. But these, the latest artists of all, belong entirely to the present century and not to that which forms the subject of this volume.

Addendum

Further Artists of Distinction

Not Mentioned by Marius

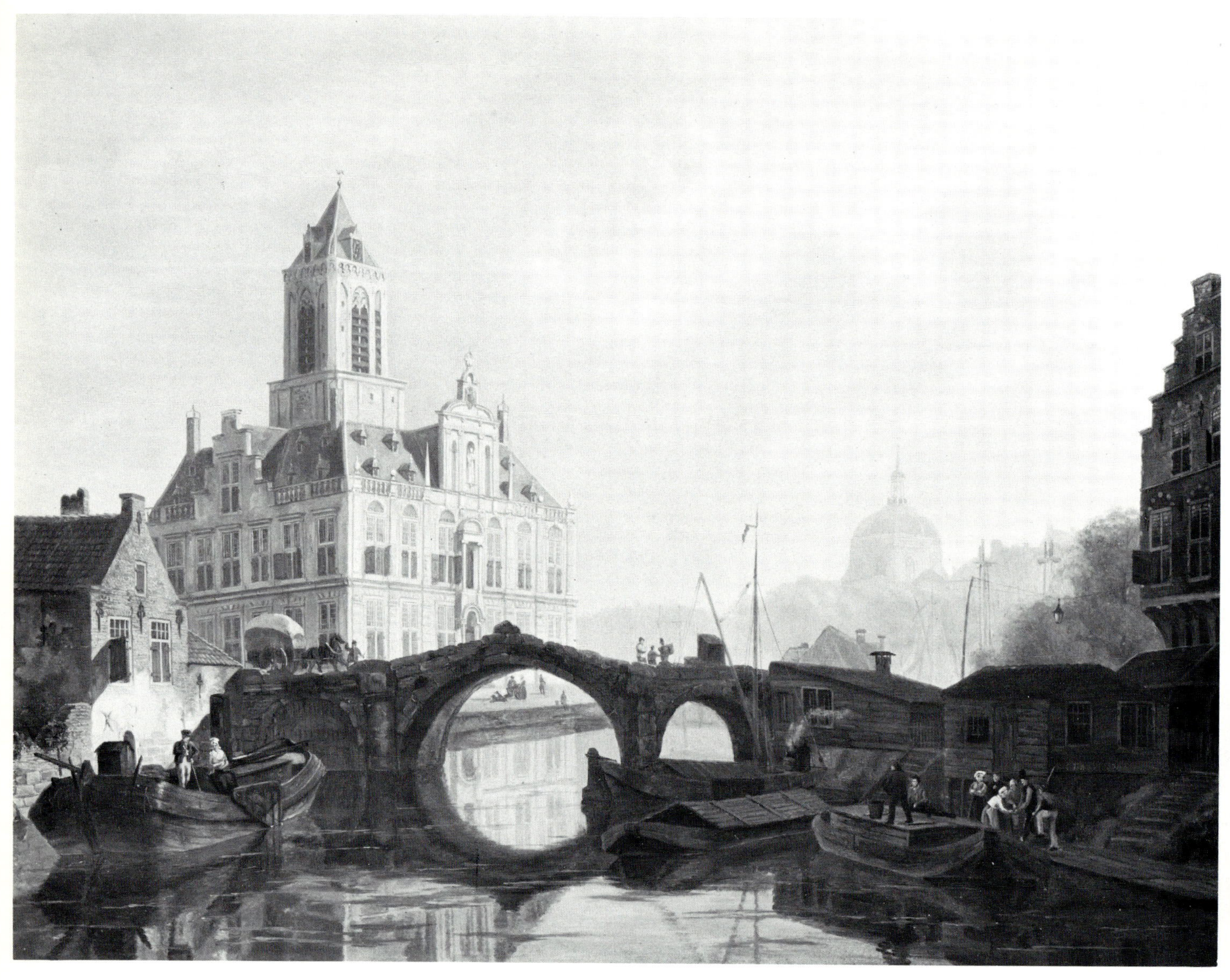

Above: **Carel Jacobus Behr (1812-1895)** – *"A View in the Hague", signed and dated 1831, 20 x 25ins.* Photograph courtesy of Richard Green.

Behr was a well known Hague painter of town views. Pupil of B.J. van Hove.

Right: **Arnoldus Bloemers (1792-1844)** – *"Still Life of Flowers", 73 x 57cms.* Photograph courtesy of Richard Green.

Bloemers followed the example of Van Huysum with his still lives of flowers and fruit. Pupil of A. Piera. He became a member of the Amsterdam Academy and the "Arti Sacrum" society of Rotterdam.

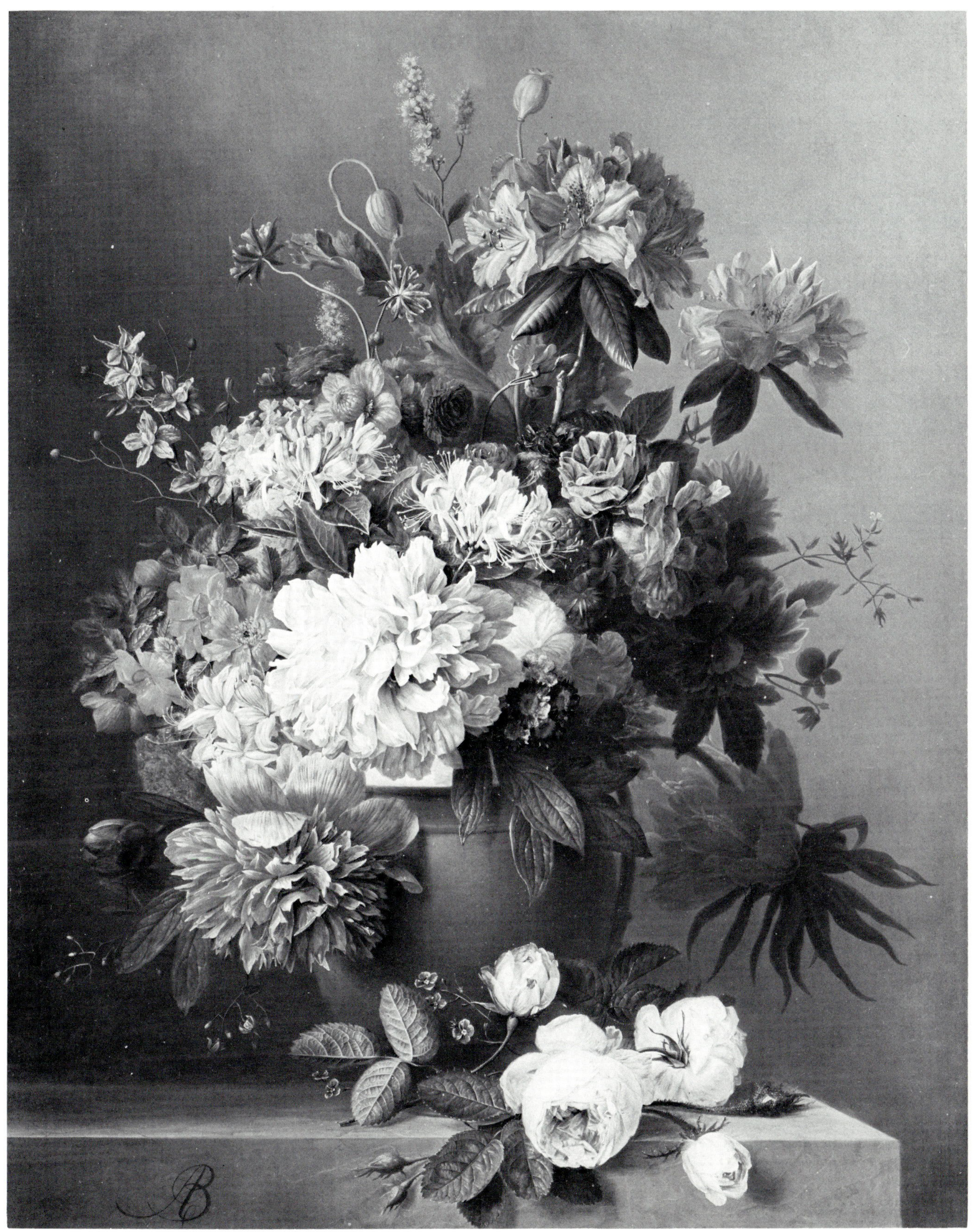

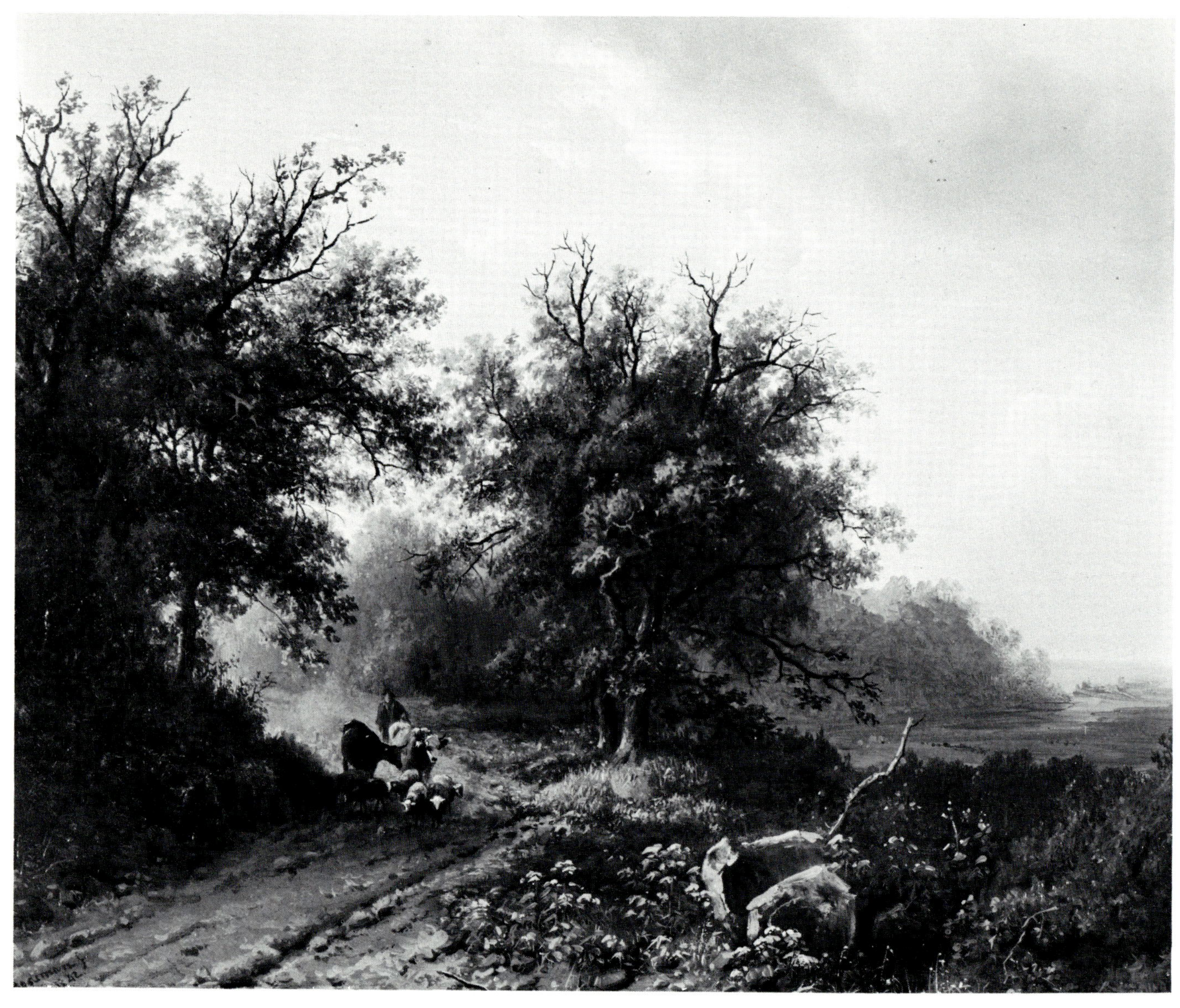

Willem Bodeman (1806-1880) – *"Shepherd, sheep and cattle in a wooded landscape", signed and dated 1842, 15 x 12½ins* Photograph courtesy of Williams & Son.

Bodeman painted woodland and mountain landscapes. A pupil of B.C. Koekkoek he travelled with him through Belgium and Germany 1827-30.

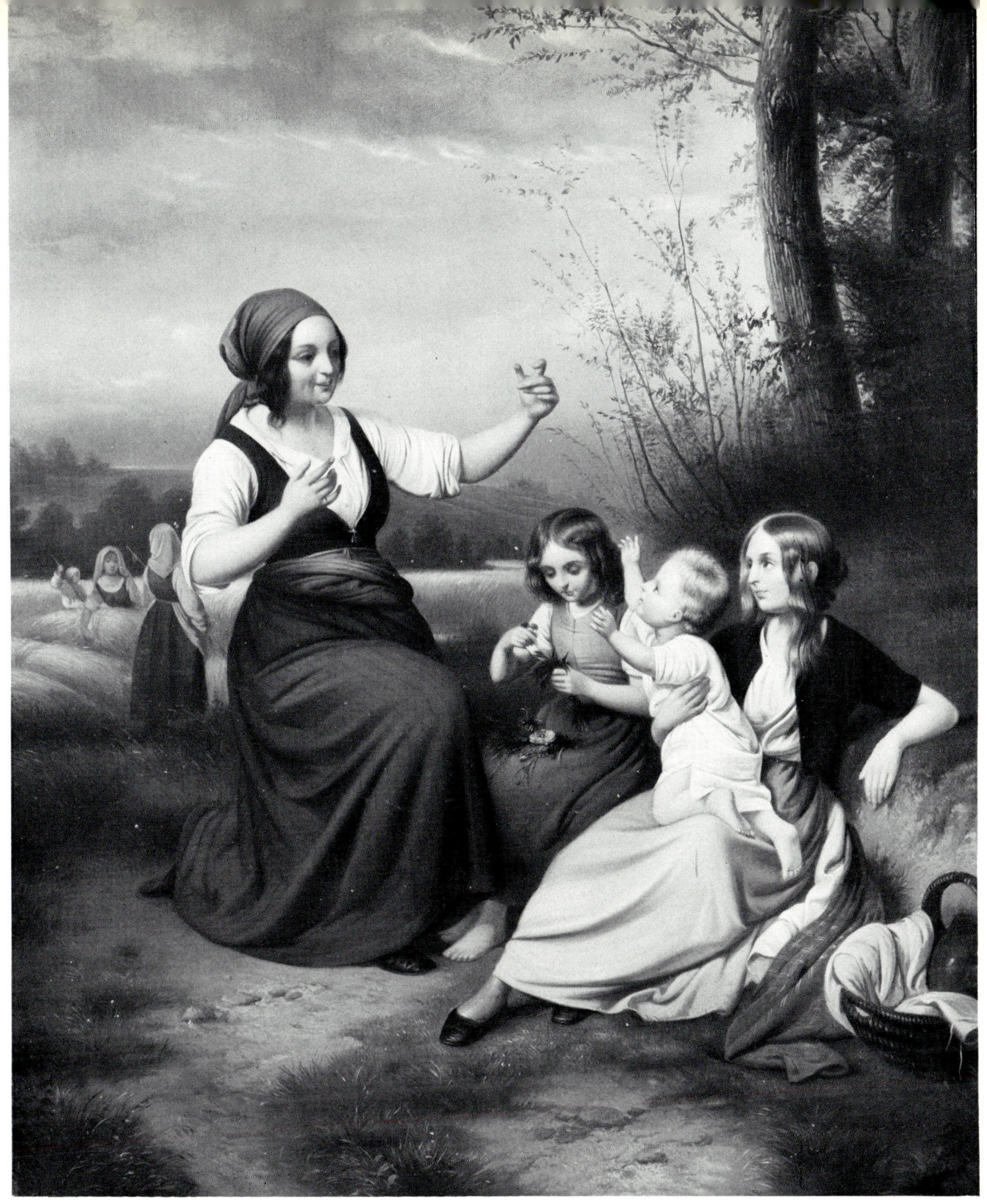

Johannes Antonius Canta (1816-1888) — *"Mother and children at the harvest field", 18 x 15ins.* Photograph courtesy of Spenser S.A.

Canta specialised in domestic scenes and landscapes with children at play. He was a member of the Amsterdam Academy.

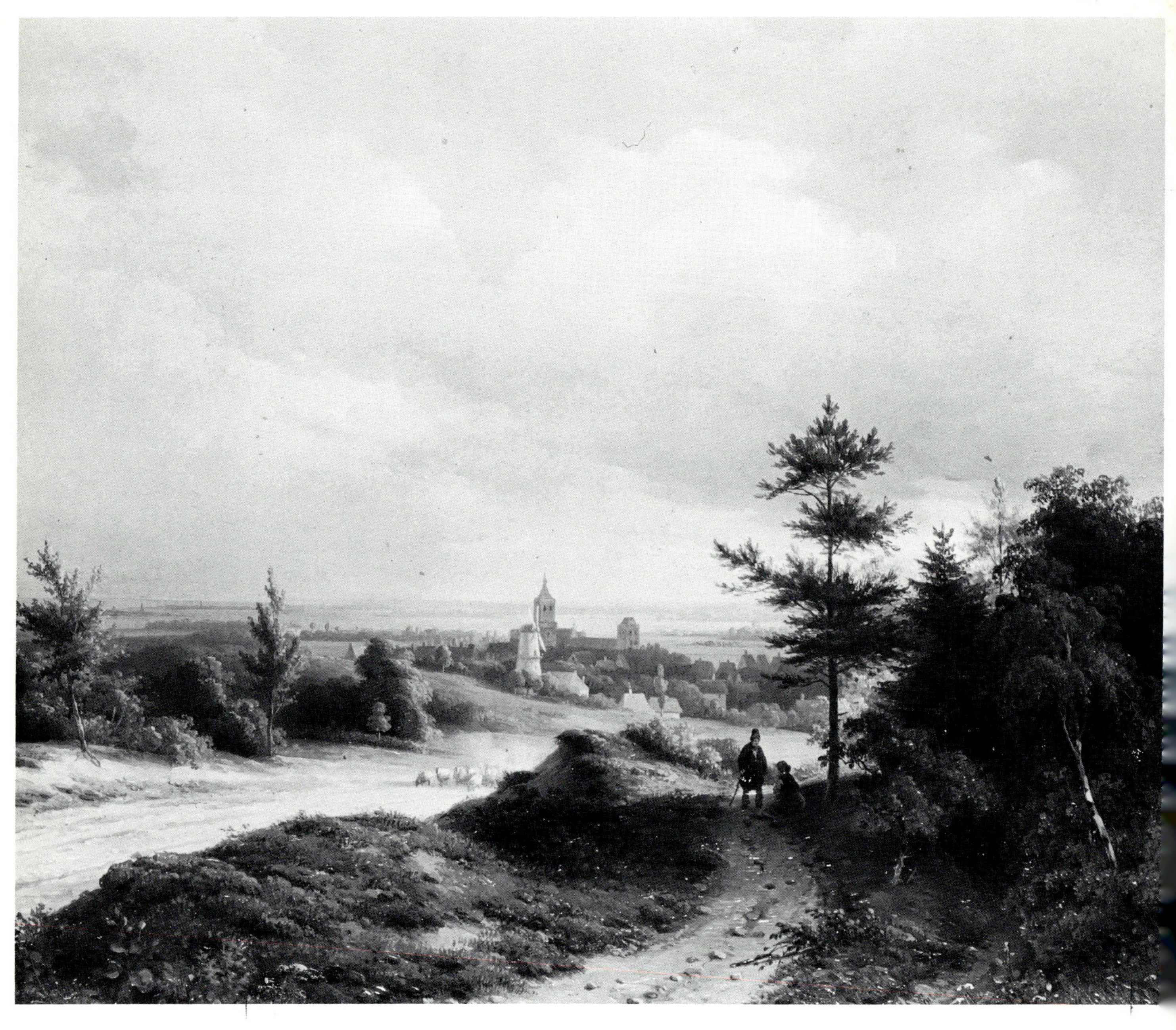

Abraham Johannes Couwenberg (1806-1844) – *"Extensive landscape with a village", 12 x 14ins.* Photograph courtesy of Spenser S.A.

Couwenberg was a landscape painter who also worked in watercolour. Member of Amsterdam Academy.

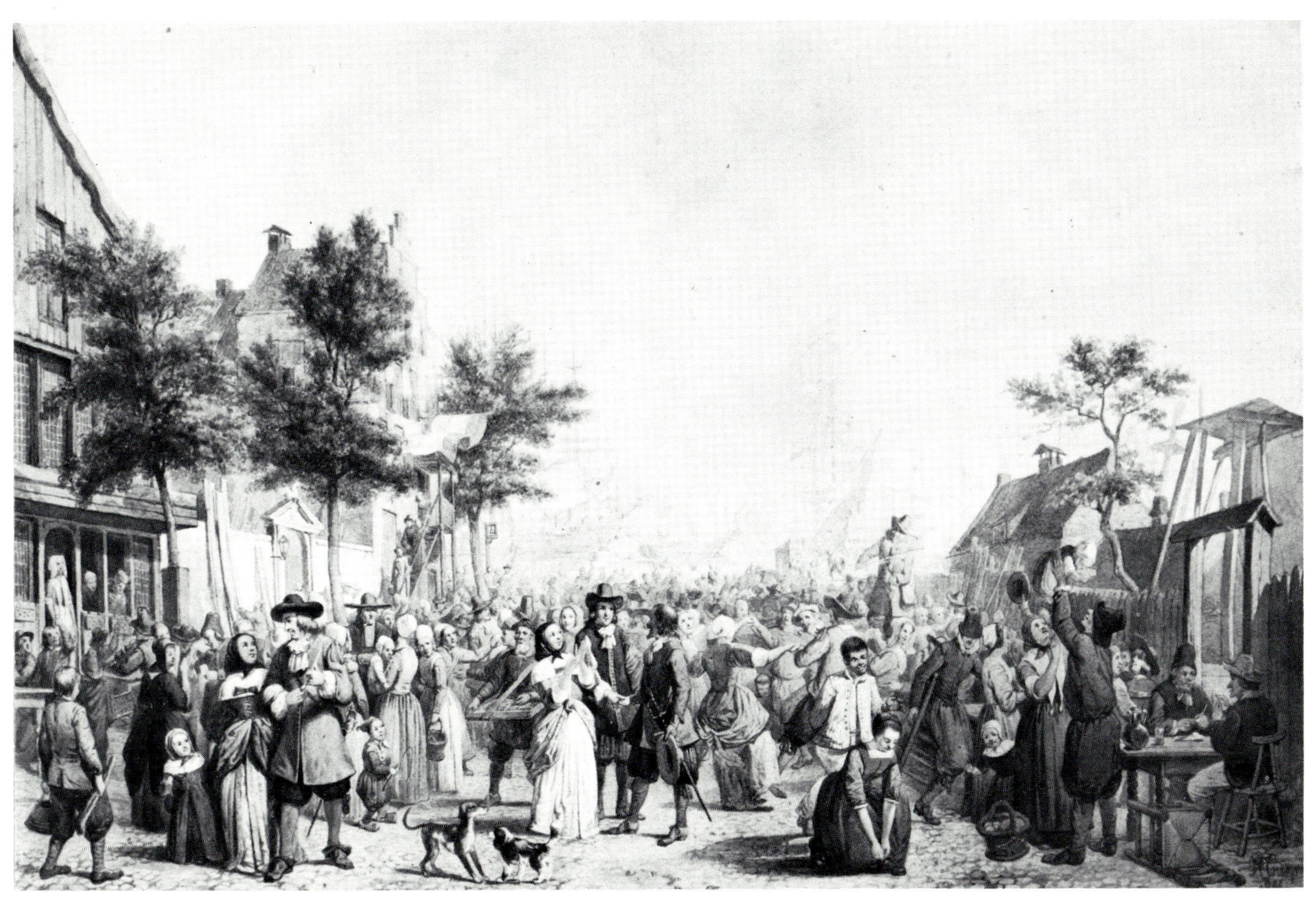

Reinier Craeyvanger, (1812-1880) — *"Street fair in a harbour town of the 17th century", signed and dated 1846, watercolour 30½ x 45½cms.* Photograph courtesy of Mak van Waay, Amsterdam.

Craeyvanger painted landscapes and townscapes, often working in watercolour or ink and sepia wash. Pupil of his brother Gijsbertus and Utrecht Drawing School. Member of "Arti et Amicitiae", Amsterdam.

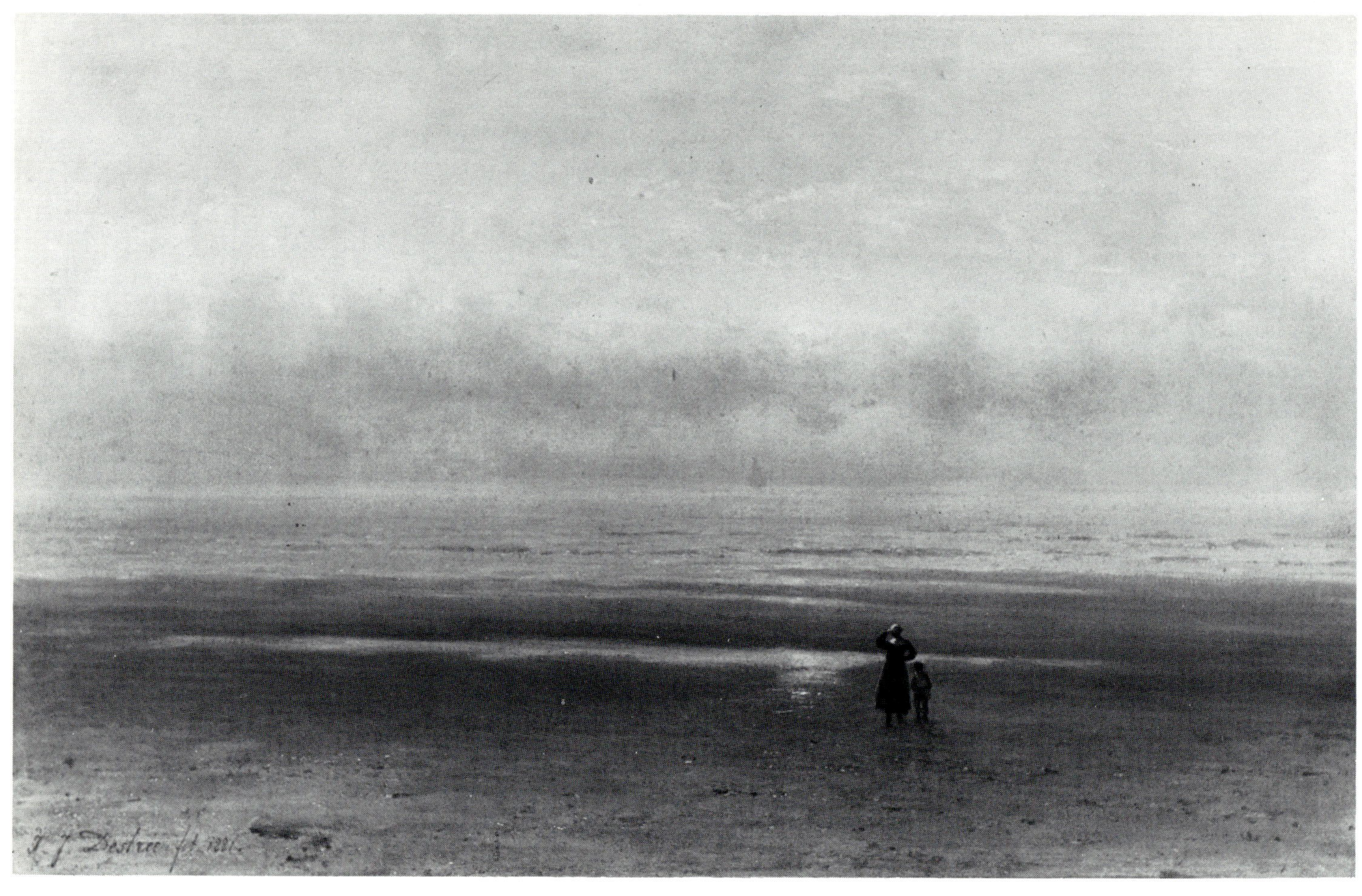

Johannes Josephus Destrée (1827-1888) — *"Beach scene at sunset", signed and dated 1881, 61½ x 100cms.* Photograph courtesy of Mak van Waay, Amsterdam.

Destrée was a landscape painter specialising in panoramic views and beach scenes. Pupil of A. Schelfhout and B.J. van Hove. He lived and worked in the Hague where he was a member of the "Pulchri Studio".

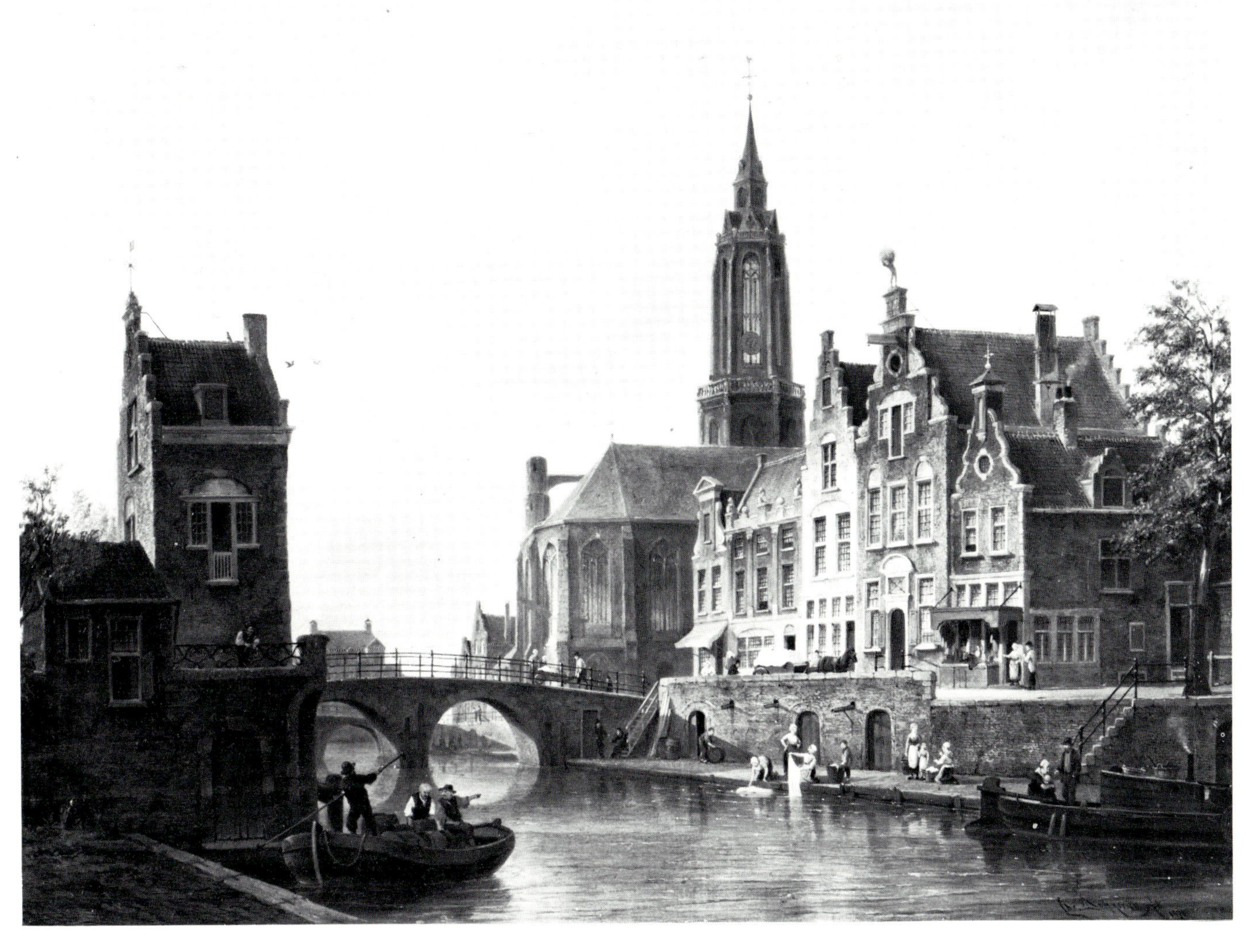

Cornelis Christiaan Dommelshuizen (1842-1928) — *"A view in Amsterdam", 23½ x 29ins.* Photograph courtesy of Sotheby & Co.

Dommelshuizen painted townscapes and marine views. He worked in America, Belgium, England and France as well as Holland. Also signed C.C. Dommershuizen, Chr. Dommelshuizen.

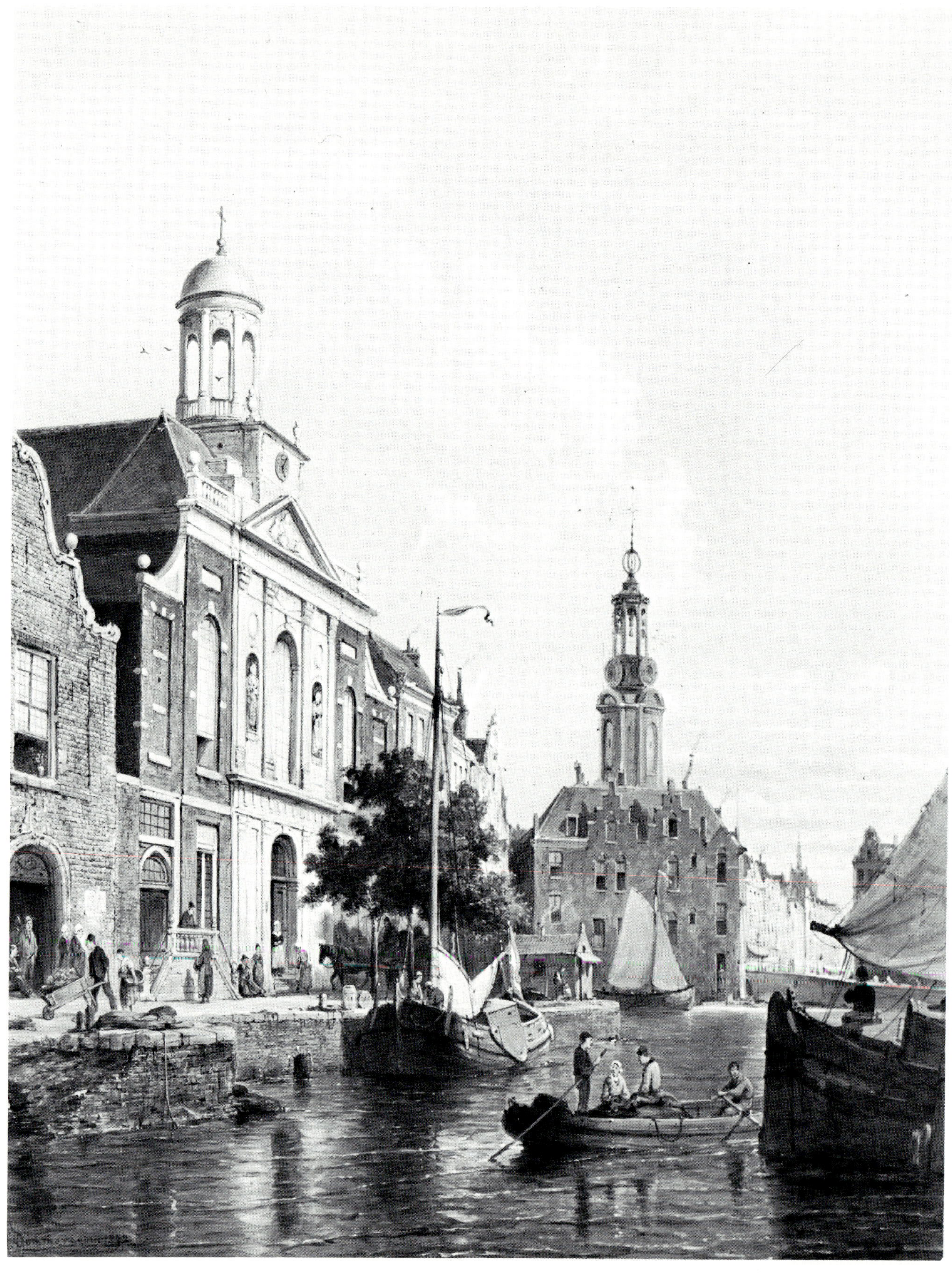

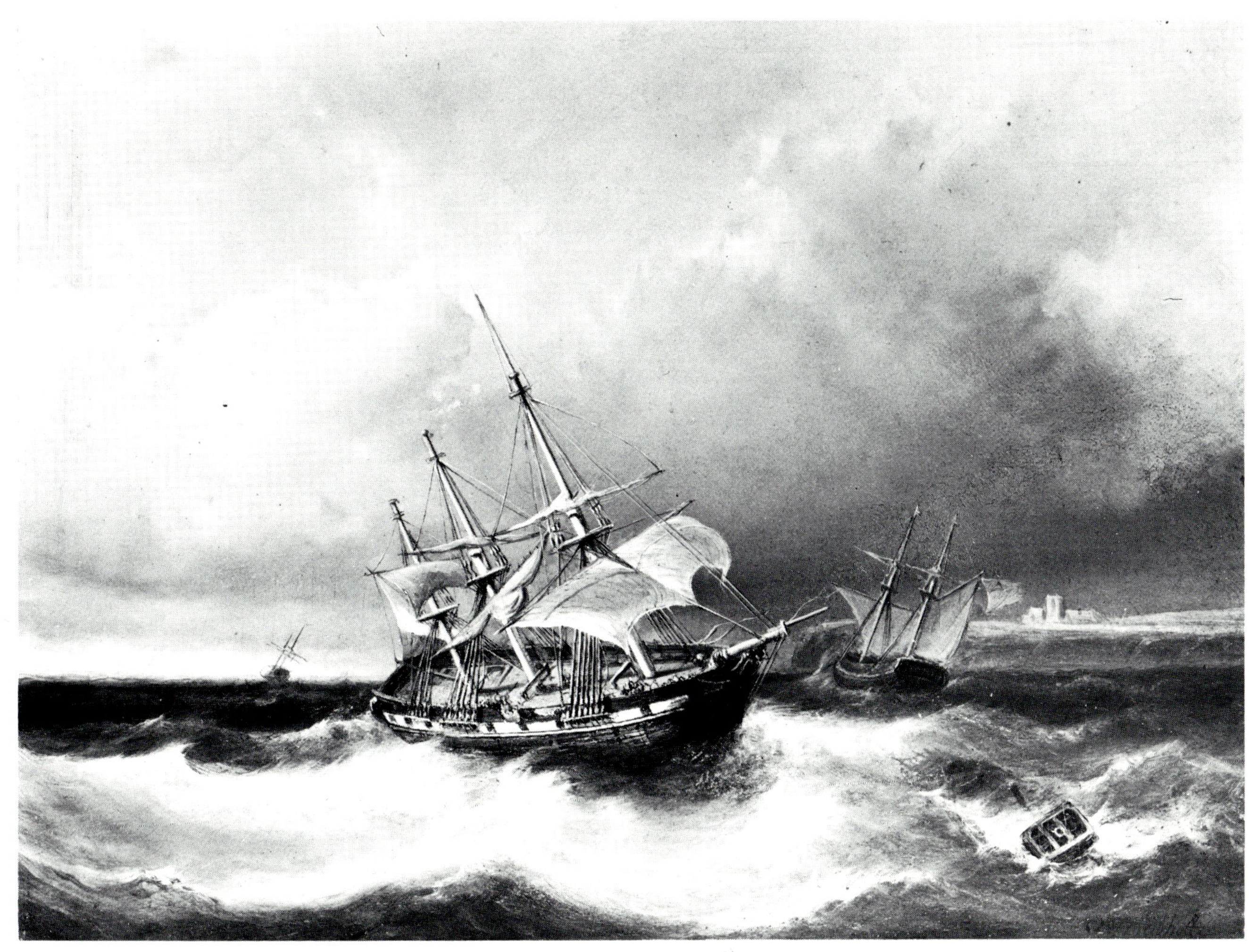

Above: **Christiaan Lodewijk Willem Dreibholtz (1799-1874)** – *"Storm at sea", 36 x 48cms.* Photograph courtesy of Mak van Waay, Amsterdam.

Dreibholtz specialised in sea and river scenes; he worked extensively in watercolour, as well as oils. Pupil of J.C. Schotel. Member of "Arti Sacrum" in Rotterdam 1832 and Amsterdam Academy 1833.

Left: **Pieter Cornelis Dommershuijzen (b.1834 d. ?)** – *"View in Amsterdam", signed and dated 1892, 20½ x 16ins.* Private collection.

P.C. Dommershuijzen painted town views, seascapes and river landscapes. He worked in Brussels and England as well as Holland. He also signed PC. Dommershuizen, P.C. Dommelshuizen, P.C. Dommershuyzen and P.C. Dommersen.

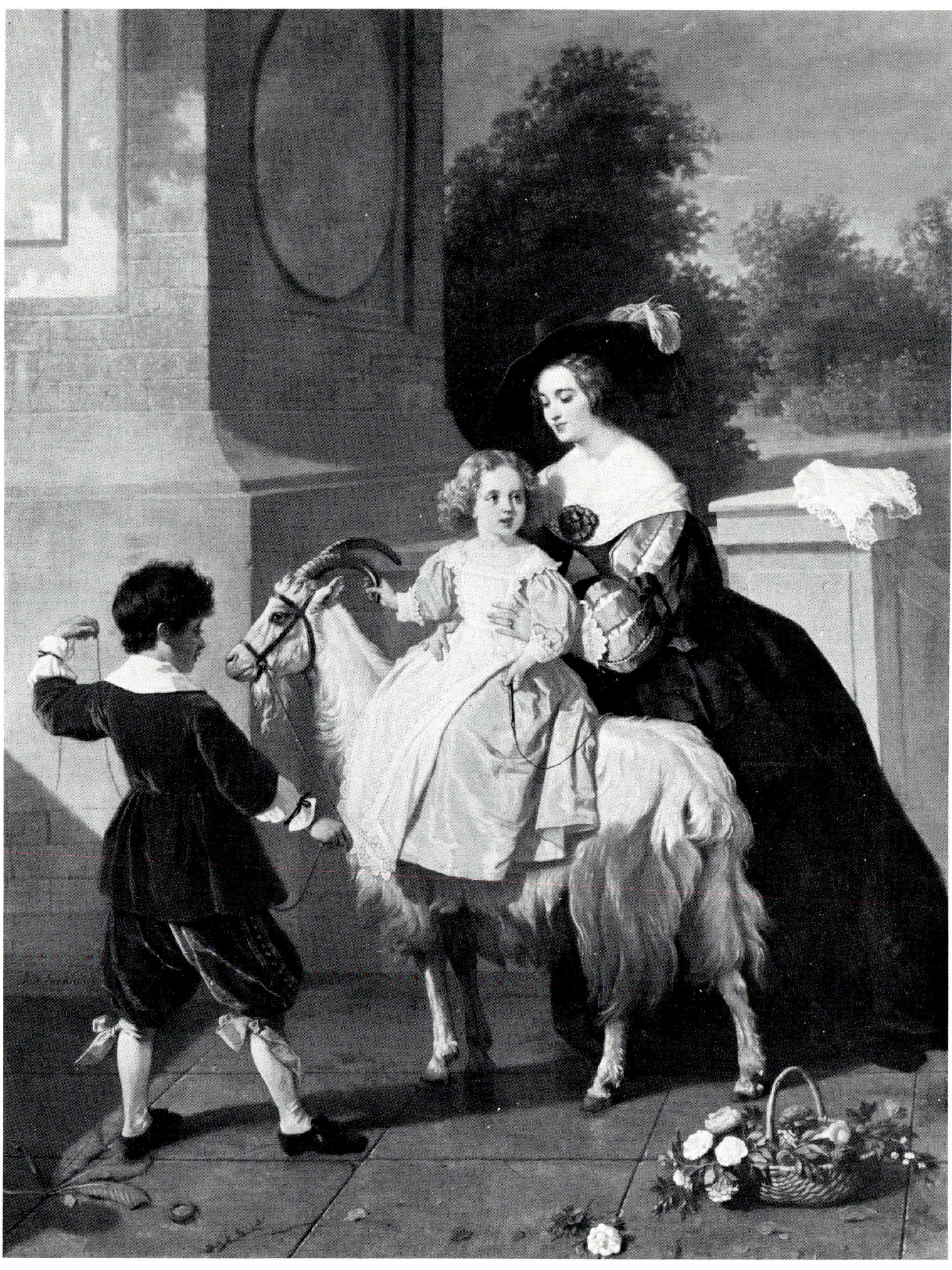

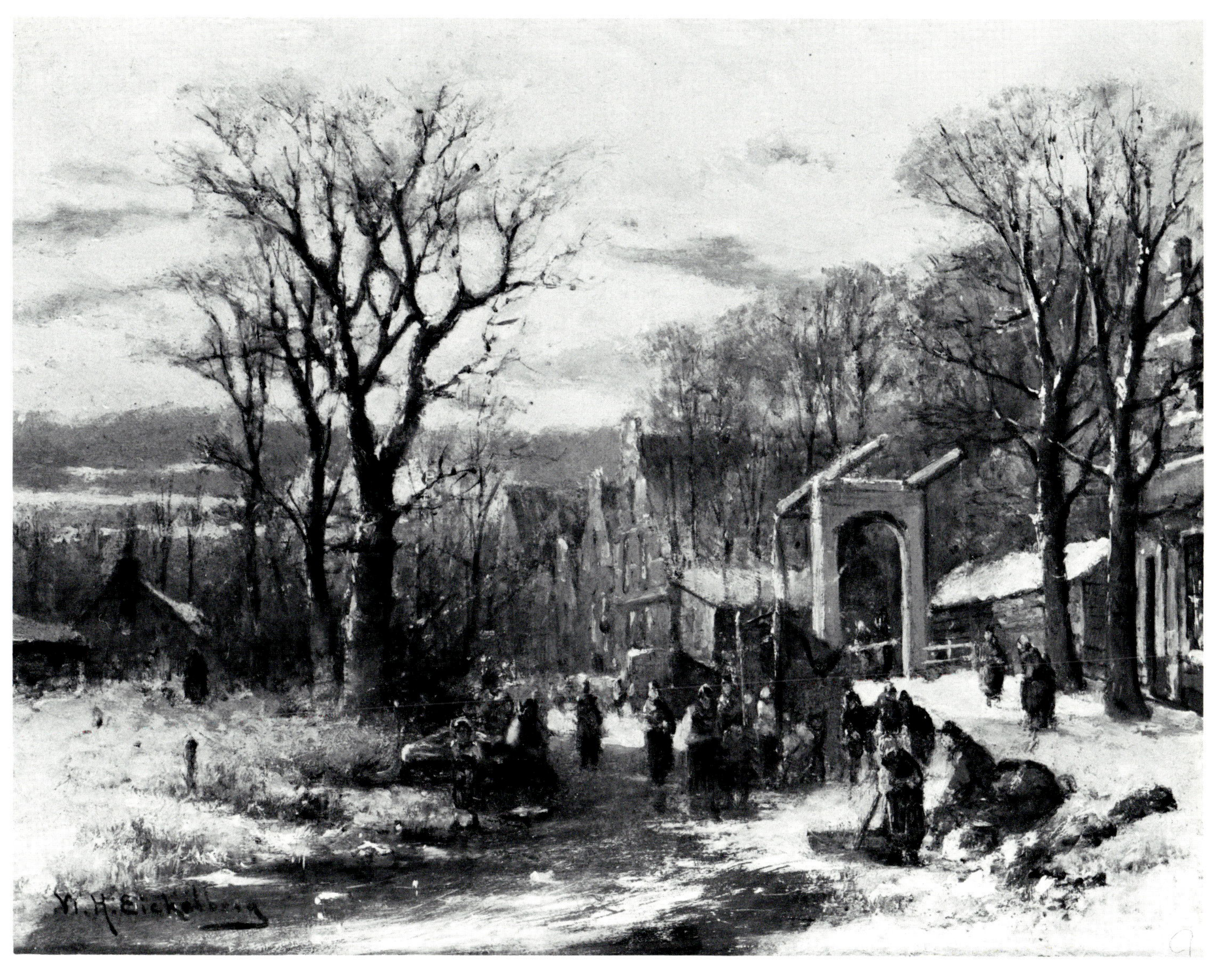

Above: **Willem Hendrik Eickelberg (1845-1920)** – *"Hilversum", 11 x 14ins.* Photograph courtesy of Spenser S.A.

Eickelberg was primarily a landscape painter though he also painted some townscapes and beach scenes. Pupil of J.D.C. Veltens and attended Amsterdam Academy.

Left: **Jacobus Josephus Eeckhout (1763-1861)** – *"A little girl on a goat with her mother and brother", 39½ x 31½ins.* Photograph courtesy of Richard Green.

Eeckhout painted portraits, genre and historical subjects. A Belgian, he was closely involved with the Dutch school. He collaborated with Andreas Schelfhout and lived in the Hague from 1831-1844.

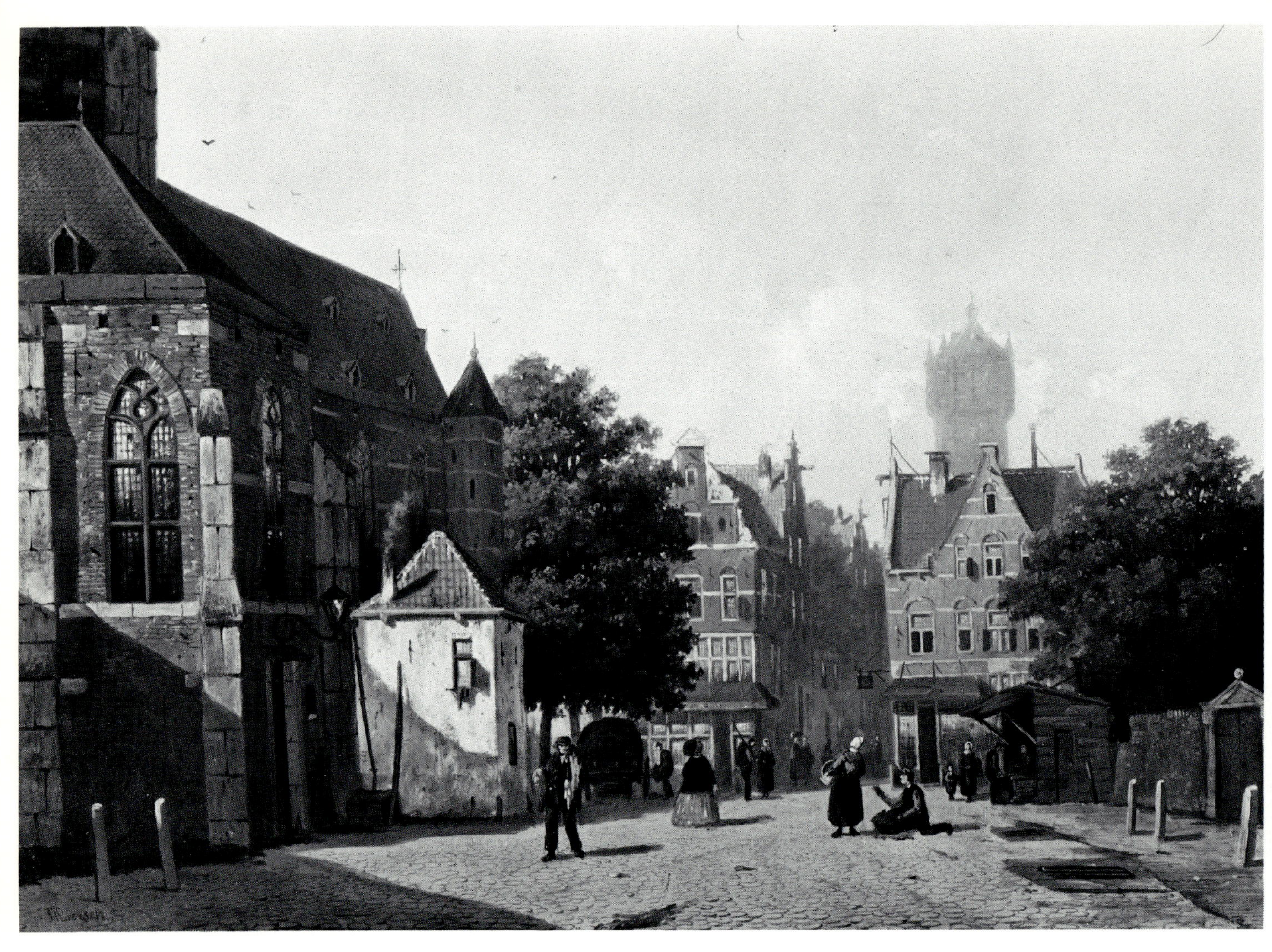

Adrianus Eversen (1818-1897) — *"View of a Dutch town", 19½ x 27¼ins.* Photograph courtesy of Richard Green.

Eversen specialised in townscapes. Pupil of C. de Kruyff and C. Springer. Member of "Arti et Amicitiae", Amsterdam 1863.

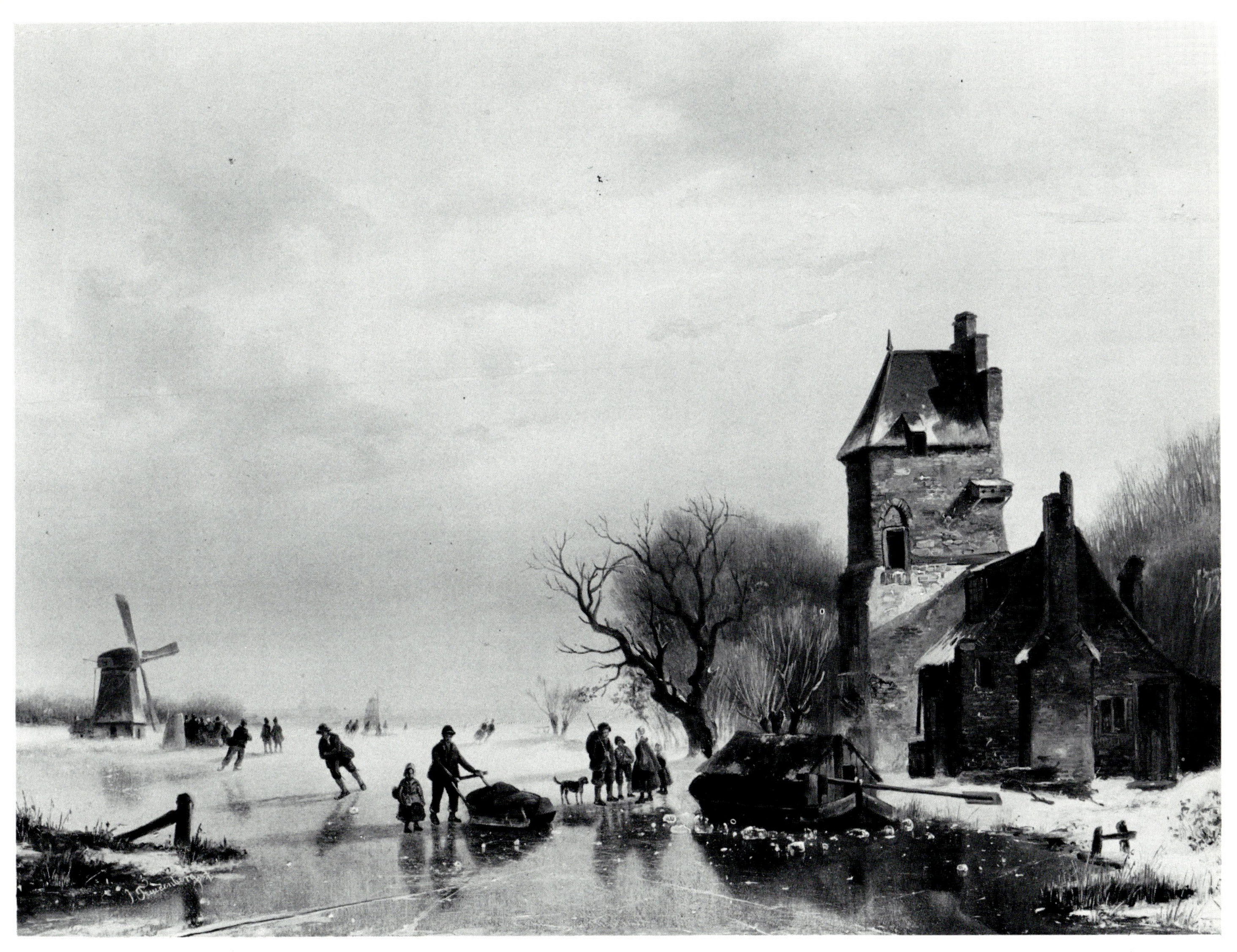

Jacobus Freudenberg (1818-1873) – *"Winter landscape", 21¼ x 15½ins.* Photograph courtesy of Richard Green.

Freudenberg was a Haarlem landscape painter.

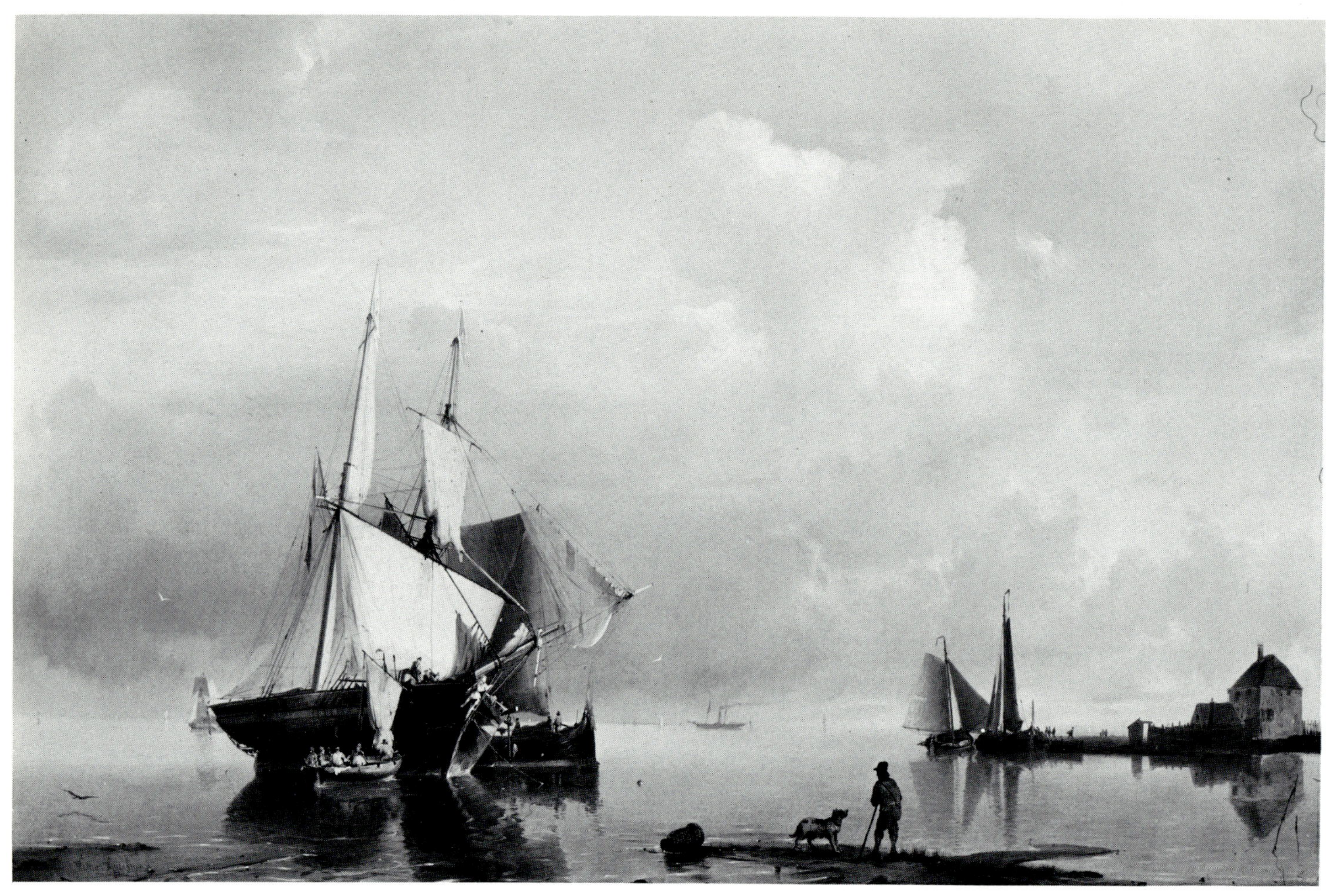

Above: **Warner Gijselman (b.1827 d. ?)** – *"Sailing barges and other shipping in an estuary", 24½ x 35½ins.* Photograph courtesy of Richard Green.

Gijselman painted landscapes and marine views. He also made finished drawings and lithographs. Studied Amsterdam Academy 1845-1849. He moved to London in 1860.

Right: **Charles Joseph (Carel Jozeph) Grips (1825-1920)** – *"The seamstress", 18 x 14ins.* Photograph courtesy of Richard Green.

Grips painted genre and figure pieces, especially kitchen interiors, also portraitist. Studied Antwerp Academy and with J.H. van Grootvelt. Father and teacher of F.A.M. Grips and E.M. Grips.

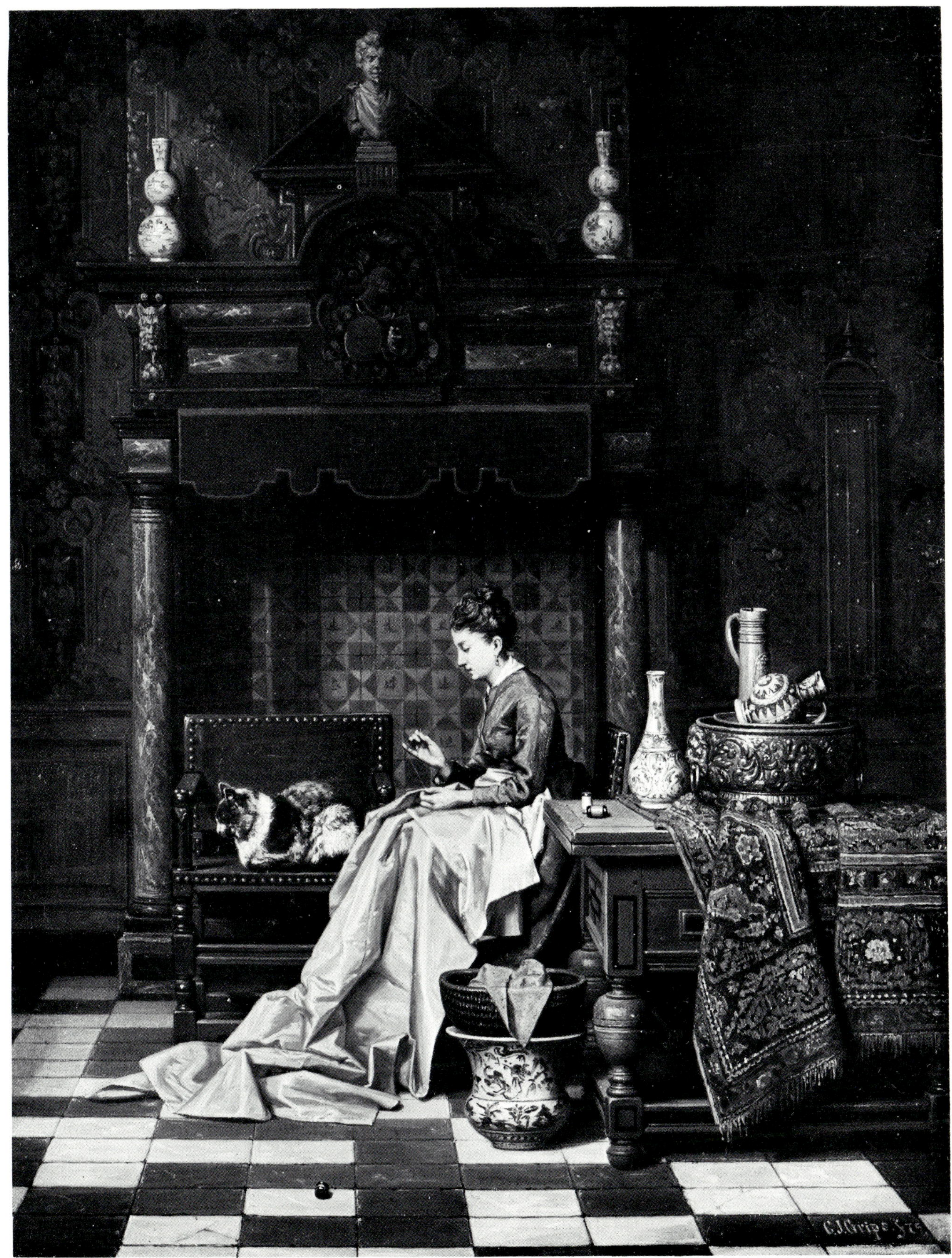

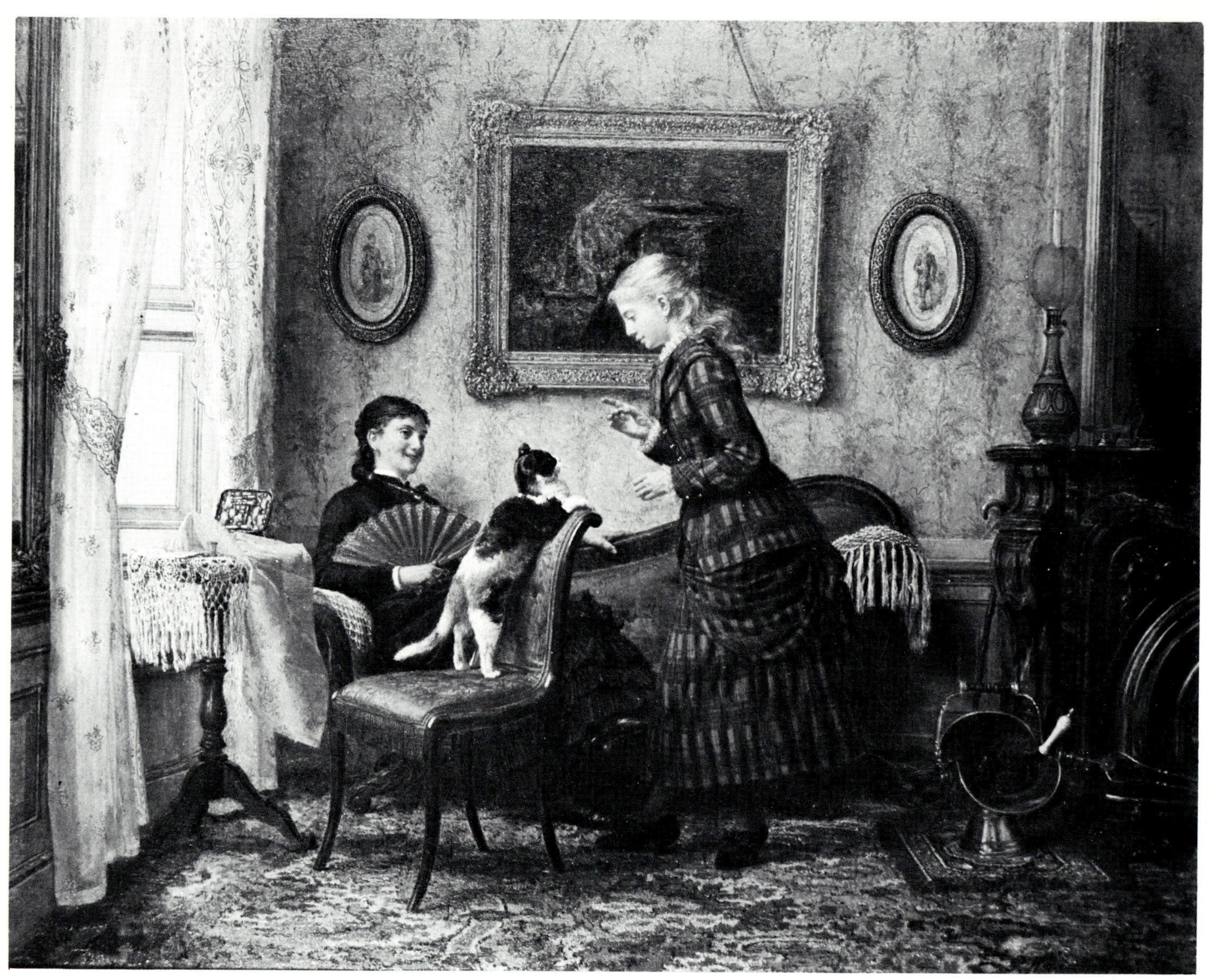

Pieter Haaxman (1854-1937) – *"Two girls playing with a cat", 19½ x 25½cms.* Photograph courtesy of Mak van Waay, Amsterdam.

Haaxman painted portraits, still lives and genre scenes. Studied the Hague Academy and with H.F.K. ten Kate. Member of "Pulchri Studio" in the Hague and "Arti et Amicitiae", Amsterdam.

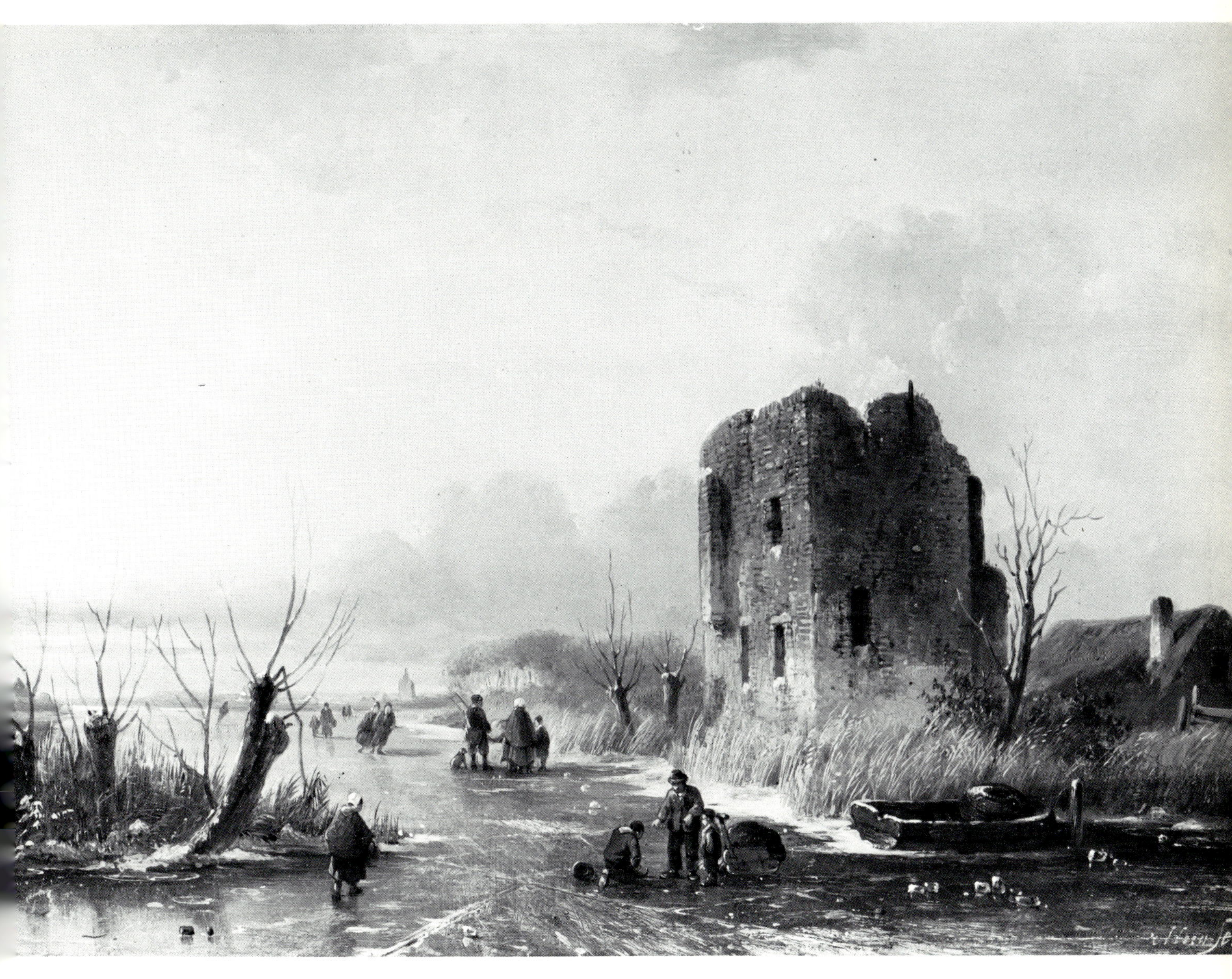

Cornelis Petrus t'Hoen (1814-1880) — *"Frozen river scene", 10¼ x 14ins.* Photograph courtesy of Richard Green.

Hoen was a landscape painter. Pupil of A. Schelfhout, A. Waldorp and G.A. Roth. Studied Hague Academy. He started out as a merchant and amateur painter. 1840 member of Amsterdam Academy. His wife, G.W. Buys was also an artist.

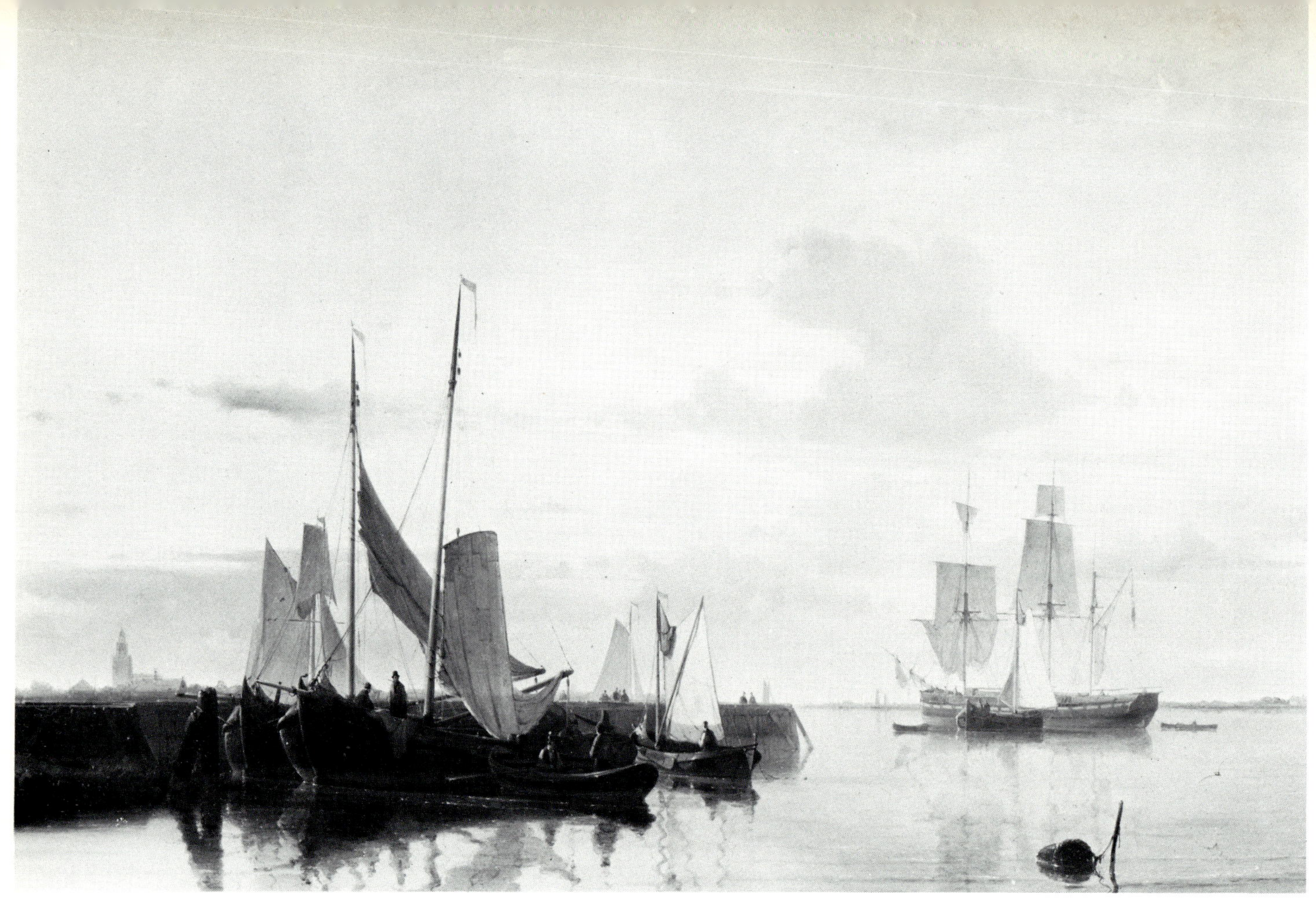

Abraham Hulk (1813-1897) – *"Fishing vessels in a calm estuary, off a jetty", 23½ x 33½ins.* Photograph courtesy of Richard Green.

Abraham Hulk was chiefly a sea painter, also some portraits. Studied Amsterdam Academy and with J. A.Daiwaille. Visited North America 1833-34 returning to Holland. Moved to London 1870. His brother J.F. Hulk Snr. and his son Hendrik were his pupils. The landscapist Abraham Hulk Jnr. was also his son and worked mainly in England.

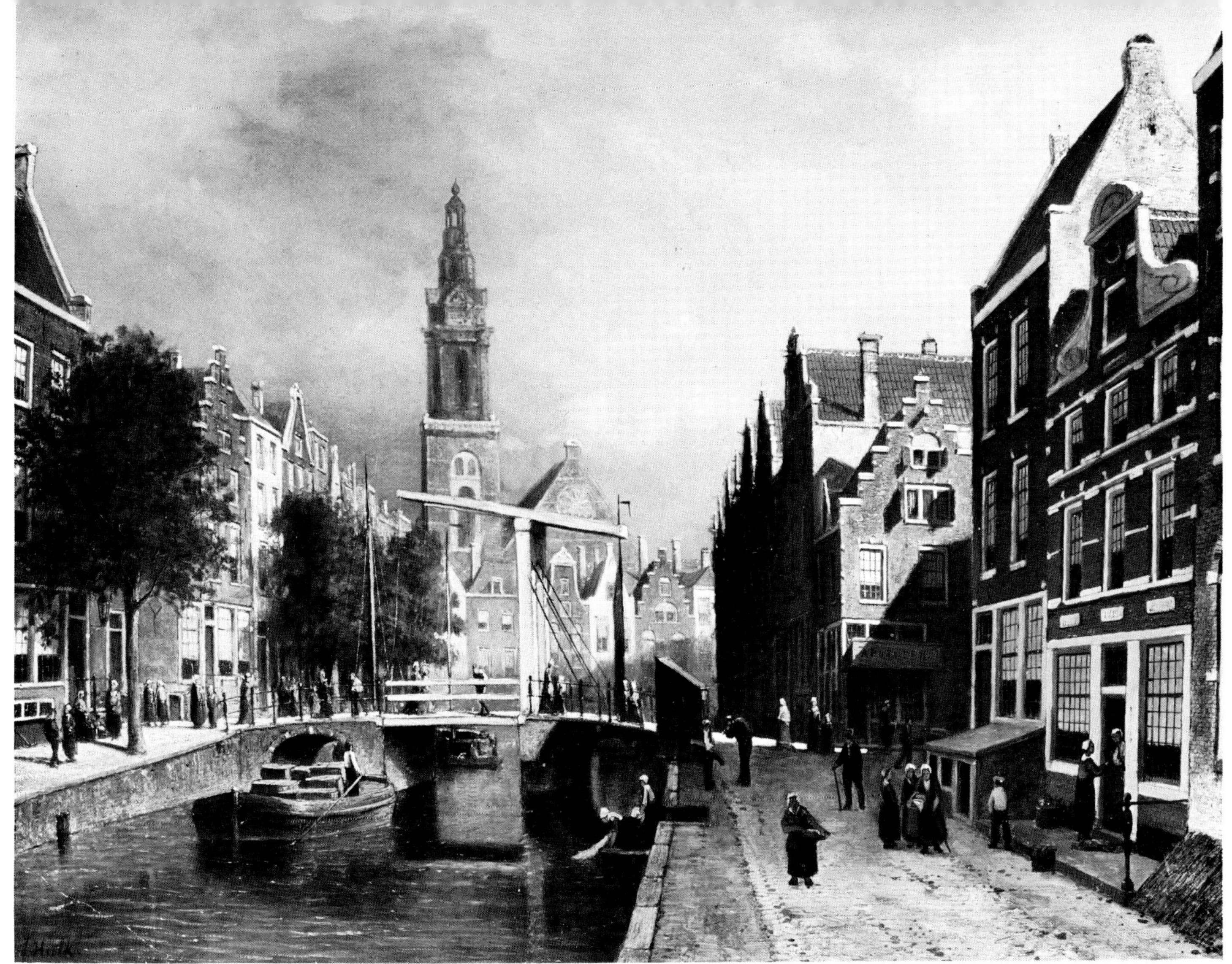

Johannes Frederik Hulk Snr. (1829-1911) – *"View of Amsterdam", 25 x 31ins.* Photograph courtesy of Spenser S.A.

J.F. Hulk specialised in town and village scenes with a few marine views. Pupil of brother A. Hulk Snr., K. Karsen and Amsterdam Academy. His son J.F. Hulk Jnr., a marine and sporting artist, was his pupil.

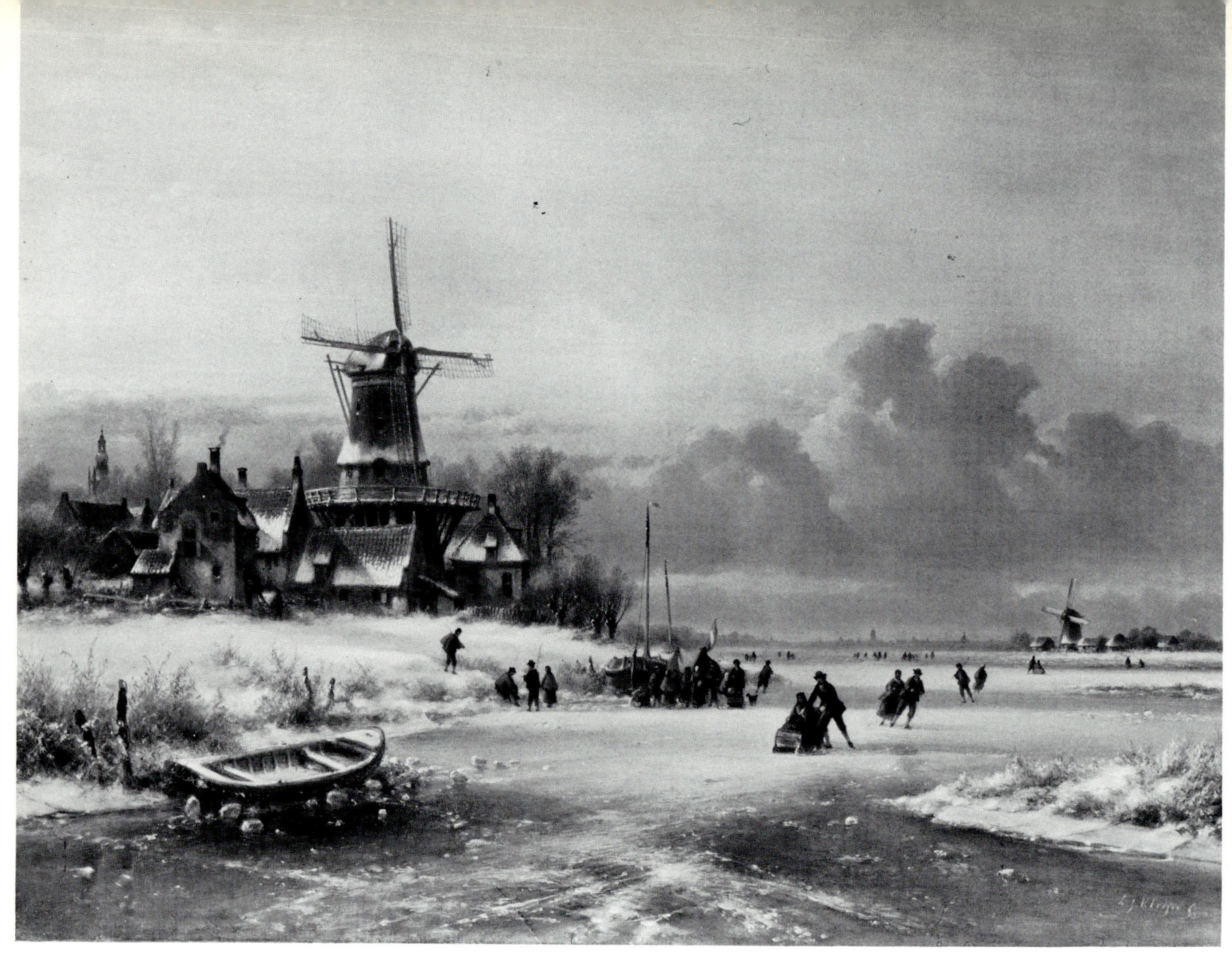

Lodewijk Johannes Kleijn (1817-1897) – *"Frozen river scene with figures skating, a windmill and village nearby"*, 28 x 36ins. Photograph courtesy of Richard Green.

Kleijn was a Hague landscape painter specialising in snow scenes. Pupil of A. Schelfhout. He should not be confused with the younger painter of the same name.

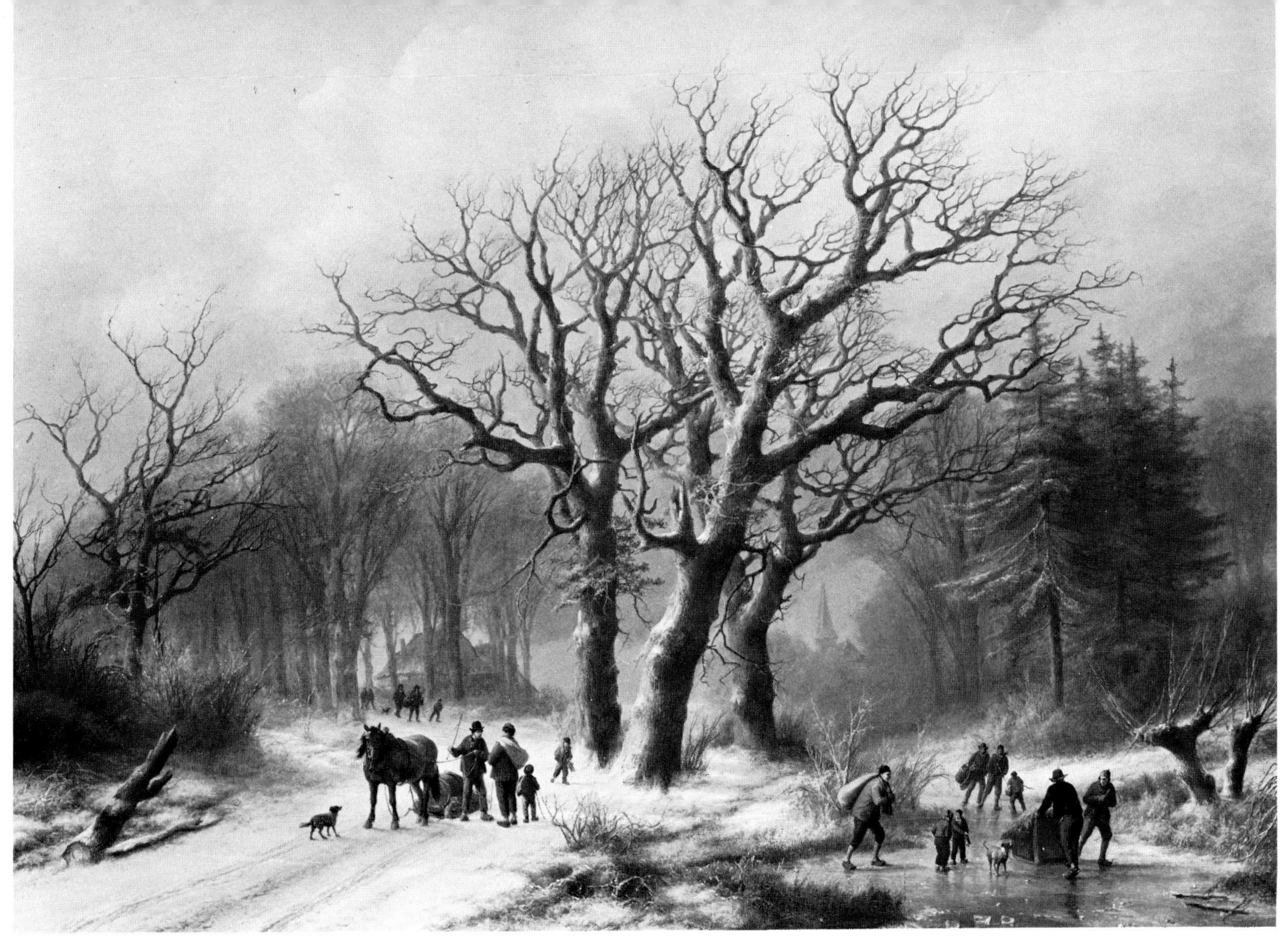

Johann Bernard Klombeck (also Clombeek) (1815-1893) – *"Winter landscape" painted in collaboration with Belgian artist Eugène Verboeckhoven, signed by both artists and dated 1873, 35½ x 47¾ins.* Photograph courtesy of Richard Green.

Klombeck was a landscapist and specialised in forest scenes. He often collaborated with Verboeckhoven who would have painted the figures in the above. Pupil of B.C. Koekkoek. Worked mainly in Kleef.

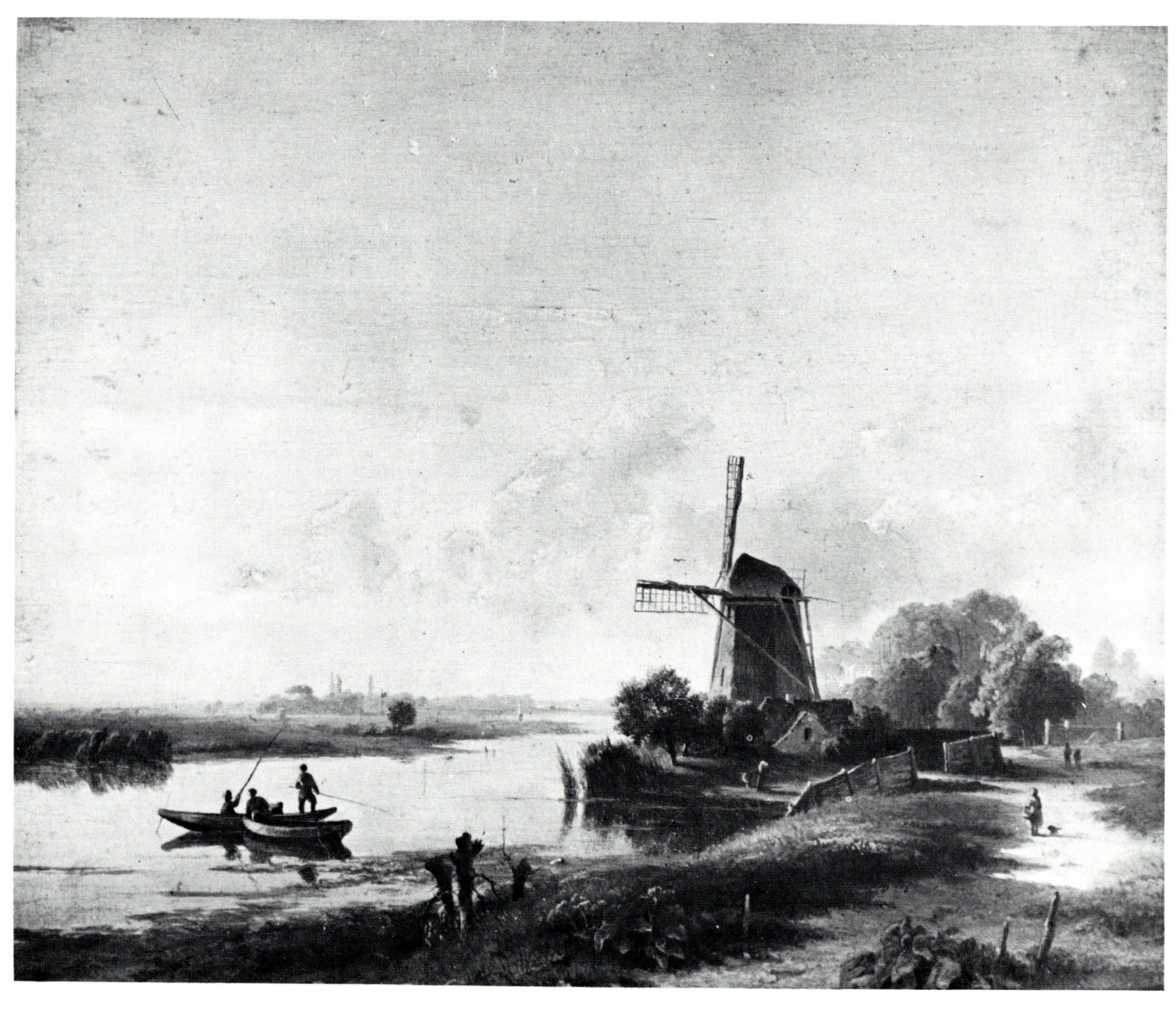

Pieter Lodewijk Kluyver (1816-1900) – *"Landscape with windmill", 23½ x 27½cms.* Photograph courtesy of Mak van Waay, Amsterdam.

Kluyver was an Amsterdam landscapist. Pupil of M. de Root.

Koekkoek Family Tree

The Koekkoek dynasty of artists stretches from the 18th to the 20th century. The repetition of names and the continuation of a family style can make their work hard to distinguish. The family tree will prove a useful aid.

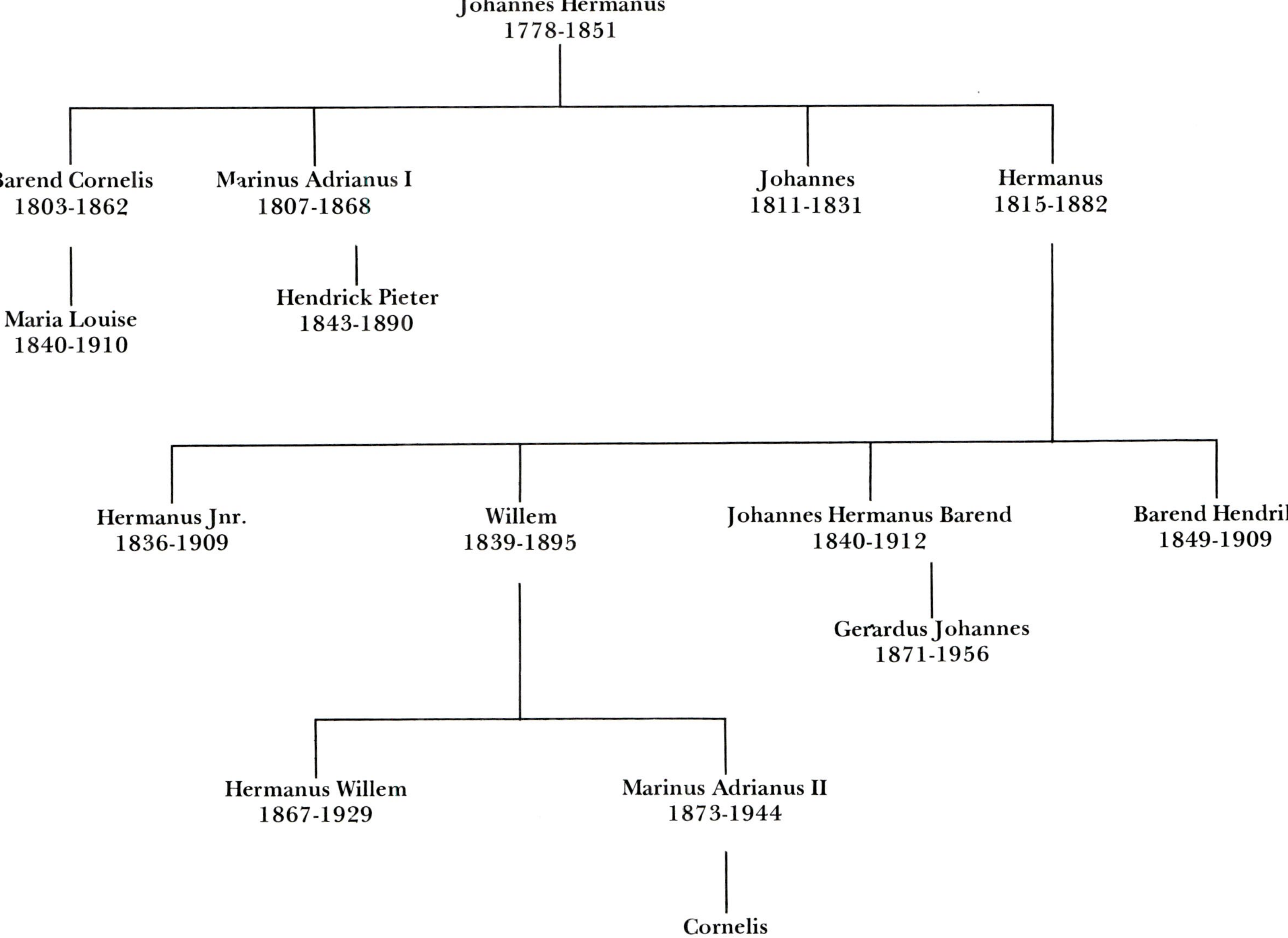

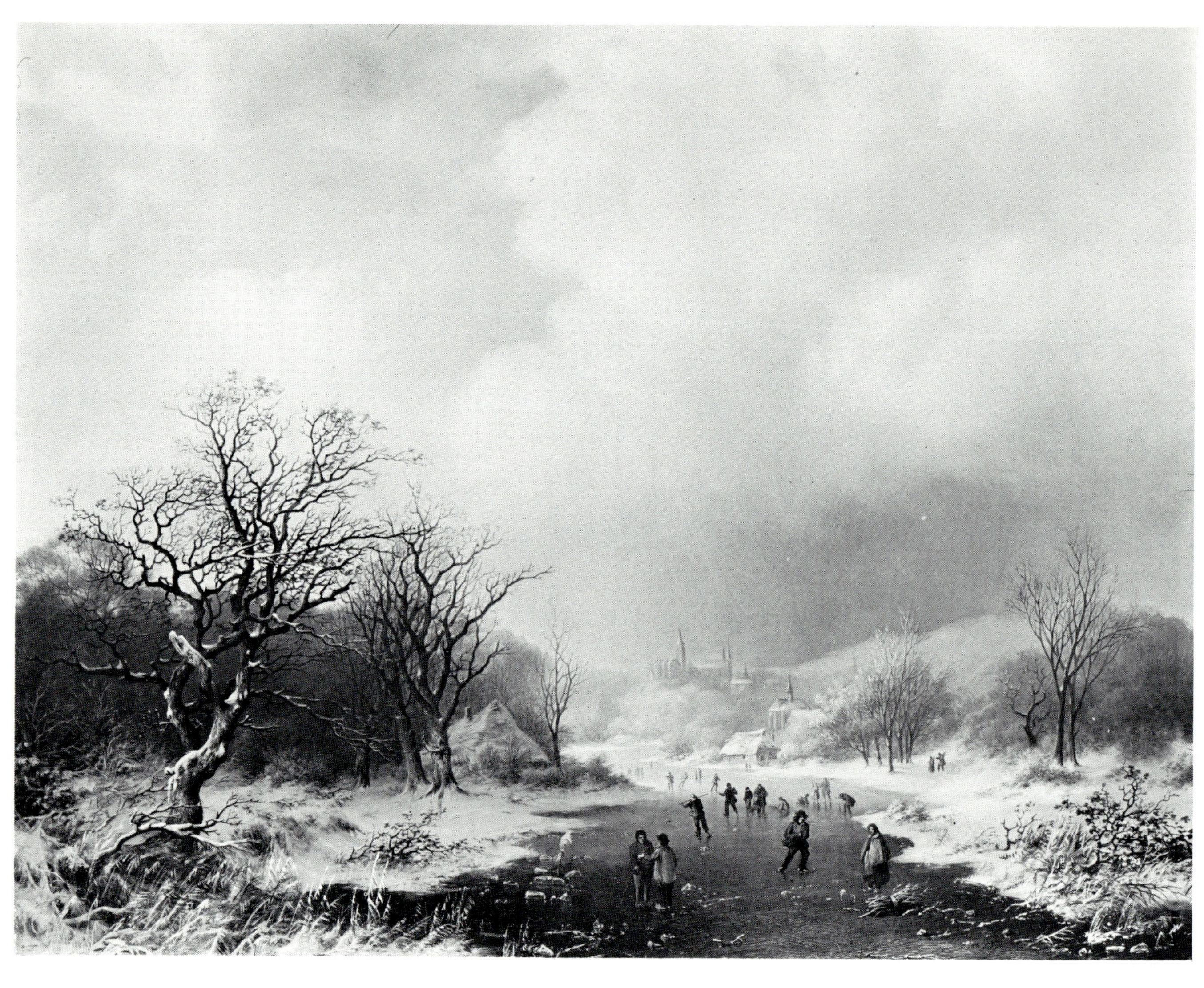

Barend Cornelis Koekkoek (1803-1862) – *"Dutch skating scene", 38 x 34ins.* Photograph courtesy of Spenser S.A.

Barend Cornelis was the leading landscapist of the Dutch Romantic school. He specialised in effects of light, icebound winter trees and the sparkle of high summer. Studied Middleburg drawing school and with his father J.H. Koekkoek, also attending Amsterdam Academy. His wife Elis Therese Daiwaille was also an artist. He had many pupils including his brother Marinus Adrianus.

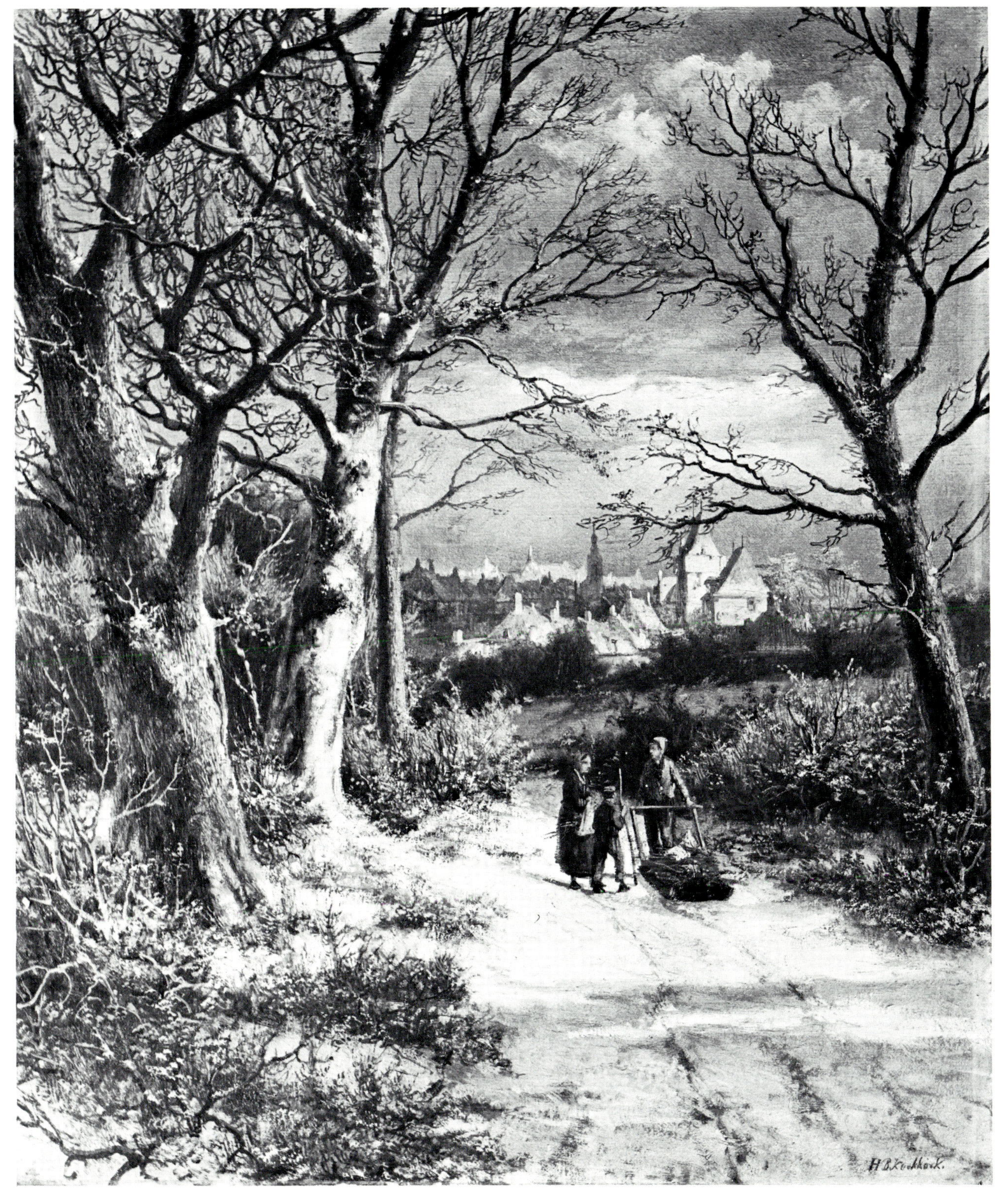

Barend Hendrik (or Hendrik Barend) Koekkoek (1849-1909) – *"Collecting wood", 75 x 61cms.* Photograph courtesy of Mak van Waay.

Barend Hendrik was Hermanus Koekkoek's youngest son. He painted landscapes, specialising in woodland scenes. He moved to London in 1882.

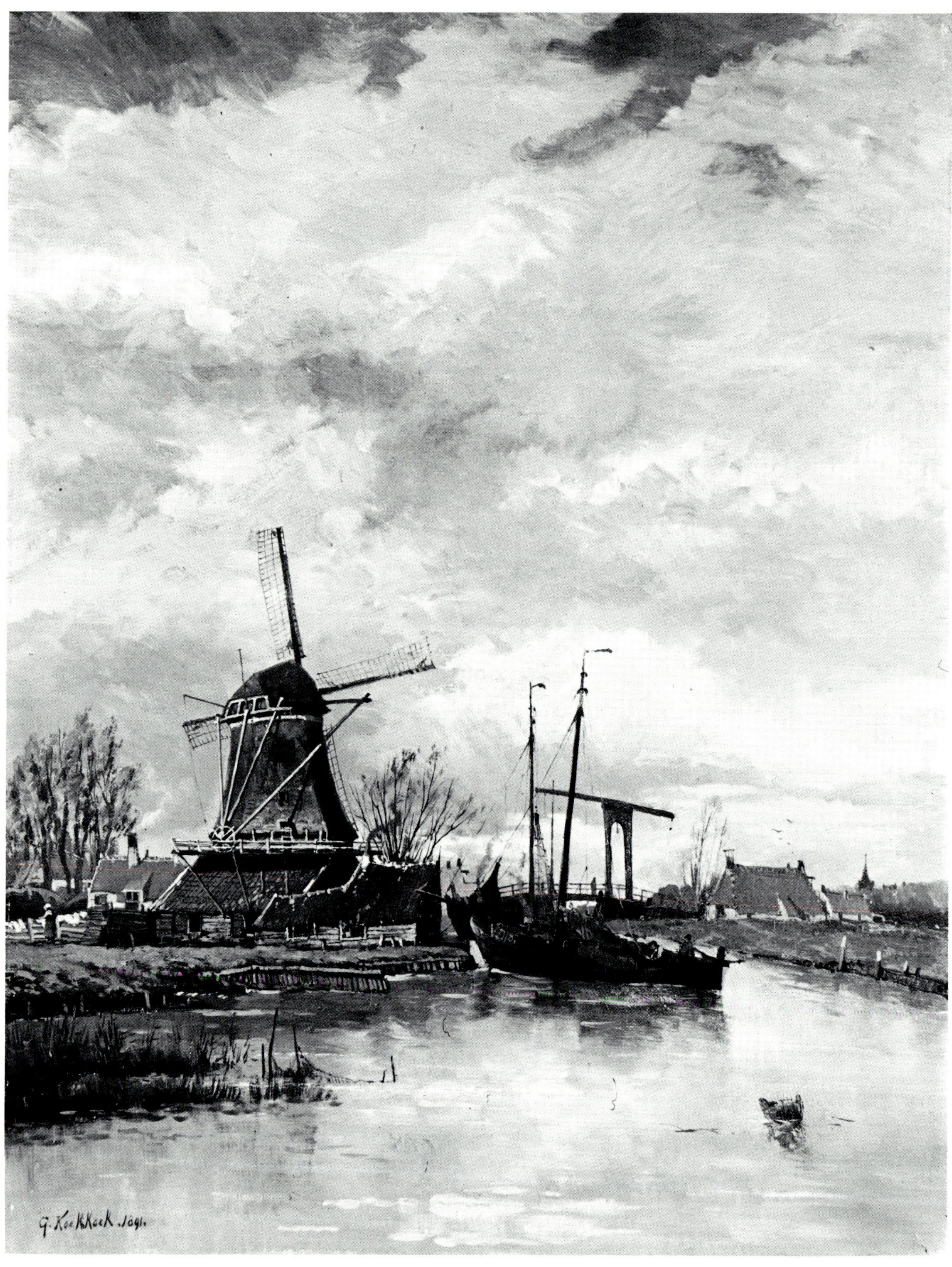
G. Koekkoek 1891.

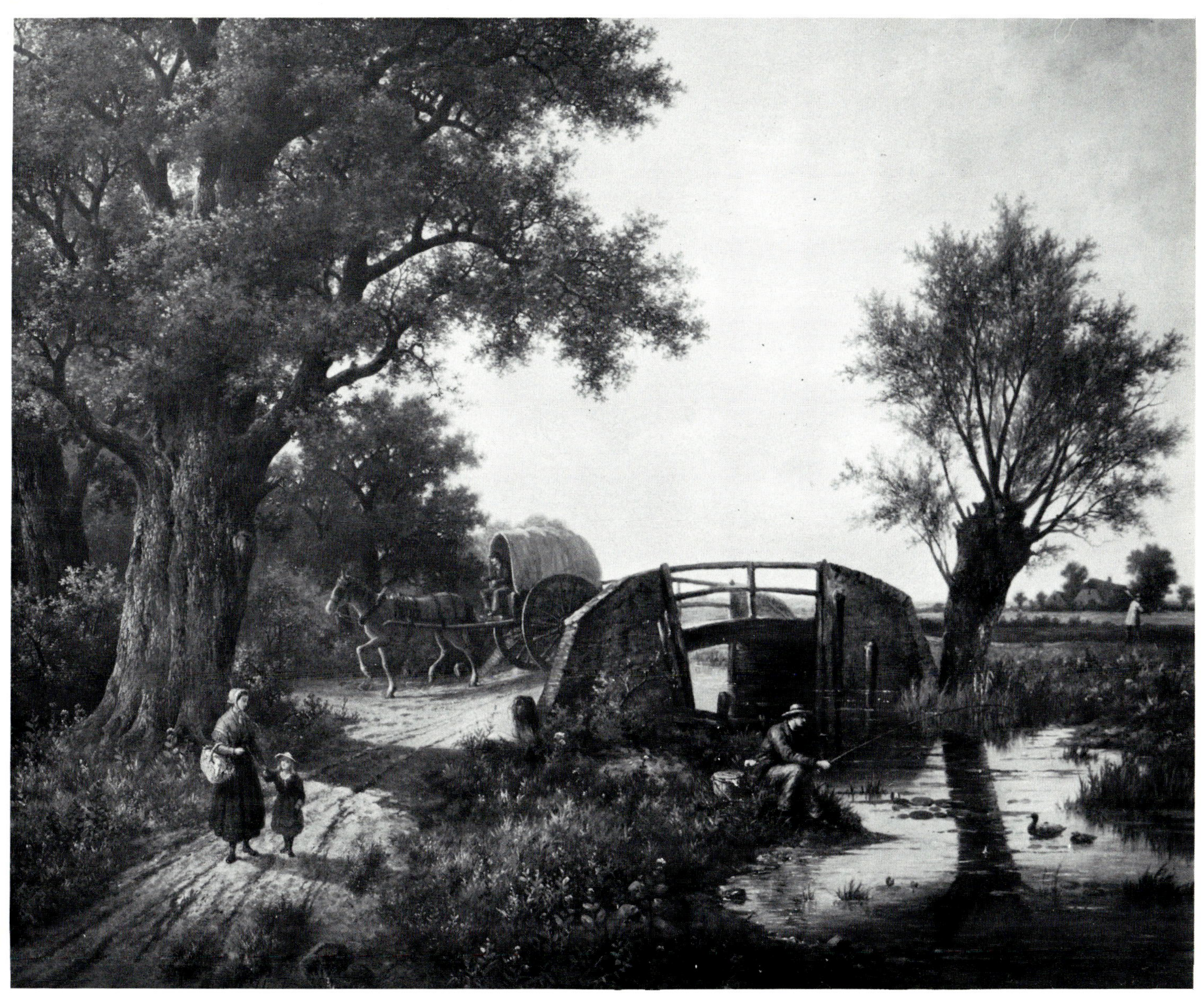

Above: **Hendrik Pieter (Pieter Hendrik) Koekkoek (1843-1890)** – *"Dutch river landscape", 44 x 56ins.* Photograph courtesy of M. Newman Ltd.

Hendrik Pieter was the son of Marinus Adrianus. He was a landscape painter and probably moved to England.

Left: **Gerardus Johannes (Gerard) Koekkoek (1871-1956)** – *"Dutch landscape with a windmill", signed and dated 1891, 84 x 64cms.* Photograph courtesy of Mak van Waay.

Gerard was the son of J.H.B. Koekkoek. A landscapist, he studied with his father, H.W. Jansen and P. Dupont. Member of "Laren-Blaricum" and "Arti et Amicitiae" of Amsterdam.

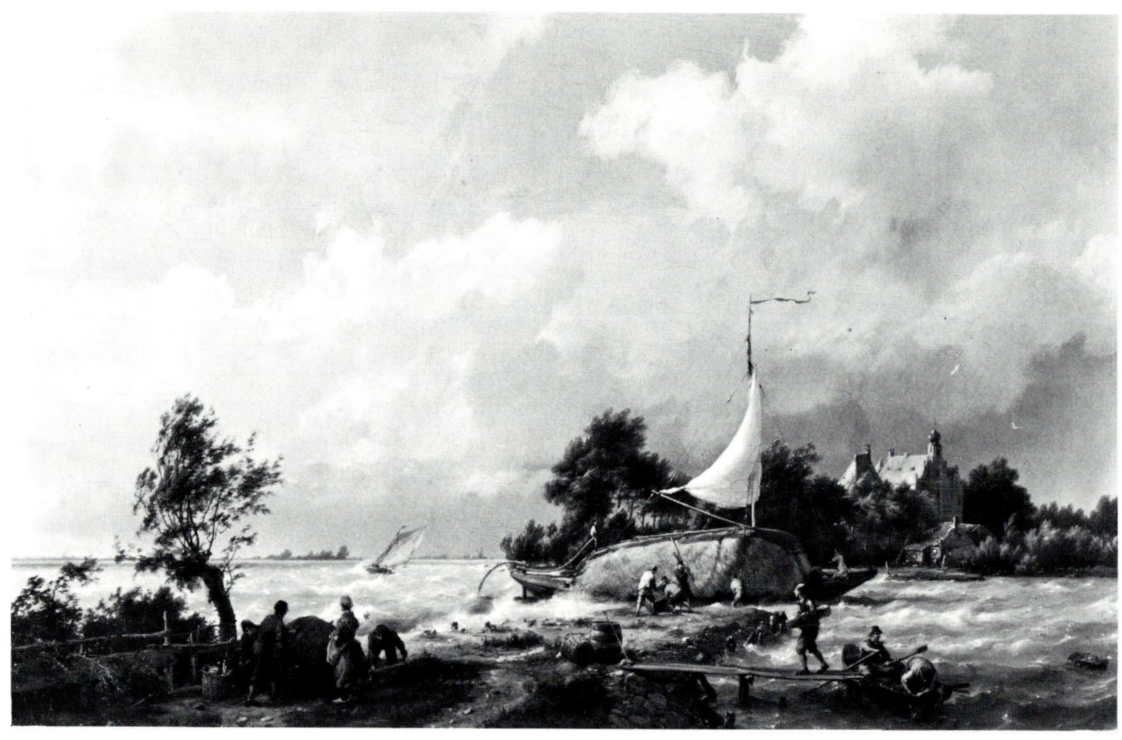

Above: **Hermanus Koekkoek (1815-1882)** – *"River estuary with a hay barge", 14 x 22½ins.* Photograph courtesy of Christie, Manson and Woods.

Hermanus was the youngest son of Johannes Hermanus and probably stands second in importance only to Barend Cornelis who was his eldest brother. He painted sea and riverscapes. Member of Amsterdam Academy 1840.

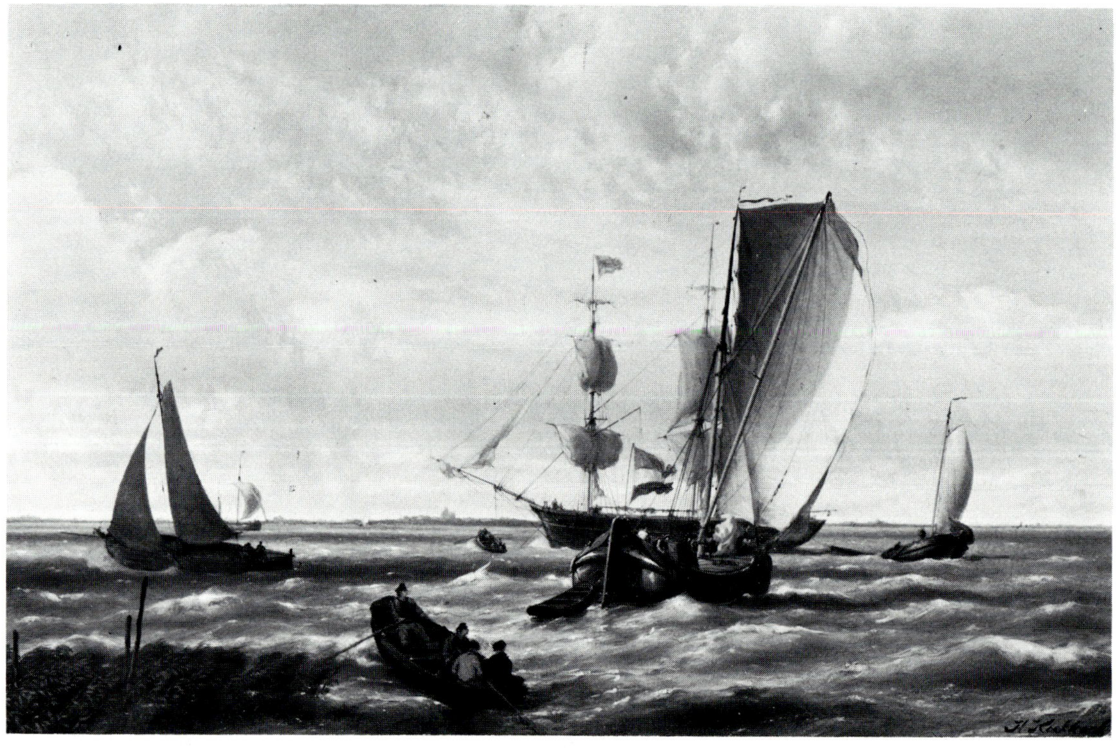

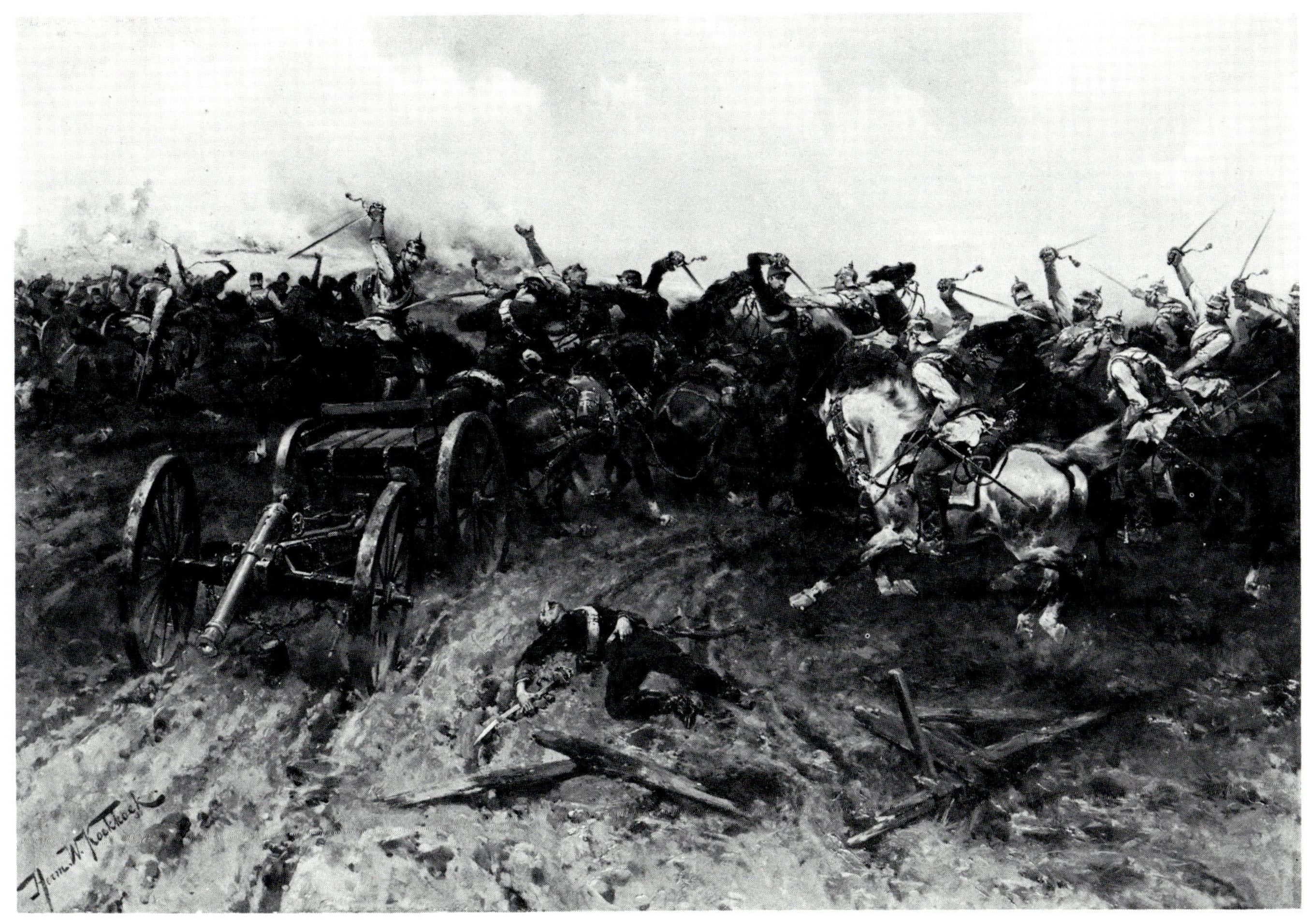

Above: **Hermanus Willem Koekkoek (1867-1929)** – *"A Cavalry engagement during the Franco-Prussian war", 34 x 49ins.* Photograph courtesy of Sotheby & Co.

Hermanus Willem was the son of Willem Koekkoek. He specialised in military pictures, particularly cavalry charges. He divided his time between Holland and London, working as illustrator for both The Illustrated London News and The Sketch.

Left: **Hermanus Koekkoek Jnr. (1836-1909)** – *"On the Zuiderzee", 25 x 16ins.* Photograph courtesy of Spenser S.A.

Hermanus Jnr. was the eldest son of Hermanus Snr. A pupil of his father he mainly painted seascapes.

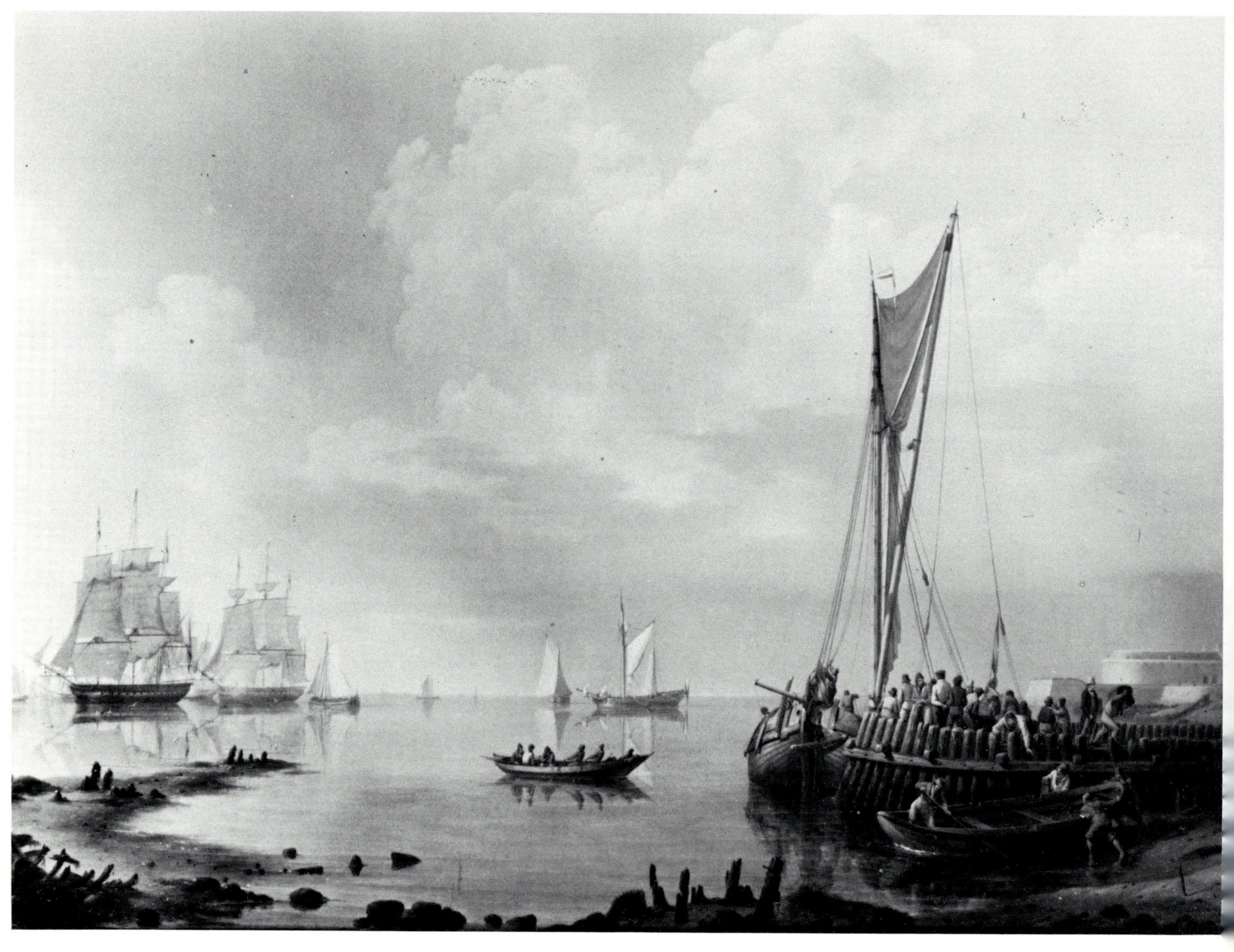

Johannes Hermanus Koekkoek (1778-1851) — *"Shipping in a calm estuary", signed and dated 1836, 24 x 32½ins.* Photograph courtesy of Sotheby & Co.

Johannes Hermanus was the father of the Koekkoek dynasty of painters. He painted sea and river scenes. Studied Middleburg under T. Gaal.

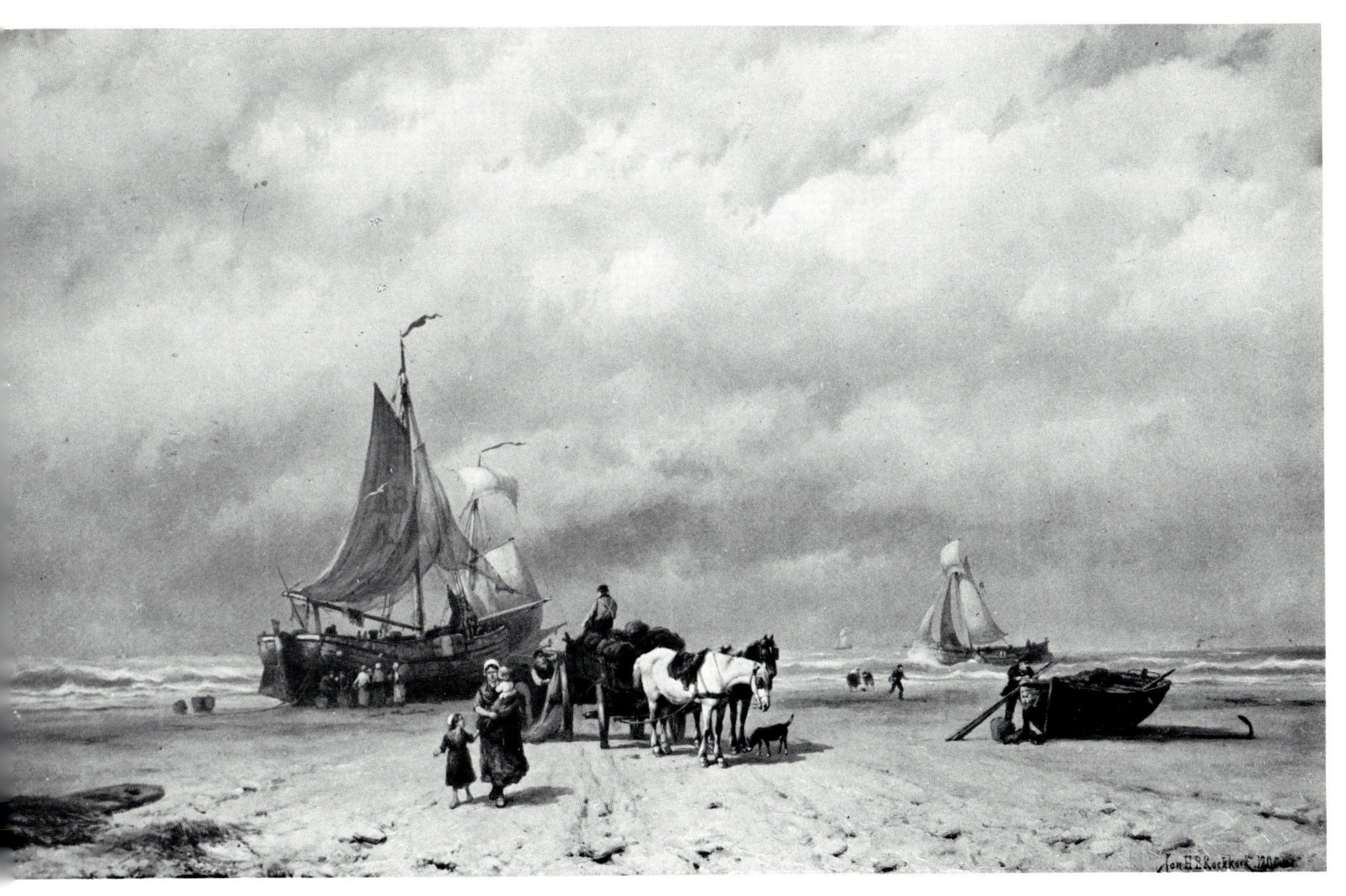

Johannes Hermanus Barend Koekkoek (1840-1912) — *"Fishermen on the beach", signed and dated 1890, 79 x 129cms.* Photograph courtesy of Mak van Waay, Amsterdam.

Johannes Hermanus Barend was the son of Hermanus. Pupil of his father, he painted landscapes and seascapes. Member of "Arti et Amicitiae" of Amsterdam.

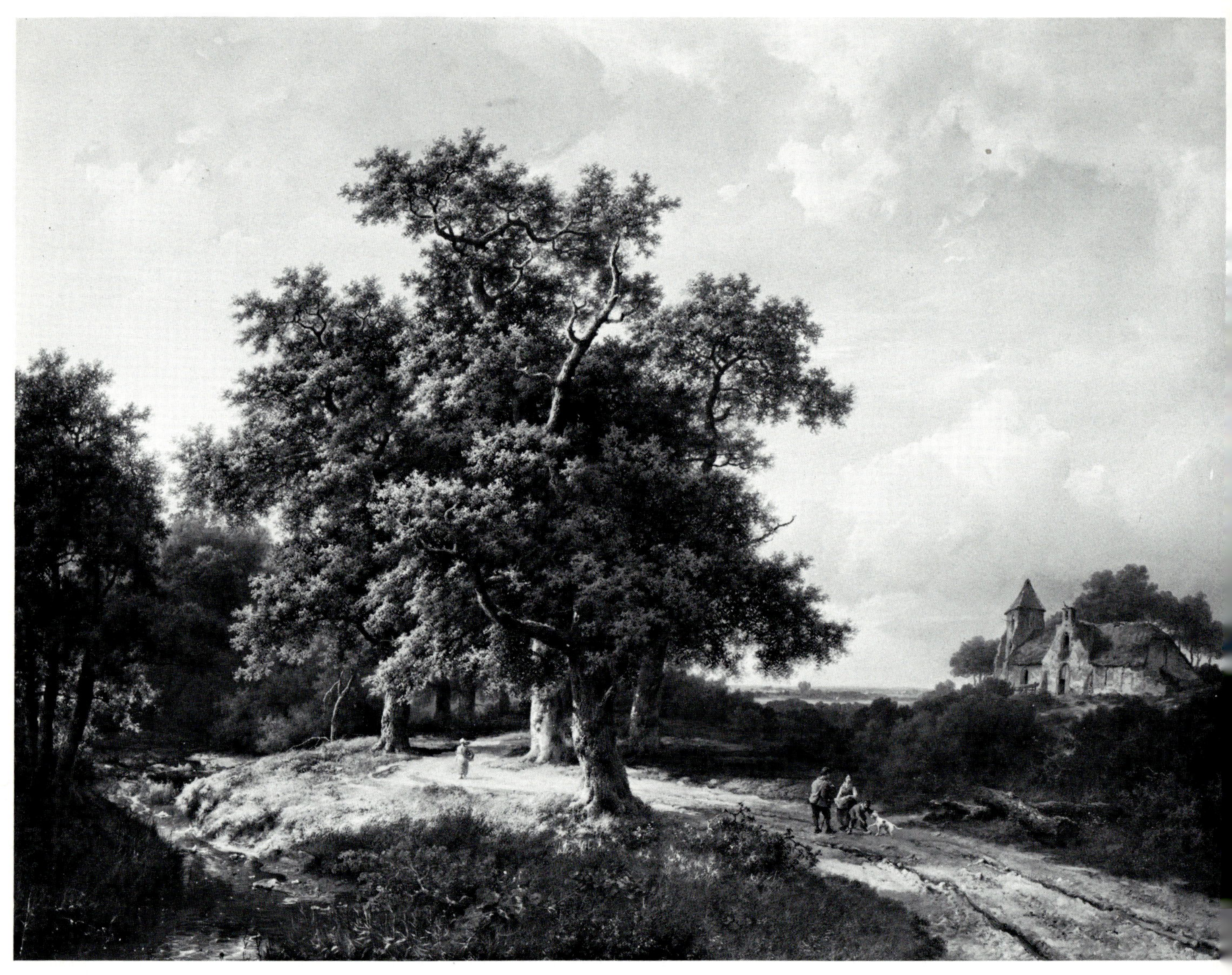

Marinus Adrianus Koekkoek (1807-1868) — *"Wooded landscape with figures on a path", signed and dated 1857, 30 x 40½ins.* Photograph courtesy of Richard Green.

Marinus Adrianus was the son of Johannes Hermanus and his pupil. He painted wooded landscapes somewhat similar to his brother Barend Cornelis. On occasion he collaborated with the Belgian artist Eugène Verboeckhoven.

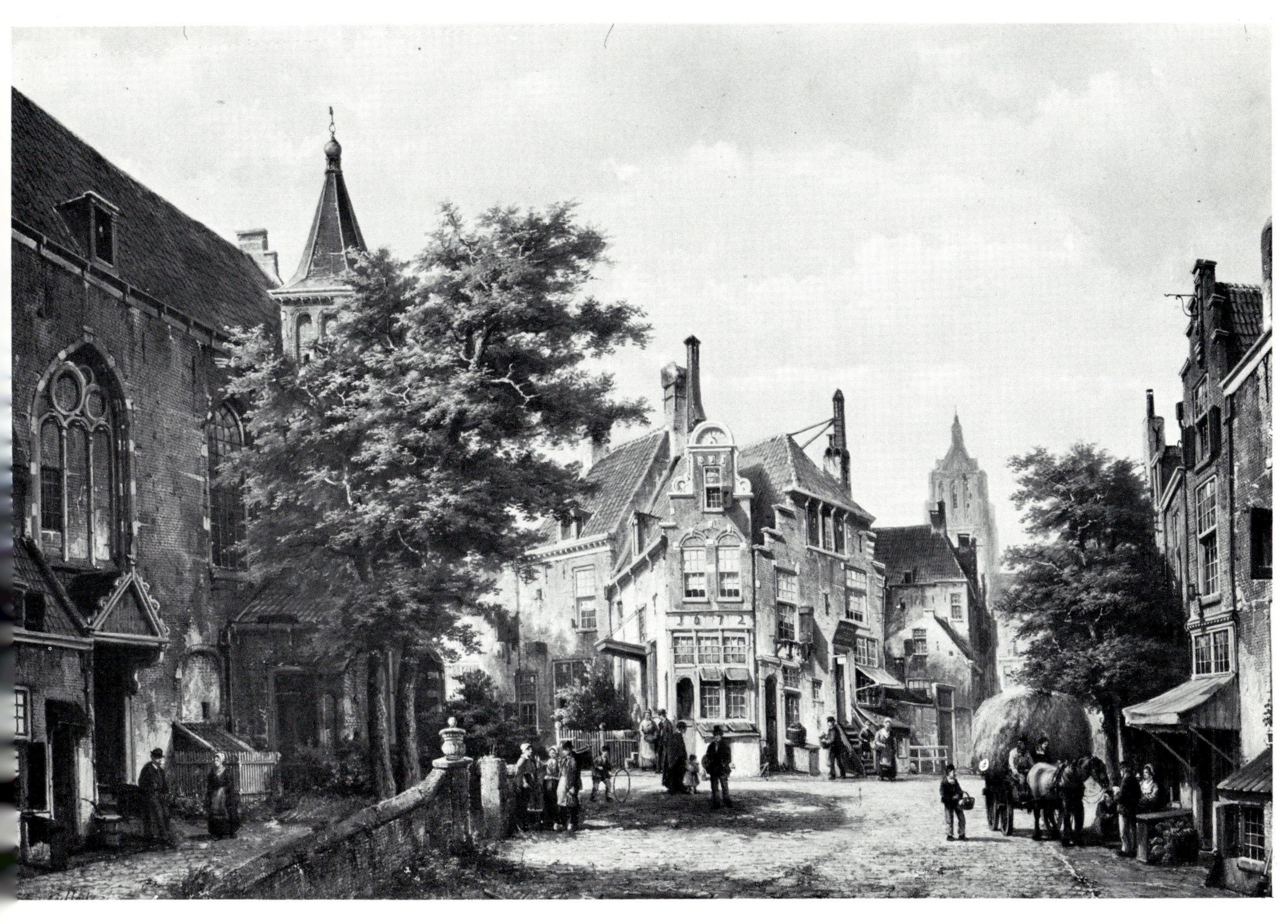

Willem Koekkoek (1839-1895) -- *"Street in a Dutch town".* Photograph courtesy of MacConnal Mason.

Willem was the son of Hermanus Koekkoek. He was the most distinguished townscapist of the family. Pupil of his father.

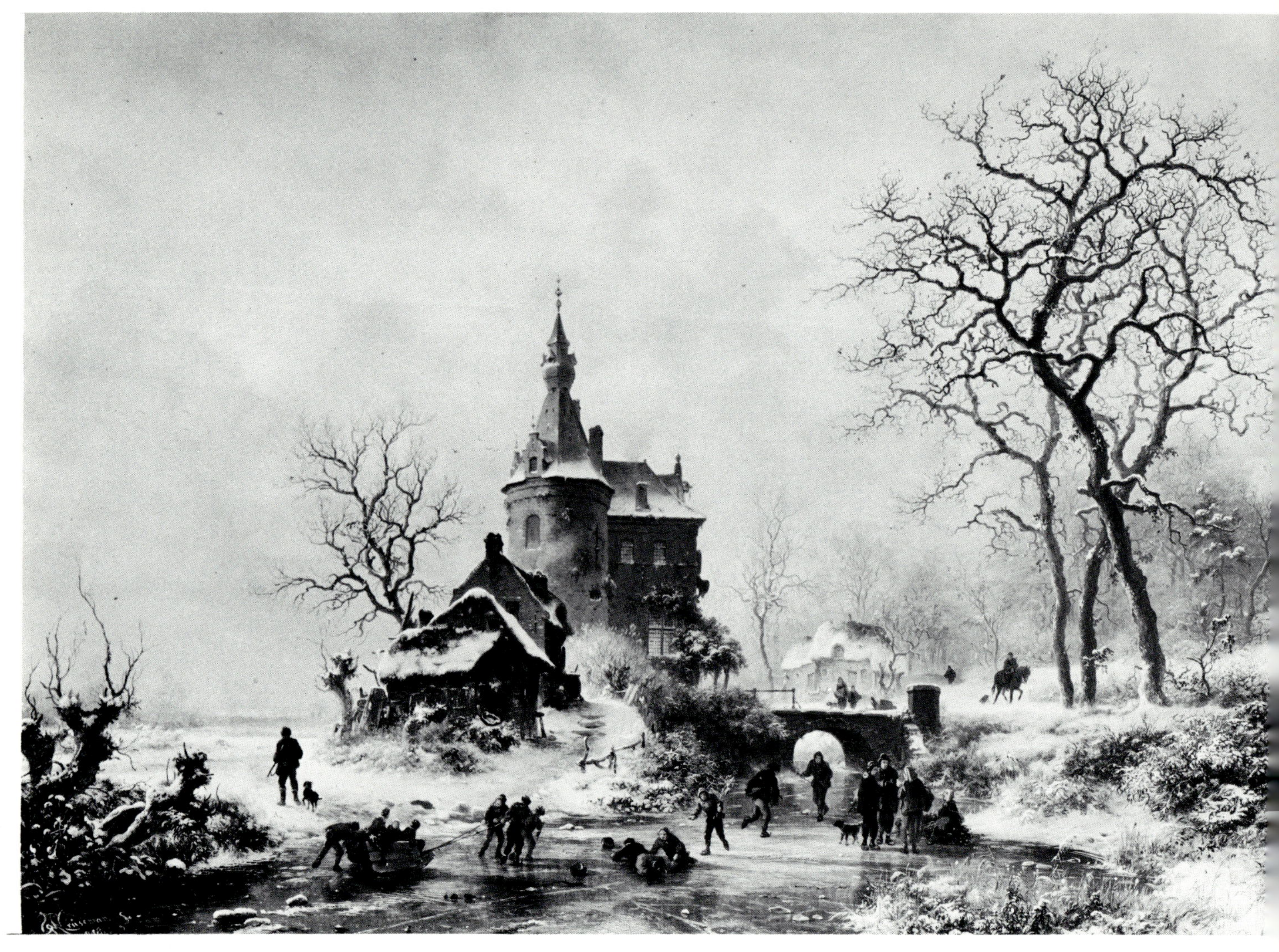

Frederik Marinus Kruseman (1816-1882) – *"Frozen river landscape", signed and dated 1848.*Photograph courtesy of MacConnal Mason.

Kruseman was primarily a landscapist, treating both summer and winter subjects, though he also painted a few still lives. He was a pupil of B.C. Koekkoek, among others, whose influence is clearly discernible in his work. For the last 20 or so years of his life he worked in the environs of Brussels.

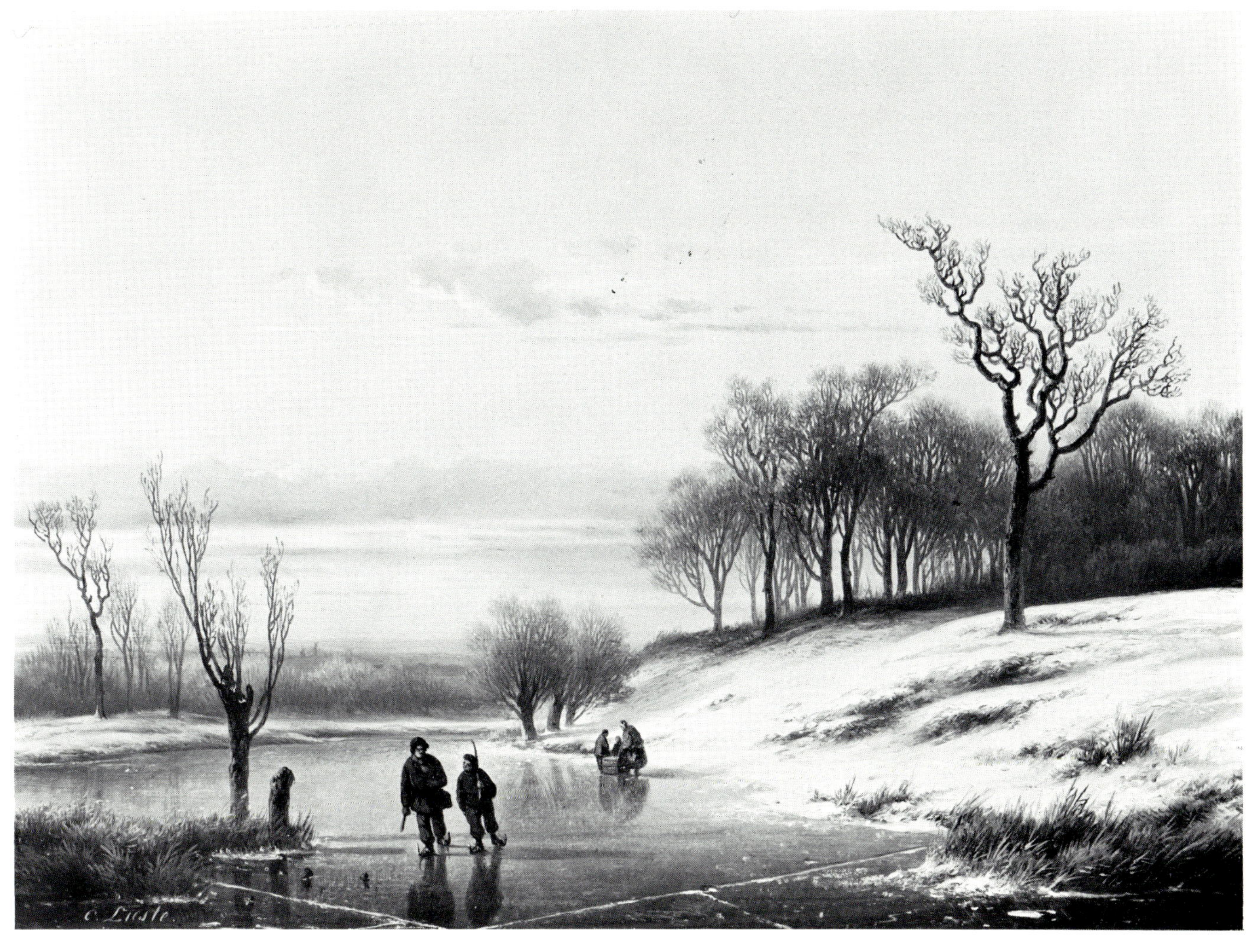

Cornelis Lieste (1817-1861) – *"Winter landscape", 11½ x 15¼ins.* Photograph courtesy of Richard Green.

Lieste was a landscapist and lithographer. Pupil of J. Reekers, N.J. Roosenboom. H.van de Sande Bakhuyzen and E. Verboeckhoven. Also studied in Belgium and Germany.

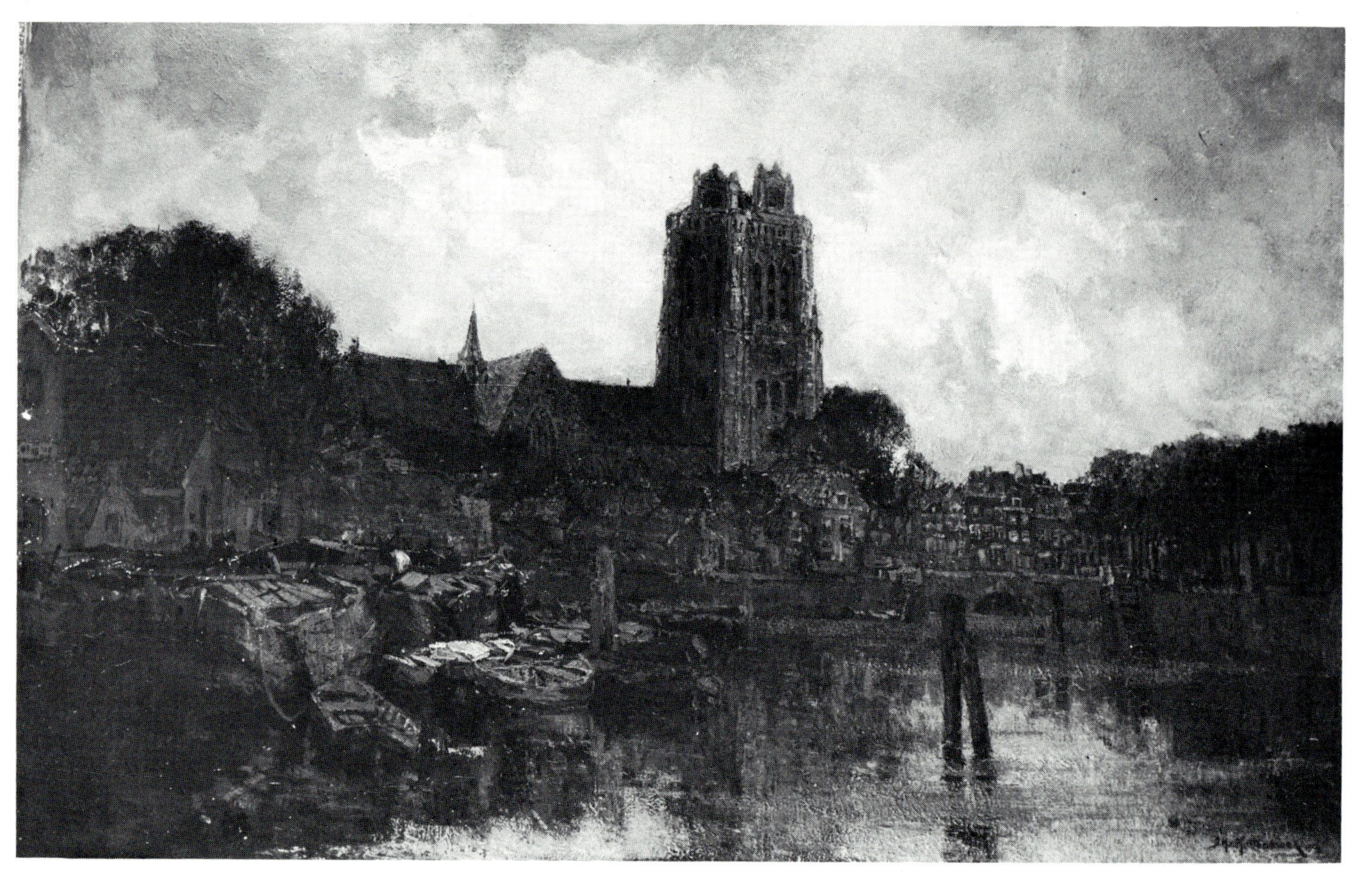

Johan Hendrik van Mastenbroek (1875-1945) – *"Town scene with boats", 82½ x 128½cms.* Photograph courtesy of Mak van Waay.

Mastenbroek specialised in ports, shipping and townscapes. He often worked in watercolour, also etched. Son of Johannes (Jan) van Mastenbroek, a cattle painter. Worked in Paris and London as well as Holland.

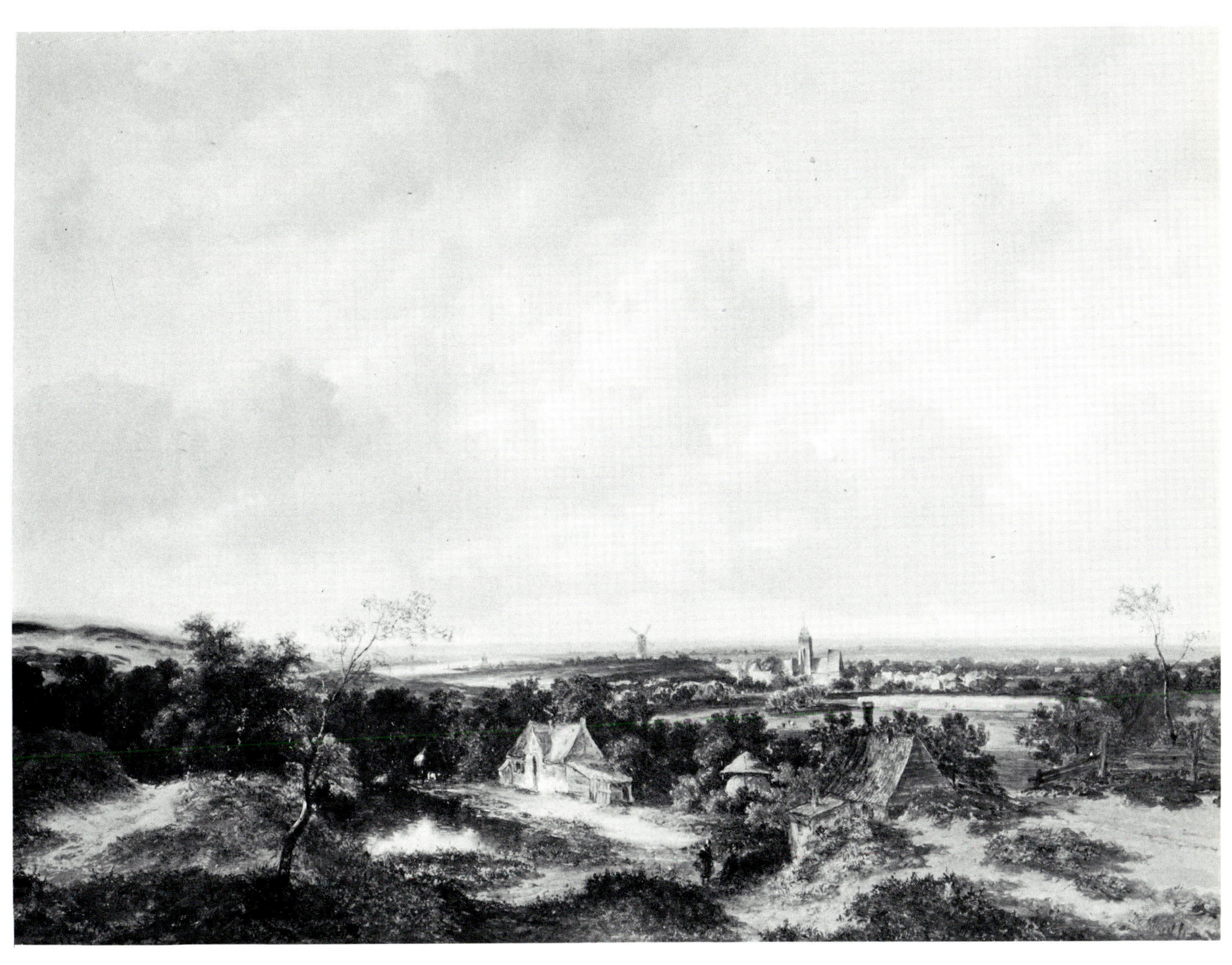

Jan Evert Morel Snr. (1769-1808) — *"Extensive summer landscape".* Photograph courtesy of MacConnal Mason.

Morel was a still life painter and landscapist. Pupil of J. Linthorst and D. van der Aa in the Hague. Also worked for short time with carriage painter D. van Jijl of Amsterdam.

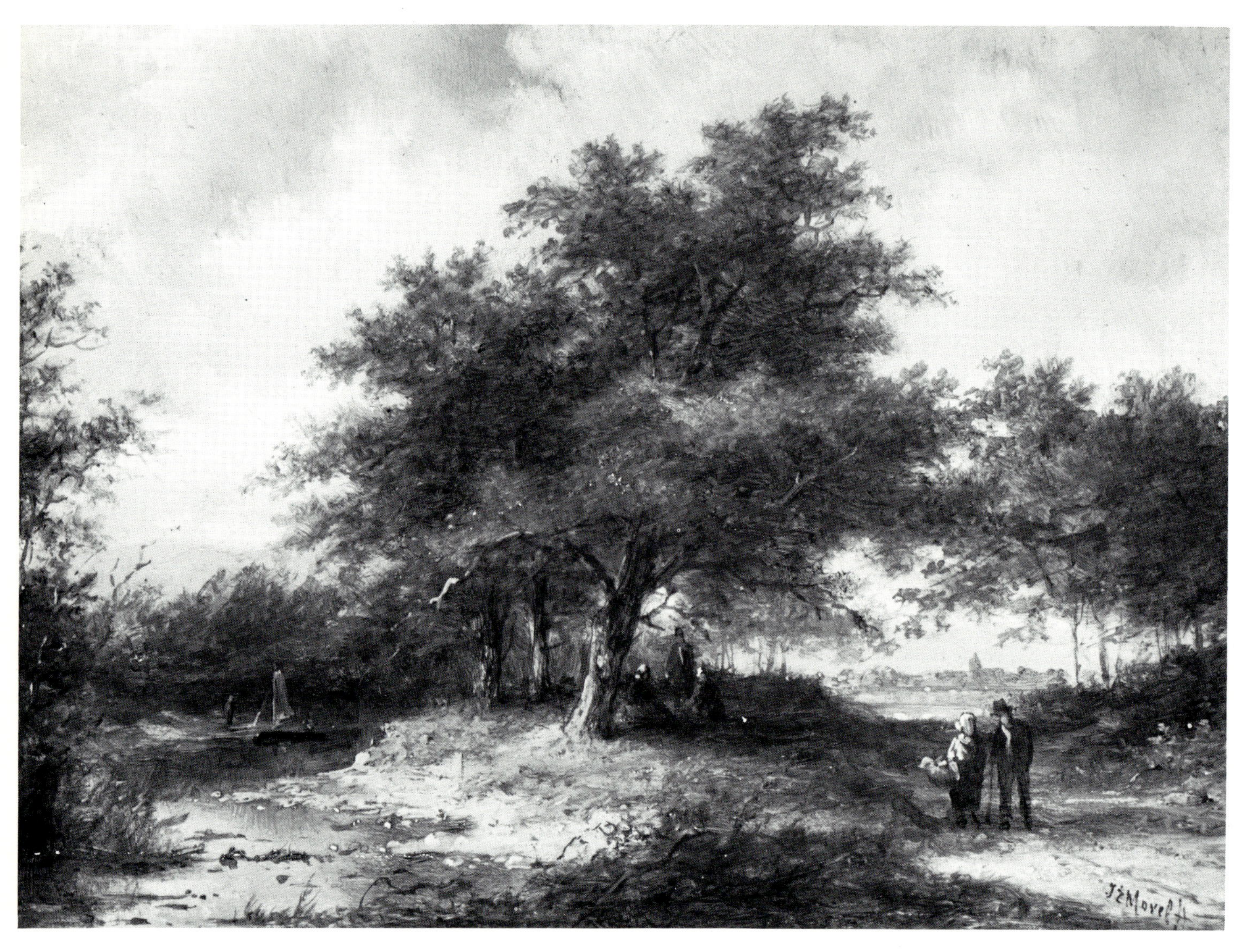

Jan Evert Morel Jnr. (1835-1905) – "*Woodland scene*". Photograph courtesy of Richard Green.

Morel was a landscapist and drawing master. Son and probably pupil of C.J. Morel. Worked mainly in Amsterdam.

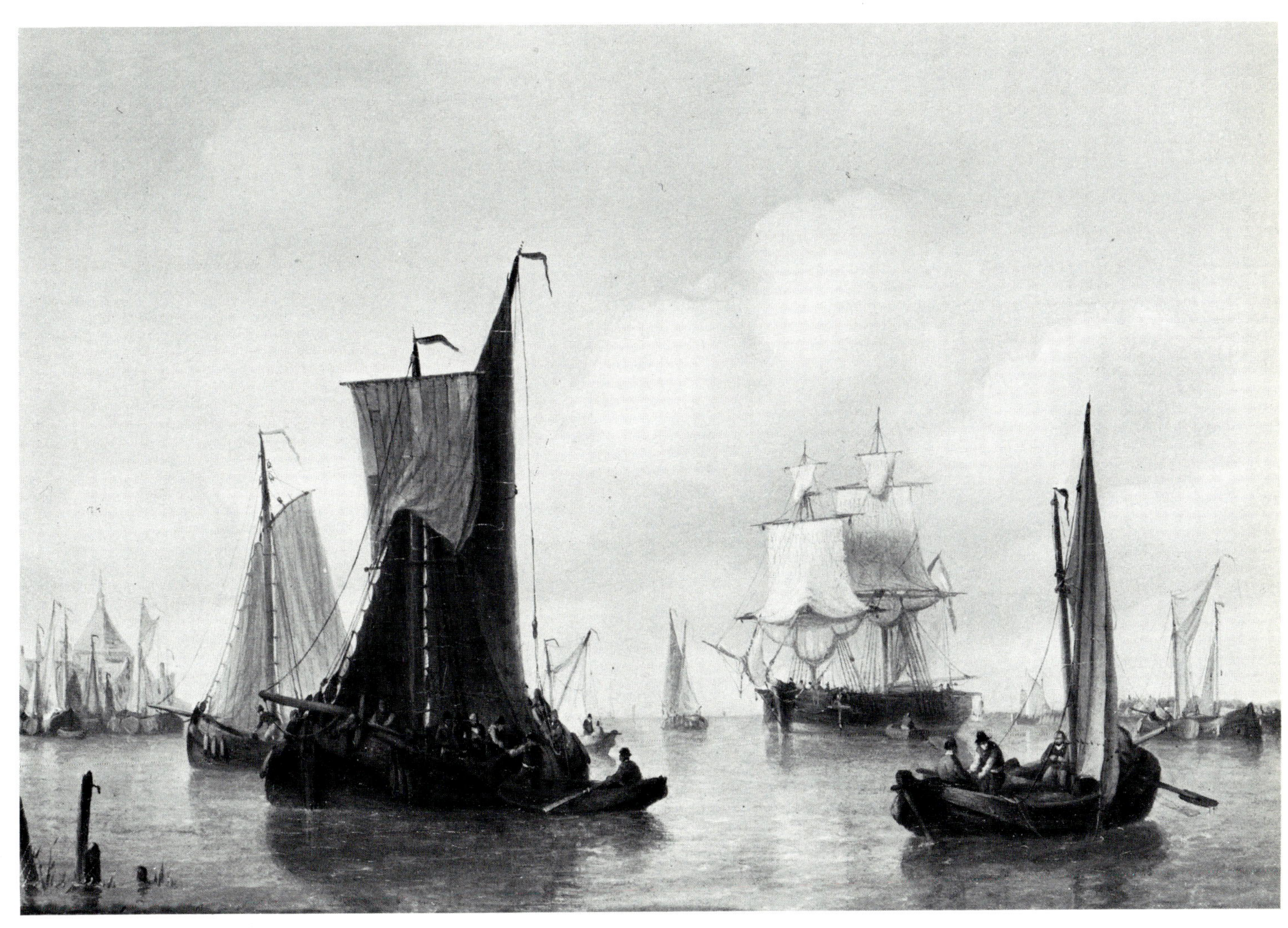

George Willem (Called Witzel) Opdenhoff (1807-1873) – *"Dutch vessels at anchor", 13½ x 18½ins.* Photograph courtesy of Spenser S.A.

Opdenhoff painted marine views, river and townscapes. Pupil of A. Schelfhout and J.C. Schotel.

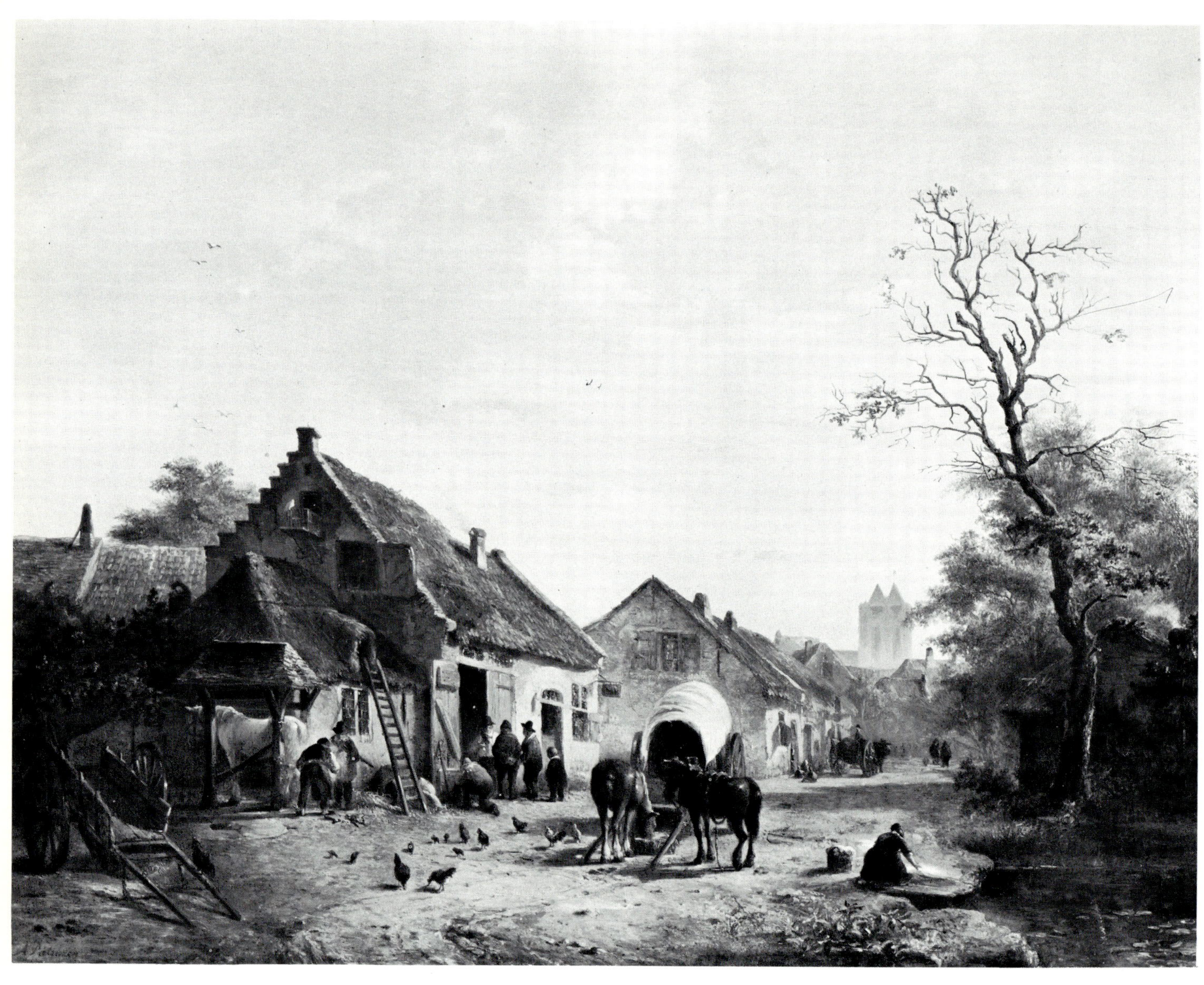

Abraham van der Wayen Pieterszen (1817-1888) – *"A village street scene", 26 x 34ins.* Photograph courtesy of Richard Green.
Pieterszen was a landscapist. Studied Middleburg drawing school and Antwerp Academy under Ivan Regemorter.

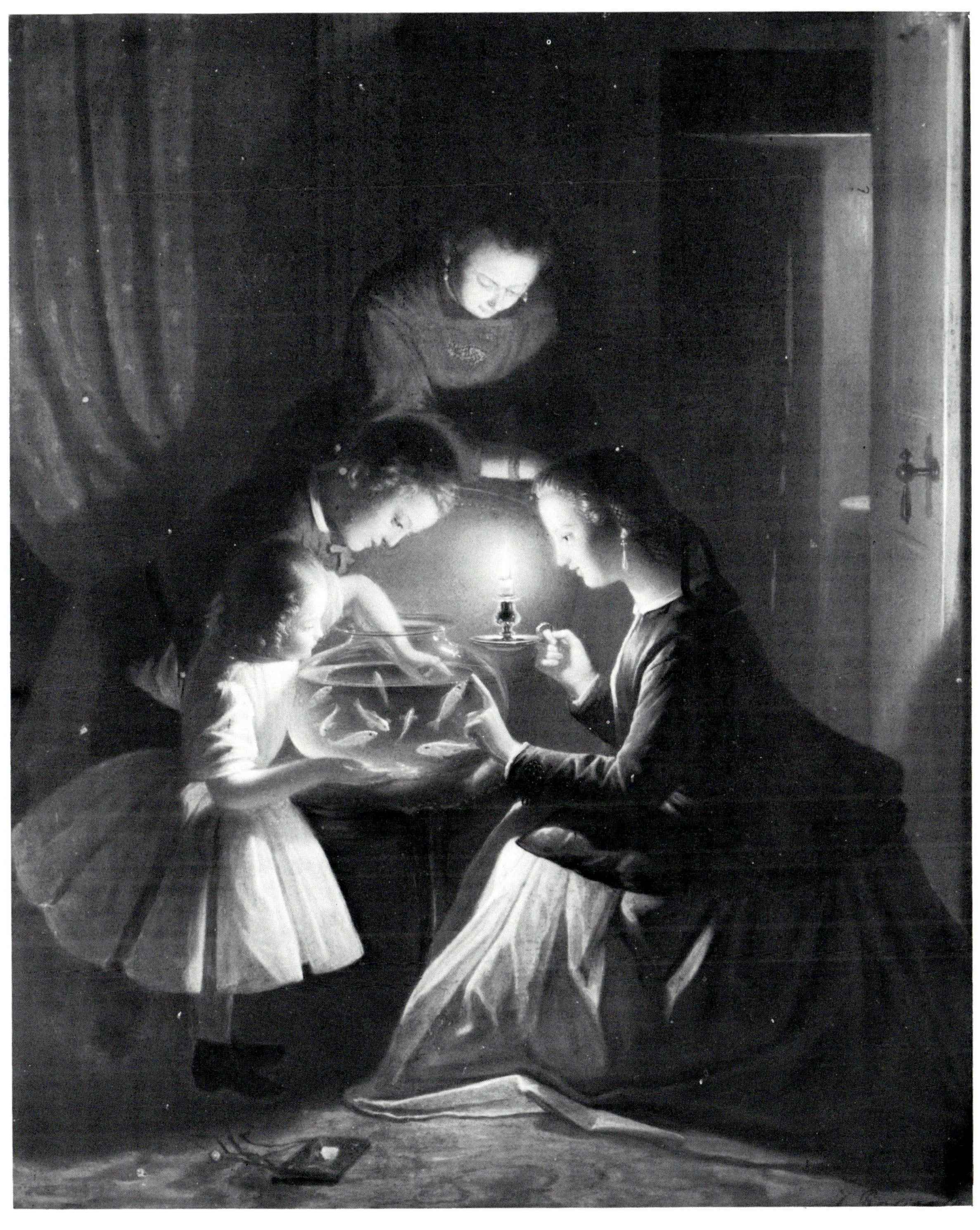

Johannes Rosierse (1818-1901) – *"The goldfish bowl", 33½ by 27¾cms.* Photograph courtesy of Mak van Waay, Amsterdam.

Rosierse painted interiors with figures, mostly by candle or lamp light. Started life as shop assistant, then studied with M. Versteeg and J. Boshamer. Lived and worked Dordrecht where he was an honorary member of "Pictura".

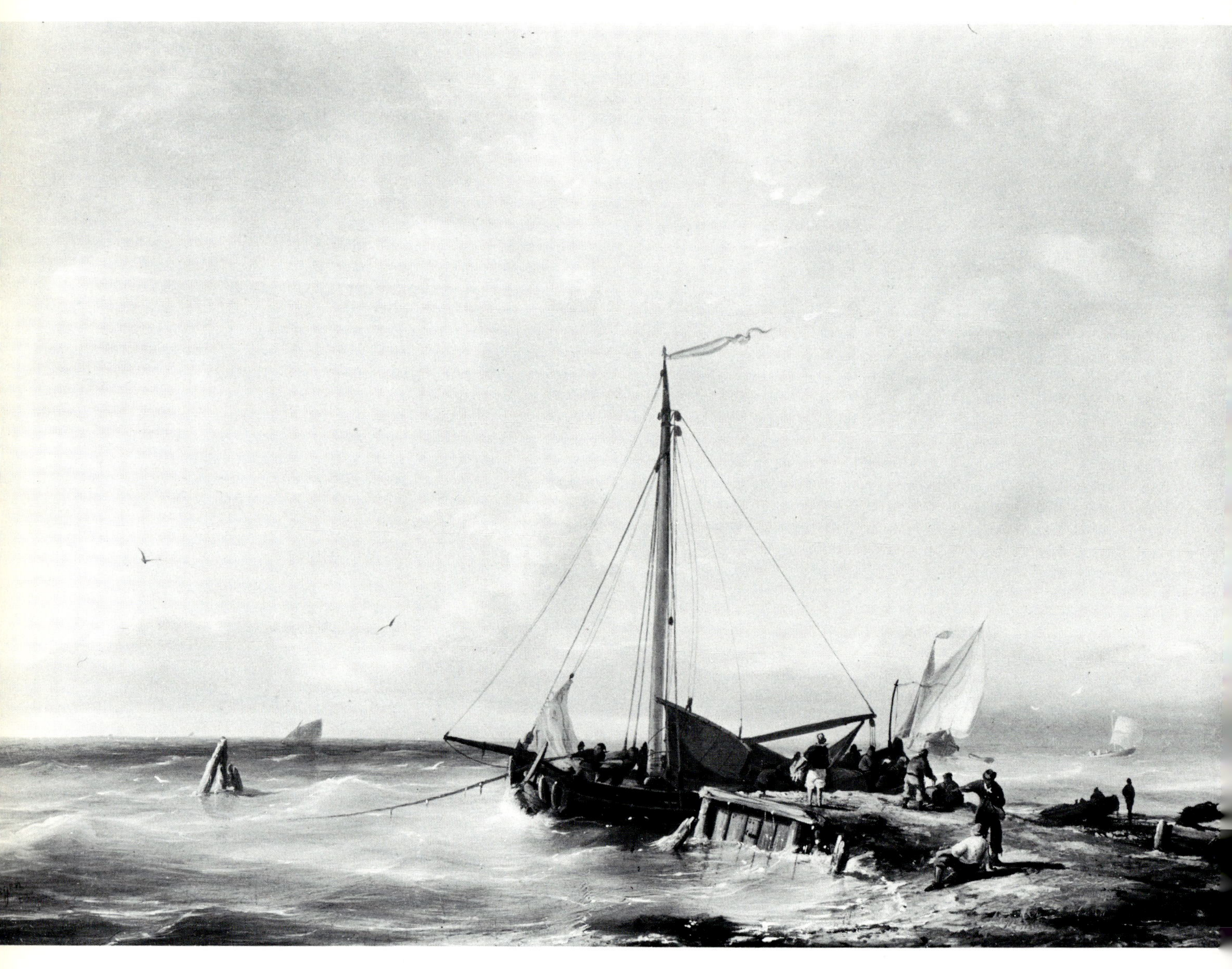

Nicolas Riegen (1827-1889) – *"Dutch coastal scene with a fishing boat hoisting sails", 12 x 16ins.* Photograph courtesy of Richard Green.

Riegen painted landscapes and marine views.

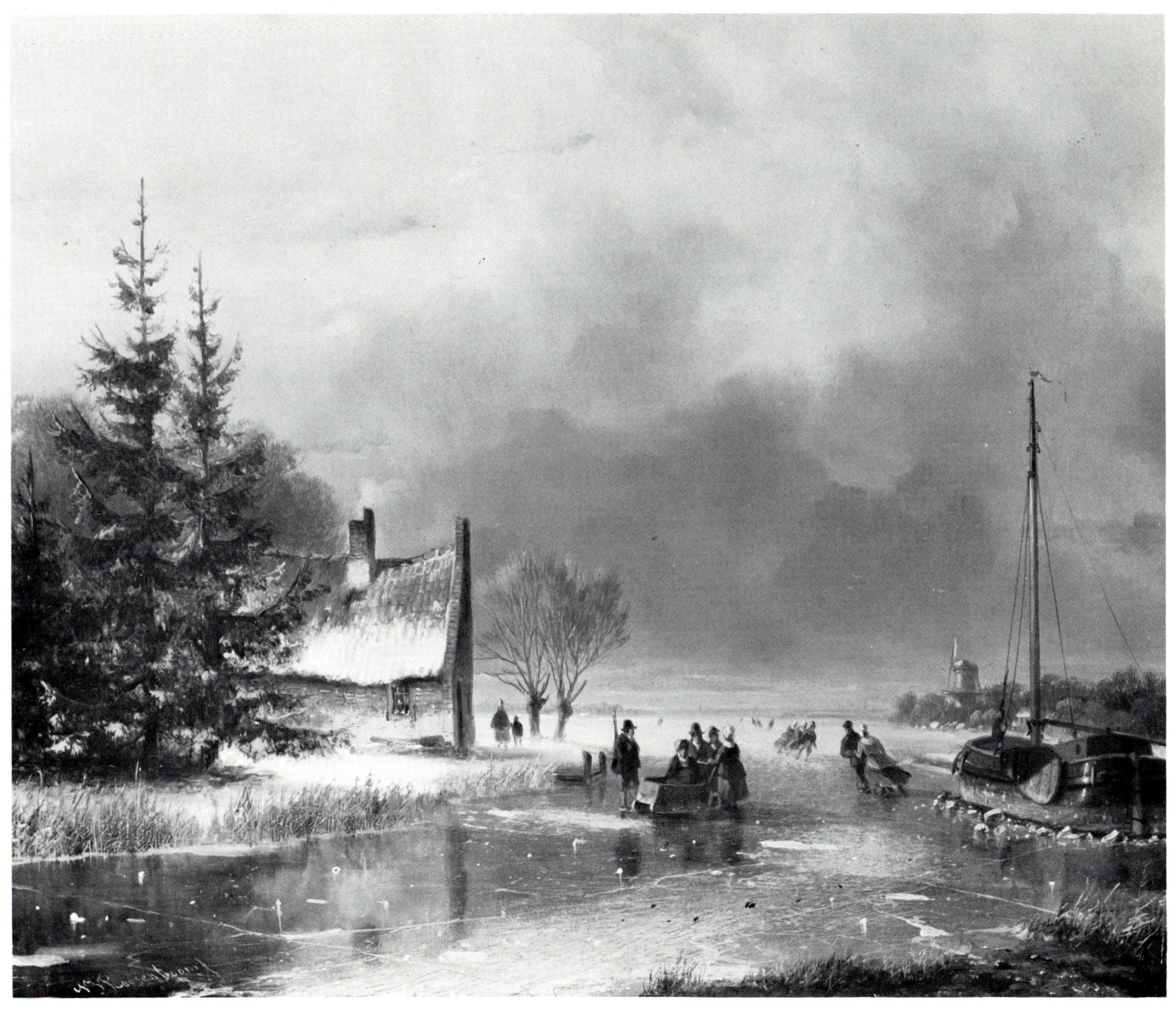

Nicolas Jan Roosenboom (b.1808 d. ?) – *"Dutch winter scene with skaters on ice", 17 x 24ins.* Photograph courtesy of Richard Green.

Roosenboom was a landscape painter. Pupil of A. Schelfhout. He was working in the Hague in 1889 but the precise date of his death does not seem to be known. He had many pupils including F.M. Kruseman and C. Liests.

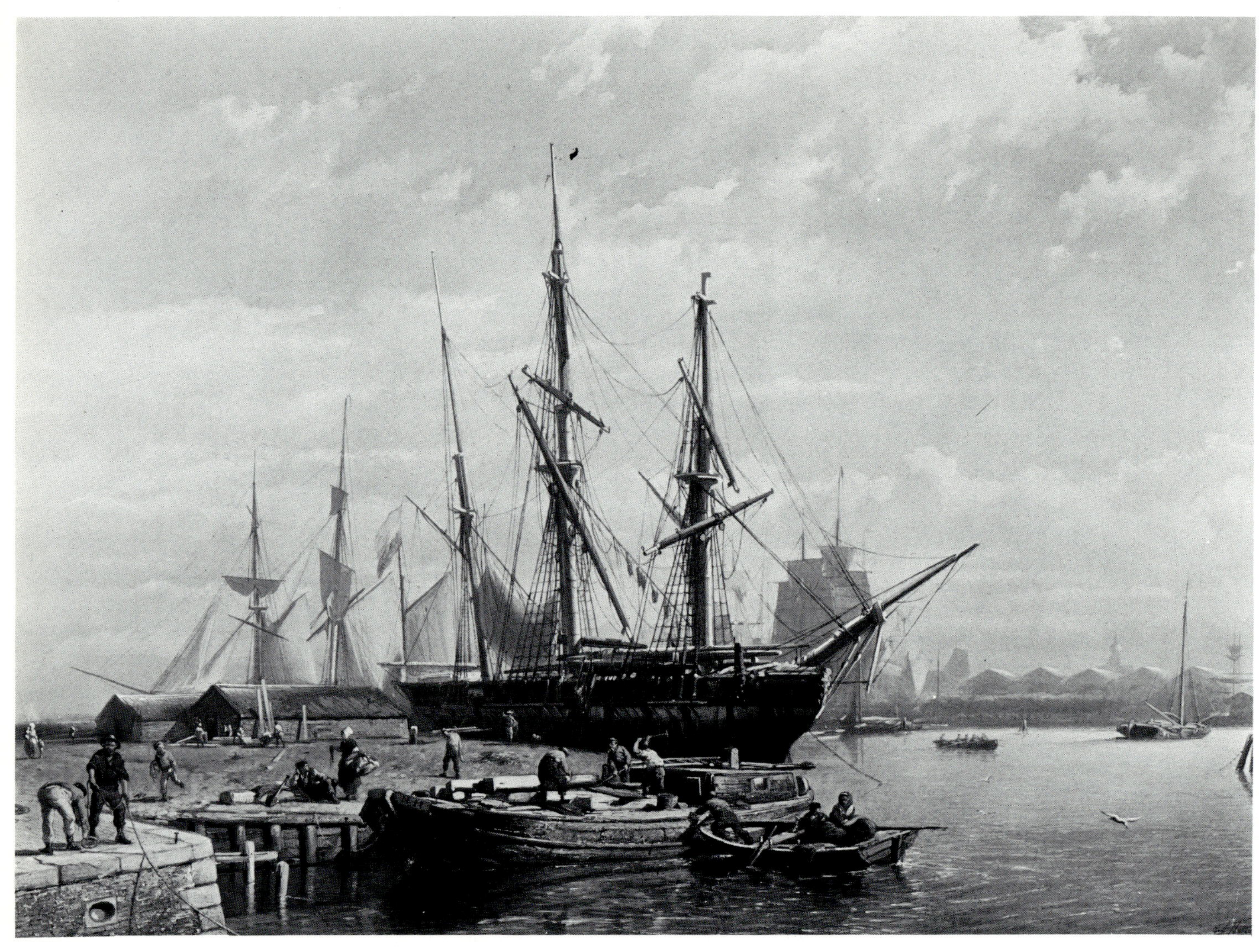

Johan Adolph Rust (1828-1915) – *"Dutch sailing ships at anchor in a river estuary", 17 x 24ins.* Photograph courtesy of Richard Green.

Rust painted town, sea and river views. Pupil of his uncle Cornelis Springer. Lived and worked Amsterdam where he was a member of "Arti et Amicitiae".

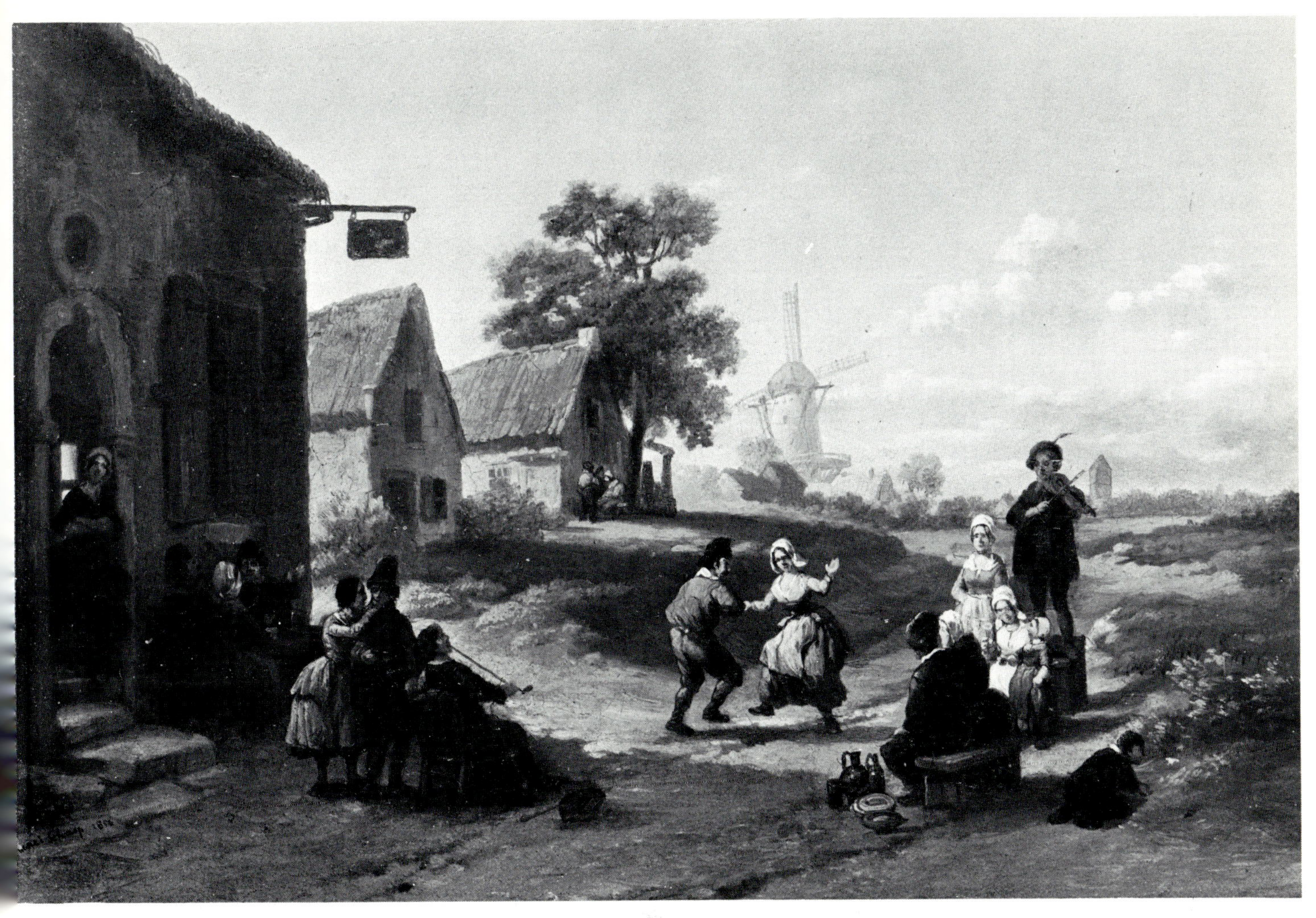

Henri Adolphe Schaep (1826-1870) – *"Merrymaking", signed and dated 1856, 7 x 10ins.* Photograph courtesy of Spenser S.A.
Schaep was a marine painter, landscapist and etcher.

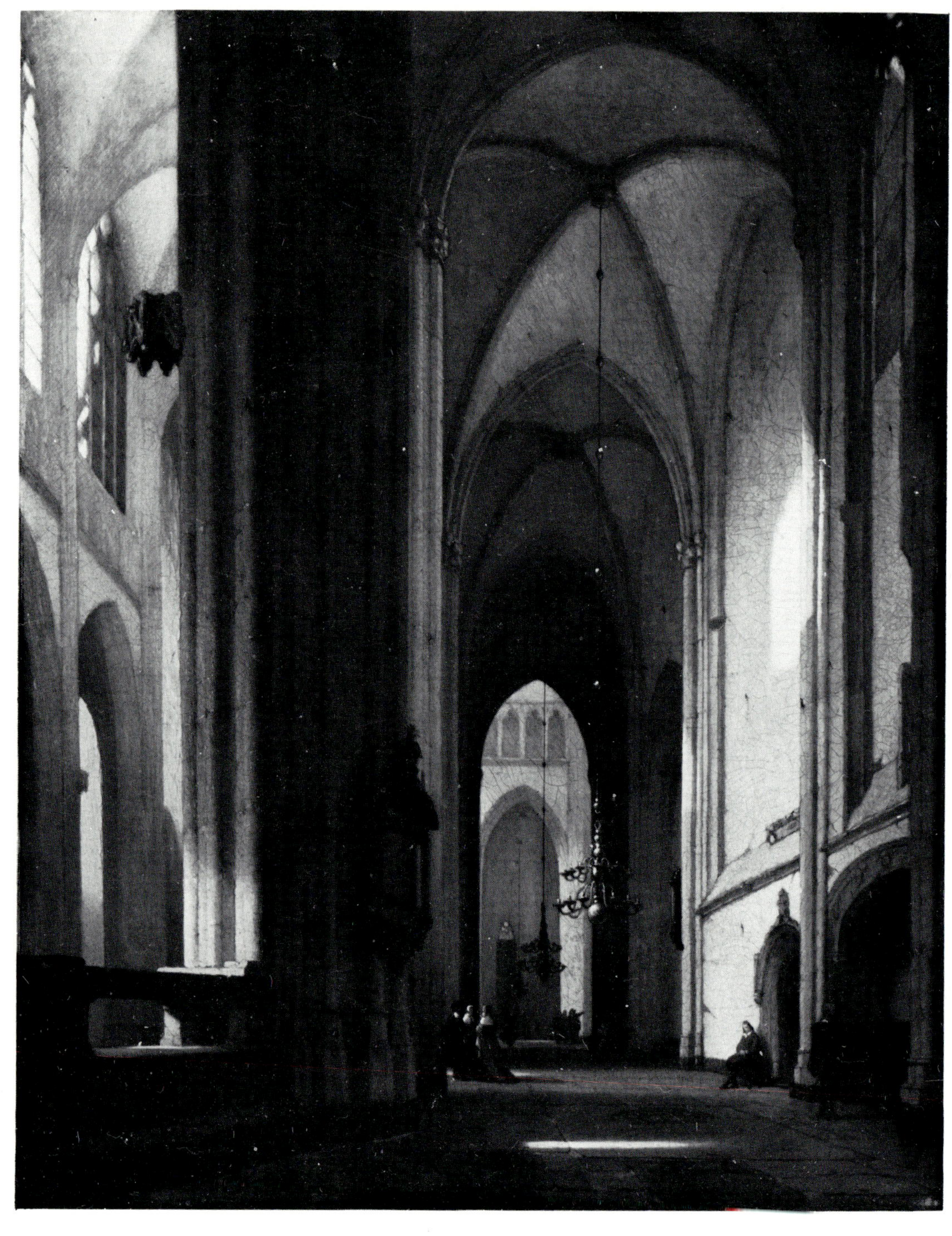

Jan Jacob Schenkel (1829-1900) — *"Interior of a Dutch cathedral", 30½ x 24½ins.* Photograph courtesy of Sotheby & Co.

Schenkel was an architectural painter, also some kitchen interiors. He worked mainly in Amsterdam. Pupil of V. Bing and J. Braet von Uberfeldt.

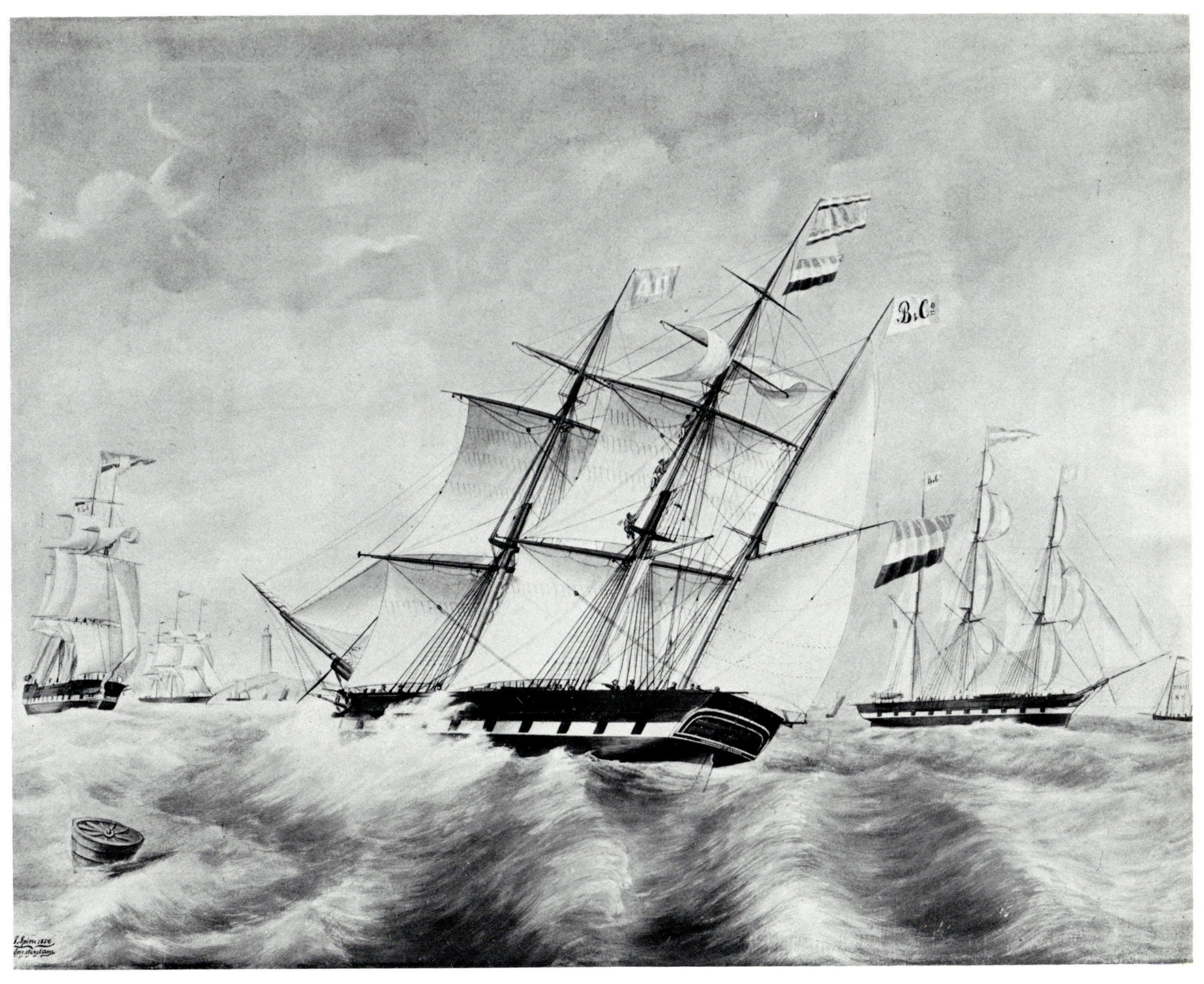

Jacobus Spin (1806-1875) – *"Shipping near the Isle of Texel", signed and dated 1856, watercolour, 20 x 27ins.* Photograph courtesy of Spenser S.A.

Spin worked mainly in watercolour and is recorded as an artist in the Amsterdam register.

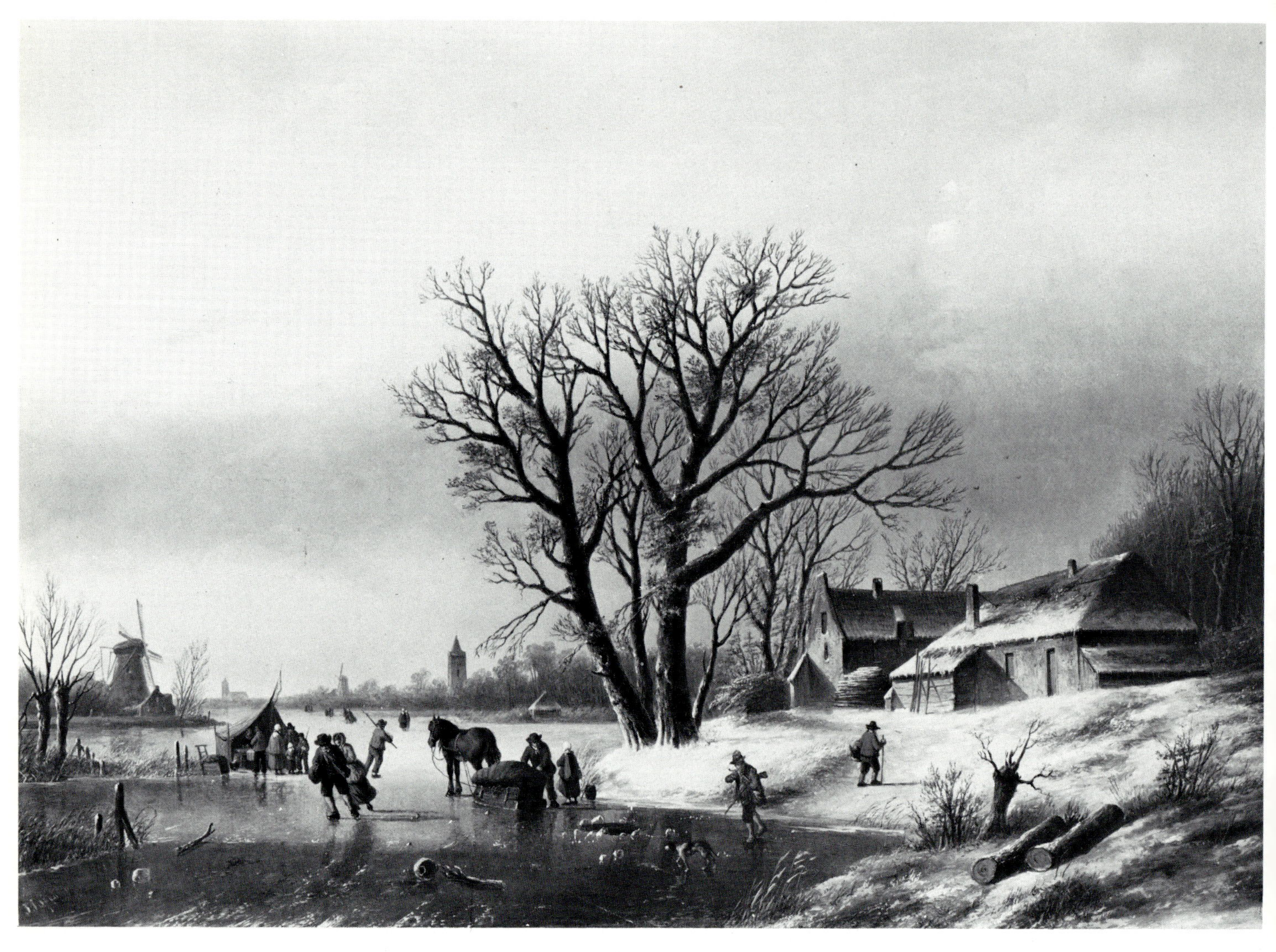

Above: **Jan Jacob Spöhler (1811-1866)** – *"Dutch winter scene", 26 x 36ins.* Photograph courtesy of Spenser S.A.

J.J. Spöhler was a landscapist, treating both summer and winter scenes. Pupil of J.W. Pieneman. Member of Amsterdam Academy 1845. J.J.C. Spöhler and J.F. Spöhler were his sons.

Right: **Johannes Franciscus Spöhler (1853-1894)** – *"Dutch canal scene", 8 x 6ins.* Photograph courtesy of Richard Green.

J.F. Spöhler painted town and village scenes with figures. He was the son of J.J. Spöhler and worked mainly in Amsterdam.

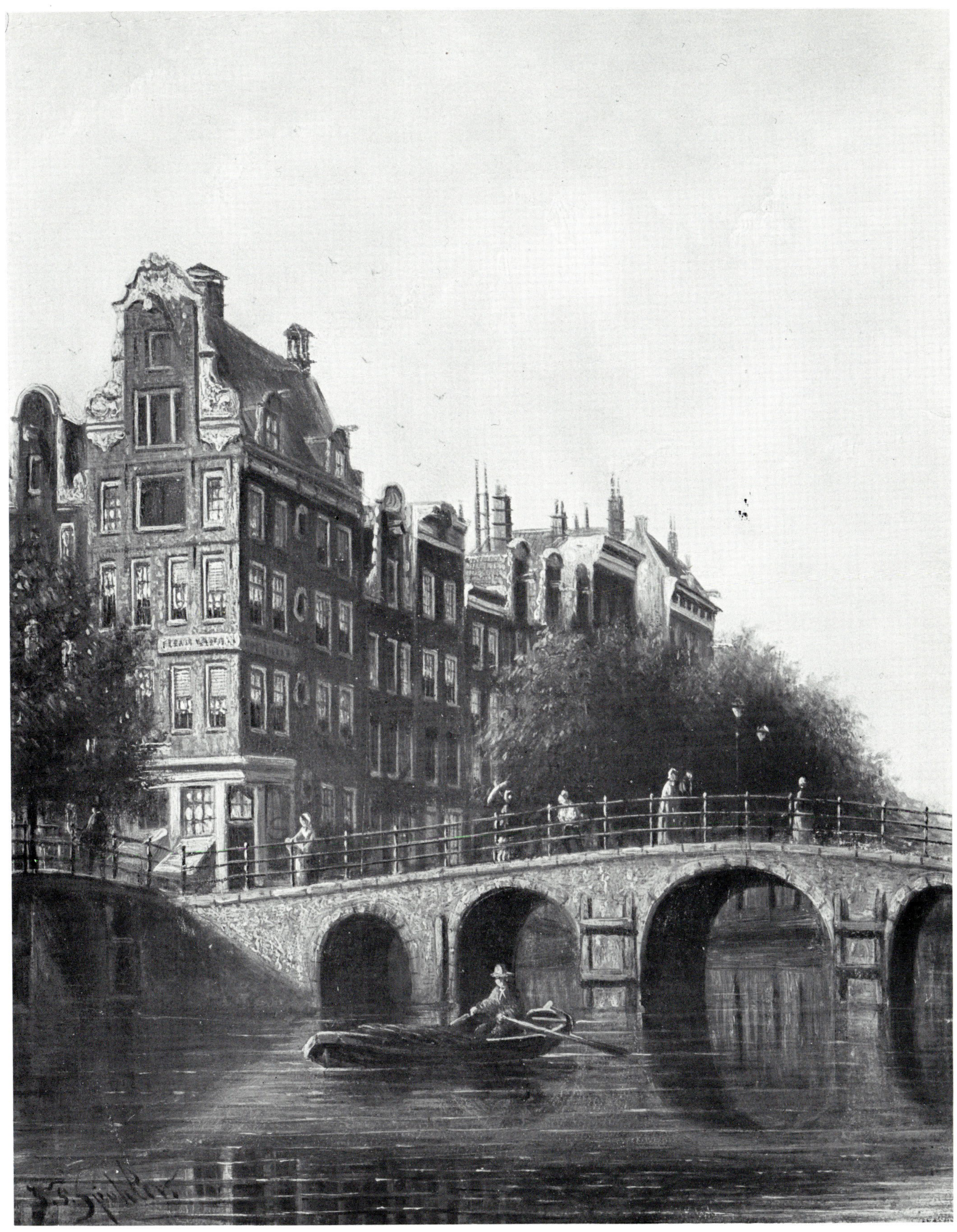

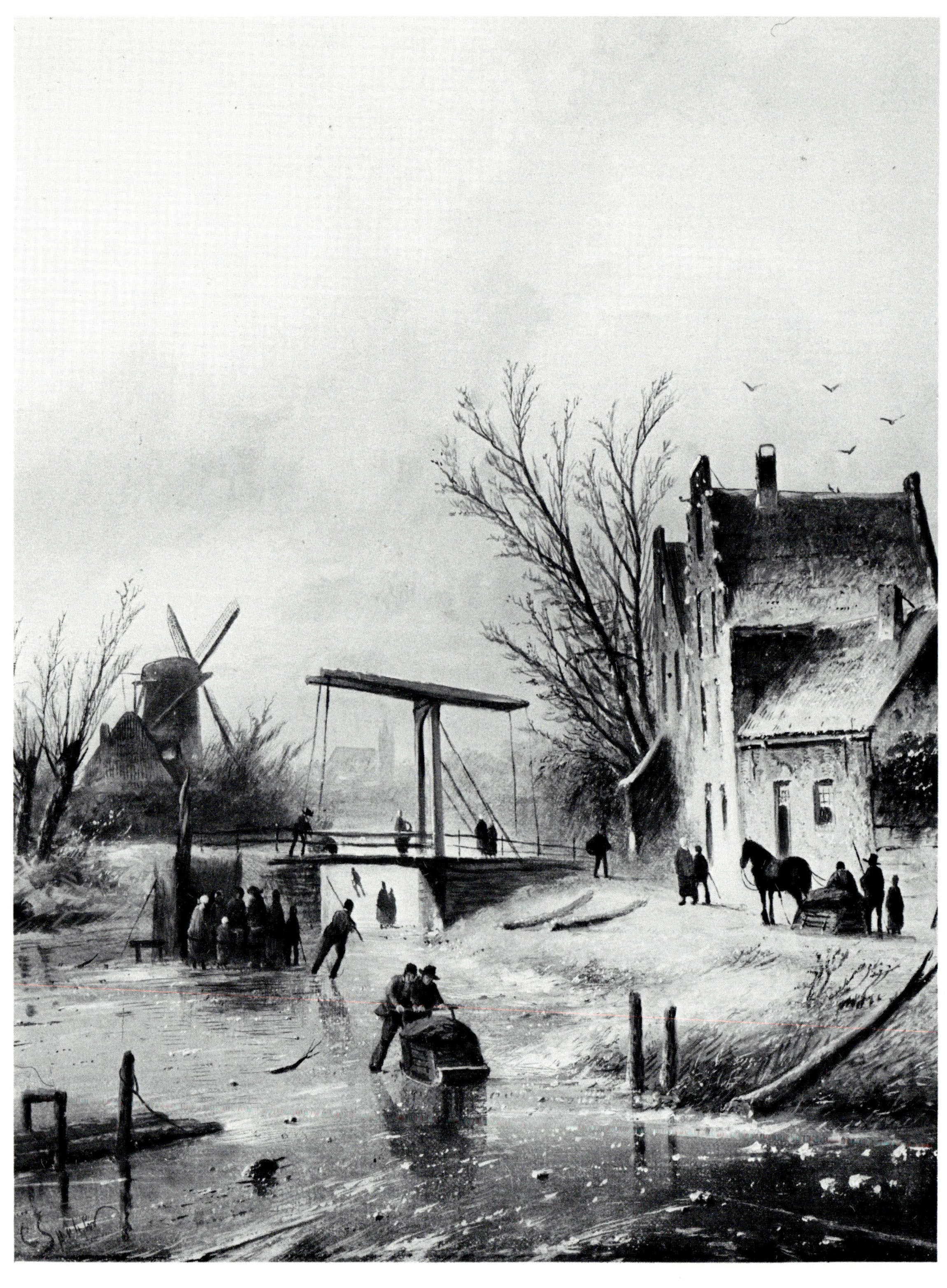

Jacob Jan Coenraad Spöhler (1827-1923) – *"Frozen river scene".* Photograph courtesy of MacConnal Mason.

J.J.C. Spöhler was the son and pupil of J.J. Spöhler; his landscape technique is close to that of his father.

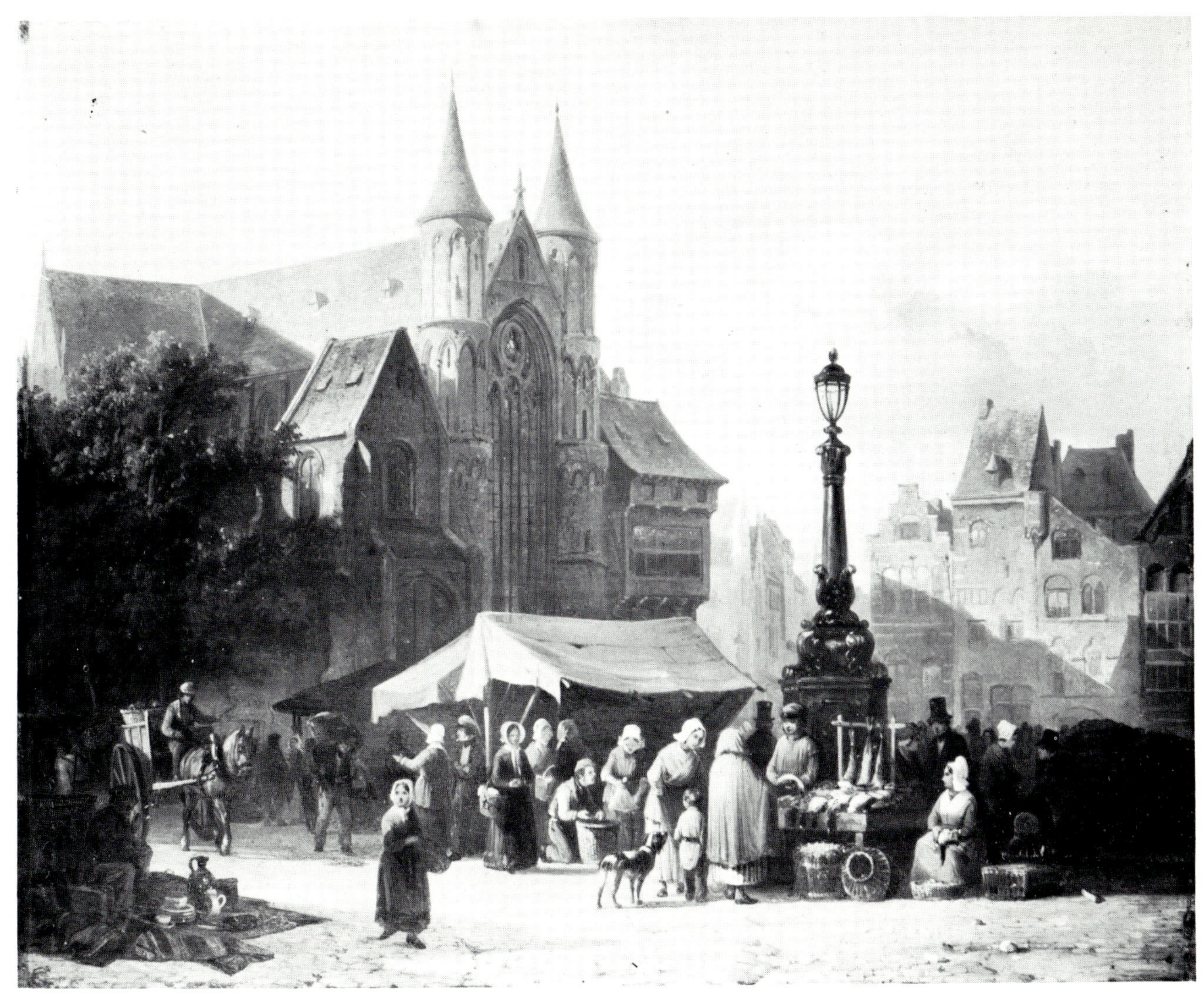

Cornelis Springer (1817-1891) – *"Street market in a Dutch town", signed with monogram and dated '50, 35.5 x 44cms.* Photograph courtesy of Sotheby & Co.

Springer was a leading townscapist of the mid-century. Studied Amsterdam Academy, also under J. van der Stok, H.G. ten Cate and K. Karsen. Member of "Felix Meritis", Amsterdam.

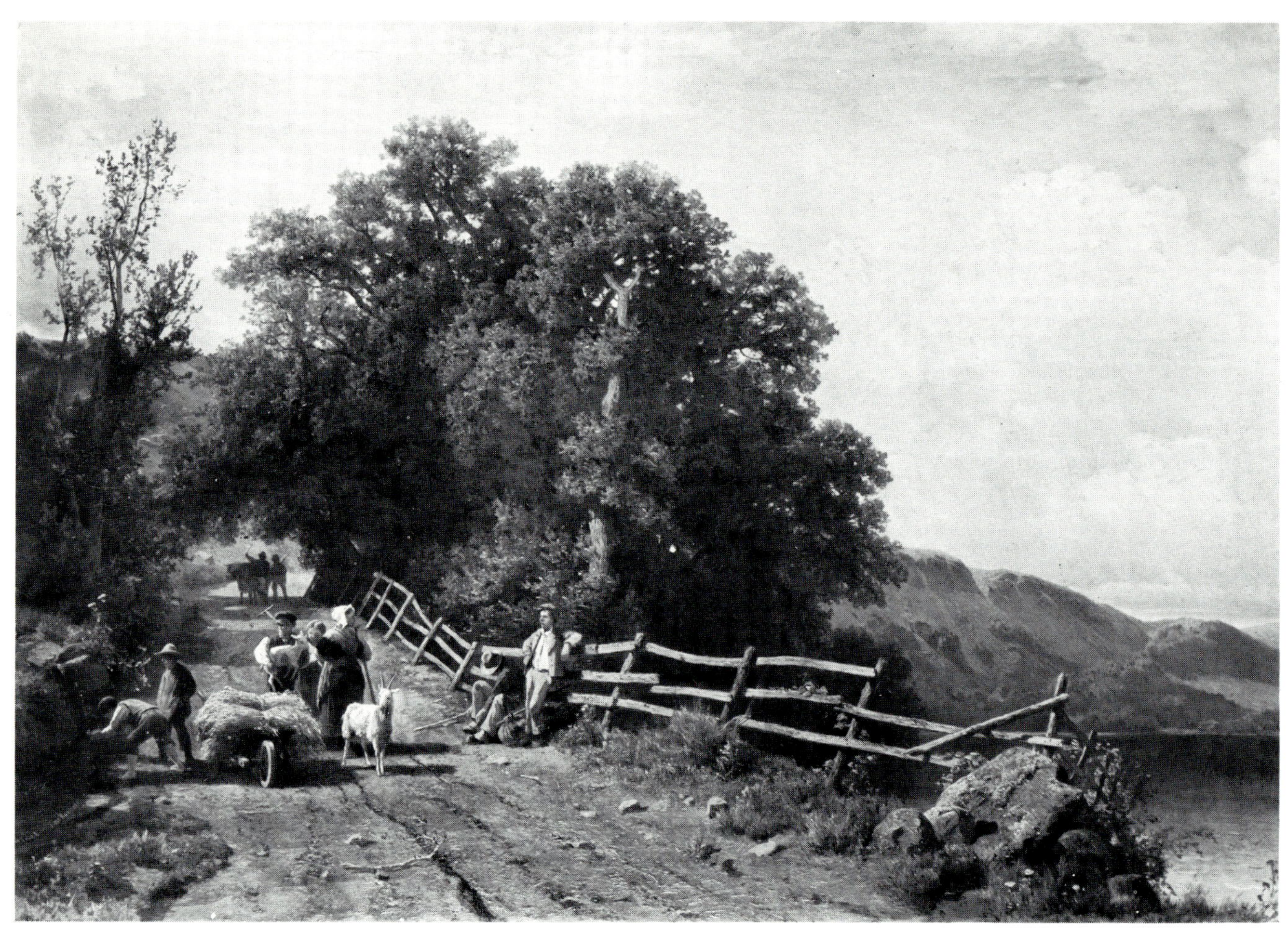

Jacobus Nicolaas Tjarda van Starckenborgh Stachouwer Jnr. (1817-1891) – *"Landscape with flowers, goat and haycart", 36 x 50½ins.* Photograph courtesy of Richard Green.

Starckenborgh was a landscape painter. Studied Amsterdam Academy of which he was later a member. Worked Düsseldorf and Wiesbaden as well as Holland. Visited North America 1849-50. Signed J.N. van Starkenborgh.

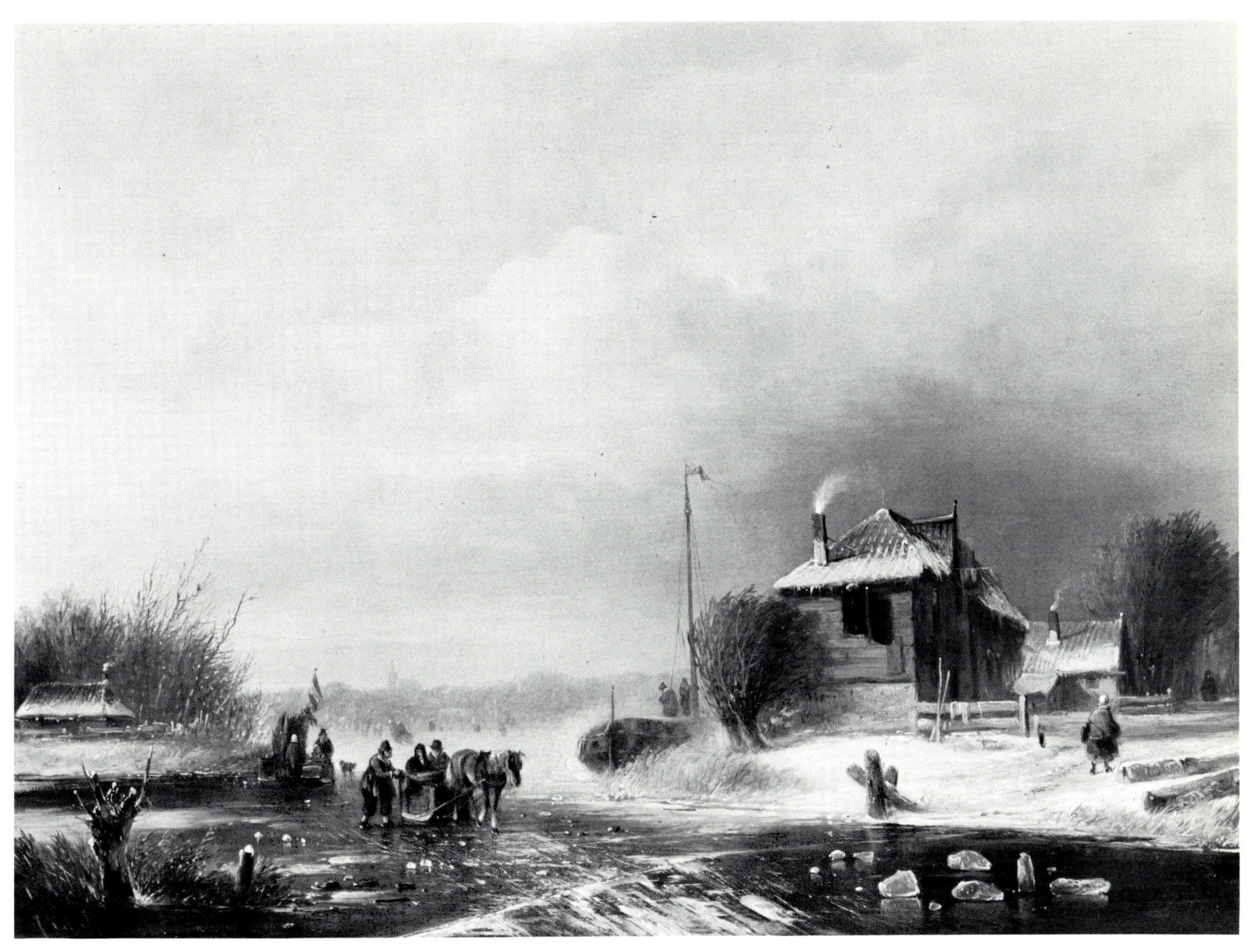

Jacobus van der Stok (1794/95-1864) — *"Dutch river landscape in winter", signed and dated '51, 12¼ x 16¾ins.* Photograph courtesy of Richard Green.

Stok was a landscapist. Pupil of A.J. Besters. C. Springer and his daughter Jacoba van der Stok (a flower painter) were among his pupils.

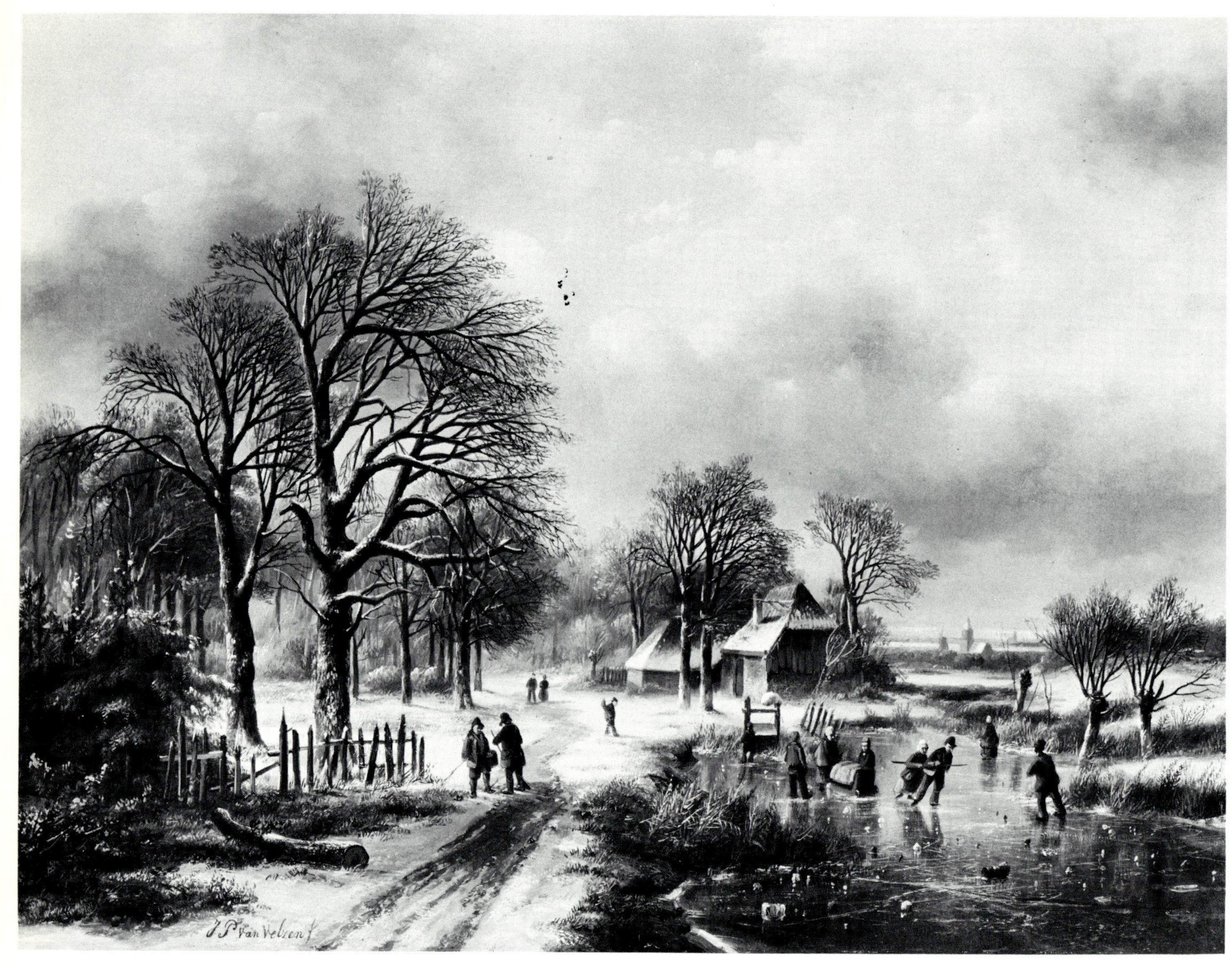

Johannes Petrus Velzen (1816-1853) — *"Winter landscape with children skating", 20½ x 28ins.* Photograph courtesy of Richard Green

Velzen painted both winter and summer landscapes. Pupil of N.J. Roosenboom. Having worked in Haarlem and Amsterdam he spent the latter part of his life in Belgium (from 1844).

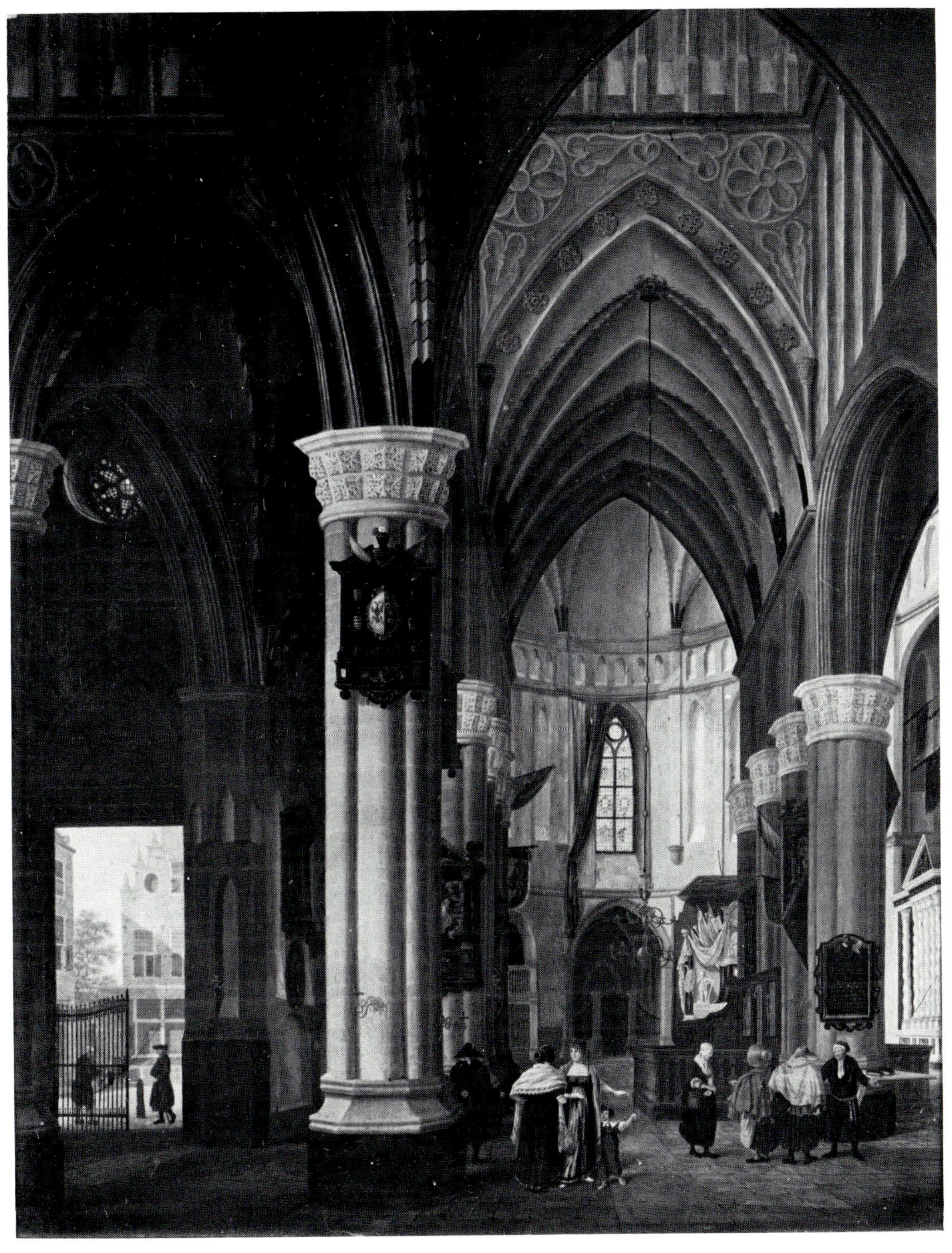

Hendrik Verheijen (1768-1849) – *"Interior of a Cathedral", 21 x 16½ins.* Photograph courtesy of Sotheby & Co.

Hendrik Verheijen lived and worked in Utrecht.

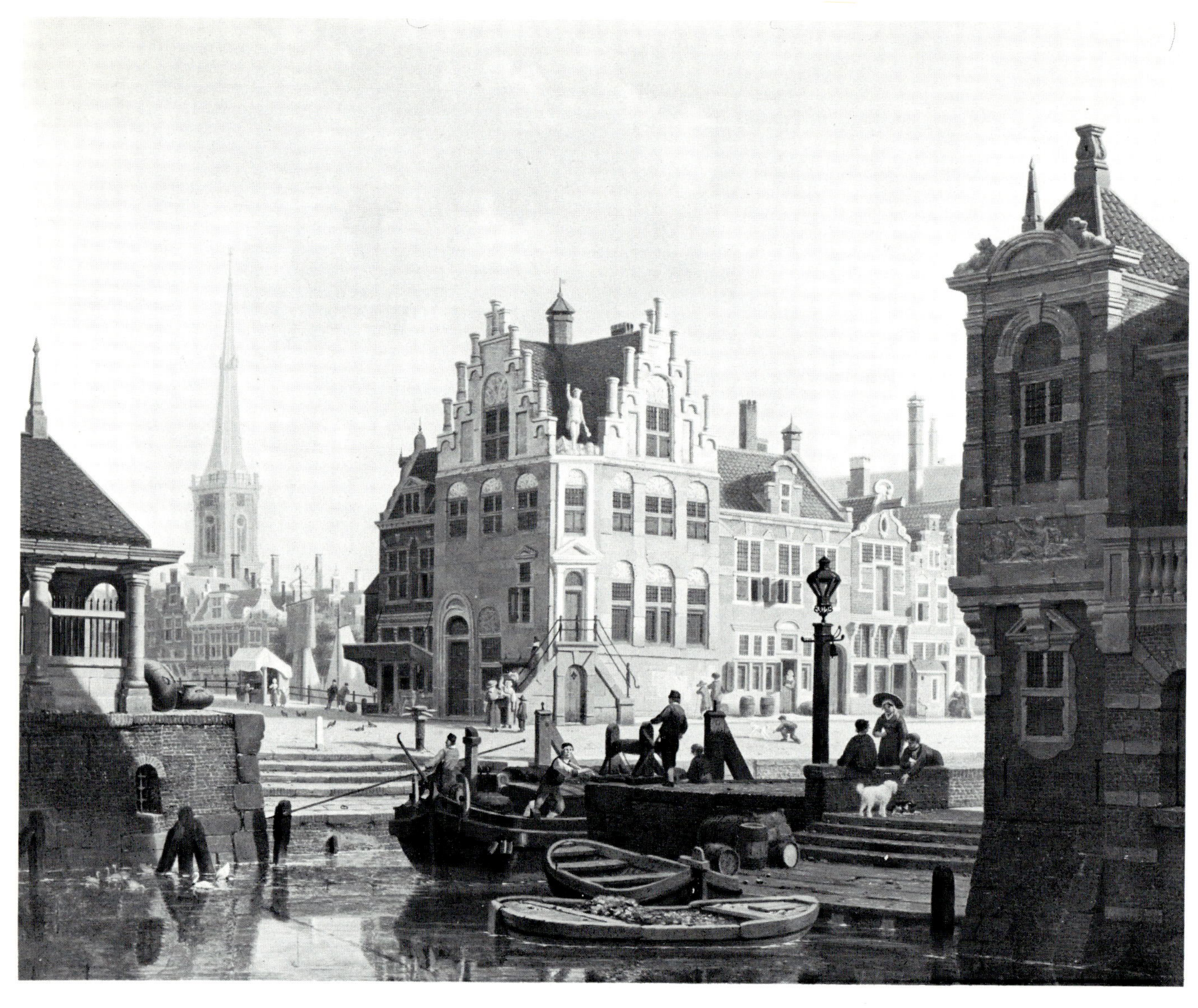

Jan Hendrik Verheijen (1778-1846) – *"Canal scene with boats, figures and buildings", 18¾ x 15½ins.* Photograph courtesy of Williams & Son.

Verheijen painted townscapes, landscapes and portraits. Pupil of carriage and ornamental painter N. Osti at Utrecht.

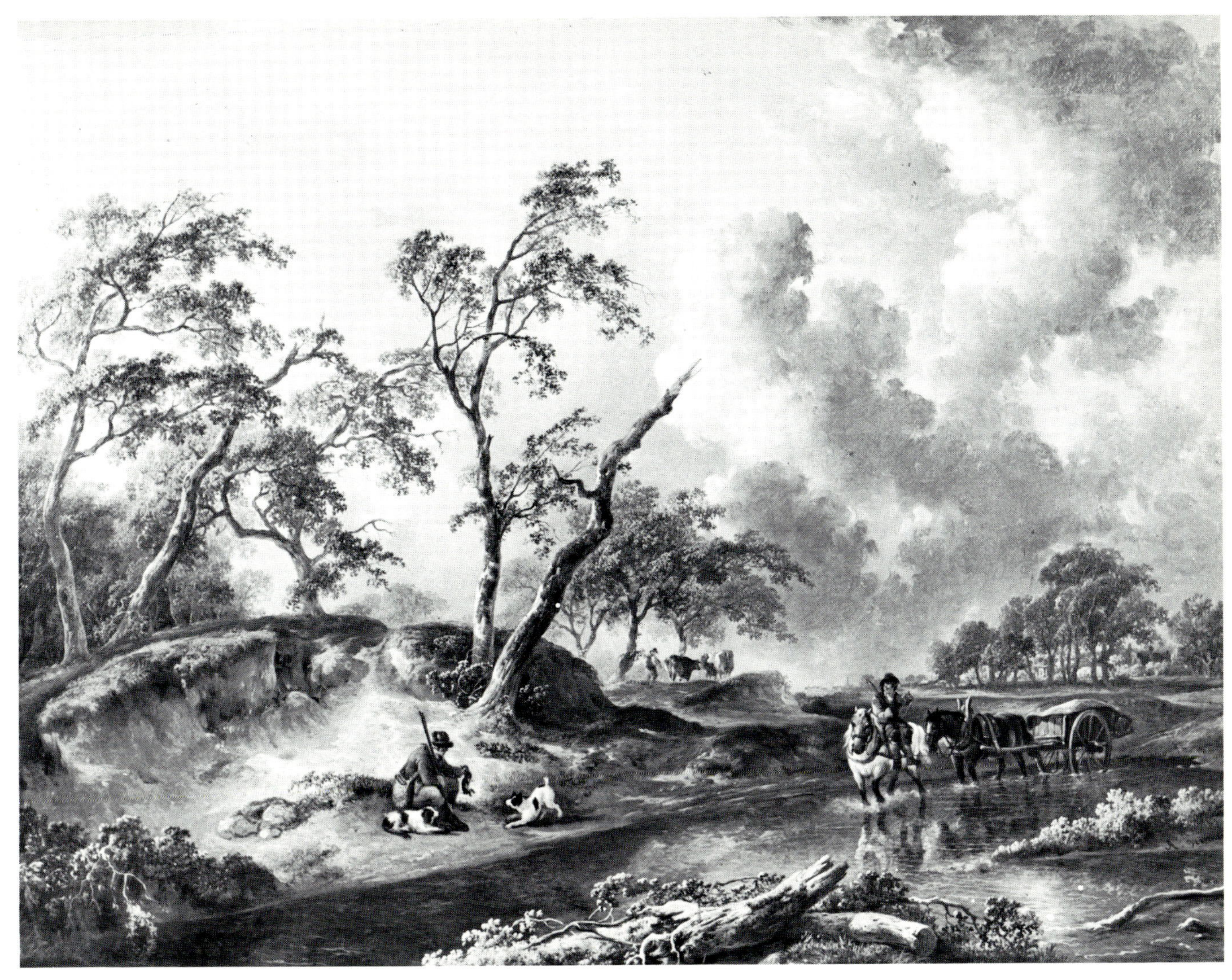

Andries Vermeulen (1763-1814) – *"Summer landscape with huntsmen resting by a stream", 21 x 27ins.* Photograph courtesy of King and Chasemore, Pulborough.

Vermeulen painted ice scenes and summer landscapes with figures. Pupil of his father Cornelis Vermeulen.

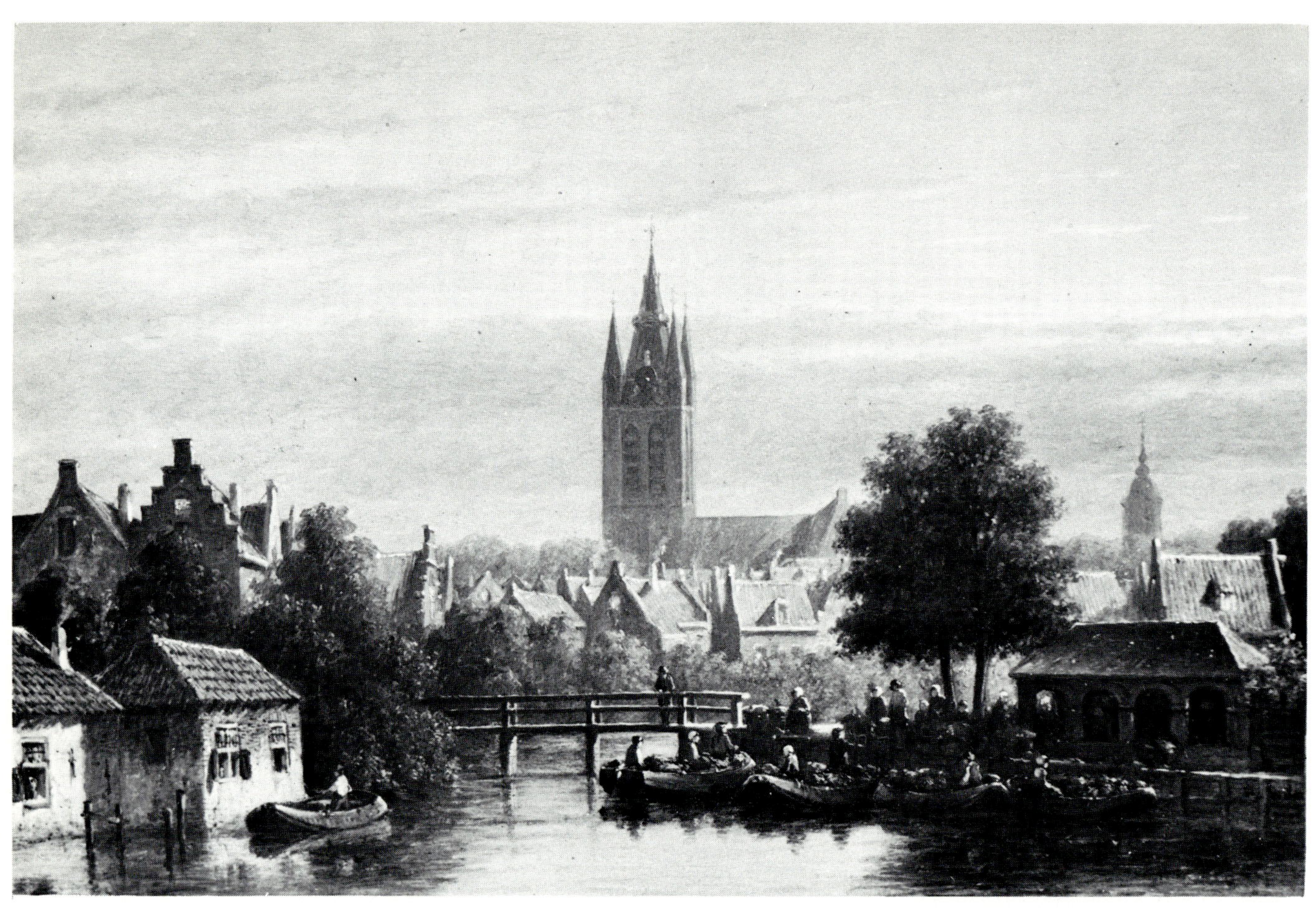

Petrus Gerardus Vertin (1819-1893) – *"Landscape with boats", 27 x 41cms.* Photograph courtesy of Mak van Waay, Amsterdam.
Vertin painted landscapes and town scenes. Studied the Hague Academy under B.J. van Hove. Lived and worked in the Hague.

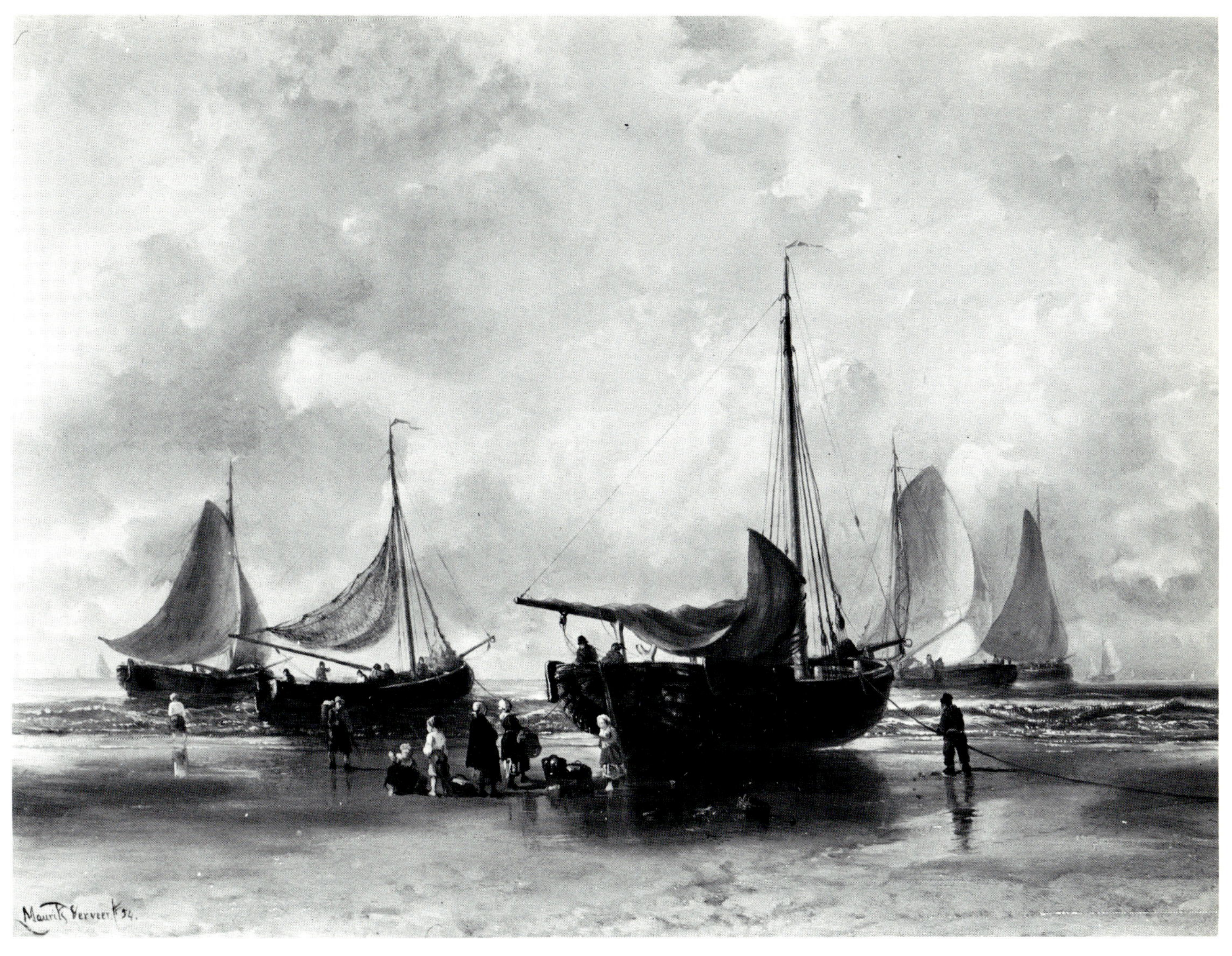

Mozes Leonardus (Mauritz) Verveer (1817-1903) — *"Sailing vessels with figures", signed and dated '54, 13¾ x 18½ins.* Photograph courtesy of Richard Green.

Verveer was a marine artist, photographer and wood engraver. He painted many beach and shipping scenes in collaboration with his brother Samuel Leonardus. Lived and worked in the Hague.

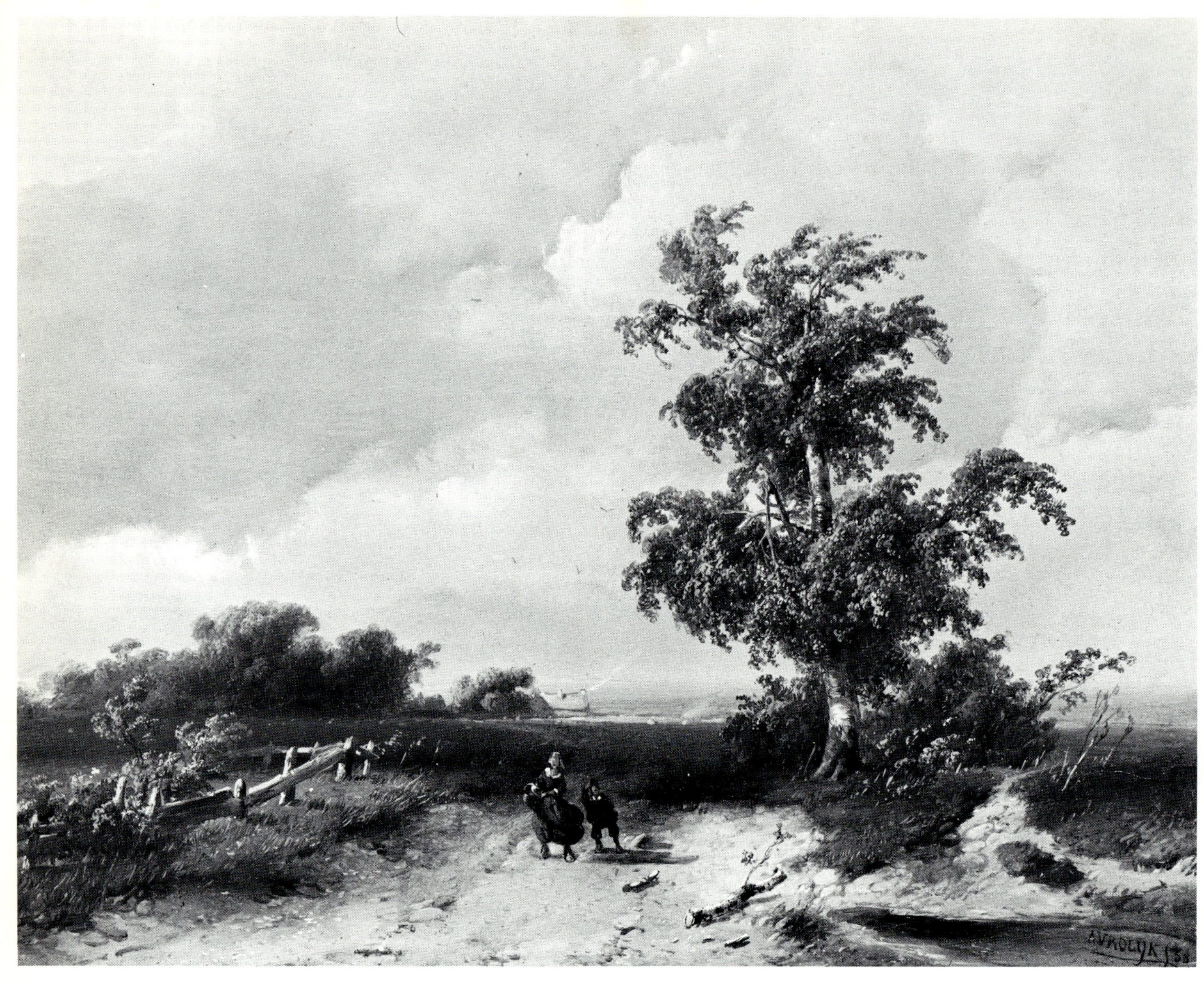

Jacobus Adrianus Vrolijk (1834-1862) – *"Windswept landscape", signed and dated 1858, 12½ x 10ins.* Photograph courtesy of Spenser S.A.

Vrolijk painted landscapes and town scenes. Pupil of A. Schelfhout. Johannes Martinus (or Jan) Vrolyk, the landscape and animal painter, was his brother and pupil.

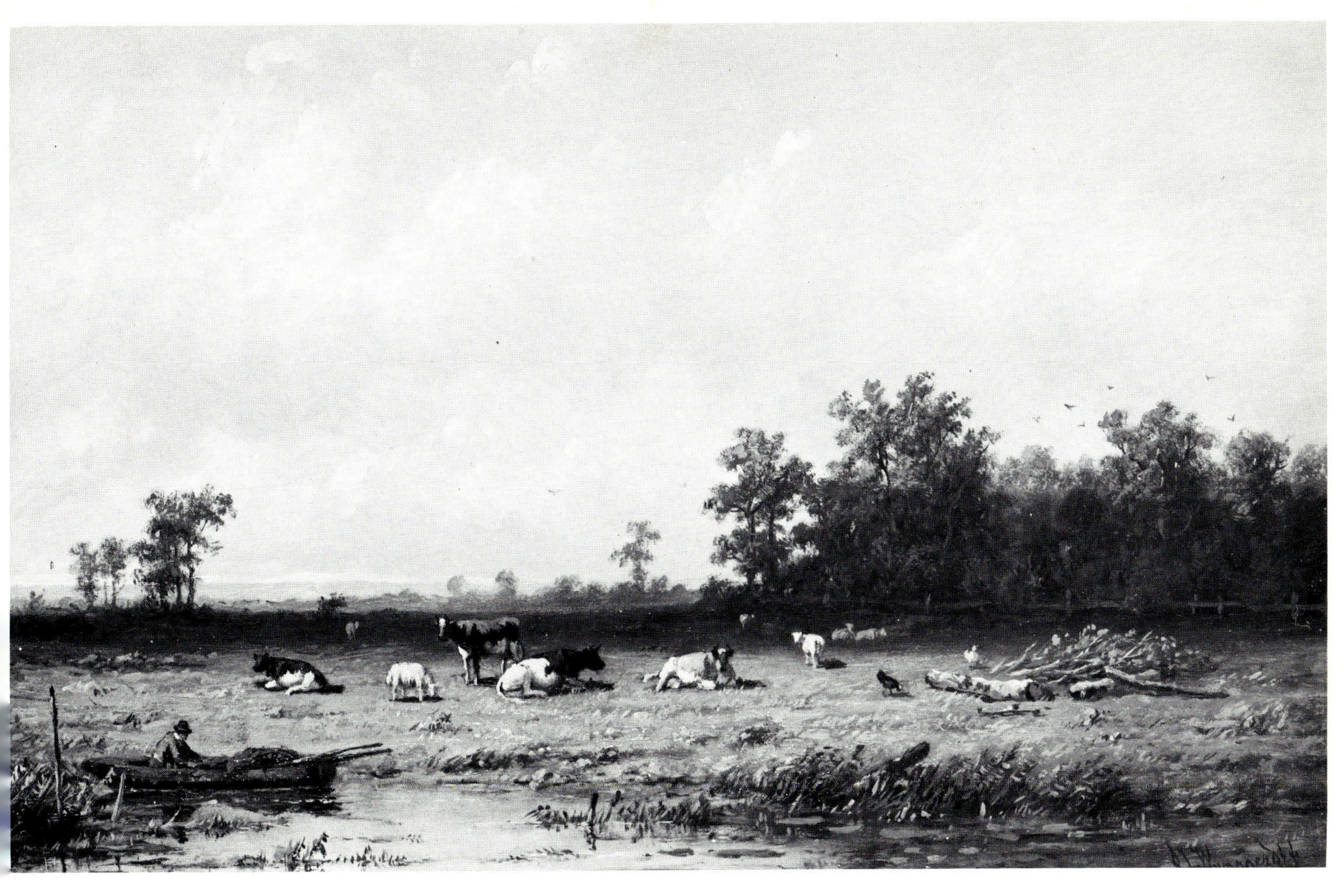

Anthonie Jacobus van Wijngaerdt (1808-1887) – *"Summer landscape", 12 x 16ins.* Photograph courtesy of Spenser S.A.
Wijngaerdt was a landscape painter and etcher. Pupil of J. de Meijer. Also studied Germany and Belgium.

Index of Artists

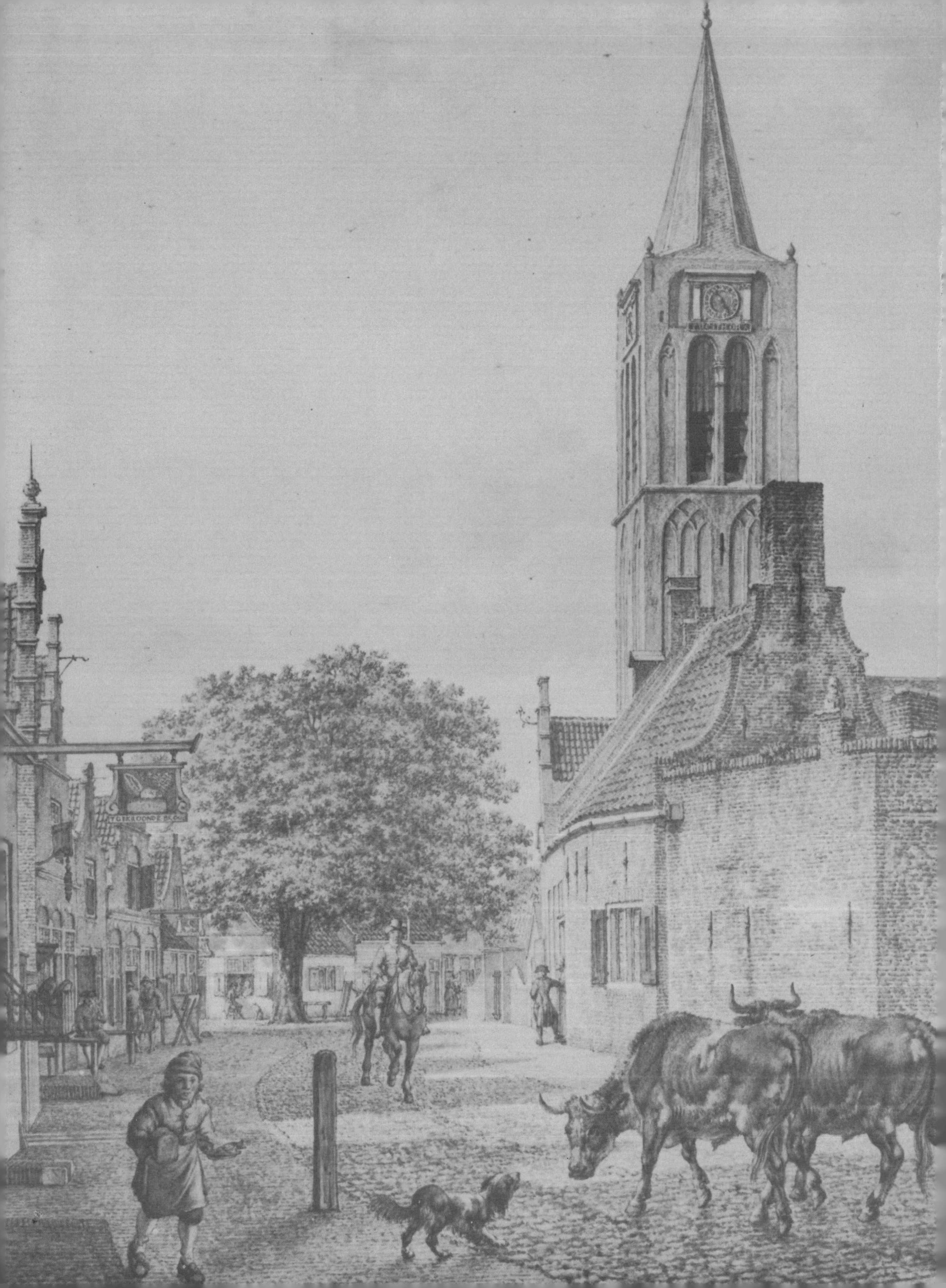